I am Here!

Volume 1

Ema Toyama

Translated and adapted by
Joshua Weeks

Lettered by
North Market Street Graphics

DEL REY

Ballantine Books * New York

A Del Rey Manga/Kodansha Trade Paperback Original

I Am Here! volume 1 copyright © 2007 Ema Toyama
I Am Here! volume 2 copyright © 2008 Ema Toyama
I Am Here! volume 3 copyright © 2008 Ema Toyama
English translation copyright © 2010 Ema Toyama

Published in the United States by Del Rey, an imprint of The Random House Publishing Group, a division of Random House, Inc., New York.

DEL REY is a registered trademark and the Del Rey colophon is a trademark of Random House, Inc.

Publication rights arranged through Kodansha Ltd.

First published in Japan in 2007–2008 by Kodansha Ltd., Tokyo, as *Ko Ko Ni Iru Yo* volumes 1, 2, and 3.

ISBN 978-0-345-52243-6

Printed in the United States of America

www.delreymanga.com

9 8 7 6 5 4 3 2

Translator/Adapter: Joshua Weeks
Lettering: North Market Street Graphics

CONTENTS

Honorifics Explained

Throughout the Del Rey Manga books, you will find Japanese honorifics left intact in the translations. For those not familiar with how the Japanese use honorifics and, more important, how they differ from American honorifics, we present this brief overview.

Politeness has always been a critical facet of Japanese culture. Ever since the feudal era, when Japan was a highly stratified society, use of honorifics—which can be defined as polite speech that indicates relationship or status—has played an essential role in the Japanese language. When addressing someone in Japanese, an honorific usually takes the form of a suffix attached to one's name (example: "Asuna-san"), is used as a title at the end of one's name, or appears in place of the name itself (example: "Negi-sensei," or simply "Sensei!").

Honorifics can be expressions of respect or endearment. In the context of manga and anime, honorifics give insight into the nature of the relationship between characters. Many English translations leave out these important honorifics and therefore distort the feel of the original Japanese. Because Japanese honorifics contain nuances that English honorifics lack, it is our policy at Del Rey not to translate them. Here, instead, is a guide to some of the honorifics you may encounter in Del Rey Manga.

-san: This is the most common honorific and is equivalent to Mr., Miss, Ms., or Mrs. It is the all-purpose honorific and can be used in any situation where politeness is required.

-sama: This is one level higher than "-san" and is used to confer great respect.

-dono: This comes from the word "tono," which means "lord." It is an even higher level than "-sama" and confers utmost respect.

-kun: This suffix is used at the end of boys' names to express familiarity or endearment. It is also sometimes used by men among friends, or when addressing someone younger or of a lower station.

-chan: This is used to express endearment, mostly toward girls. It is also used for little boys, pets, and even among lovers. It gives a sense of childish cuteness.

Bozu: This is an informal way to refer to a boy, similar to the English terms "kid" and "squirt."

Sempai/
Senpai: This title suggests that the addressee is one's senior in a group or organization. It is most often used in a school setting, where underclassmen refer to their upperclassmen as "sempai." It can also be used in the workplace, such as when a newer employee addresses an employee who has seniority in the company.

Kohai: This is the opposite of "sempai" and is used toward underclassmen in school or newcomers in the workplace. It connotes that the addressee is of a lower station.

Sensei: Literally meaning "one who has come before," this title is used for teachers, doctors, or masters of any profession or art.

-[blank]:   This is usually forgotten in these lists, but it is perhaps the most significant difference between Japanese and English. The lack of honorific means that the speaker has permission to address the person in a very intimate way. Usually, only family, spouses, or very close friends have this kind of permission. Known as *yobisute*, it can be gratifying when someone who has earned the intimacy starts to call one by one's name without an honorific. But when that intimacy hasn't been earned, it can be very insulting.

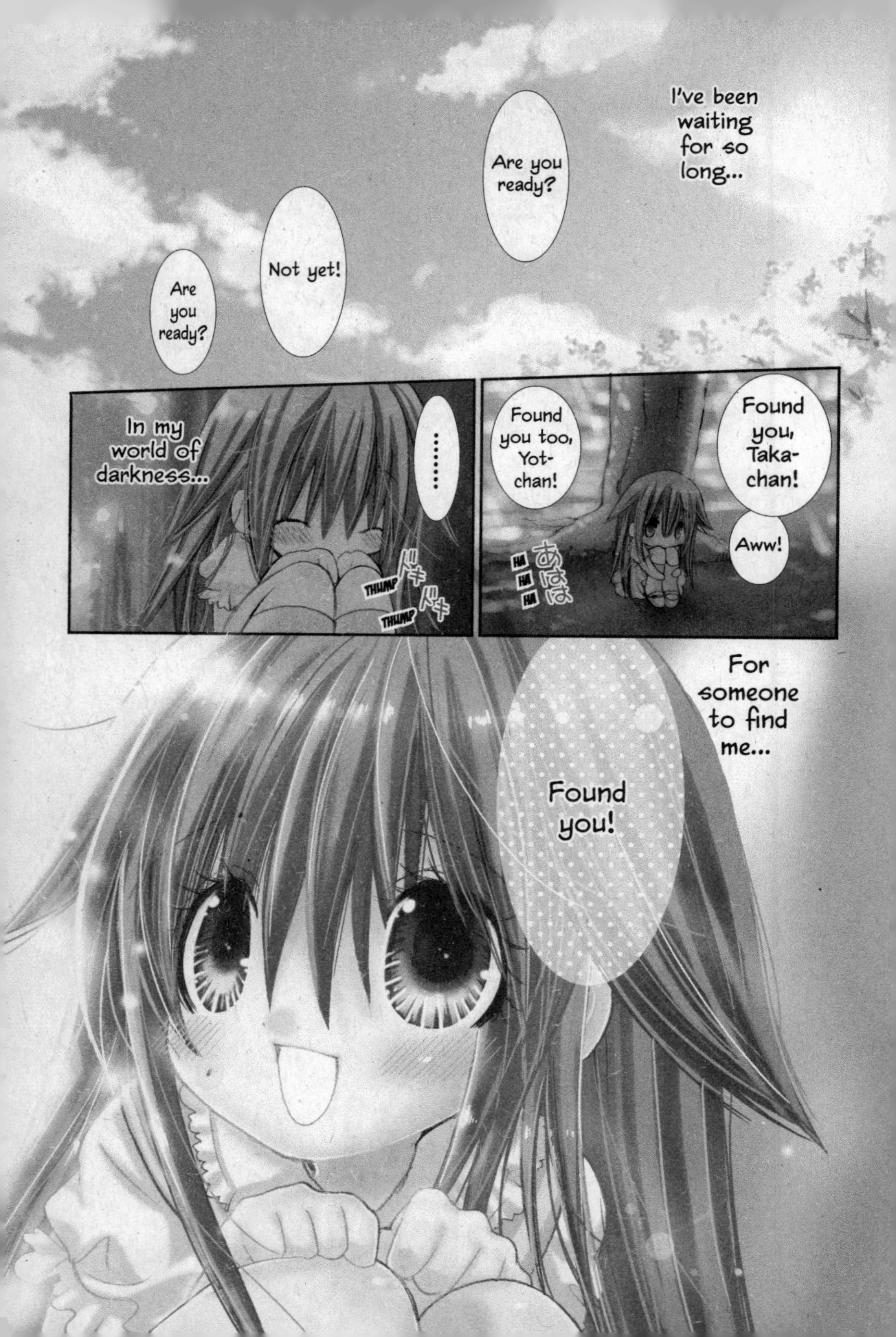

I've been waiting for so long...
Are you ready?
Not yet!
Are you ready?
Found you, Taka-chan!
Aww!
Found you too, Yot-chan!
あはは
HA HA HA
......
In my world of darkness...
ドキ THUMP
ドキ THUMP
For someone to find me...
Found you!

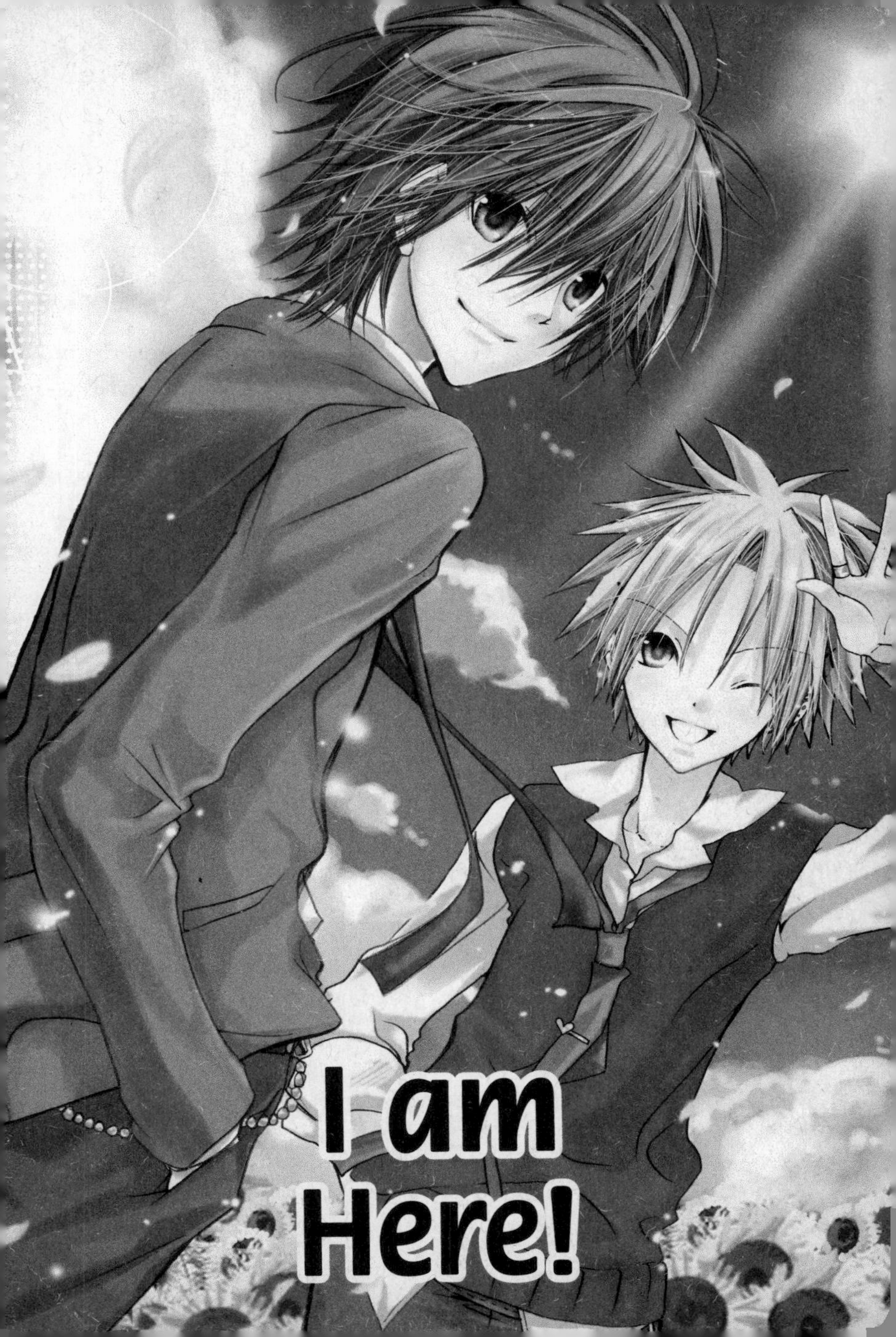
I am
Here!

Diary 1 A Sunflower and the Sun

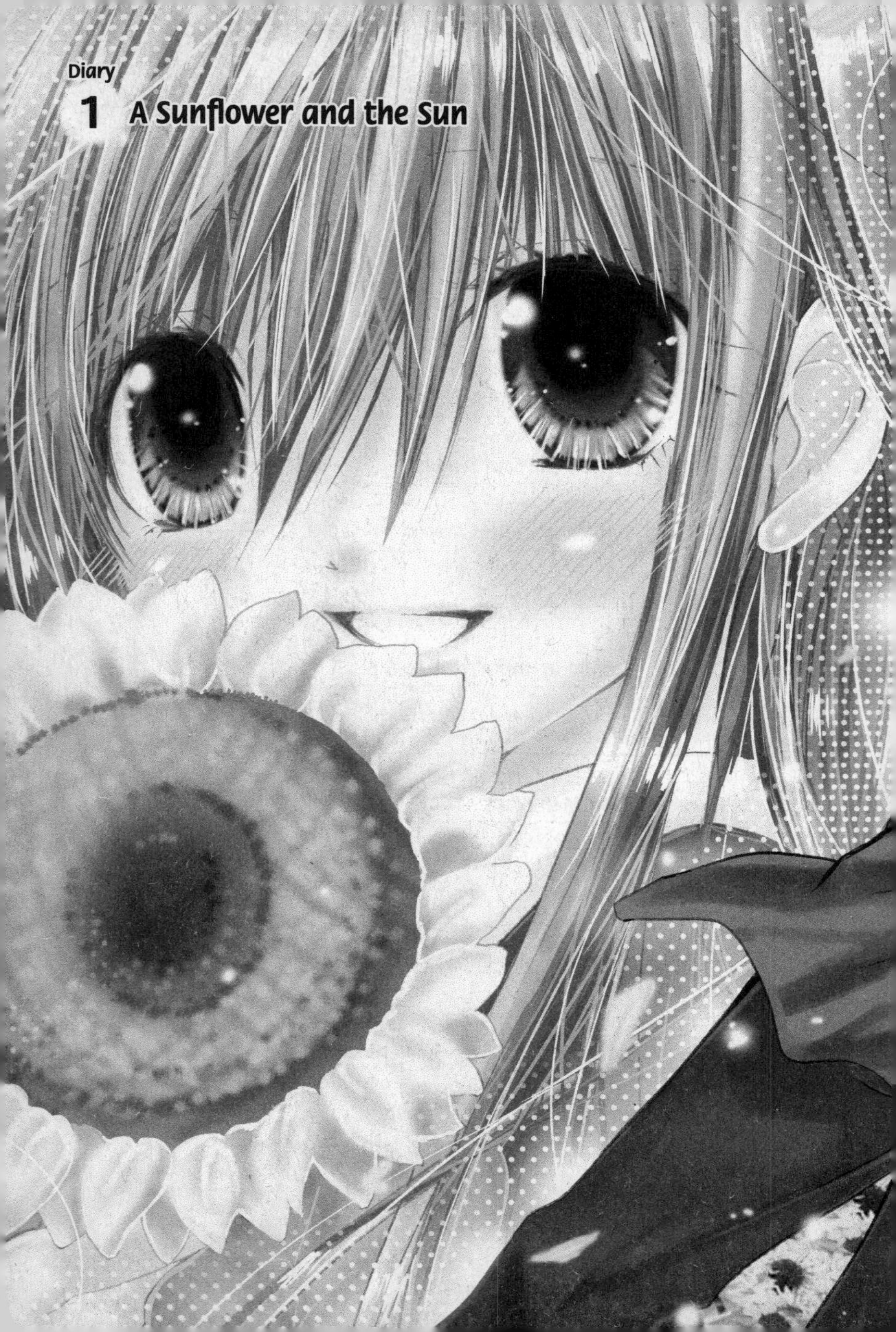

I am Here!

CONTENTS

I wonder what happiness is.

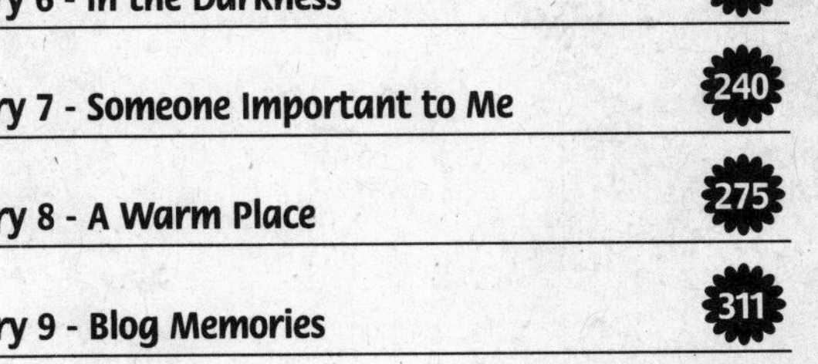

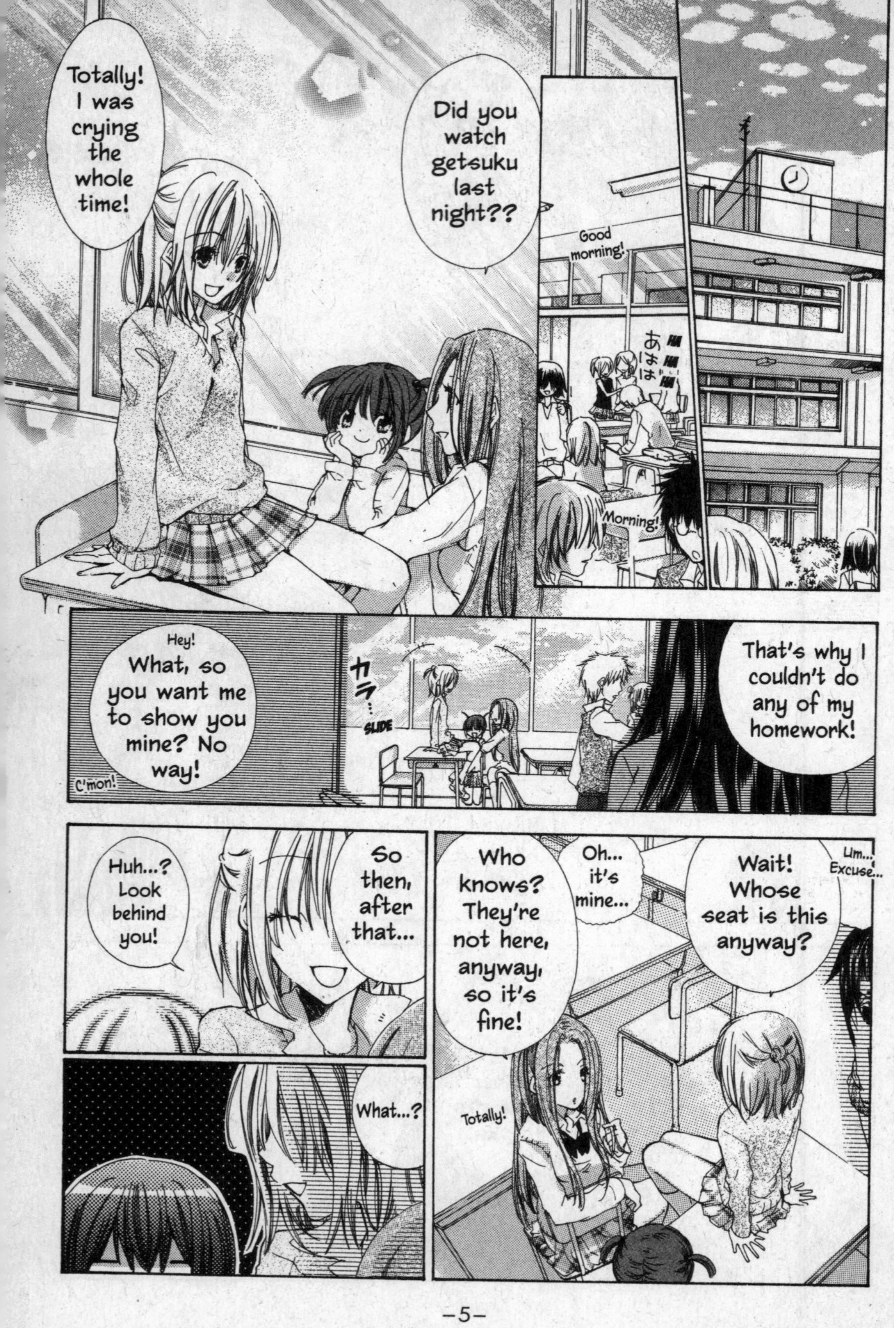

Good morning!
あはは
HA HA HA
Morning!
Did you watch getsuku last night??
Totally! I was crying the whole time!
That's why I couldn't do any of my homework!
カラ…
SLIDE
Hey!
What, so you want me to show you mine? No way!
C'mon!
Um... Excuse...
Wait! Whose seat is this anyway?
Oh... it's mine...
Who knows? They're not here, anyway, so it's fine!
Totally!
So then, after that...
Huh...? Look behind you!
What...?

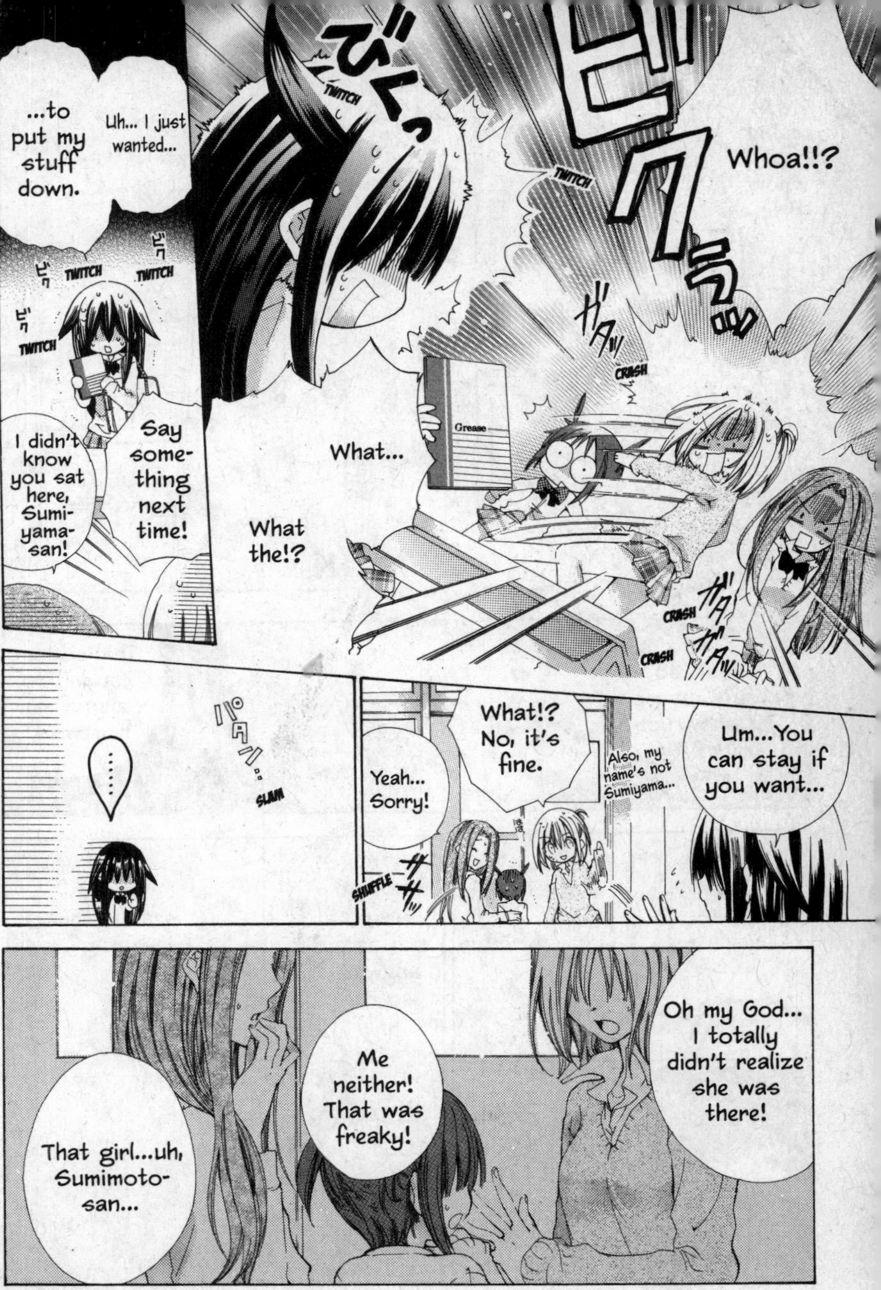

ビクッ
TWITCH
Whoa!!?
びくっ
TWITCH
ガタッ
CRASH
ガタ
CRASH
ガタッ
CRASH
Grease
What...
What the!?
Uh... I just wanted...
...to put my stuff down.
TWITCH
TWITCH
TWITCH
Say some- thing next time!
I didn't know you sat here, Sumi- yama- san!
Um...You can stay if you want...
Also, my name's not Sumiyama...
What!? No, it's fine.
Yeah... Sorry!
SHUFFLE
パタン
SLAM
......
Oh my God... I totally didn't realize she was there!
Me neither! That was freaky!
That girl...uh, Sumimoto- san...

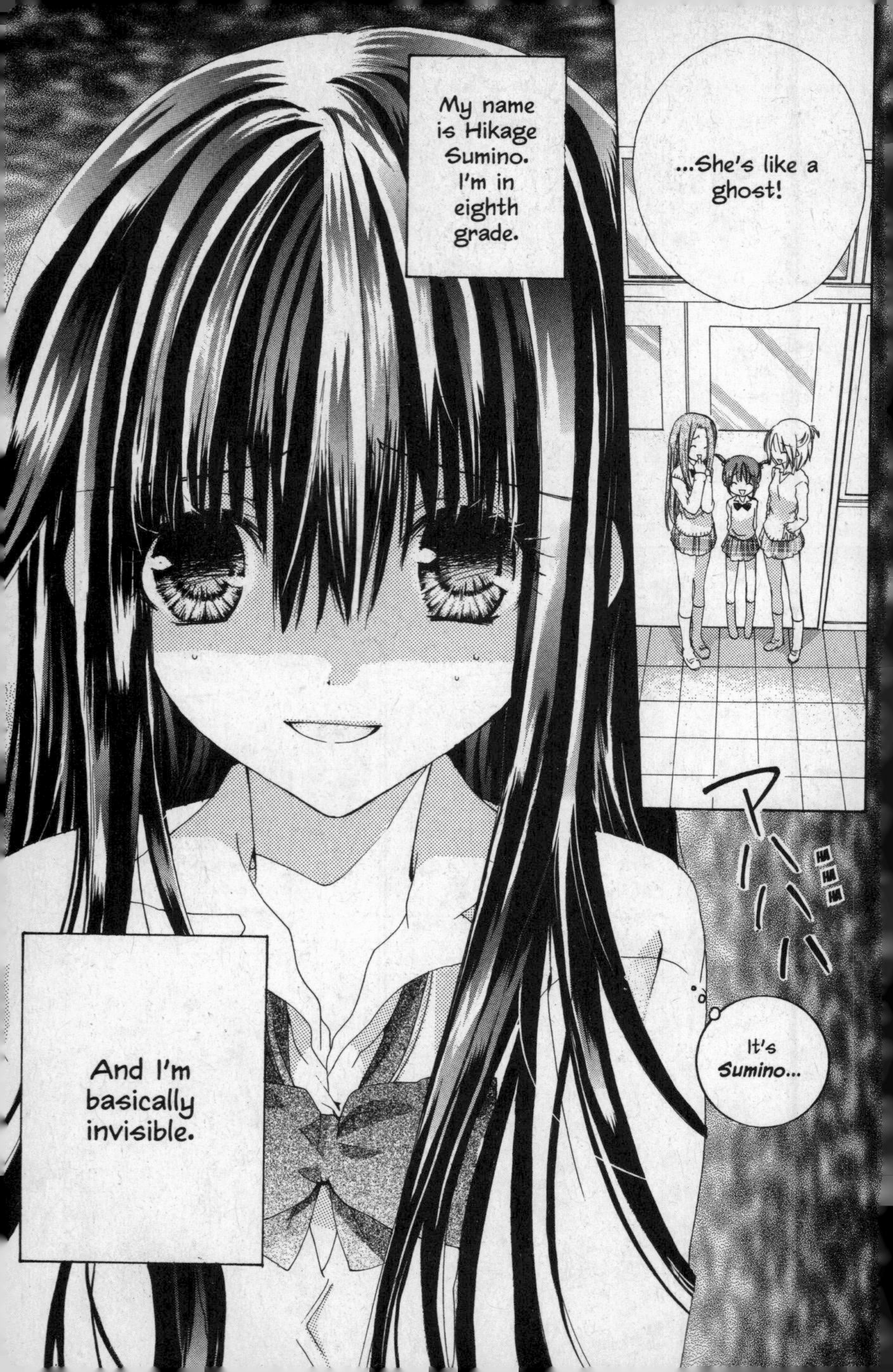
...She's like a ghost!
HA HA HA
It's Sumino...
My name is Hikage Sumino. I'm in eighth grade.
And I'm basically invisible.

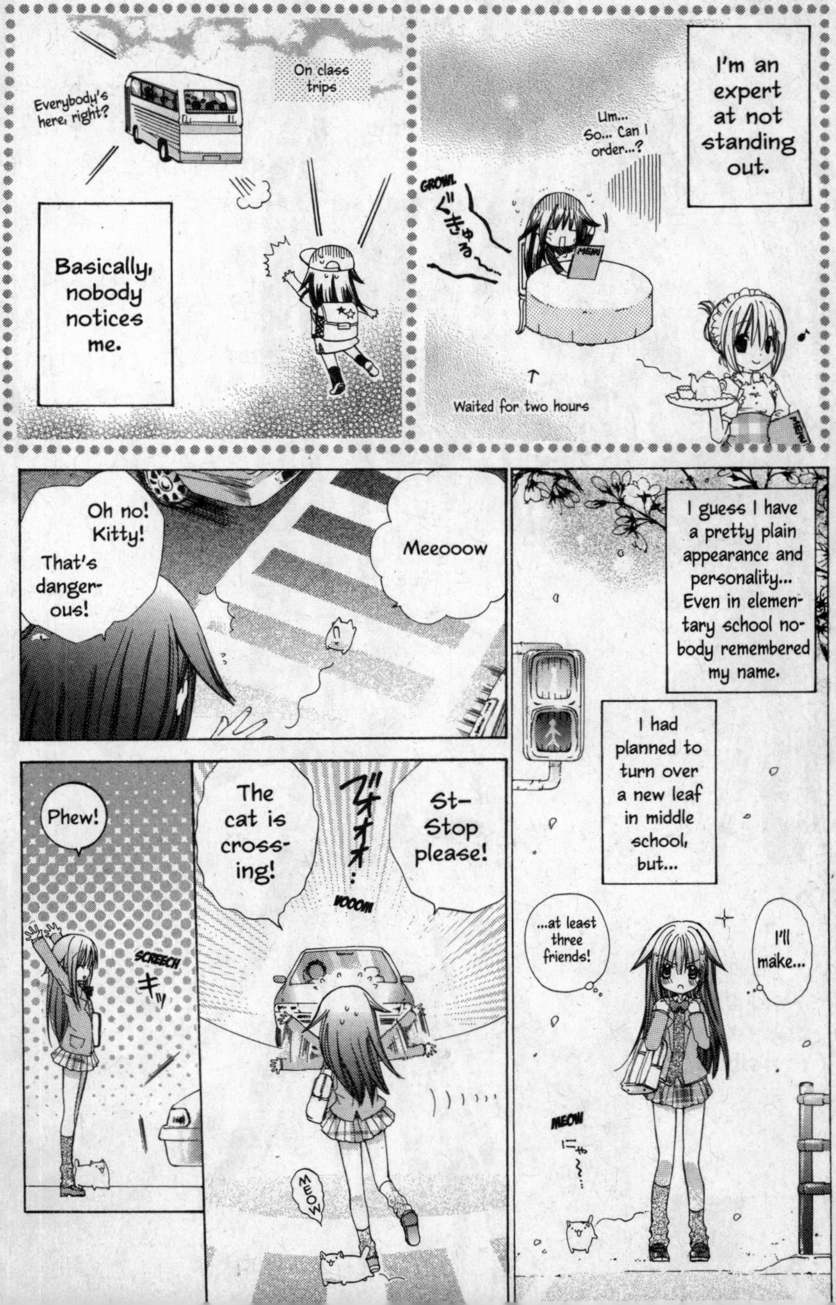
I'm an expert at not standing out.
Um... So... Can I order...?
GROWL
ぐきゅるる~
Waited for two hours
On class trips
Everybody's here, right?
Basically, nobody notices me.
I guess I have a pretty plain appearance and personality... Even in elementary school nobody remembered my name.
I had planned to turn over a new leaf in middle school, but...
I'll make...
...at least three friends!
MEOW
にゃ~...
Meeooow
Oh no! Kitty!
That's danger-ous!
St- Stop please!
ブォオオ...
The cat is cross-ing!
VOOOM
MEOW
Phew!
SCREECH
キッ

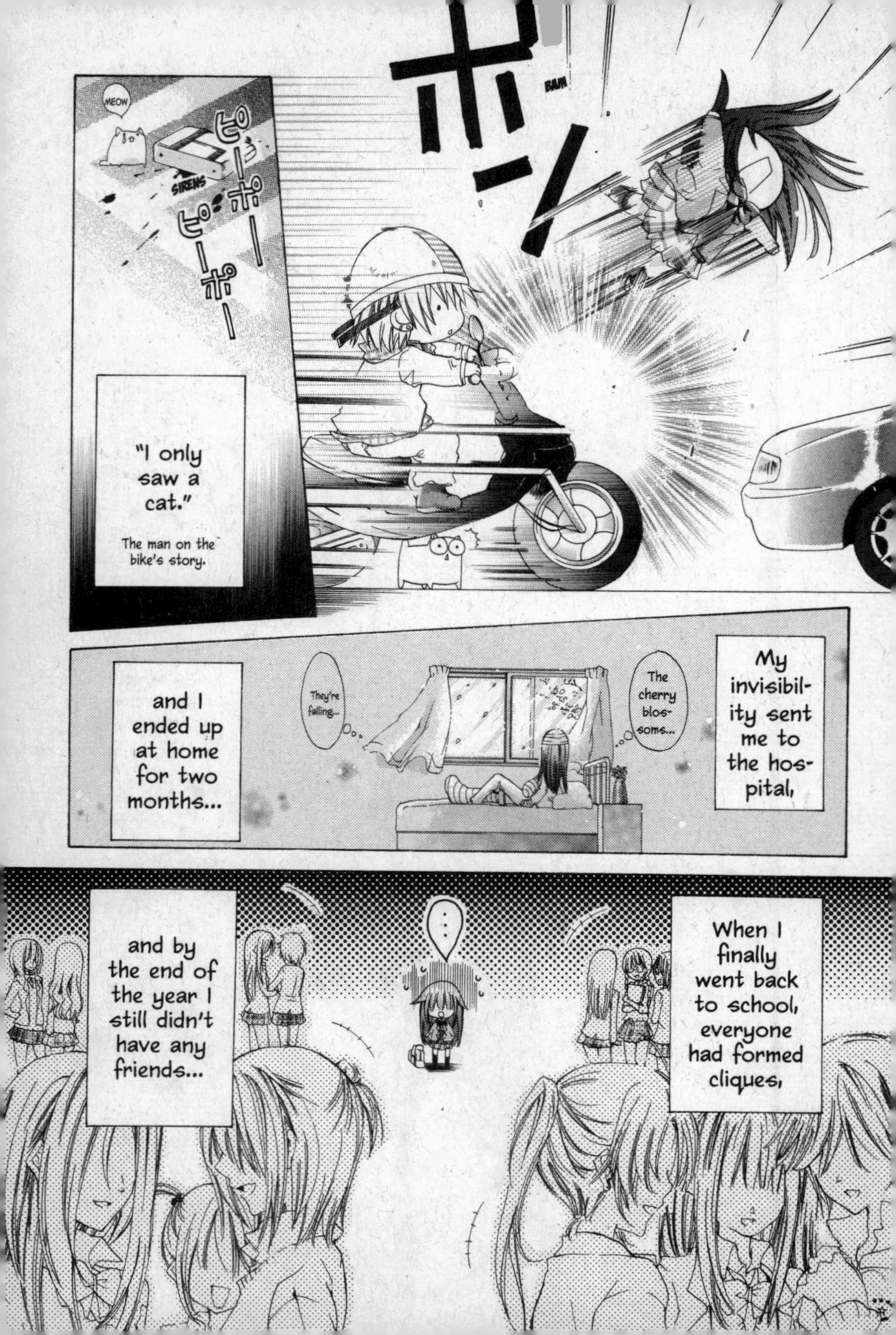

ポーン
BAM
MEOW
ピーポーピーポー
SIRENS
"I only saw a cat."
The man on the bike's story.
My invisibility sent me to the hospital,
The cherry blossoms...
They're falling...
and I ended up at home for two months...
When I finally went back to school, everyone had formed cliques,
...
and by the end of the year I still didn't have any friends...

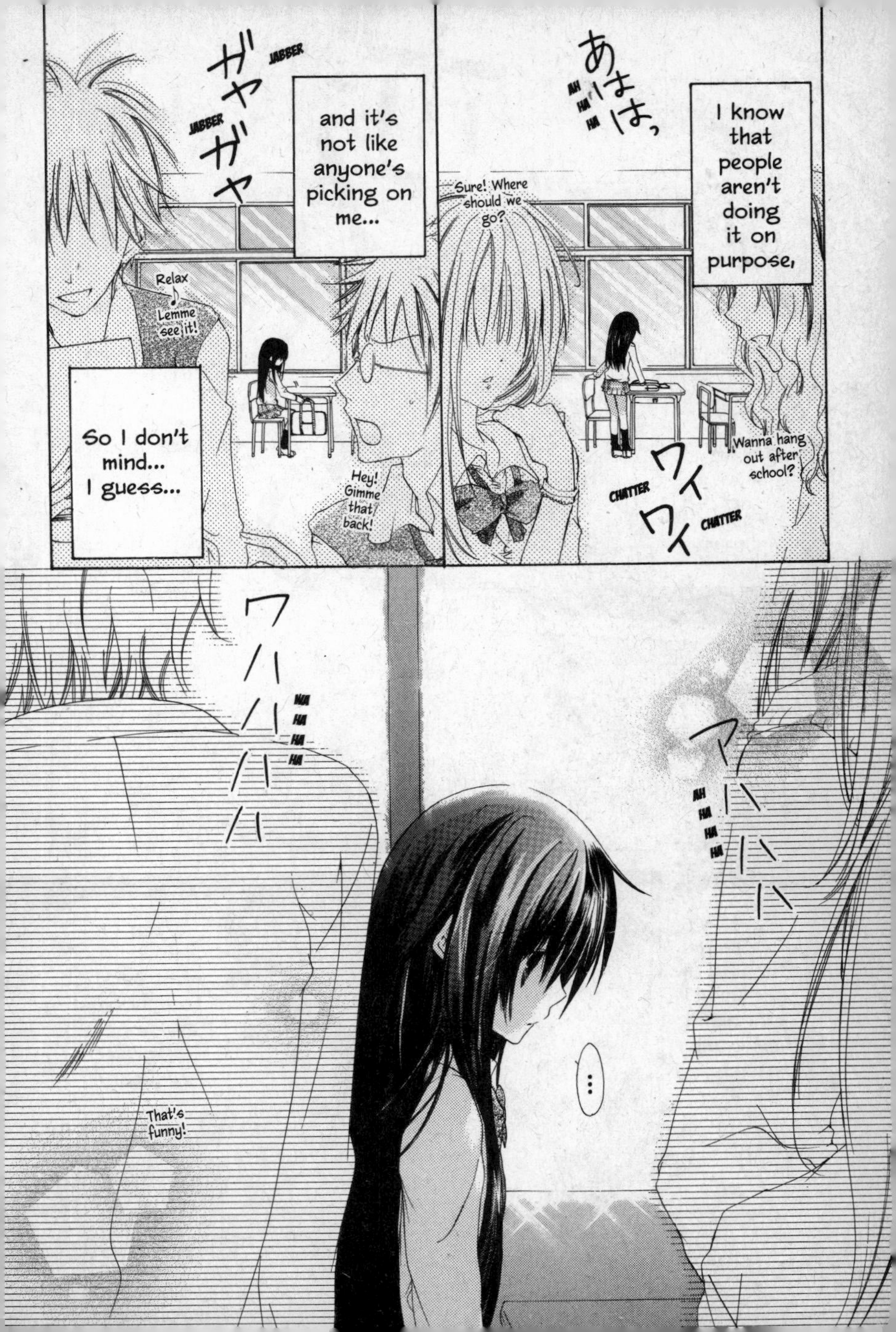
I know that people aren't doing it on purpose,
あはは、
AH HA HA
Sure! Where should we go?
Wanna hang out after school?
ワイワイ
CHATTER CHATTER
and it's not like anyone's picking on me...
ガヤガヤ
JABBER JABBER
Hey! Gimme that back!
Relax ♪ Lemme see it!
So I don't mind... I guess...
アーハハハ
AH HA HA HA
...
ワハハハハ
HA HA HA HA
That's funny!

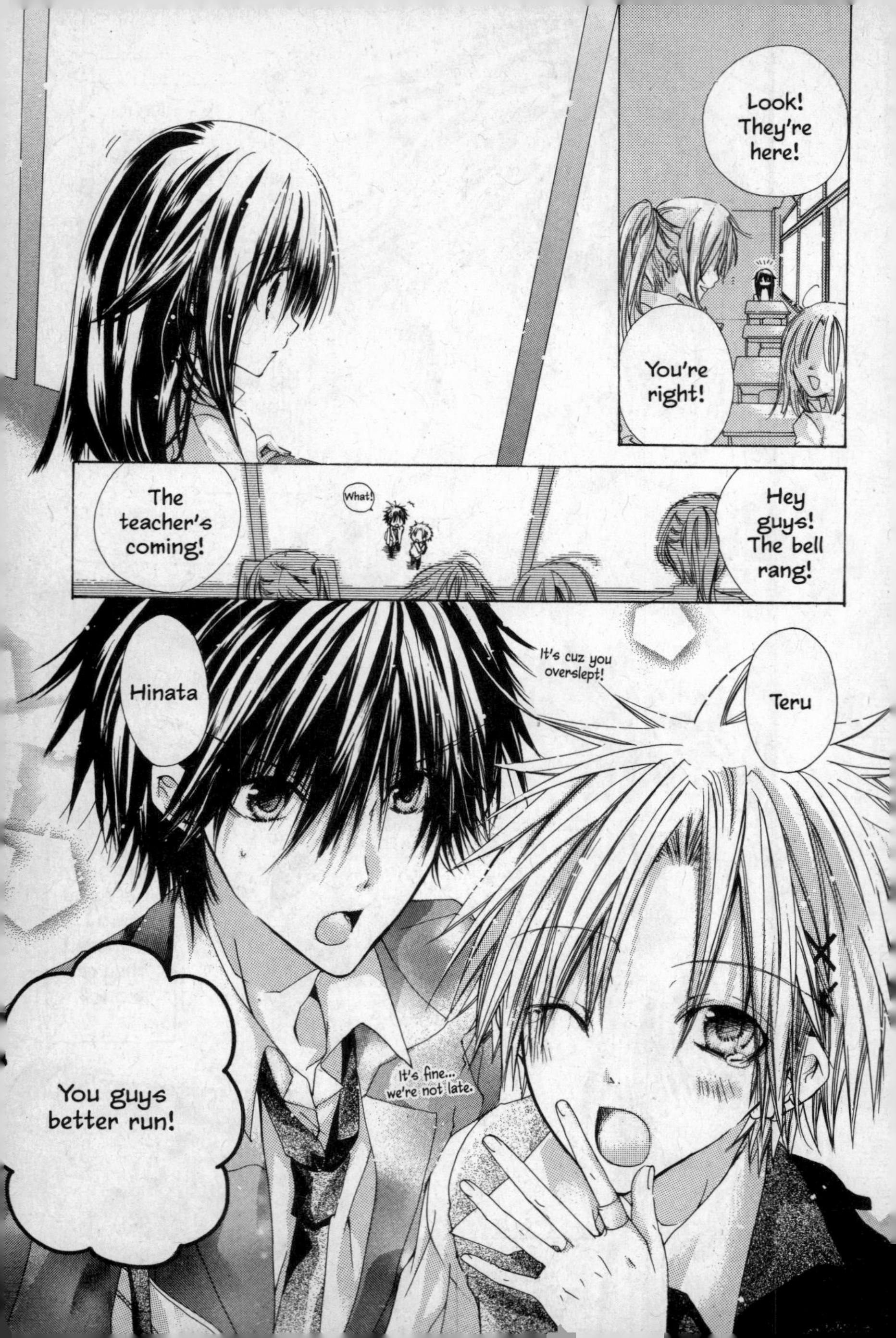
Look! They're here!
You're right!
Hey guys! The bell rang!
What!
The teacher's coming!
Teru
It's cuz you overslept!
Hinata
It's fine... we're not late.
You guys better run!

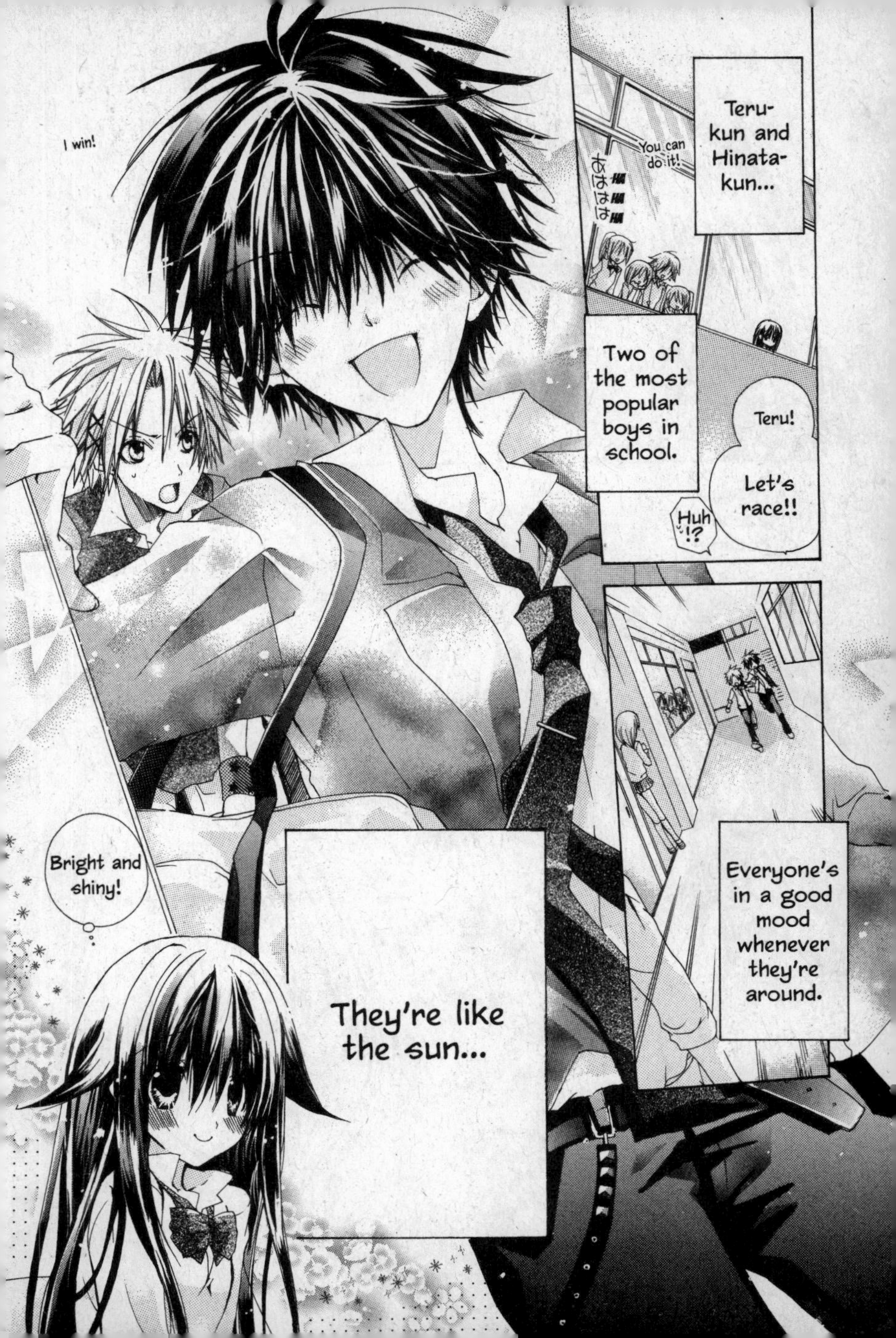

Teru-kun and Hinata-kun...
You can do it!
あははは HA HA HA
Two of the most popular boys in school.
Teru!
Let's race!!
Huh!?
Everyone's in a good mood whenever they're around.
I win!
They're like the sun...
Bright and shiny!

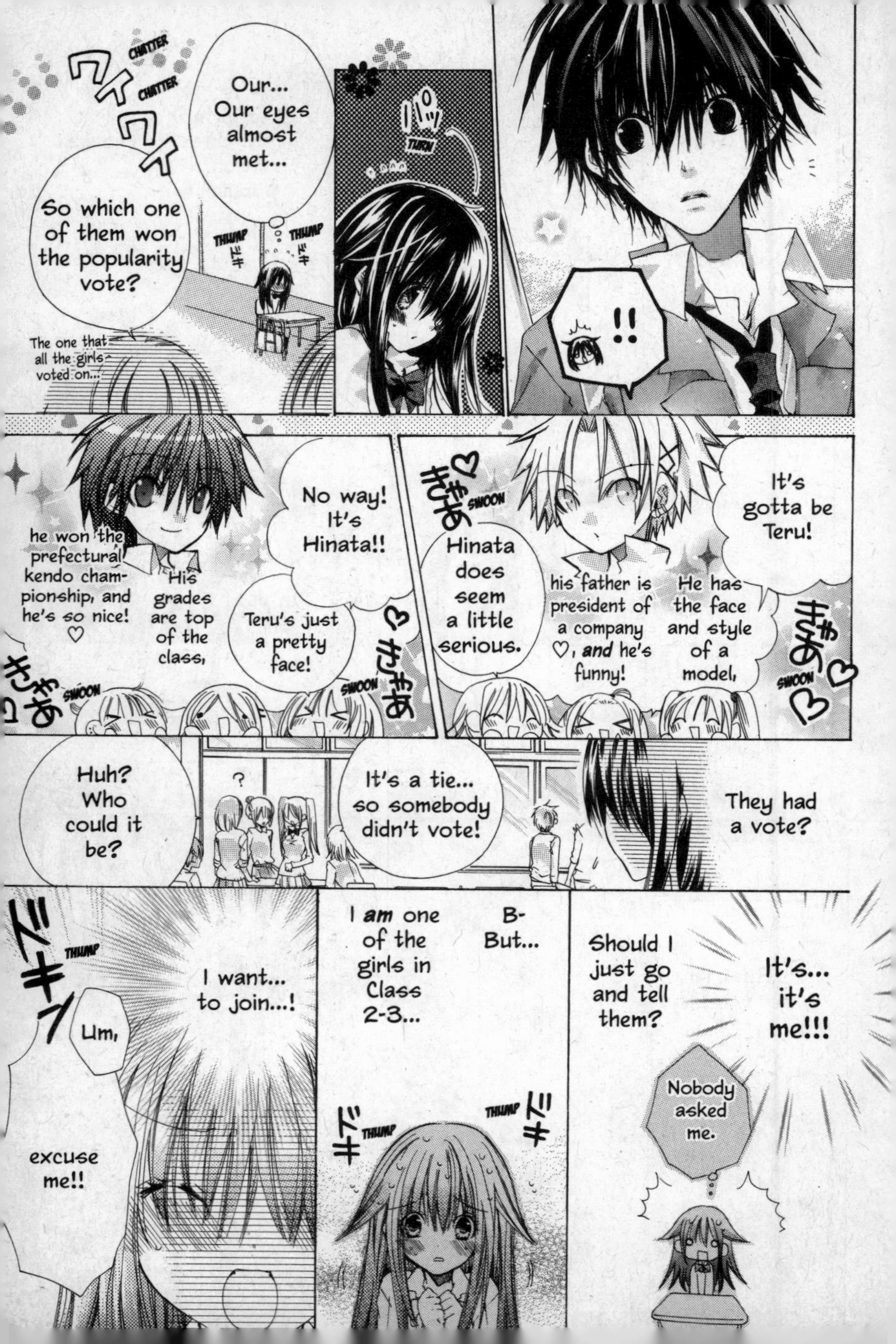
!!
TURN
Our... Our eyes almost met...
CHATTER
CHATTER
THUMP
THUMP
So which one of them won the popularity vote?
The one that all the girls voted on...
It's gotta be Teru!
He has the face and style of a model,
his father is president of a company ♡, and he's funny!
SWOON
Hinata does seem a little serious.
SWOON
No way! It's Hinata!!
His grades are top of the class,
he won the prefectural kendo championship, and he's so nice! ♡
Teru's just a pretty face!
SWOON
SWOON
They had a vote?
It's a tie... so somebody didn't vote!
?
Huh? Who could it be?
It's... it's me!!!
Should I just go and tell them?
Nobody asked me.
B-But...
I *am* one of the girls in Class 2-3...
THUMP
THUMP
I want... to join...!
THUMP
Um,
excuse me!!

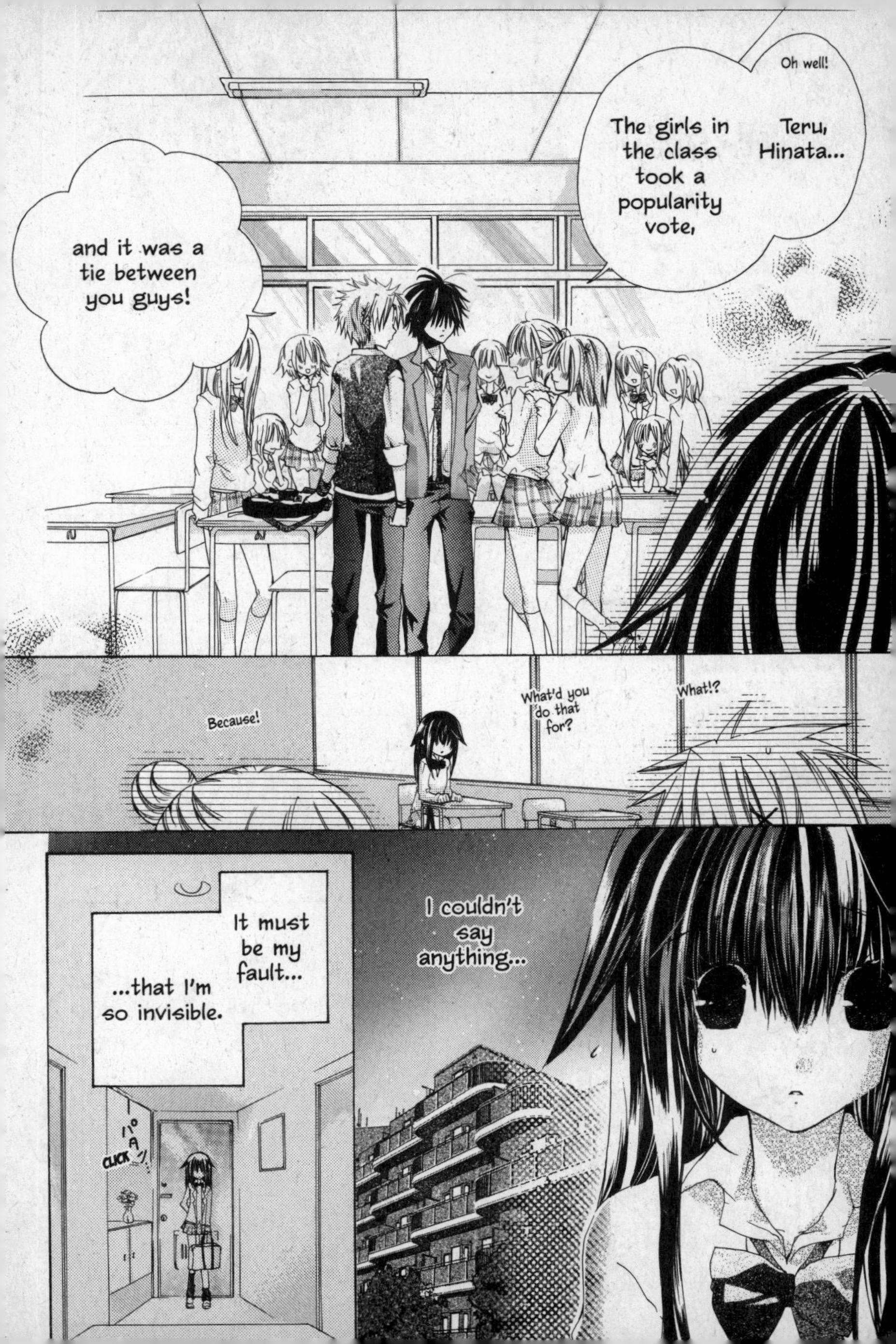

Oh well!
Teru, Hinata...
The girls in the class took a popularity vote,
and it was a tie between you guys!
What!?
What'd you do that for?
Because!
I couldn't say anything...
It must be my fault...
...that I'm so invisible.
CLICK

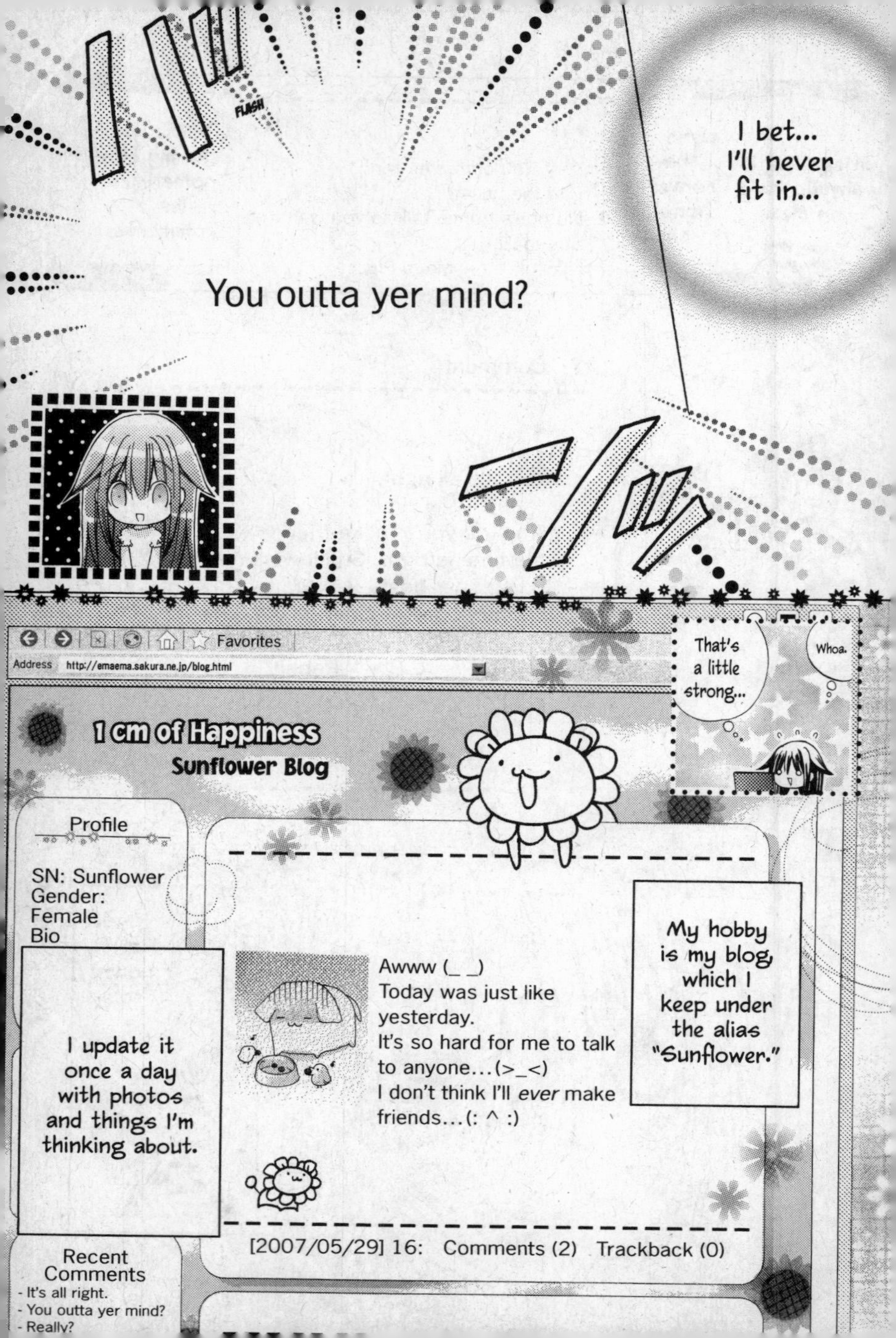

I bet... I'll never fit in...
FLASH
You outta yer mind?
Whoa.
That's a little strong...
Favorites
Address http://emaema.sakura.ne.jp/blog.html
1 cm of Happiness
Sunflower Blog
My hobby is my blog, which I keep under the alias "Sunflower."
Profile
SN: Sunflower
Gender: Female
Bio
I update it once a day with photos and things I'm thinking about.
Awww (_ _)
Today was just like yesterday.
It's so hard for me to talk to anyone…(>_<)
I don't think I'll *ever* make friends…(: ^ :)
[2007/05/29] 16: Comments (2) Trackback (0)
Recent Comments
- It's all right.
- You outta yer mind?
- Really?

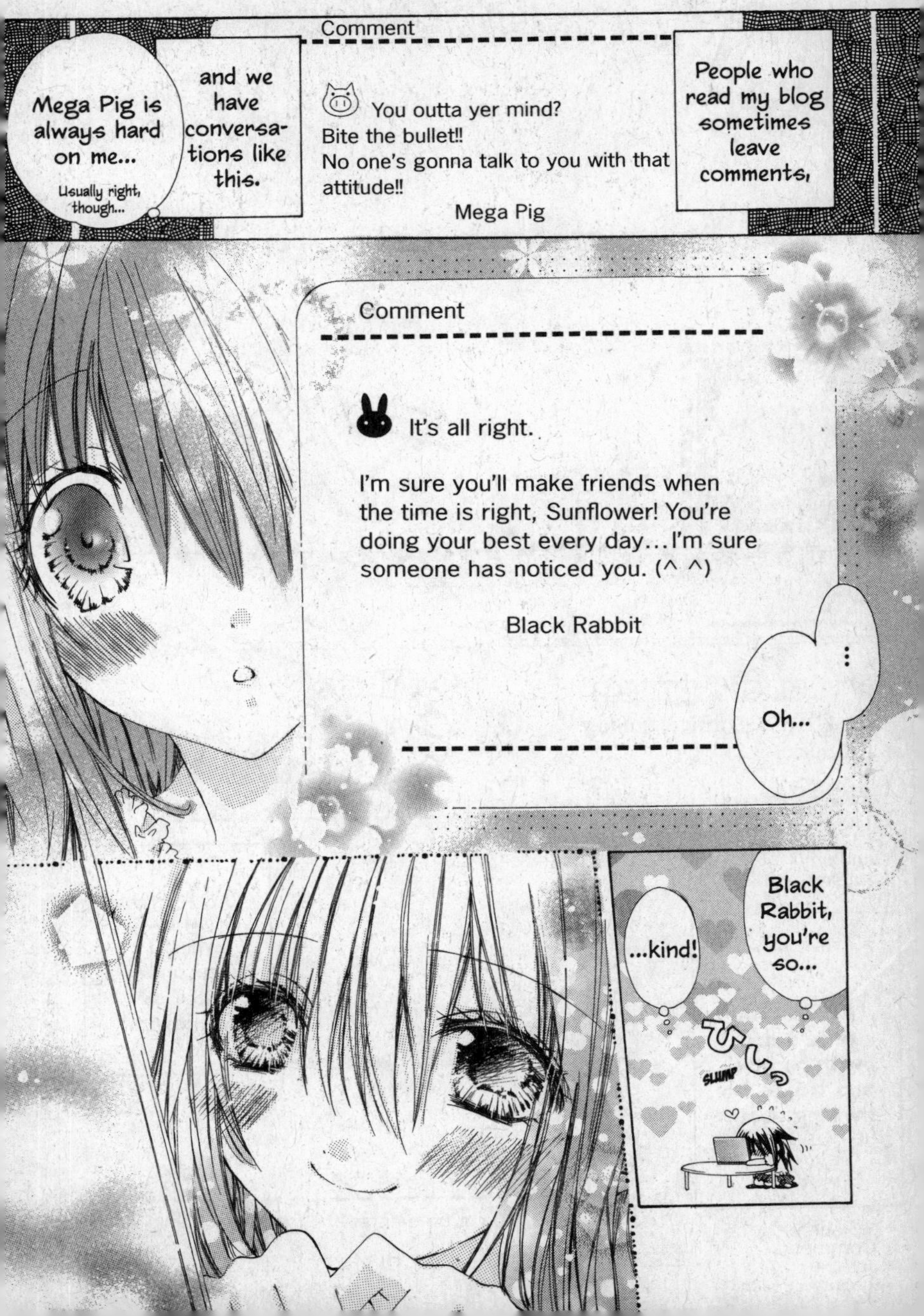
People who read my blog sometimes leave comments,
Comment
You outta yer mind?
Bite the bullet!!
No one's gonna talk to you with that attitude!!
Mega Pig
and we have conversations like this.
Mega Pig is always hard on me...
Usually right, though...
Comment
It's all right.
I'm sure you'll make friends when the time is right, Sunflower! You're doing your best every day...I'm sure someone has noticed you. (^ ^)
Black Rabbit
...
Oh...
Black Rabbit, you're so...
...kind!
SLUMP

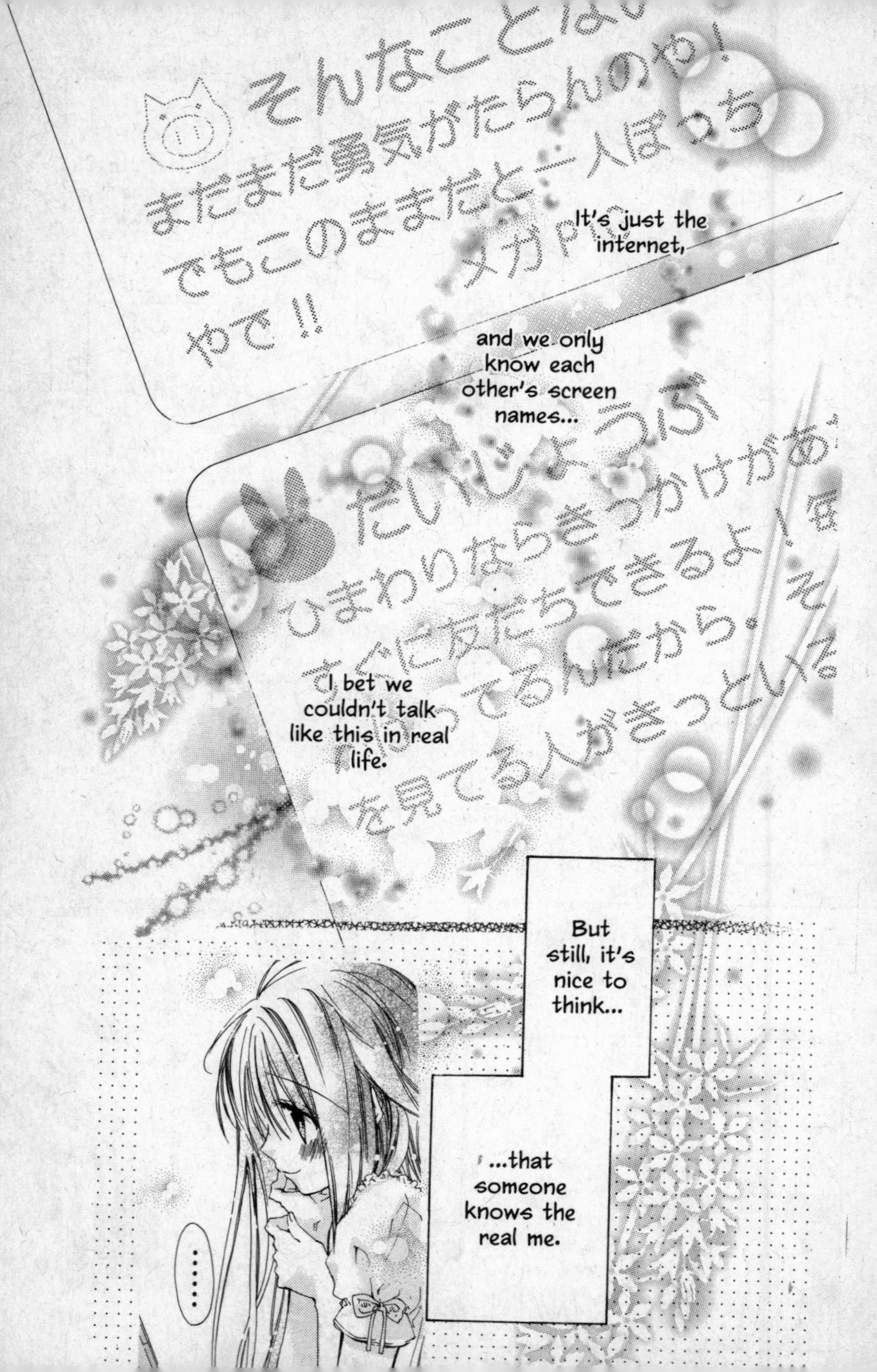

まだまだ勇気がたらんのや!
でもこのままだと一人ぼっち
やで!!
It's just the internet,
and we only know each other's screen names...
だいじょうぶ
すぐに友だちできるよ!
I bet we couldn't talk like this in real life.
But still, it's nice to think...
...that someone knows the real me.
……

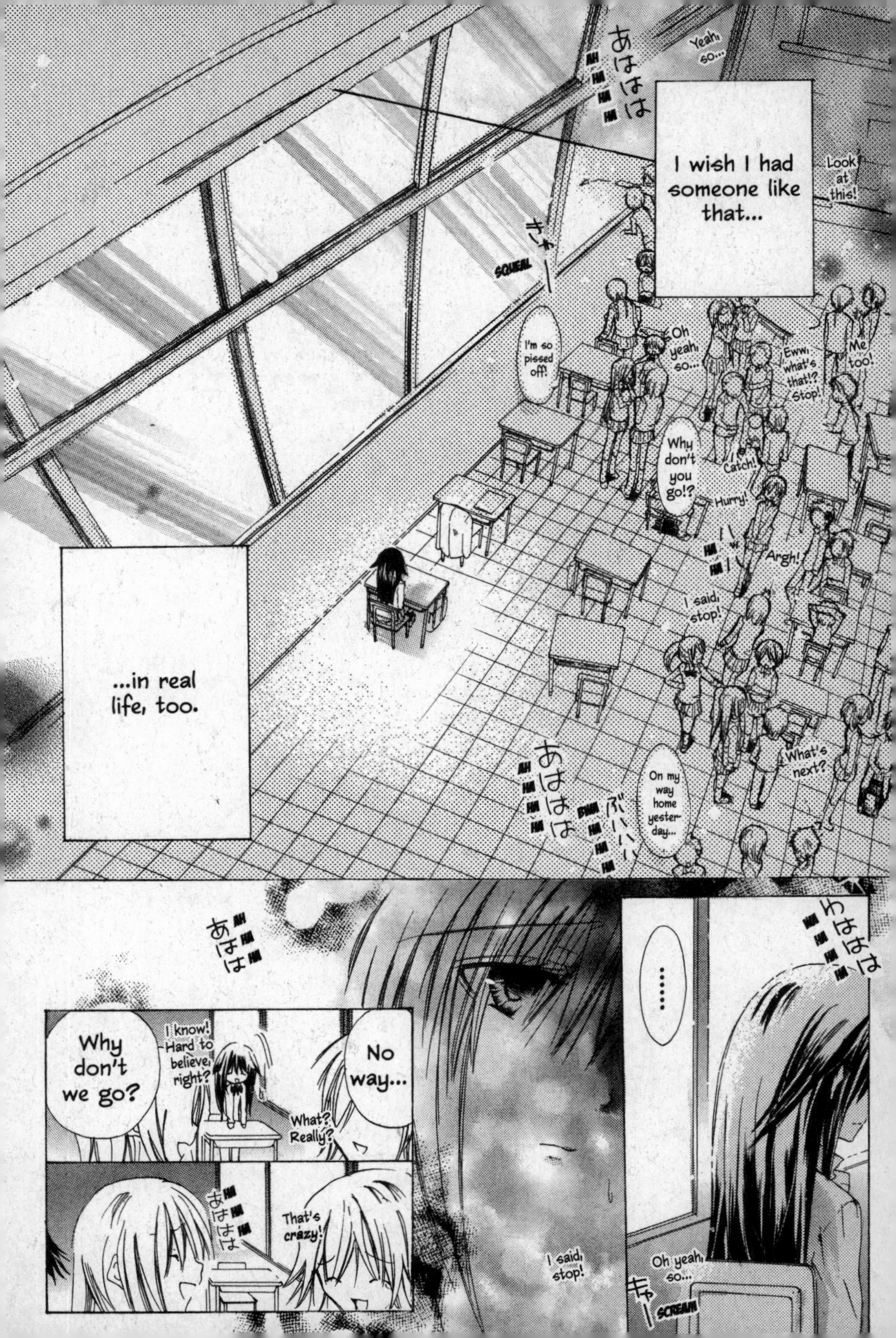
Yeah, so...
あははは
AH HA HA HA
I wish I had someone like that...
Look at this!
きゃー
SQUEAL
Me too!
Eww, what's that!? Stop!
Oh yeah, so...
I'm so pissed off!
Why don't you go!?
Catch!
Hurry!
HA HA
Argh!
I said, stop!
...in real life, too.
What's next?
On my way home yesterday...
ぶははは
BWA HA HA HA
あははは
AH HA HA HA
わははは
HA HA HA HA
......
Oh yeah, so...
キャー
SCREAM
I said, stop!
あはは
AH HA HA
No way...
What? Really?
I know! Hard to believe, right?
Why don't we go?
That's crazy!
あははは
HA HA HA

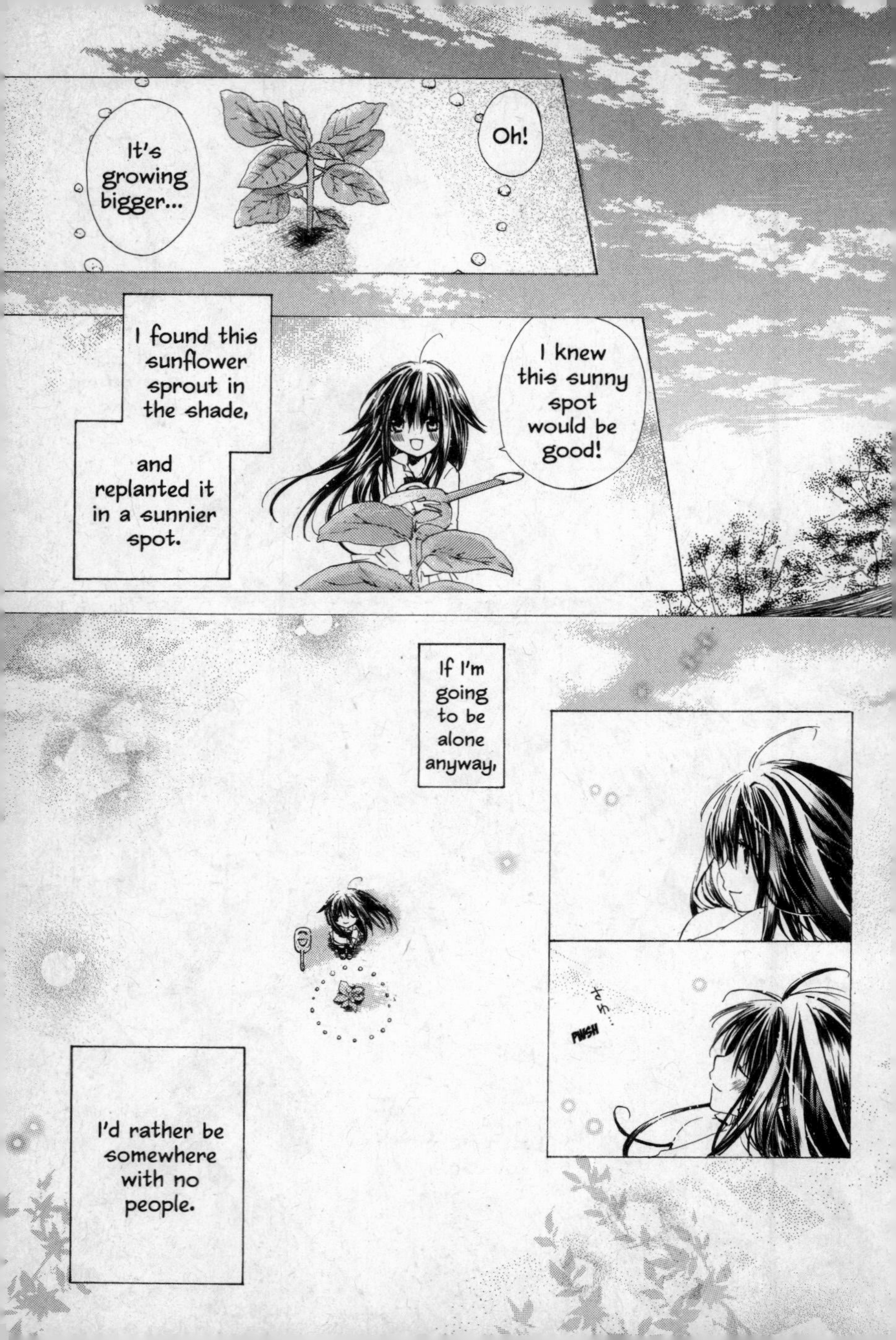
Oh!
It's growing bigger...
I knew this sunny spot would be good!
I found this sunflower sprout in the shade,
and replanted it in a sunnier spot.
さわ…
PWSH
If I'm going to be alone anyway,
I'd rather be somewhere with no people.

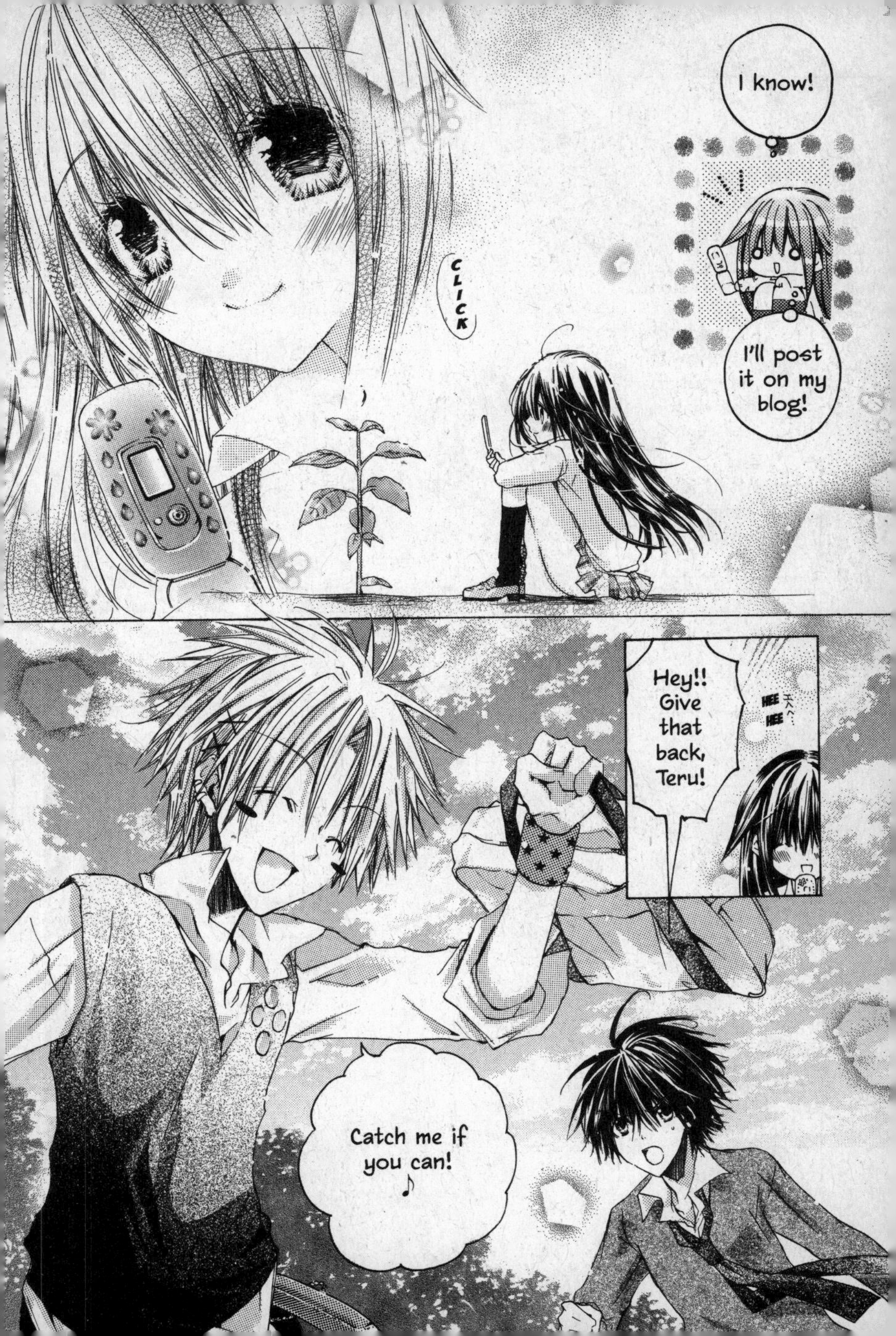
I know!
I'll post it on my blog!
CLICK
Hey!! Give that back, Teru!
HEE HEE
Catch me if you can! ♪

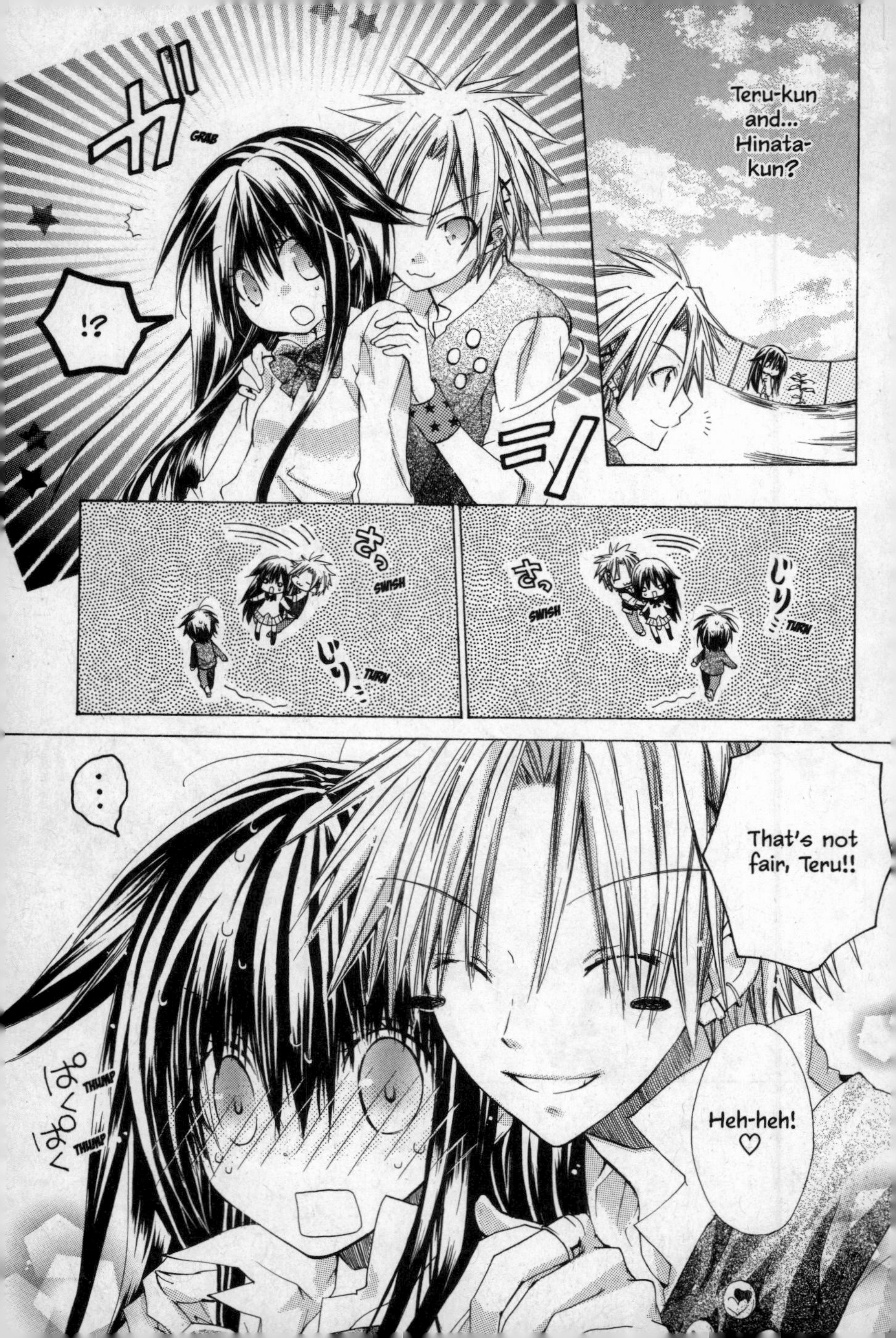

Teru-kun and... Hinata-kun?
GRAB
!?
SWISH
TURN
SWISH
TURN
That's not fair, Teru!!
Heh-heh! ♡
...
THUMP
THUMP

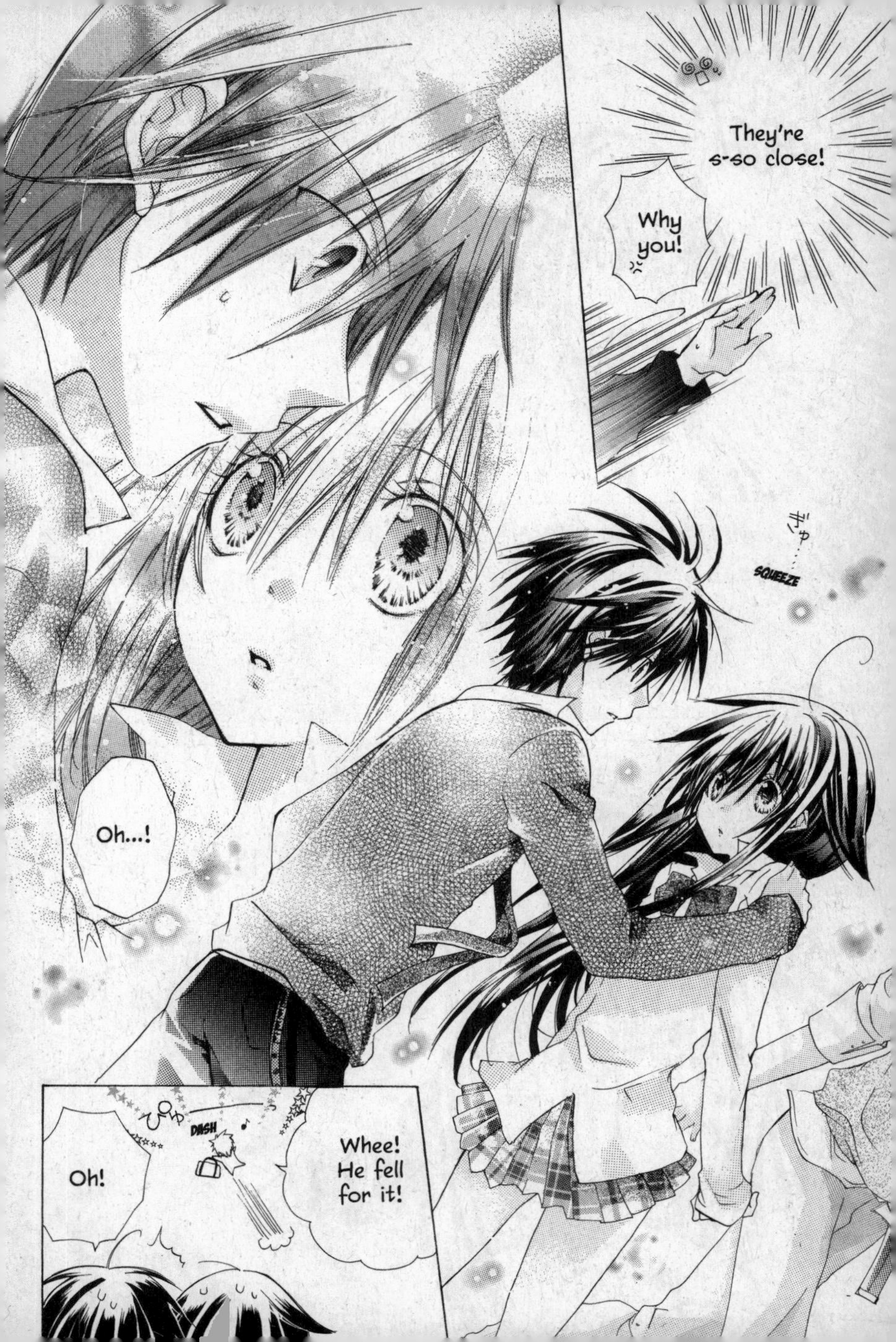
They're s-so close!
Why you!
ぎゅ…
SQUEEZE
Oh...!
Whee! He fell for it!
DASH
Oh!

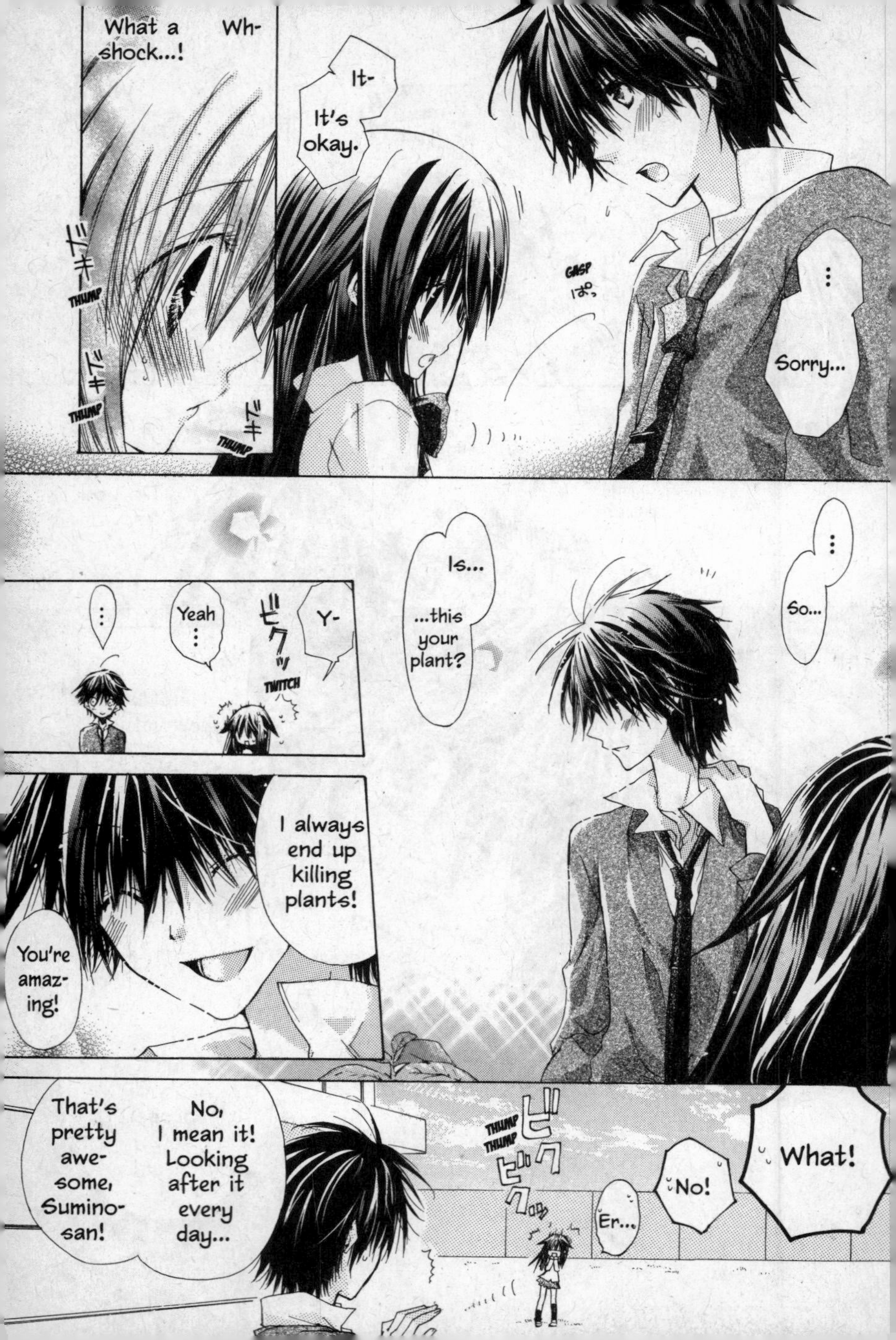

...
Sorry...
GASP
ぱっ
It-
It's okay.
Wh-
What a shock...!
ドキ
THUMP
ドキ
THUMP
ドキ
THUMP
...
So...
Is...
...this your plant?
Y-
ビクッ
TWITCH
Yeah
...
...
I always end up killing plants!
You're amazing!
What!
No!
Er...
ビクビクッ
THUMP THUMP
No, I mean it! Looking after it every day...
That's pretty awesome, Sumino-san!

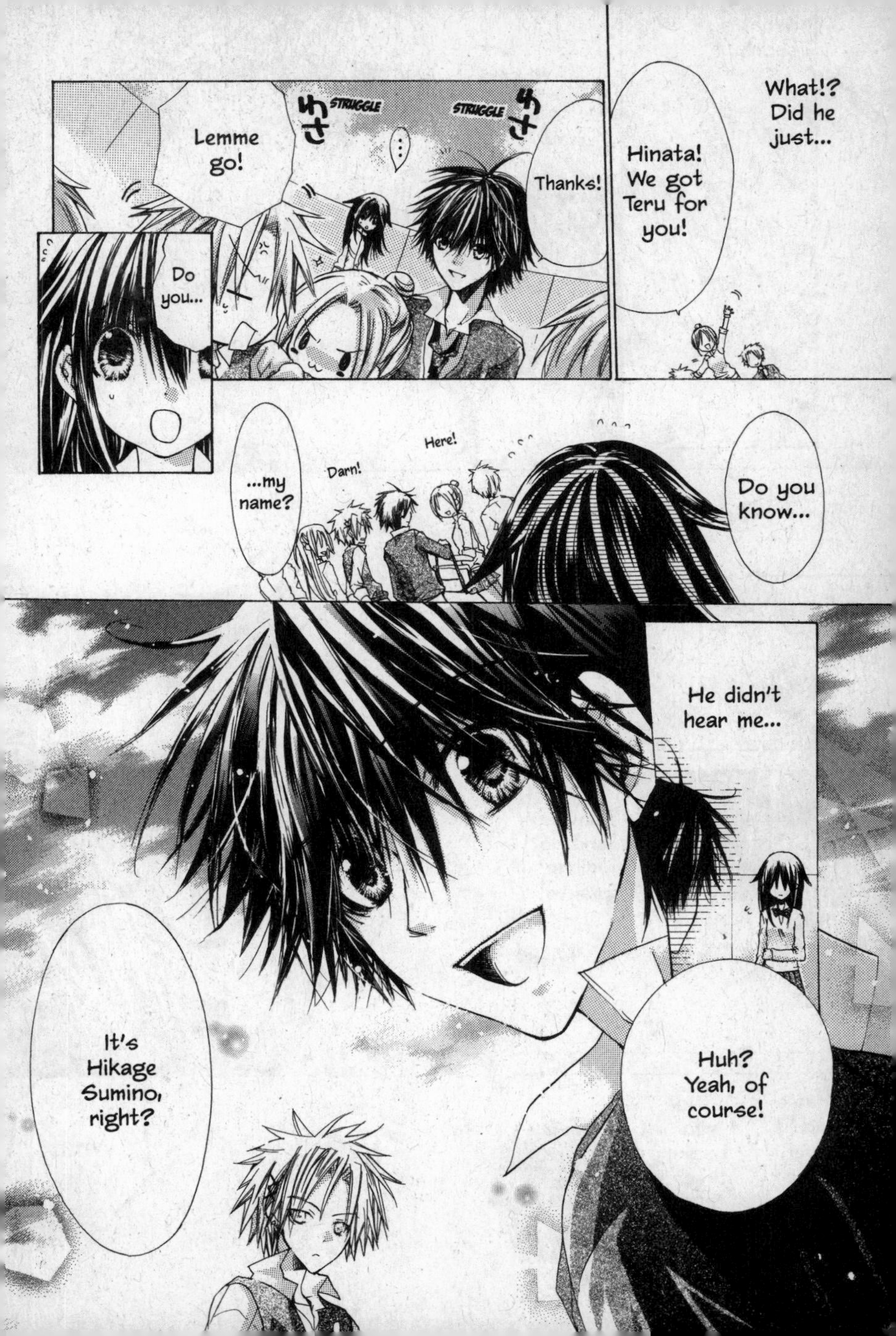
What!? Did he just...
Hinata! We got Teru for you!
ゆさ STRUGGLE
Thanks!
...
ゆさ STRUGGLE
Lemme go!
Do you...
Do you know...
Here!
Darn!
...my name?
He didn't hear me...
Huh? Yeah, of course!
It's Hikage Sumino, right?

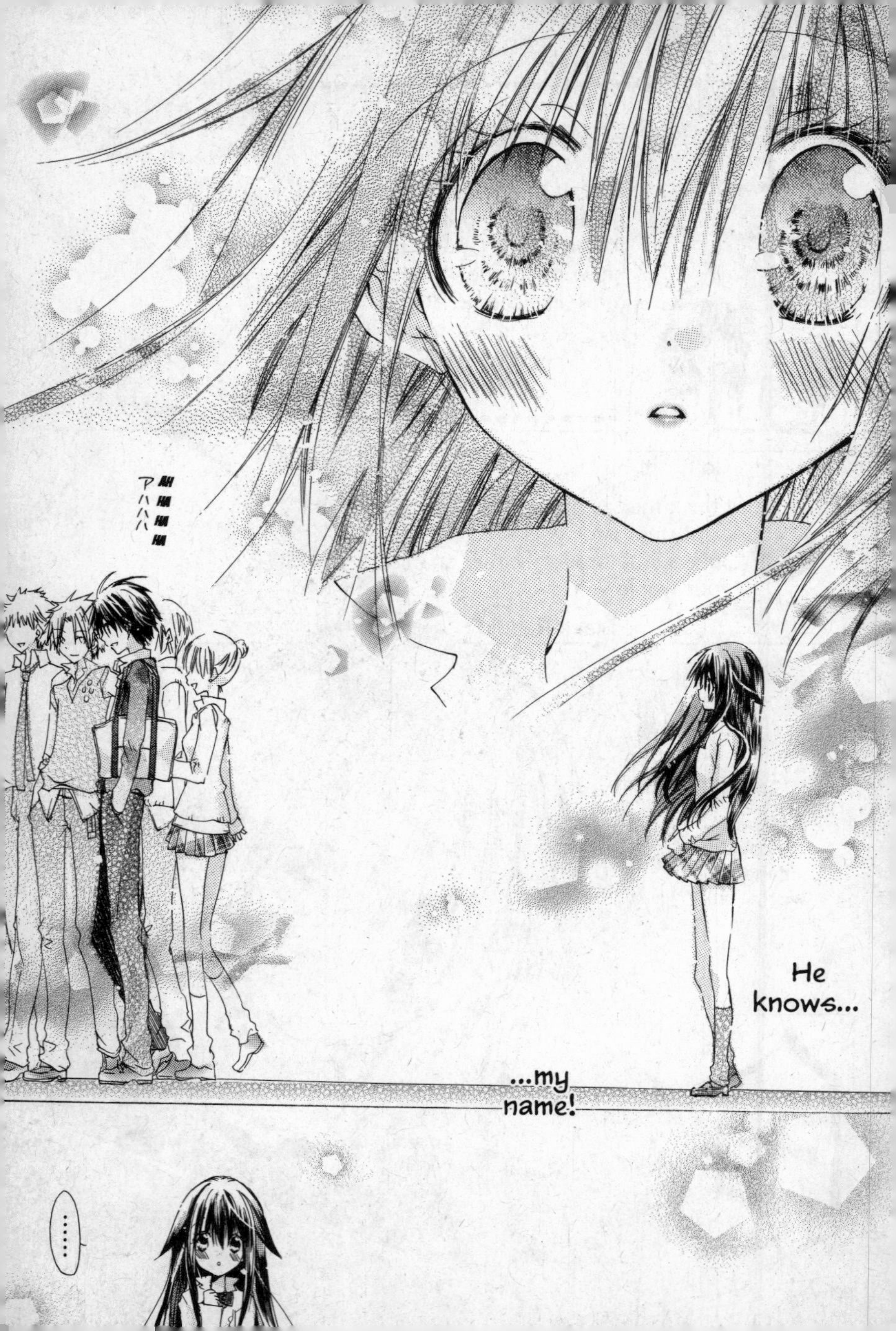
He knows...
...my name!
AH HA HA HA
アハハハ
......

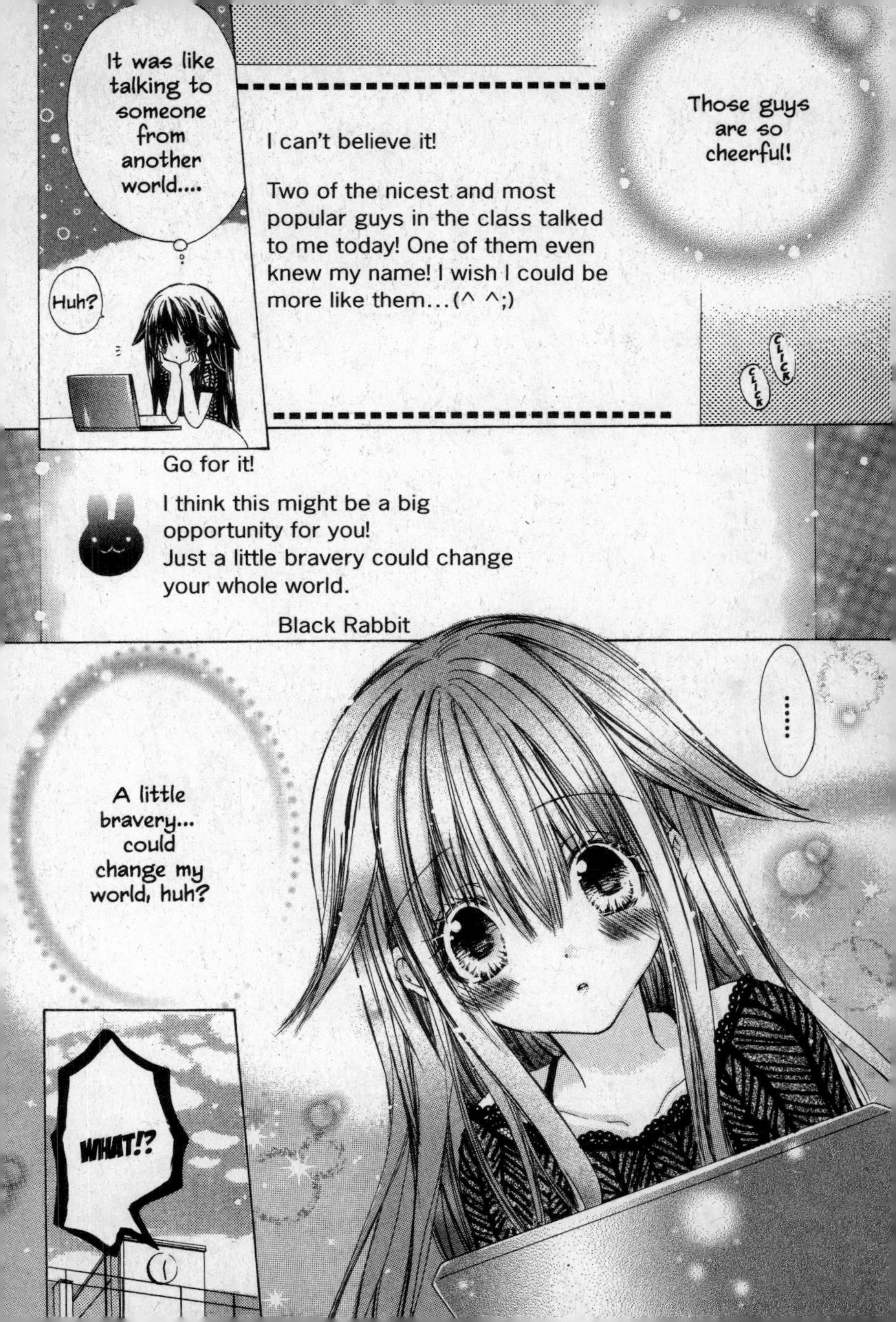
Those guys are so cheerful!
CLICK
CLICK
I can't believe it!
Two of the nicest and most popular guys in the class talked to me today! One of them even knew my name! I wish I could be more like them…(^ ^;)
It was like talking to someone from another world....
Huh?
Go for it!
I think this might be a big opportunity for you!
Just a little bravery could change your whole world.
Black Rabbit
......
A little bravery... could change my world, huh?
WHAT!?

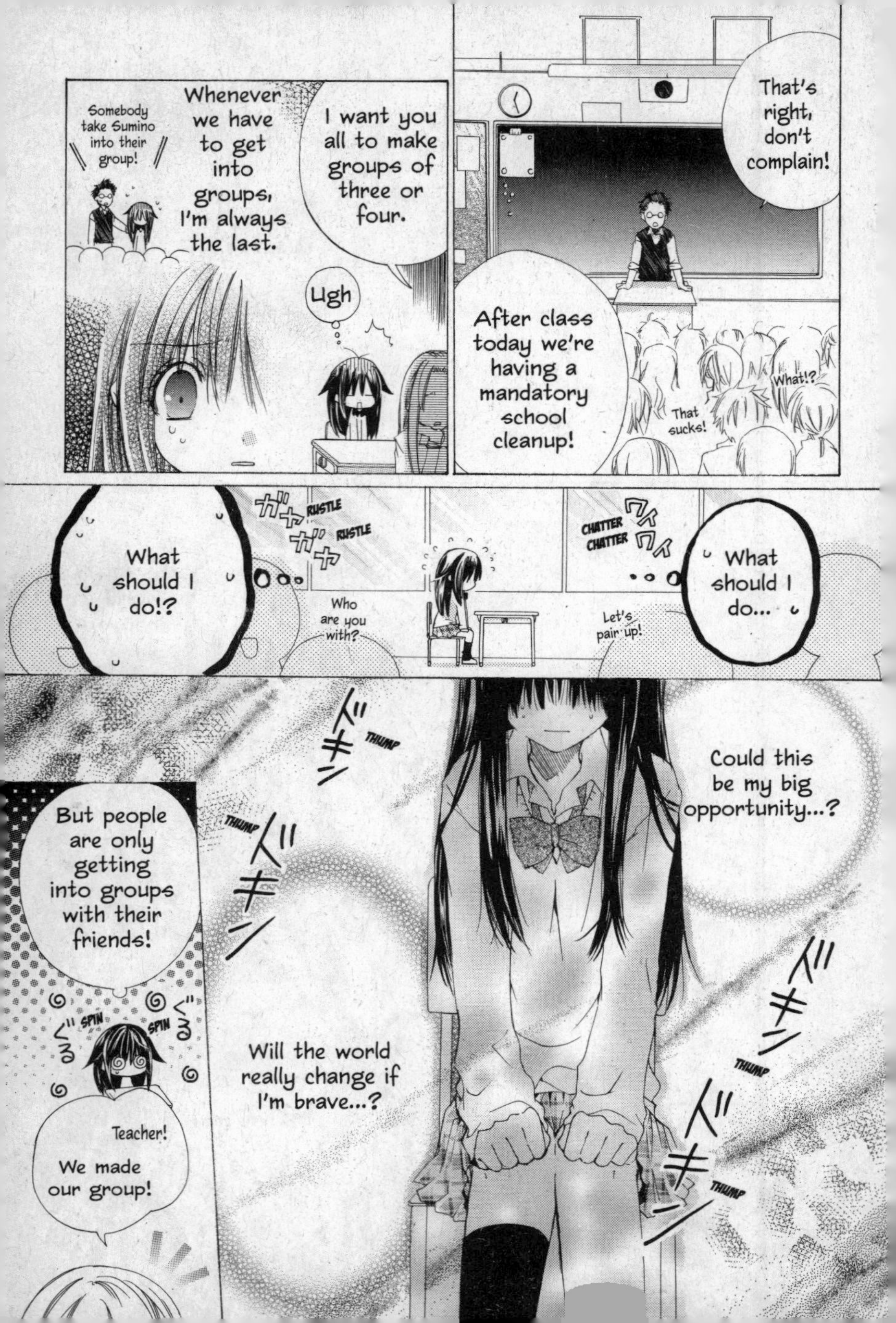
That's right, don't complain!
After class today we're having a mandatory school cleanup!
What!?
That sucks!
I want you all to make groups of three or four.
Whenever we have to get into groups, I'm always the last.
Somebody take Sumino into their group!
Ugh
What should I do...
Let's pair up!
CHATTER CHATTER
Who are you with?
RUSTLE RUSTLE
What should I do!?
Could this be my big opportunity...?
THUMP
THUMP
THUMP
THUMP
Will the world really change if I'm brave...?
But people are only getting into groups with their friends!
SPIN SPIN
Teacher!
We made our group!

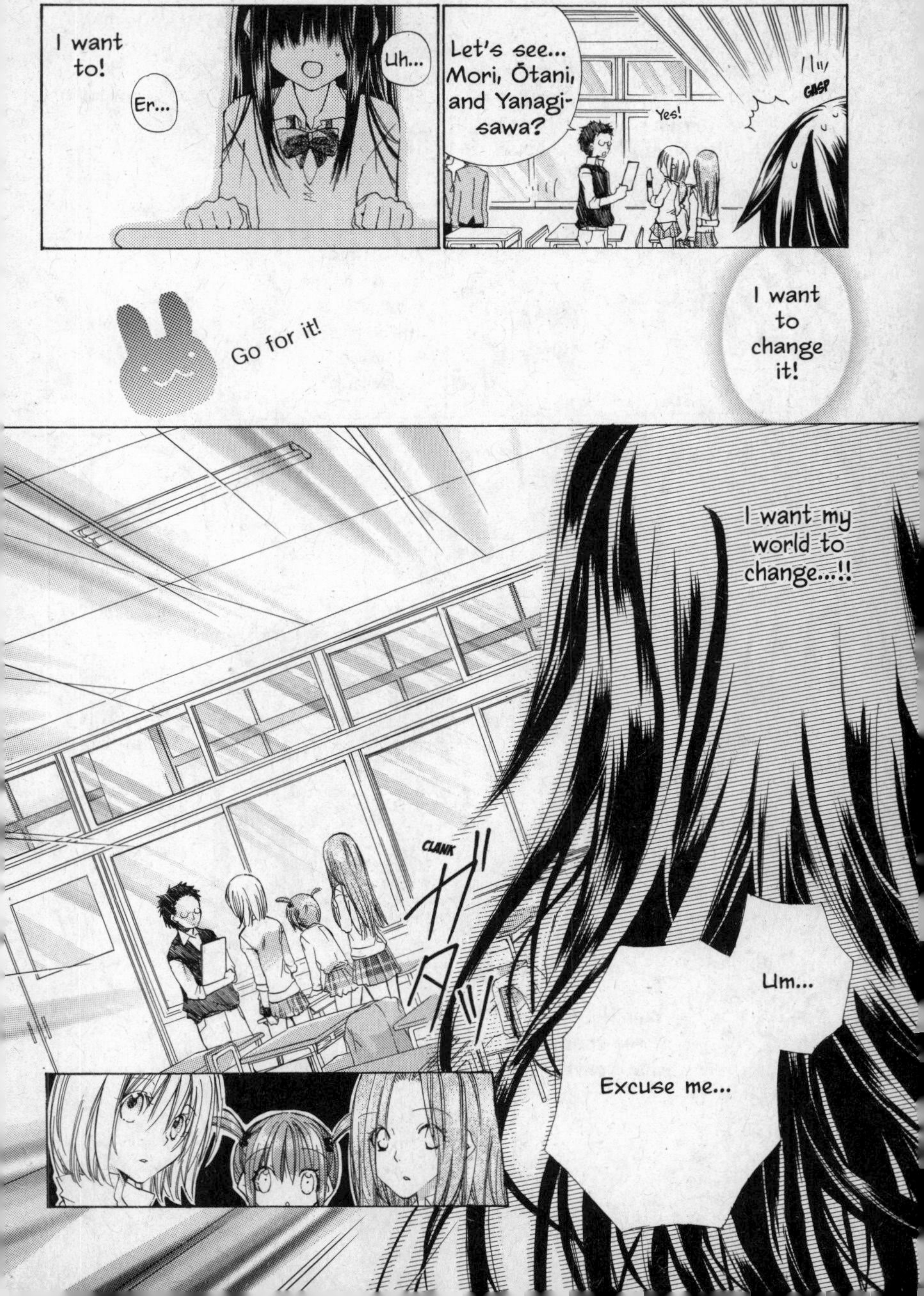
Let's see... Mori, Ōtani, and Yanagi-sawa?
Yes!
GASP
Uh...
I want to!
Er...
I want to change it!
Go for it!
I want my world to change...!!
CLANK
Um...
Excuse me...

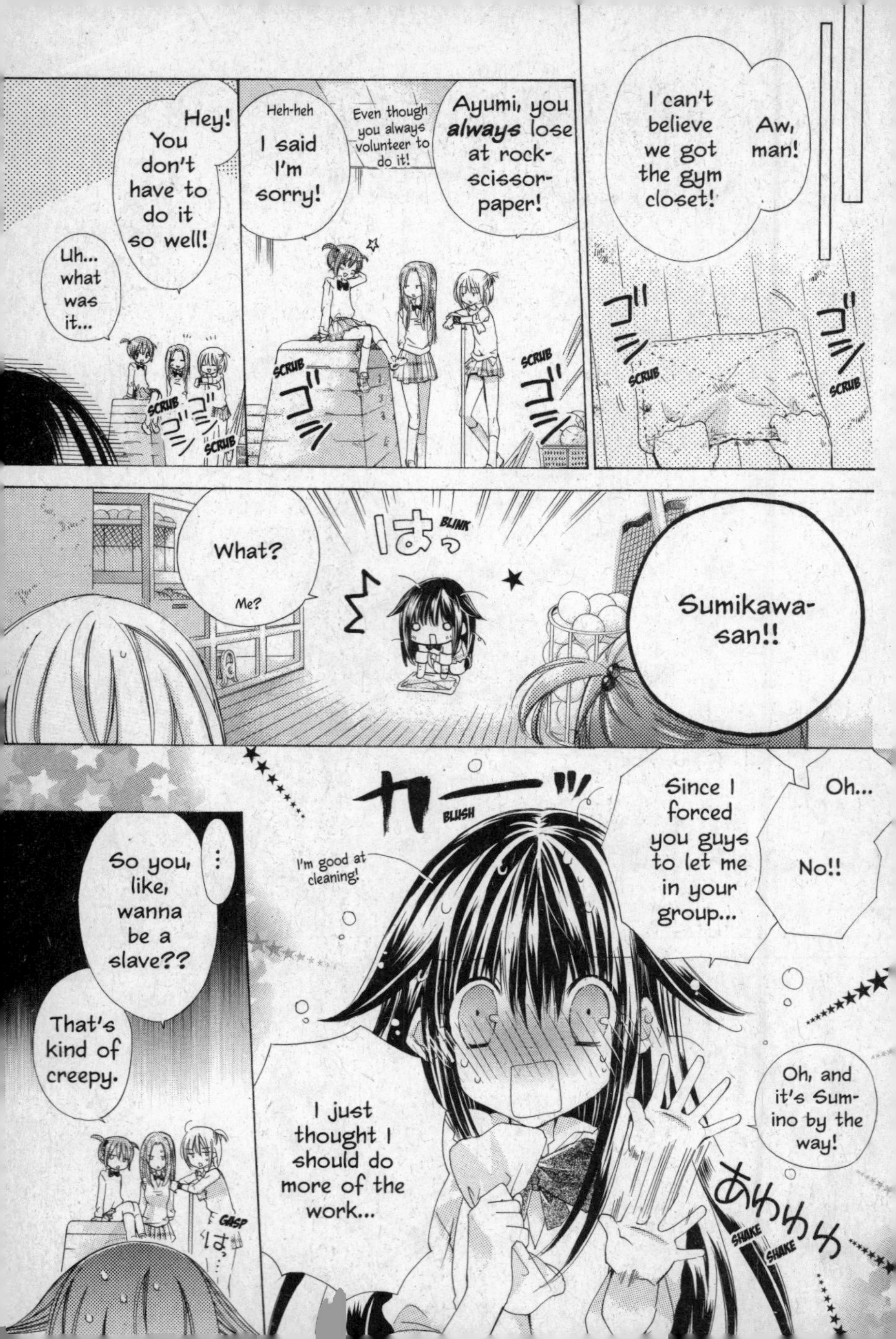
Aw, man!
I can't believe we got the gym closet!
ゴシ SCRUB
ゴシ SCRUB
Ayumi, you **always** lose at rock-scissor-paper!
Even though you always volunteer to do it!
Heh-heh I said I'm sorry!
SCRUB ゴシ
SCRUB ゴシ
Hey! You don't have to do it so well!
Uh... what was it...
SCRUB ゴシゴシ SCRUB
Sumikawa-san!!
はっ BLINK
What? Me?
Oh... No!!
Since I forced you guys to let me in your group...
カーッ BLUSH
I'm good at cleaning!
Oh, and it's Sumino by the way!
あわわわ SHAKE SHAKE
I just thought I should do more of the work...
...
So you, like, wanna be a slave??
That's kind of creepy.
GASP は,

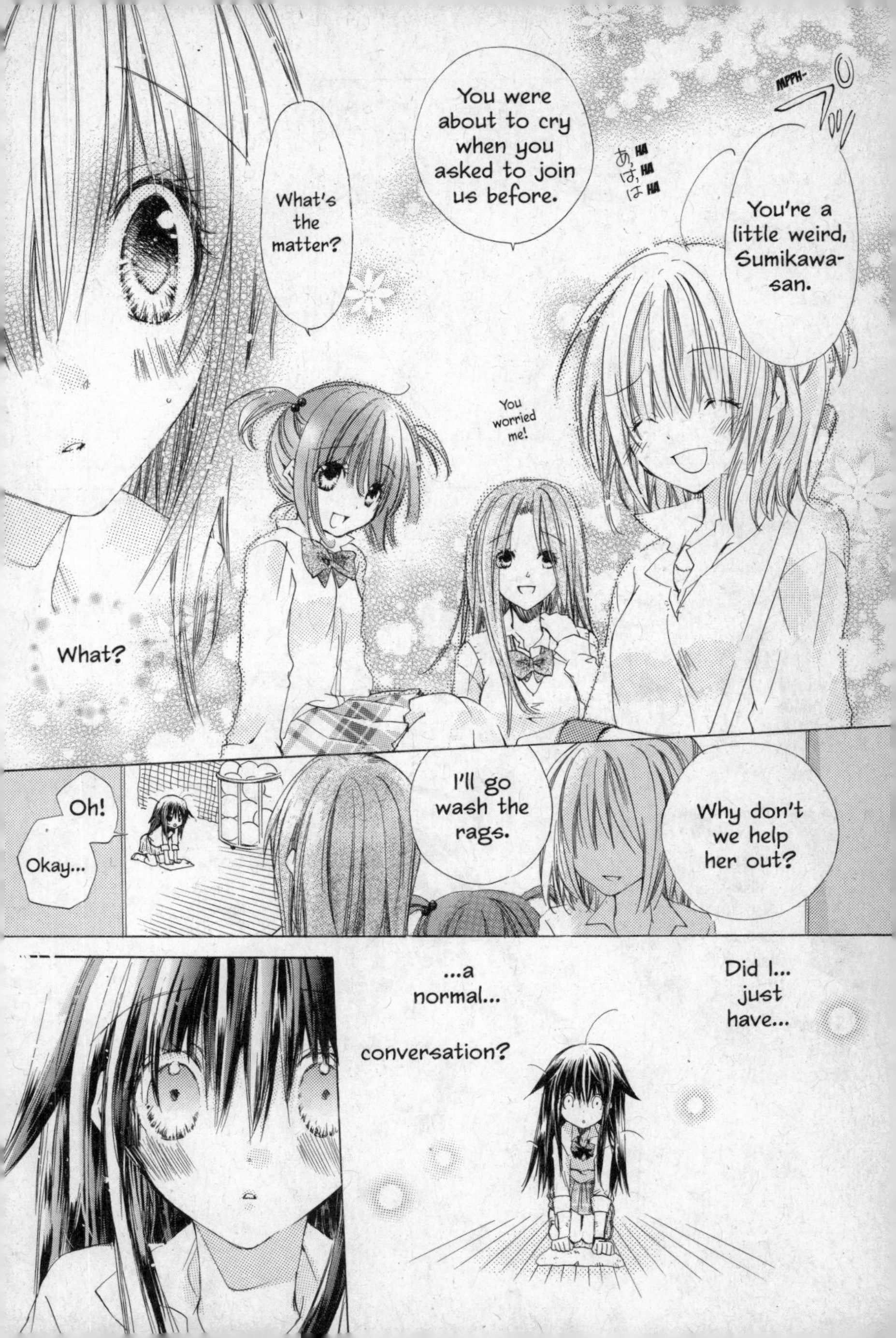
MPPH-
You're a little weird, Sumikawa-san.
あは、は HA HA HA
You were about to cry when you asked to join us before.
You worried me!
What's the matter?
What?
Why don't we help her out?
I'll go wash the rags.
Oh!
Okay...
Did I... just have...
...a normal...
conversation?

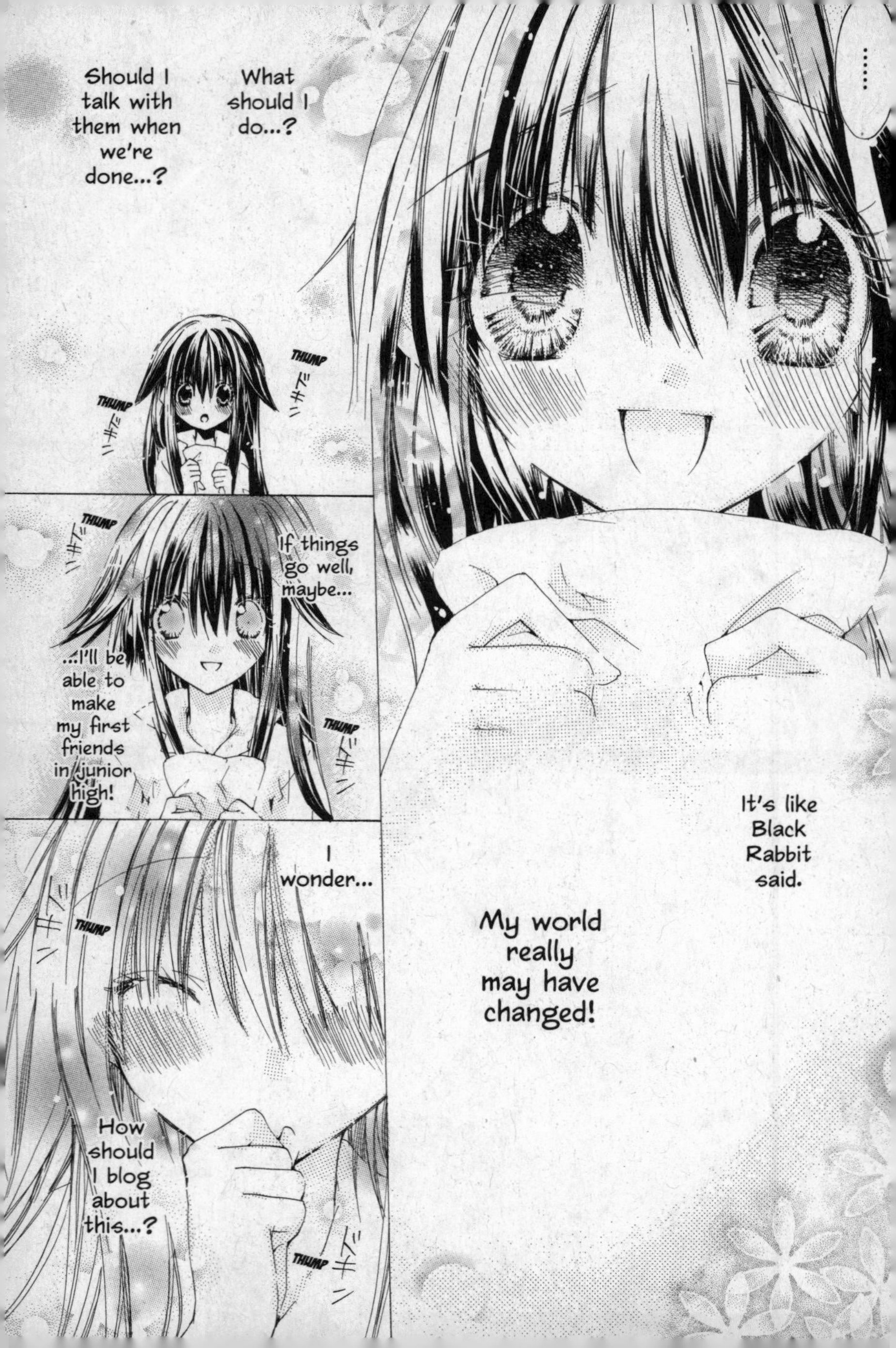
……
It's like Black Rabbit said.
My world really may have changed!
What should I do...?
Should I talk with them when we're done...?
THUMP
THUMP
If things go well, maybe...
THUMP
...I'll be able to make my first friends in junior high!
THUMP
I wonder...
THUMP
How should I blog about this...?
THUMP

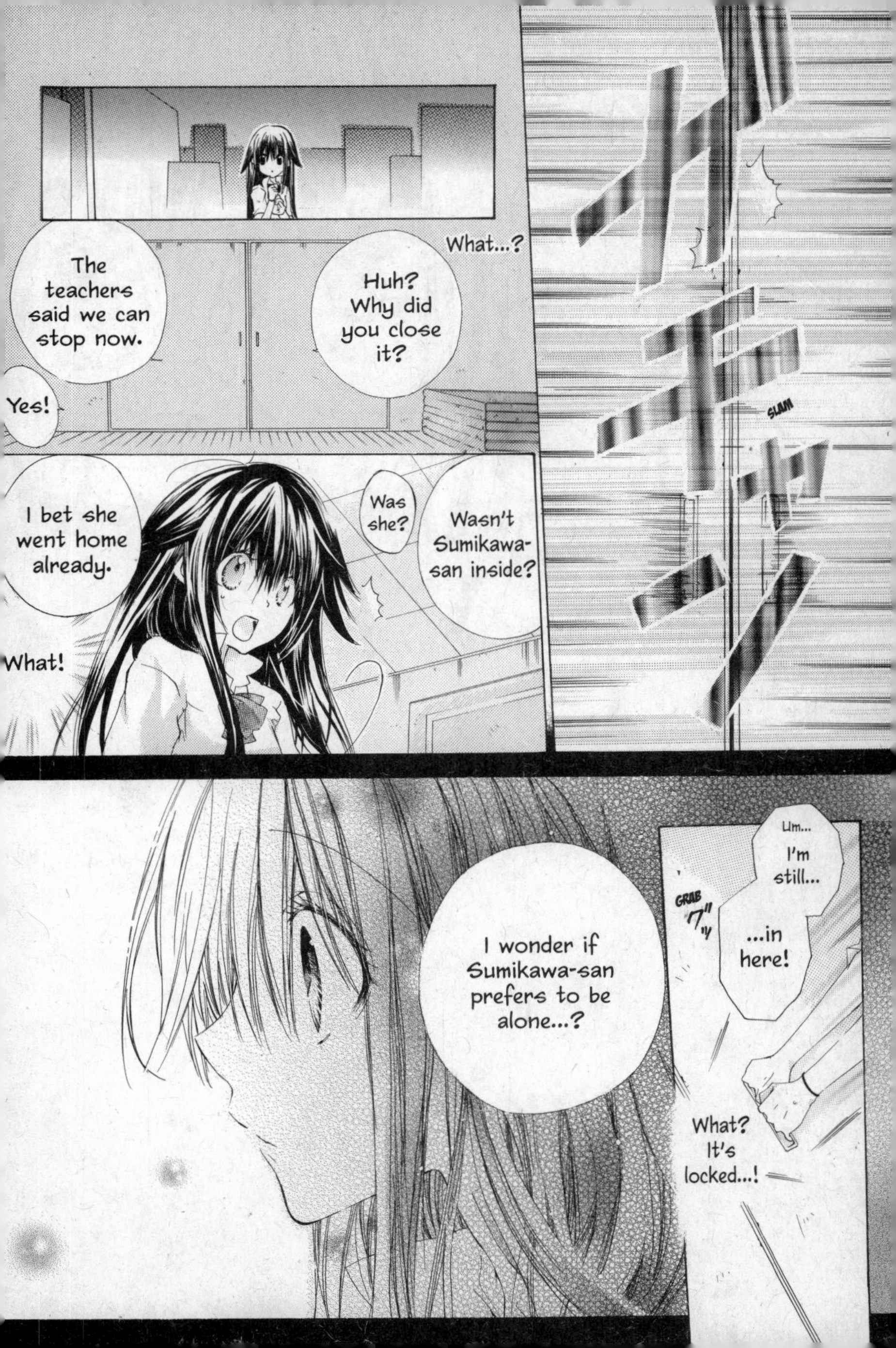
SLAM
What...?
Huh? Why did you close it?
The teachers said we can stop now.
Yes!
Wasn't Sumikawa-san inside?
Was she?
I bet she went home already.
What!
Um... I'm still...
GRAB
...in here!
What? It's locked...!
I wonder if Sumikawa-san prefers to be alone...?

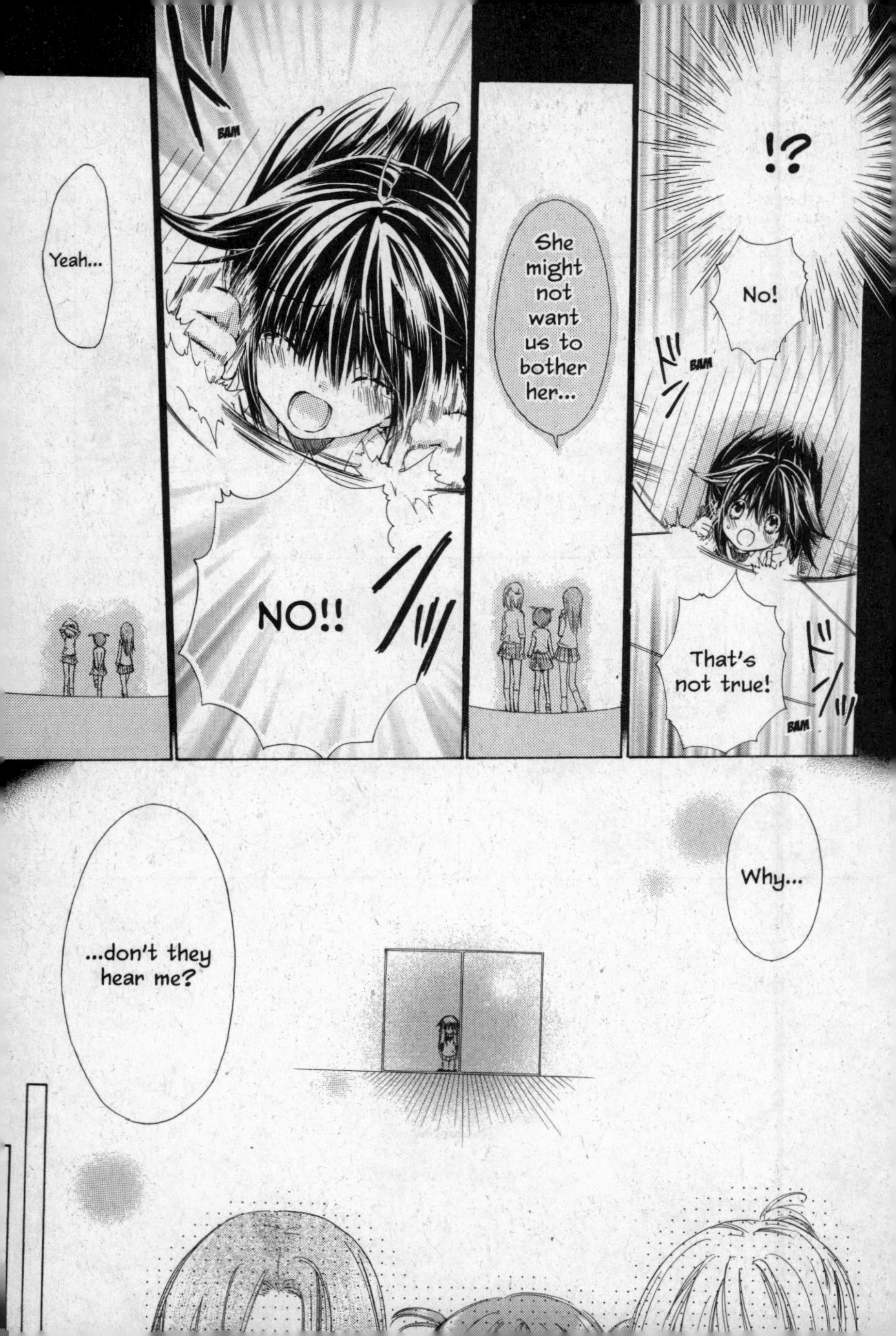

!?
No!
BAM
That's not true!
BAM
She might not want us to bother her...
BAM
NO!!
Yeah...
Why...
...don't they hear me?

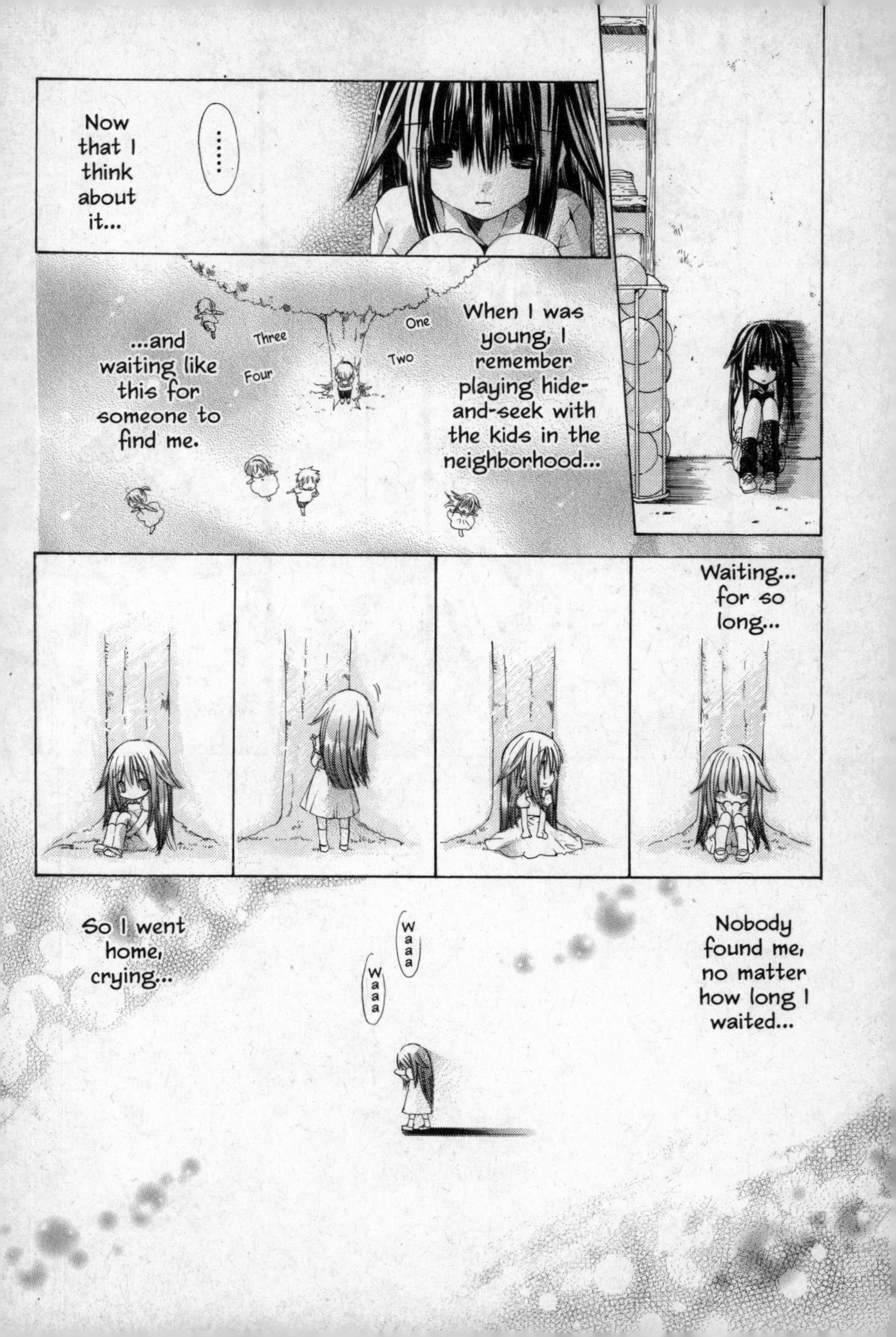
......
Now that I think about it...
When I was young, I remember playing hide-and-seek with the kids in the neighborhood...
One
Two
Three
Four
...and waiting like this for someone to find me.
Waiting... for so long...
Nobody found me, no matter how long I waited...
Waaa
Waaa
So I went home, crying...

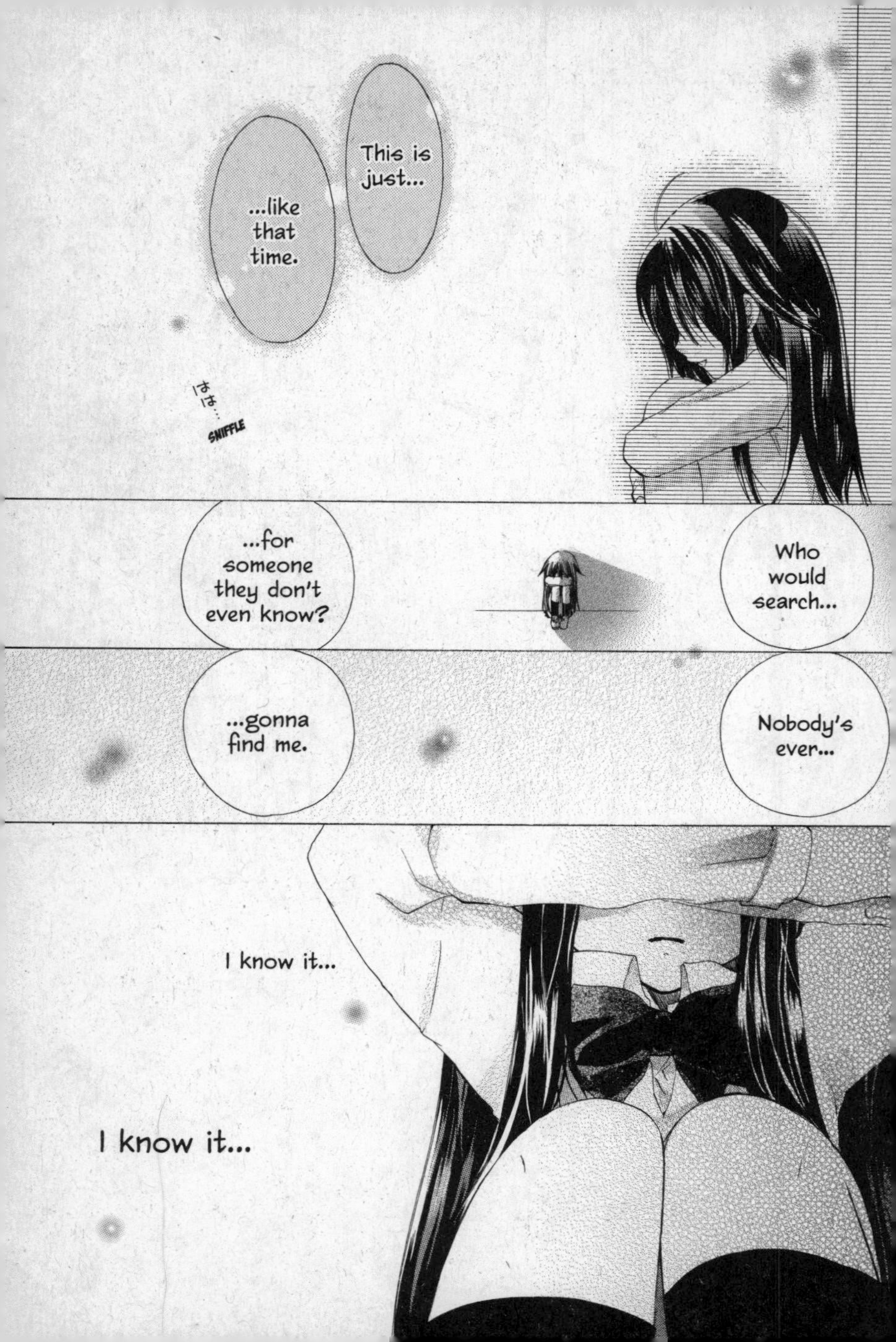
This is just...
...like that time.
はは…
SNIFFLE
Who would search...
...for someone they don't even know?
Nobody's ever...
...gonna find me.
I know it...
I know it...

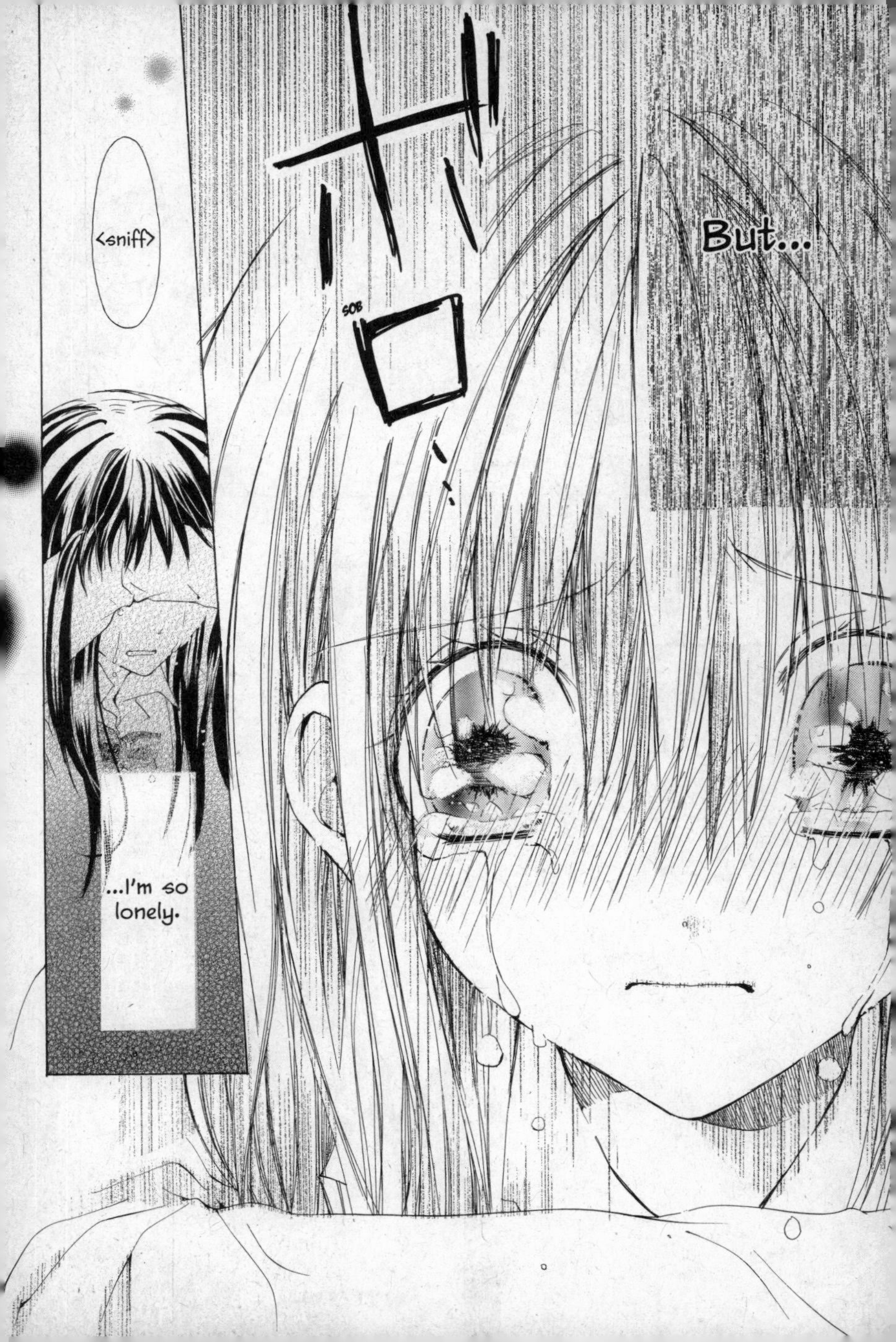
But...
ボロ
SOB
<sniff>
...I'm so lonely.

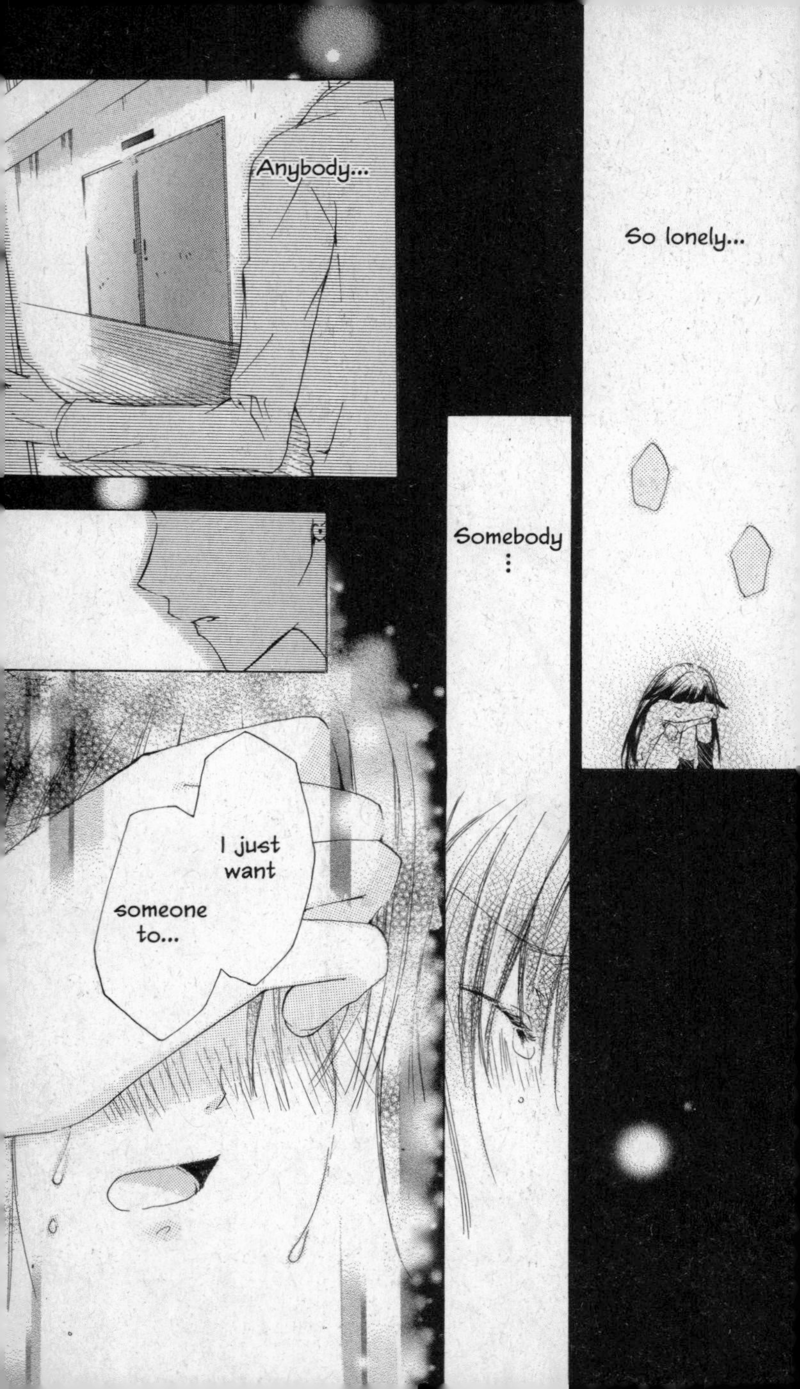
So lonely...
Somebody...
Anybody...
I just want someone to...

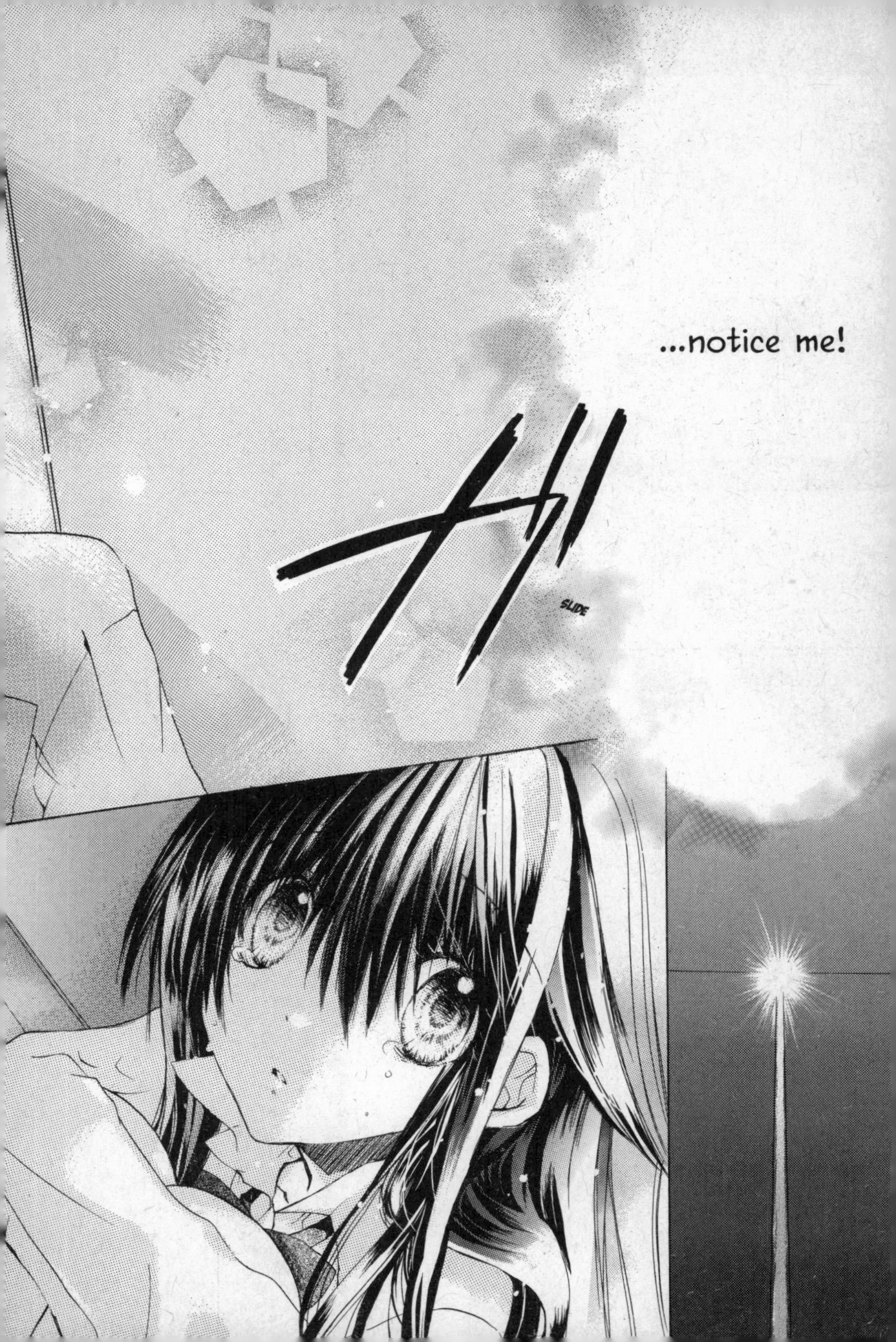
...notice me!
SLIDE

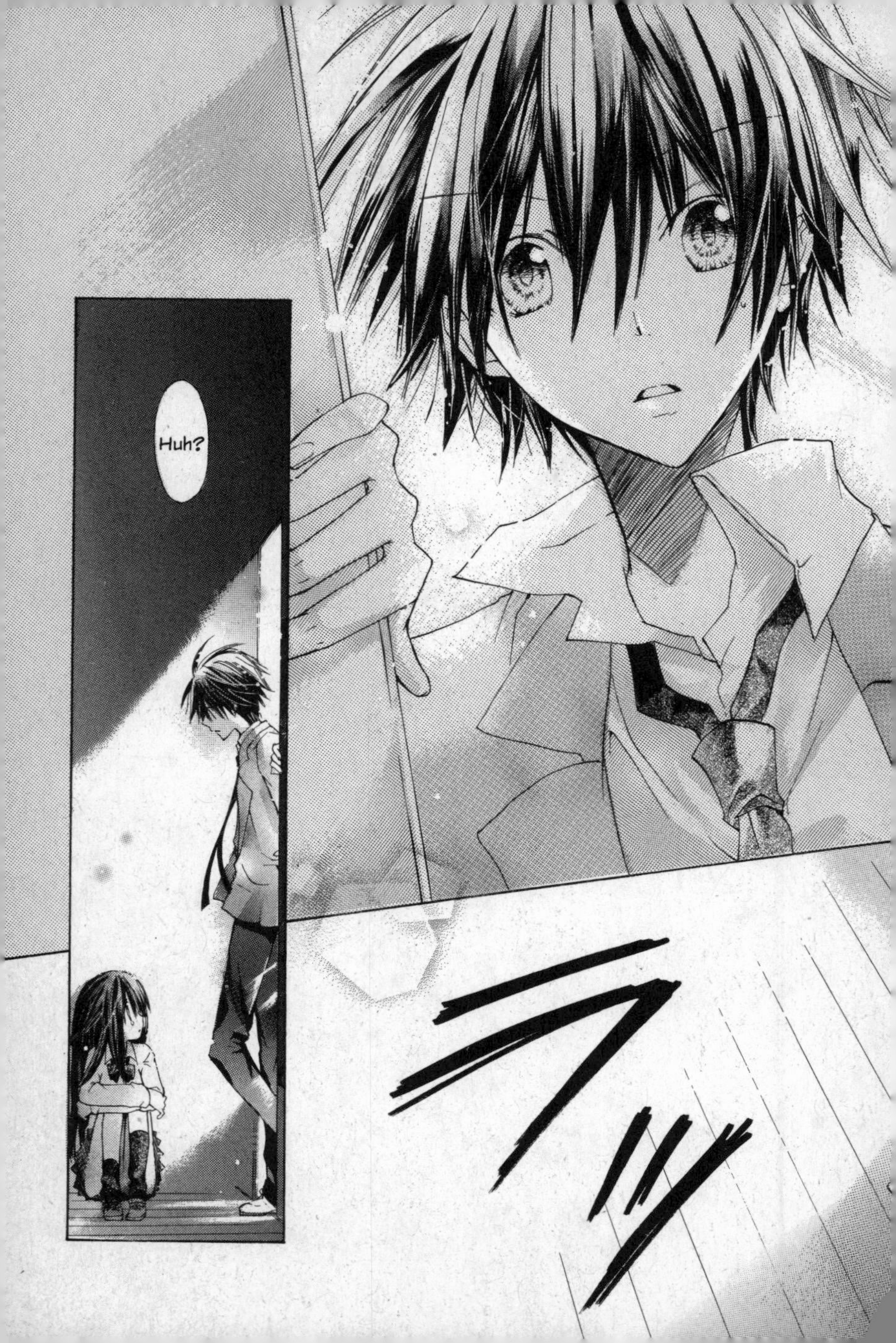
Huh?
ラッ

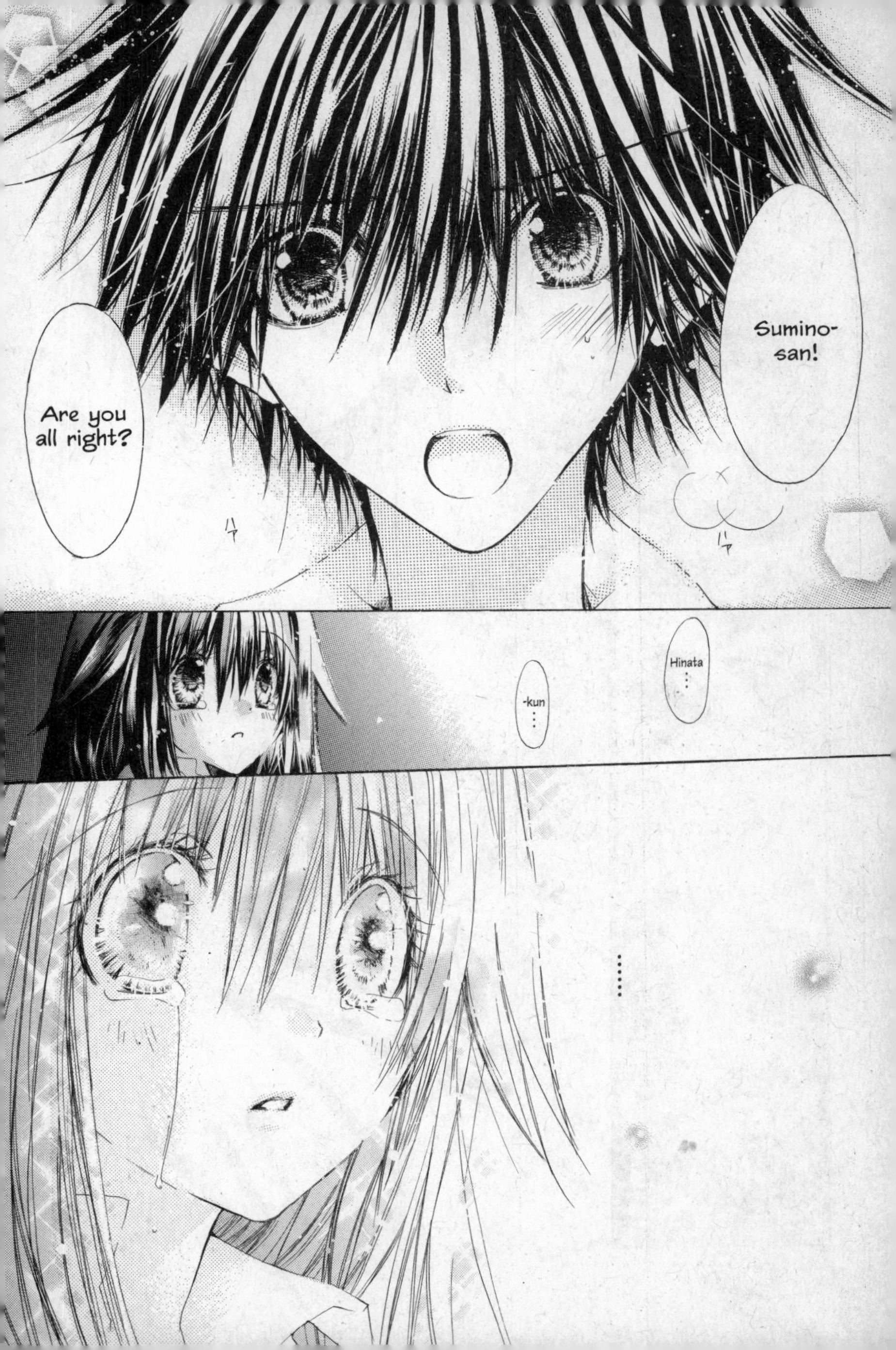
Sumino-san!
Are you all right?
Hinata...
-kun...
......

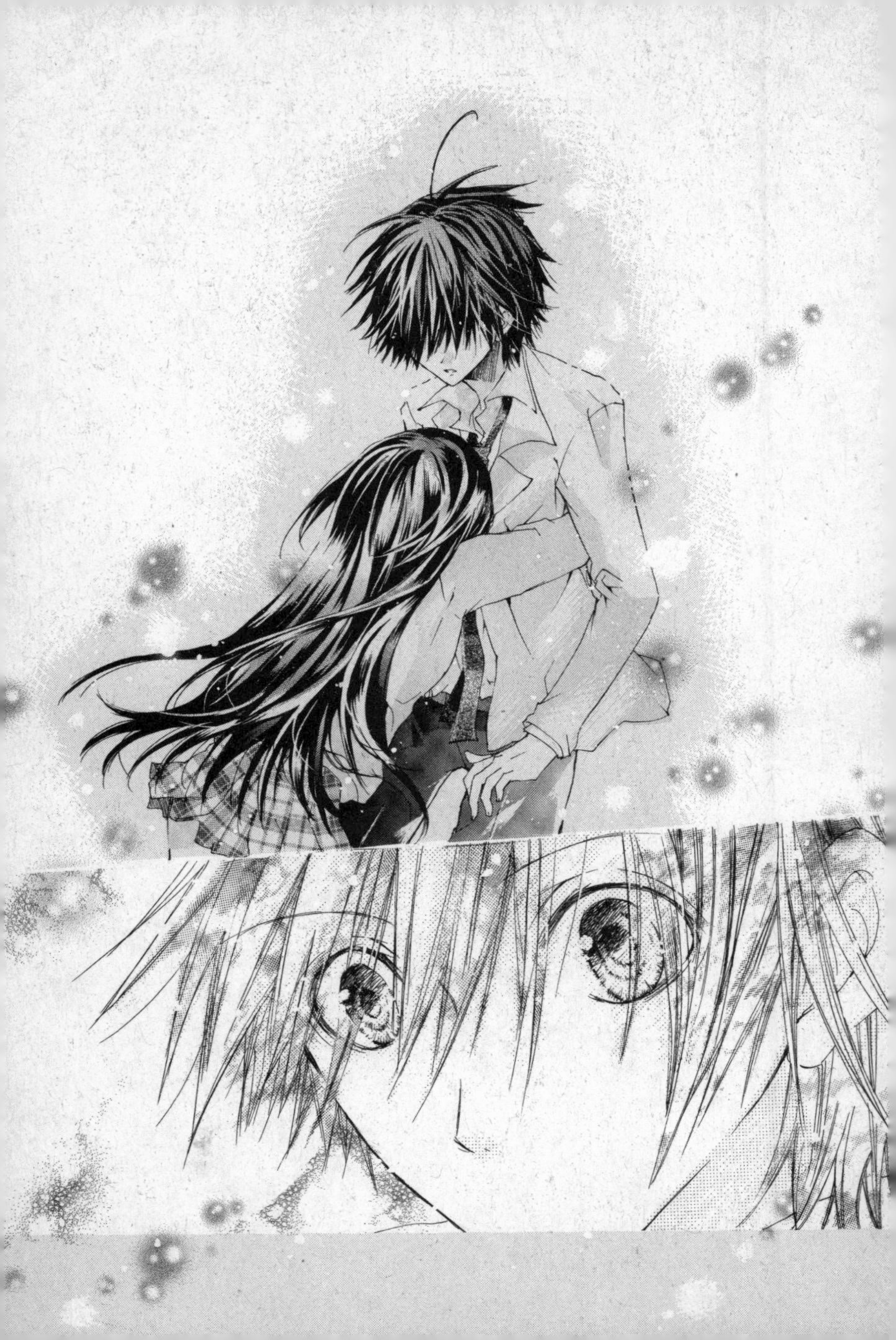

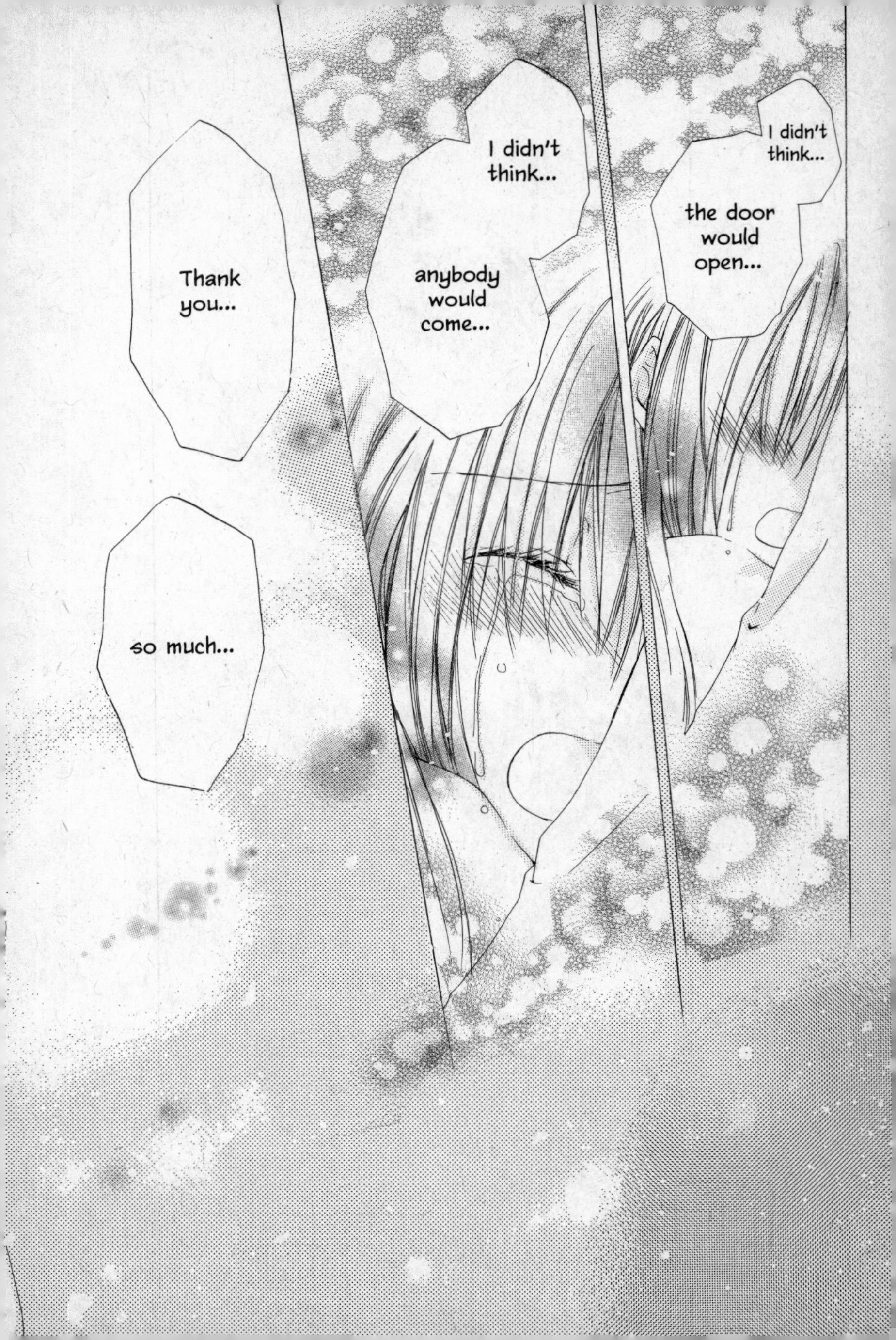
I didn't think...
the door would open...
I didn't think...
anybody would come...
Thank you...
so much...

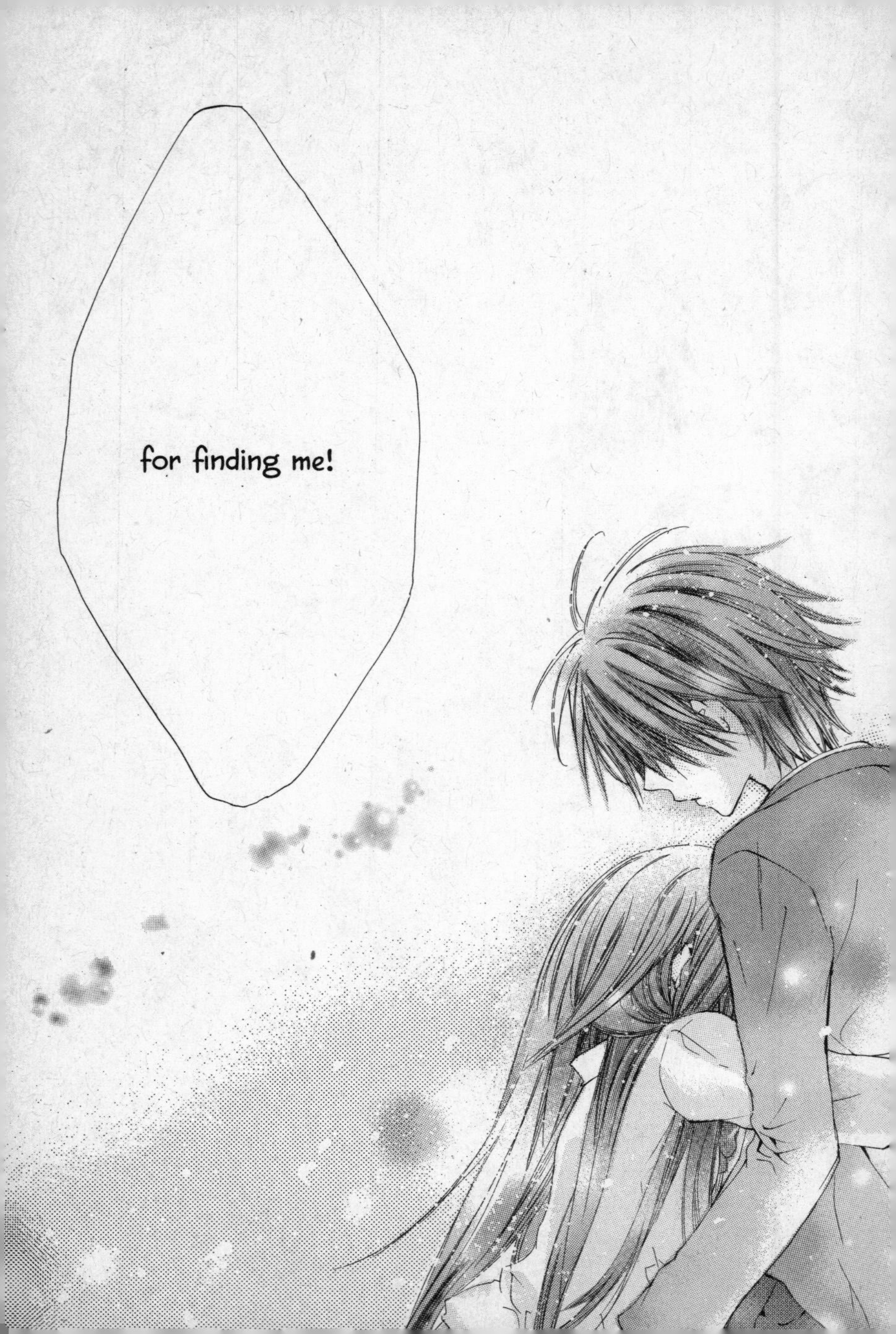
for finding me!

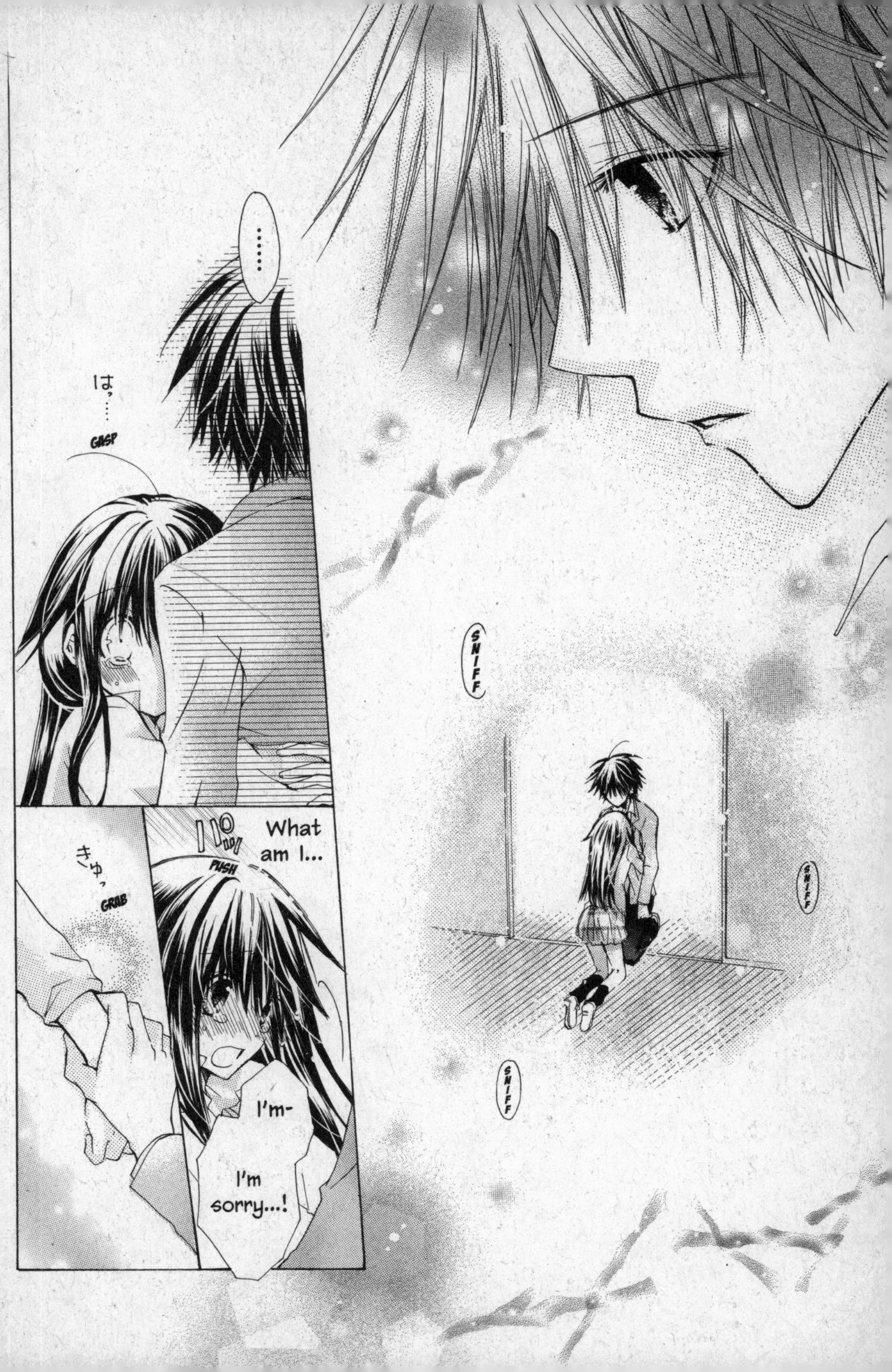
SNIFF
SNIFF
SNIFF
……
は……
GASP
What am I...
PUSH
I'm-
I'm sorry...!
きゅっ
GRAB

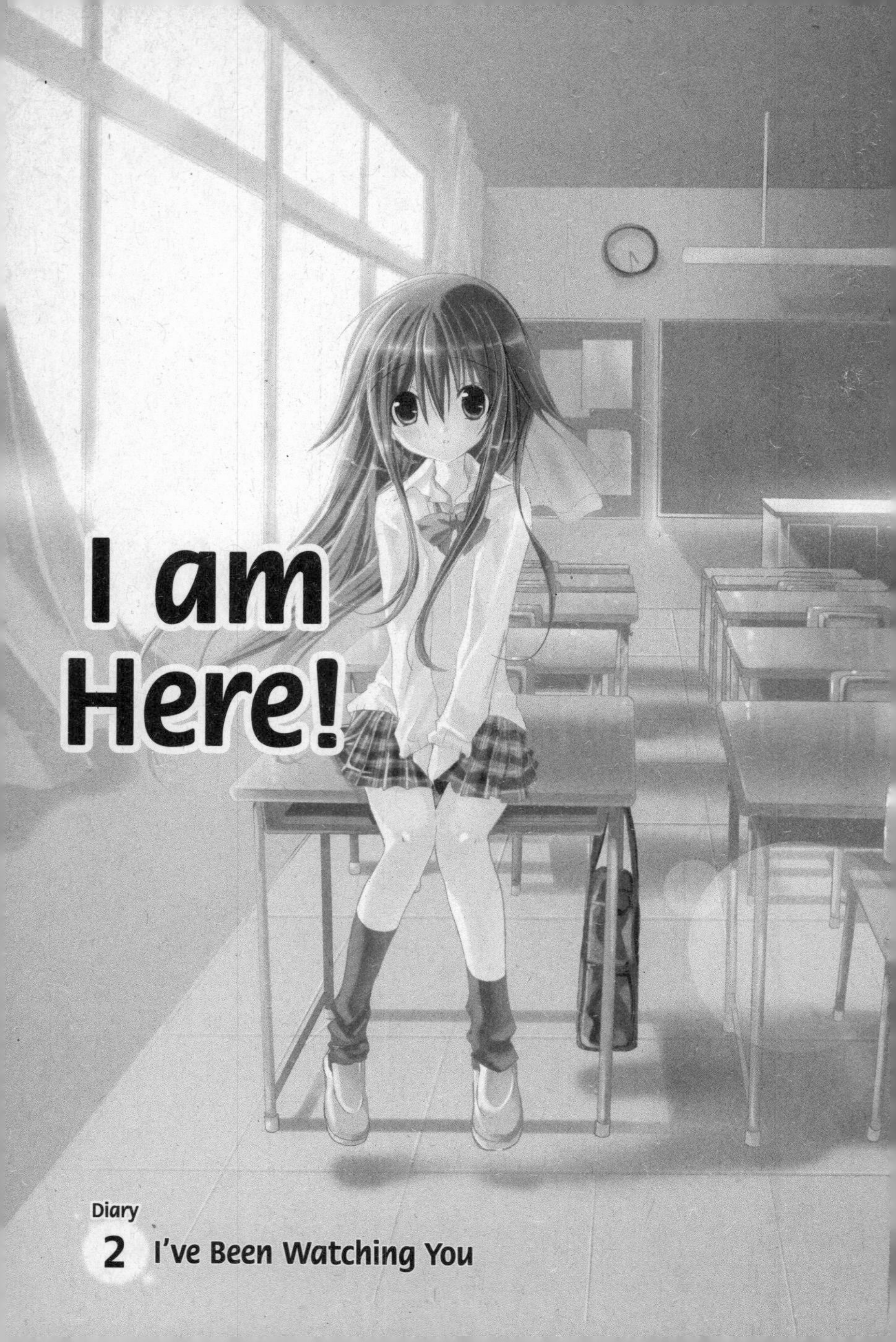
I am Here!
Diary
2 I've Been Watching You

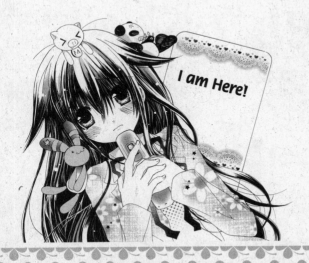

I am Here!

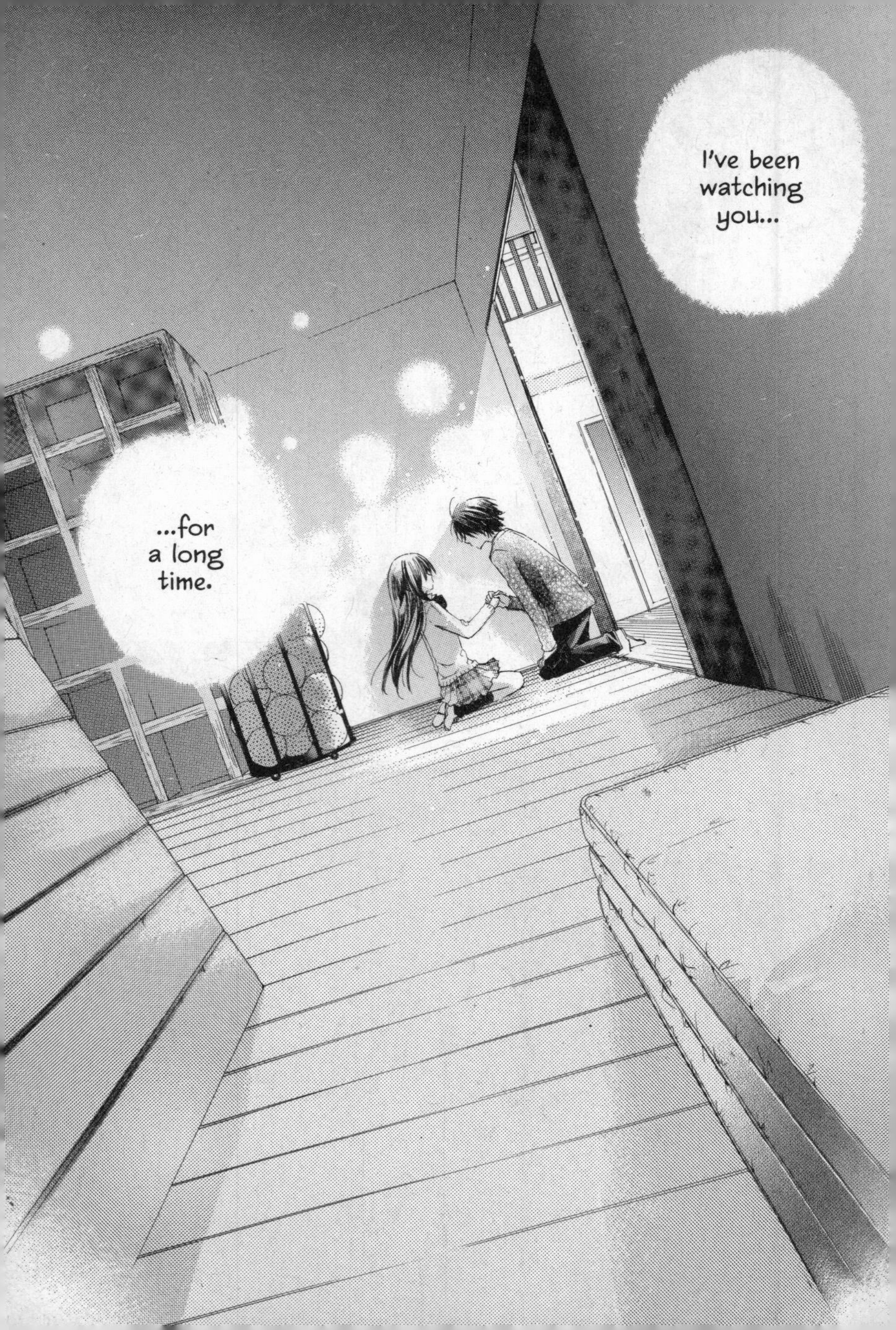
I've been watching you...
...for a long time.

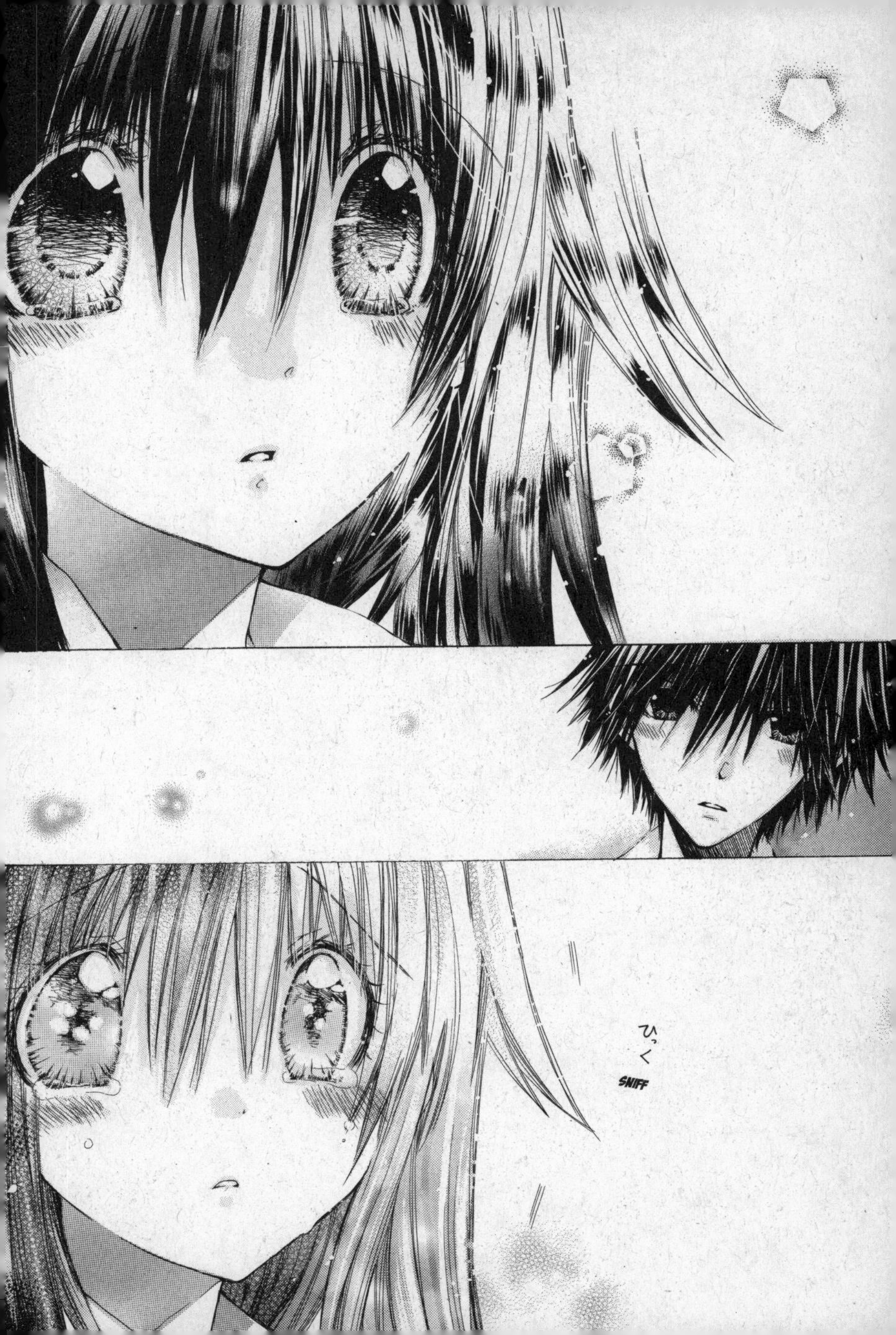
ひくっ
SNIFF

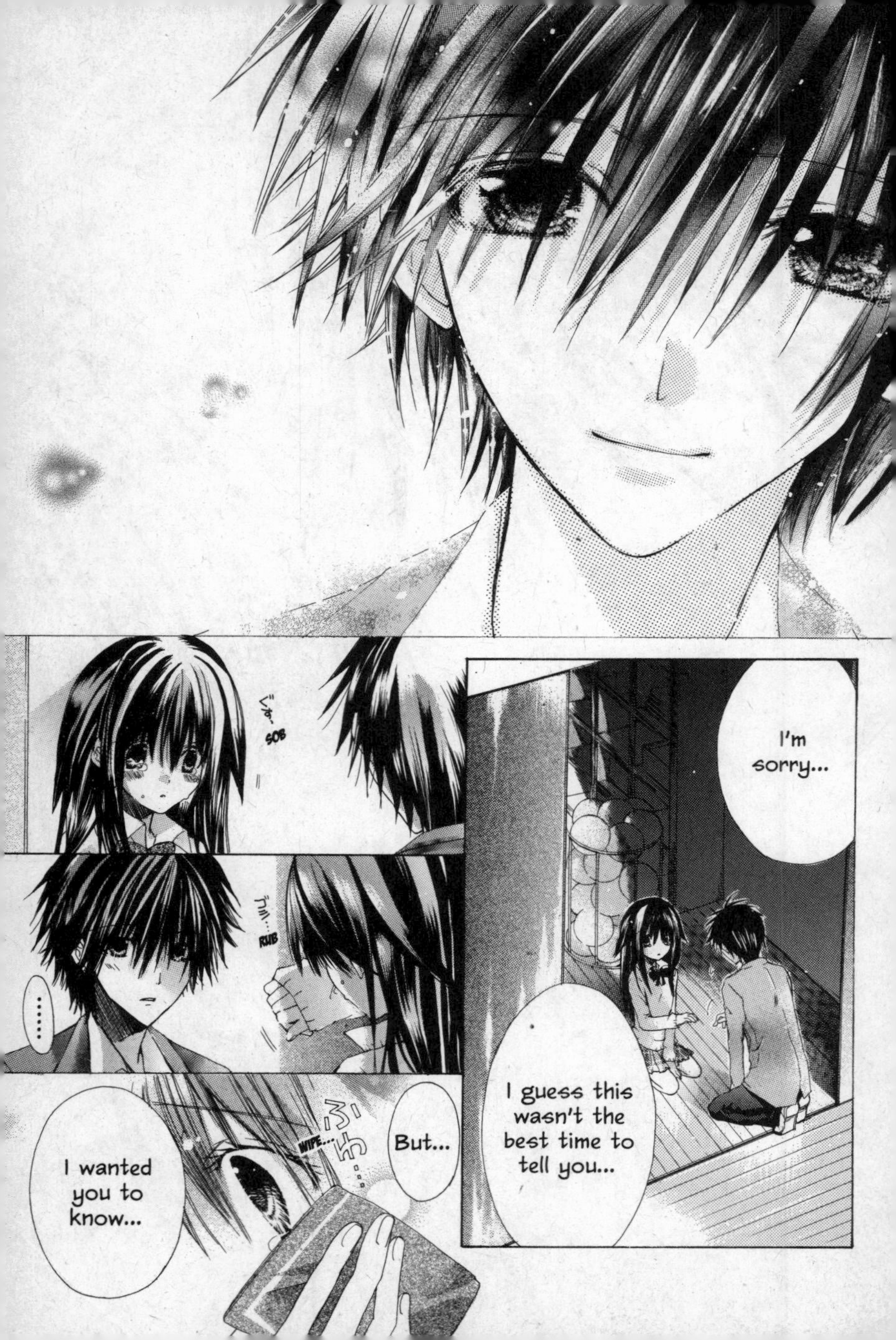
I'm sorry...
I guess this wasn't the best time to tell you...
SOB
......
RUB
But...
WIPE...
I wanted you to know...

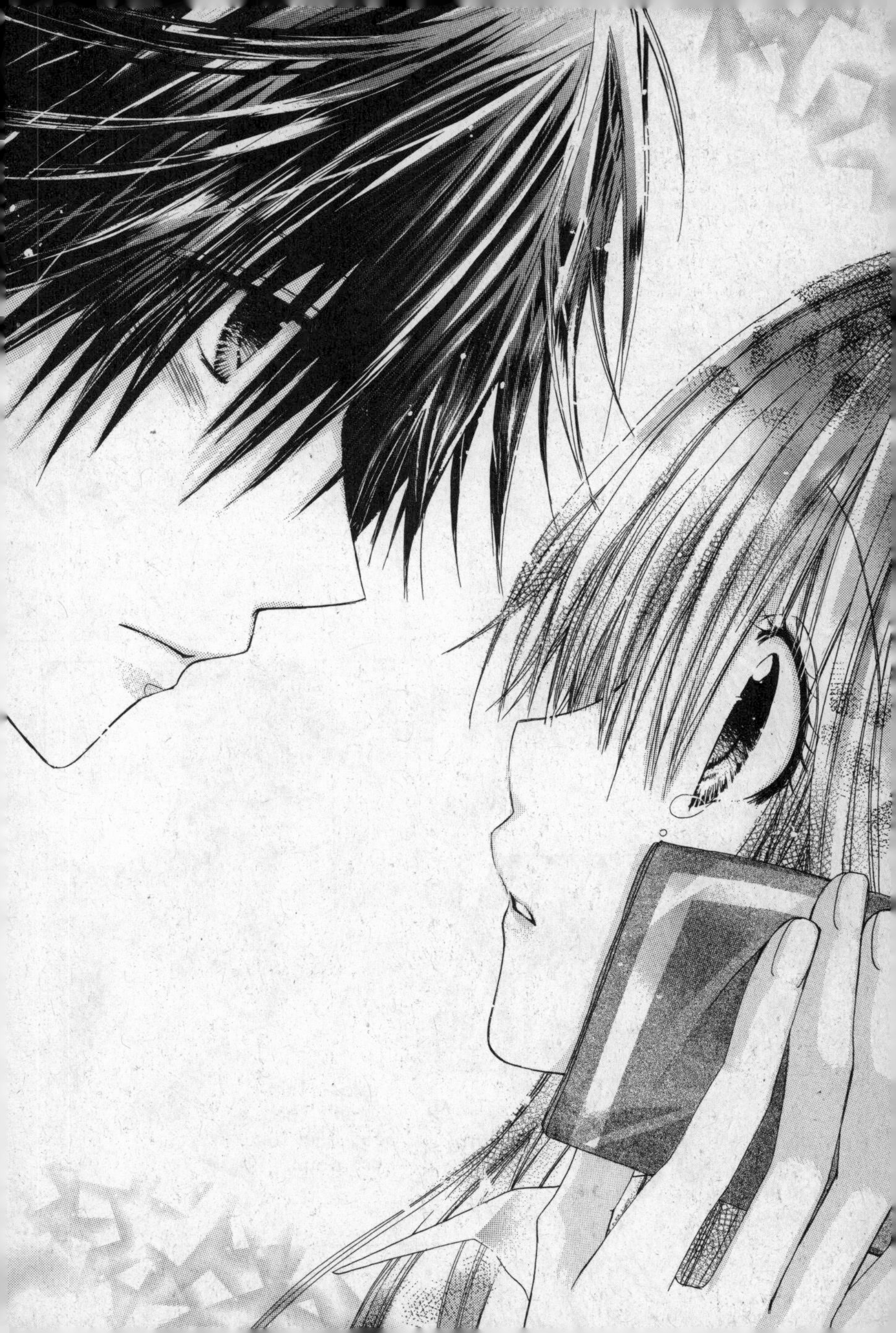

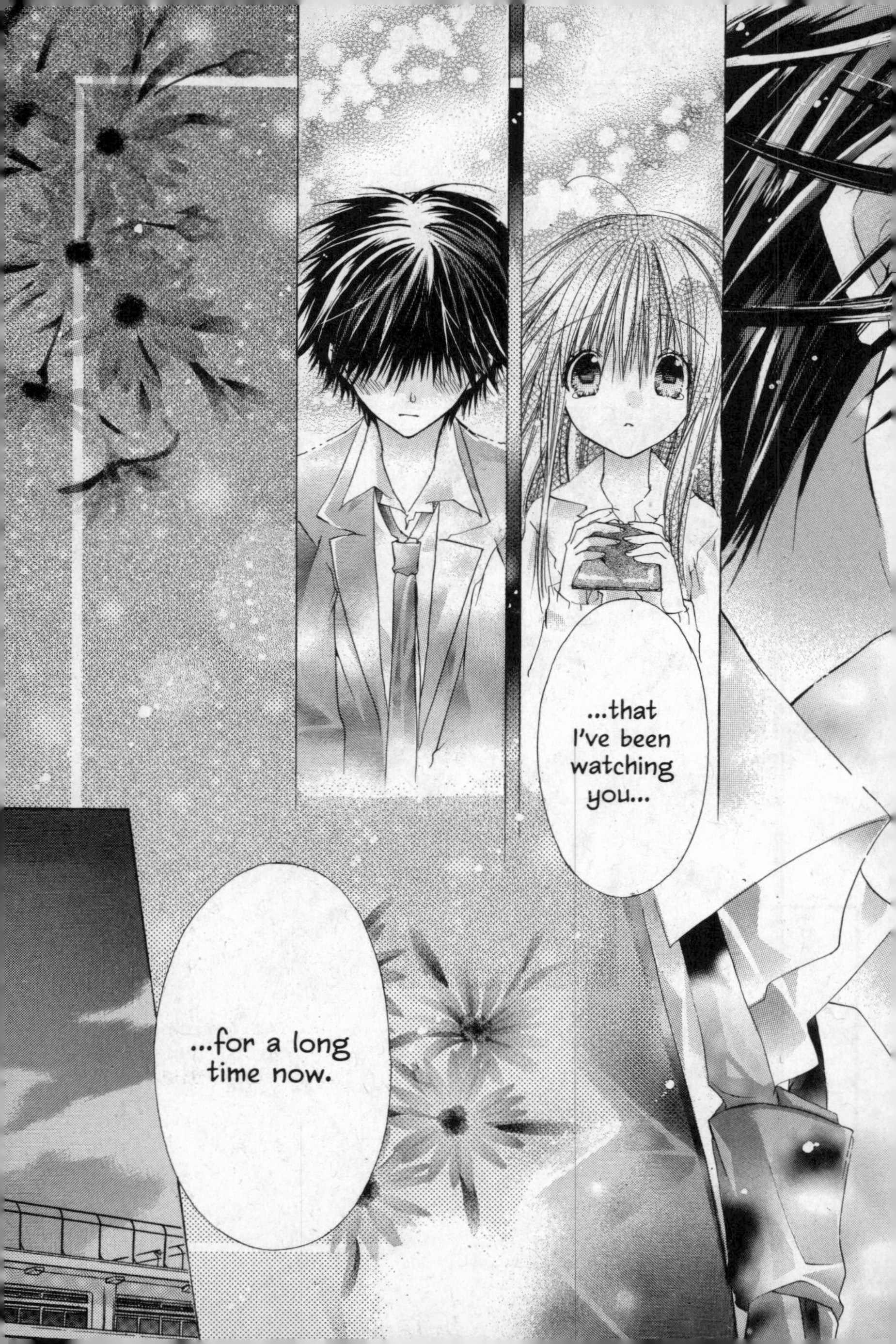
...that I've been watching you...
...for a long time now.

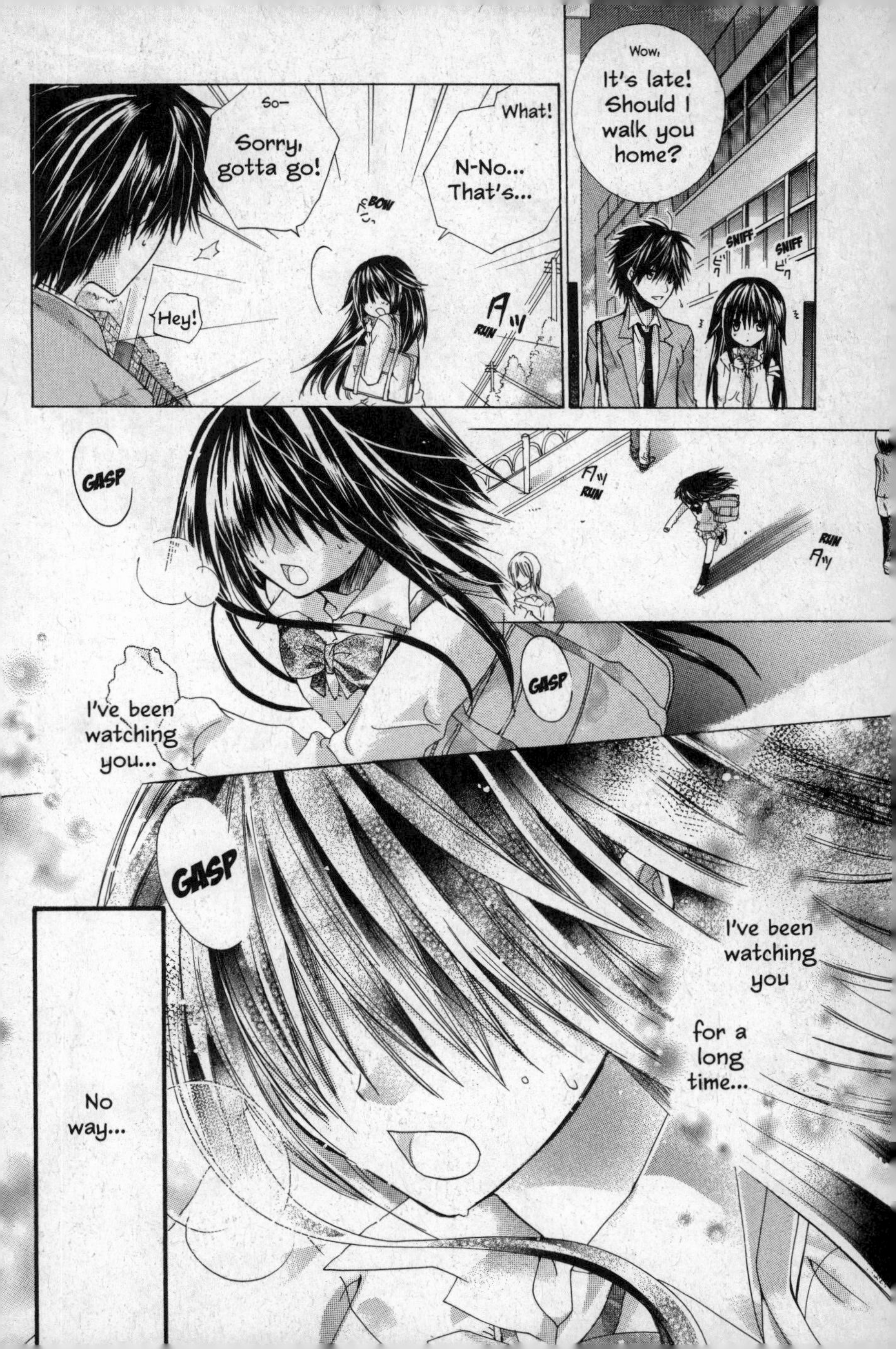
Wow,
It's late! Should I walk you home?
SNIFF
SNIFF
What!
N-No... That's...
So—
Sorry, gotta go!
BOW
RUN
Hey!
RUN
RUN
GASP
GASP
I've been watching you...
I've been watching you
for a long time...
GASP
No way...

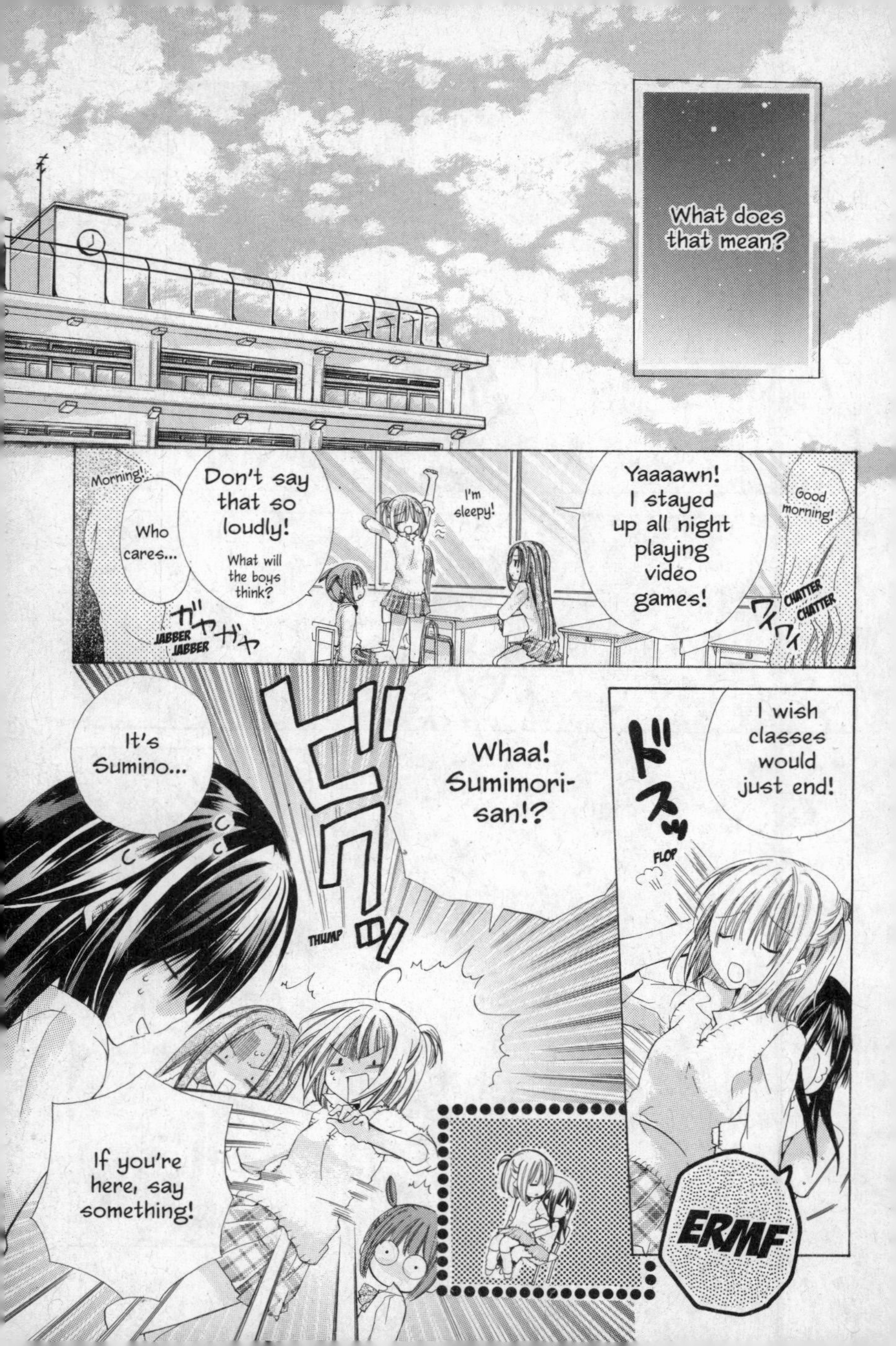

What does that mean?
Good morning!
ワイワイ
CHATTER CHATTER
Yaaaawn! I stayed up all night playing video games!
I'm sleepy!
Don't say that so loudly!
What will the boys think?
Who cares...
Morning!
ガヤガヤ
JABBER JABBER
I wish classes would just end!
ドスッ
FLOP
ERMF
Whaa! Sumimori-san!?
ビクッ
THUMP
It's Sumino...
If you're here, say something!

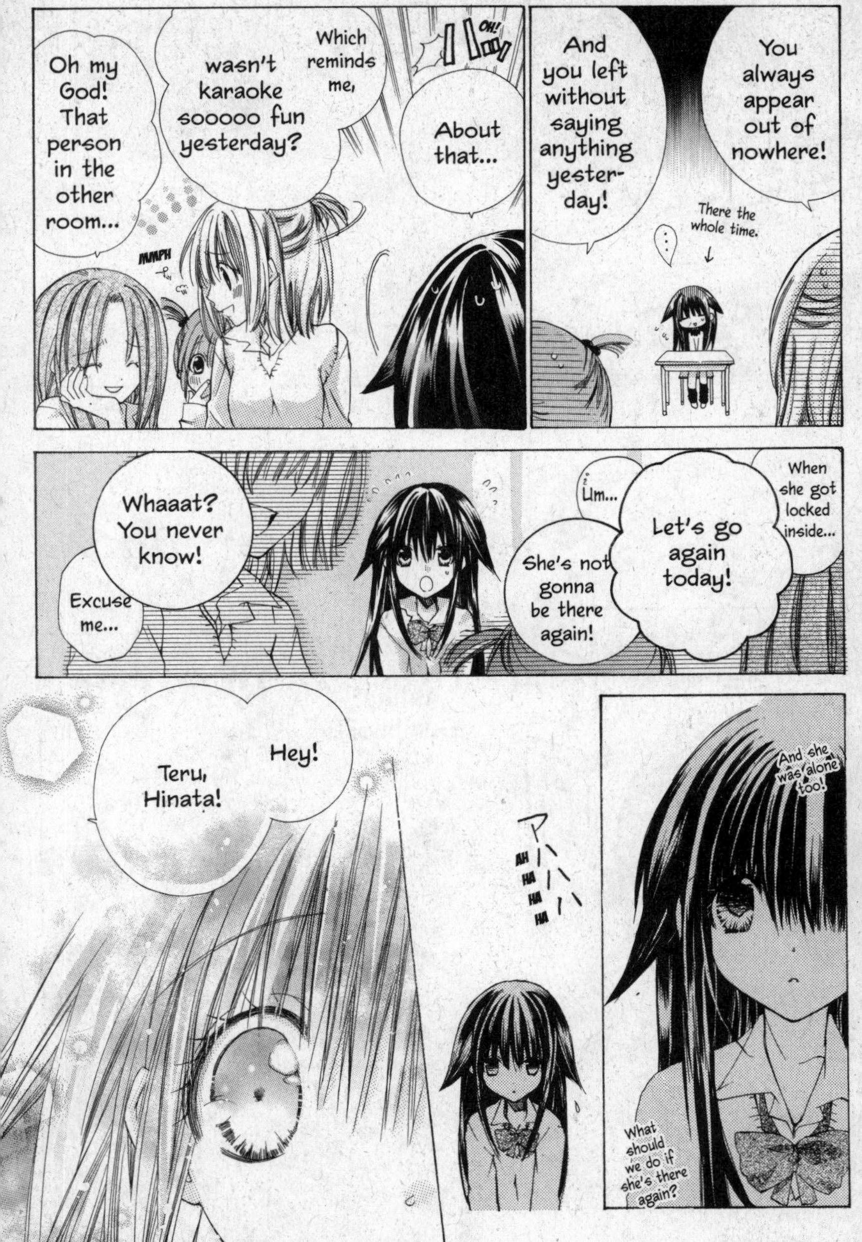
You always appear out of nowhere!
And you left without saying anything yesterday!
...
There the whole time.
OH!
About that...
Which reminds me,
wasn't karaoke sooooo fun yesterday?
Oh my God! That person in the other room...
MMPH
When she got locked inside...
Let's go again today!
Um...
She's not gonna be there again!
Whaaat? You never know!
Excuse me...
And she was alone too!
What should we do if she's there again?
AH HA HA HA
Hey!
Teru, Hinata!

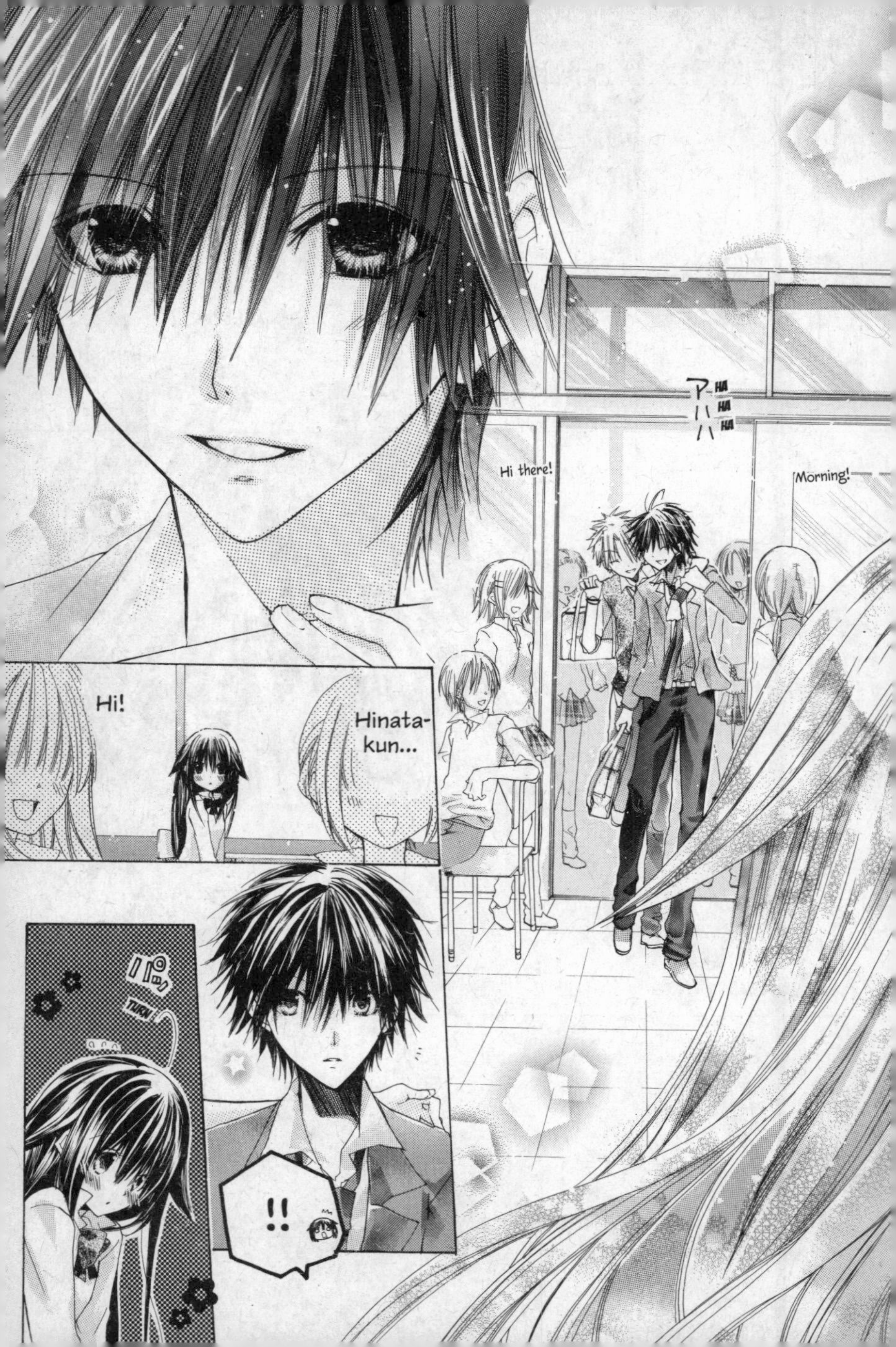

HA HA HA
Morning!
Hi there!
Hinata-kun...
Hi!
!!
TURN

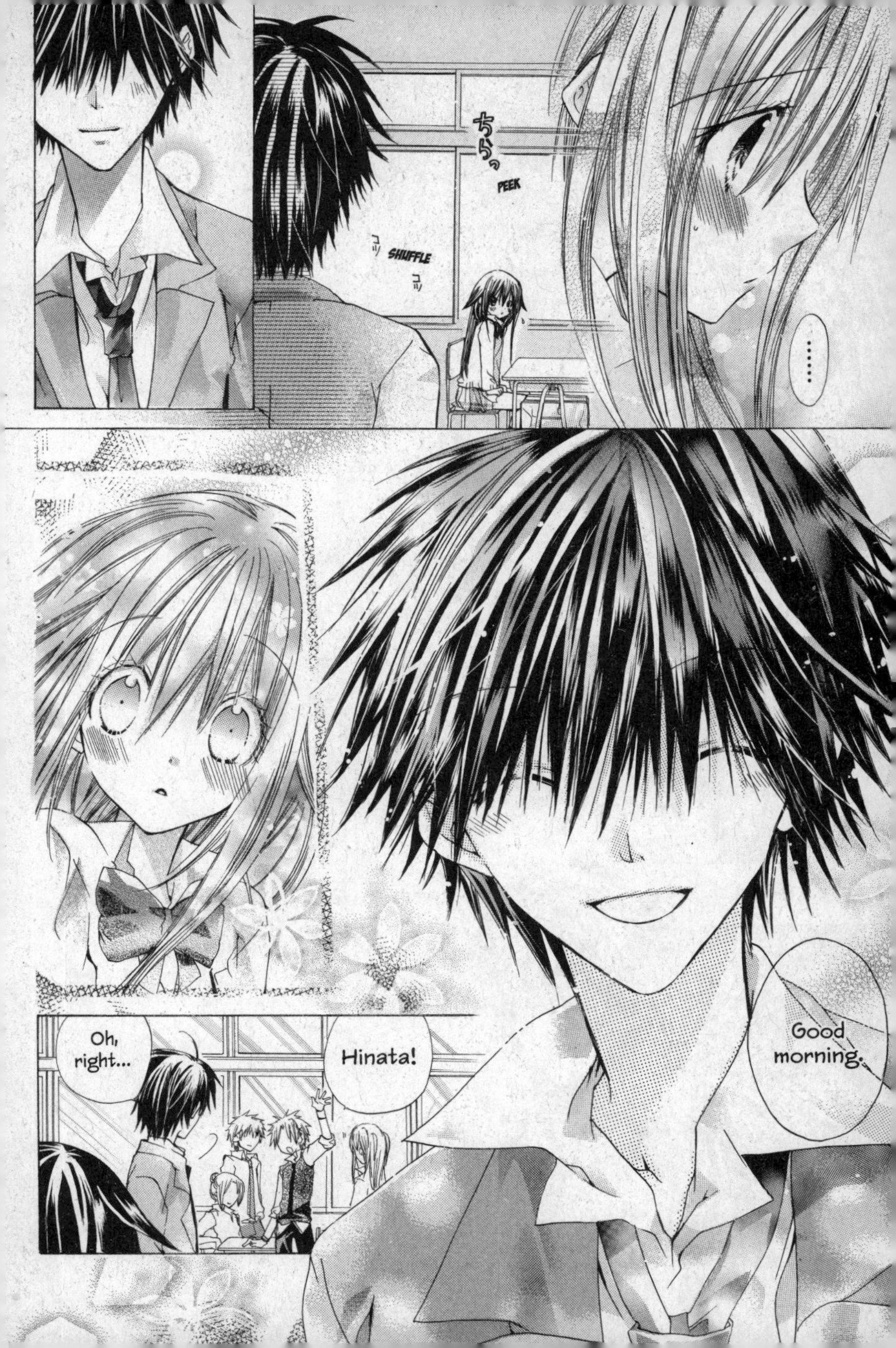
......
ちらっ
PEEK
コソ
SHUFFLE
コソ
Good morning.
Hinata!
Oh, right...

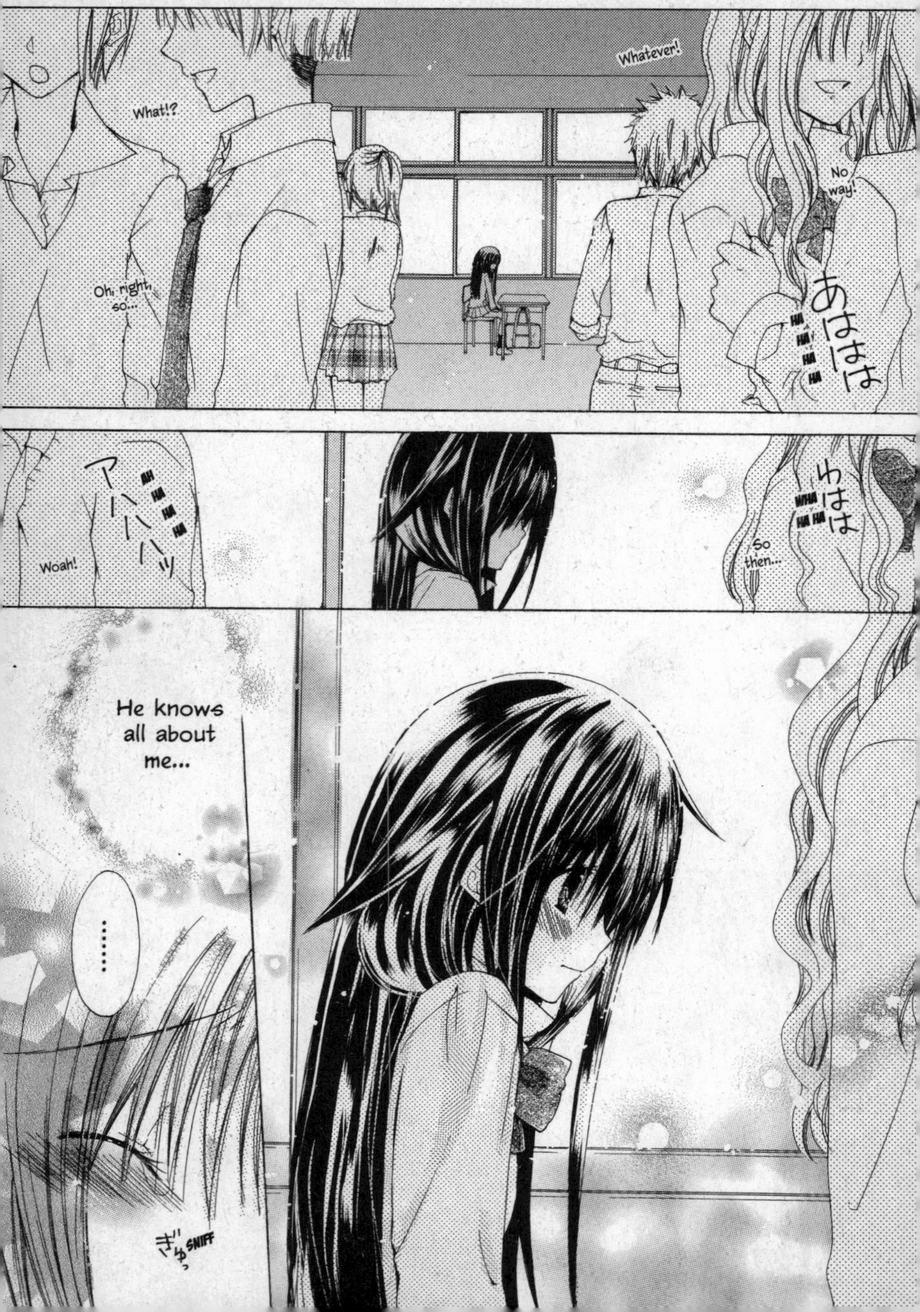
Whatever!
No way!
あははは
HA HA HA HA
What!?
Oh, right, so...
ゎはは
WHA HA HA
So then...
アハハハッ
AH HA HA HA
Woah!
He knows all about me...
......
ぎゅっ
SNIFF

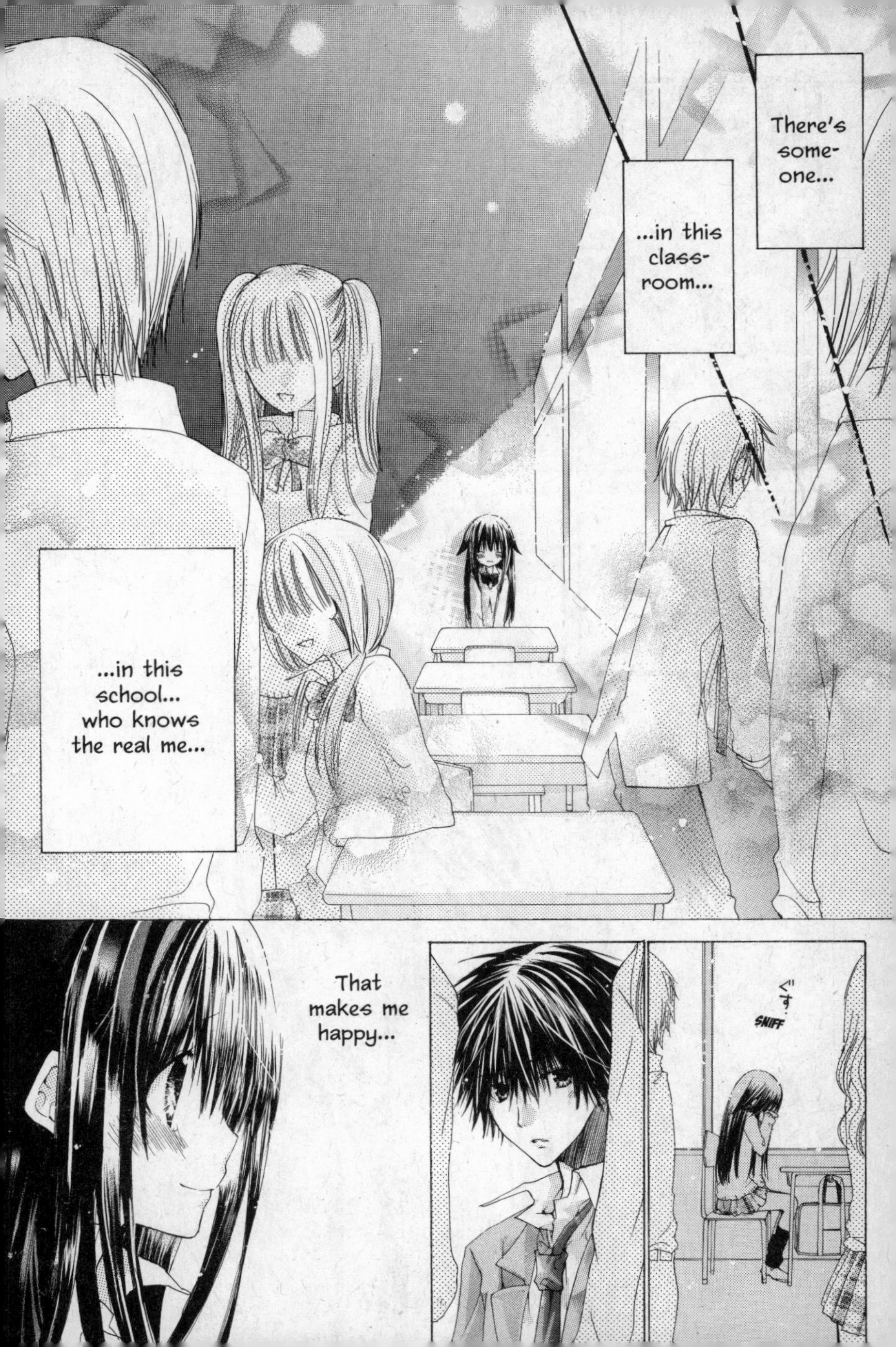
There's some-one...
...in this class-room...
...in this school... who knows the real me...
ぐす
SNIFF
That makes me happy...

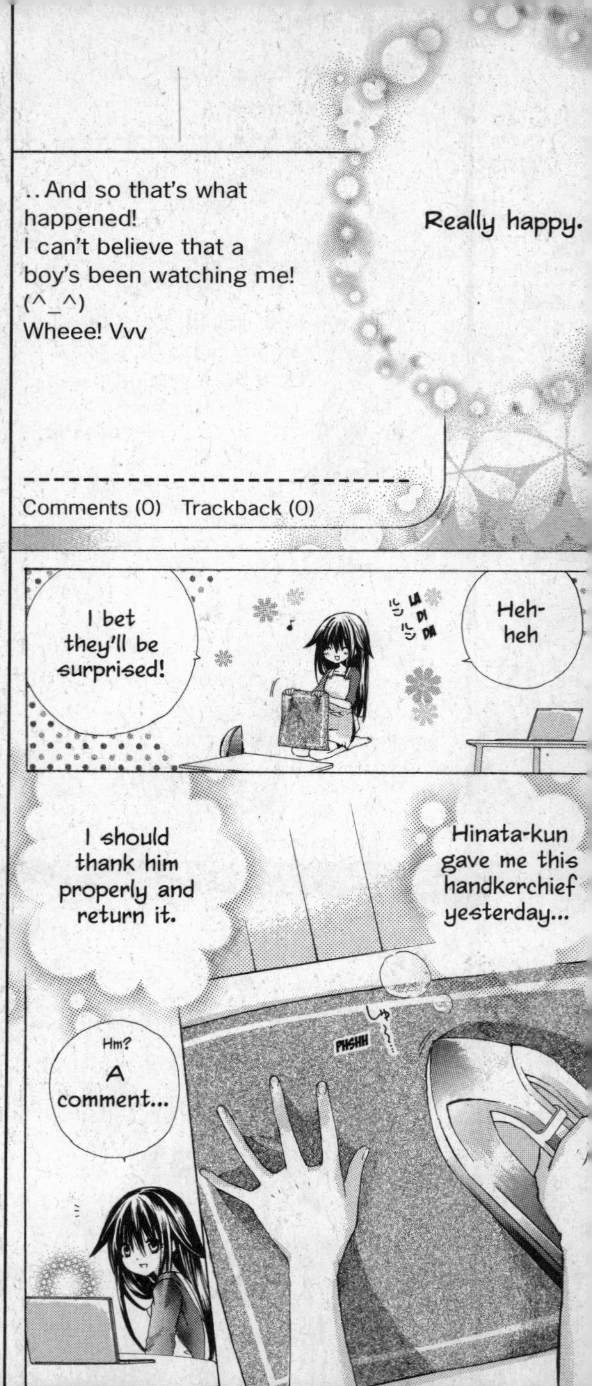
Really happy.
..And so that's what happened!
I can't believe that a boy's been watching me!
(^_^)
Wheee! Vvv
Comments (0) Trackback (0)
Heh-heh
LA DI DA
I bet they'll be surprised!
Hinata-kun gave me this handkerchief yesterday...
I should thank him properly and return it.
PHSHH
Hm?
A comment...

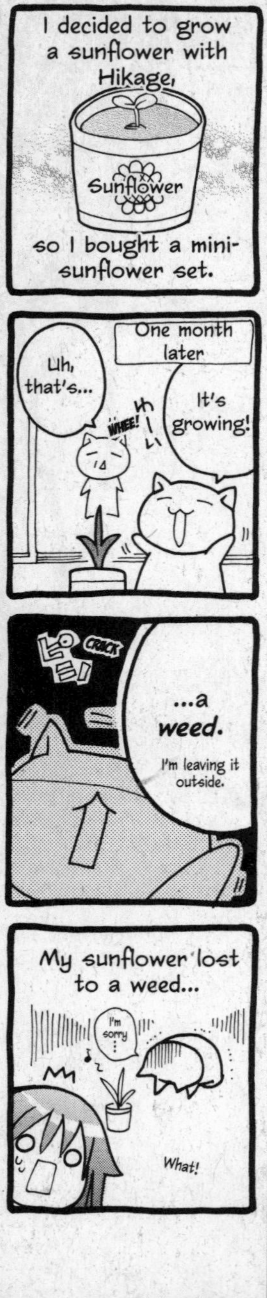
I decided to grow a sunflower with Hikage,
Sunflower
so I bought a mini-sunflower set.
One month later
It's growing!
WHEE!
Uh, that's...
CRACK
...a weed.
I'm leaving it outside.
My sunflower lost to a weed...
I'm sorry...
What!

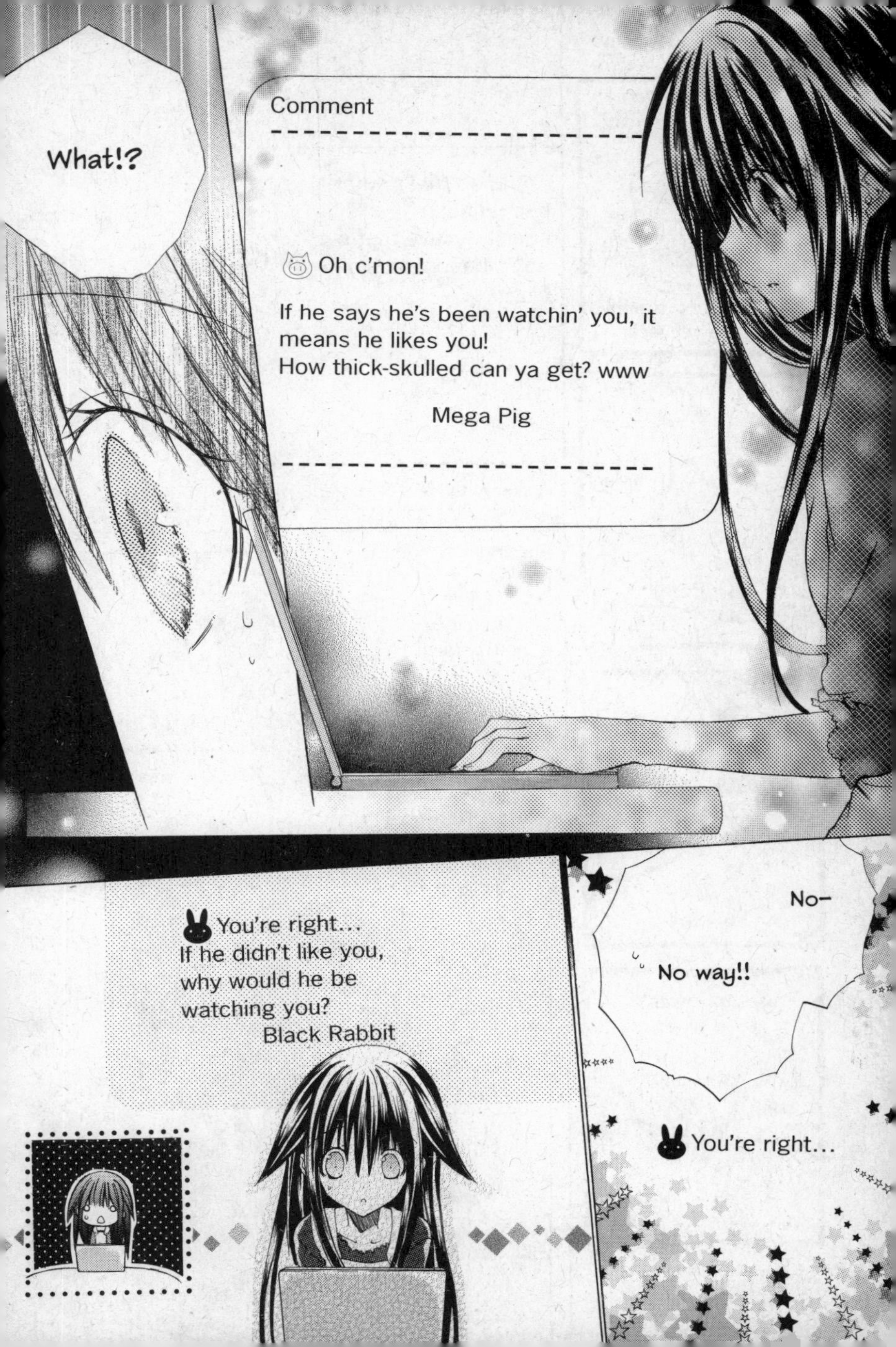
Comment
Oh c'mon!
If he says he's been watchin' you, it means he likes you!
How thick-skulled can ya get? www
Mega Pig
What!?
No–
No way!!
You're right...
You're right...
If he didn't like you,
why would he be
watching you?
Black Rabbit

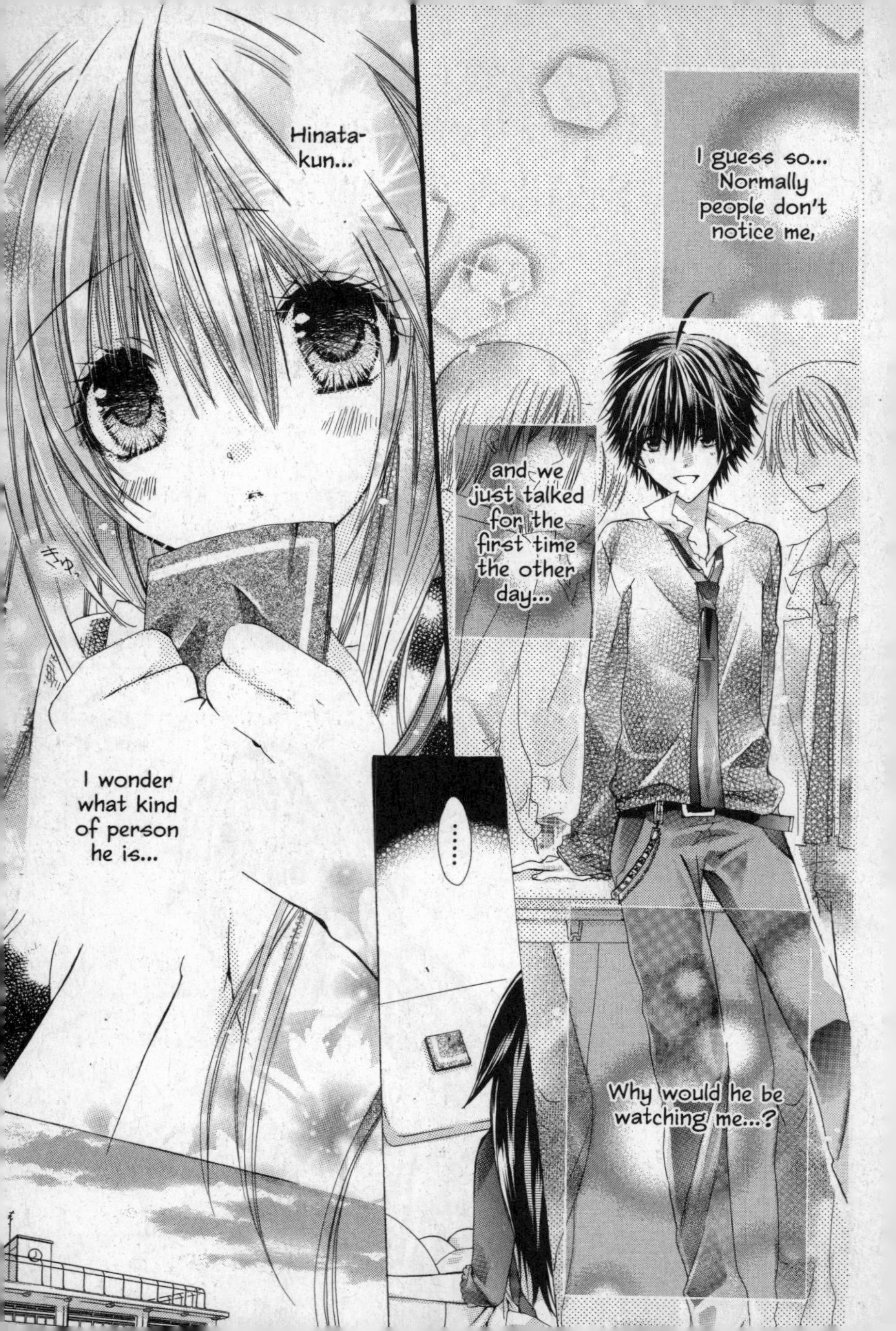
I guess so... Normally people don't notice me,
and we just talked for the first time the other day...
......
Why would he be watching me...?
Hinata-kun...
I wonder what kind of person he is...

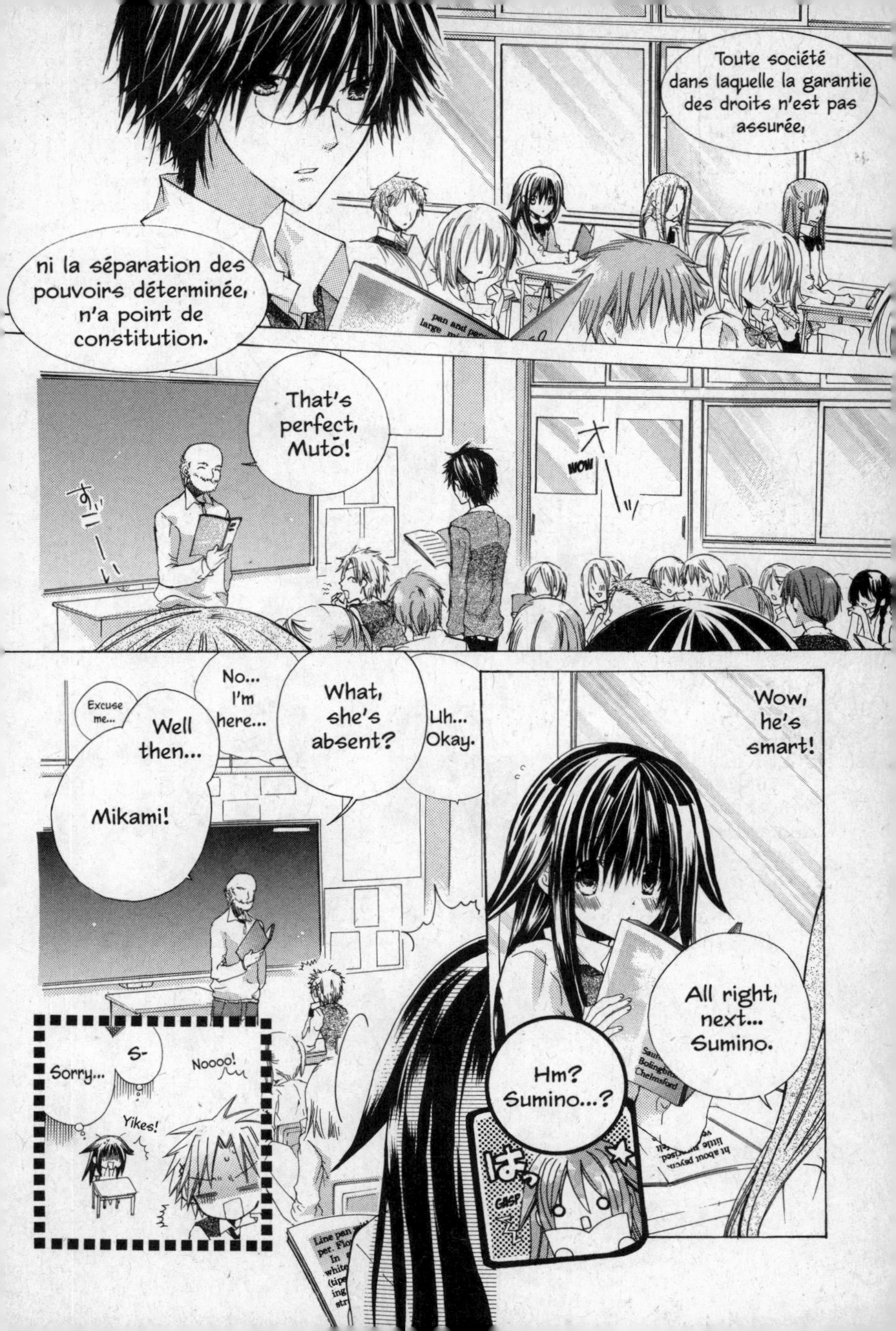
Toute société dans laquelle la garantie des droits n'est pas assurée,
ni la séparation des pouvoirs déterminée, n'a point de constitution.
WOW
That's perfect, Mutō!
Wow, he's smart!
All right, next... Sumino.
Hm? Sumino...?
GASP
Uh... Okay.
What, she's absent?
No... I'm here...
Excuse me...
Well then...
Mikami!
Noooo!
S-
Sorry...
Yikes!

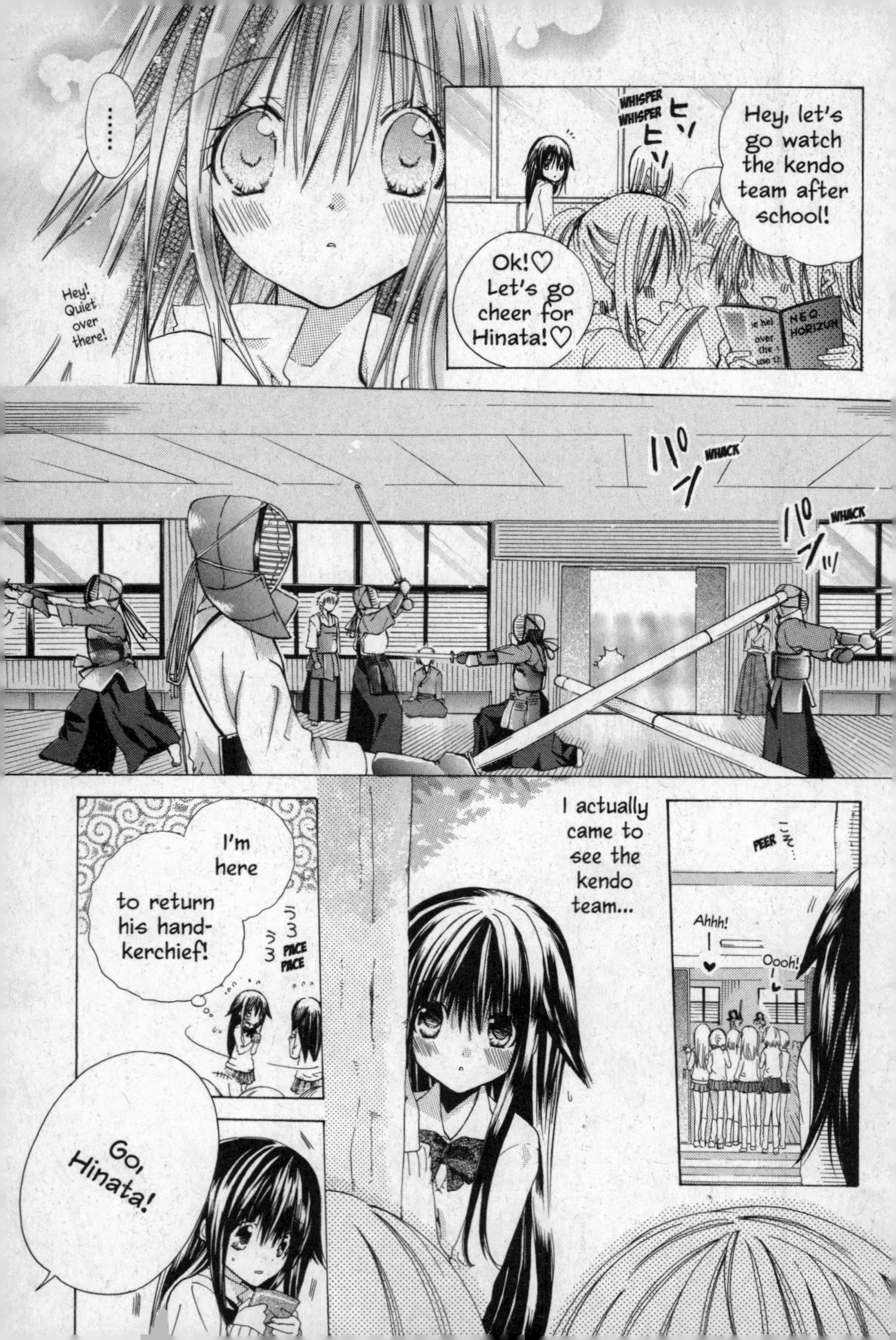
WHISPER WHISPER
Hey, let's go watch the kendo team after school!
Ok!♡ Let's go cheer for Hinata!♡
......
Hey! Quiet over there!
WHACK
WHACK
PEER
Ahhh!
Oooh!
I actually came to see the kendo team...
I'm here to return his hand-kerchief!
PACE PACE
Go, Hinata!

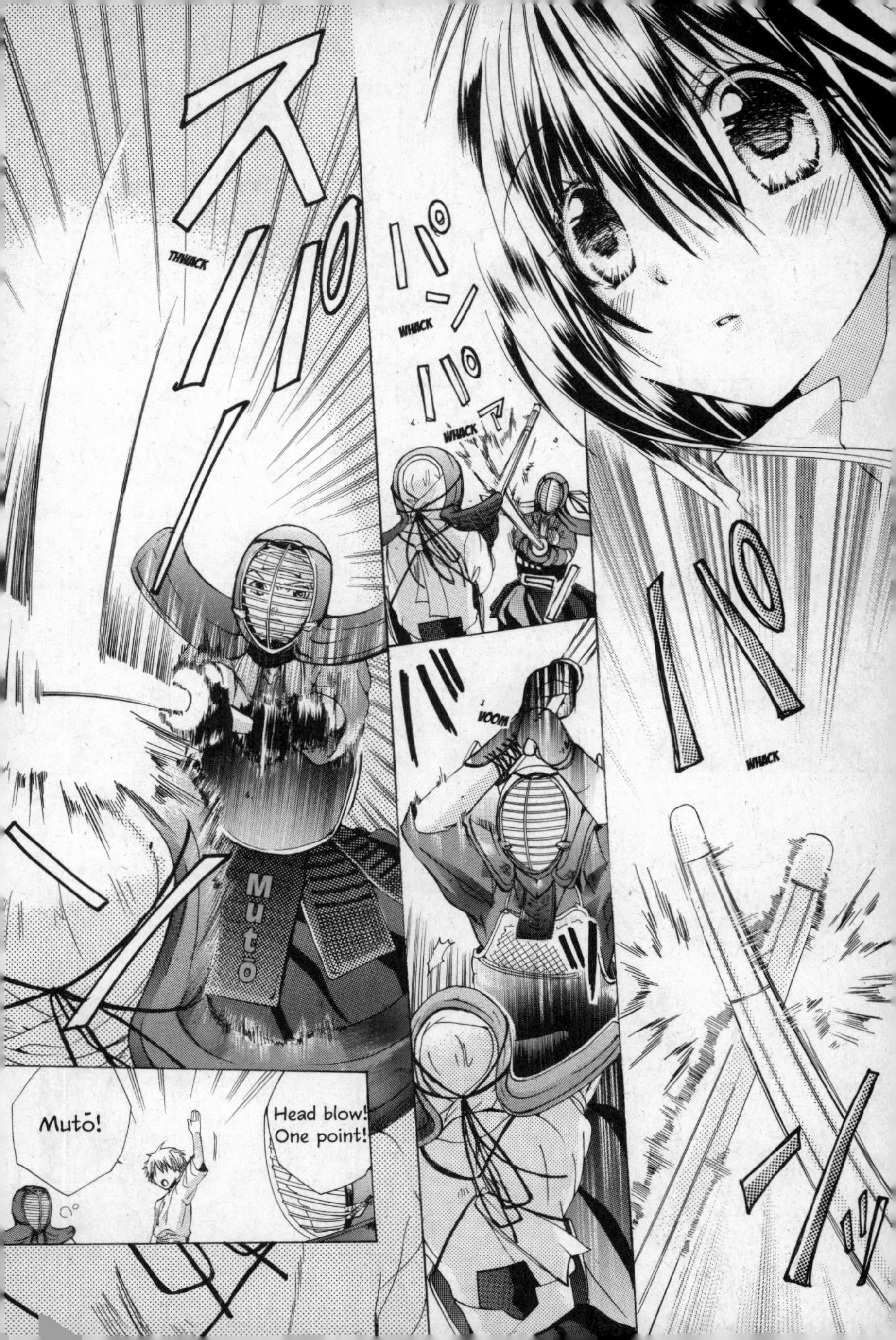
WHACK
WHACK
WHACK
VOOM
THWACK
Mutō
Head blow! One point!
Mutō!

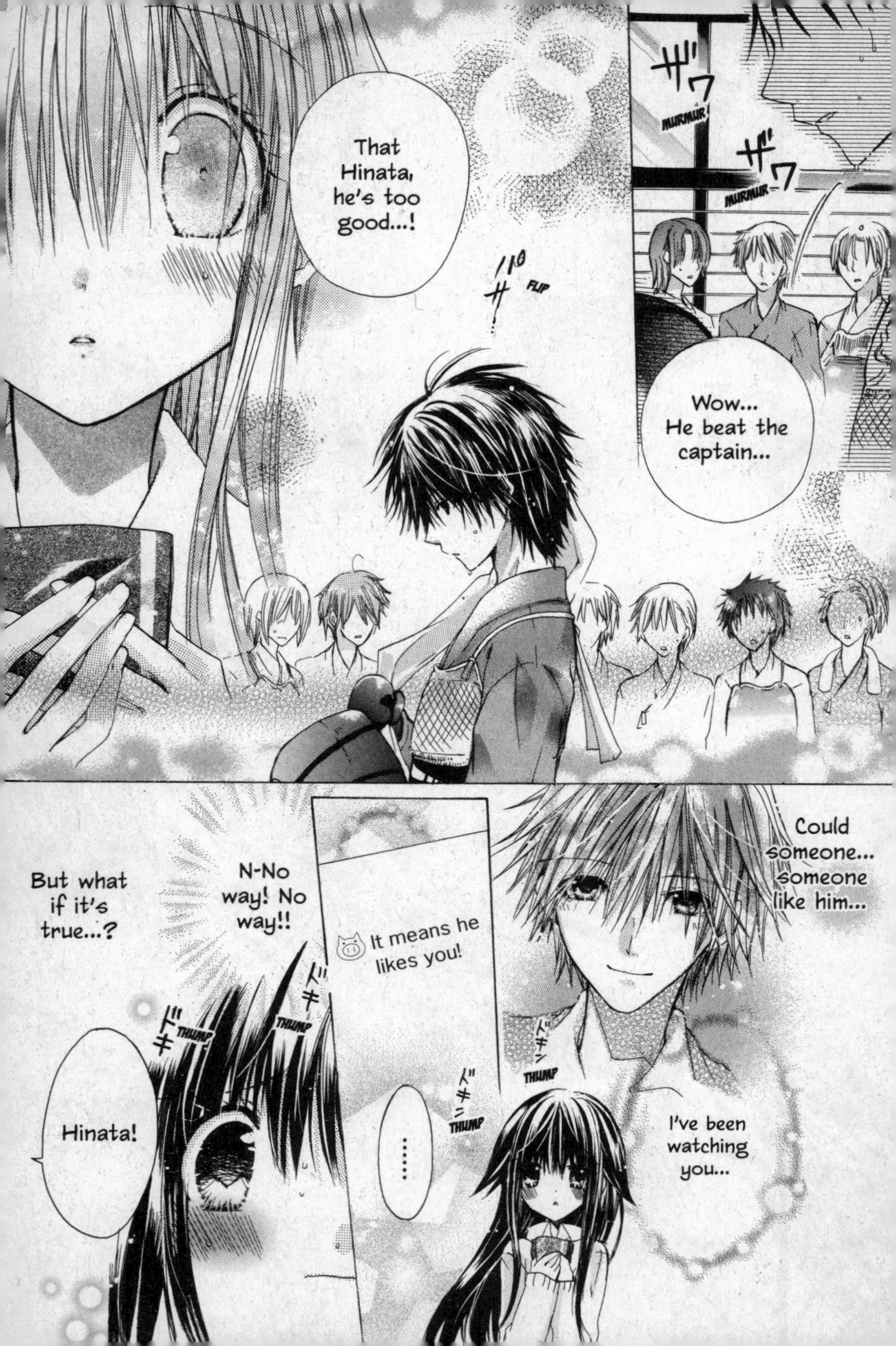
ザワ
MURMUR
ザワ
MURMUR
Wow... He beat the captain...
That Hinata, he's too good...!
パサ
FLIP
Could someone... someone like him...
I've been watching you...
ドキン
THUMP
ドキン
THUMP
......
It means he likes you!
N-No way! No way!!
But what if it's true...?
ドキ
THUMP
ドキ
THUMP
Hinata!

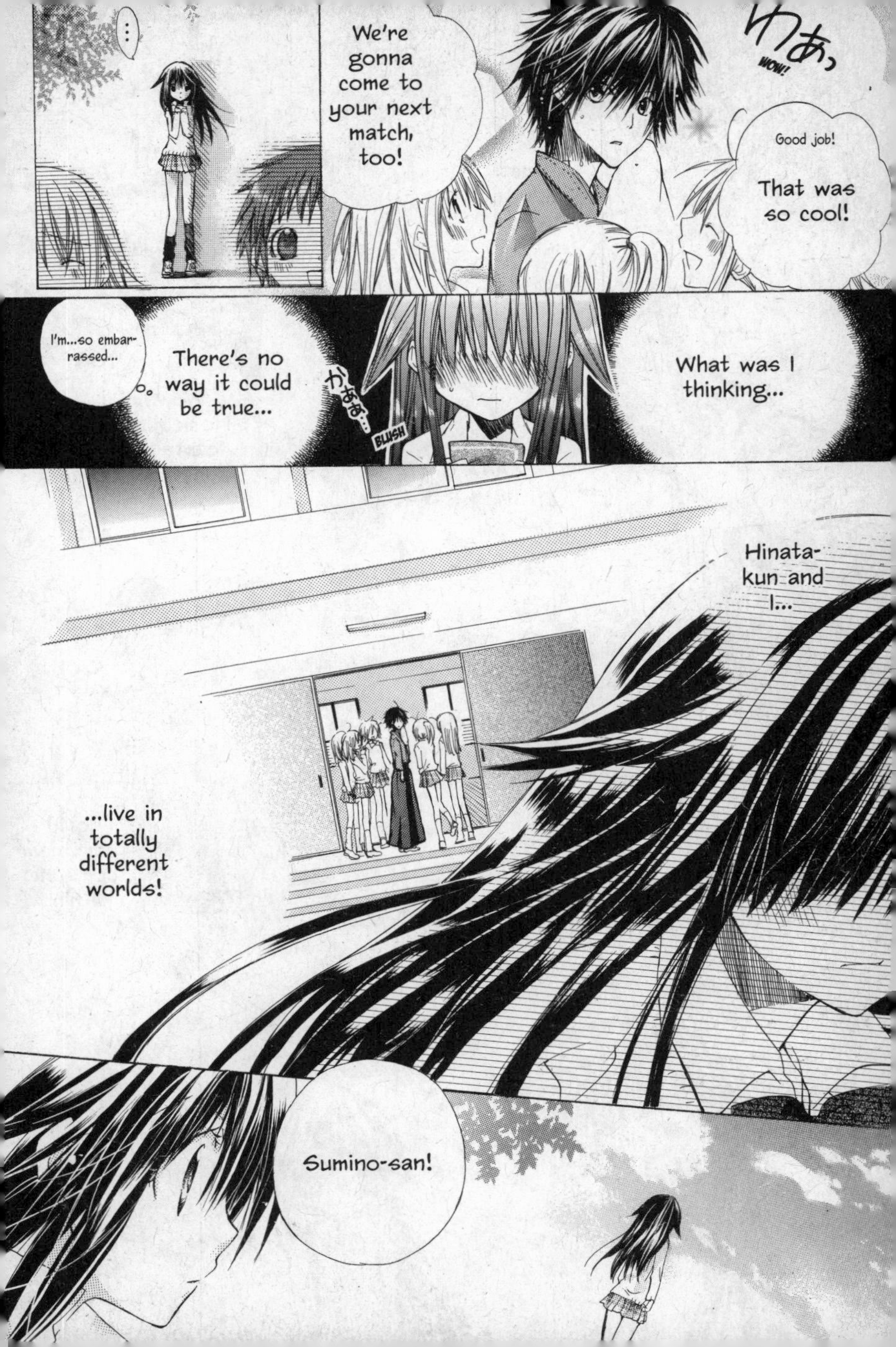
わあっ
WOW!
Good job!
That was so cool!
We're gonna come to your next match, too!
...
What was I thinking...
かあああ…
BLUSH
There's no way it could be true...
I'm...so embarrassed...
Hinata-kun and I...
...live in totally different worlds!
Sumino-san!

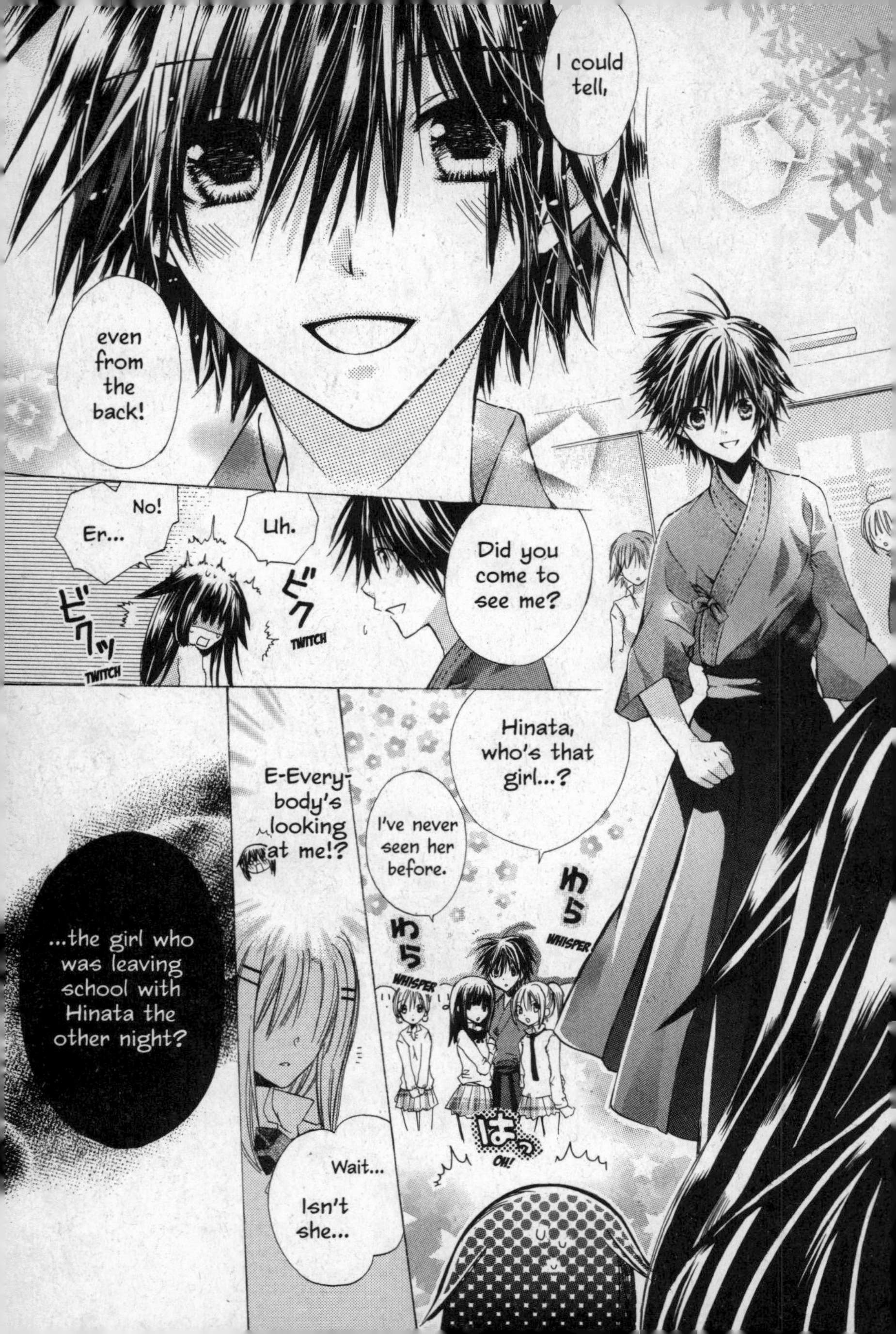

I could tell,
even from the back!
Did you come to see me?
ビク
TWITCH
Uh.
No! Er...
ビクッ
TWITCH
Hinata, who's that girl...?
I've never seen her before.
わら
WHISPER
わら
WHISPER
E-Everybody's looking at me!?
はっ
OH!
Wait... Isn't she...
...the girl who was leaving school with Hinata the other night?

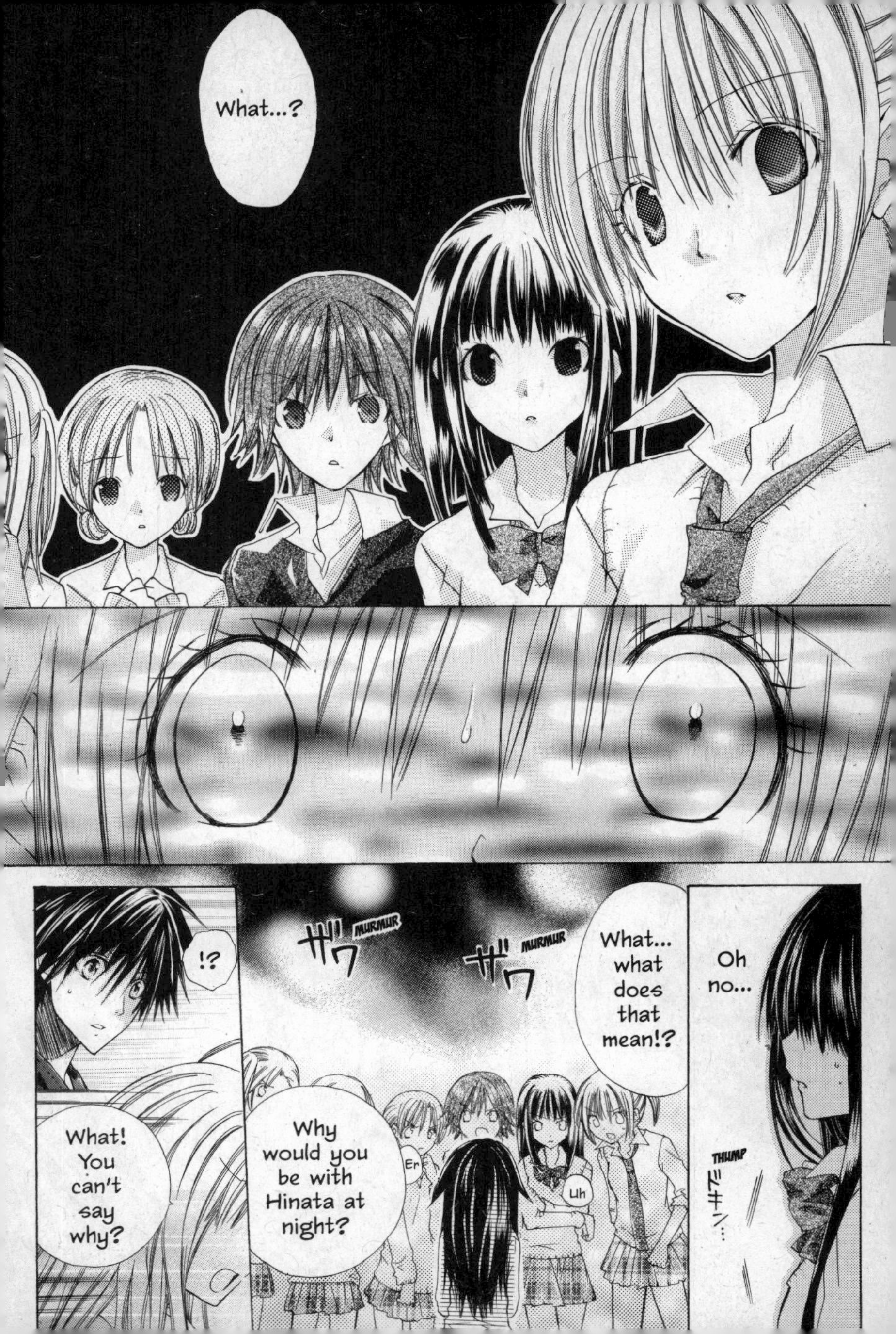
What...?
Oh no...
THUMP
ドキン…
What... what does that mean!?
ザワ MURMUR
ザワ MURMUR
!?
Uh
Er
Why would you be with Hinata at night?
What! You can't say why?

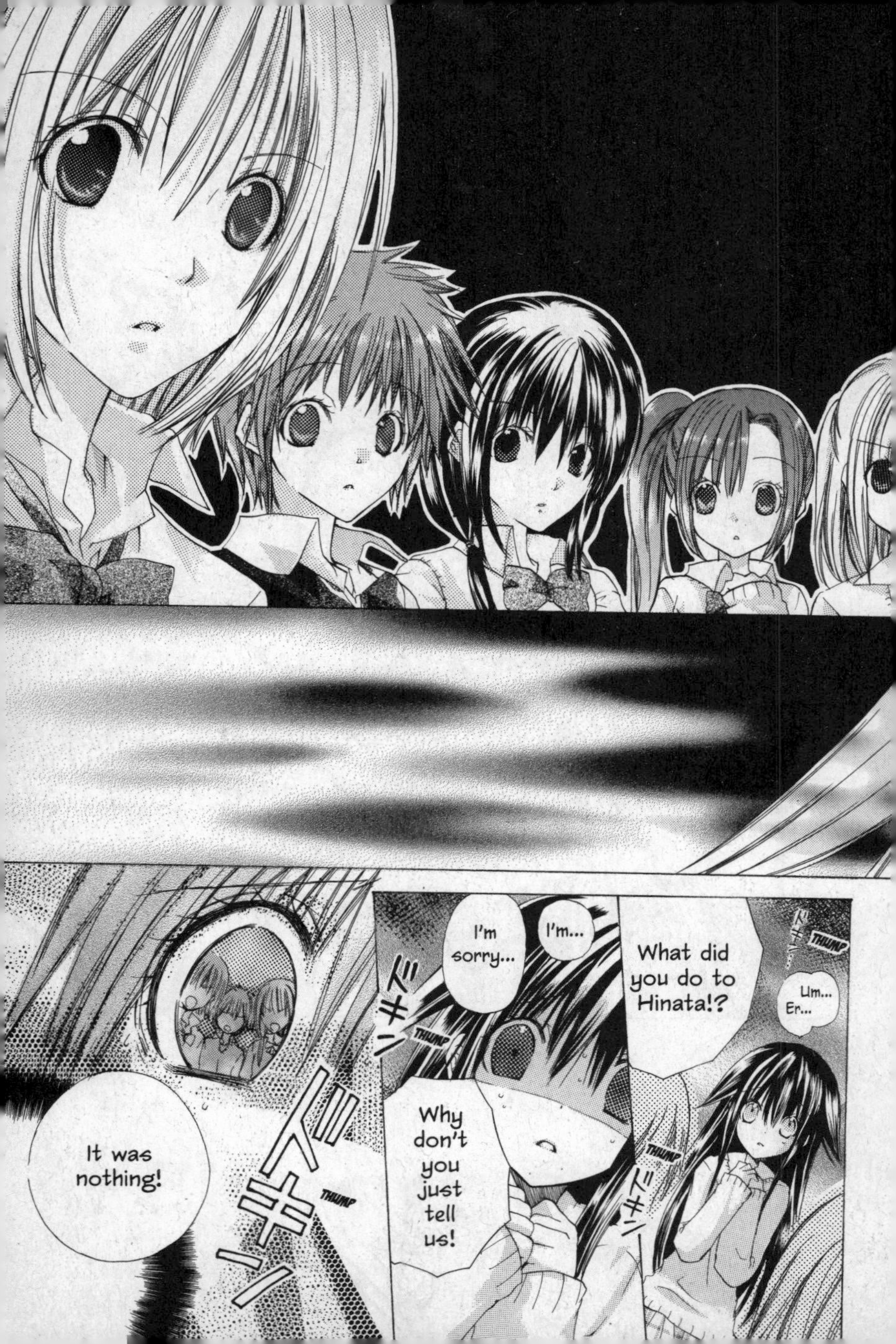
THUMP
What did you do to Hinata!?
Um... Er...
THUMP
I'm...
I'm sorry...
THUMP
Why don't you just tell us!
THUMP
It was nothing!

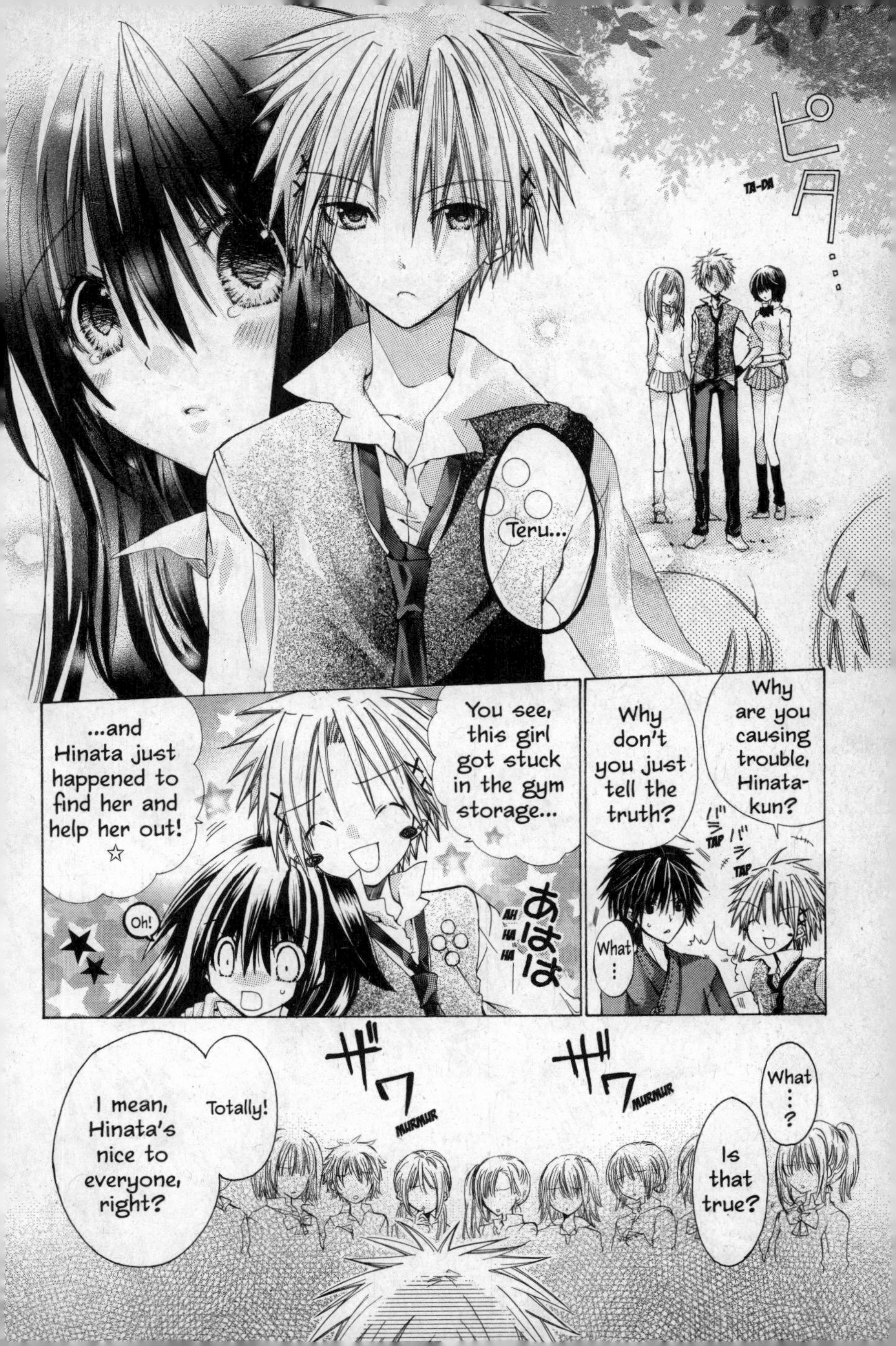
ピタ…
TA-DA
Teru...
Why are you causing trouble, Hinata-kun?
Why don't you just tell the truth?
バシ
TAP
バシ
TAP
What...
You see, this girl got stuck in the gym storage...
...and Hinata just happened to find her and help her out! ☆
あはは
AH HA HA
Oh!
ザワ
MURMUR
ザワ
MURMUR
What...?
Is that true?
Totally!
I mean, Hinata's nice to everyone, right?

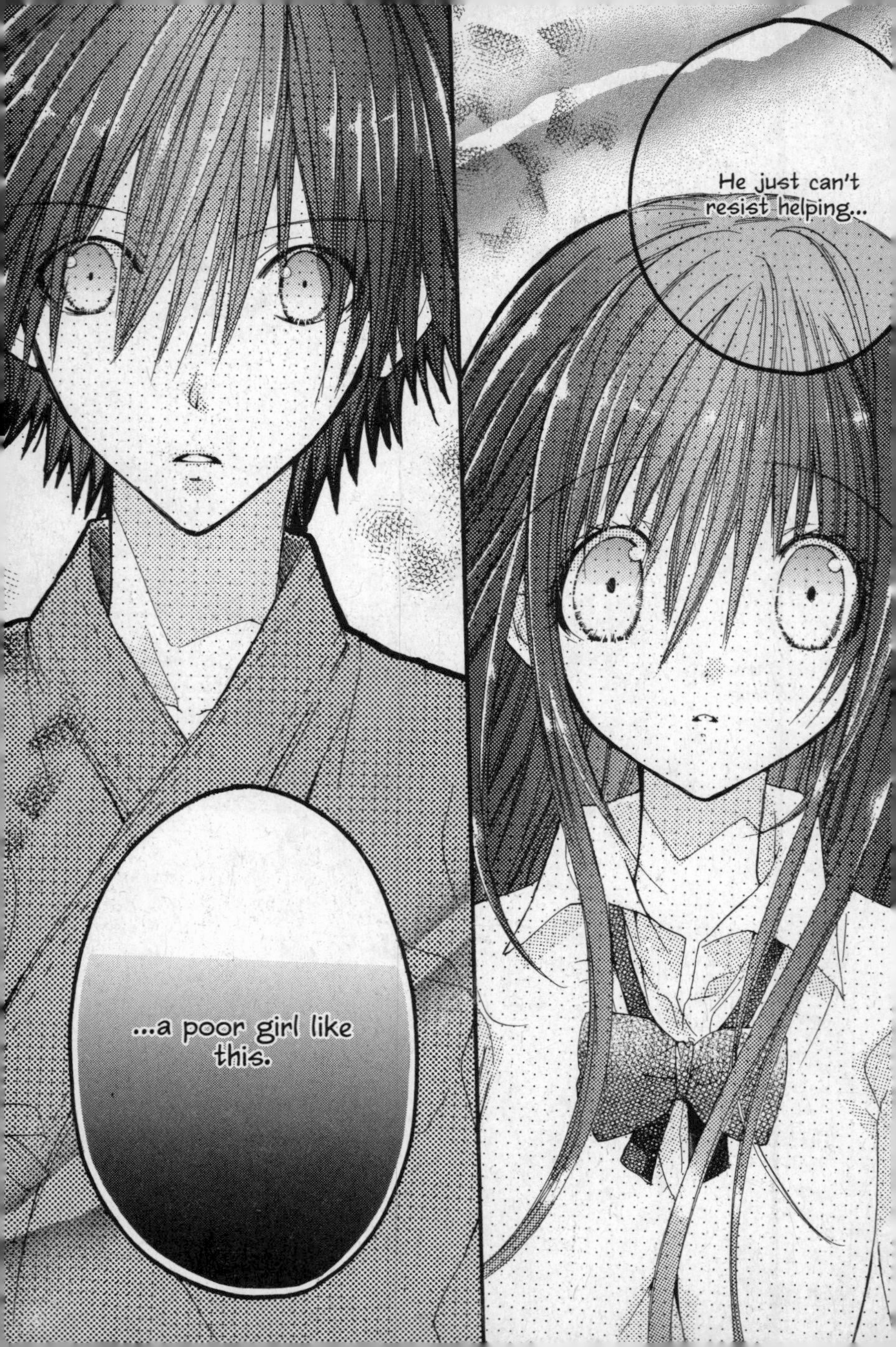
He just can't resist helping...
...a poor girl like this.

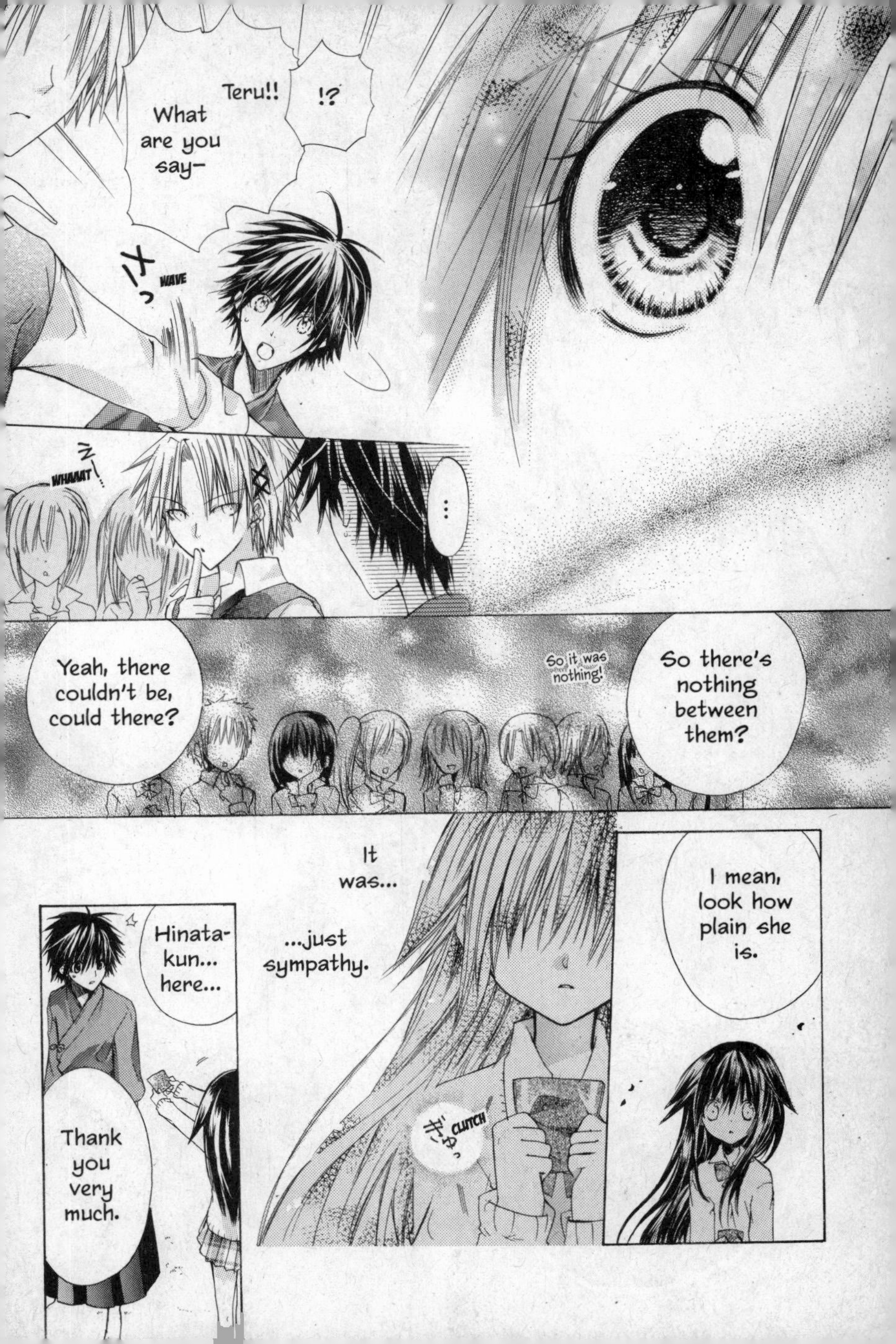

!?
Teru!! What are you say-
WAVE
...
WHAAAT
So there's nothing between them?
So it was nothing!
Yeah, there couldn't be, could there?
I mean, look how plain she is.
It was...
...just sympathy.
CLUTCH
Hinata-kun... here...
Thank you very much.

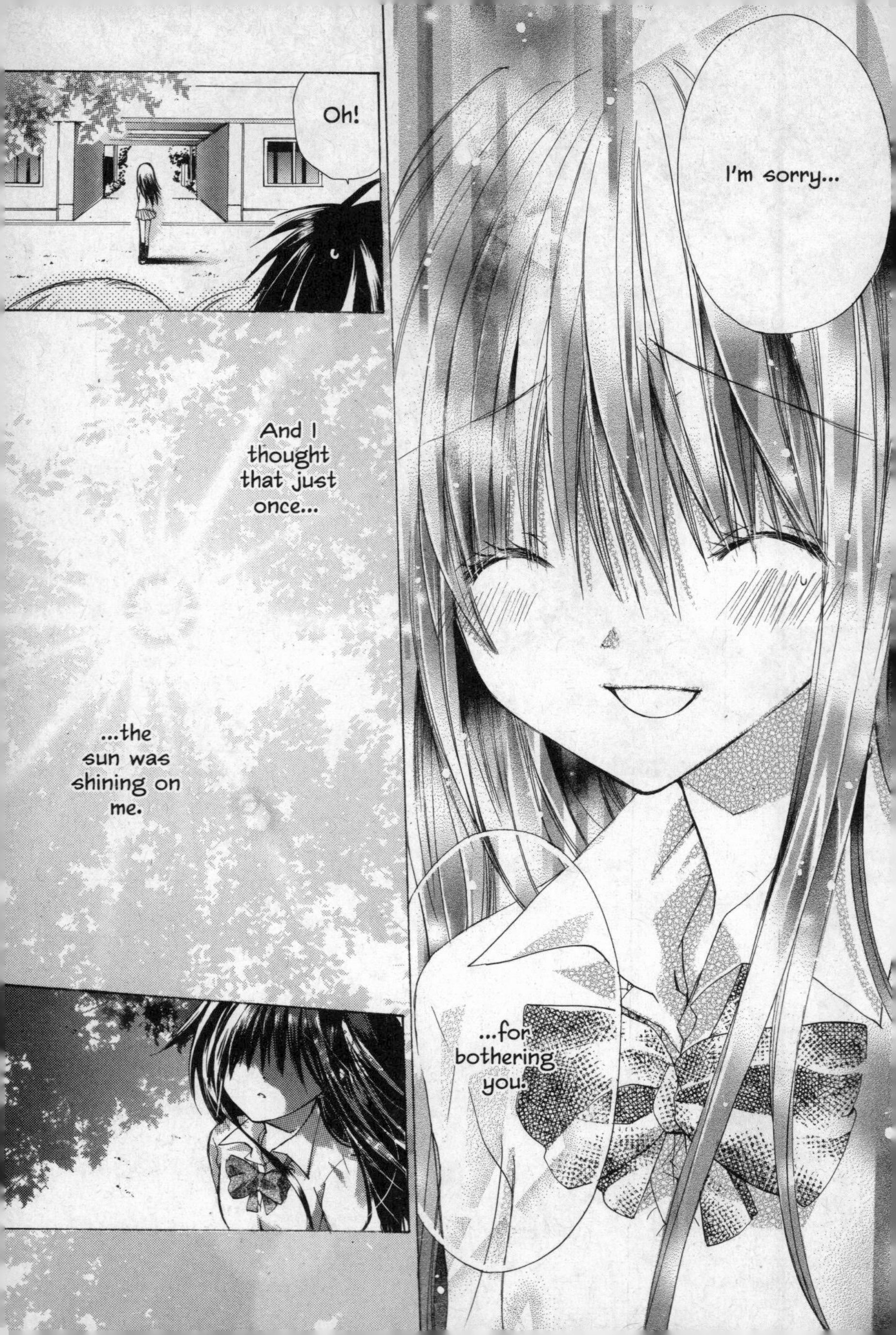
I'm sorry...
...for bothering you.
Oh!
And I thought that just once...
...the sun was shining on me.

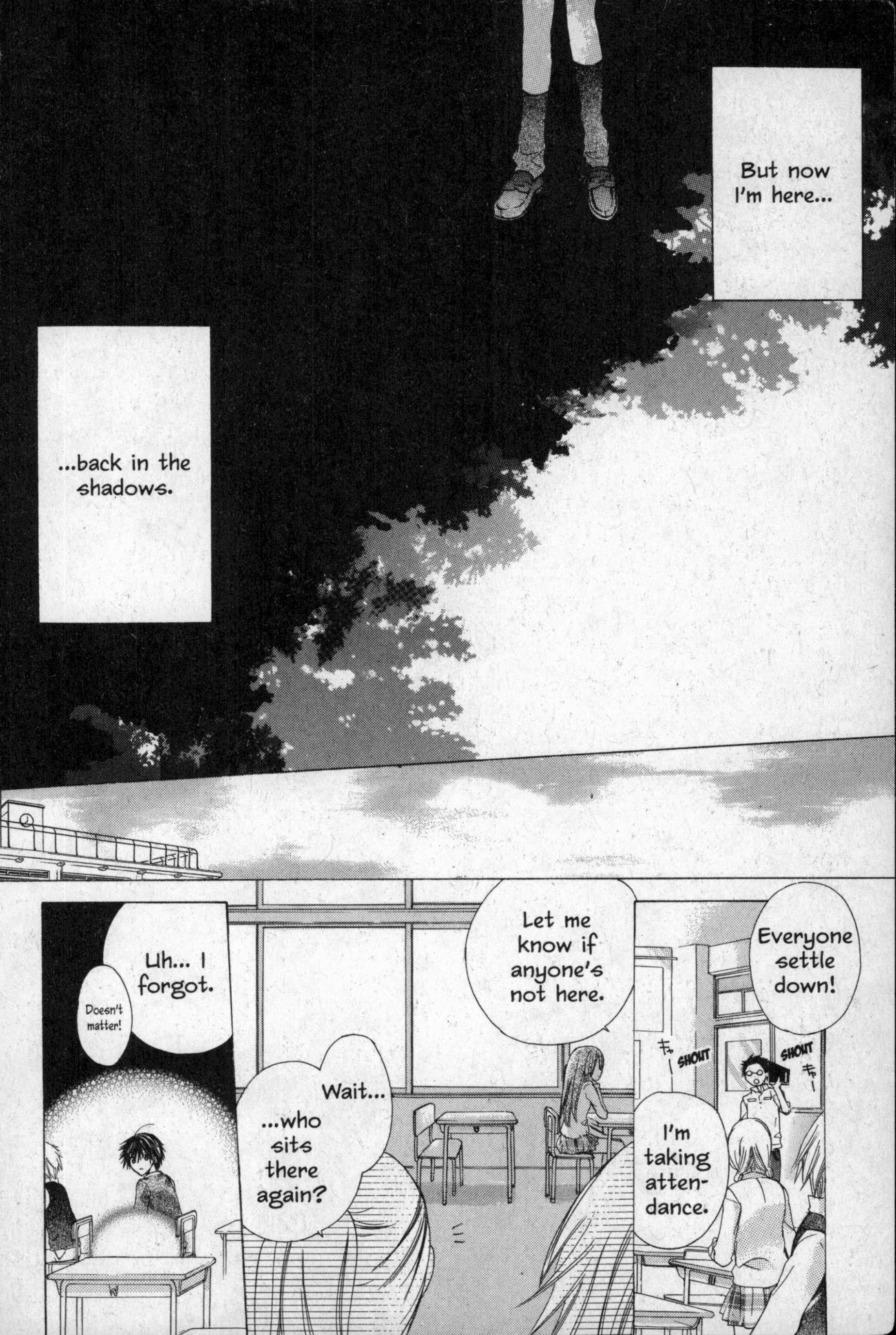
But now I'm here...
...back in the shadows.
Everyone settle down!
SHOUT
SHOUT
I'm taking atten-dance.
Let me know if anyone's not here.
Wait...
...who sits there again?
Uh... I forgot.
Doesn't matter!

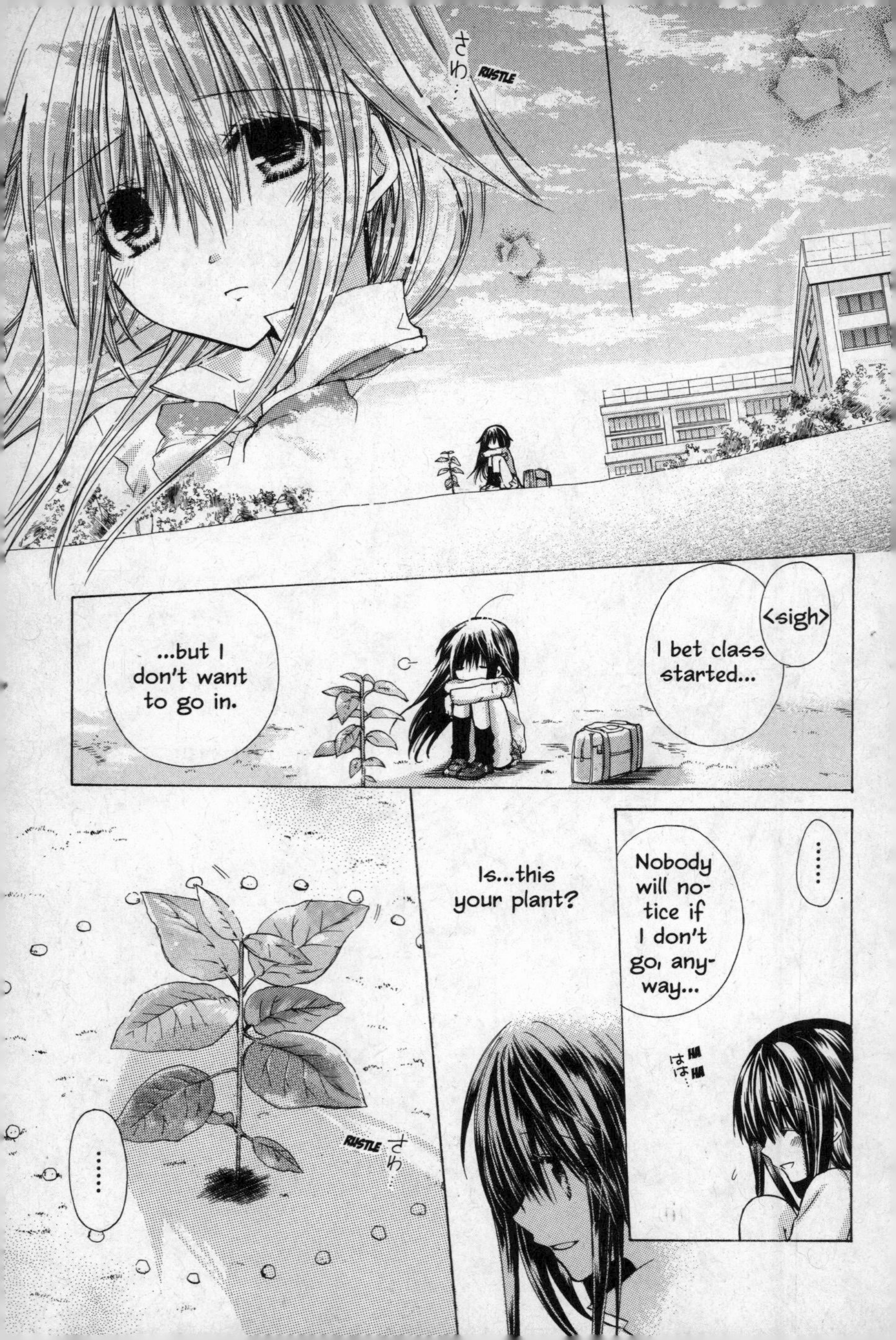
さわ…
RUSTLE
<sigh>
I bet class started...
...but I don't want to go in.
……
Nobody will no-tice if I don't go, any-way...
はは…
HA HA
Is...this your plant?
RUSTLE
さわ…
……

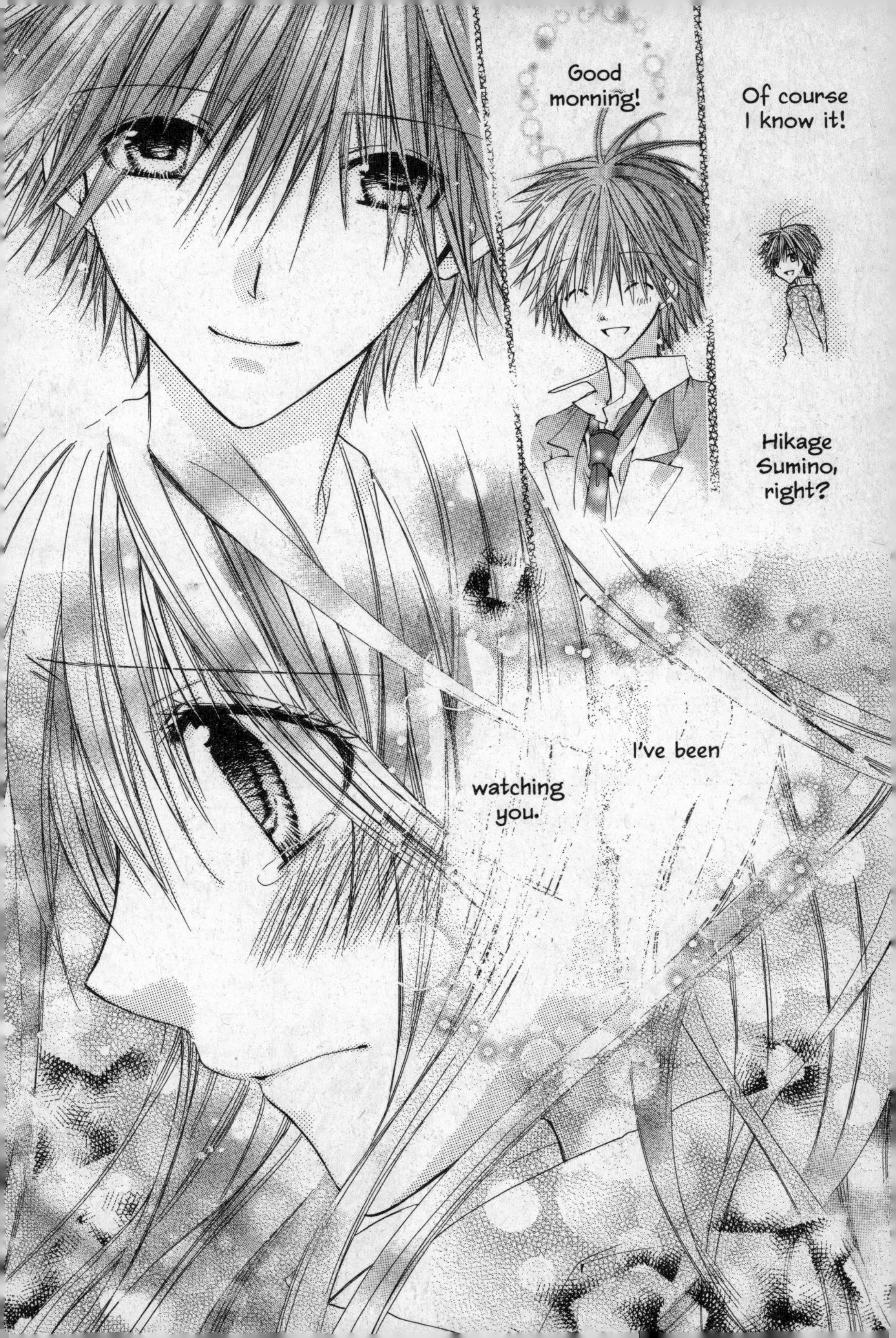
Of course I know it!
Hikage Sumino, right?
Good morning!
I've been
watching you.

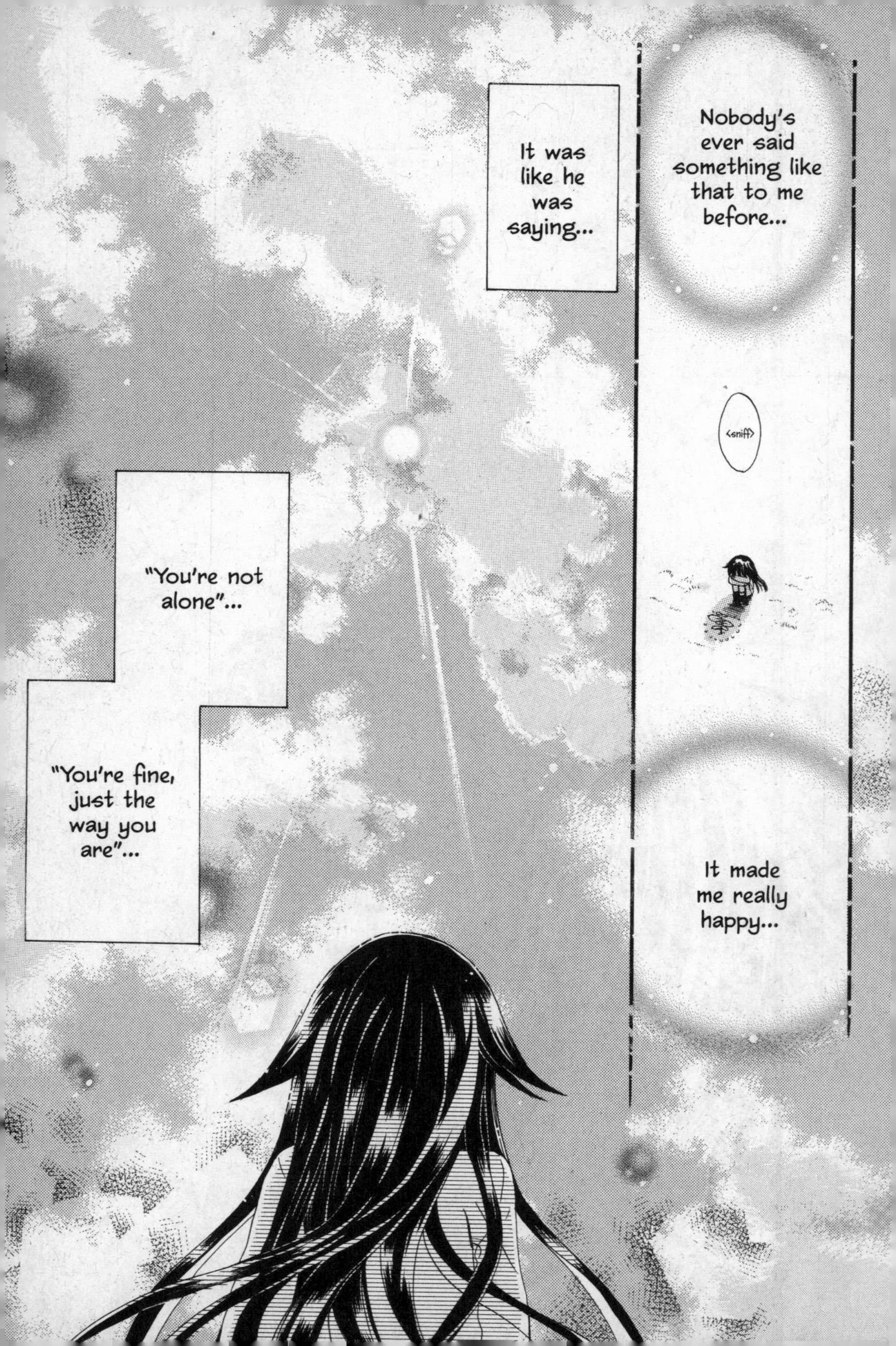
Nobody's ever said something like that to me before...
<sniff>
It made me really happy...
It was like he was saying...
"You're not alone"...
"You're fine, just the way you are"...

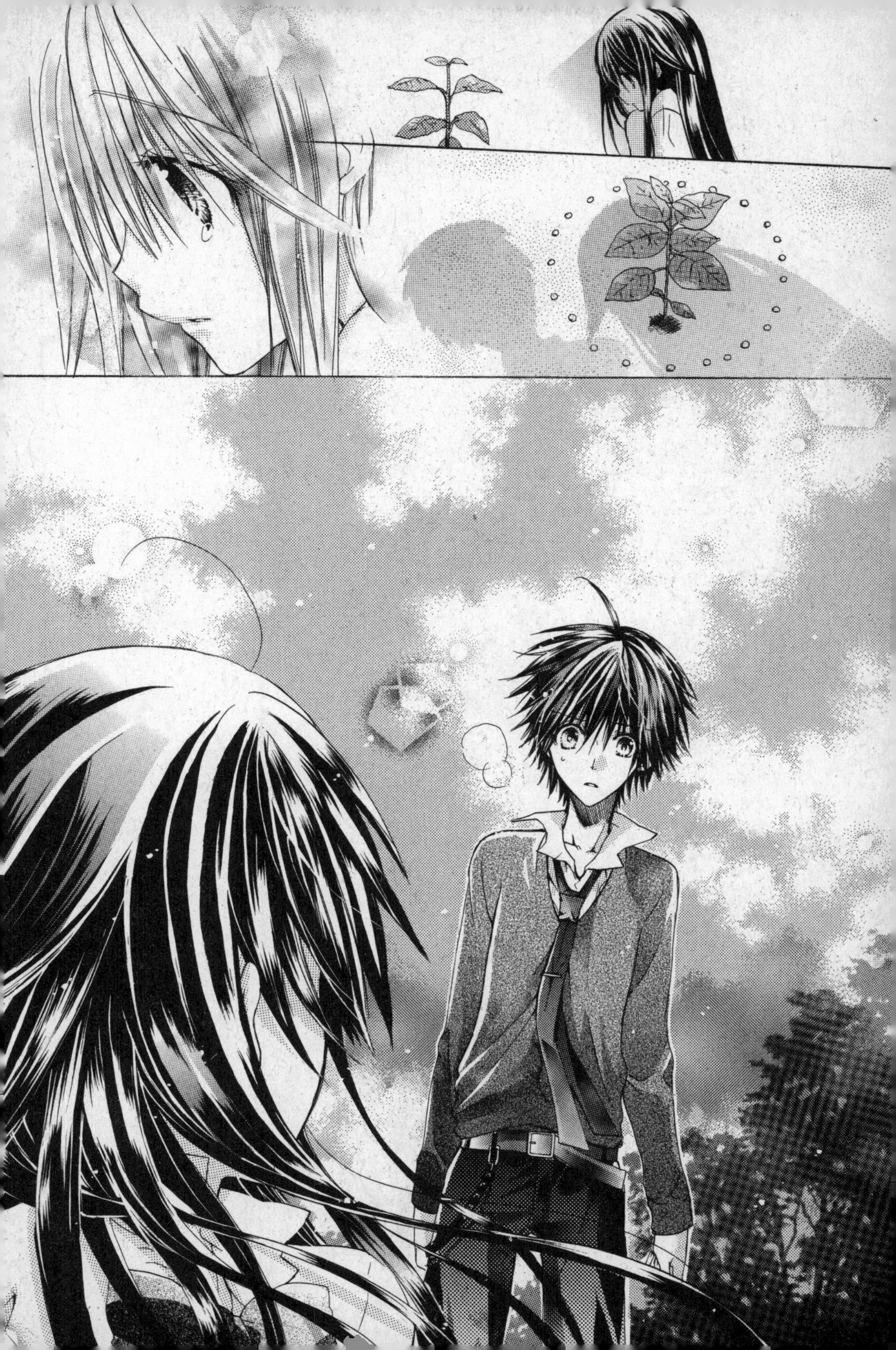

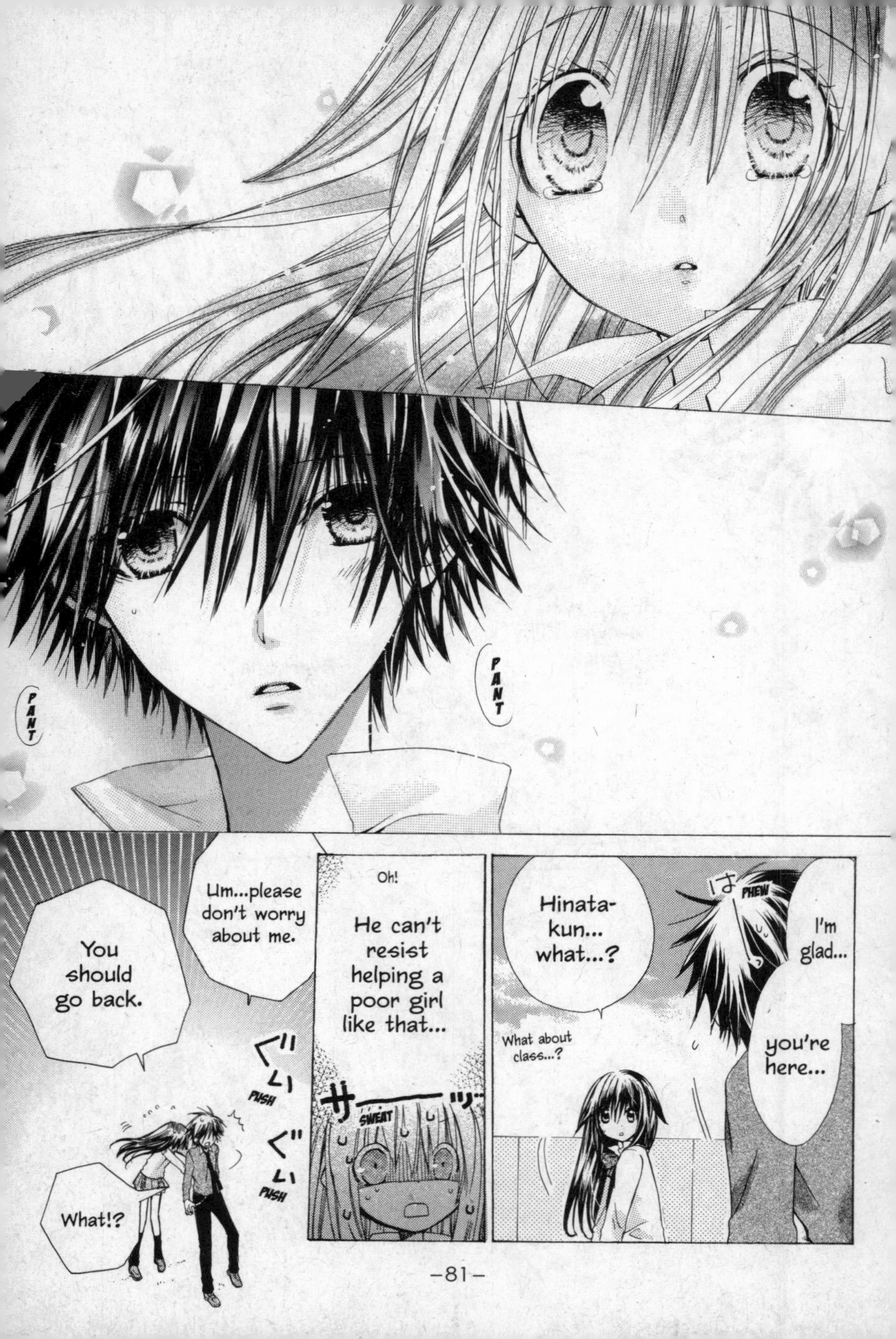
PANT
PANT
PHEW
I'm glad...
you're here...
Hinata-kun... what...?
What about class...?
Oh!
He can't resist helping a poor girl like that...
SWEAT
Um...please don't worry about me.
You should go back.
PUSH
PUSH
What!?

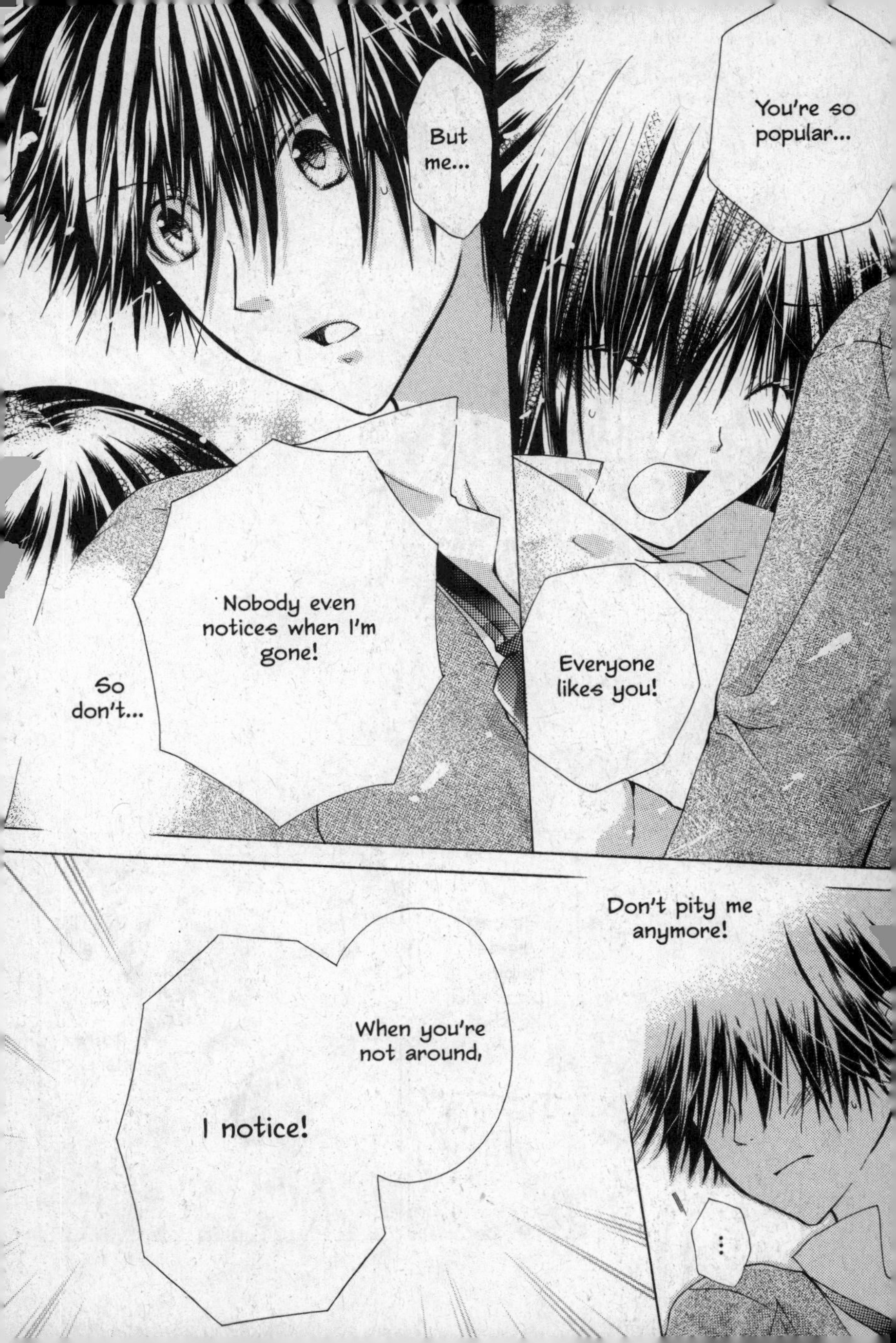
You're so popular...
Everyone likes you!
But me...
Nobody even notices when I'm gone!
So don't...
Don't pity me anymore!
When you're not around,
I notice!
...

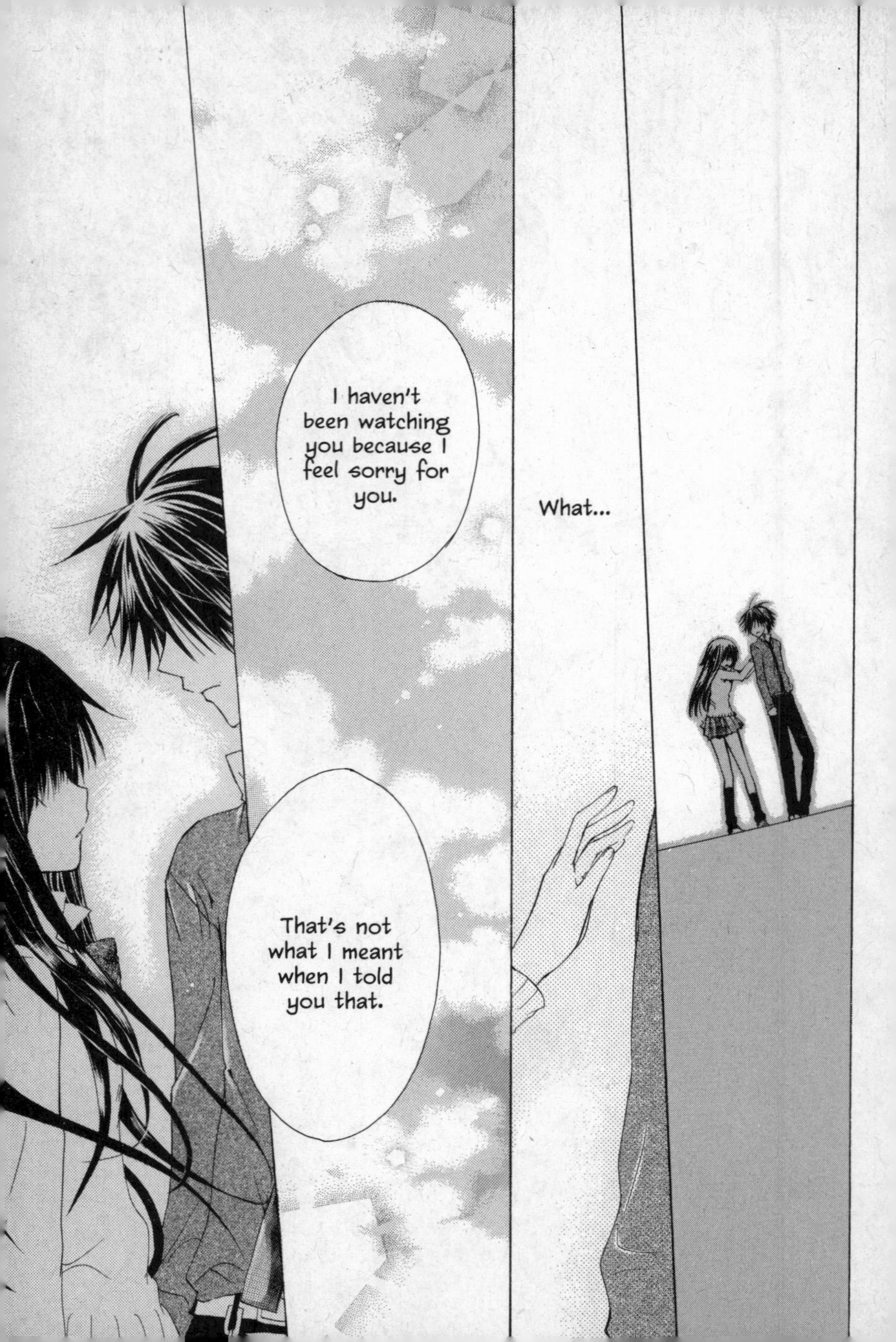
What...
I haven't been watching you because I feel sorry for you.
That's not what I meant when I told you that.

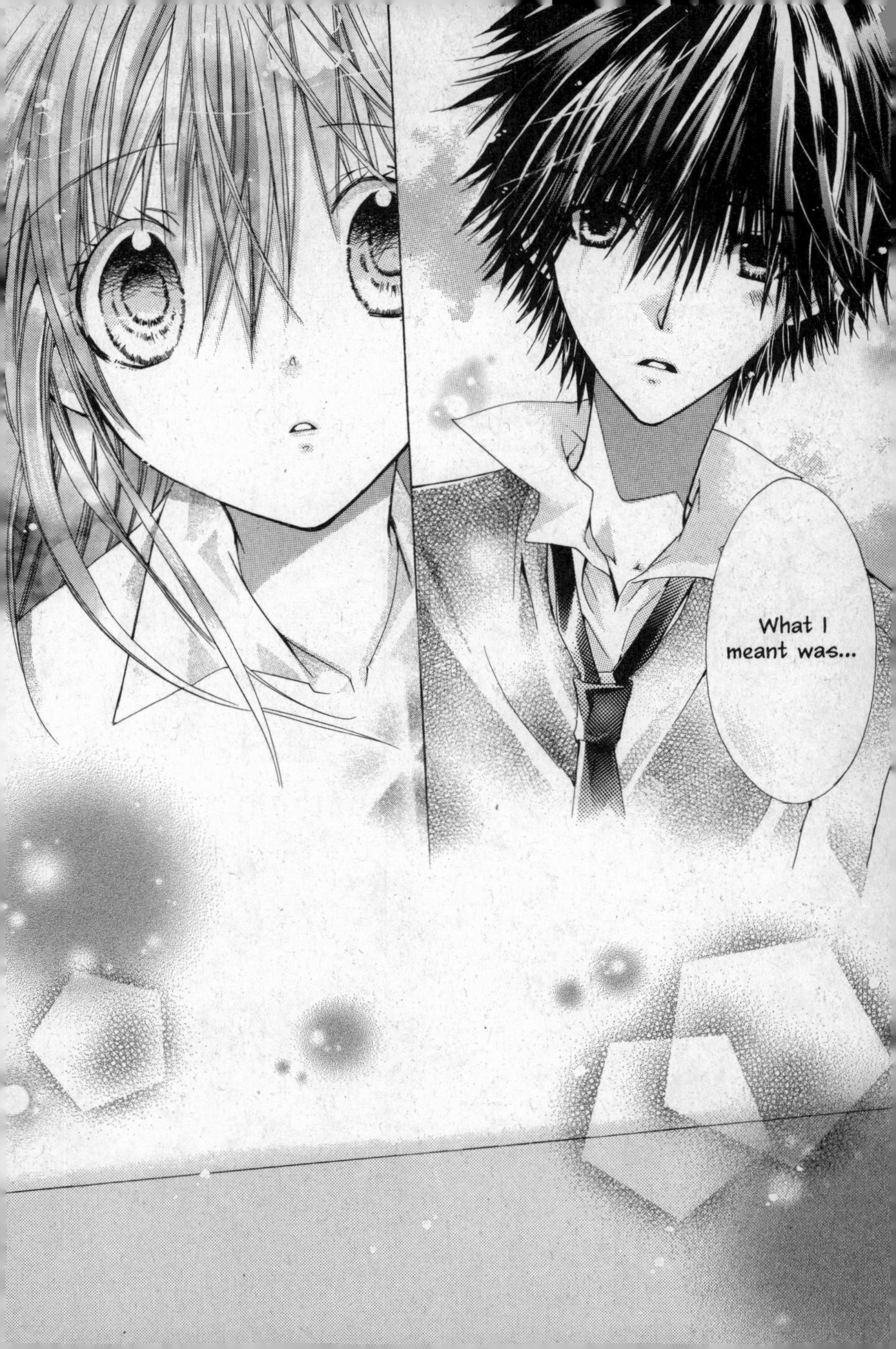
What I meant was...

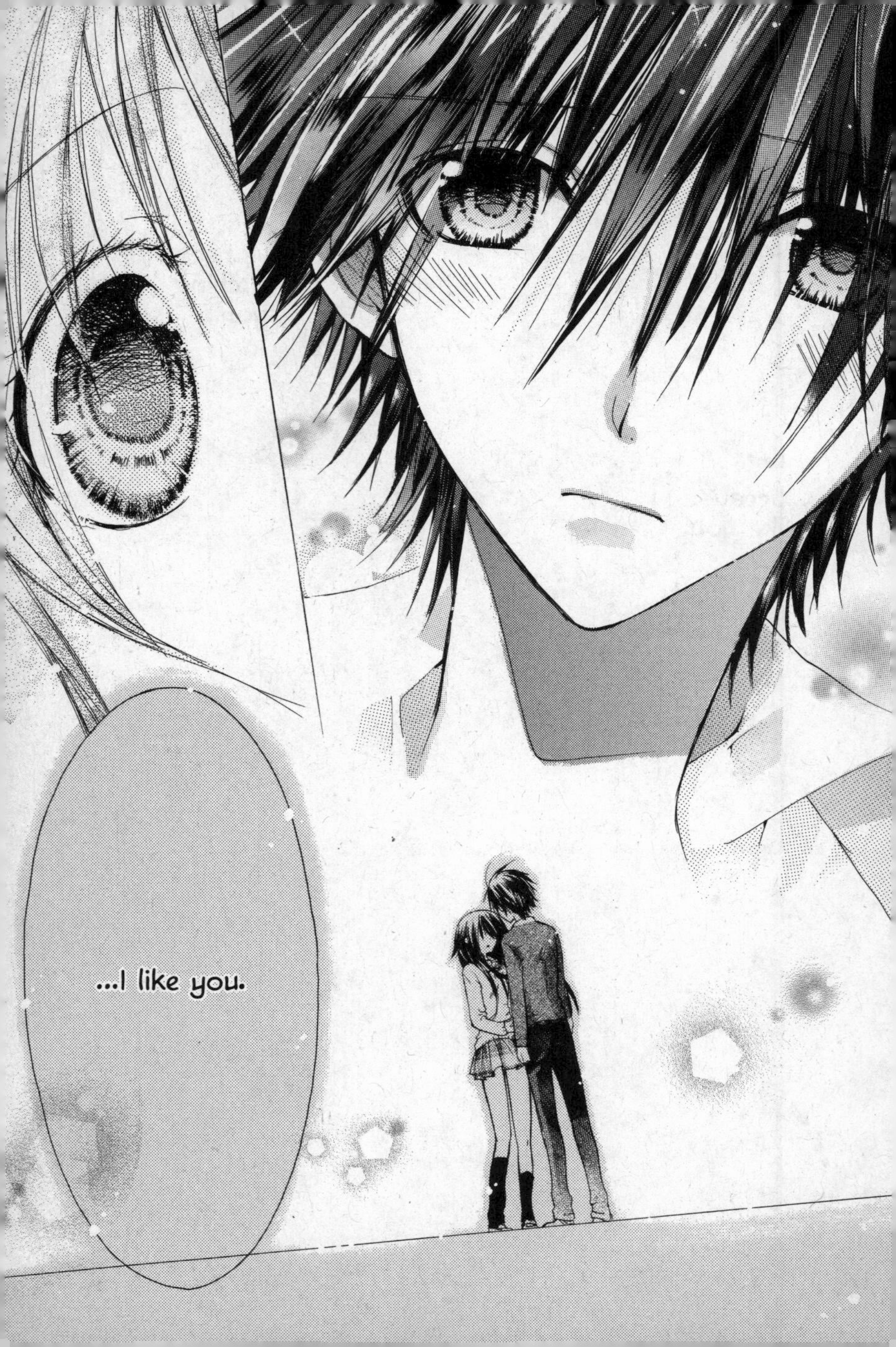
...I like you.

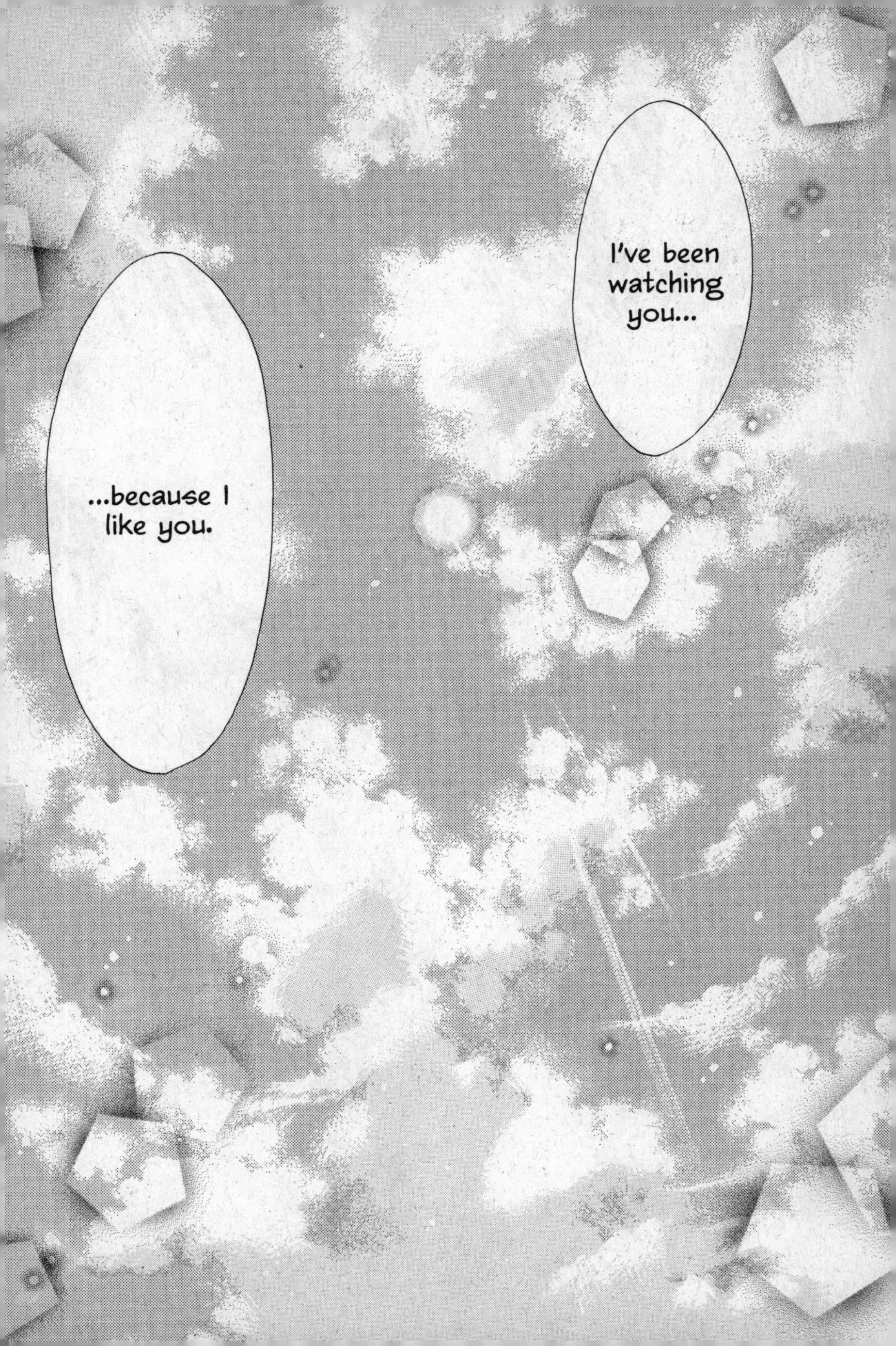
I've been watching you...
...because I like you.

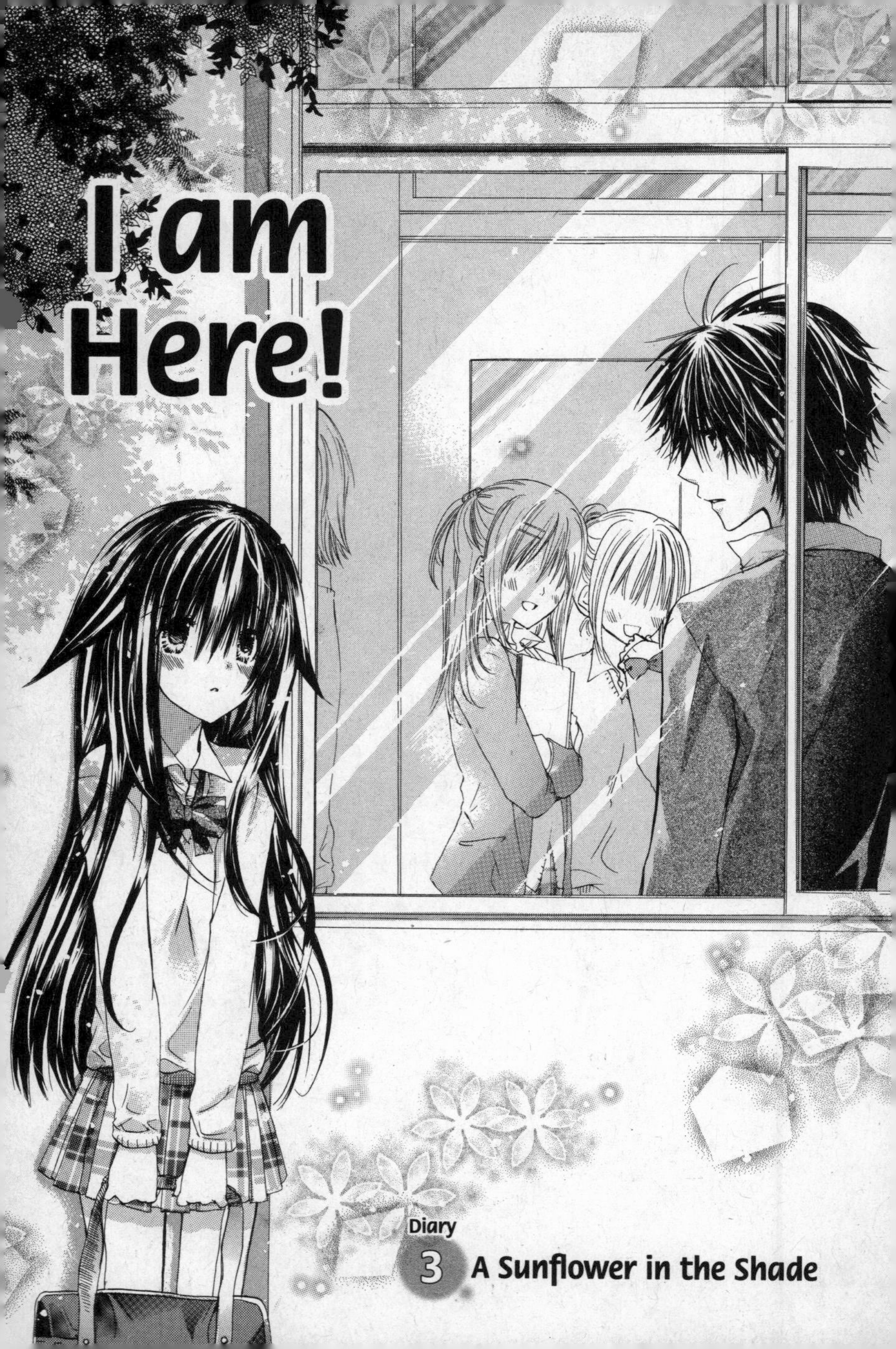
I am Here!
Diary
3 A Sunflower in the Shade

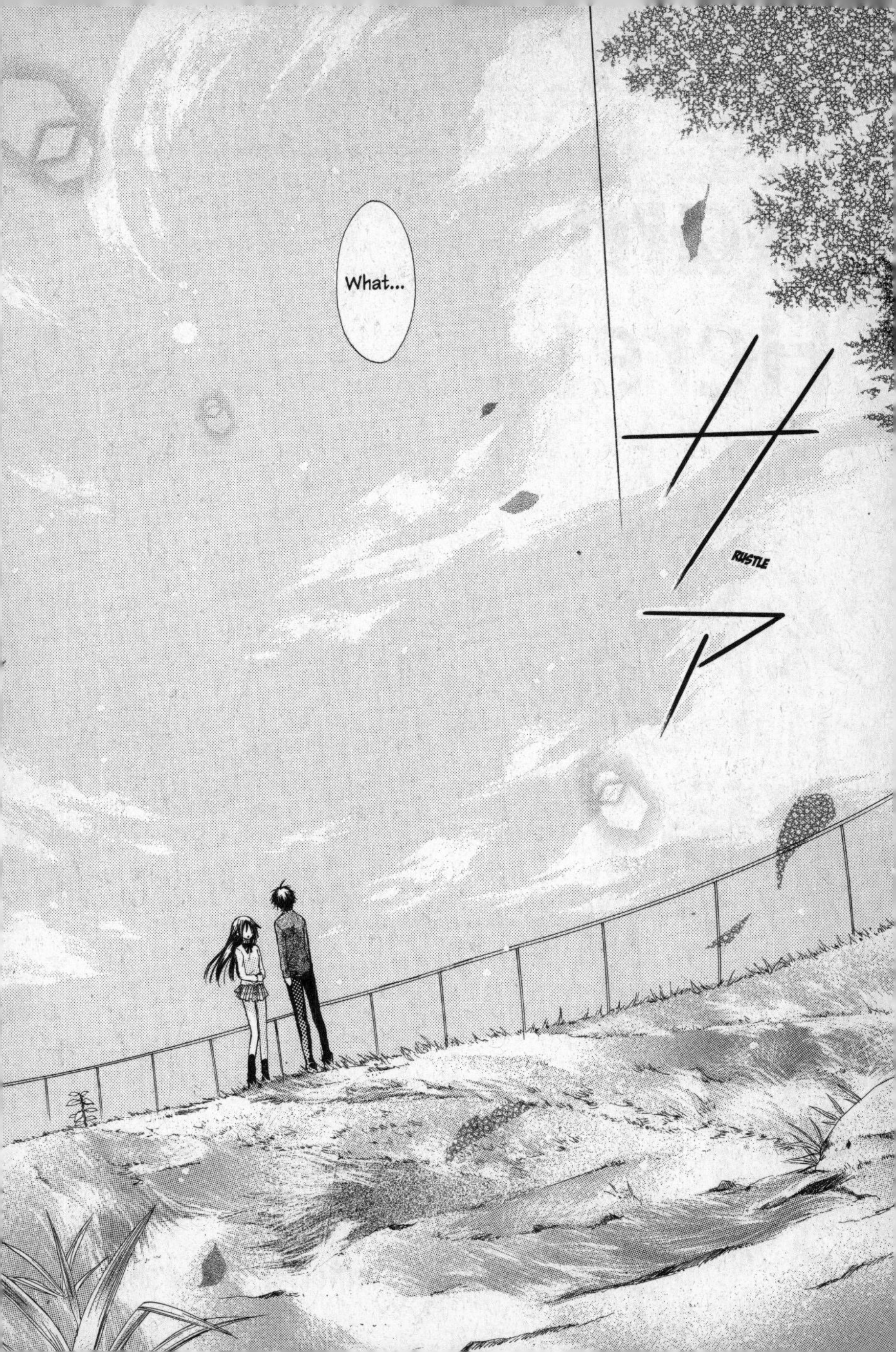
RUSTLE
What...

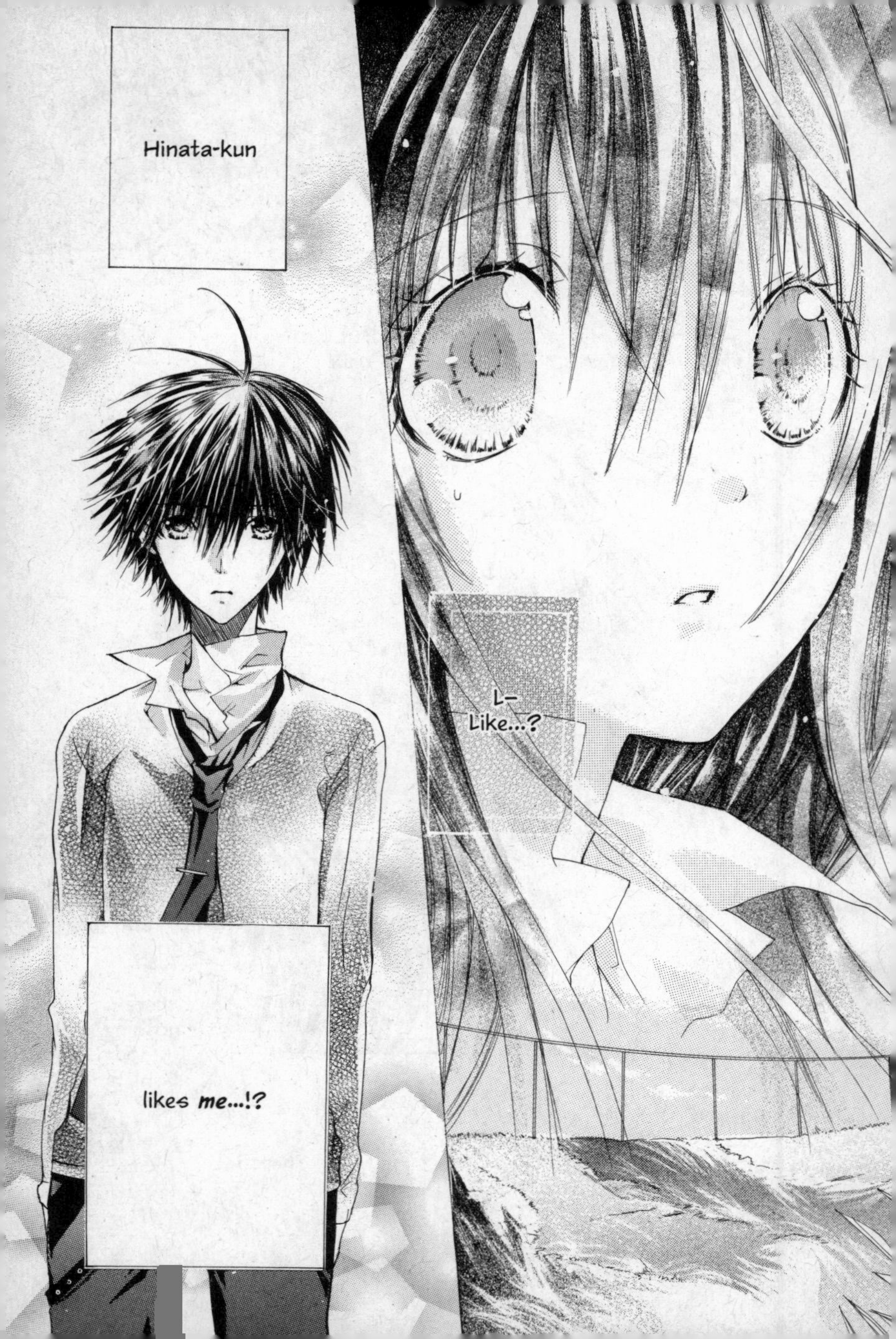
L–
Like...?
Hinata-kun
likes me...!?

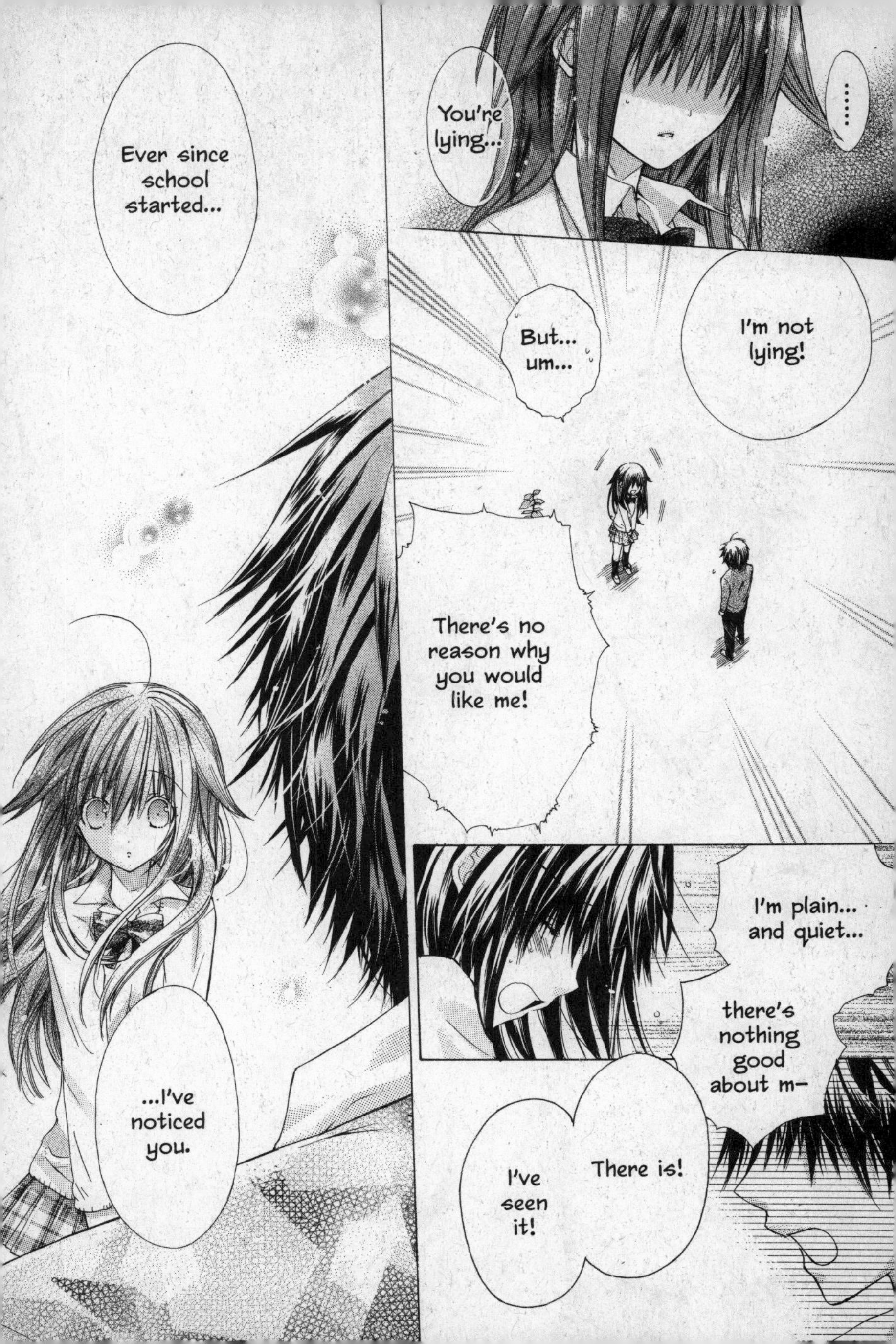
......
You're lying...!
I'm not lying!
But... um...
There's no reason why you would like me!
I'm plain... and quiet...
there's nothing good about m-
There is!
I've seen it!
Ever since school started...
...I've noticed you.

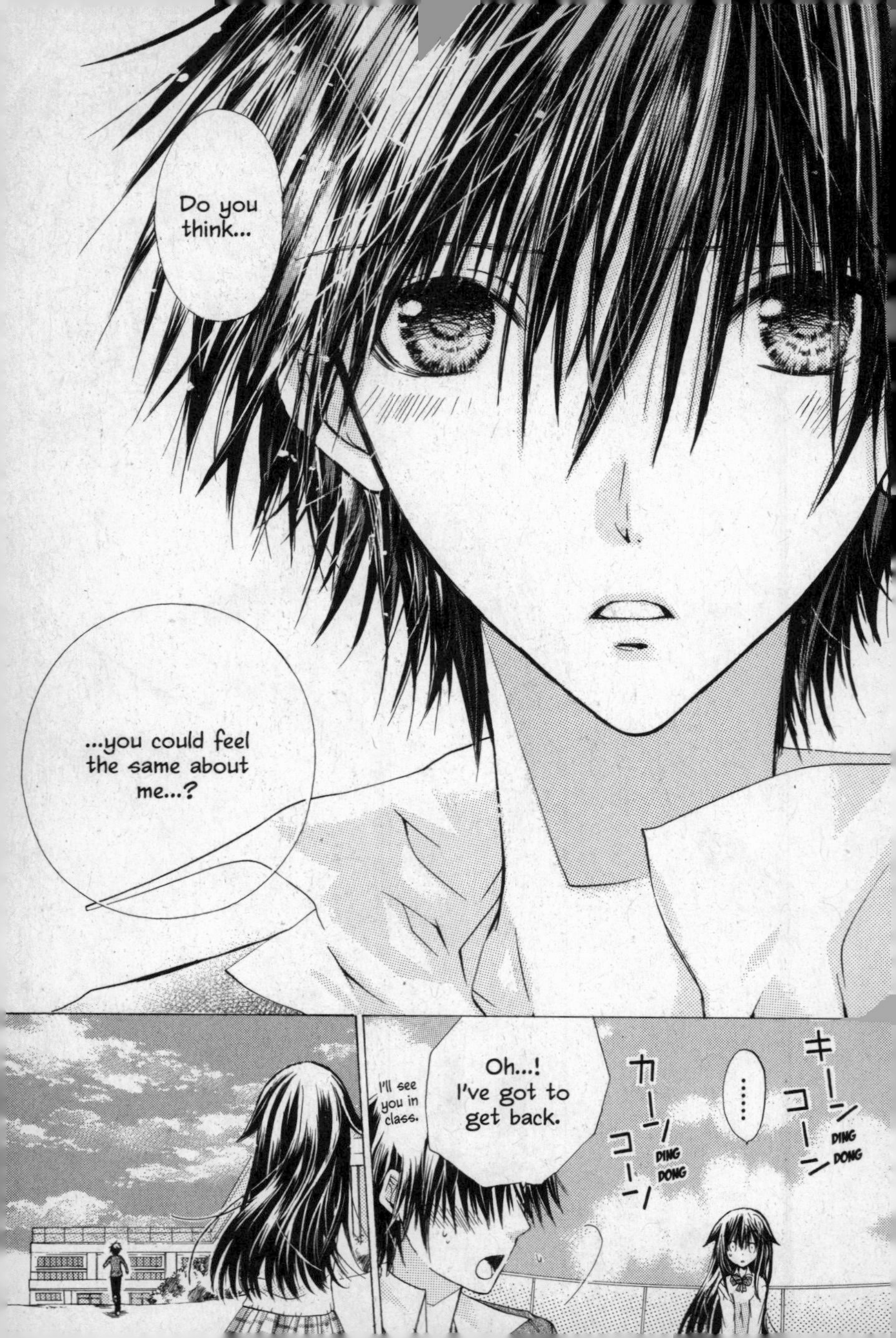
Do you think...
...you could feel the same about me...?
キーンコーン
DING DONG
カーンコーン
DING DONG
......
Oh...! I've got to get back.
I'll see you in class.

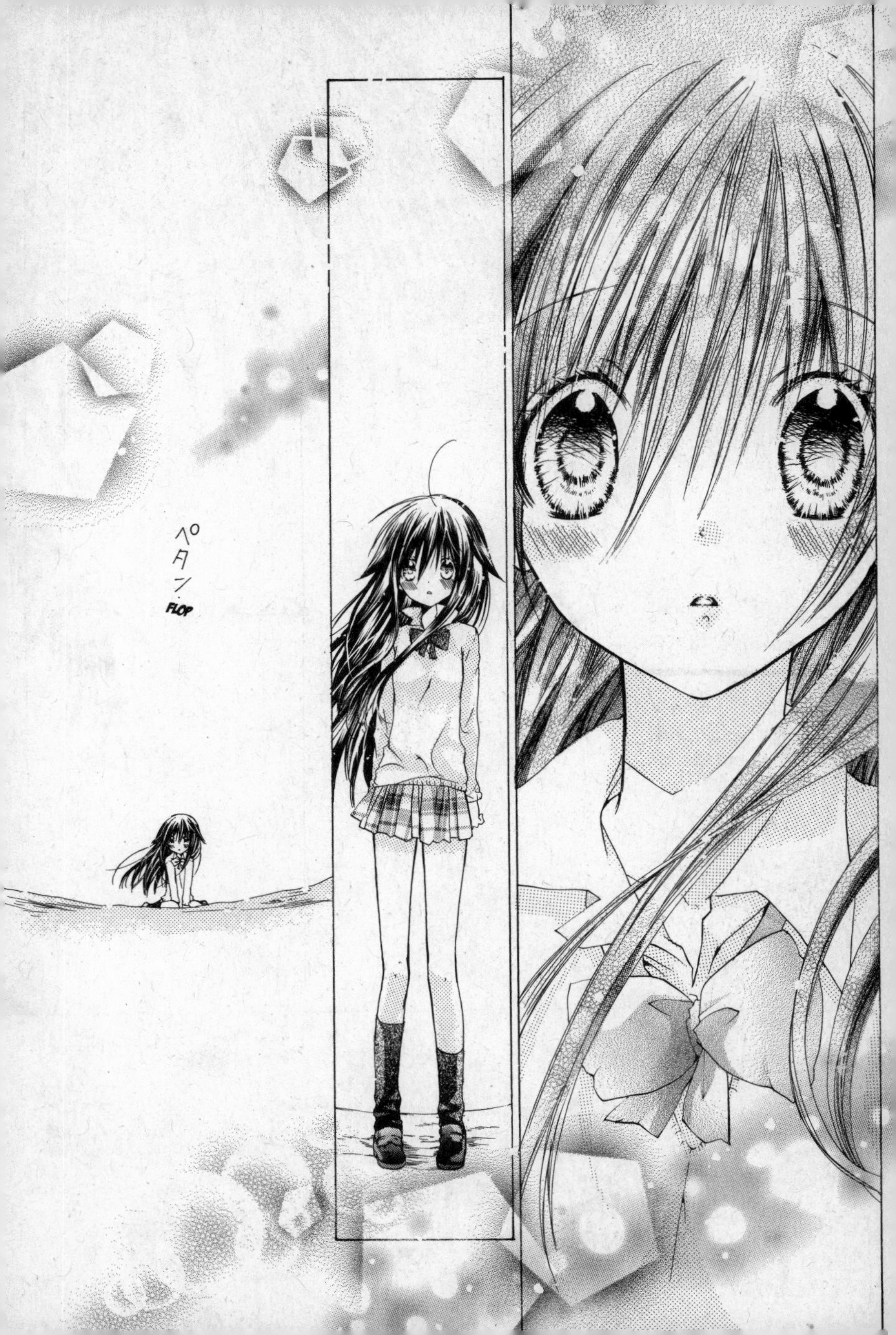
ペタン
FLOP

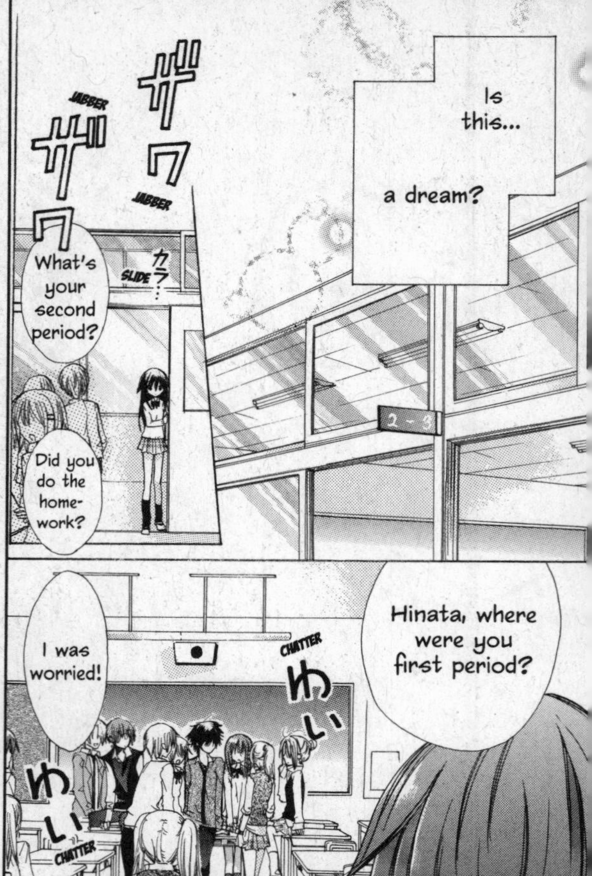

Is this...
a dream?
ザワ JABBER
ザワ JABBER
What's your second period?
SLIDE カラ...
Did you do the home-work?
Hinata, where were you first period?
CHATTER わい
I was worried!
わい CHATTER
Don't cut class by yourself.
Take me with you!
CHATTER わい
CHATTER わい
The teacher was mad!
Oh...

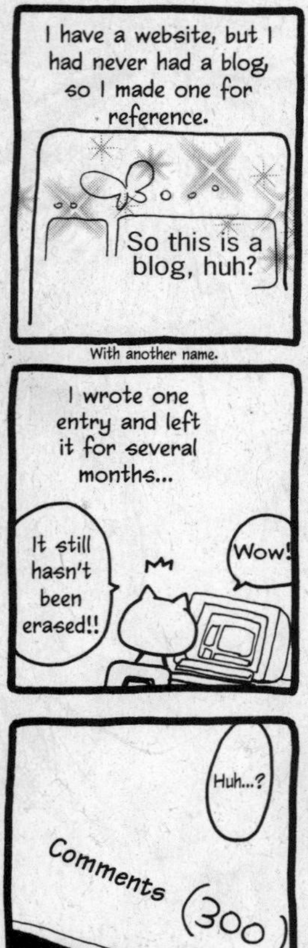

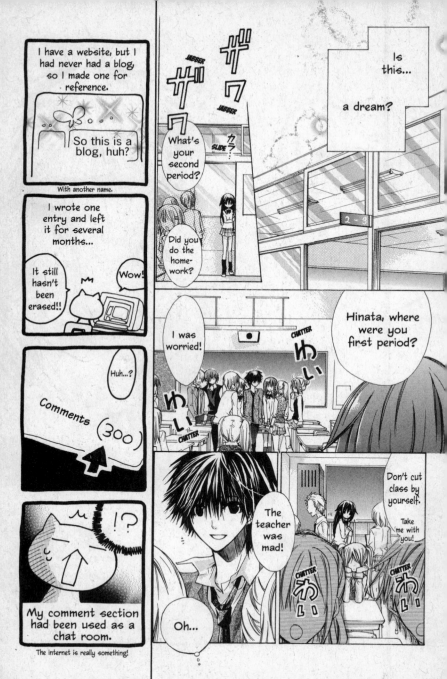

I have a website, but I had never had a blog, so I made one for reference.
So this is a blog, huh?
With another name.
I wrote one entry and left it for several months...
Wow!
It still hasn't been erased!!
Huh...?
Comments (300)
!?
My comment section had been used as a chat room.
The internet is really something!

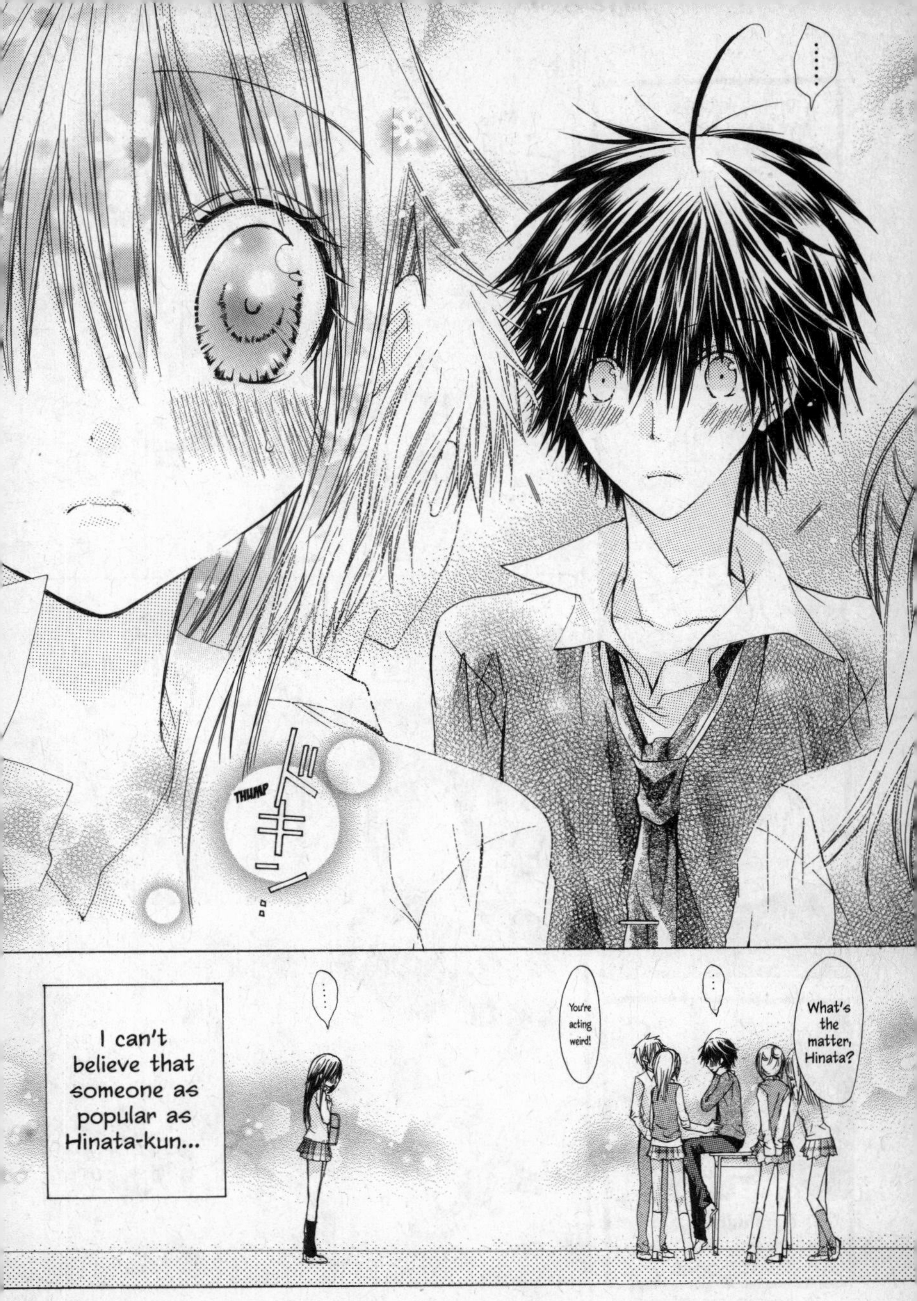
……
THUMP
What's the matter, Hinata?
…
You're acting weird!
……
I can't believe that someone as popular as Hinata-kun...

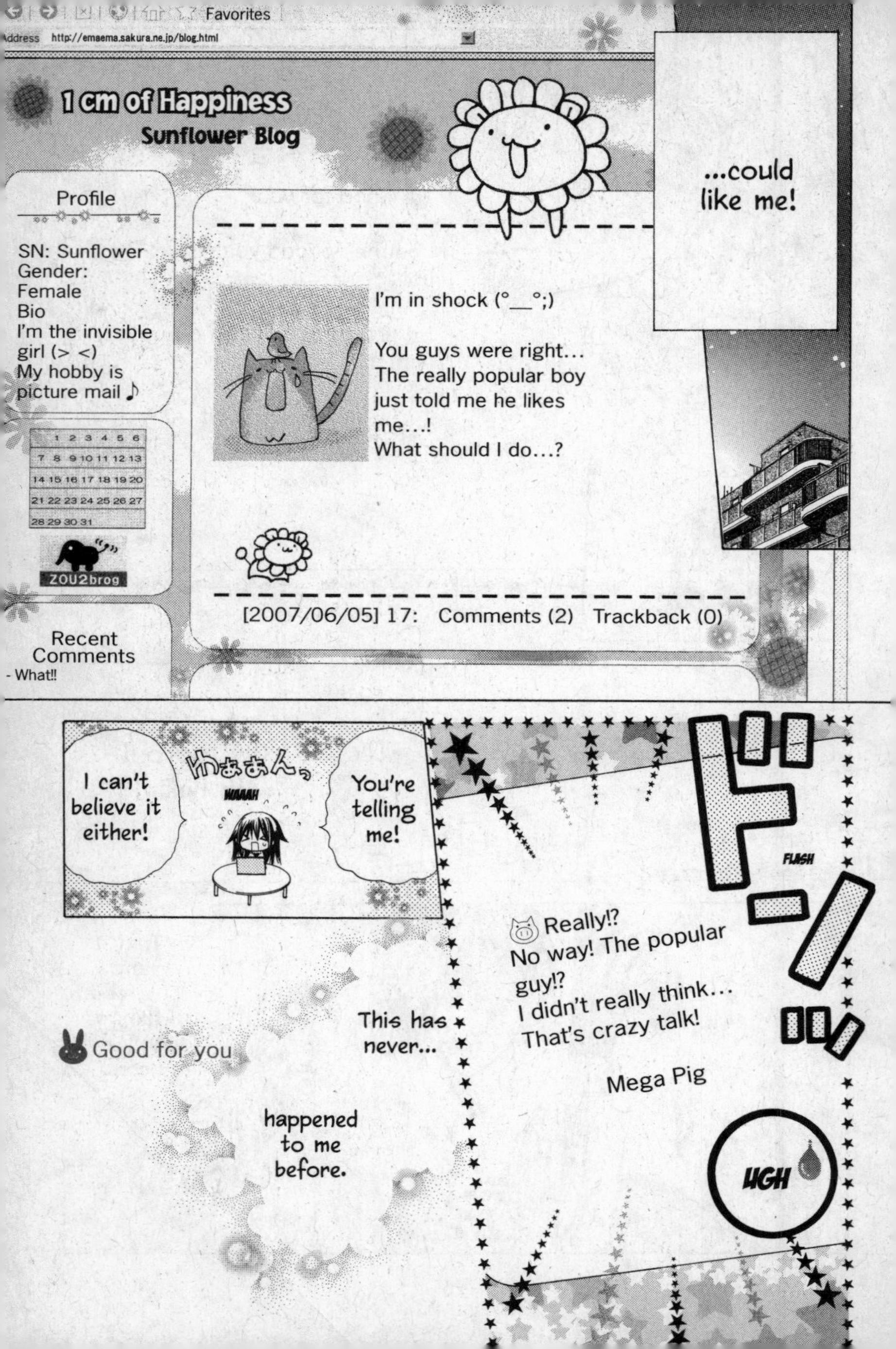

...could like me!
Favorites
Address http://emaema.sakura.ne.jp/blog.html
1 cm of Happiness
Sunflower Blog
Profile
SN: Sunflower
Gender:
Female
Bio
I'm the invisible girl (> <)
My hobby is picture mail ♪
1 2 3 4 5 6
7 8 9 10 11 12 13
14 15 16 17 18 19 20
21 22 23 24 25 26 27
28 29 30 31
ZOU2brog
I'm in shock (°__°;)
You guys were right...
The really popular boy just told me he likes me...!
What should I do...?
[2007/06/05] 17: Comments (2) Trackback (0)
Recent Comments
- What!!
FLASH
Really!?
No way! The popular guy!?
I didn't really think...
That's crazy talk!
Mega Pig
UGH
You're telling me!
WAAAH
I can't believe it either!
This has never...
happened to me before.
Good for you

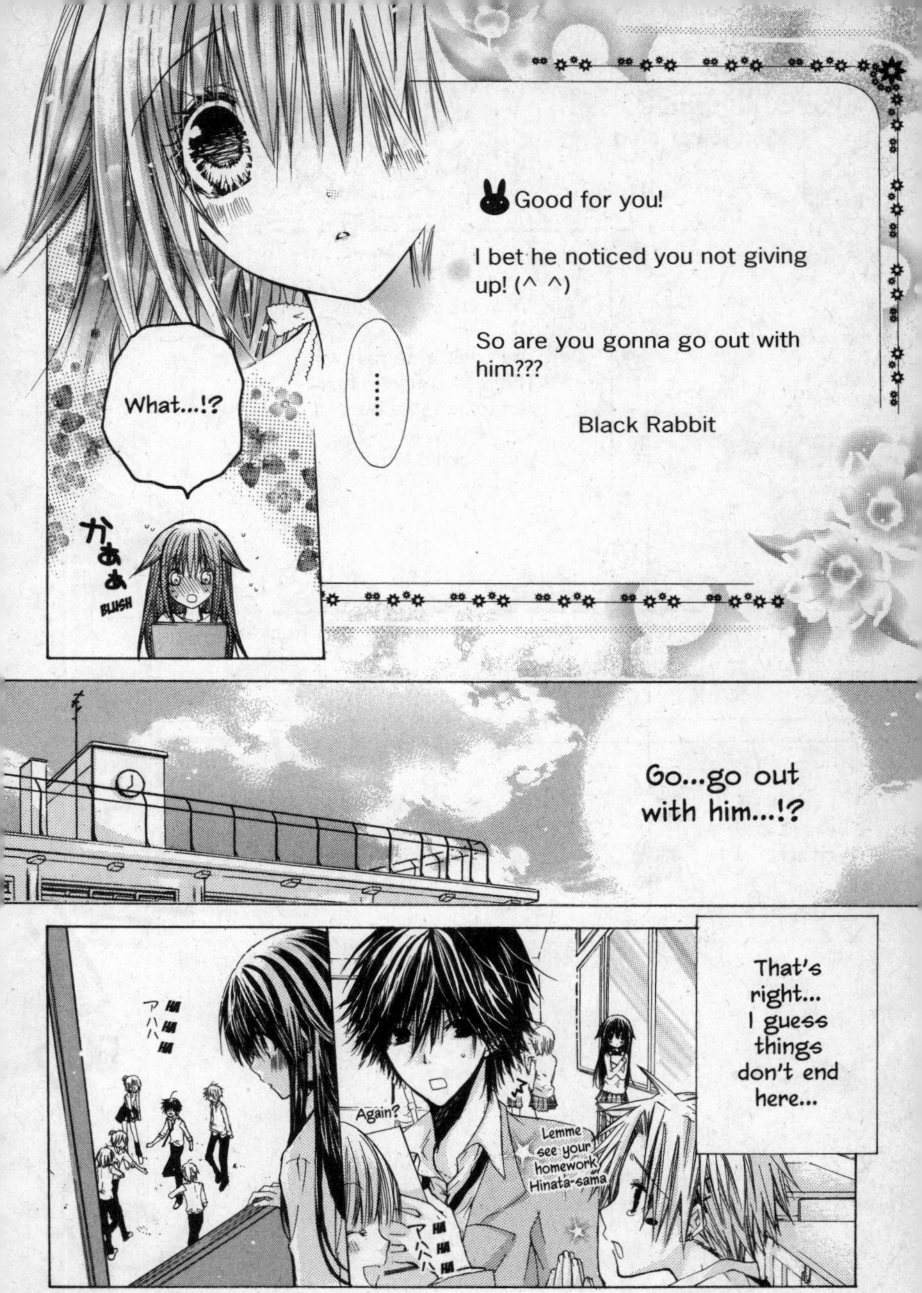
Good for you!
I bet he noticed you not giving up! (^ ^)
So are you gonna go out with him???
Black Rabbit
......
What...!?
かぁぁ BLUSH
Go...go out with him...!?
That's right... I guess things don't end here...
Lemme see your homework Hinata-sama
Again?
アハハ HA HA HA
アハハ HA HA HA

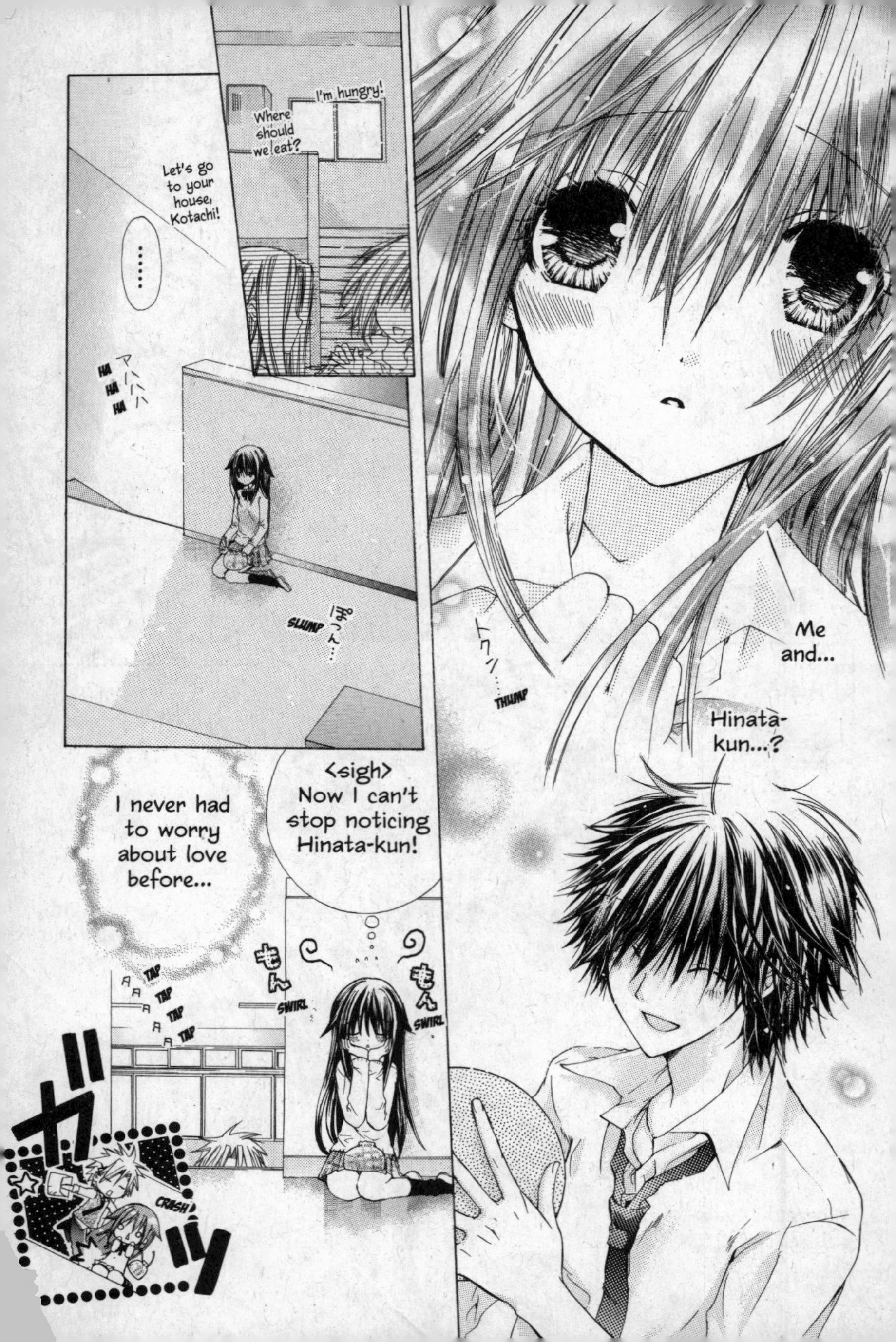
Me and...
Hinata-kun...?
THUMP
I'm hungry!
Where should we eat?
Let's go to your house, Kotachi!
......
HA HA HA
SLUMP
<sigh> Now I can't stop noticing Hinata-kun!
I never had to worry about love before...
SWIRL
SWIRL
TAP TAP TAP TAP
CRASH

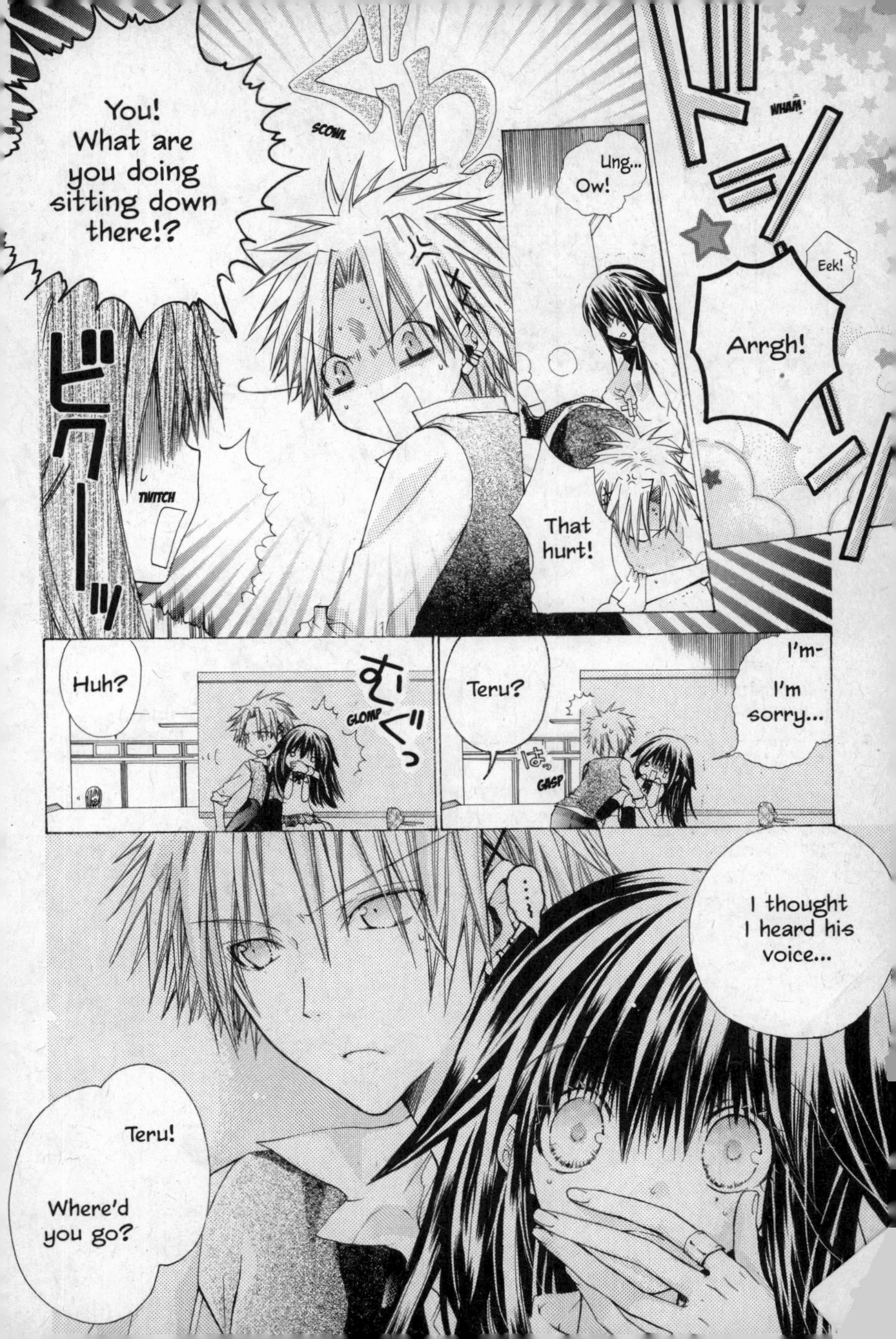
WHAM
Eek!
Arrgh!
Ung... Ow!
That hurt!
SCOWL
You! What are you doing sitting down there!?
TWITCH
I'm-
I'm sorry...
Teru?
GASP
Huh?
GLOMP
I thought I heard his voice...
...
Teru!
Where'd you go?

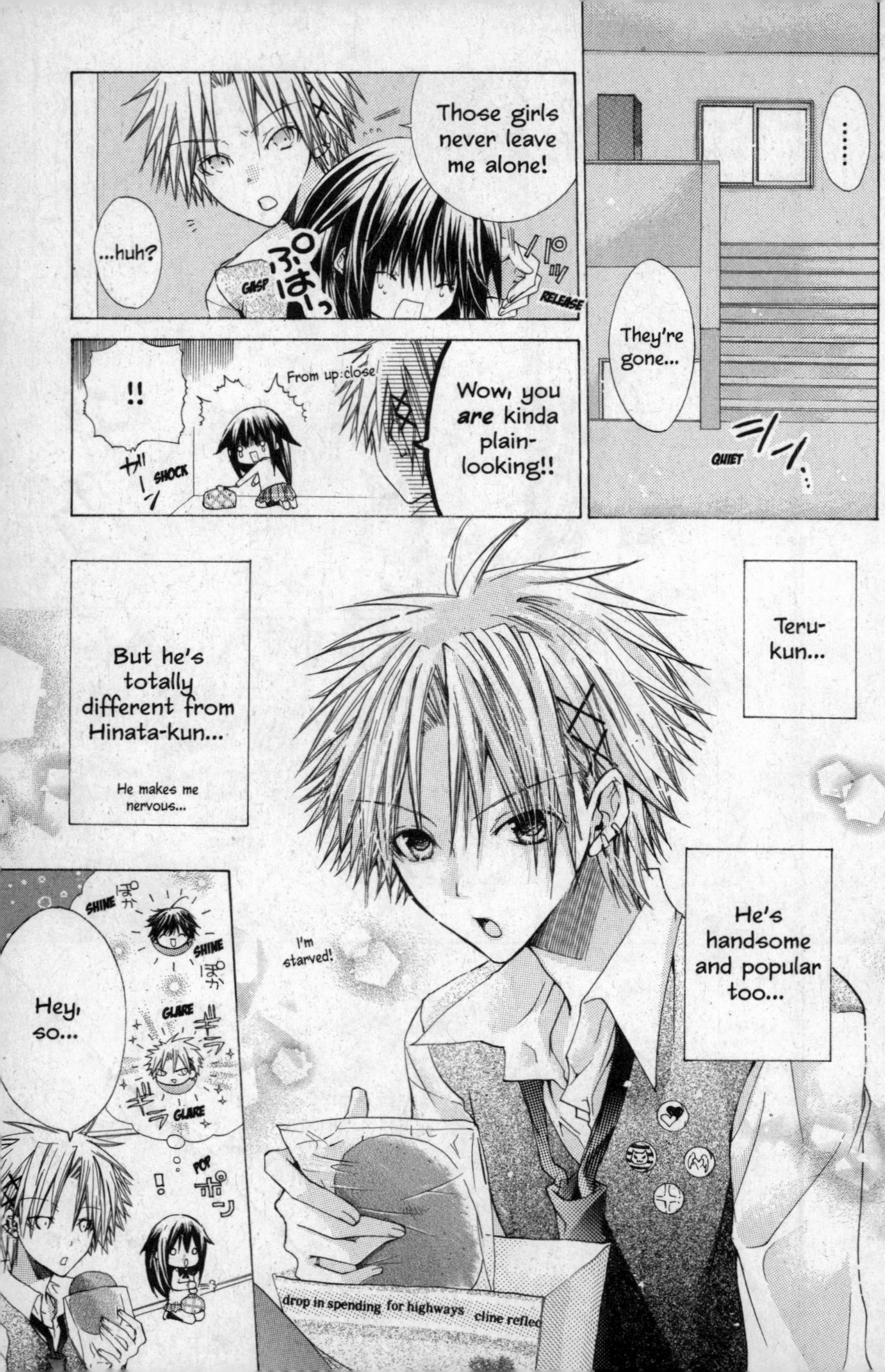
......
They're gone...
QUIET
Those girls never leave me alone!
RELEASE
パッ
GASP
ぷはーっ
...huh?
Wow, you *are* kinda plain-looking!!
From up close
!!
SHOCK
ガーン
Teru-kun...
But he's totally different from Hinata-kun...
He makes me nervous...
He's handsome and popular too...
I'm starved!
drop in spending for highways cline reflec
SHINE
ぽか
SHINE
ぽか
GLARE
ギラ
ギラ
GLARE
POP
ポン
!
Hey, so...

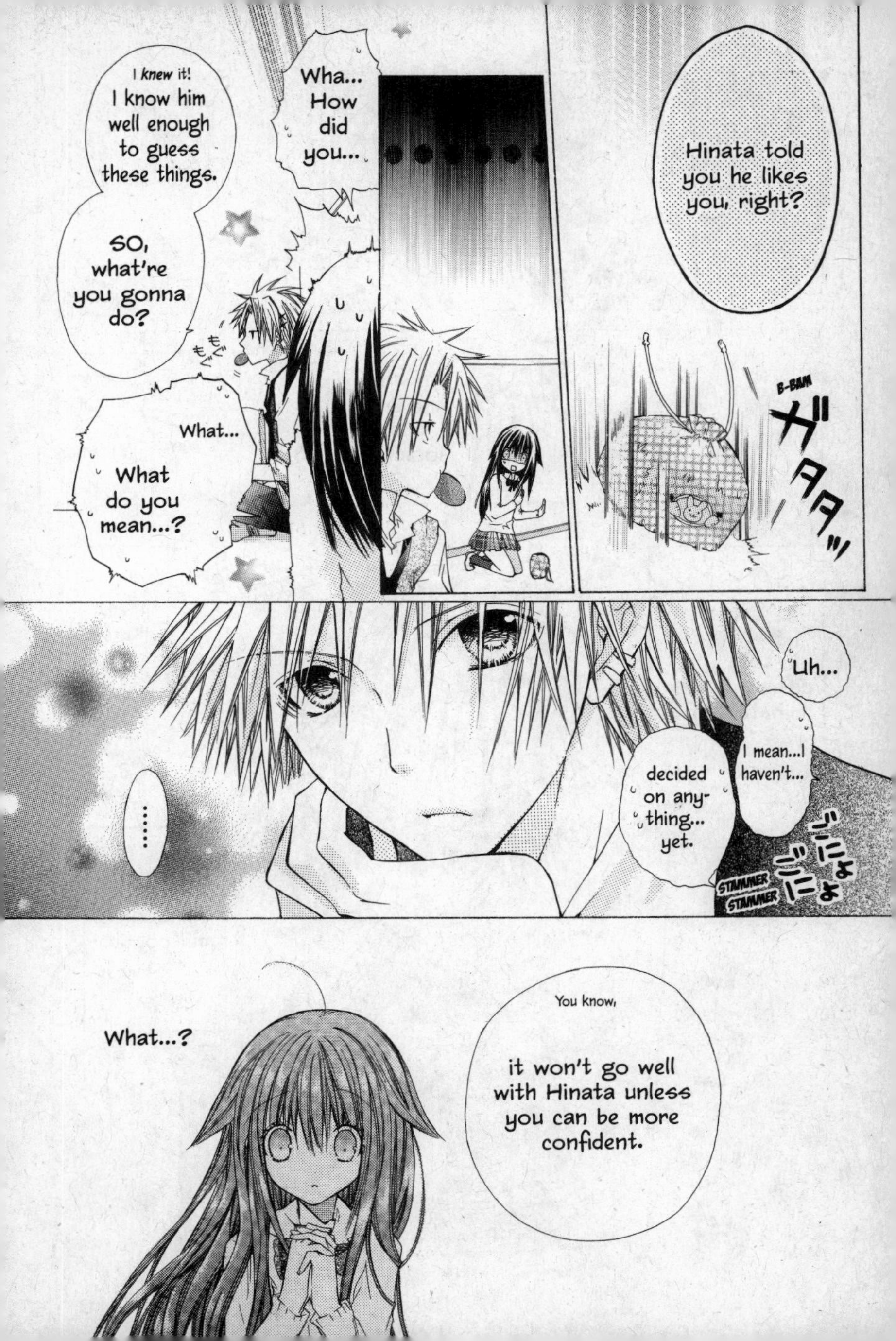
Hinata told you he likes you, right?
B-BAM
ガタタッ
Wha... How did you...
I knew it! I know him well enough to guess these things.
SO, what're you gonna do?
もぐもぐ
What... What do you mean...?
Uh...
I mean...I haven't...
decided on any-thing... yet.
STAMMER STAMMER
ごにょごにょ
......
You know, it won't go well with Hinata unless you can be more confident.
What...?

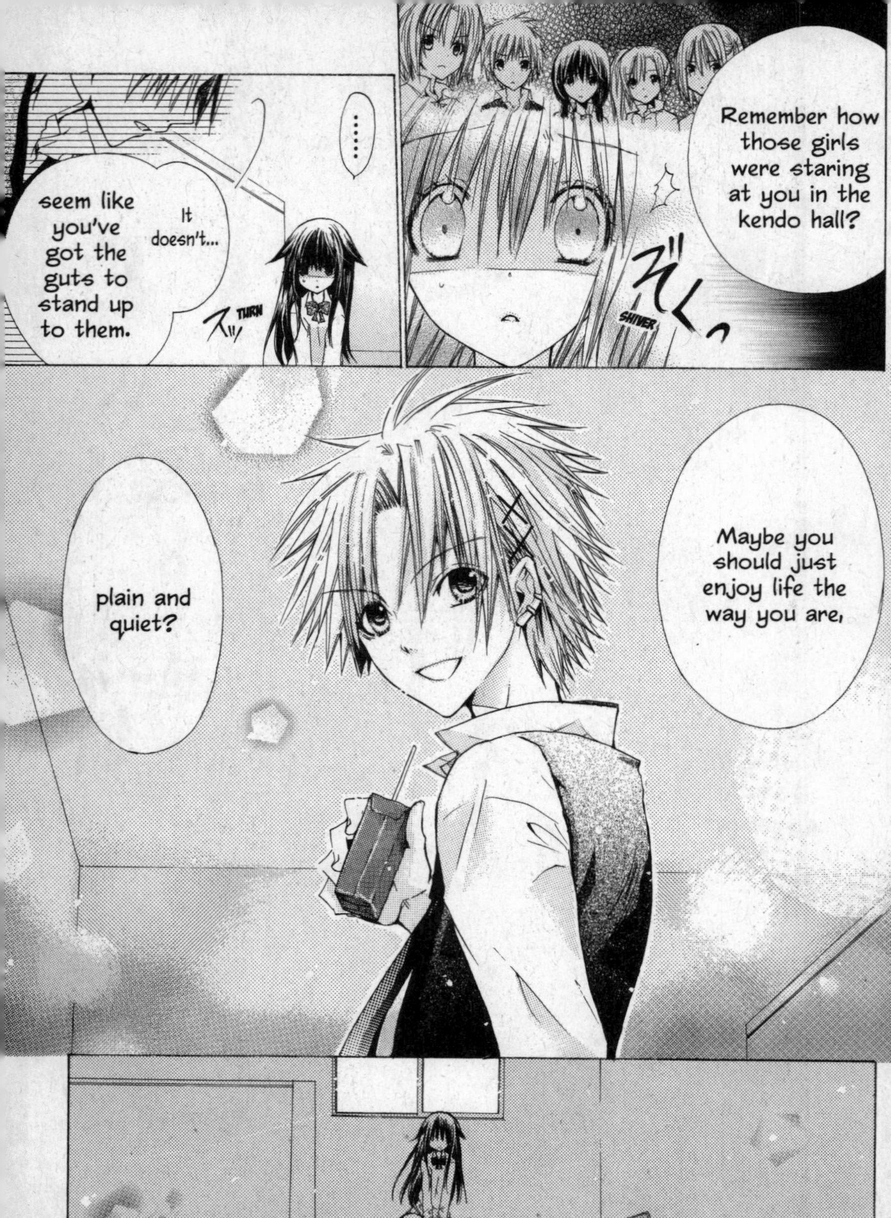
Remember how those girls were staring at you in the kendo hall?
ぞくっ
SHIVER
......
It doesn't...
seem like you've got the guts to stand up to them.
スッ
TURN
Maybe you should just enjoy life the way you are,
plain and quiet?

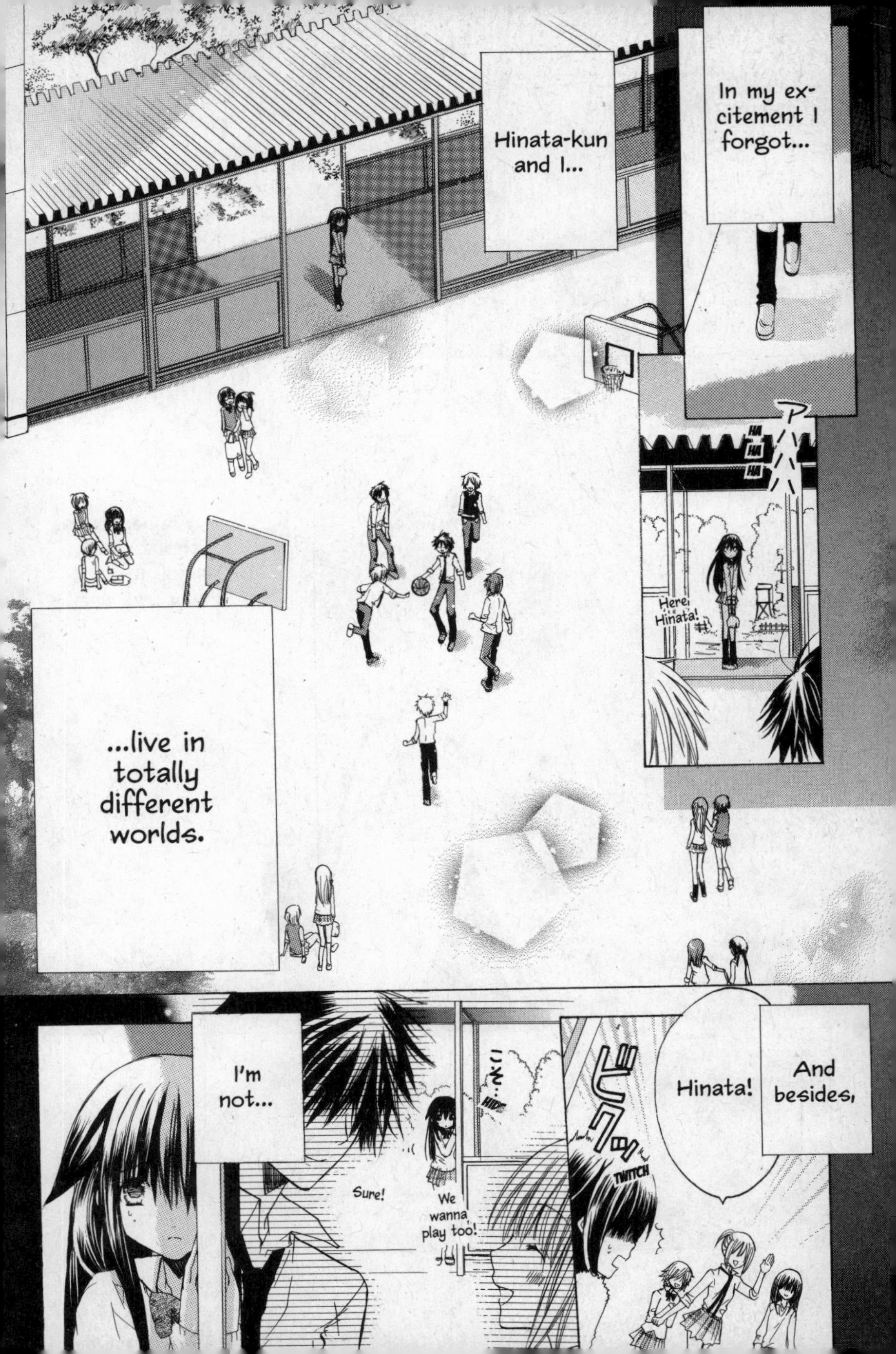

In my ex-citement I forgot...
HA
HA
HA
Here, Hinata!
Hinata-kun and I...
...live in totally different worlds.
And besides,
Hinata!
TWITCH
We wanna play too!
Sure!
I'm not...

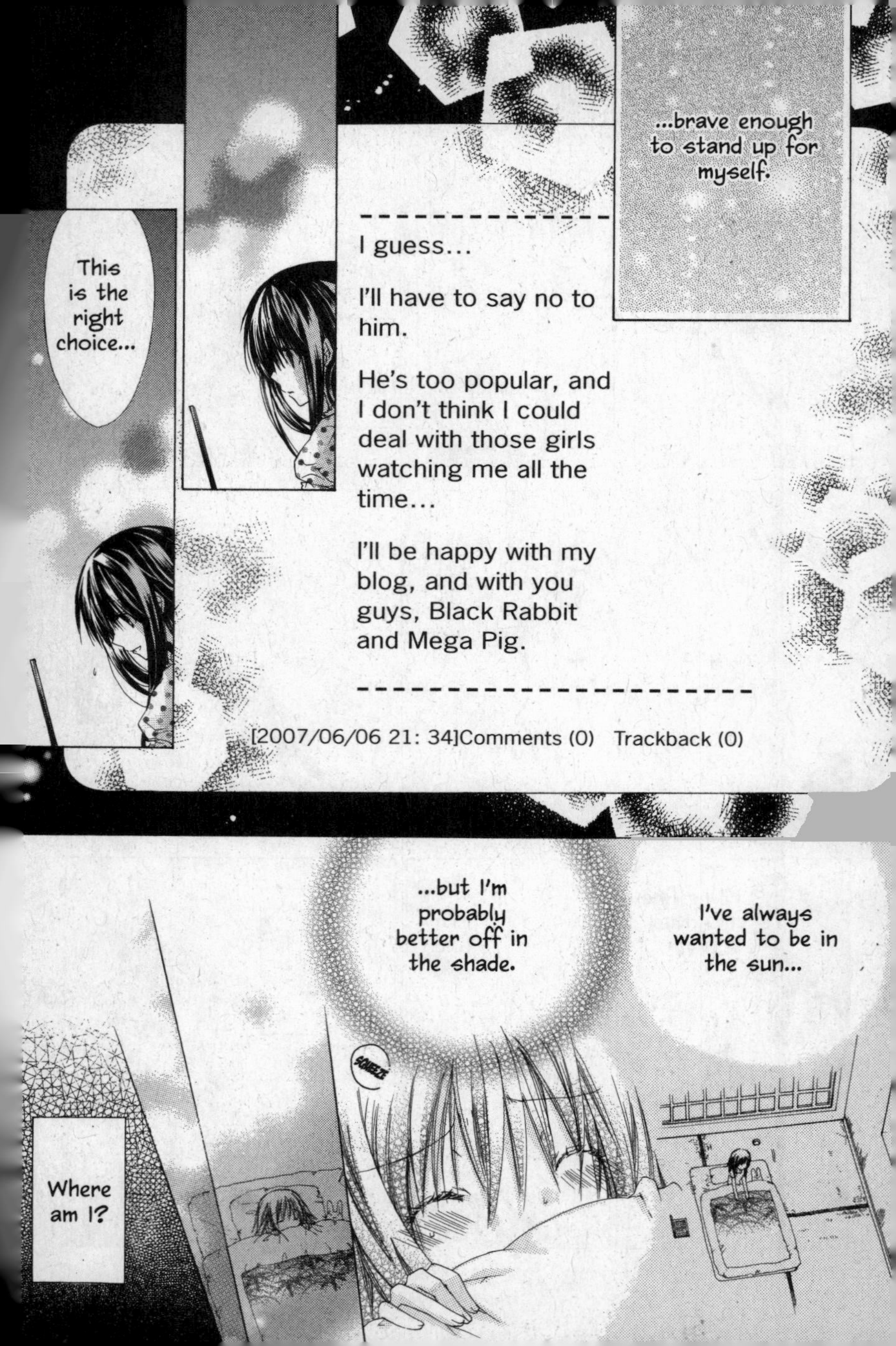
...brave enough to stand up for myself.
I guess...
I'll have to say no to him.
He's too popular, and I don't think I could deal with those girls watching me all the time...
I'll be happy with my blog, and with you guys, Black Rabbit and Mega Pig.
[2007/06/06 21: 34]Comments (0) Trackback (0)
This is the right choice...
I've always wanted to be in the sun...
...but I'm probably better off in the shade.
SQUEEZE
Where am I?

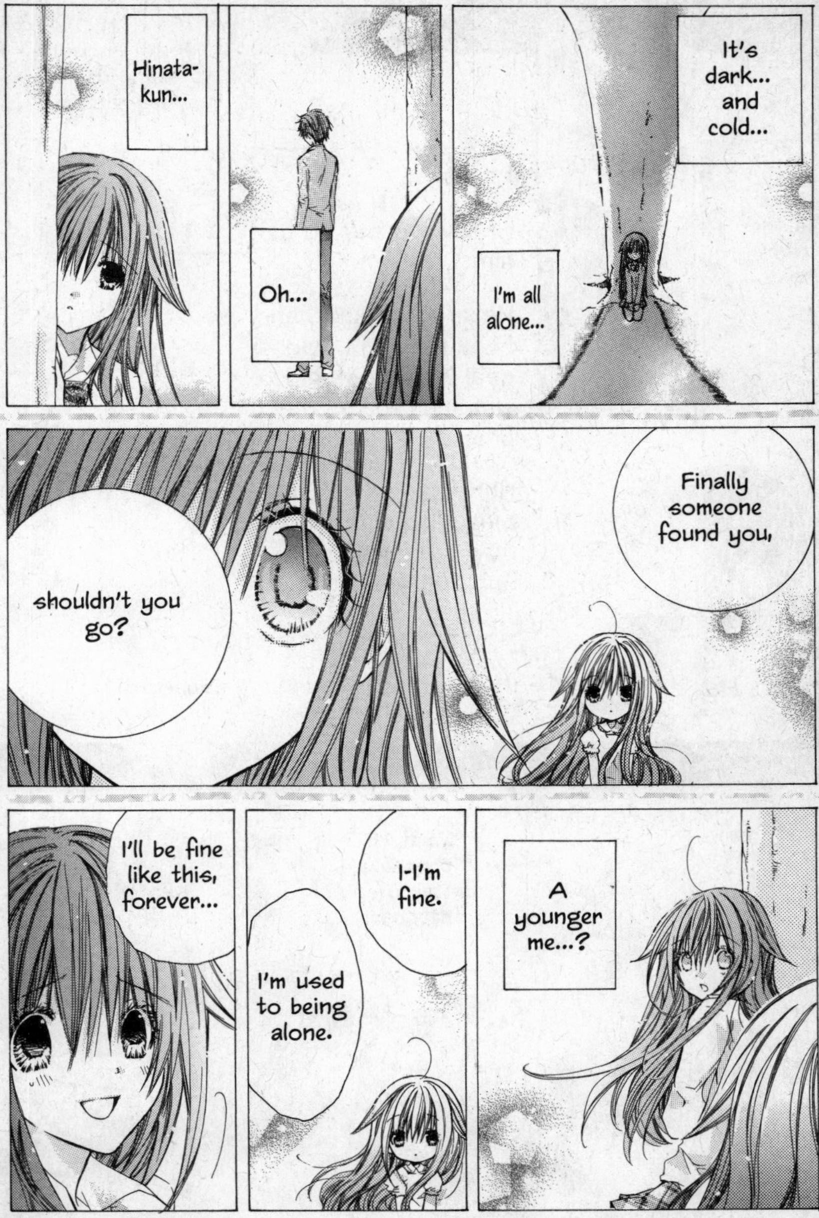
It's dark... and cold...
I'm all alone...
Oh...
Hinata-kun...
Finally someone found you,
shouldn't you go?
A younger me...?
I-I'm fine.
I'm used to being alone.
I'll be fine like this, forever...

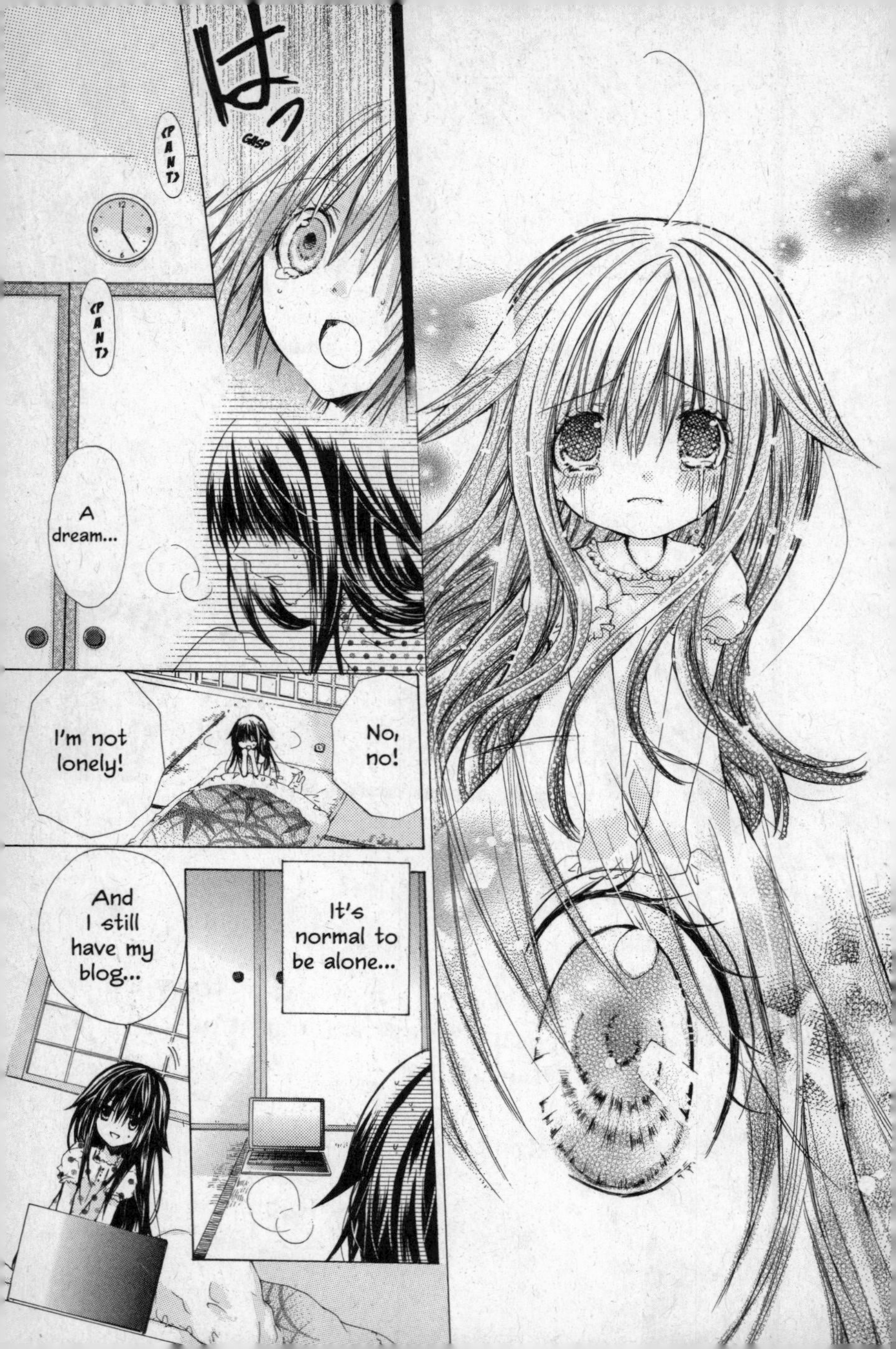
はっ
GASP
‹PANT›
‹PANT›
A dream...
No, no!
I'm not lonely!
It's normal to be alone...
And I still have my blog...

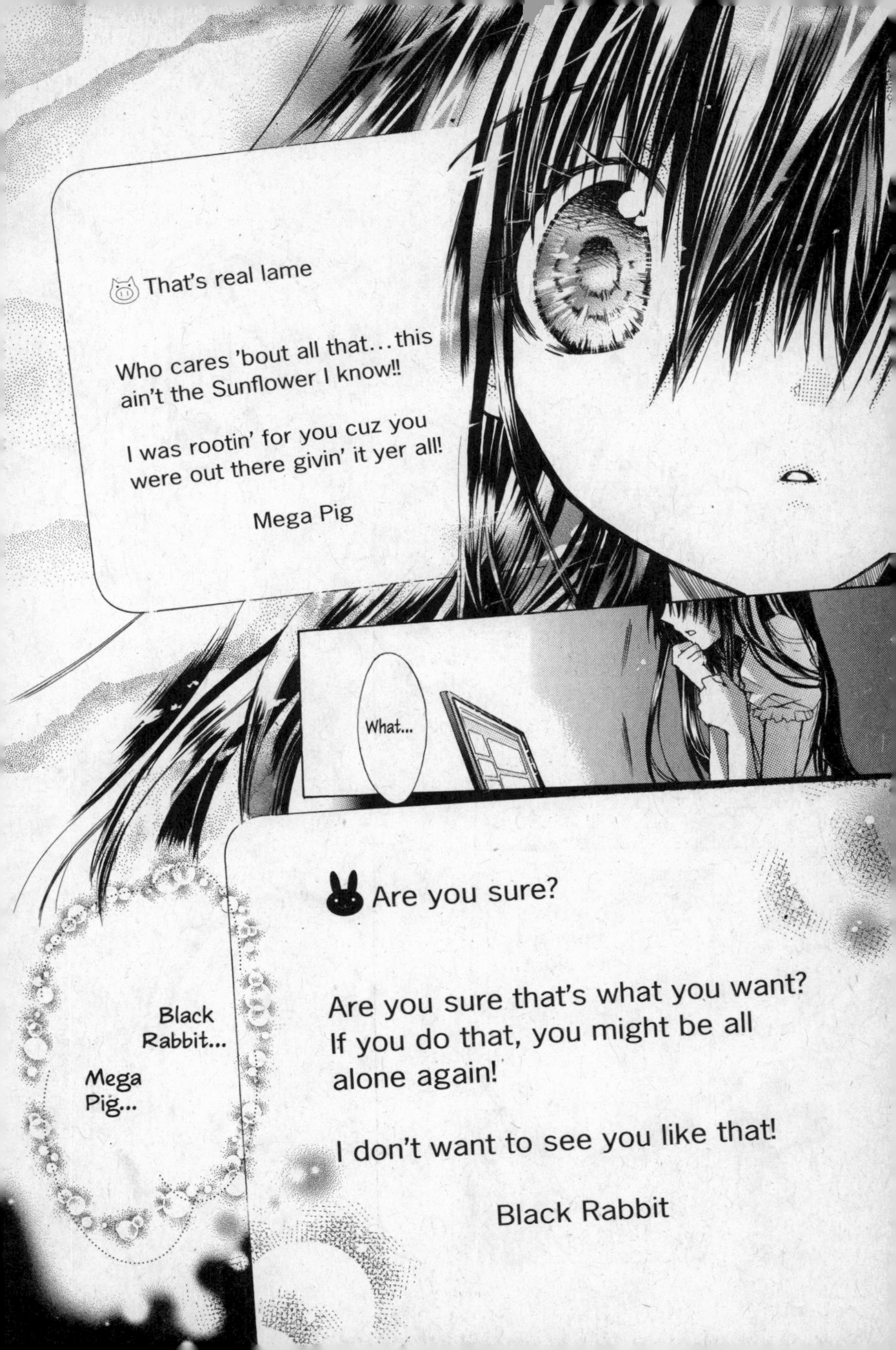
That's real lame
Who cares 'bout all that... this ain't the Sunflower I know!!
I was rootin' for you cuz you were out there givin' it yer all!
Mega Pig
What...
Are you sure?
Are you sure that's what you want? If you do that, you might be all alone again!
I don't want to see you like that!
Black Rabbit
Black Rabbit...
Mega Pig...

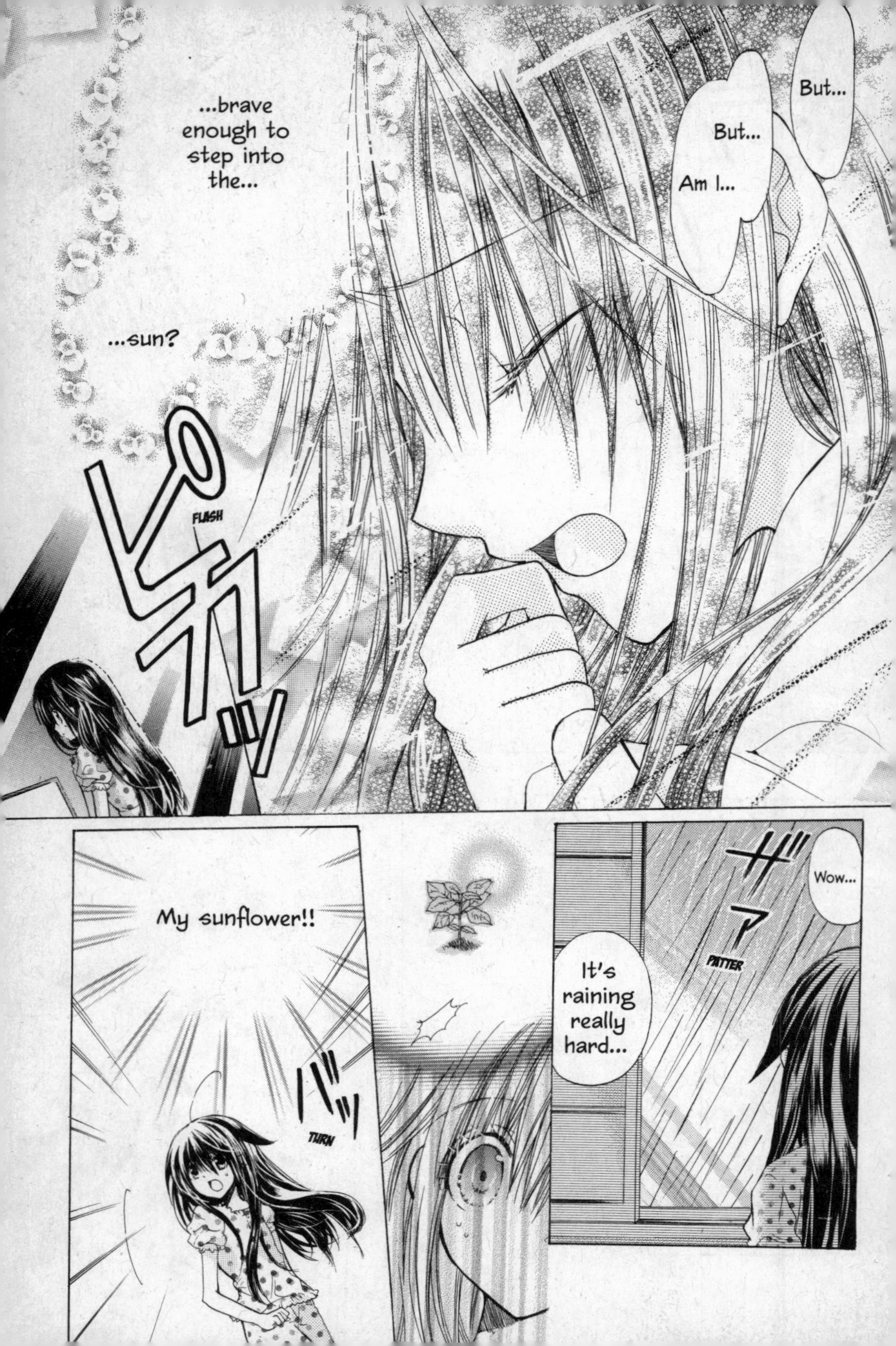
But...
But...
Am I...
...brave enough to step into the...
...sun?
FLASH
Wow...
PATTER
It's raining really hard...
My sunflower!!
TURN

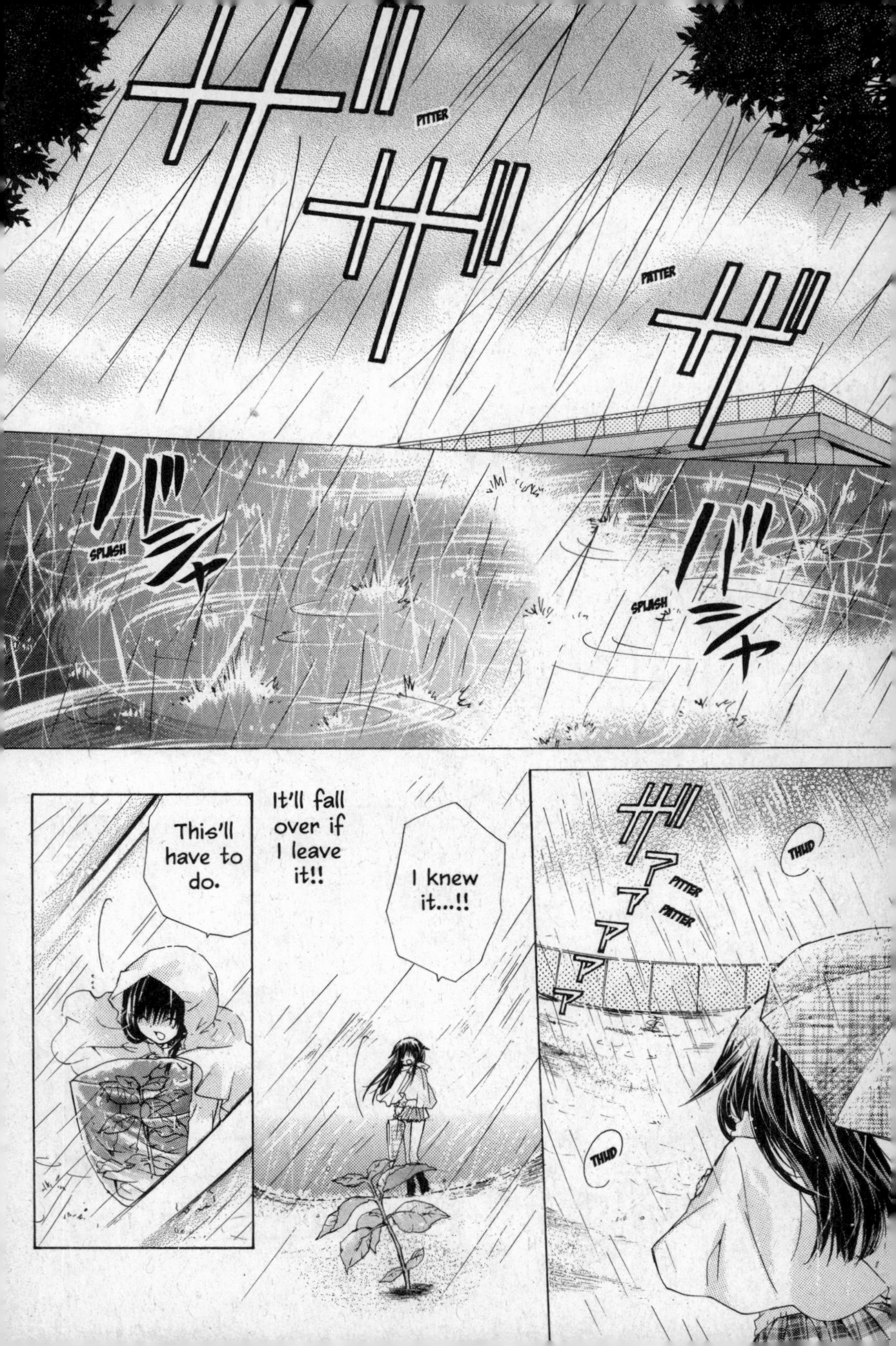
ザザザ
PATTER
PITTER
バシャ
SPLASH
バシャ
SPLASH
ザァァァァァ
PITTER
PATTER
THUD
THUD
I knew it...!!
It'll fall over if I leave it!!
This'll have to do.

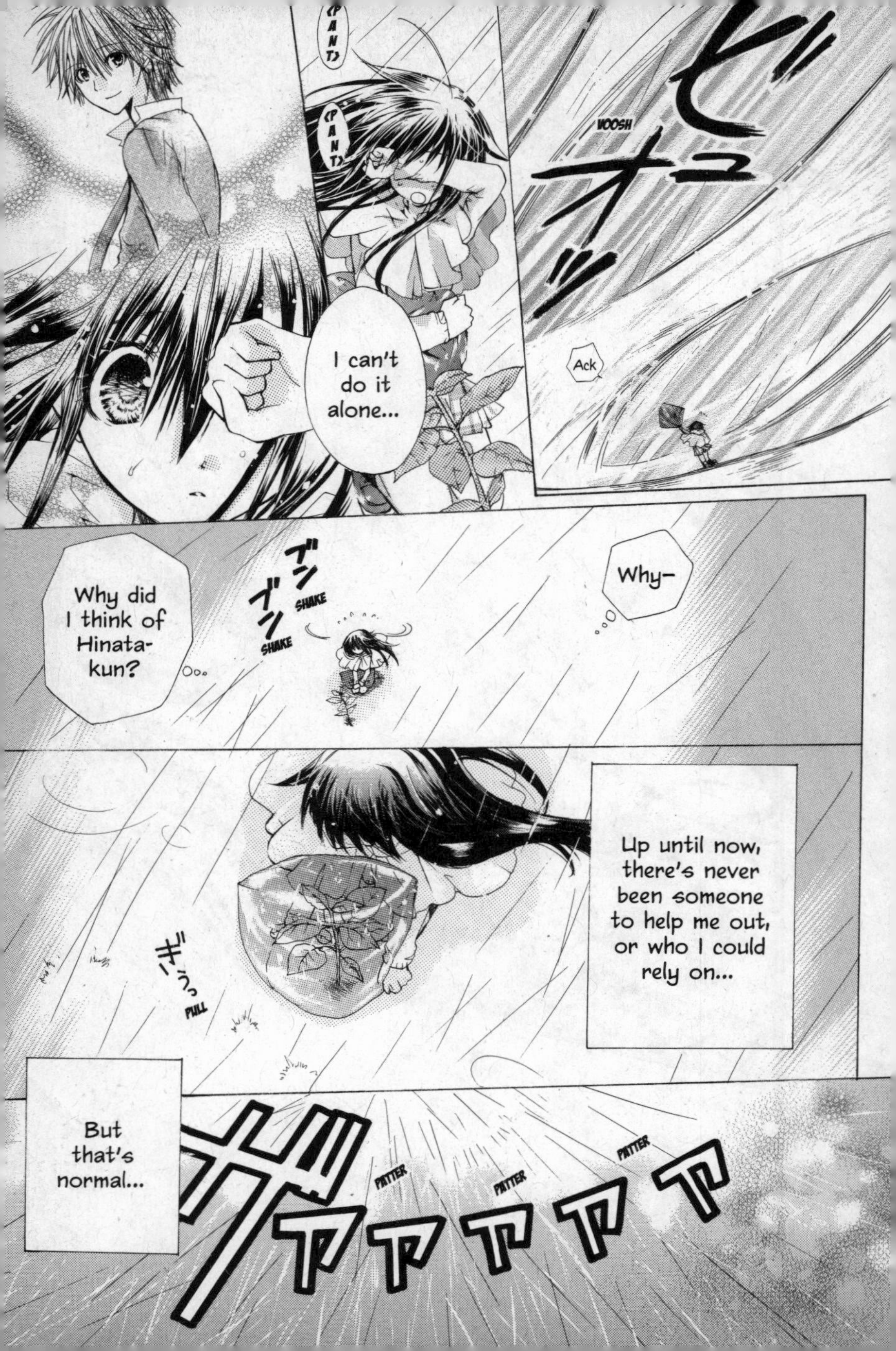
VOOSH
Ack
<PANT>
<PANT>
I can't do it alone...
Why-
SHAKE
SHAKE
Why did I think of Hinata-kun?
Up until now, there's never been someone to help me out, or who I could rely on...
PULL
PATTER
PATTER
PATTER
But that's normal...

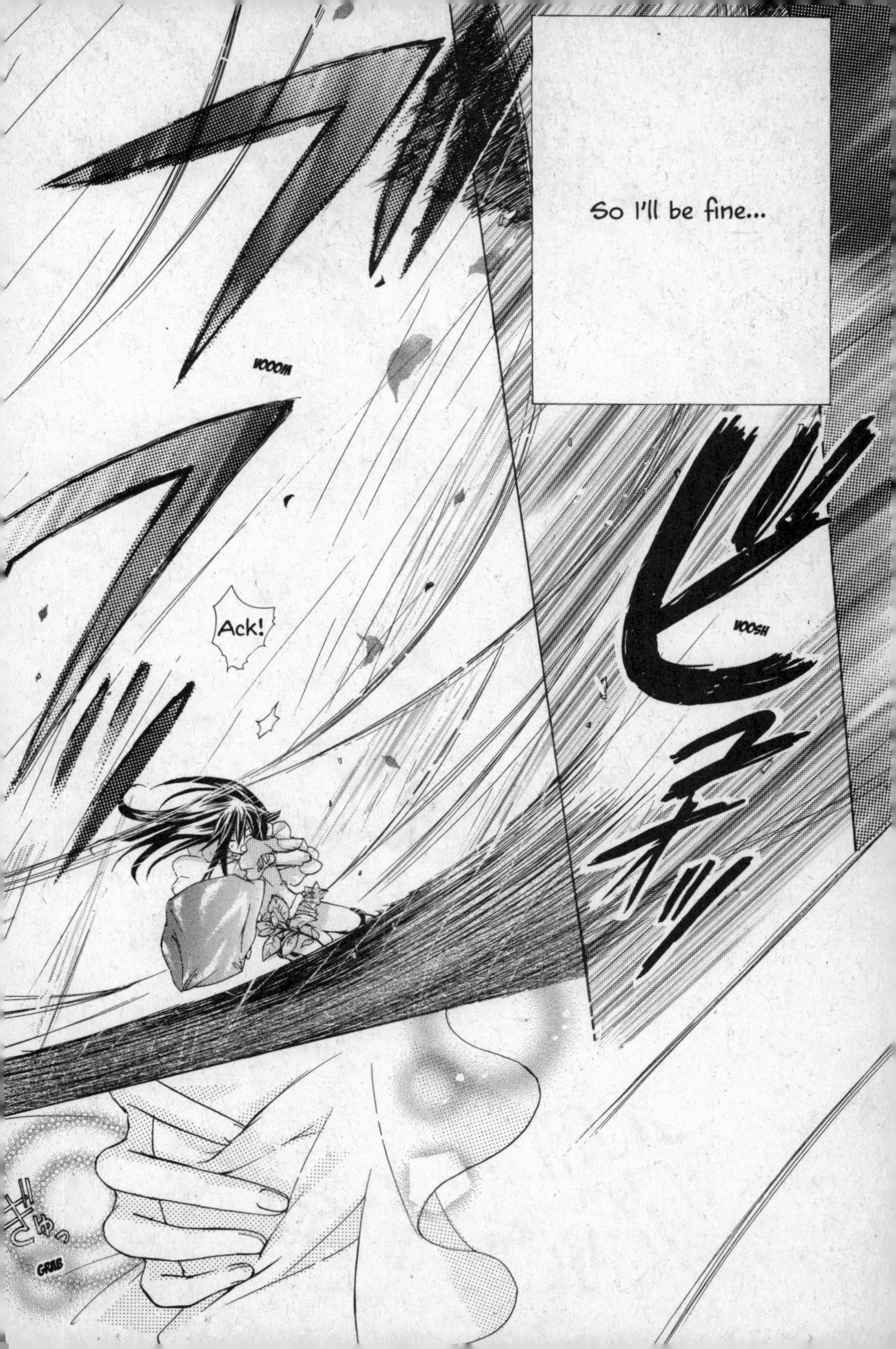
So I'll be fine...
VOOSH
VOOOM
Ack!
GRAB

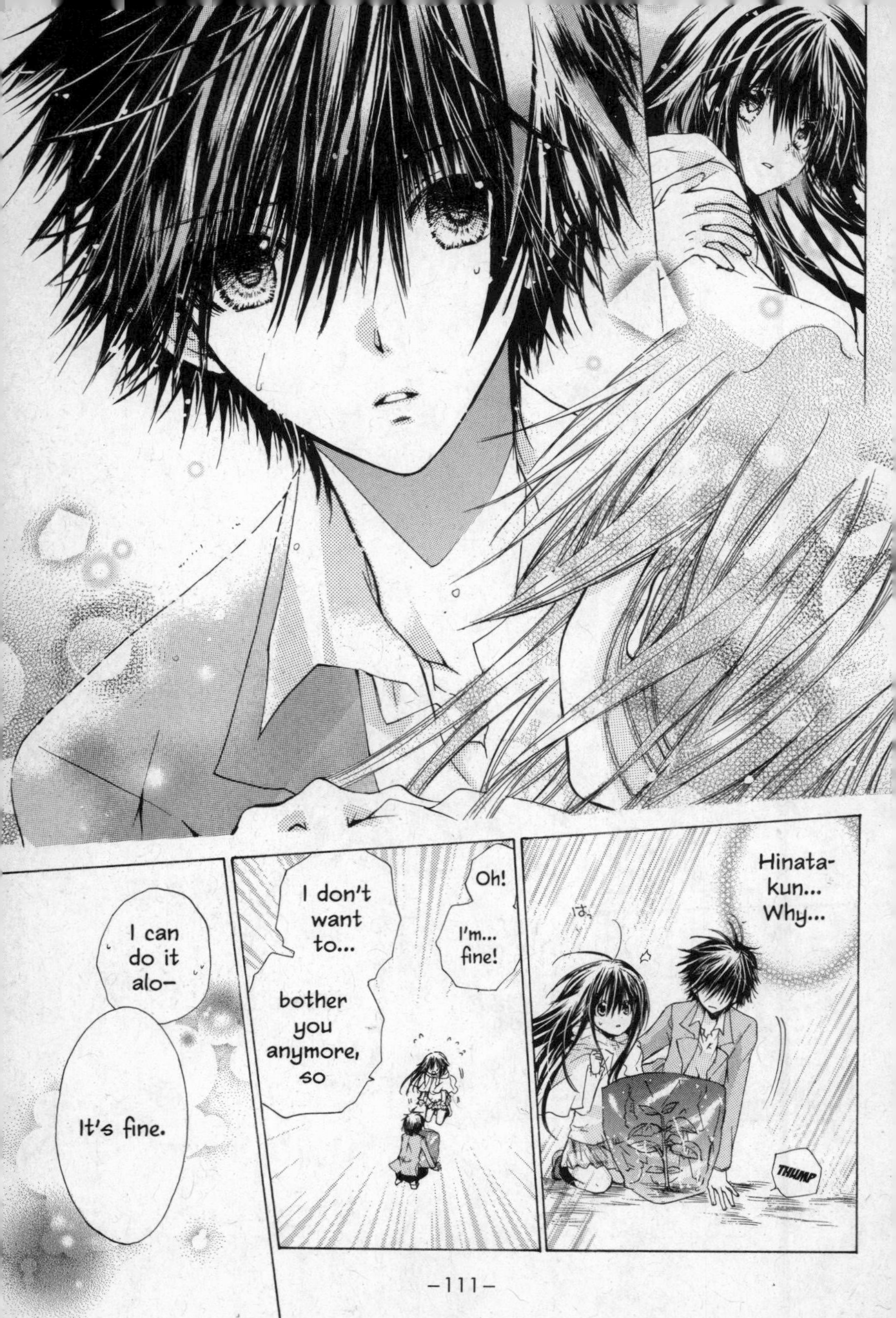
Hinata-kun... Why...
はっ
THUMP
Oh!
I'm... fine!
I don't want to...
bother you anymore, so
I can do it alo-
It's fine.

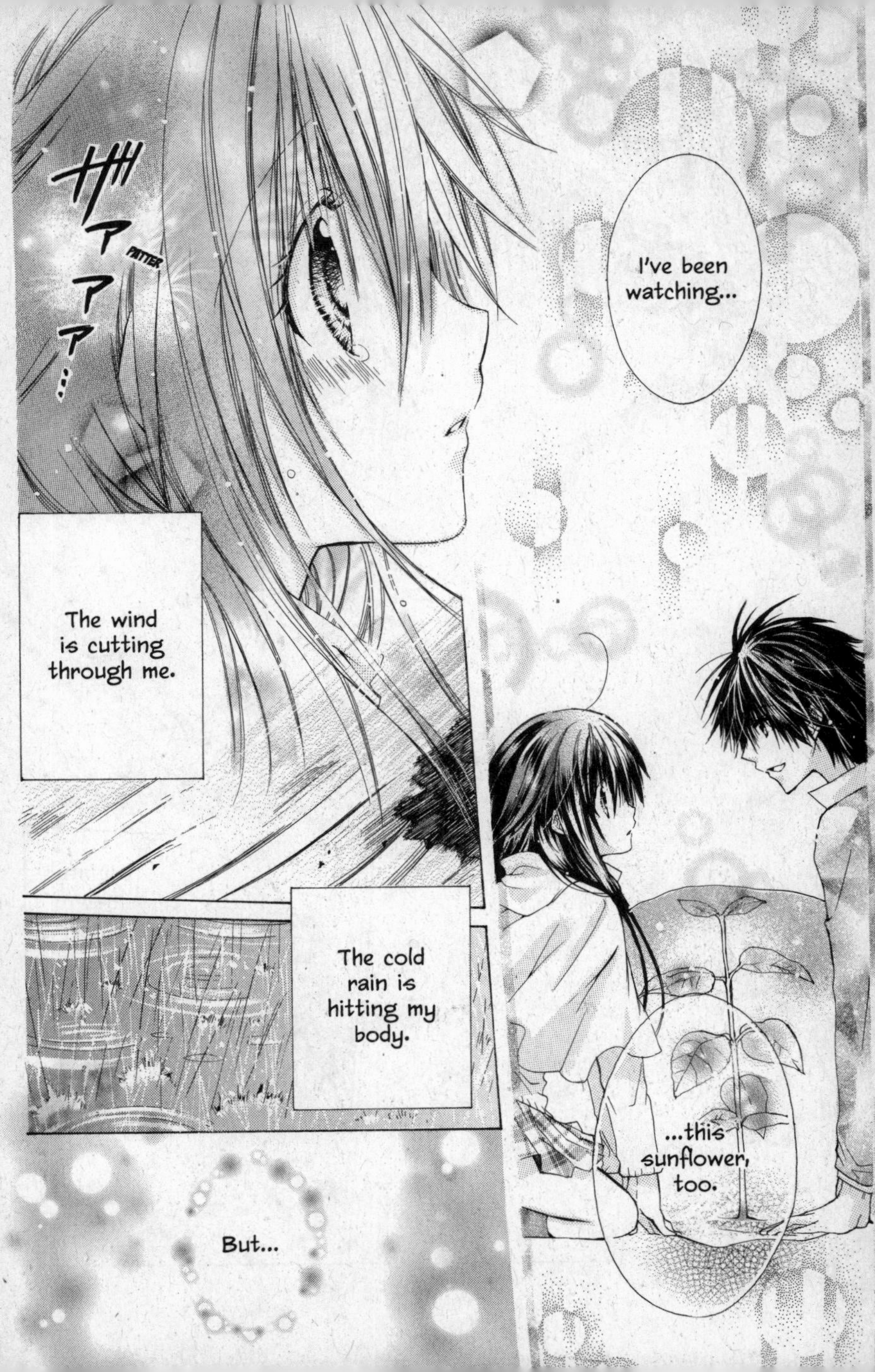
I've been watching...
...this sunflower, too.
ザァァァ…
PATTER
The wind is cutting through me.
The cold rain is hitting my body.
But...

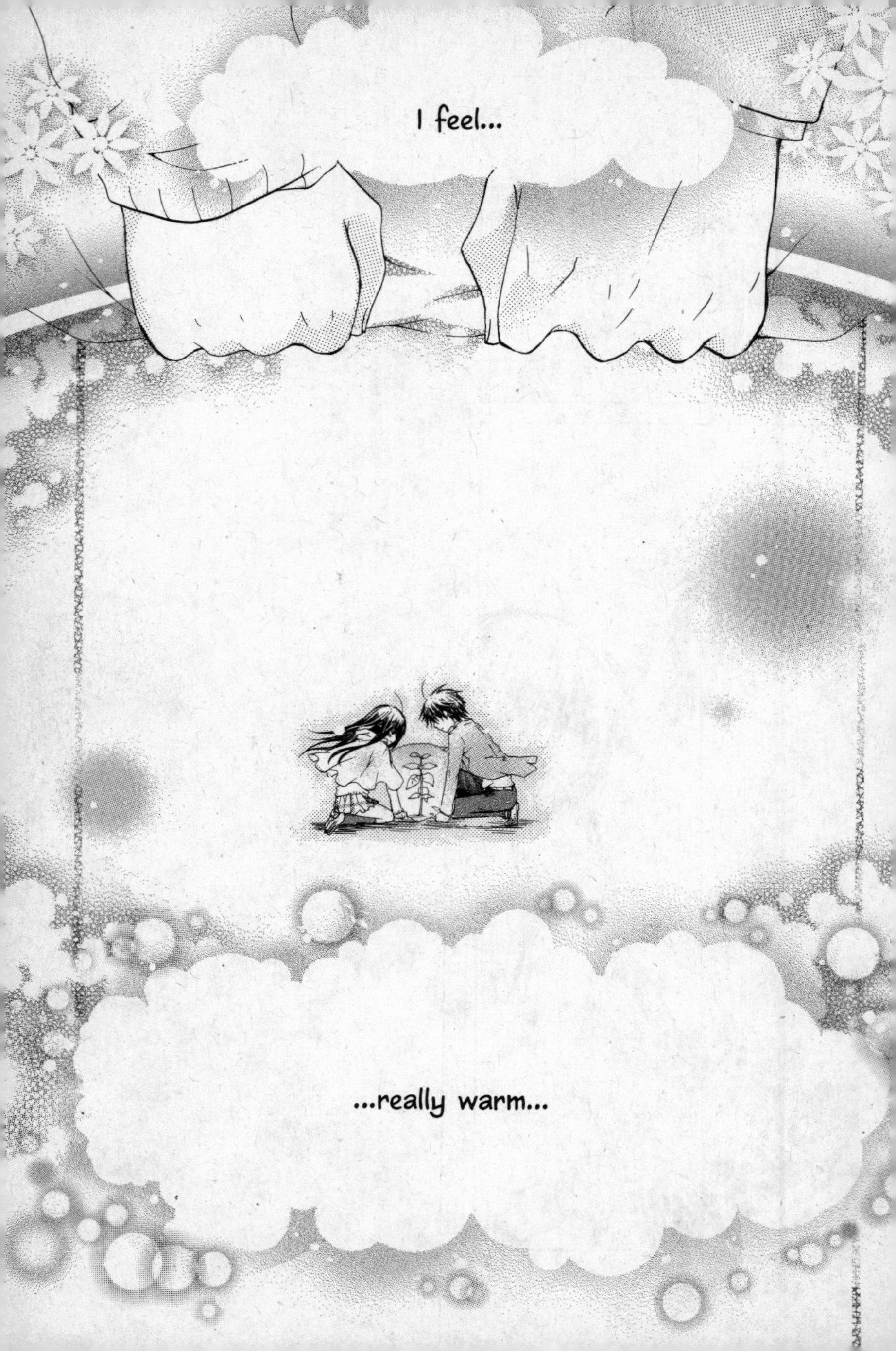
I feel...
...really warm...

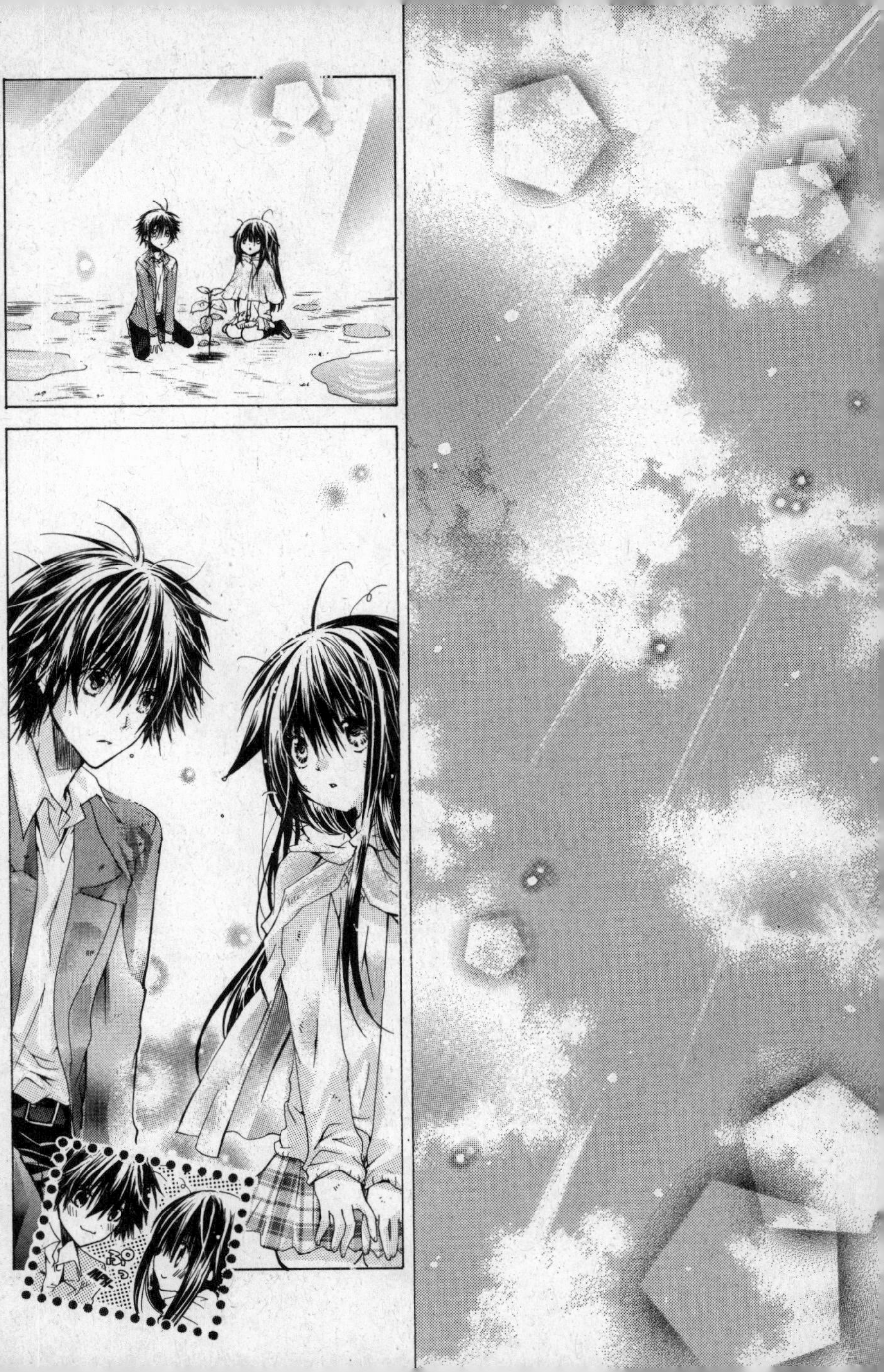
MPH-

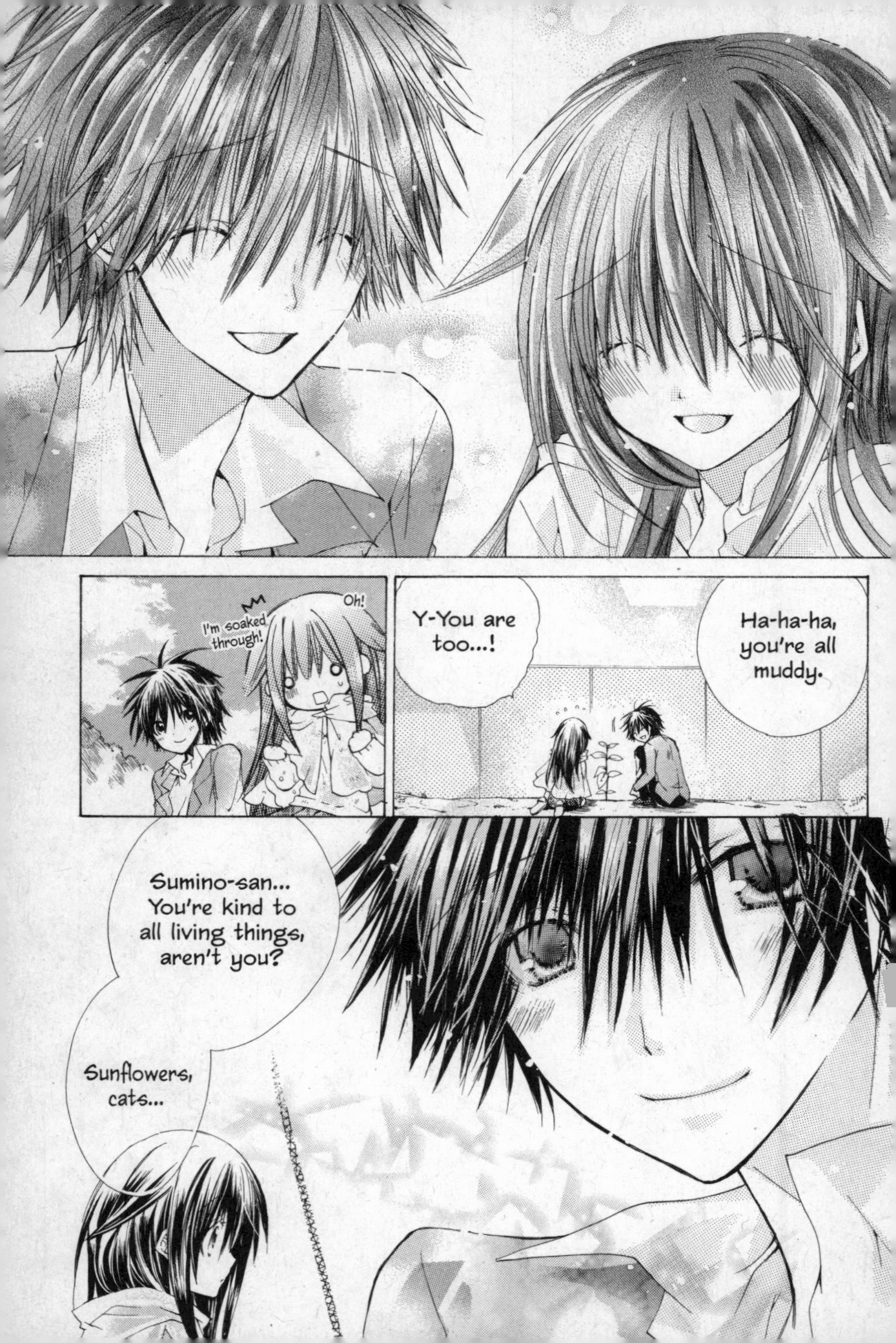
Ha-ha-ha, you're all muddy.
Y-You are too...!
Oh!
I'm soaked through!
Sumino-san... You're kind to all living things, aren't you?
Sunflowers, cats...

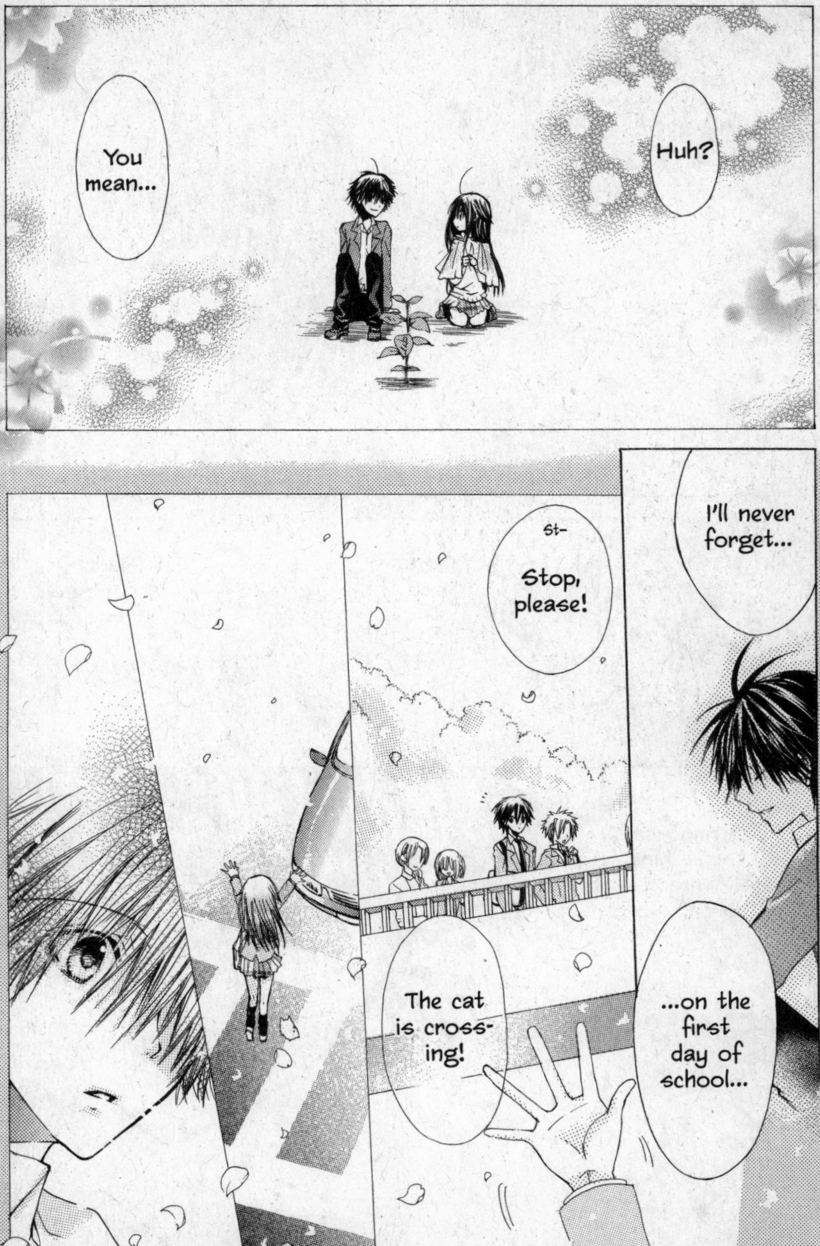
Huh?
You mean...
I'll never forget...
...on the first day of school...
St-
Stop, please!
The cat is crossing!

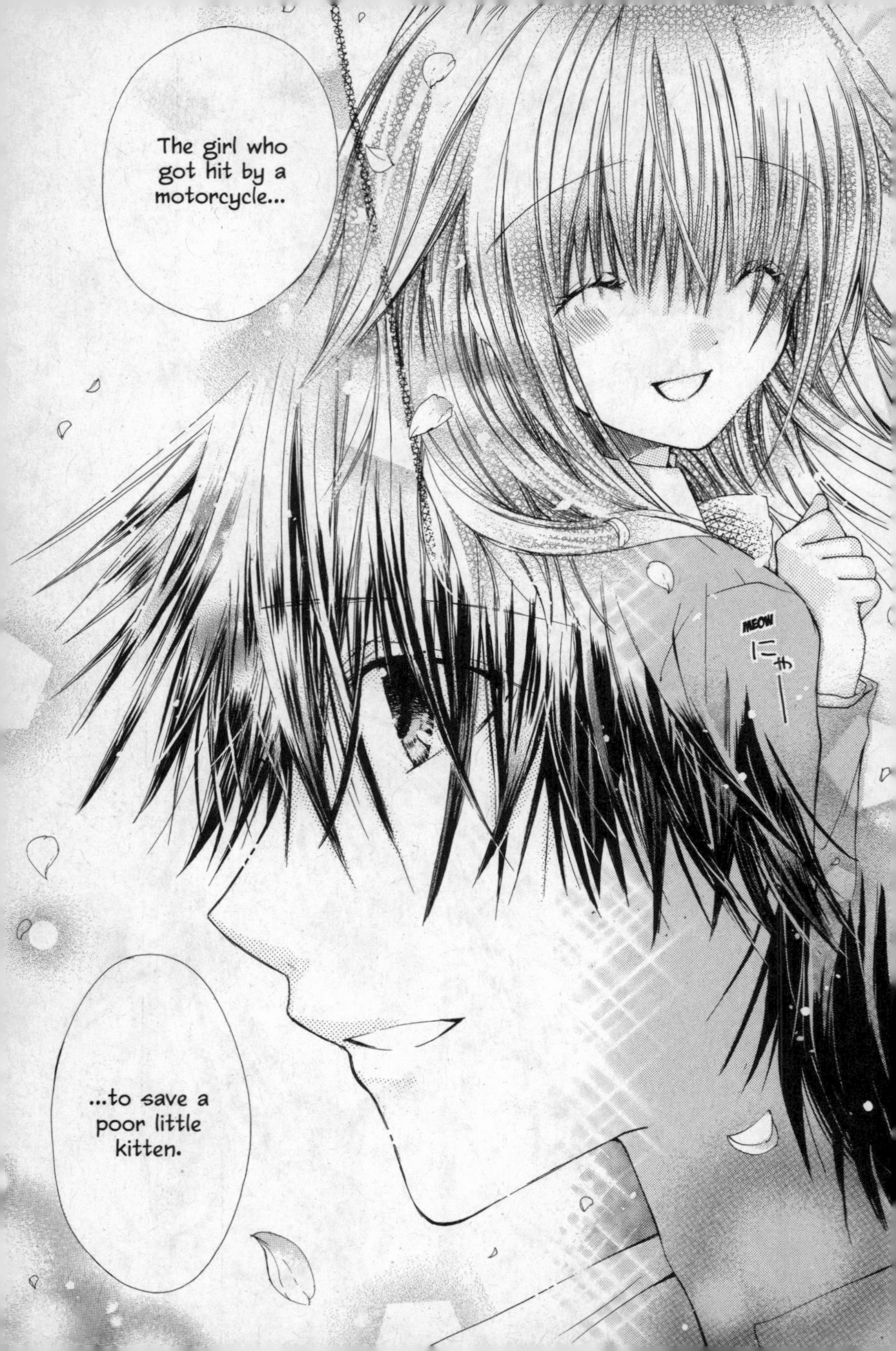
MEOW
にゃー
The girl who got hit by a motorcycle...
...to save a poor little kitten.

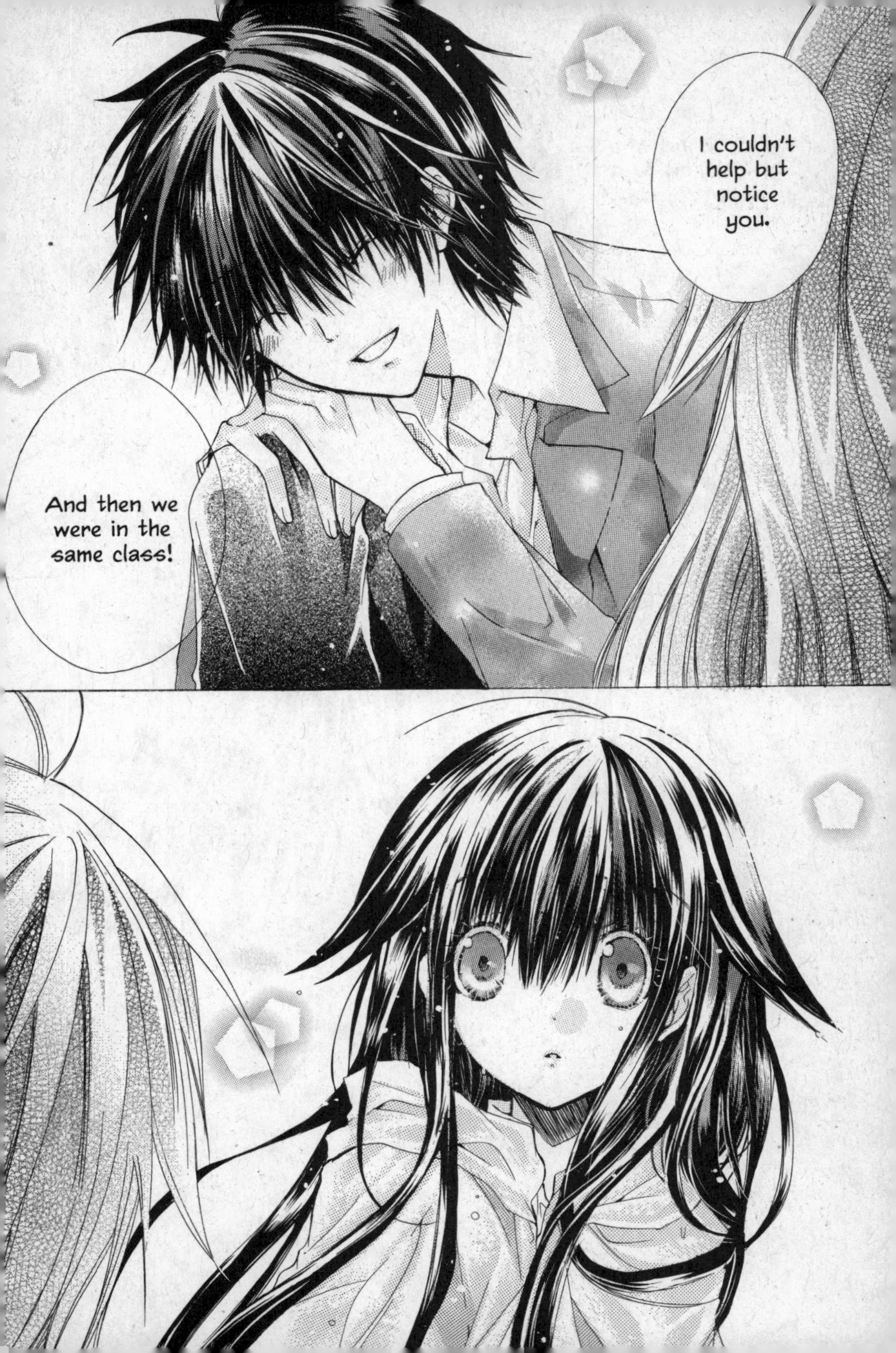
I couldn't help but notice you.
And then we were in the same class!

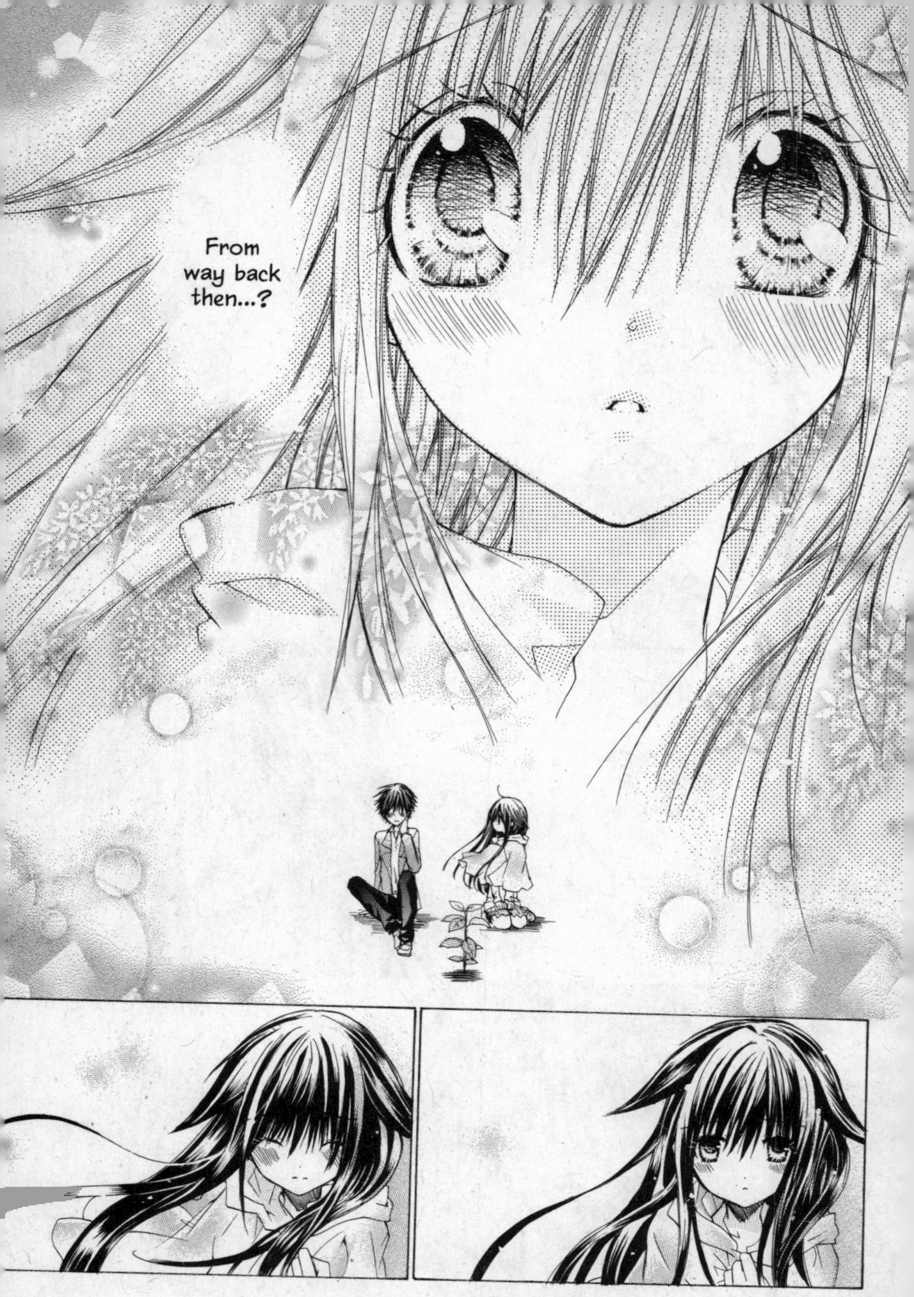
From way back then...?

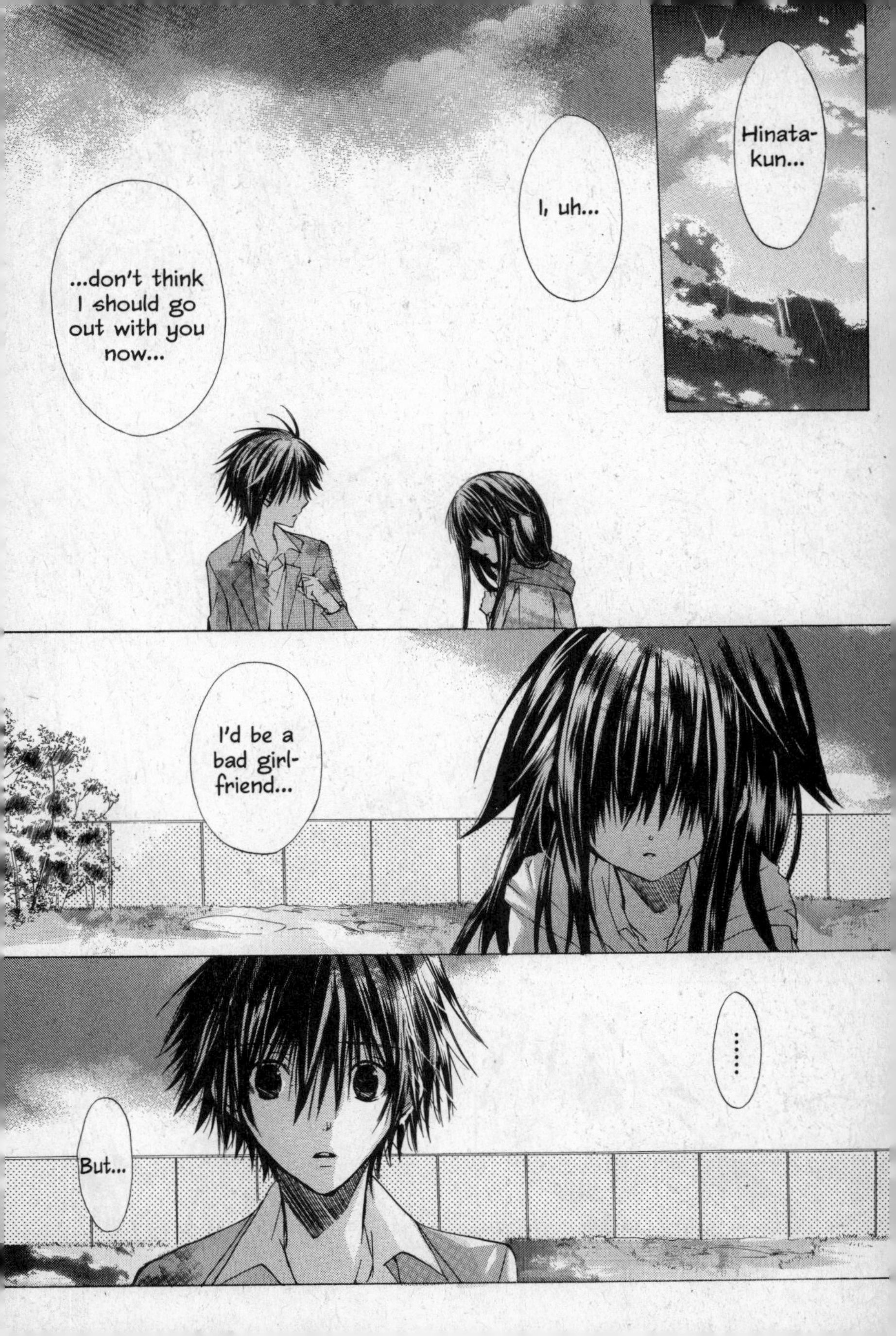
Hinata-kun...
I, uh...
...don't think I should go out with you now...
I'd be a bad girl-friend...
......
But...

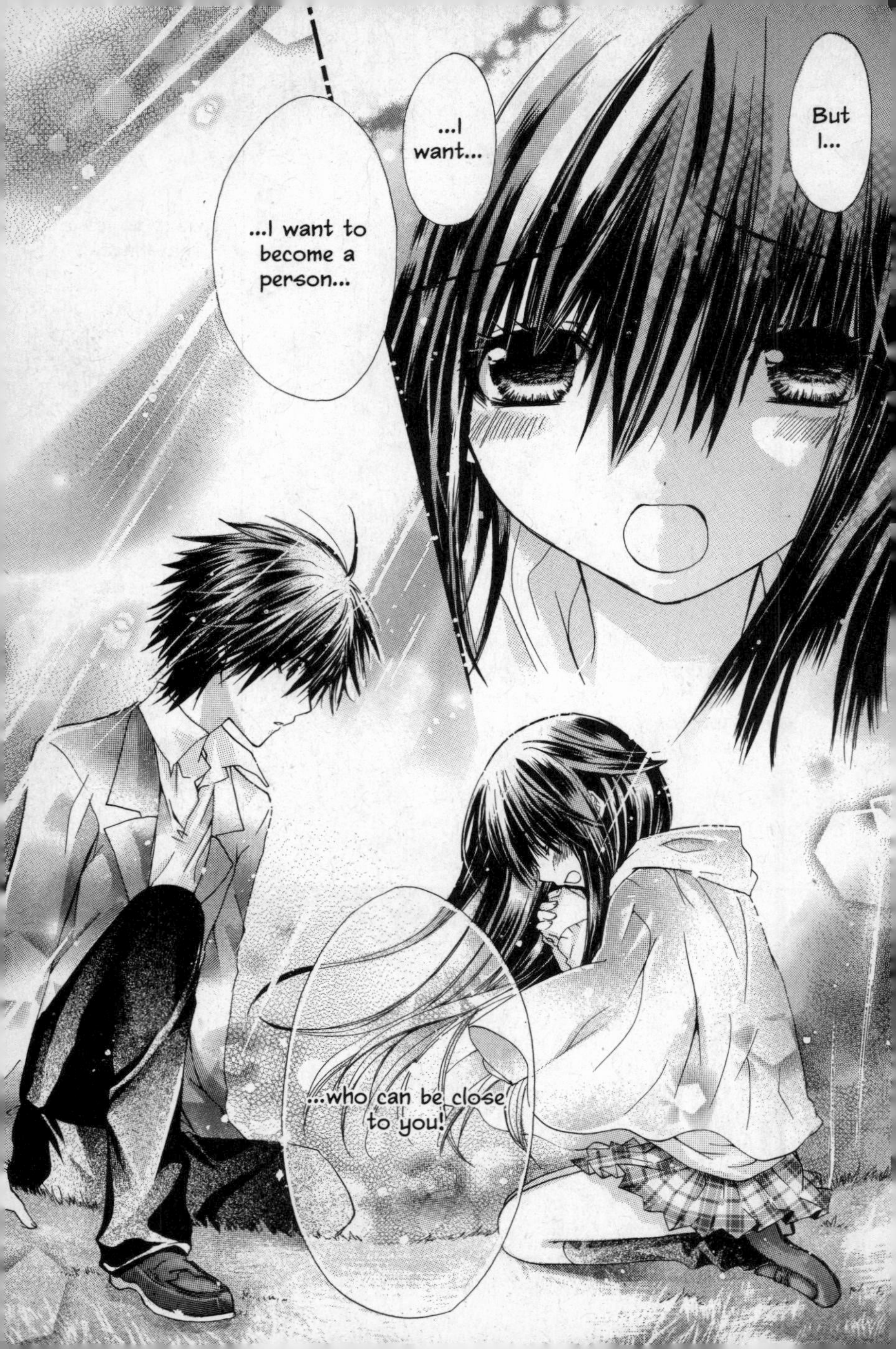
But I...
...I want...
...I want to become a person...
...who can be close to you!

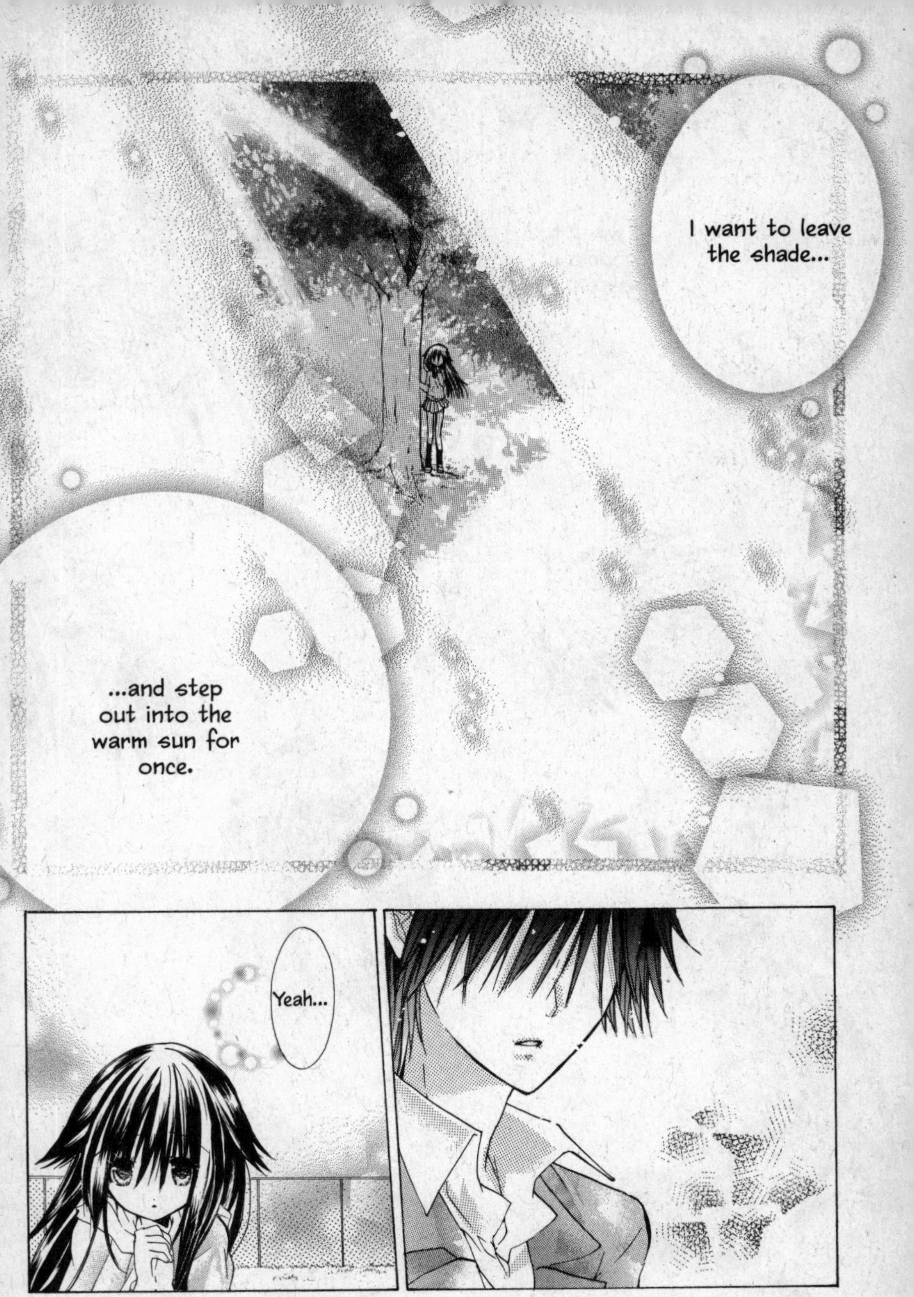
I want to leave the shade...
...and step out into the warm sun for once.
Yeah...

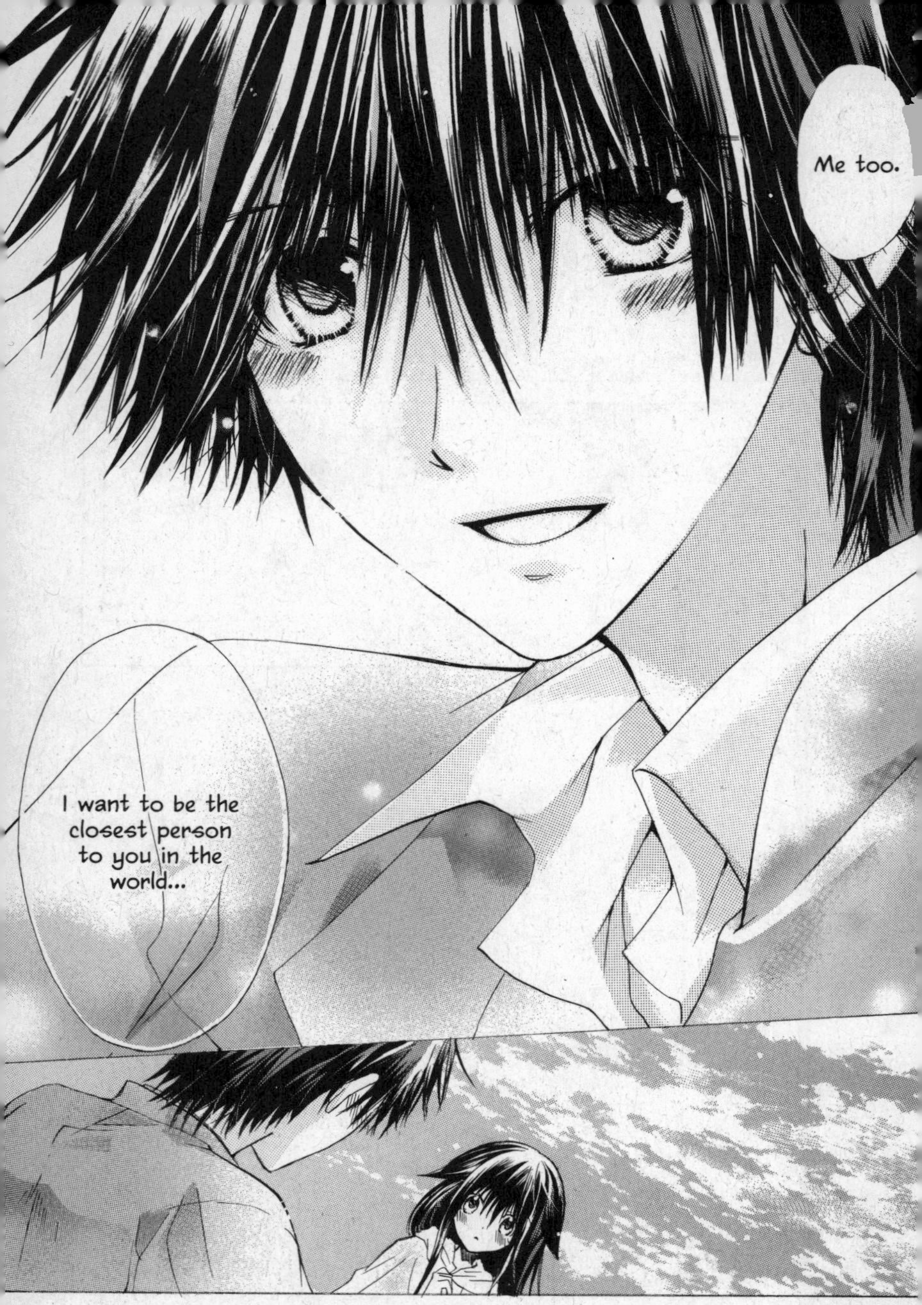
Me too.
I want to be the closest person to you in the world...

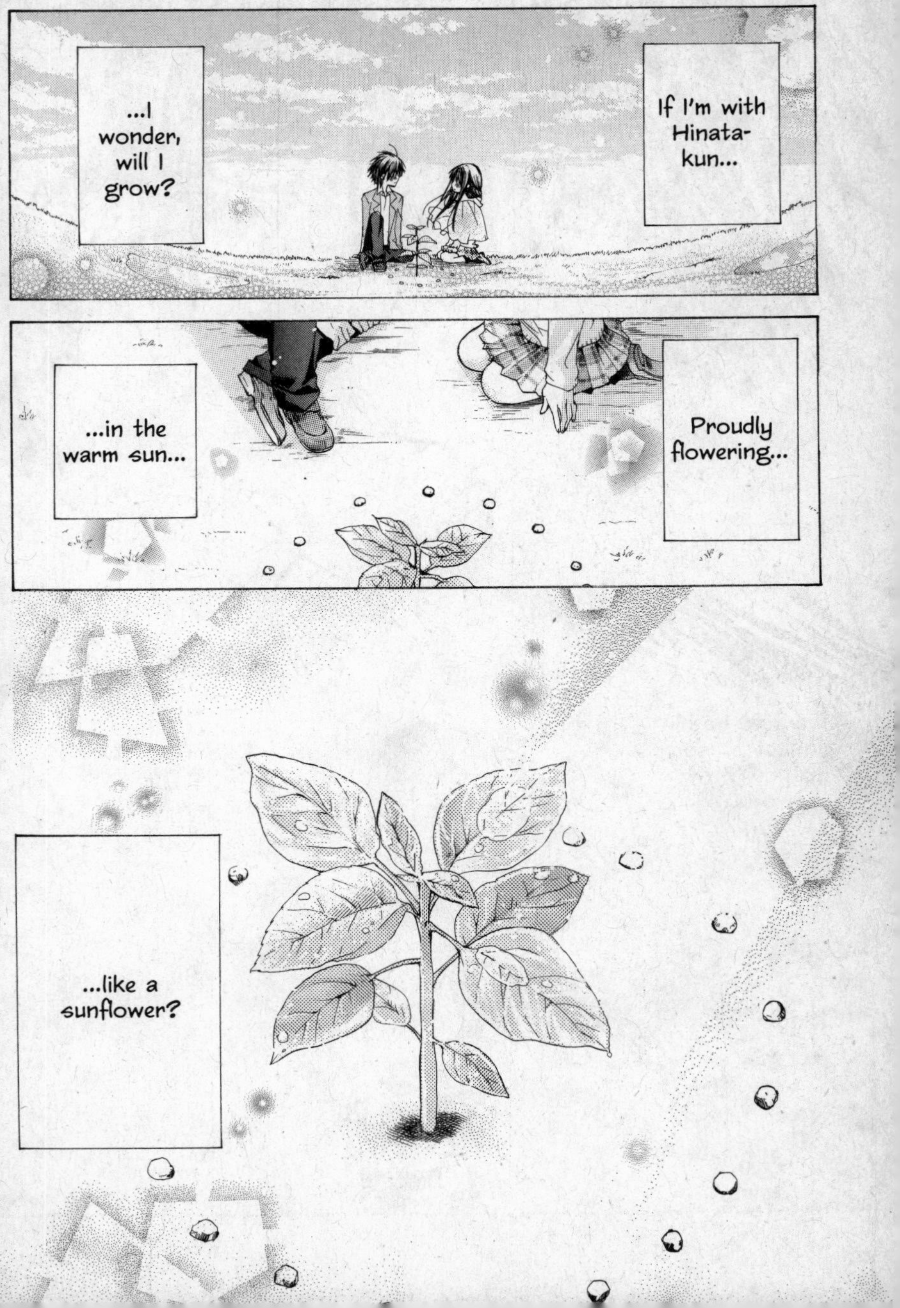
If I'm with Hinata-kun...
...I wonder, will I grow?
Proudly flowering...
...in the warm sun...
...like a sunflower?

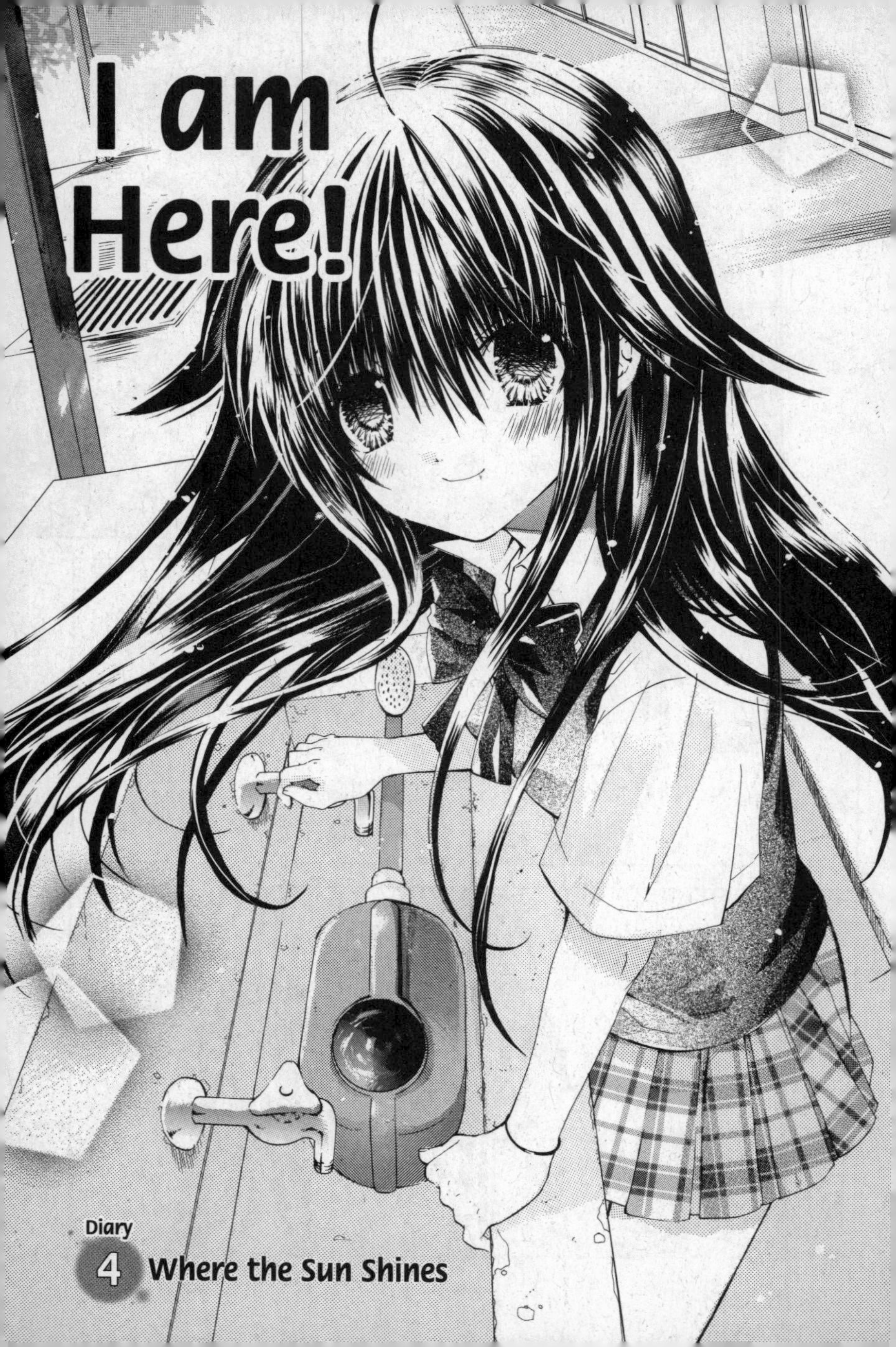
I am Here!
Diary
4 Where the Sun Shines

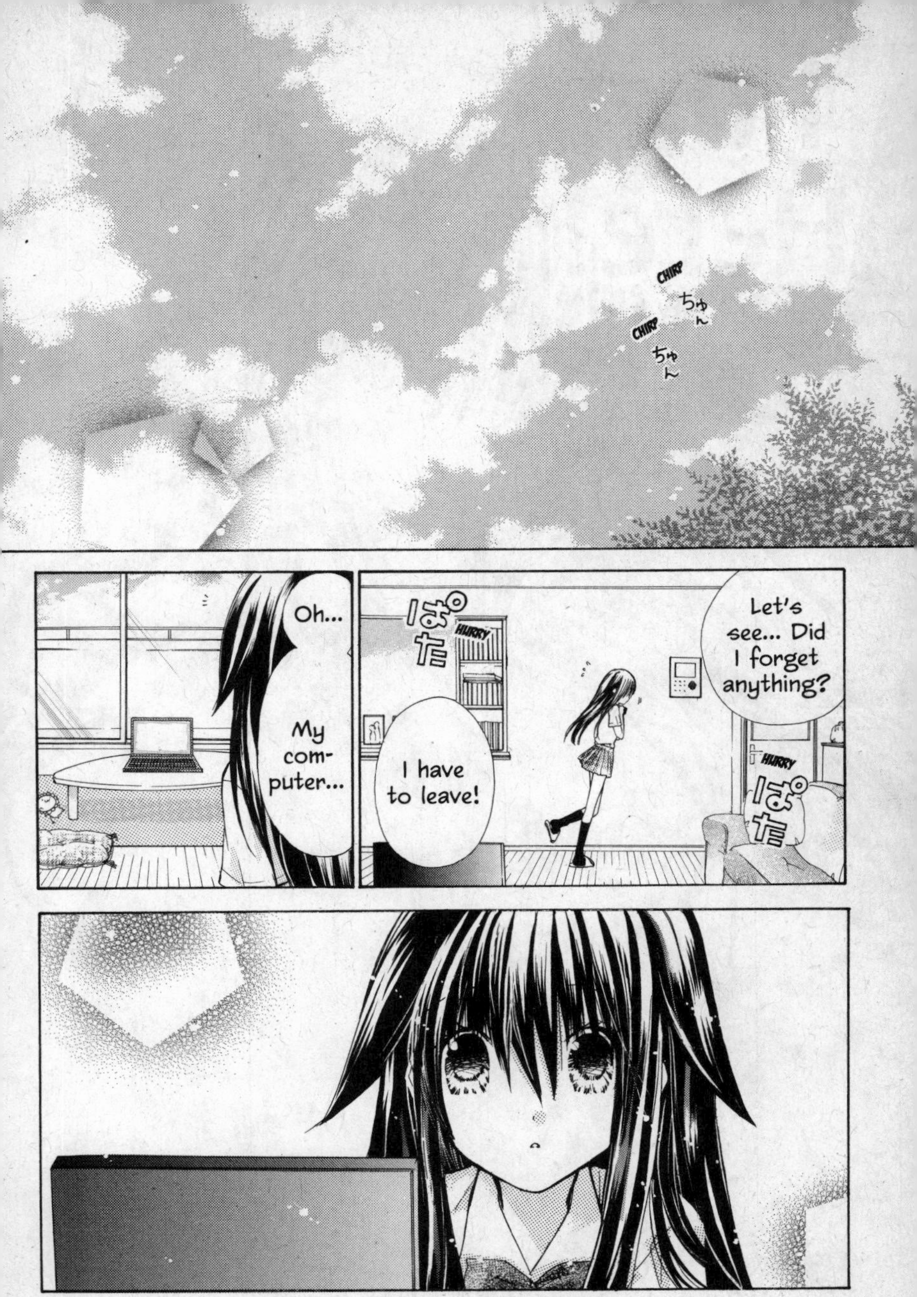
CHIRP
ちゅん
CHIRP
ちゅん
Let's see... Did I forget anything?
HURRY
ぱた
I have to leave!
HURRY
ぱた
Oh...
My computer...

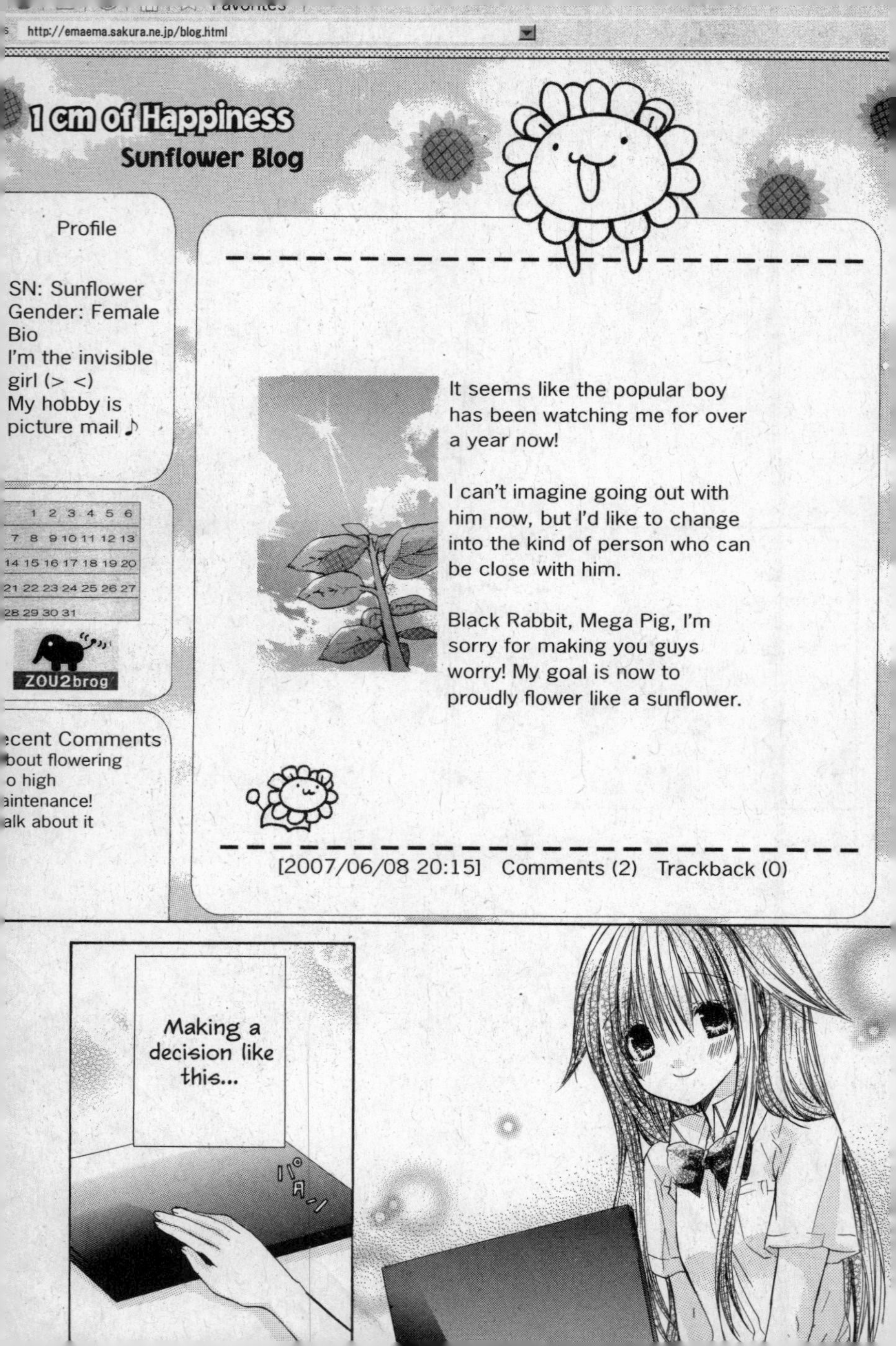

http://emaema.sakura.ne.jp/blog.html
1 cm of Happiness
Sunflower Blog
Profile
SN: Sunflower
Gender: Female
Bio
I'm the invisible girl (> <)
My hobby is picture mail ♪
1 2 3 4 5 6
7 8 9 10 11 12 13
14 15 16 17 18 19 20
21 22 23 24 25 26 27
28 29 30 31
ZOU2brog
ecent Comments
bout flowering
o high
aintenance!
alk about it
It seems like the popular boy has been watching me for over a year now!
I can't imagine going out with him now, but I'd like to change into the kind of person who can be close with him.
Black Rabbit, Mega Pig, I'm sorry for making you guys worry! My goal is now to proudly flower like a sunflower.
[2007/06/08 20:15] Comments (2) Trackback (0)
Making a decision like this...

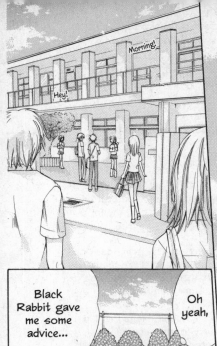

Hey!

Morning!

...feels like a big first step!

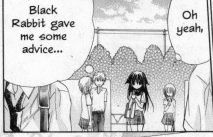

Black Rabbit gave me some advice...

Oh yeah,

I'm leaving!

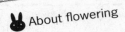 About flowering

Try to be bright! Why don't you start by trying to say hi to people?
(^ ^)/

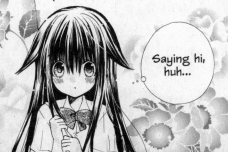

Saying hi, huh...

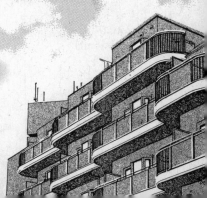

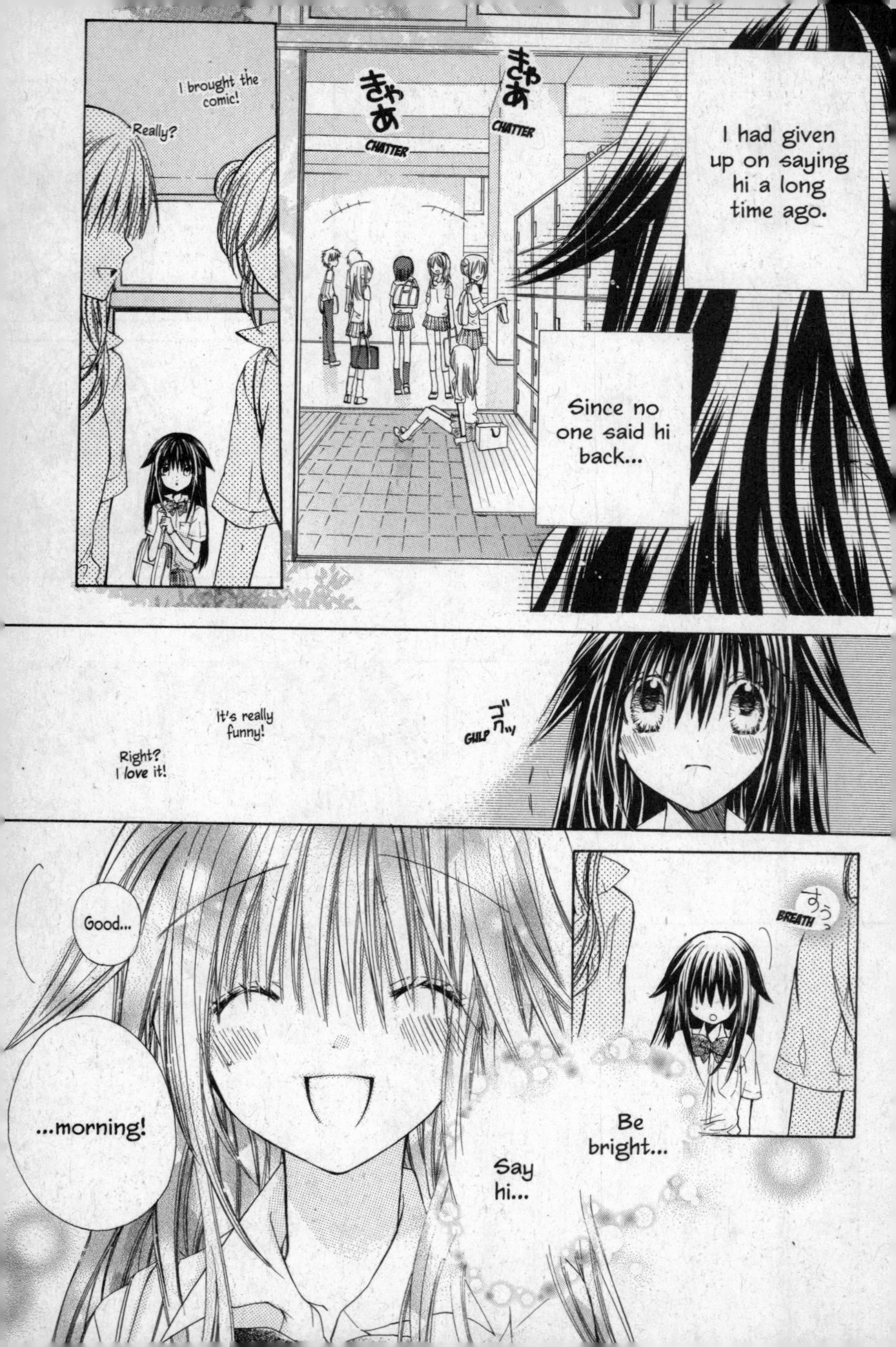
I had given up on saying hi a long time ago.
Since no one said hi back...
きゃあ
CHATTER
きゃあ
CHATTER
I brought the comic!
Really?
ゴクッ
GULP
It's really funny!
Right? I love it!
すぅっ
BREATH
Be bright...
Say hi...
Good...
...morning!

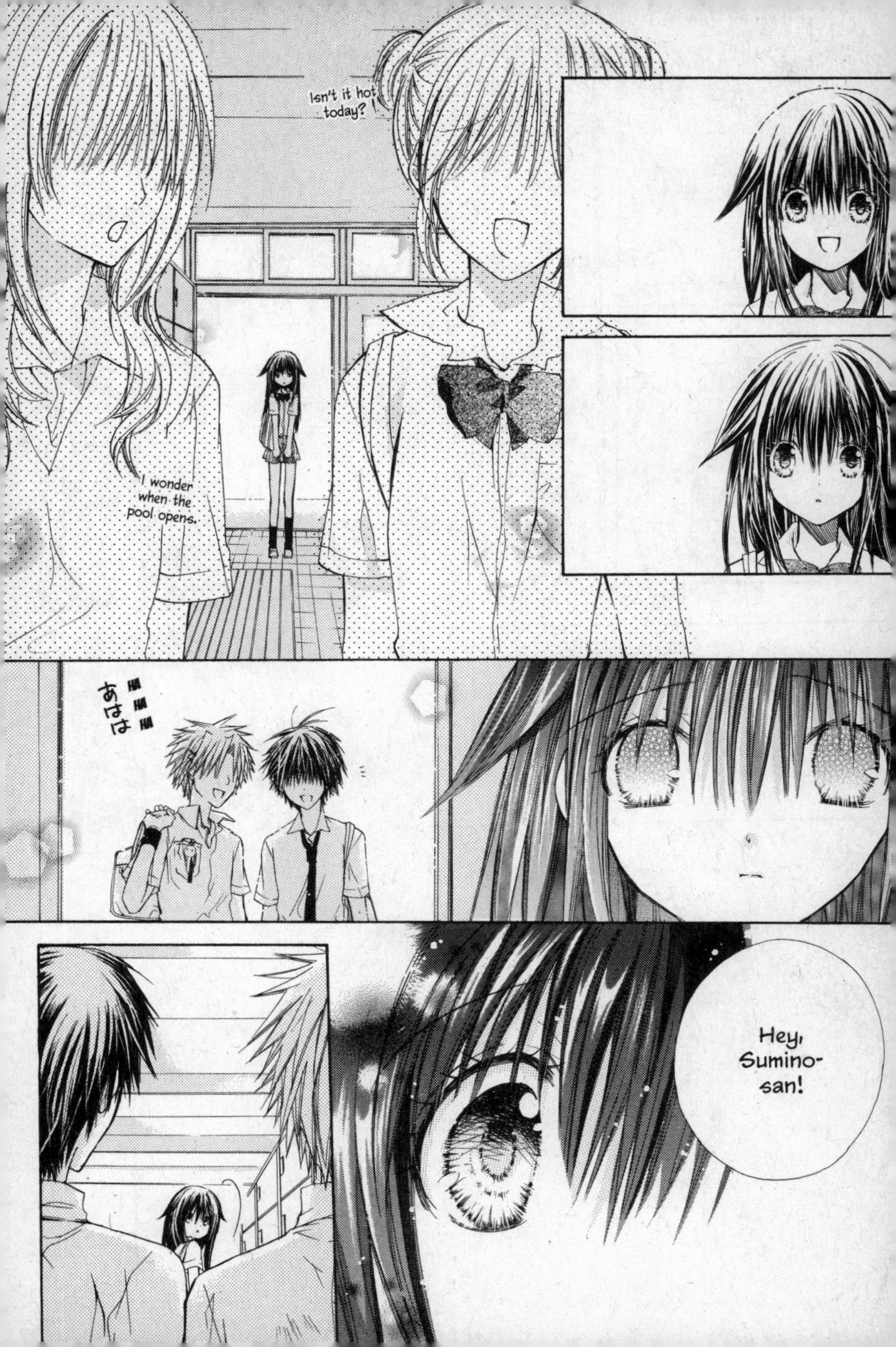
Isn't it hot today?
I wonder when the pool opens.
あはは HA HA HA
Hey, Sumino-san!

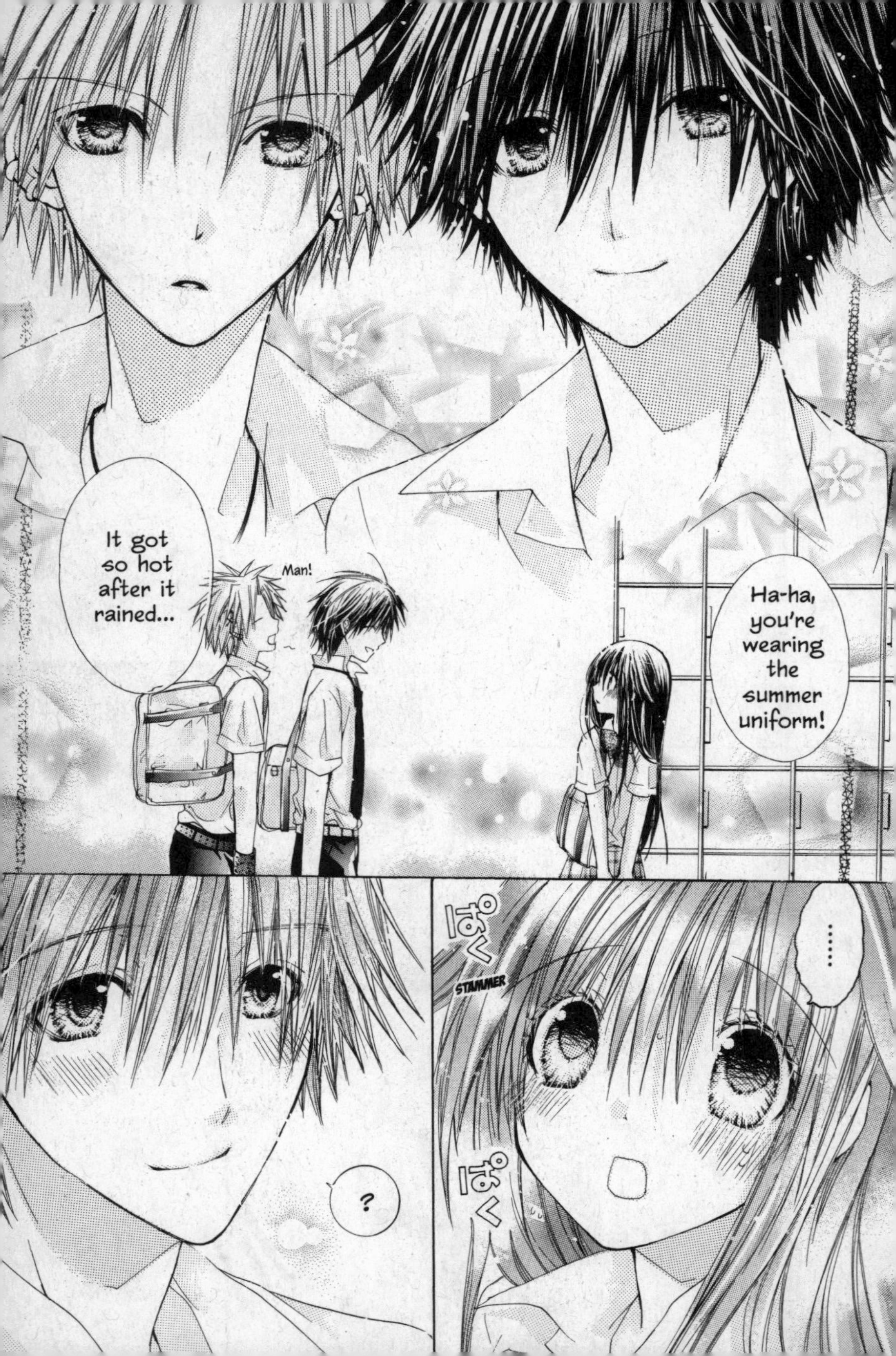
Ha-ha, you're wearing the summer uniform!
Man!
It got so hot after it rained...
......
ぱく
STAMMER
ぱく
?

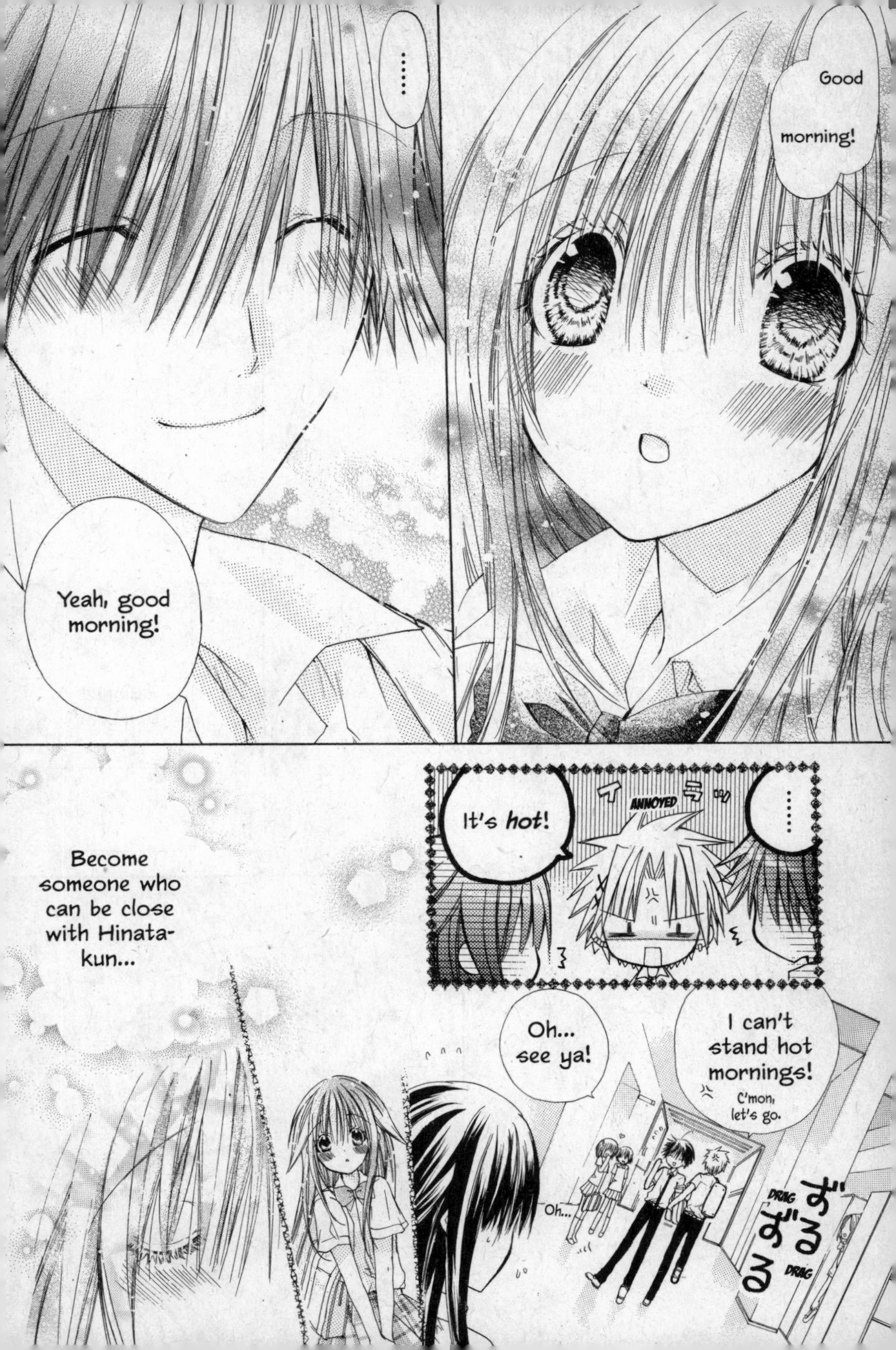
Good morning!
......
Yeah, good morning!
......
イラッ
ANNOYED
It's hot!
I can't stand hot mornings!
C'mon, let's go.
Oh... see ya!
ずるずる
DRAG
DRAG
Oh...
Become someone who can be close with Hinata-kun...

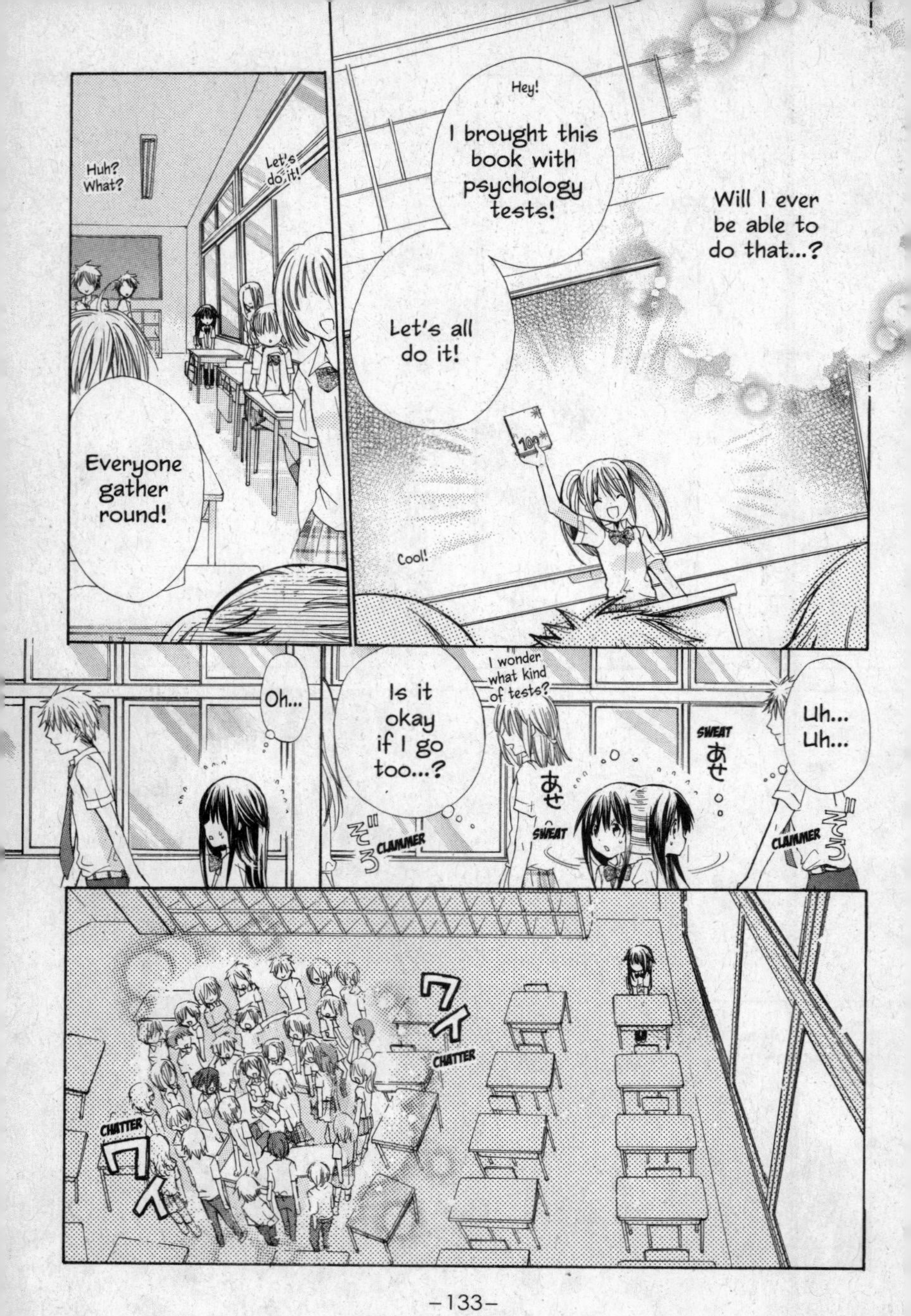
Will I ever be able to do that...?
Hey!
I brought this book with psychology tests!
Let's all do it!
Cool!
Let's do it!
Huh? What?
Everyone gather round!
Uh... uh...
ぞろ CLAMMER
あせ SWEAT
あせ SWEAT
I wonder what kind of tests?
Is it okay if I go too...?
ぞろ CLAMMER
Oh...
ワイ CHATTER
ワイ CHATTER

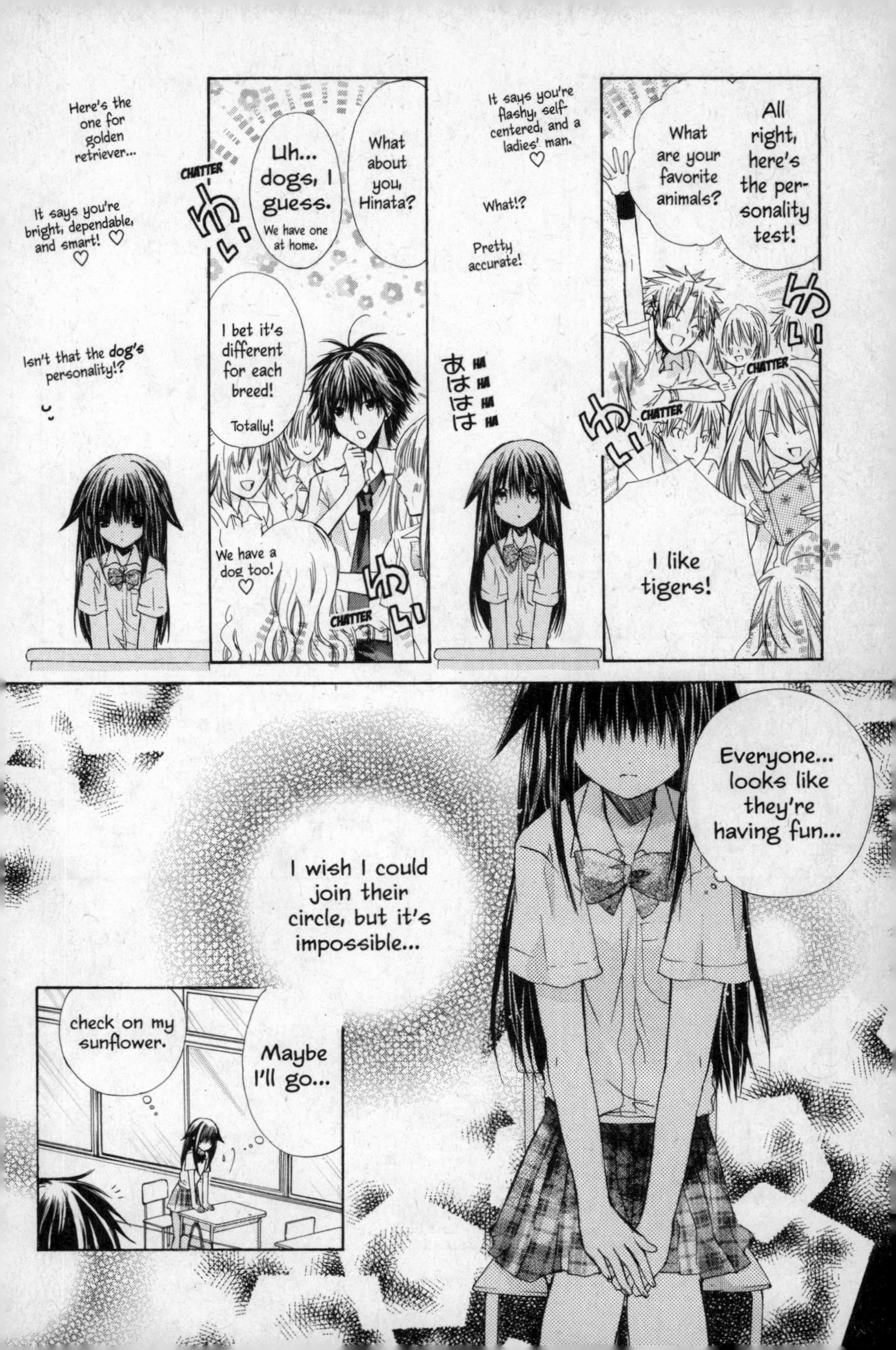
All right, here's the per-sonality test!
What are your favorite animals?
CHATTER
CHATTER
I like tigers!
It says you're flashy, self-centered, and a ladies' man. ♡
What!?
Pretty accurate!
あははは HA HA HA HA
What about you, Hinata?
Uh... dogs, I guess. We have one at home.
CHATTER
I bet it's different for each breed!
Totally!
We have a dog too! ♡
CHATTER
Here's the one for golden retriever...
It says you're bright, dependable, and smart! ♡ ♡
Isn't that the dog's personality!?
Everyone... looks like they're having fun...
I wish I could join their circle, but it's impossible...
Maybe I'll go...
check on my sunflower.

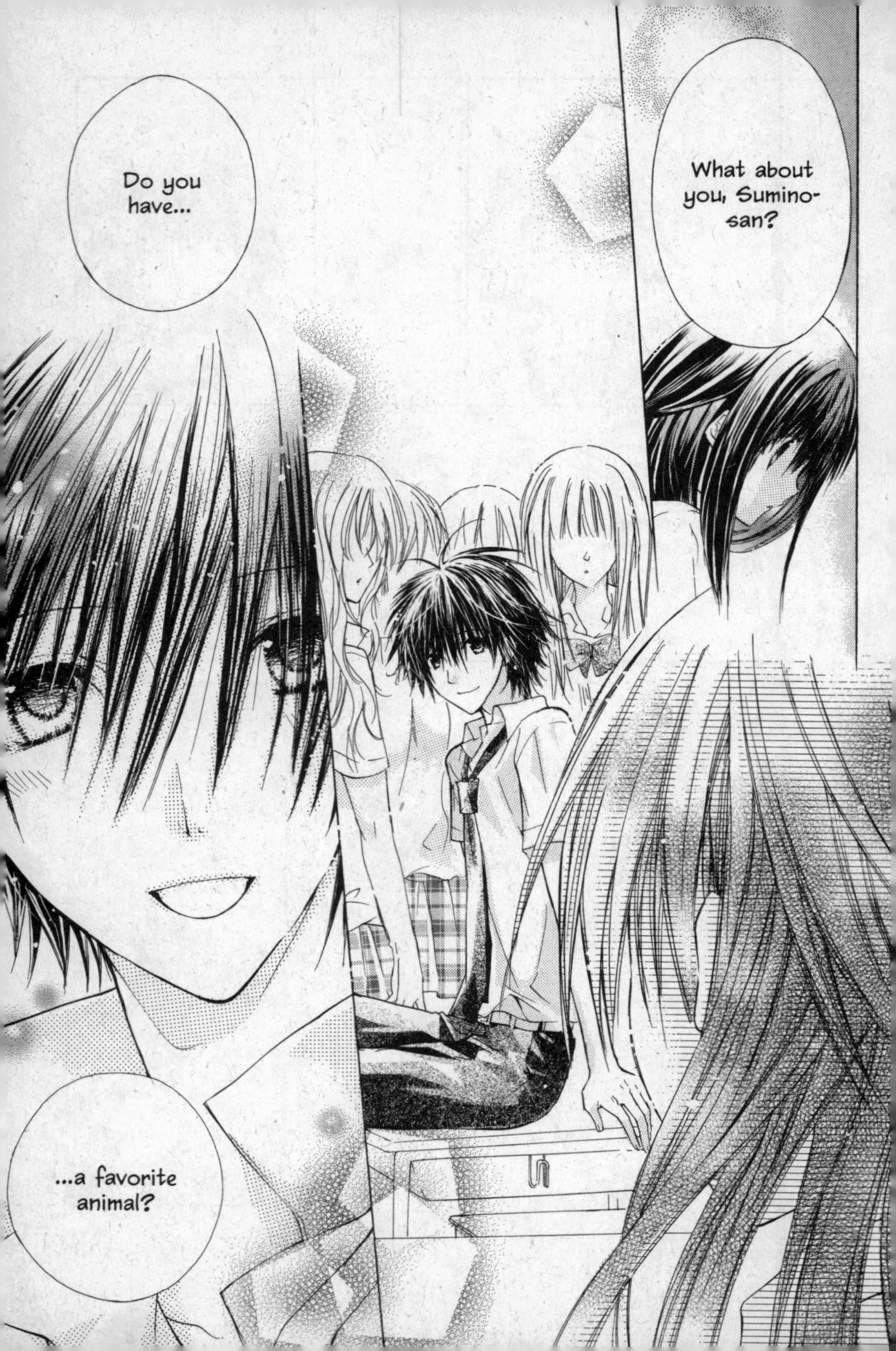
What about you, Sumino-san?
Do you have...
...a favorite animal?

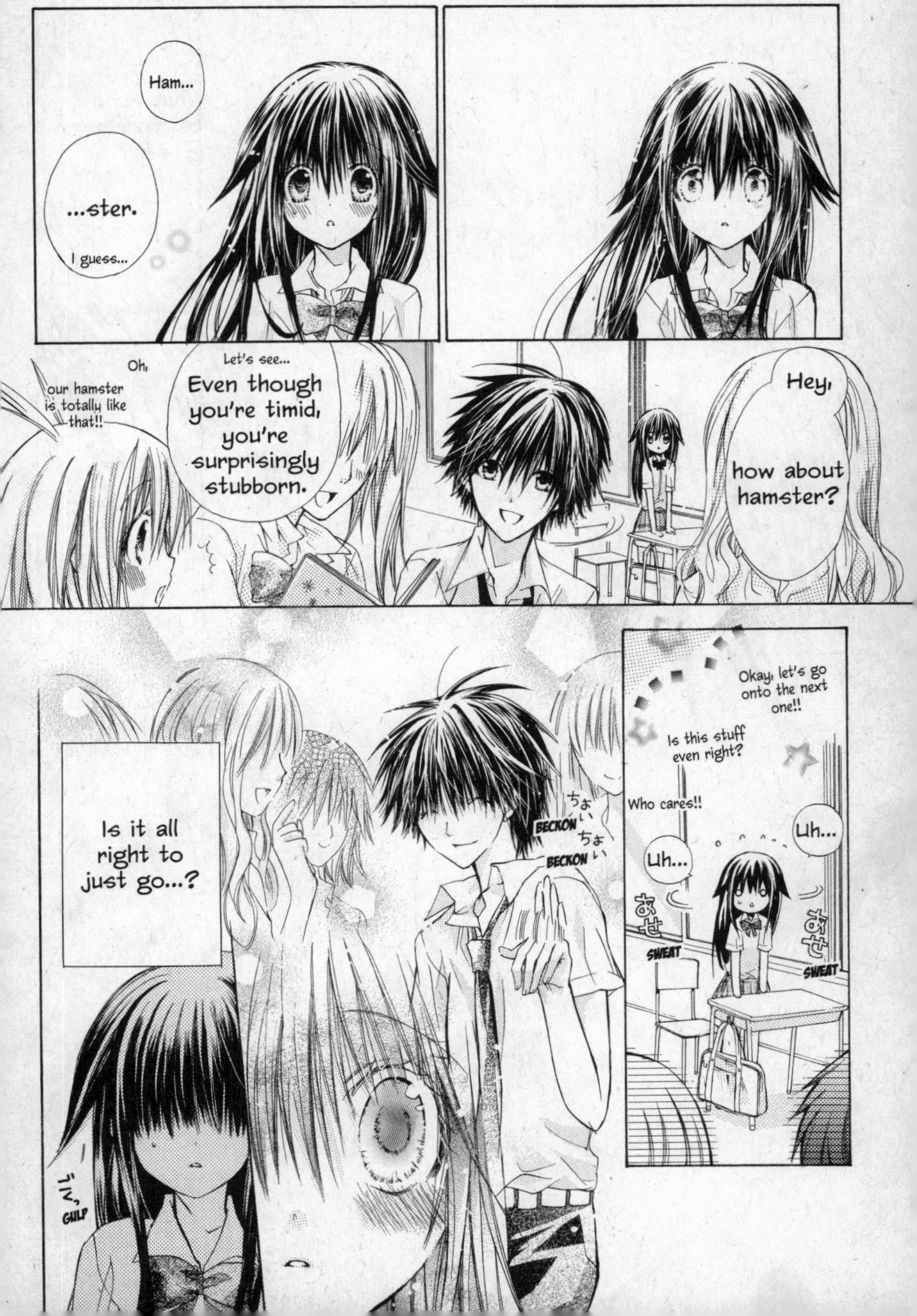
Ham...
...ster.
I guess...
Hey,
how about hamster?
Let's see...
Even though you're timid, you're surprisingly stubborn.
Oh, our hamster is totally like that!!
Okay, let's go onto the next one!!
Is this stuff even right?
Who cares!!
Uh...
Uh...
SWEAT
SWEAT
BECKON
BECKON
Is it all right to just go...?
GULP

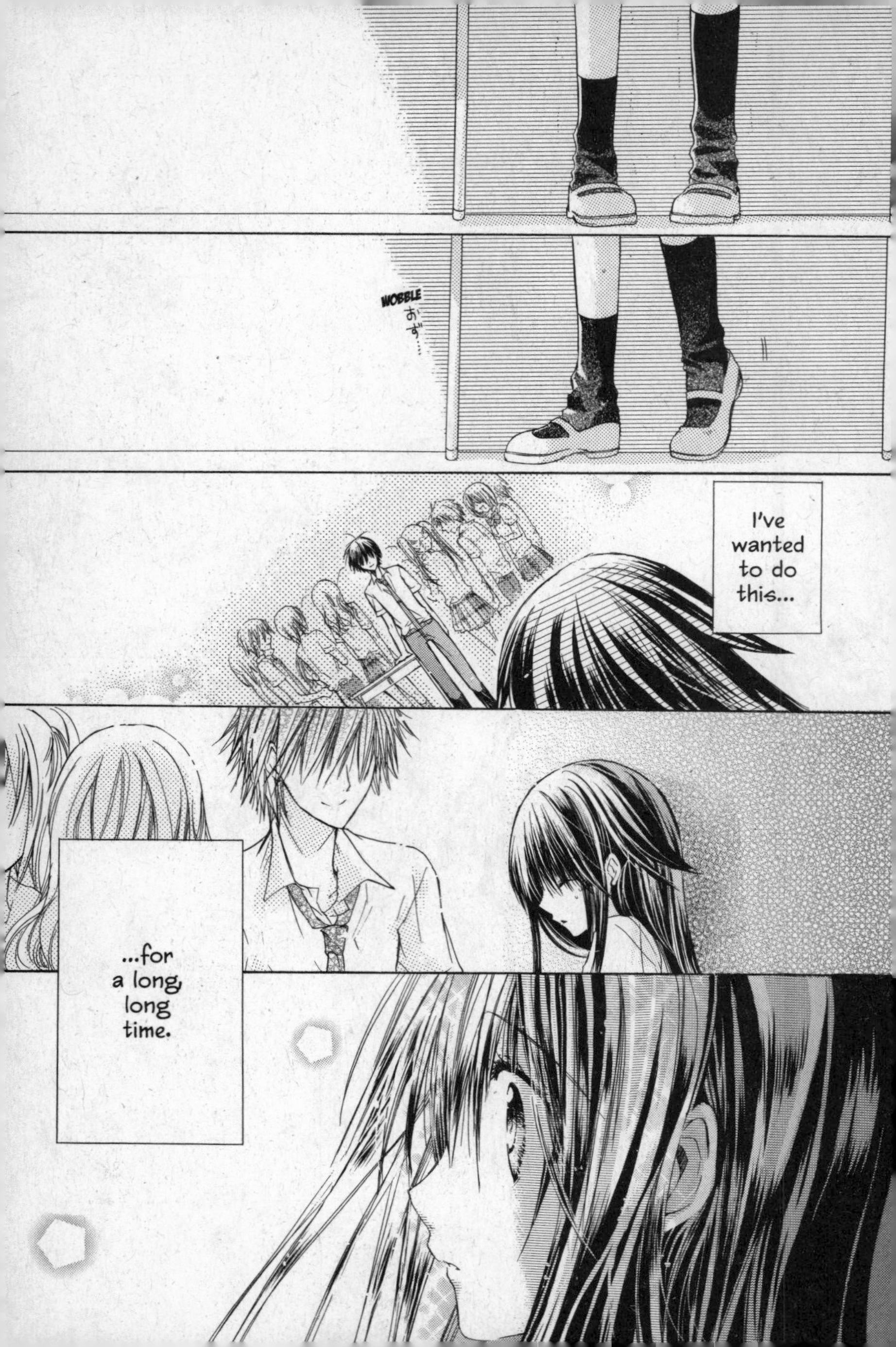

WOBBLE
おず…
I've wanted to do this...
...for a long, long time.

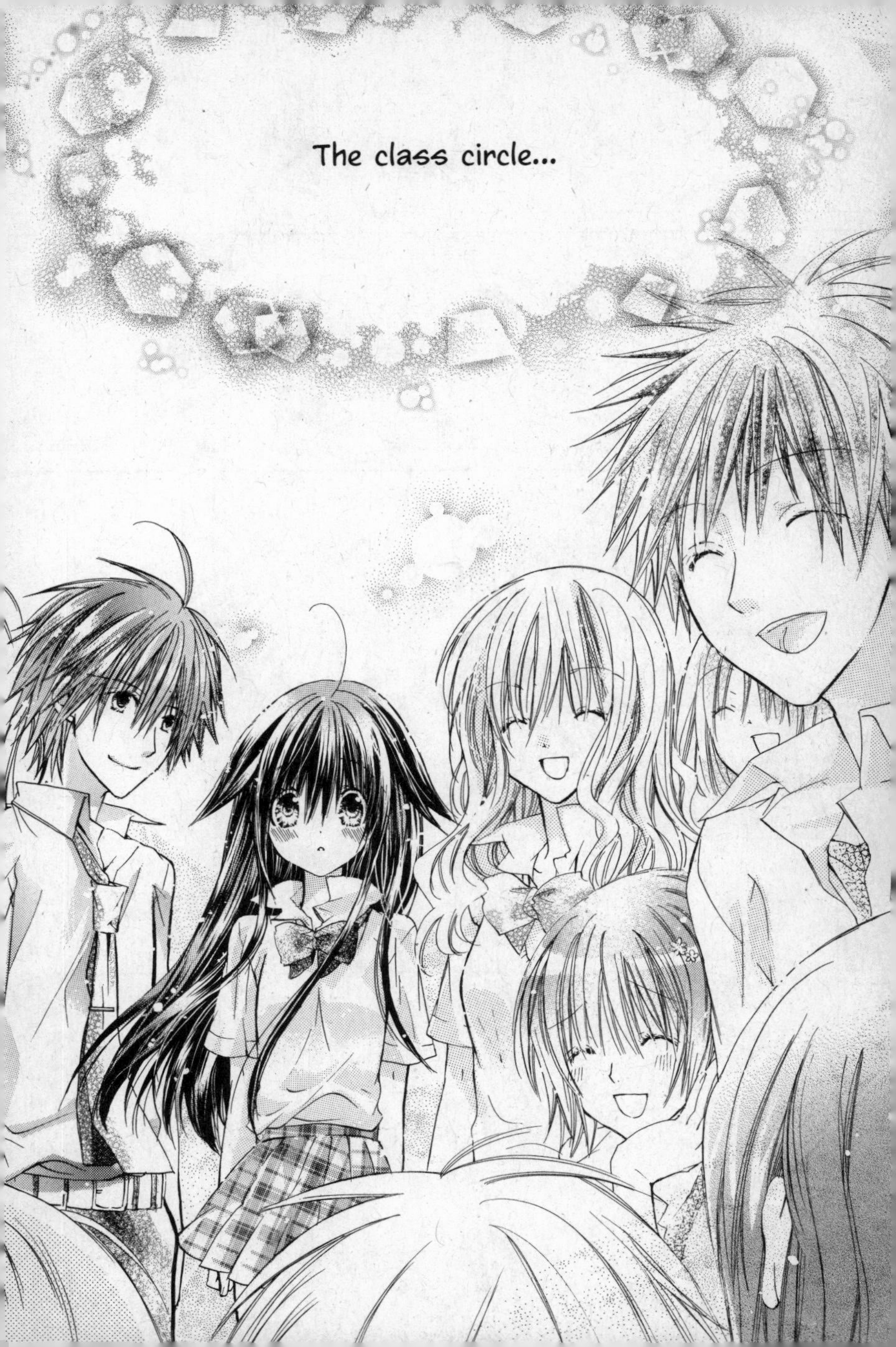
The class circle...

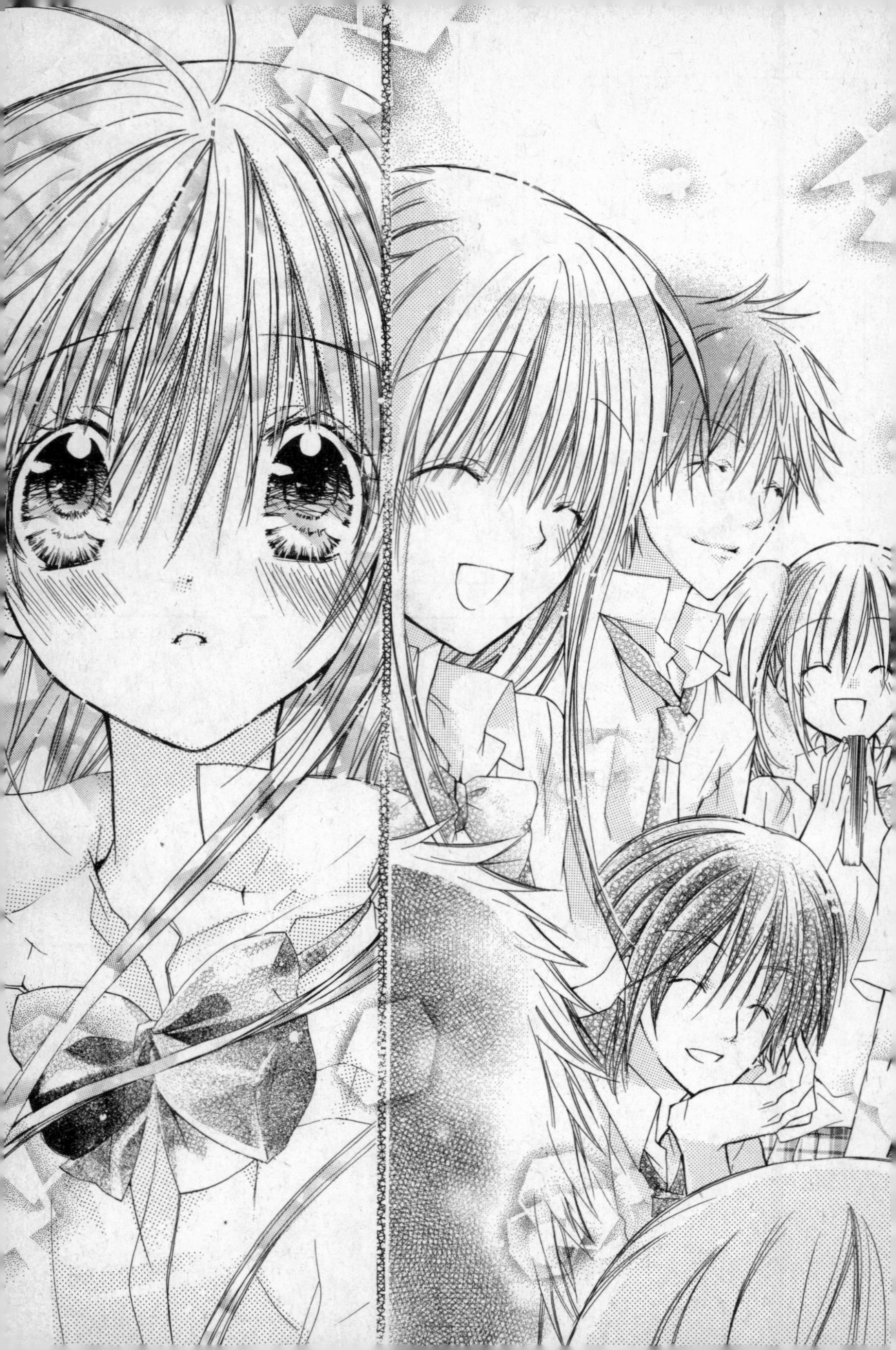

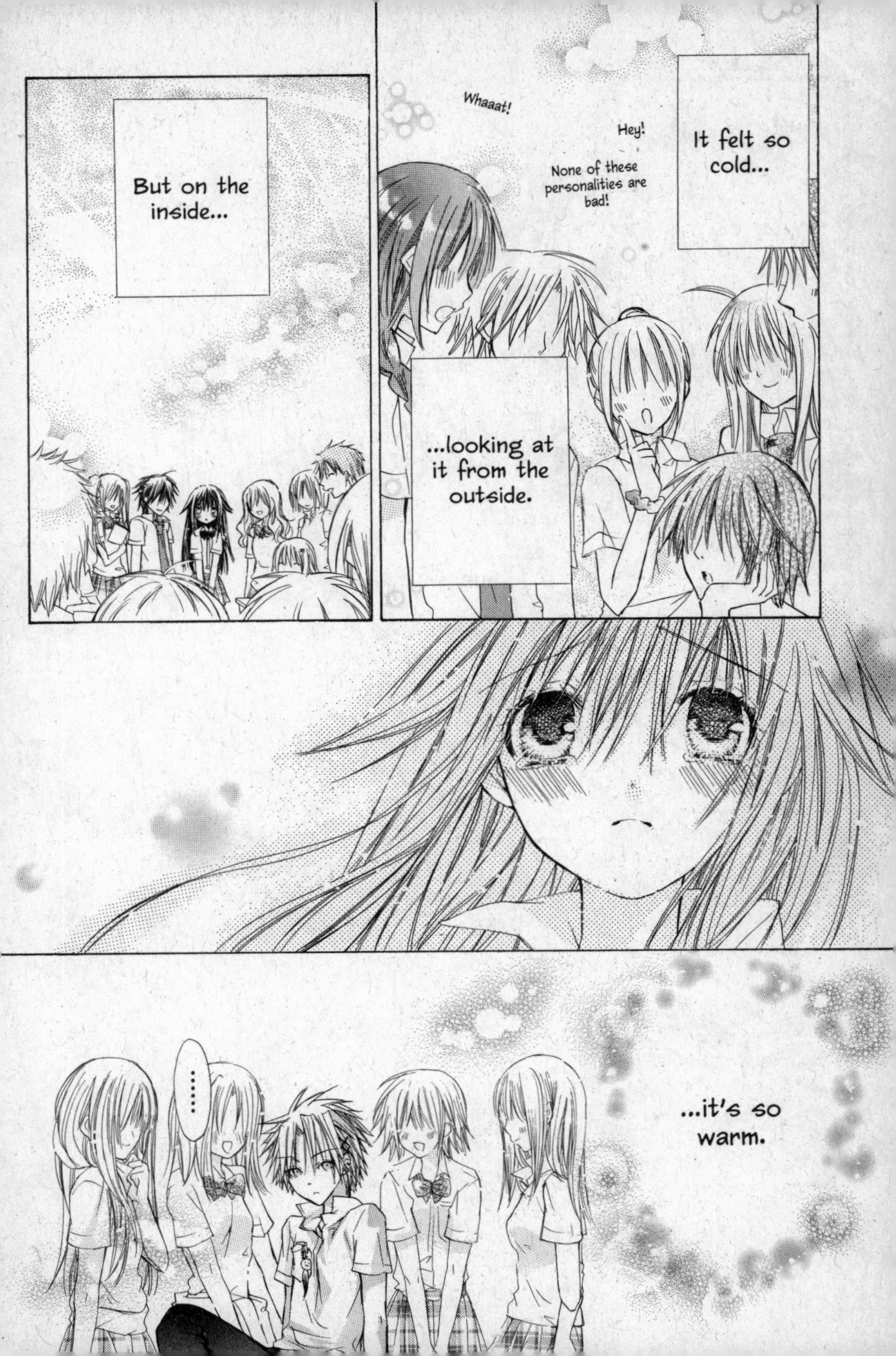
It felt so cold...
Hey!
Whaaat!
None of these personalities are bad!
...looking at it from the outside.
But on the inside...
...it's so warm.
......

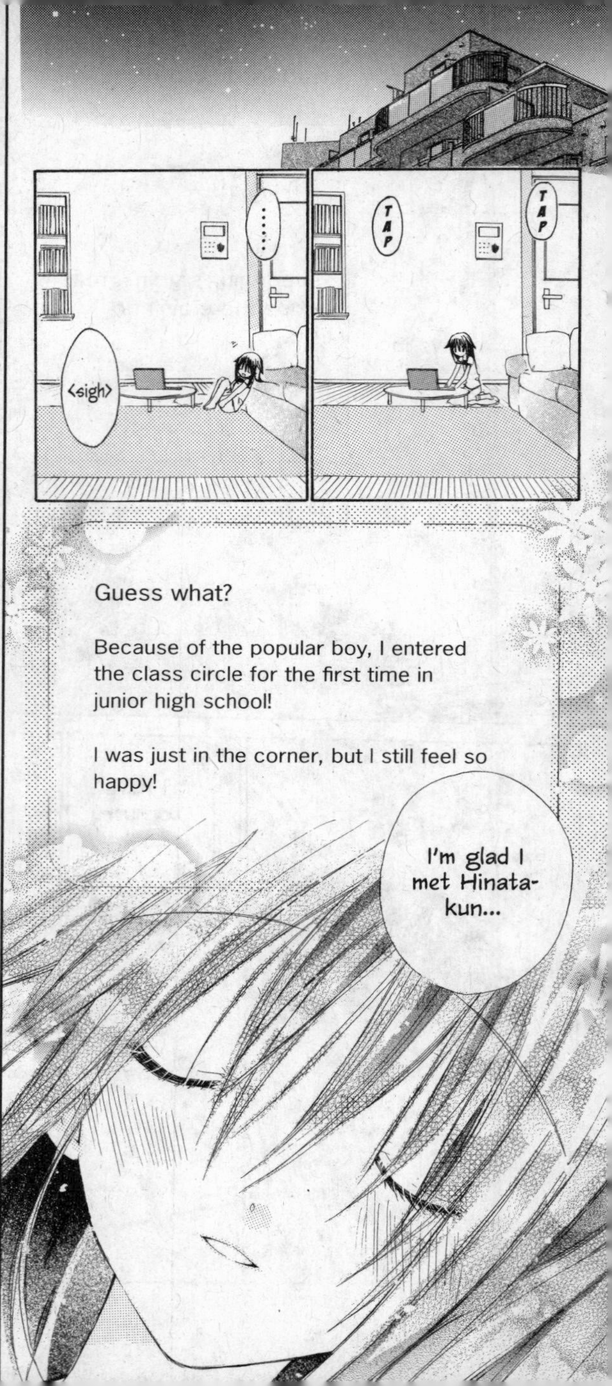
TAP
TAP
......
<sigh>
Guess what?
Because of the popular boy, I entered the class circle for the first time in junior high school!
I was just in the corner, but I still feel so happy!
I'm glad I met Hinata-kun...

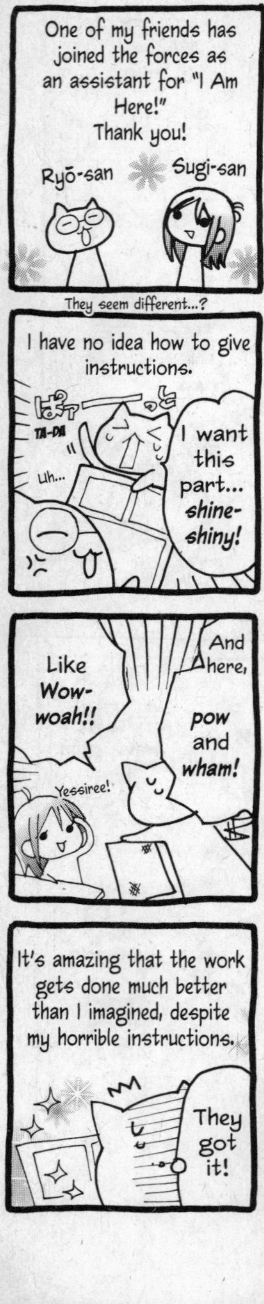
One of my friends has joined the forces as an assistant for "I Am Here!" Thank you!
Ryō-san
Sugi-san
They seem different...?
I have no idea how to give instructions.
TA-DA
I want this part... shine-shiny!
Uh...
Like Wow-woah!!
And here, pow and wham!
Yessiree!
It's amazing that the work gets done much better than I imagined, despite my horrible instructions.
They got it!

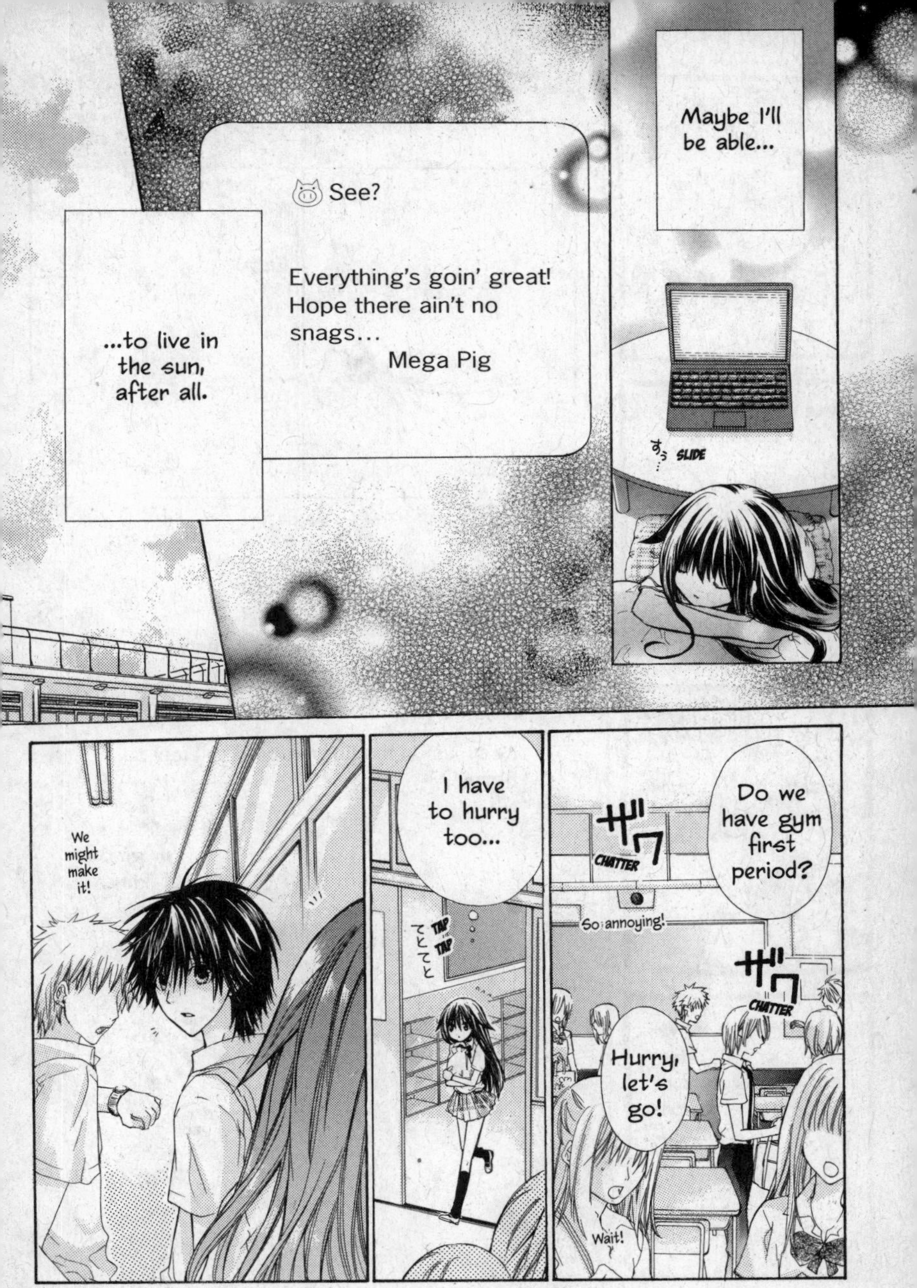
Maybe I'll be able...
すぅ SLIDE
See?
Everything's goin' great! Hope there ain't no snags...
Mega Pig
...to live in the sun, after all.
Do we have gym first period?
ザワ CHATTER
So annoying!
ザワ CHATTER
Hurry, let's go!
Wait!
I have to hurry too...
てとてと TAP TAP
We might make it!

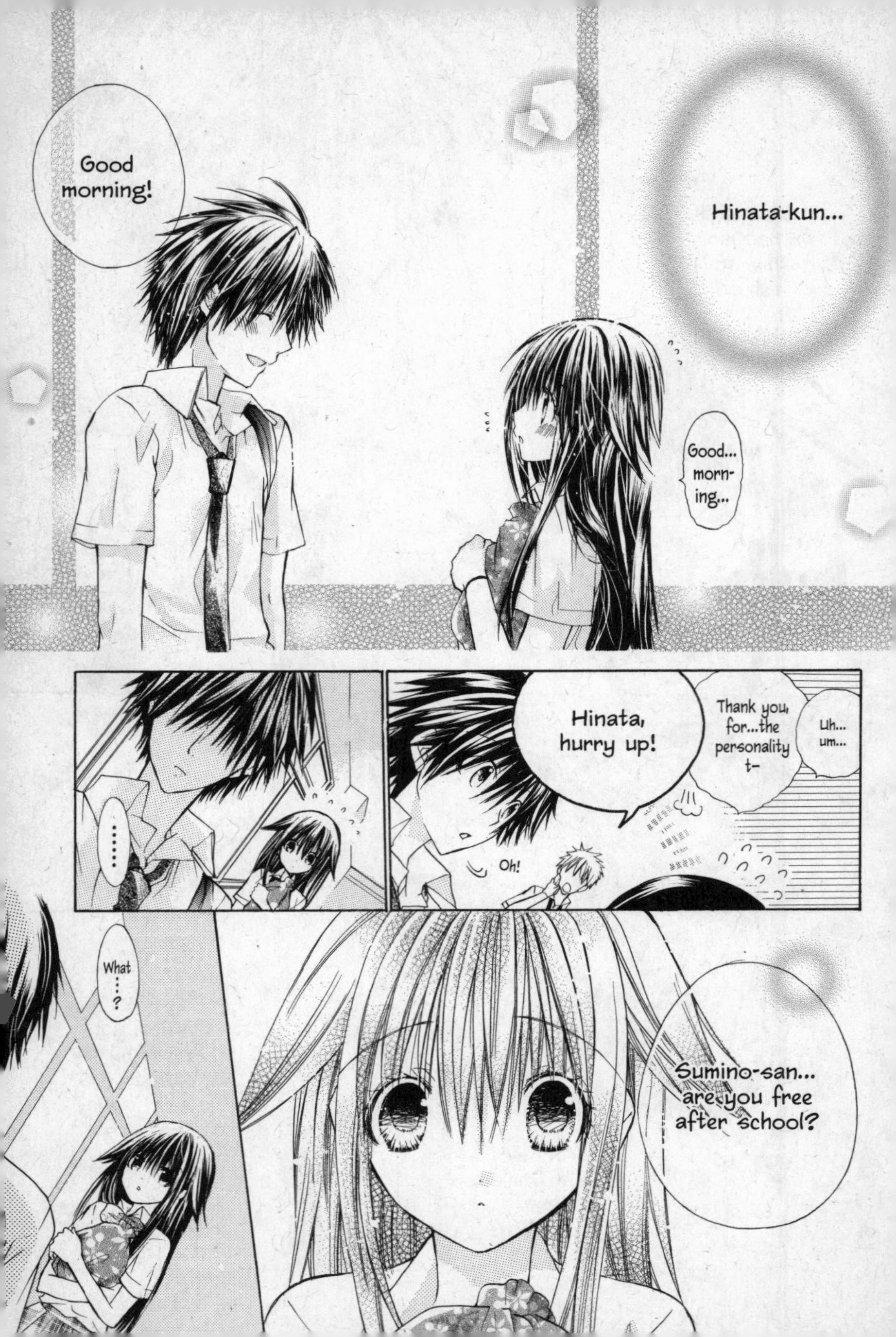
Hinata-kun...
Good morning!
Good... morn-ing...
Uh... um...
Thank you, for...the personality t-
Hinata, hurry up!
Oh!
......
Sumino-san... are you free after school?
What...?

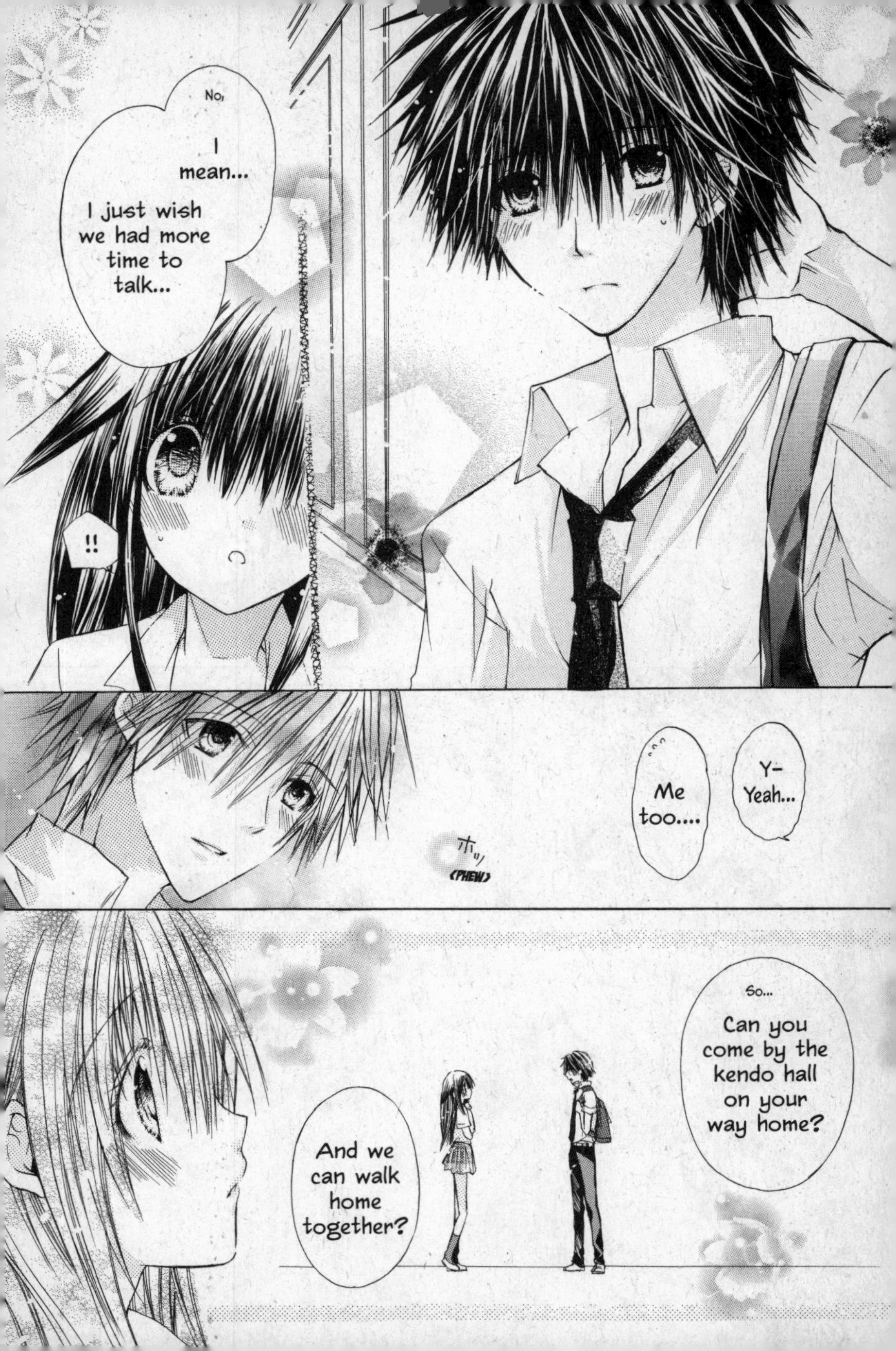
No,
I mean...
I just wish we had more time to talk...
!!
Y- Yeah...
Me too....
ホッ
(PHEW)
So...
Can you come by the kendo hall on your way home?
And we can walk home together?

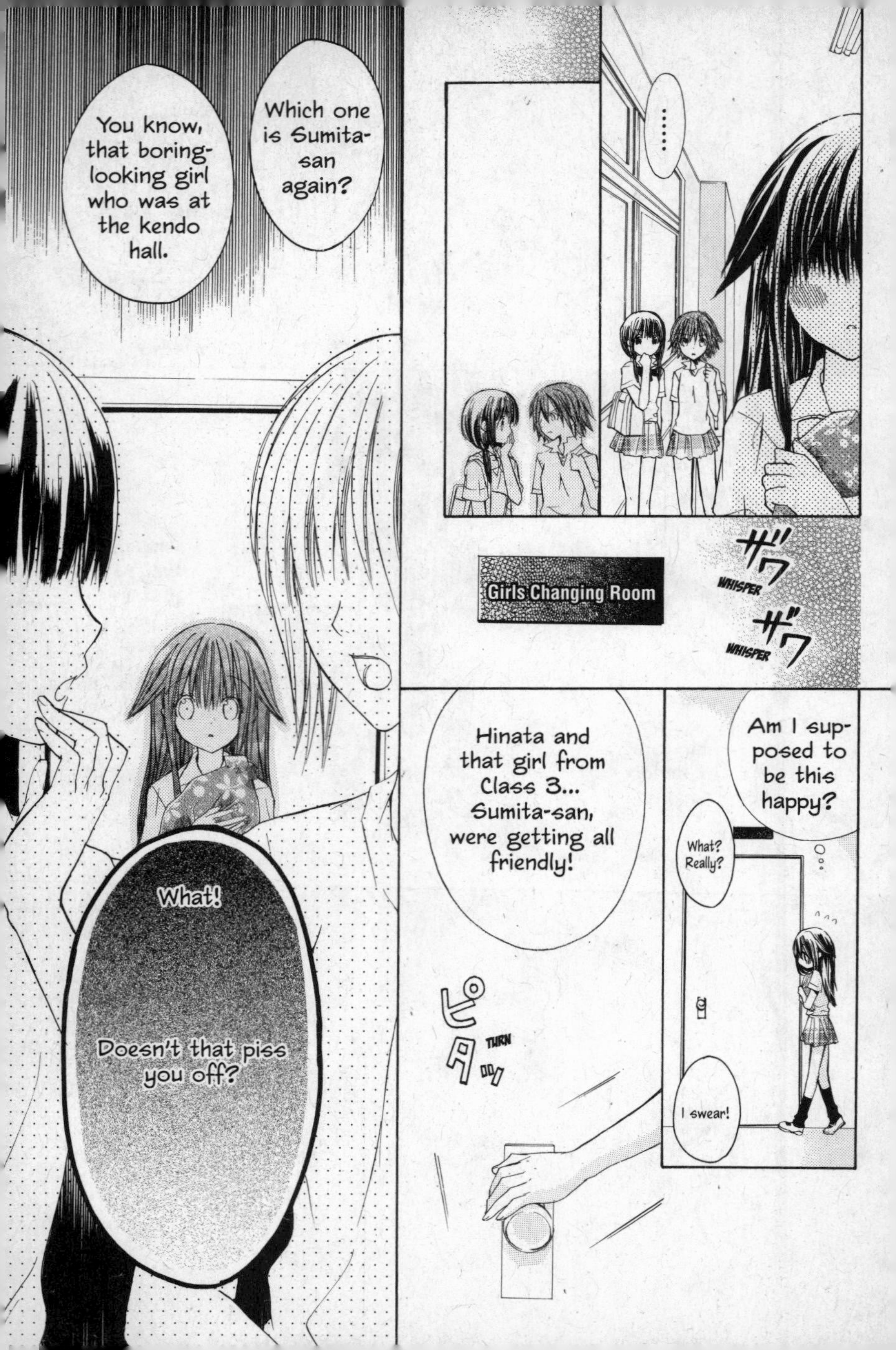
......
ザワ WHISPER
ザワ WHISPER
Girls Changing Room
Am I supposed to be this happy?
Hinata and that girl from Class 3... Sumita-san, were getting all friendly!
What? Really?
I swear!
ピタッ TURN
Which one is Sumita-san again?
You know, that boring-looking girl who was at the kendo hall.
What!
Doesn't that piss you off?

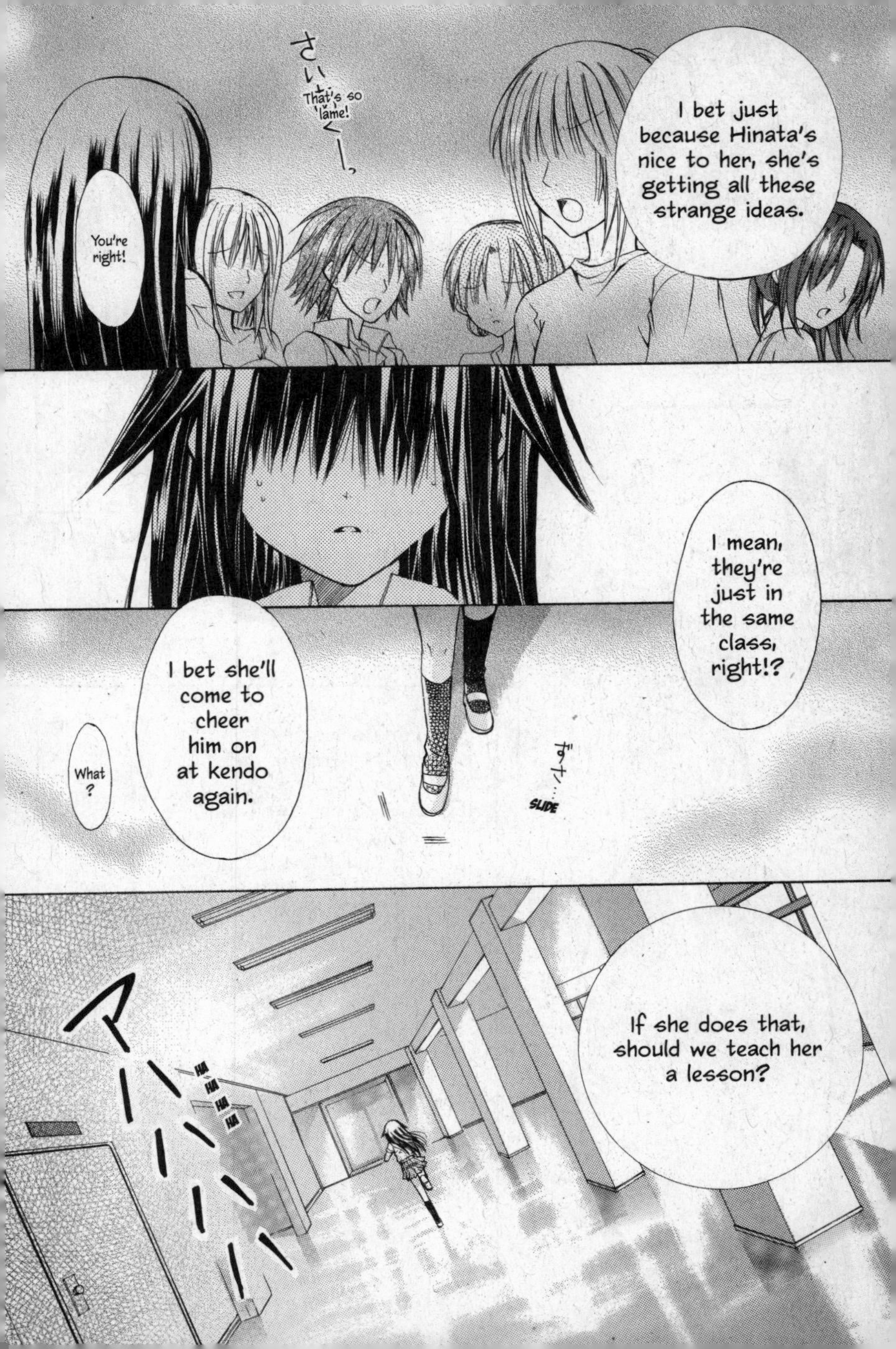
I bet just because Hinata's nice to her, she's getting all these strange ideas.
That's so lame!
You're right!
I mean, they're just in the same class, right!?
SLIDE
I bet she'll come to cheer him on at kendo again.
What?
If she does that, should we teach her a lesson?
HA HA HA HA

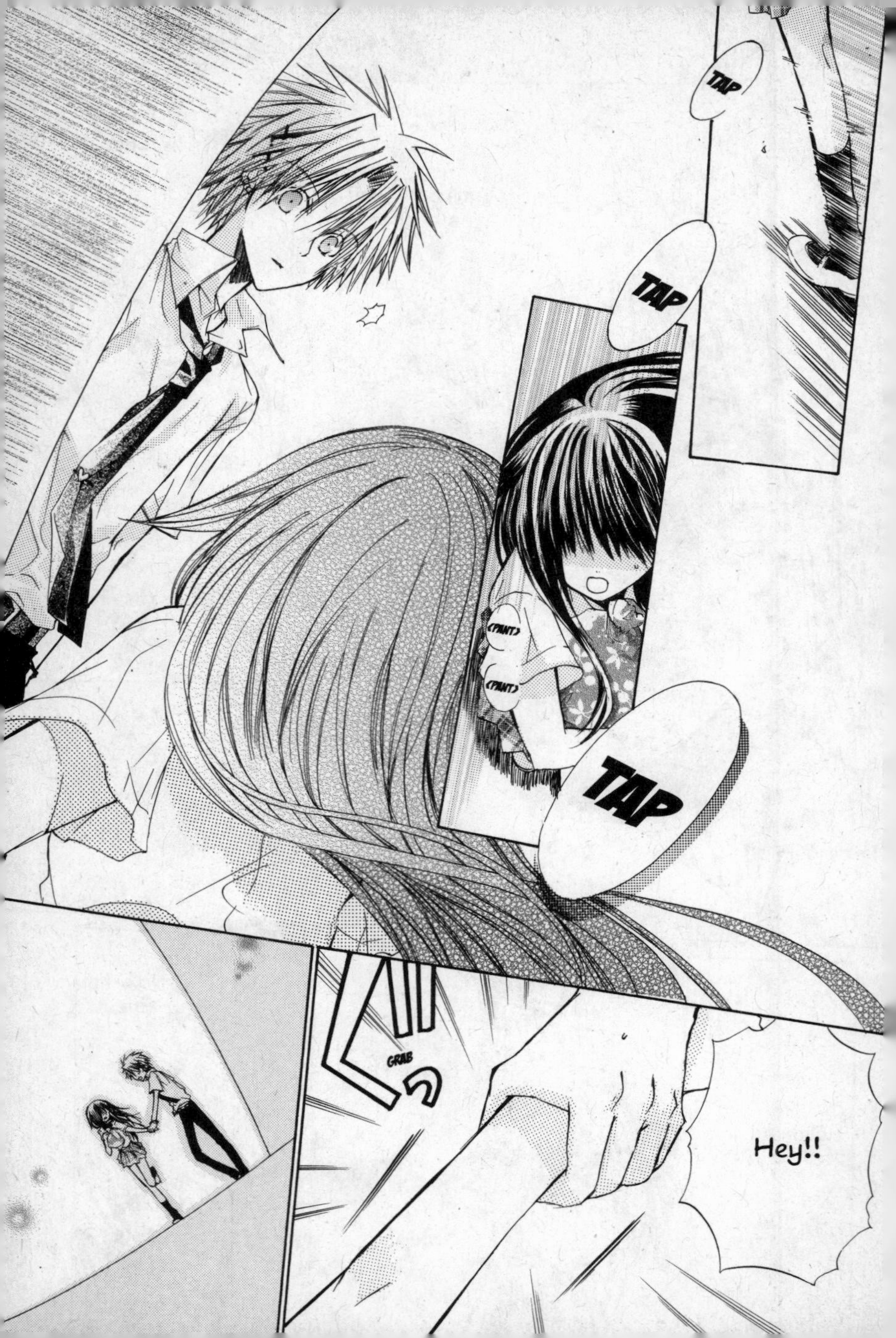
TAP
TAP
<PANT>
<PANT>
TAP
Hey!!
GRAB

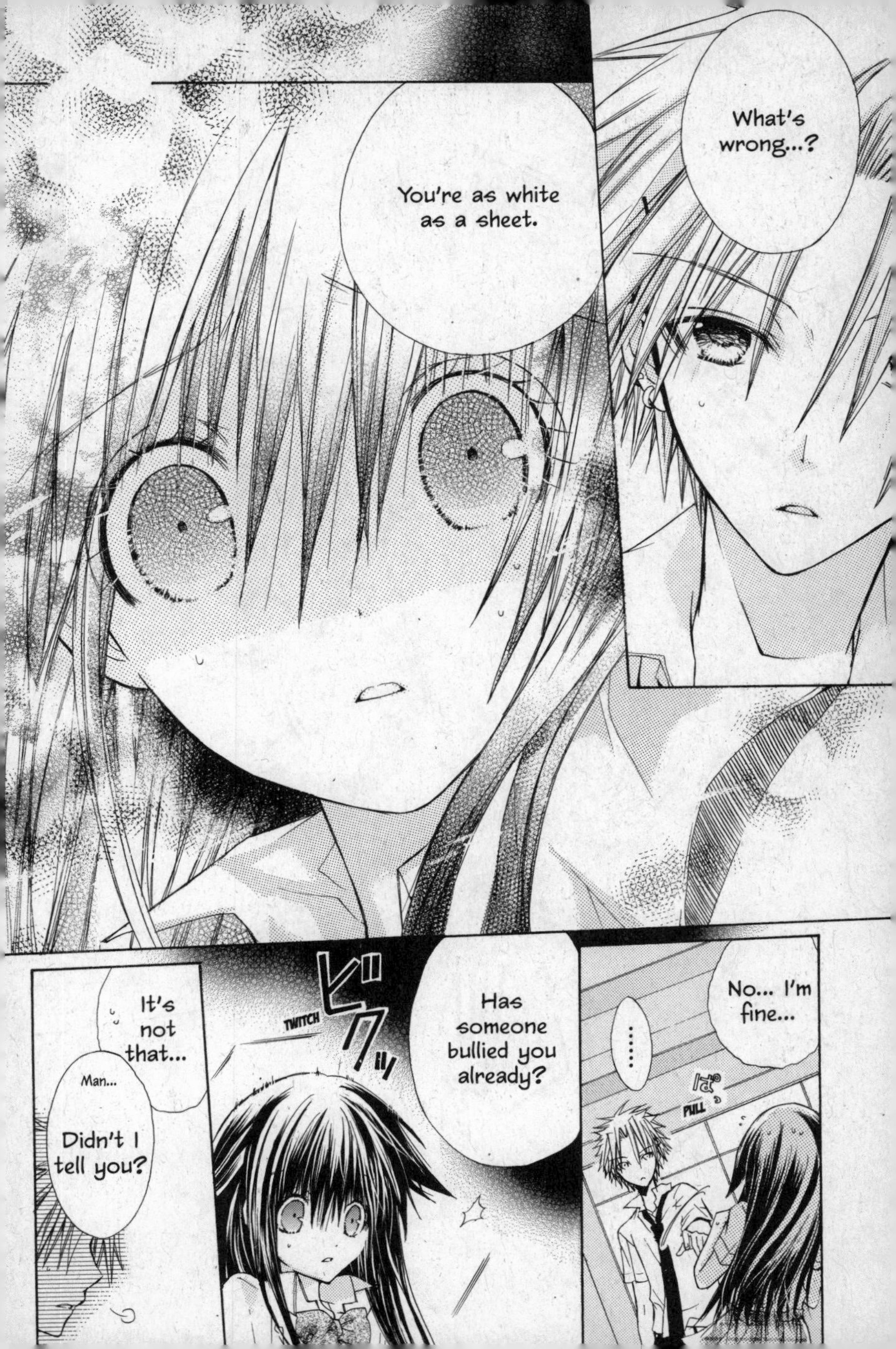
What's wrong...?
You're as white as a sheet.
No... I'm fine...
......
ぱっ
PULL
Has someone bullied you already?
ビクッ
TWITCH
It's not that...
Man...
Didn't I tell you?

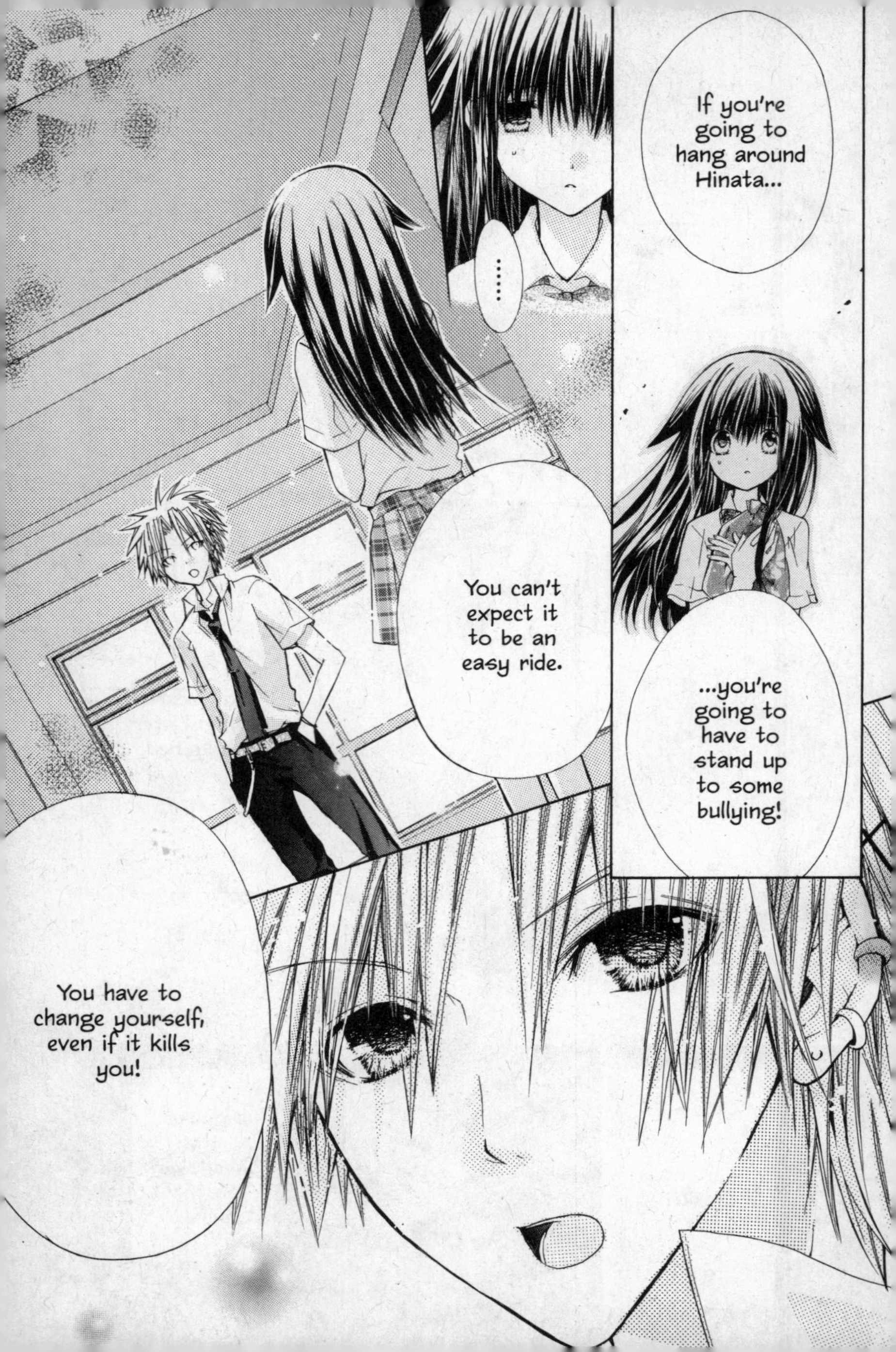
If you're going to hang around Hinata...
...you're going to have to stand up to some bullying!
.....
You can't expect it to be an easy ride.
You have to change yourself, even if it kills you!

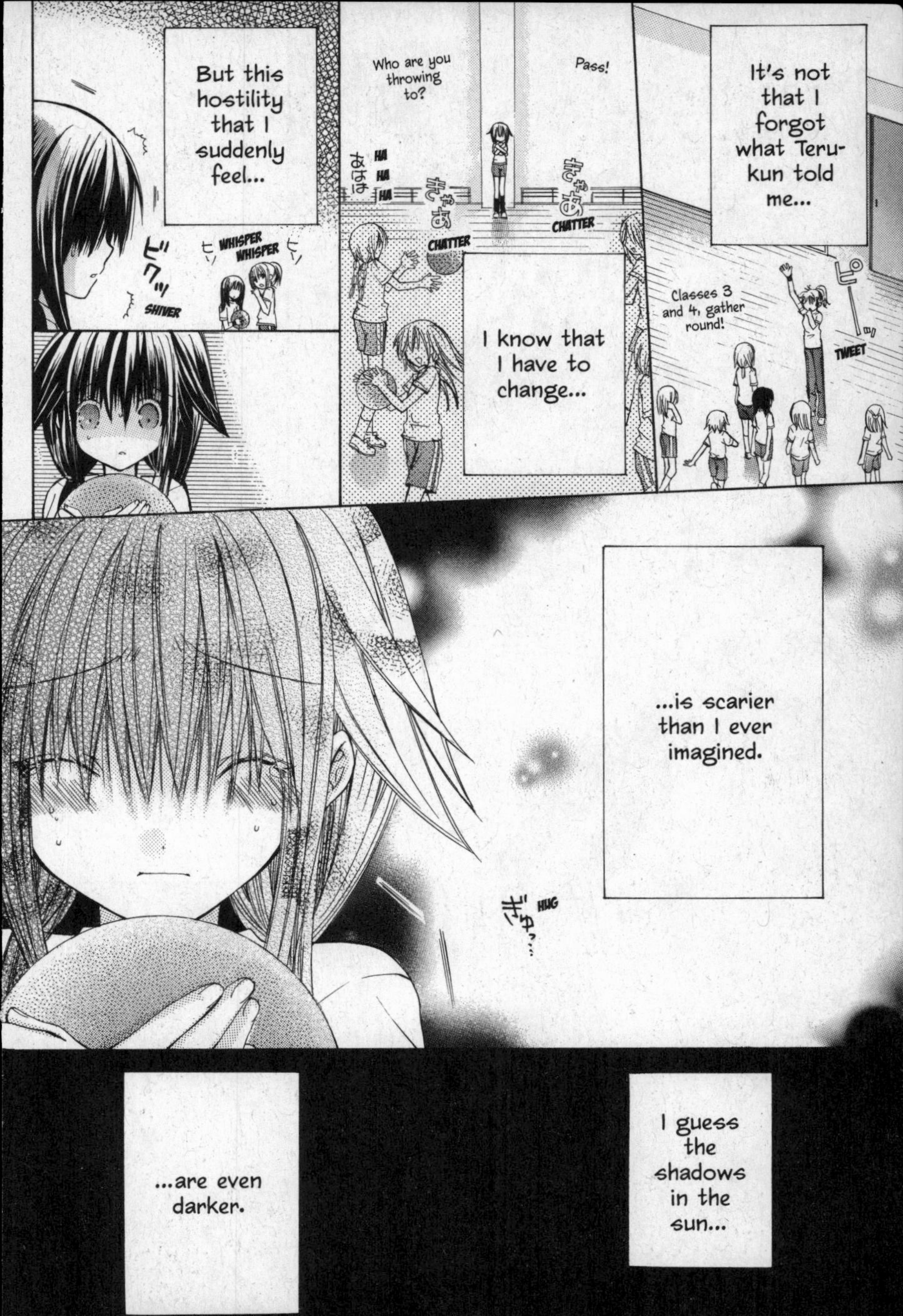

It's not that I forgot what Teru-kun told me...
TWEET
Classes 3 and 4, gather round!
Pass!
Who are you throwing to?
CHATTER
CHATTER
HA HA HA
I know that I have to change...
But this hostility that I suddenly feel...
WHISPER WHISPER
SHIVER
...is scarier than I ever imagined.
HUG
I guess the shadows in the sun...
...are even darker.

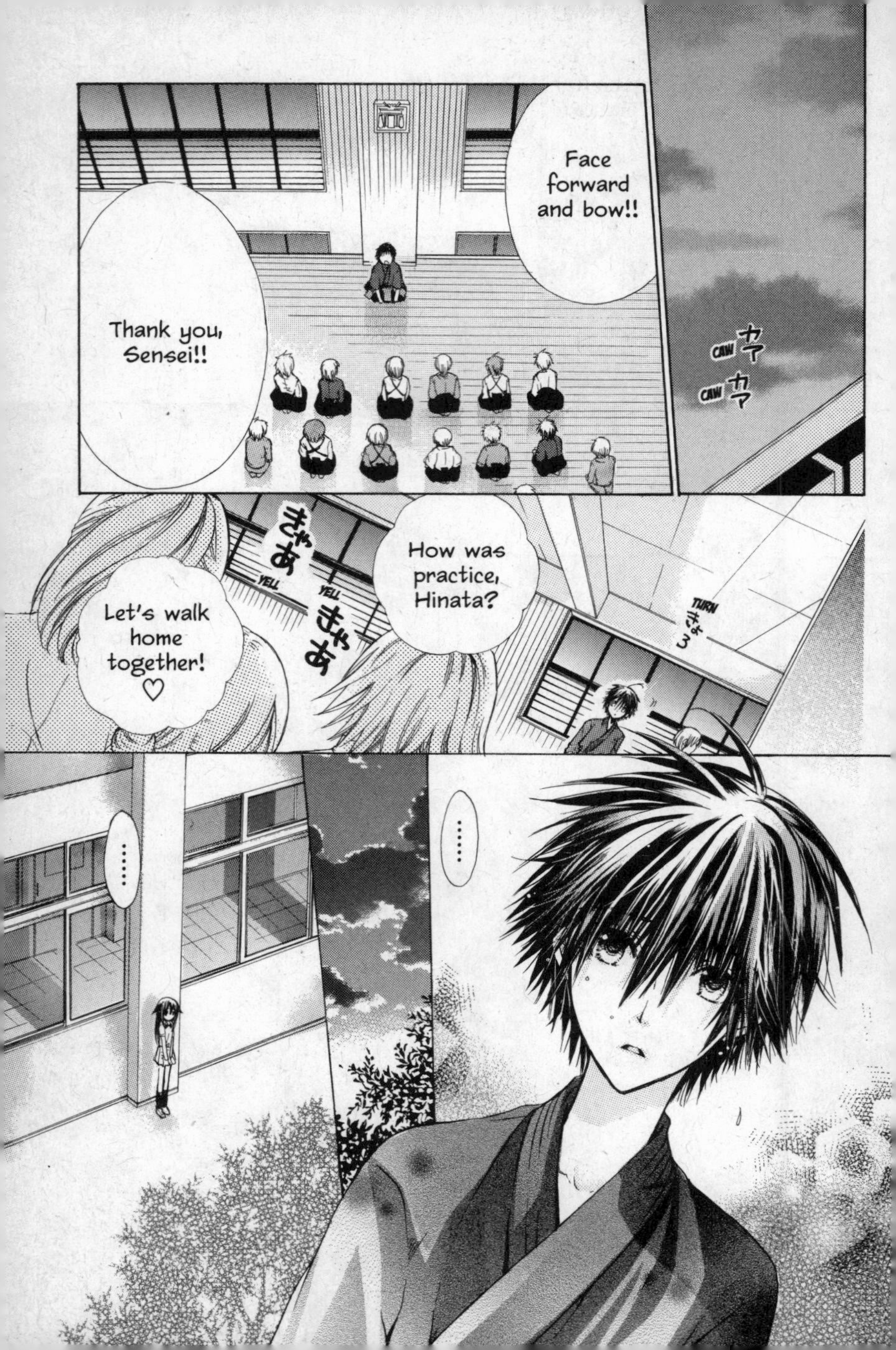

CAW カァ
CAW カァ
Face forward and bow!!
Thank you, Sensei!!
TURN きょろ
How was practice, Hinata?
きゃあ YELL
きゃあ YELL
Let's walk home together! ♡
......
......

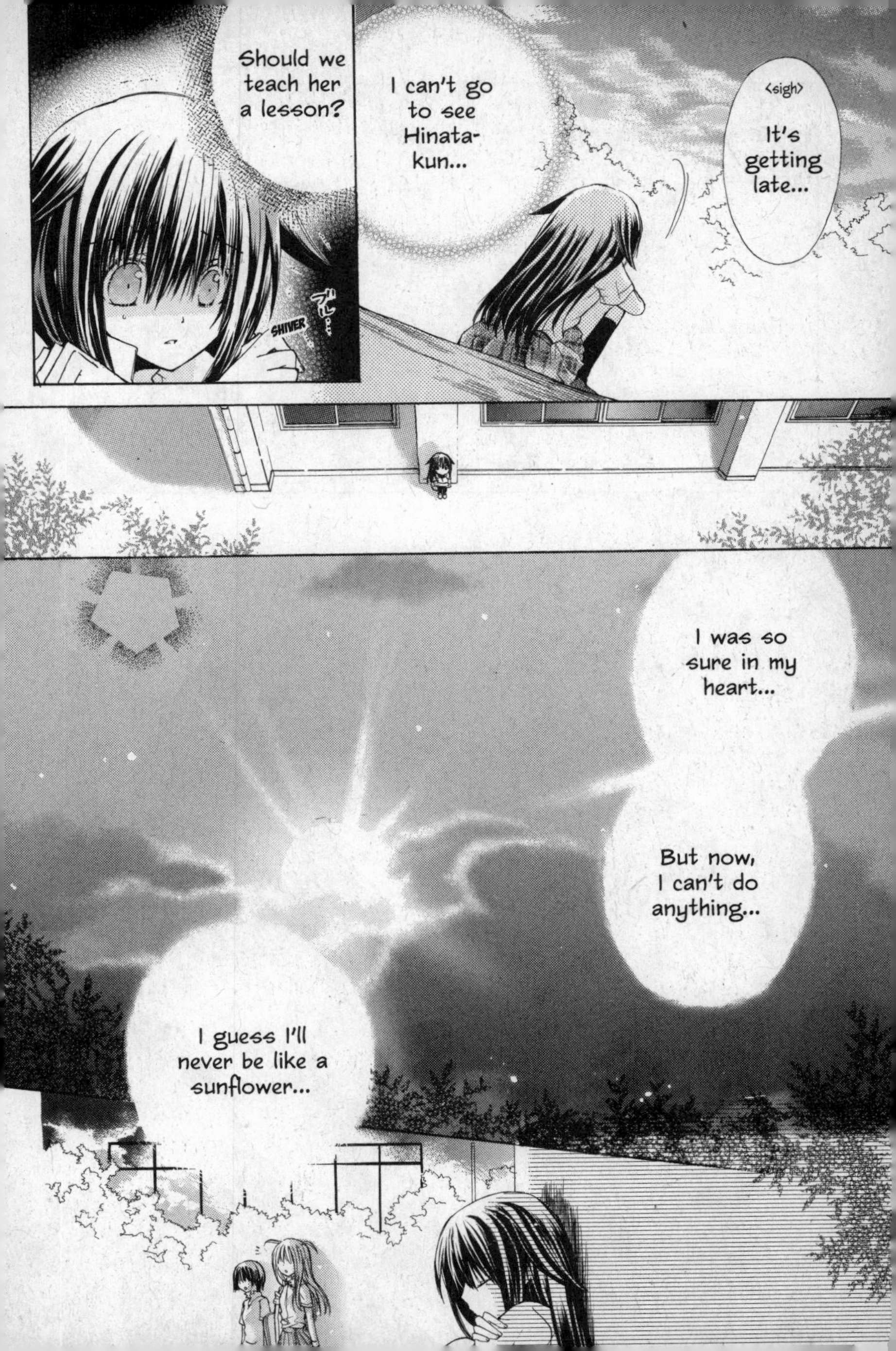
<sigh>
It's getting late...
I can't go to see Hinata-kun...
Should we teach her a lesson?
ブル…
SHIVER
I was so sure in my heart...
But now, I can't do anything...
I guess I'll never be like a sunflower...

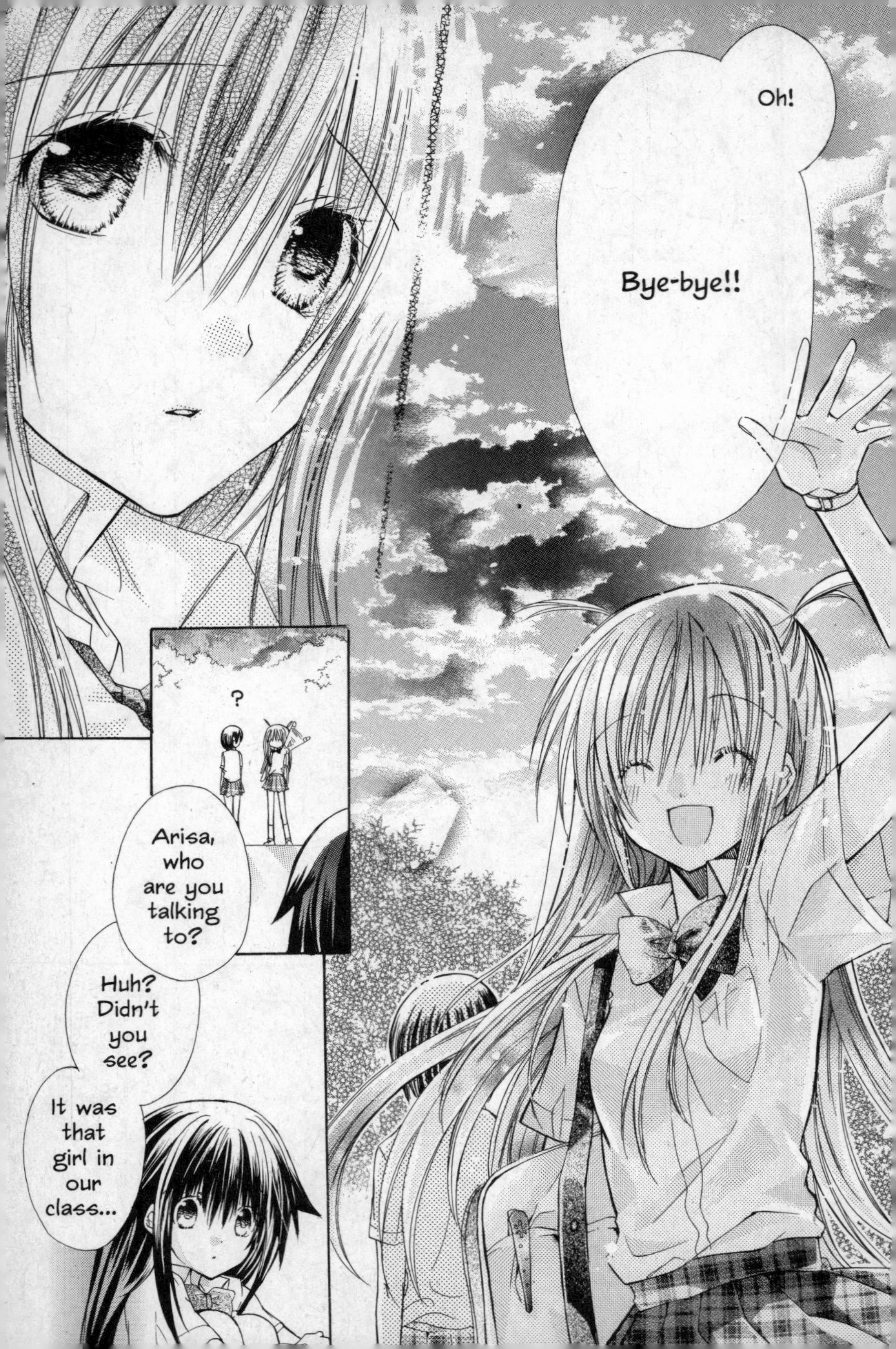
Oh!
Bye-bye!!
?
Arisa, who are you talking to?
Huh? Didn't you see?
It was that girl in our class...

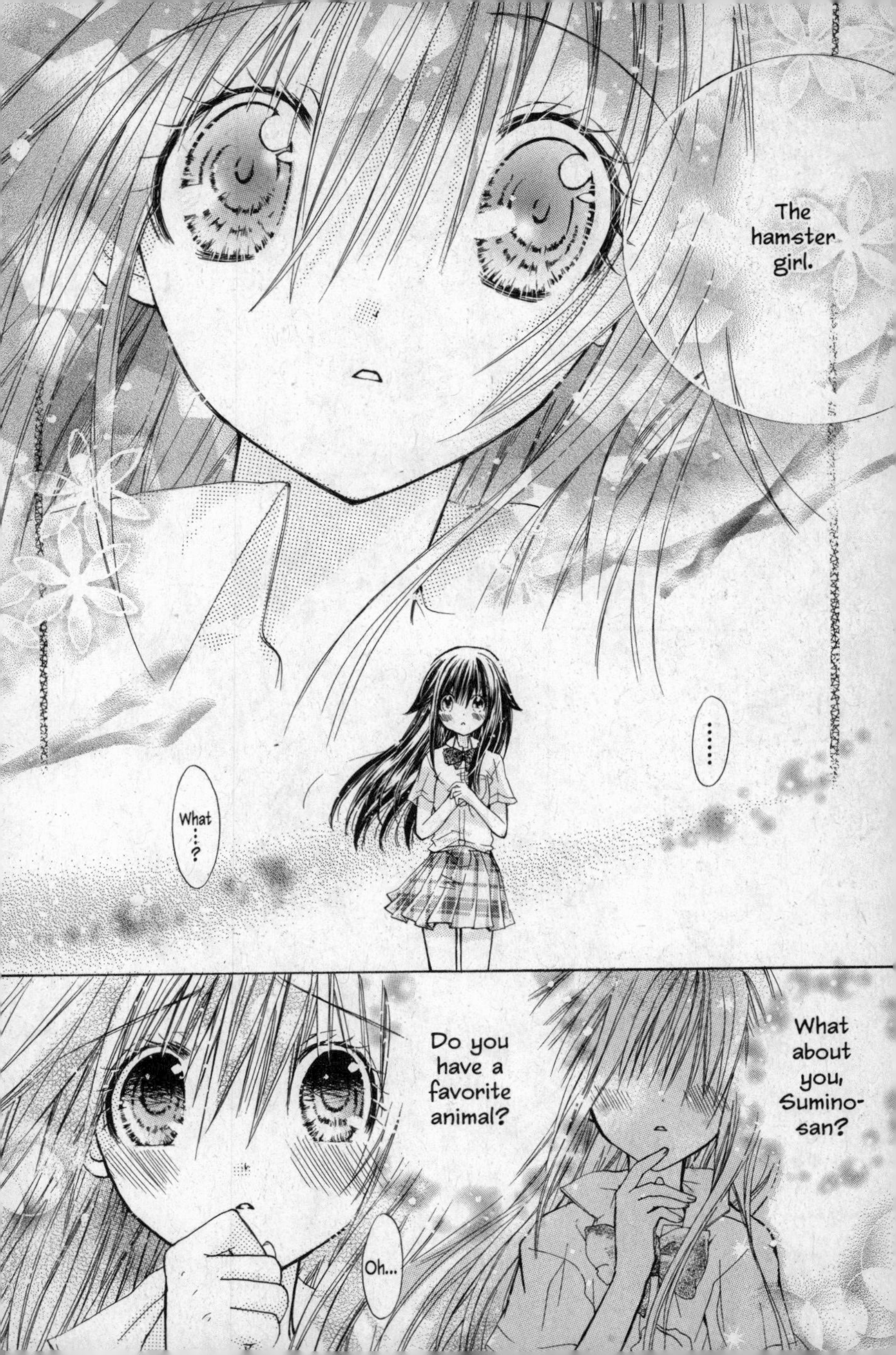
The hamster girl.
......
What...?
What about you, Sumino-san?
Do you have a favorite animal?
Oh...

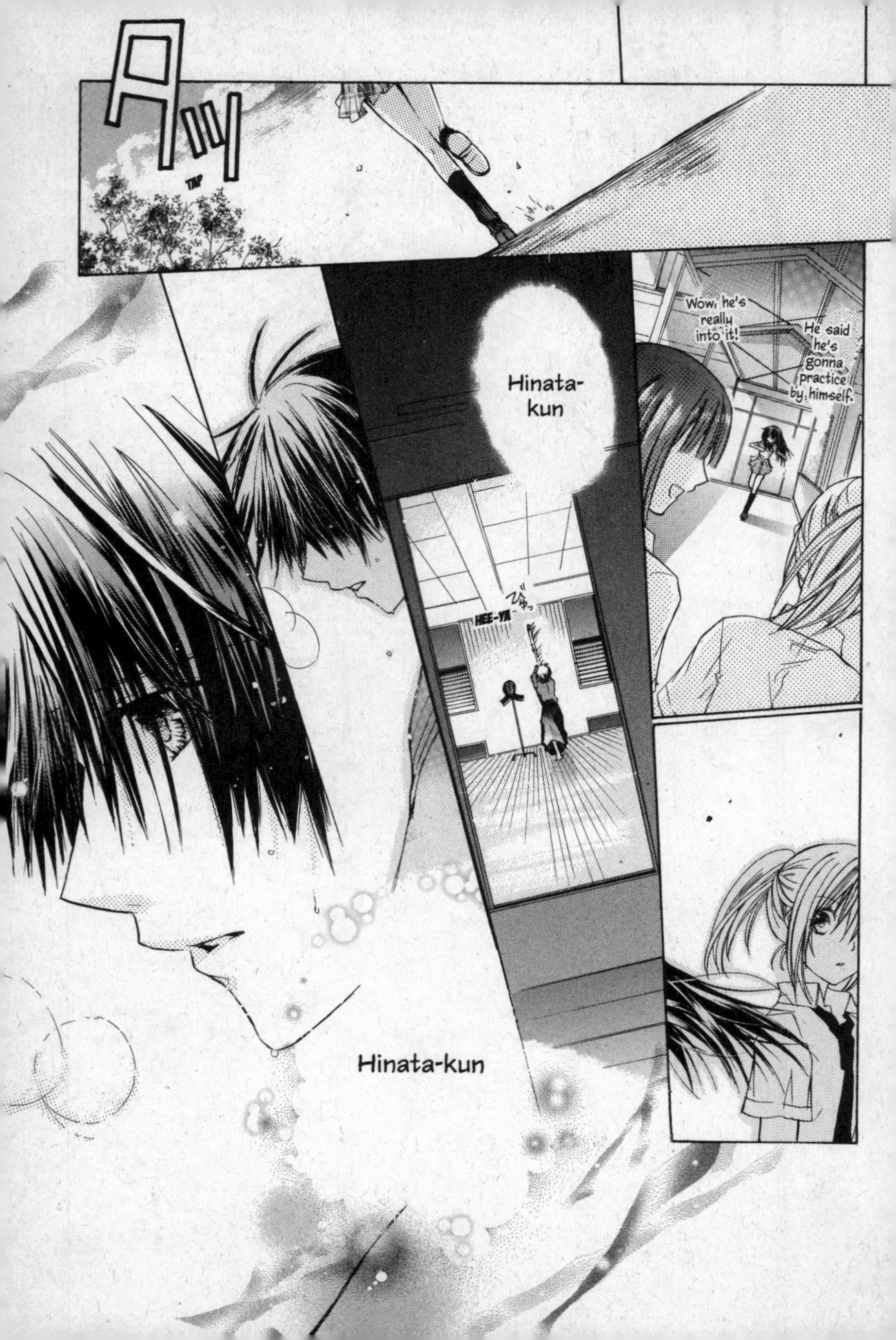
TAP
He said he's gonna practice by himself.
Wow, he's really into it!
Hinata-kun
HEE-YA
Hinata-kun

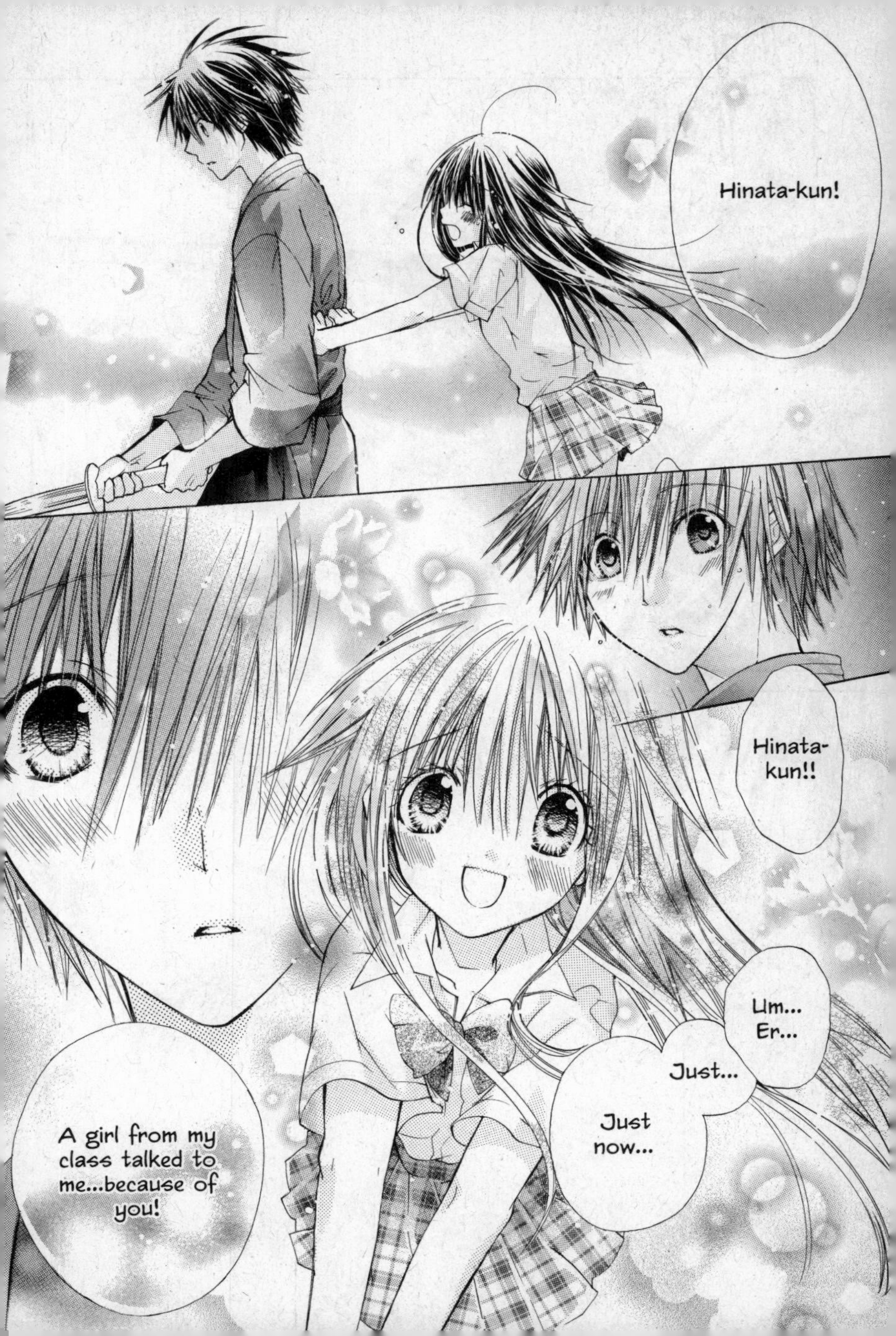
Hinata-kun!
Hinata-kun!!
Um... Er...
Just...
Just now...
A girl from my class talked to me...because of you!

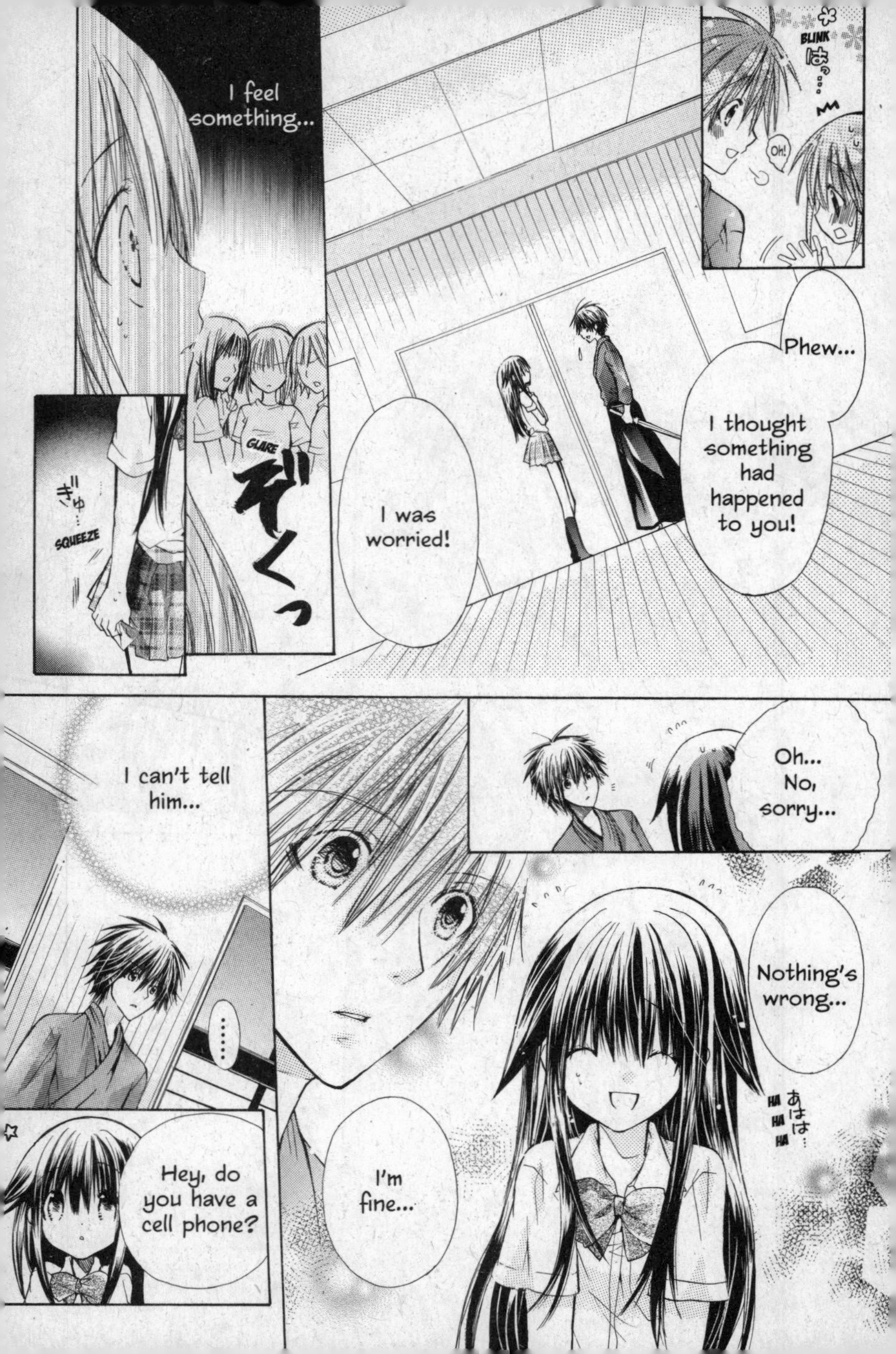
BLINK
はっ...
Oh!
Phew...
I thought something had happened to you!
I was worried!
I feel something...
GLARE
ぞくっ
ぎゅ...
SQUEEZE
Oh... No, sorry...
Nothing's wrong...
HA HA HA
あはは...
I'm fine...
I can't tell him...
......
Hey, do you have a cell phone?

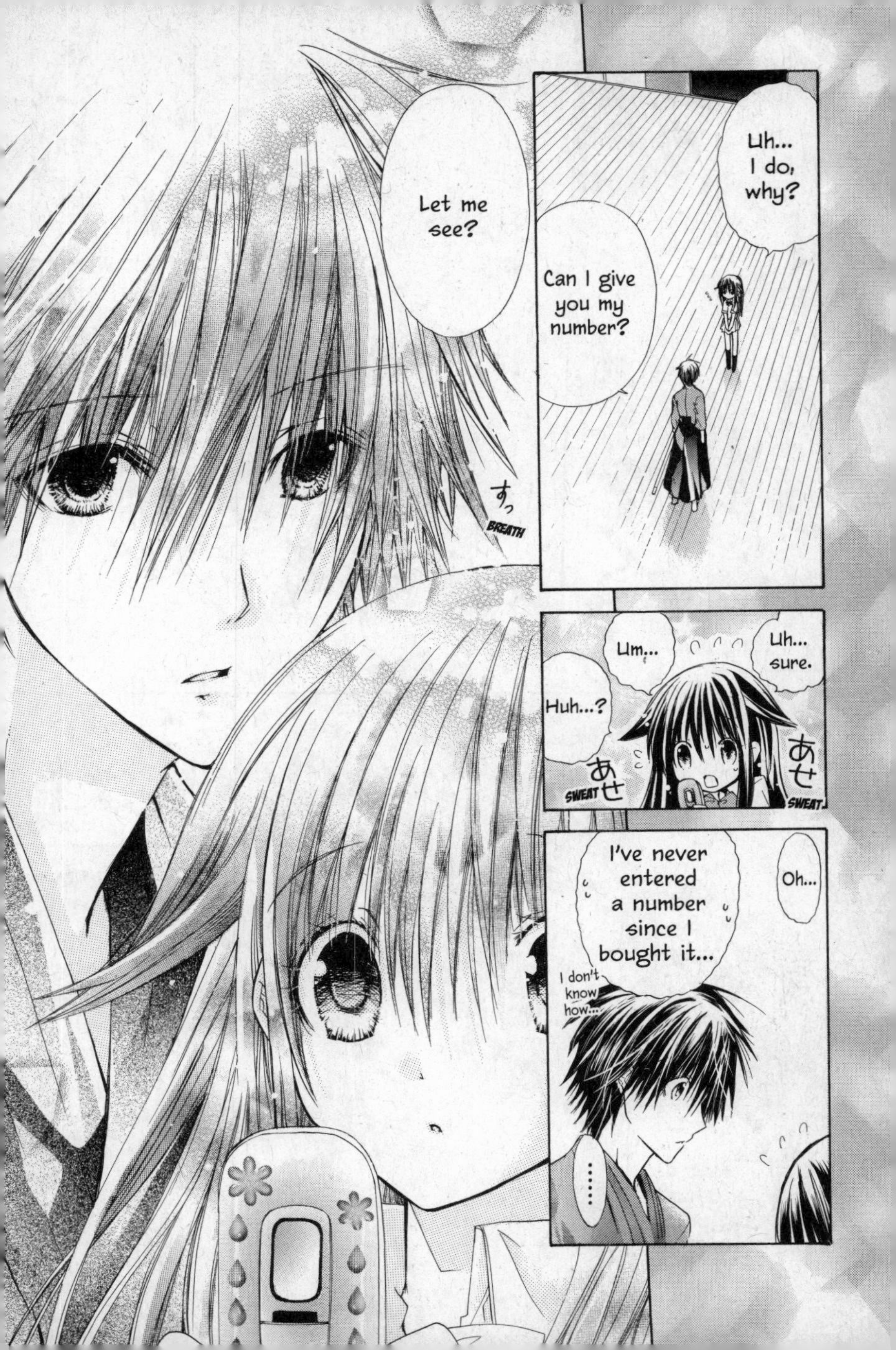
Uh... I do, why?
Can I give you my number?
Uh... sure.
Um...
Huh...?
あせ SWEAT
あせ SWEAT
Oh...
I've never entered a number since I bought it...
I don't know how...
......
Let me see?
すっ BREATH

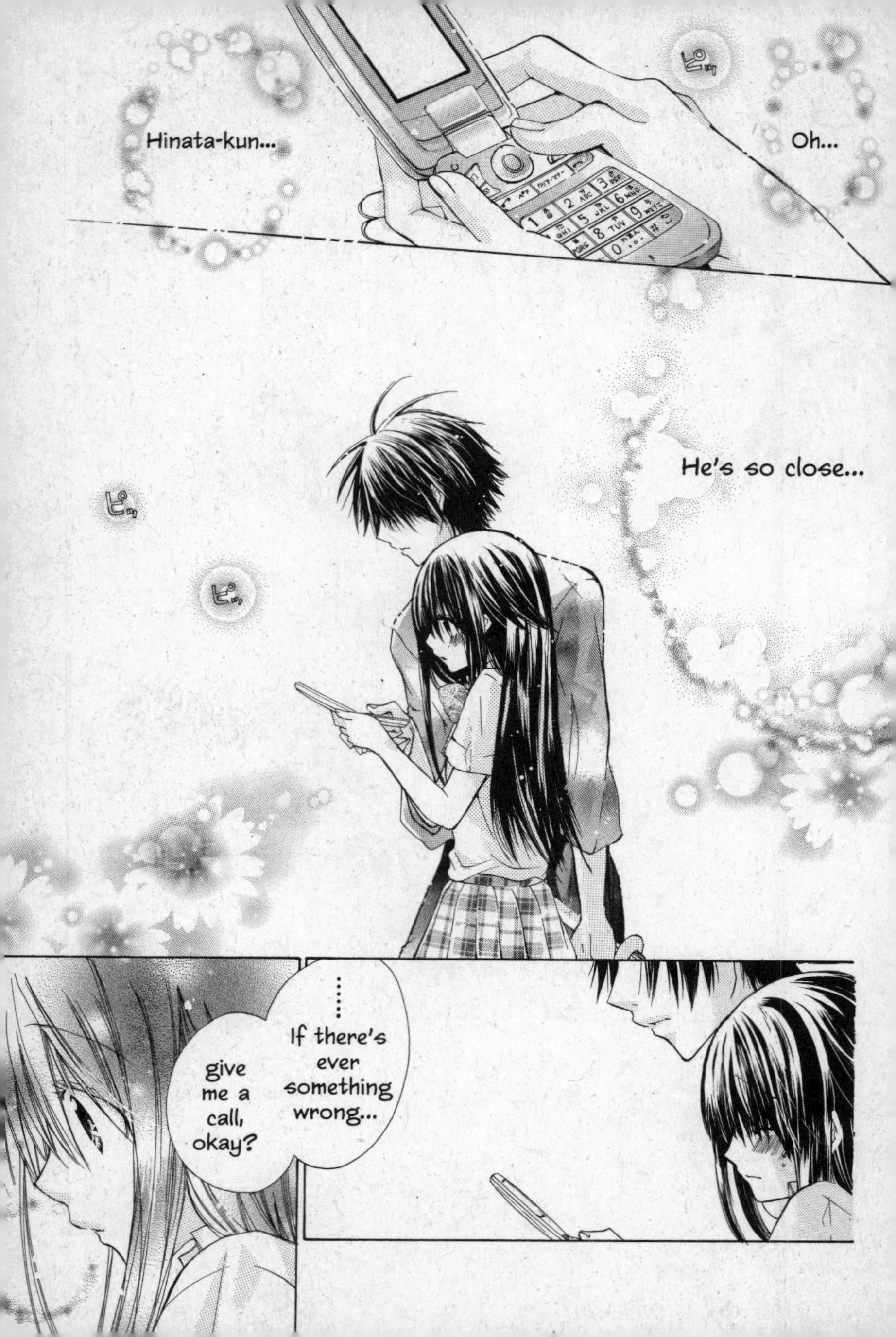
Oh...
Hinata-kun...
ピッ
He's so close...
ピッ
ピッ
......
If there's ever something wrong...
give me a call, okay?

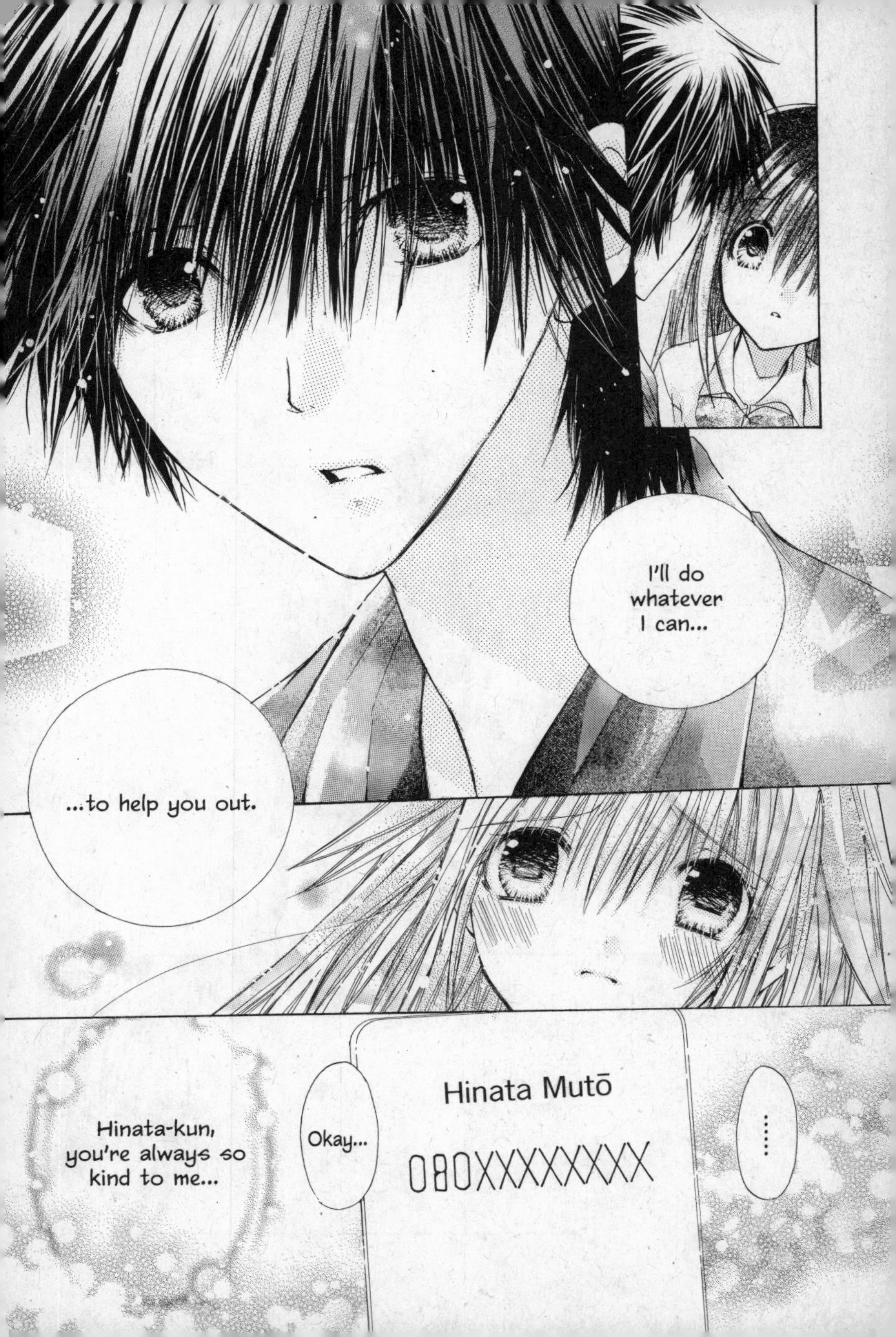
I'll do whatever I can...
...to help you out.
......
Hinata Mutō
080XXXXXXXX
Okay...
Hinata-kun, you're always so kind to me...

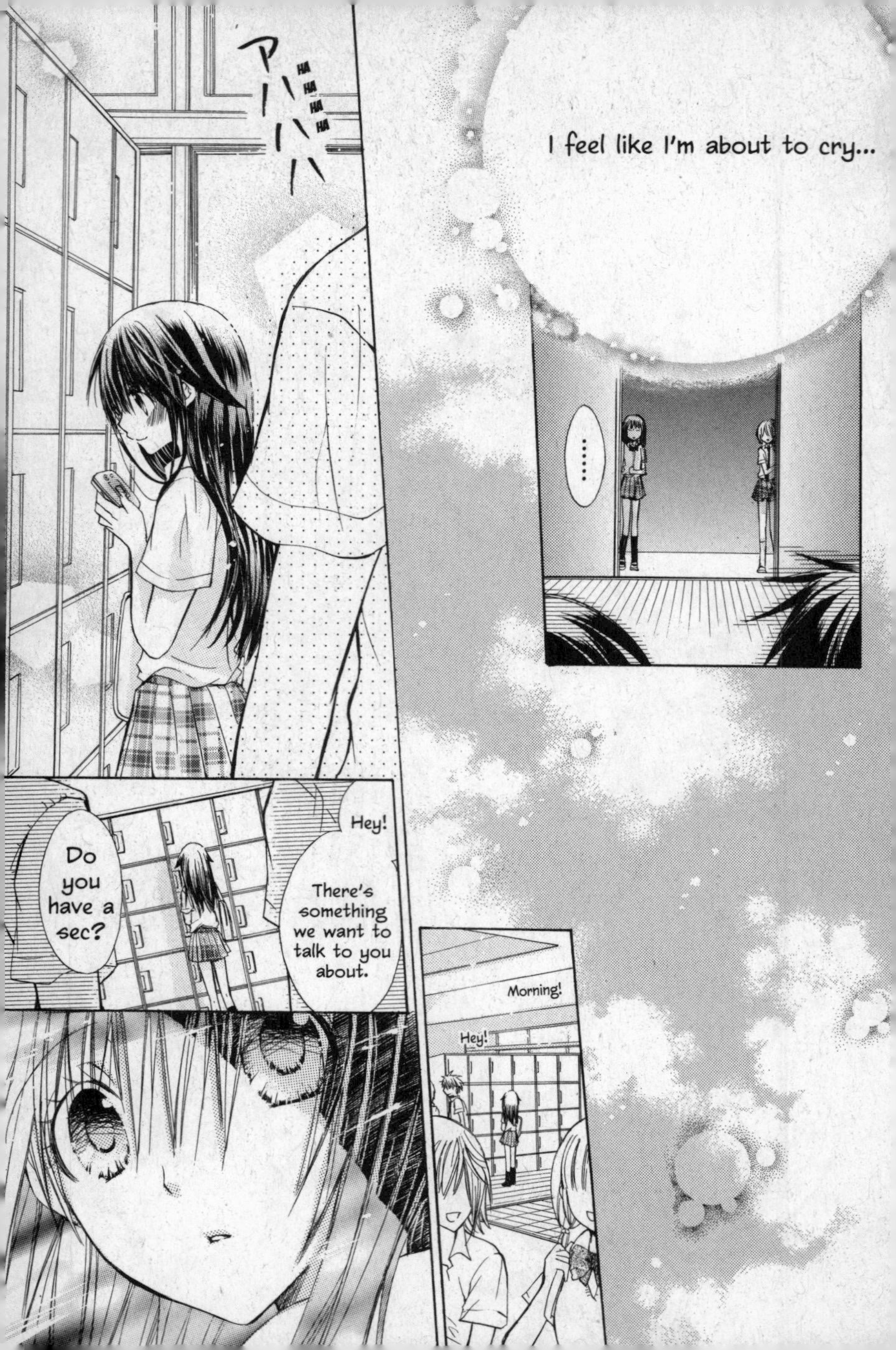
I feel like I'm about to cry...
......
アハハハ
HA HA HA HA
Hey!
There's something we want to talk to you about.
Do you have a sec?
Morning!
Hey!

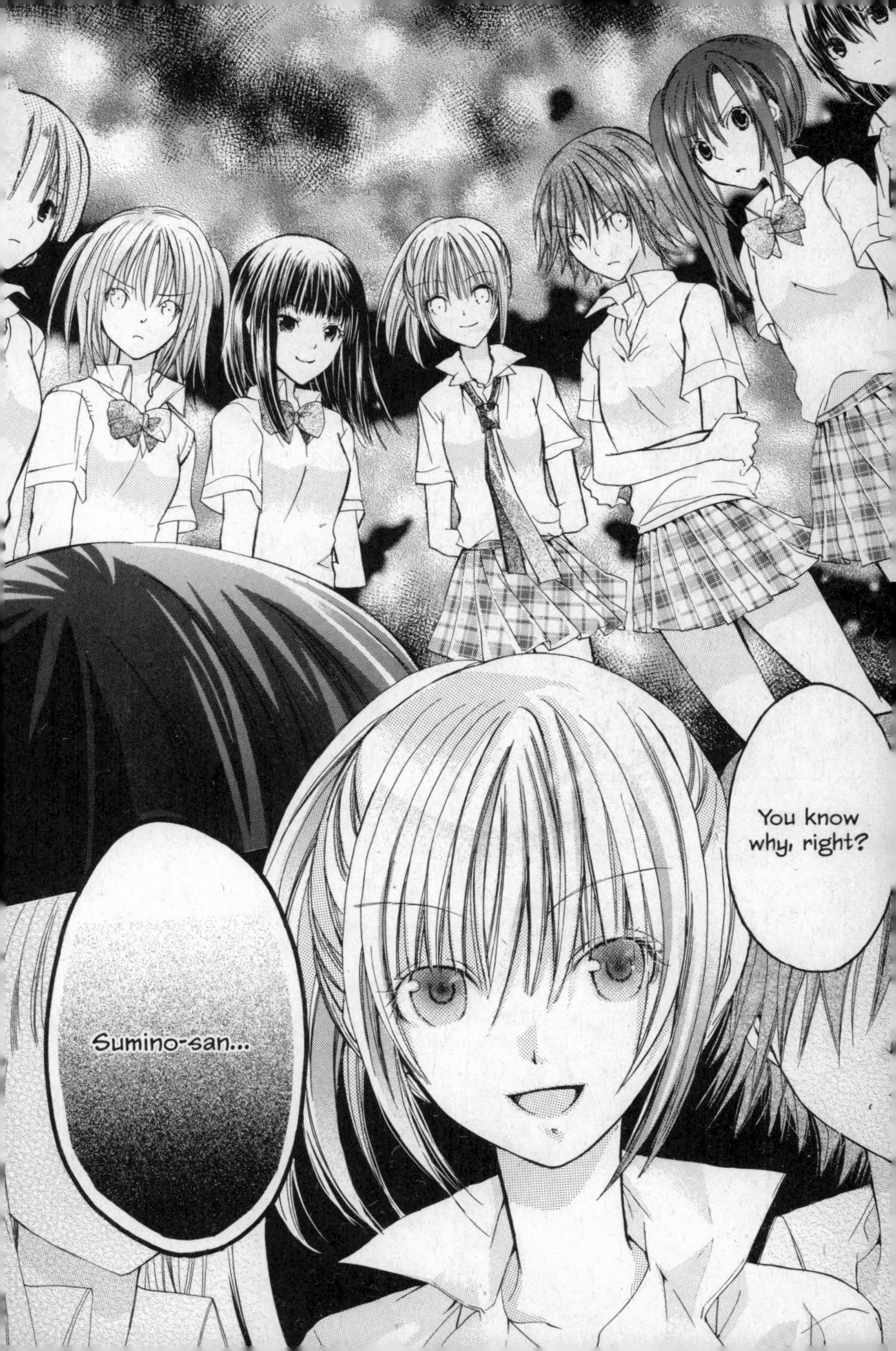
You know why, right?
Sumino-san...

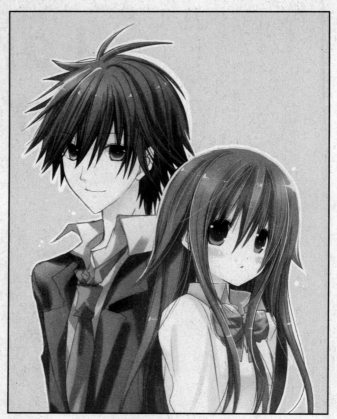

Ema Tōyama

I think my Hikage-quotient is pretty high. A boy who was in my class for two years asked me "what's your name again?" on our graduation day.

That sucks. It's hard to know how to respond.

I dedicate this comic to all the people who've had experiences like that, and all the people who sometimes feel lonely.

PROFILE
Born May 23
Gemini
Blood Type B

I am Here!

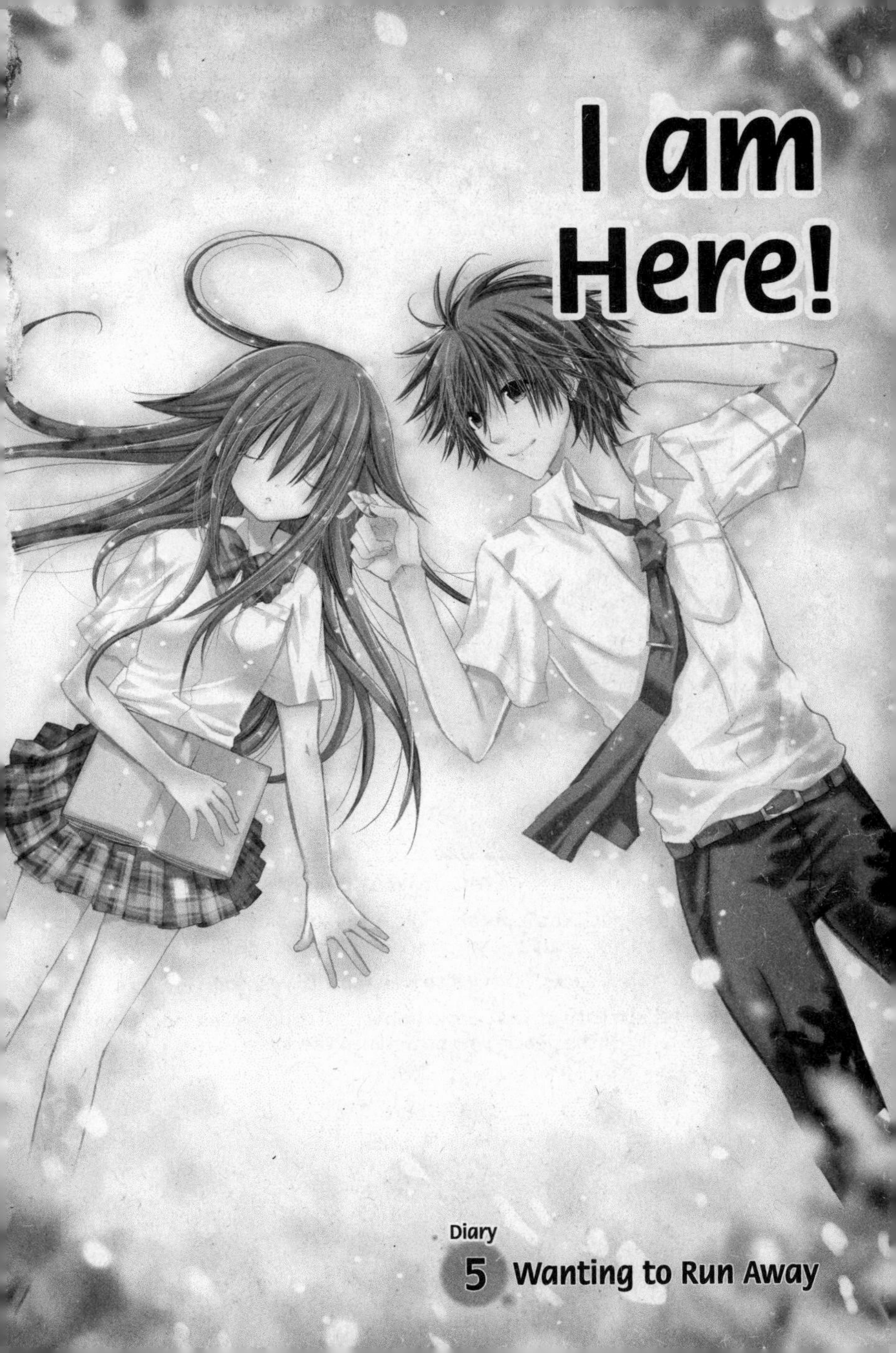

Diary 5 Wanting to Run Away

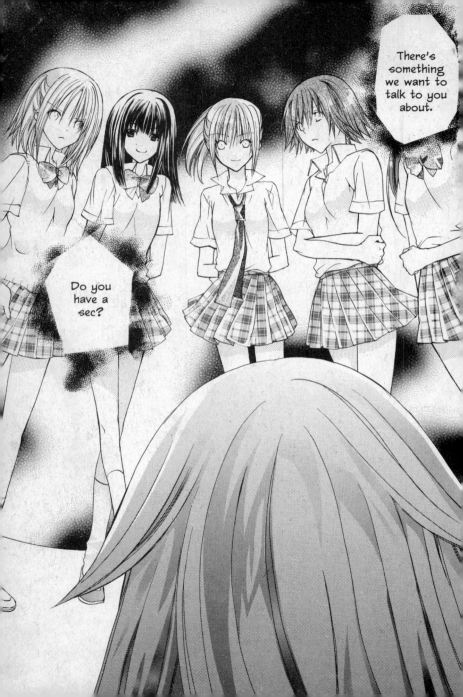

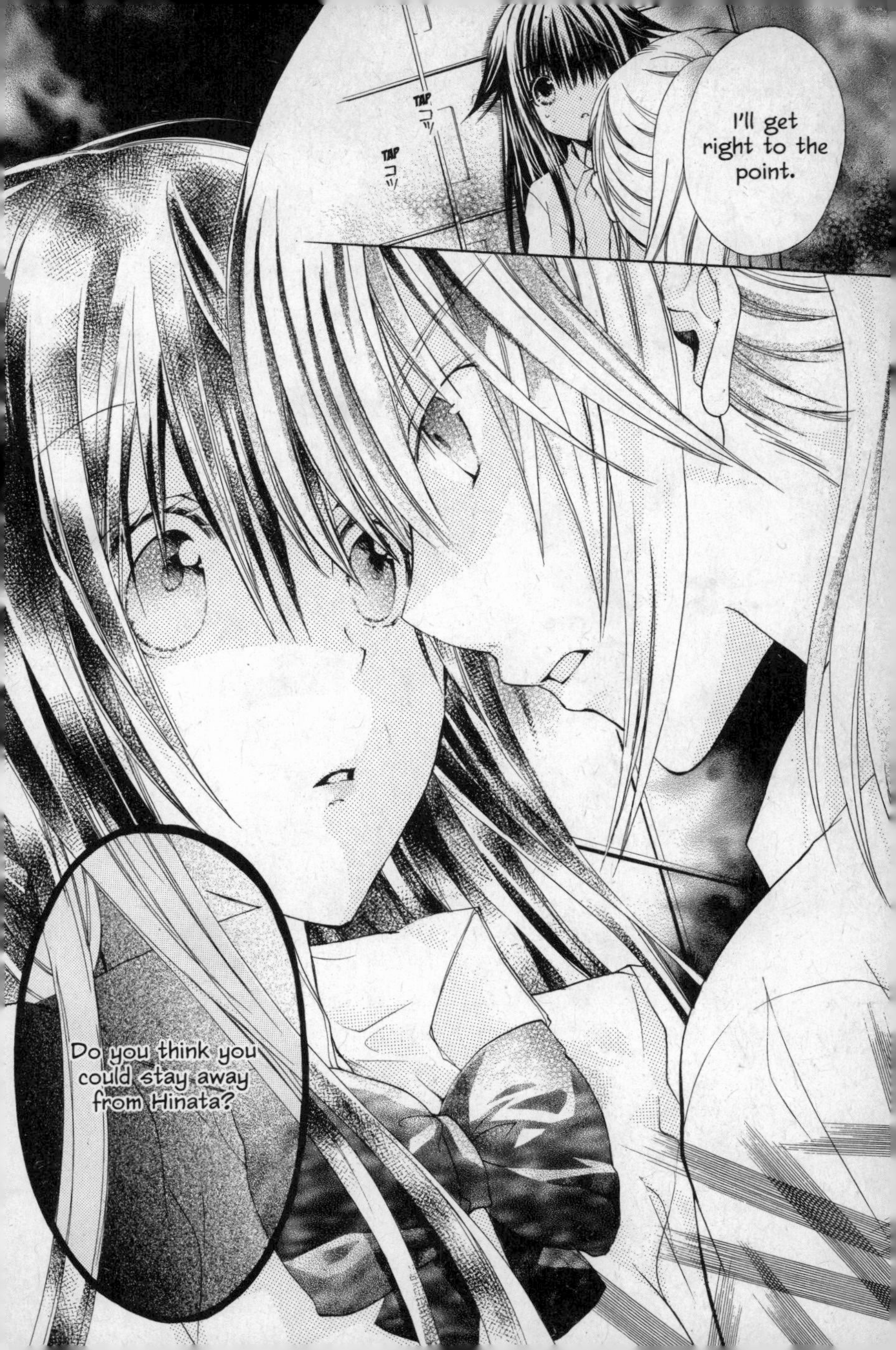
I'll get right to the point.
TAP コツ
TAP コツ
Do you think you could stay away from Hinata?

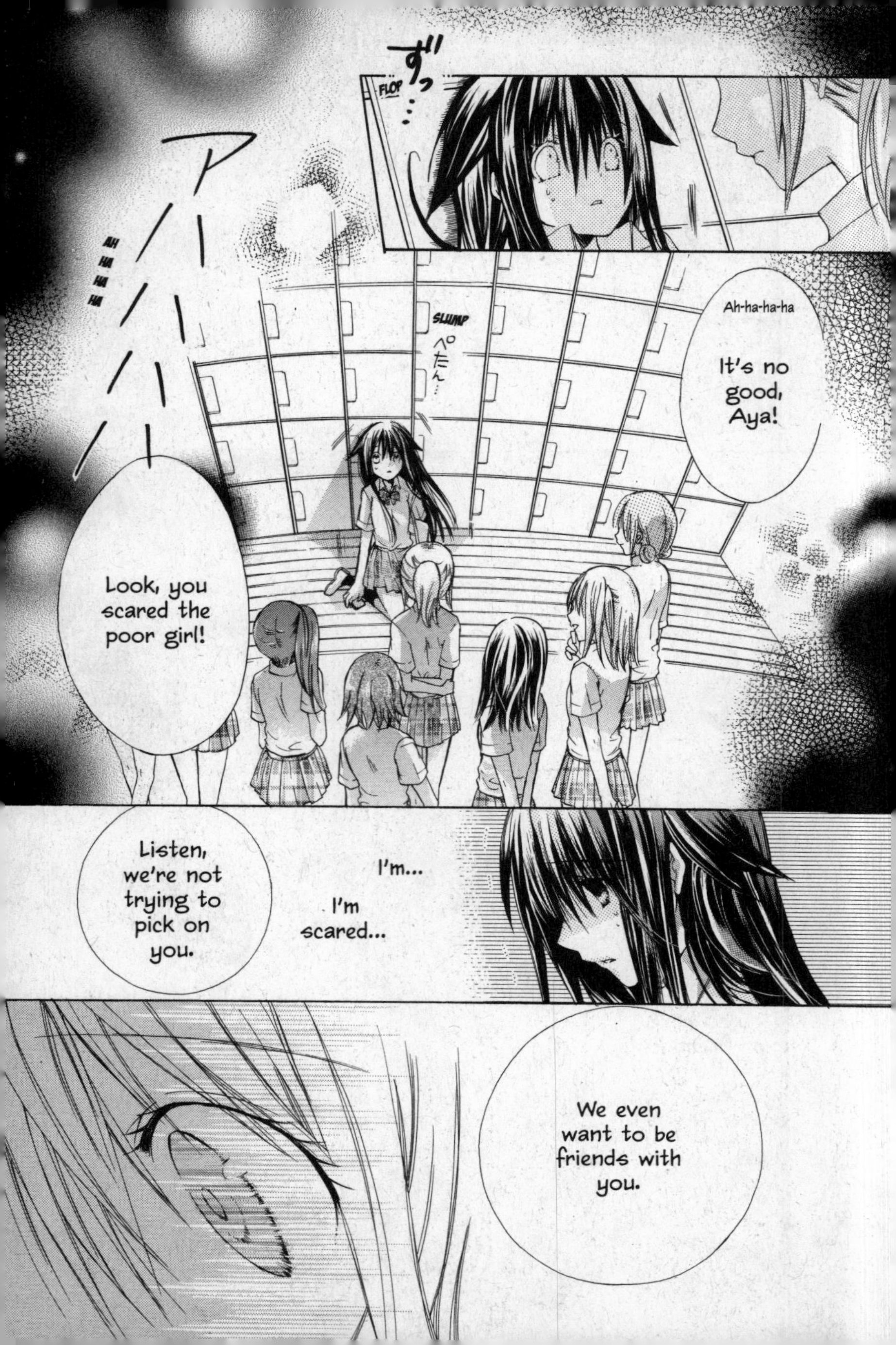
FLOP
ずっ…
Ah-ha-ha-ha
It's no good, Aya!
SLUMP
ぺたん…
アーハハハ
AH HA HA HA
Look, you scared the poor girl!
I'm...
I'm scared...
Listen, we're not trying to pick on you.
We even want to be friends with you.

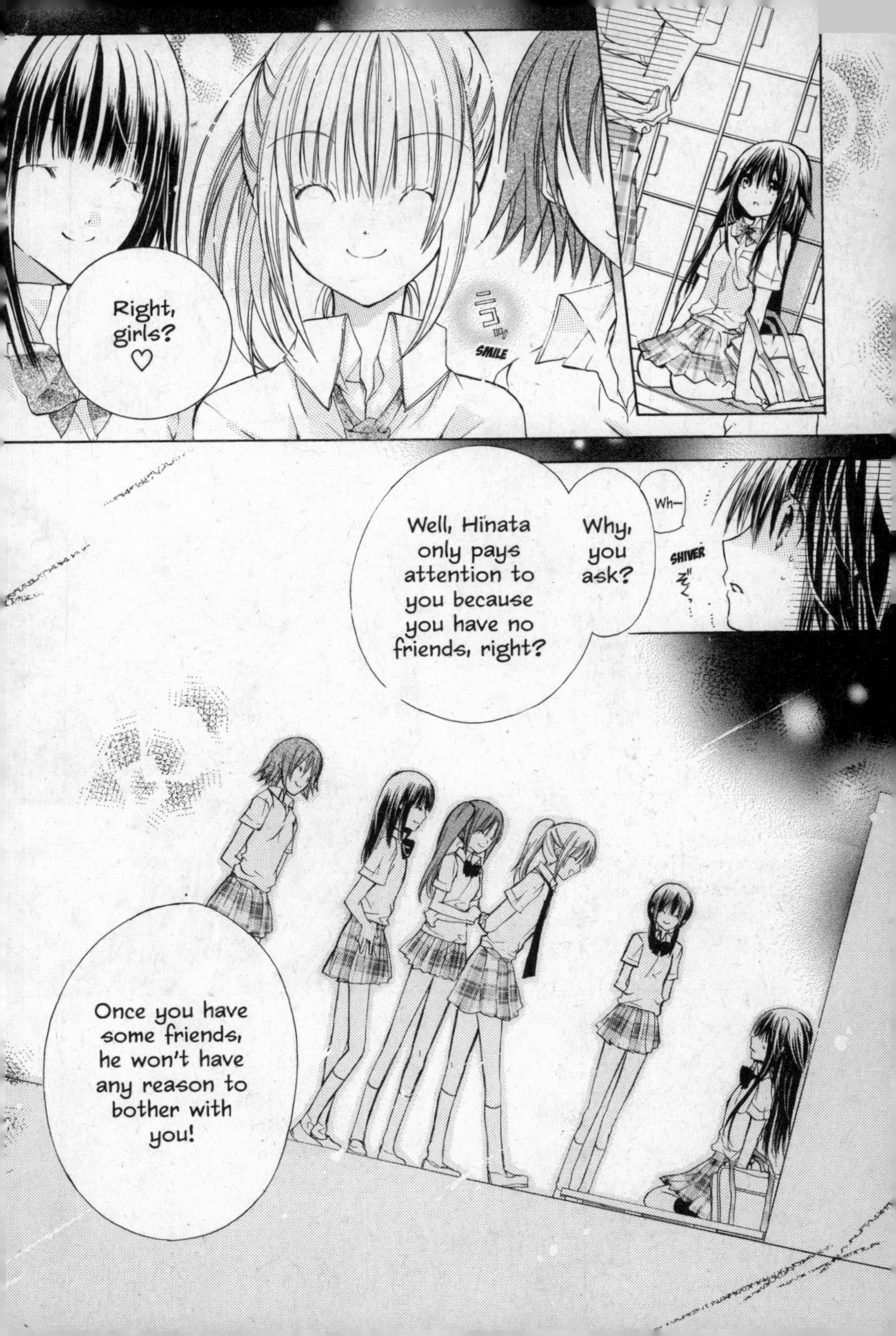
ニコッ
SMILE
Right, girls? ♡
Wh—
ぞく
SHIVER
Why, you ask?
Well, Hinata only pays attention to you because you have no friends, right?
Once you have some friends, he won't have any reason to bother with you!

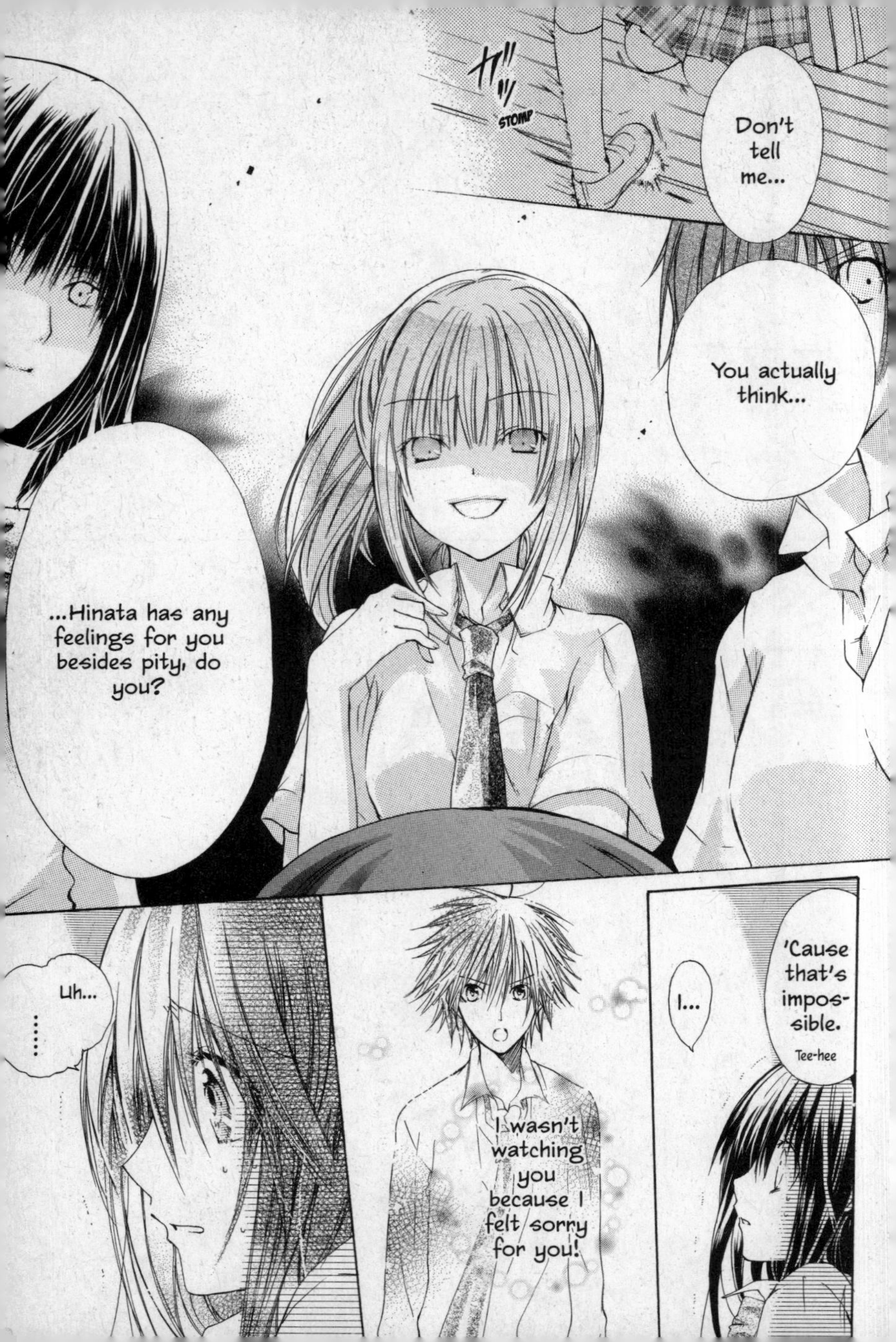
STOMP
Don't tell me...
You actually think...
...Hinata has any feelings for you besides pity, do you?
'Cause that's impos-sible.
Tee-hee
I...
I wasn't watching you because I felt sorry for you!
Uh...
......

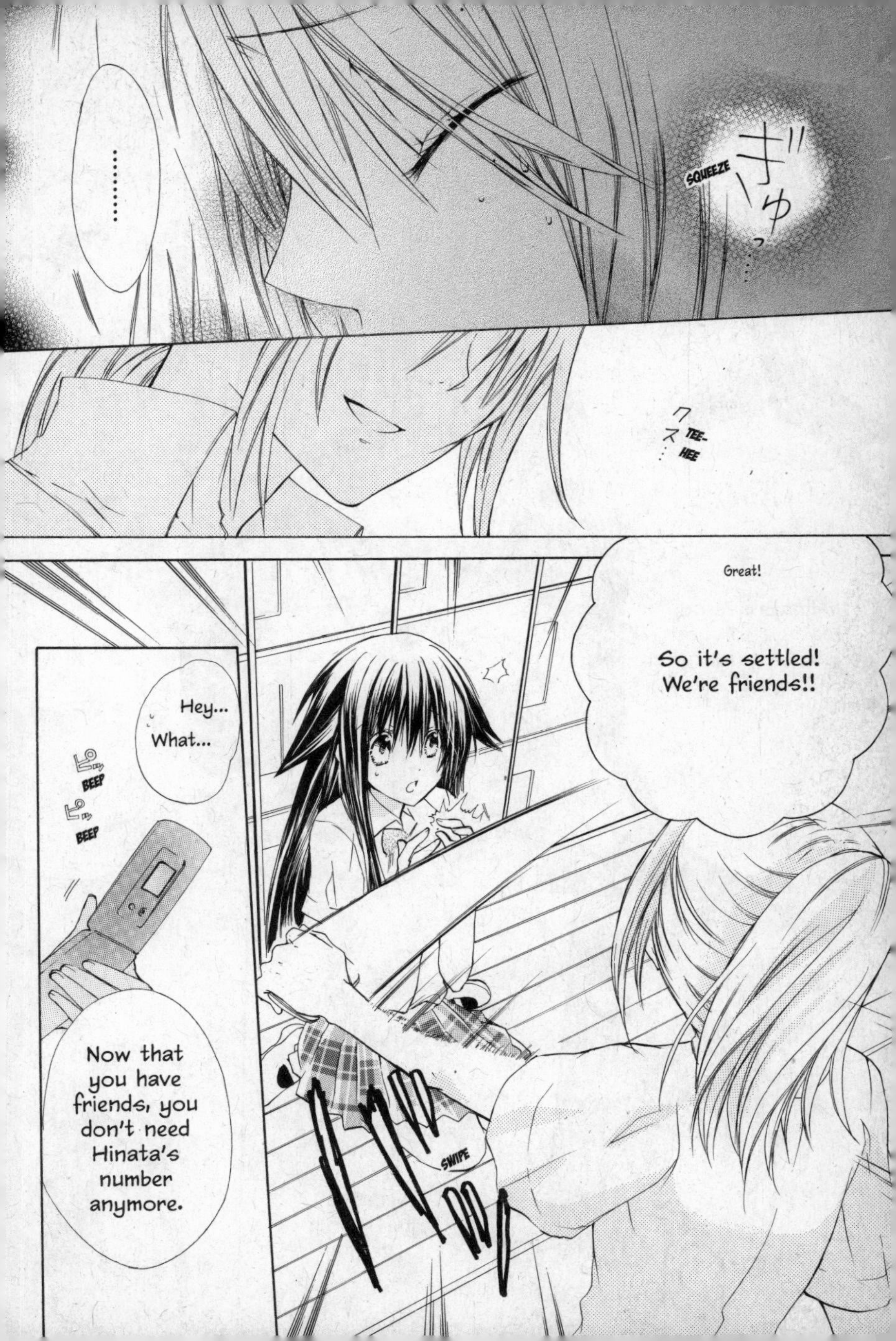
......
ぎゅっ
SQUEEZE
クス...
TEE-HEE
Great!
So it's settled! We're friends!!
Hey... What...
ピッ
BEEP
ピッ
BEEP
Now that you have friends, you don't need Hinata's number anymore.
SWIPE

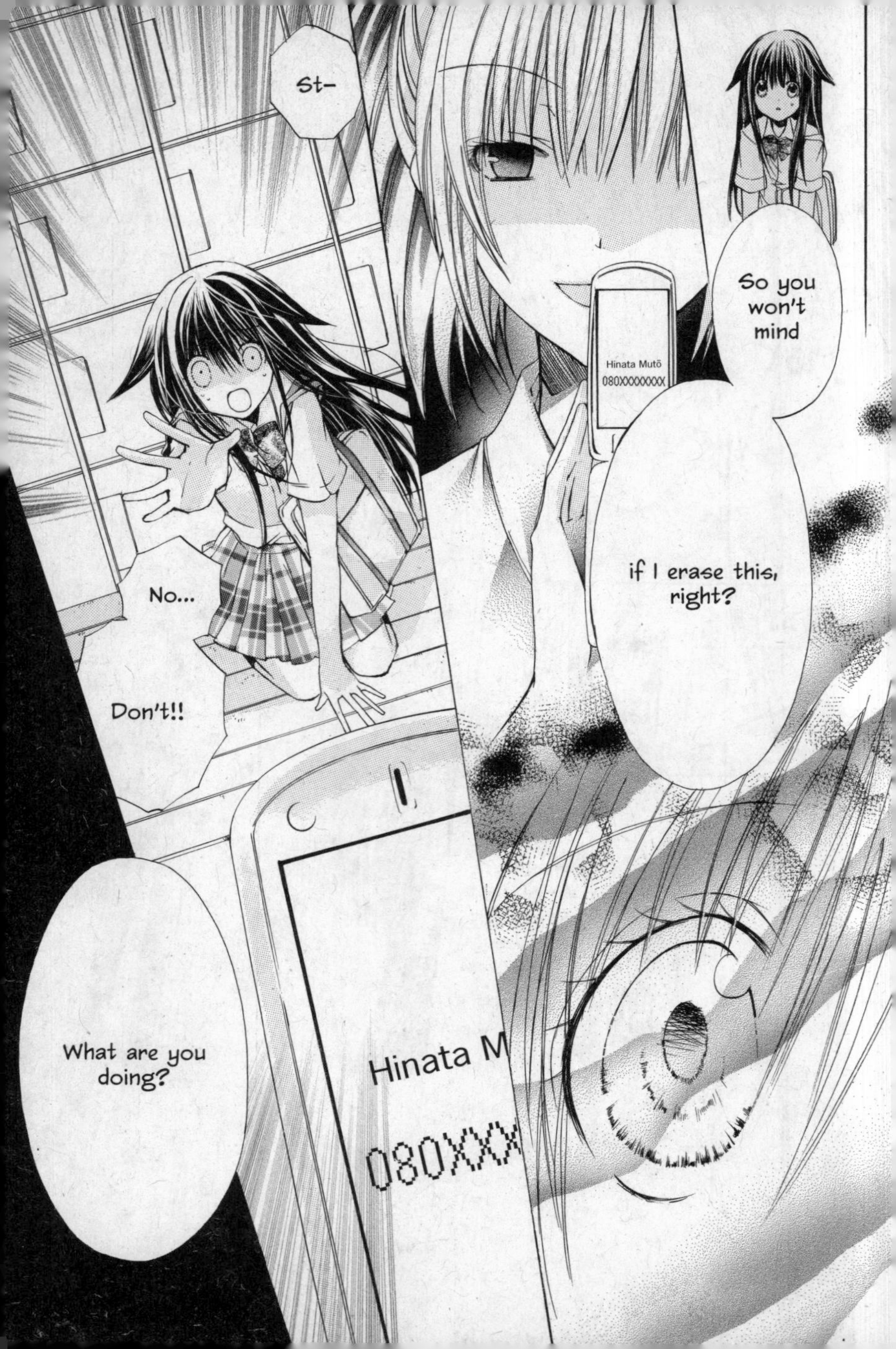
So you won't mind
if I erase this, right?
Hinata Mutō
080XXXXXXXX
St-
No...
Don't!!
Hinata M
080XXX
What are you doing?

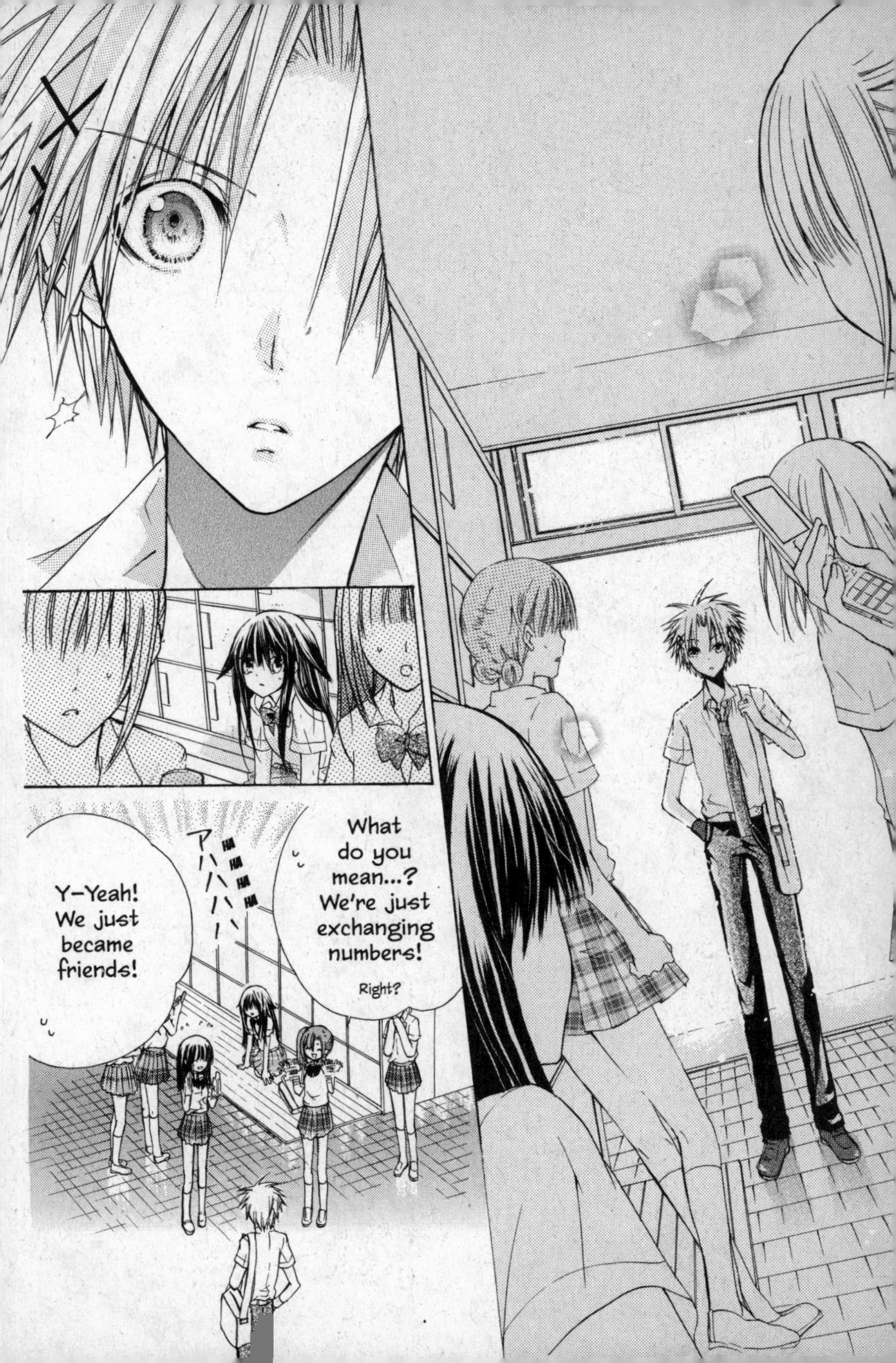

What do you mean...? We're just exchanging numbers!
Right?
HA HA HA HA
Y-Yeah! We just became friends!

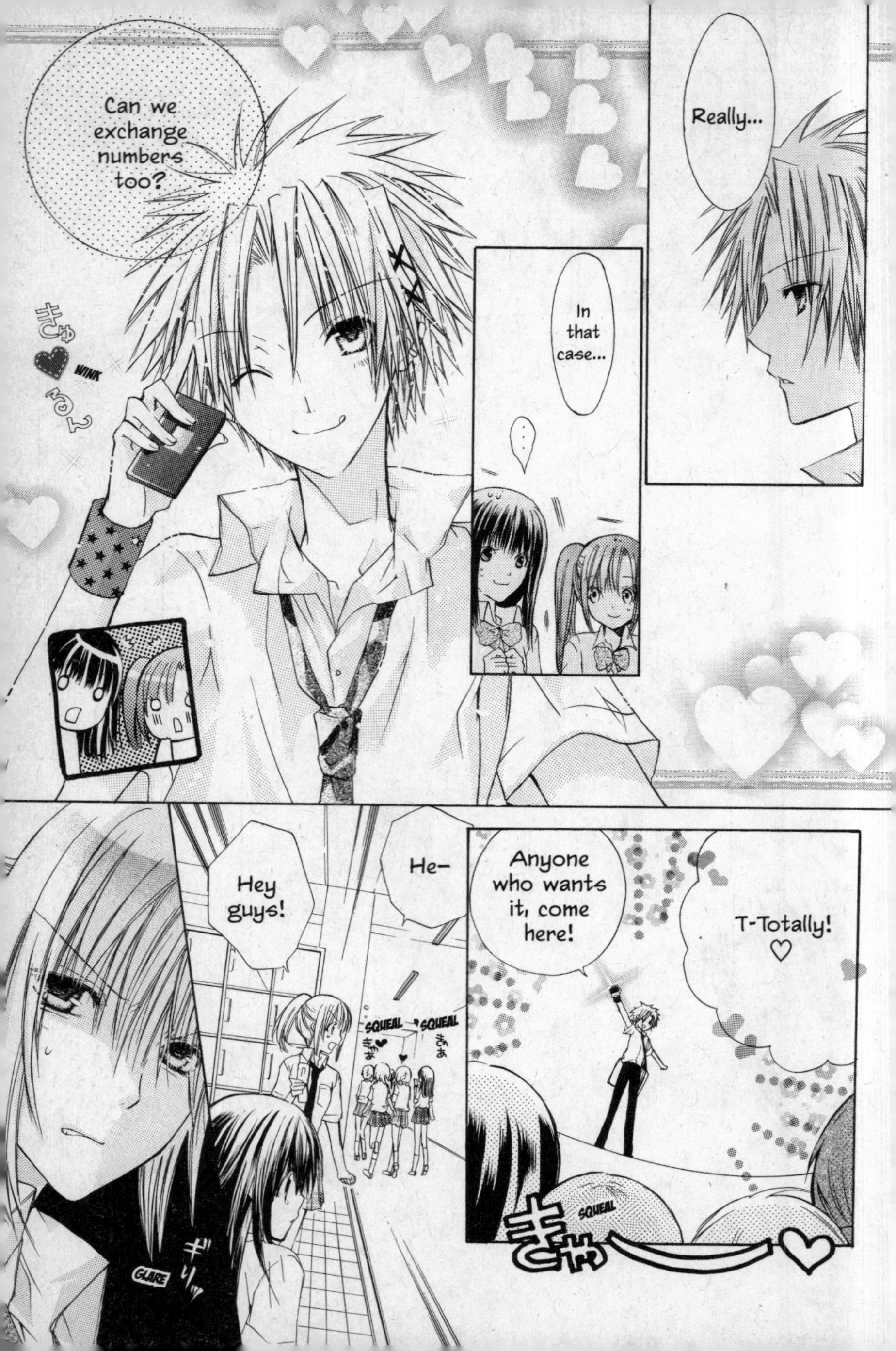
Really...
In that case...
...
Can we exchange numbers too?
きゅるん
WINK
Anyone who wants it, come here!
T-Totally! ♡
SQUEAL
きゃー♡
He-
Hey guys!
SQUEAL
きゃ♥
SQUEAL
きゃあ
GLARE
ギリッ

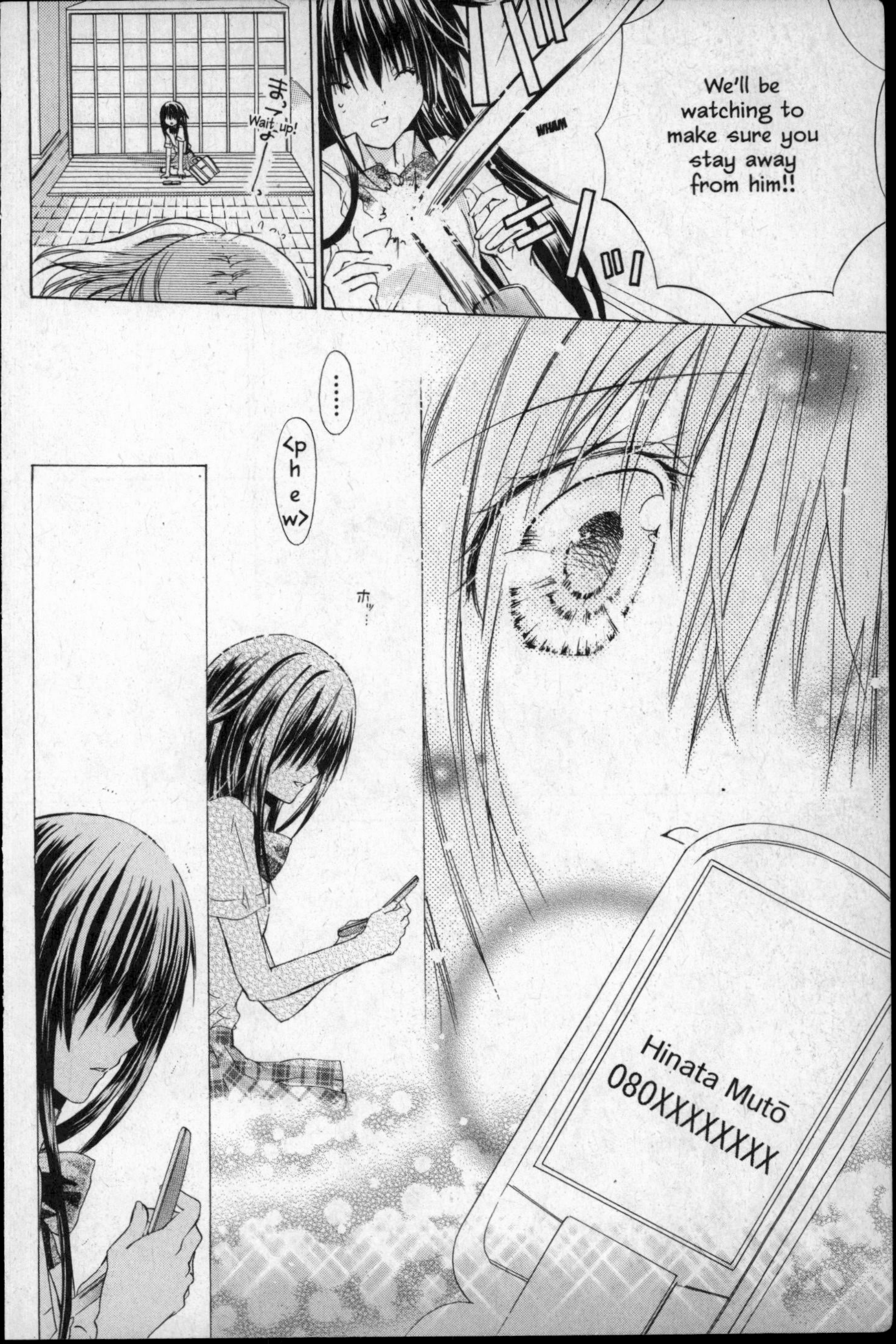
We'll be watching to make sure you stay away from him!!
WHAM
Wait up!
......
<phew>
Hinata Mutō
080XXXXXXXX

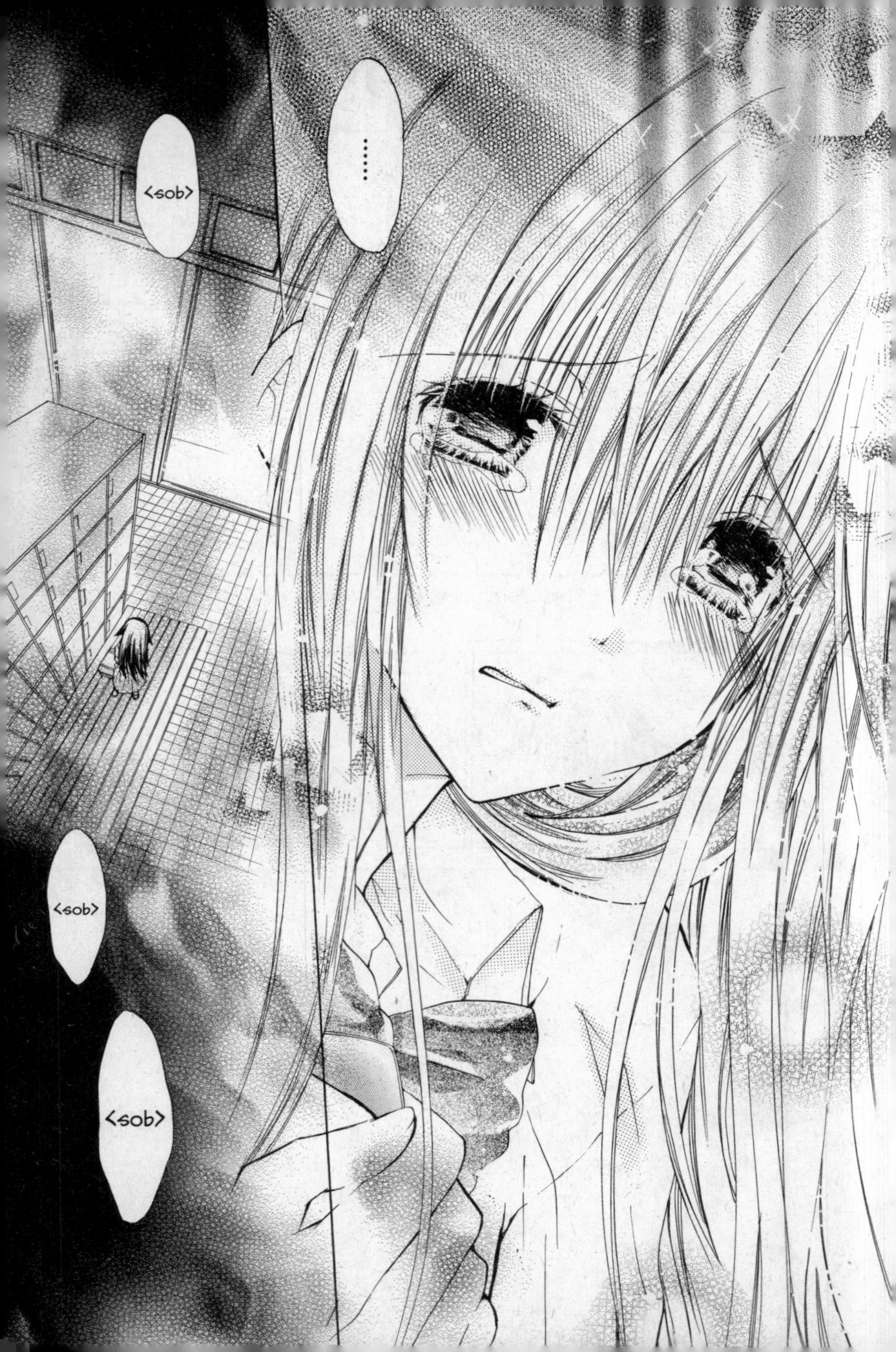
......
<sob>
<sob>
<sob>

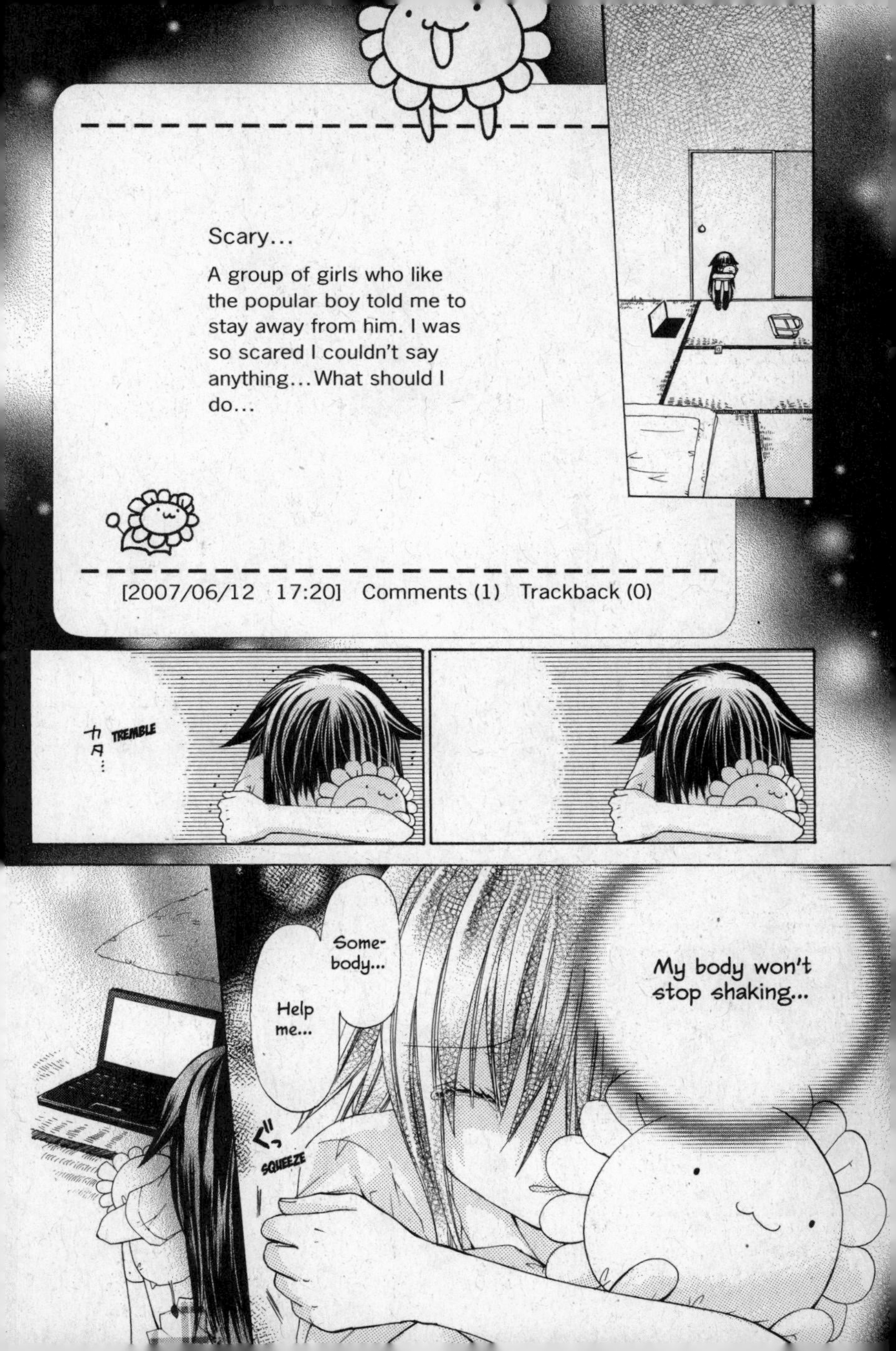
Scary...
A group of girls who like the popular boy told me to stay away from him. I was so scared I couldn't say anything...What should I do...
[2007/06/12 17:20] Comments (1) Trackback (0)
TREMBLE
My body won't stop shaking...
Some-body... Help me...
SQUEEZE

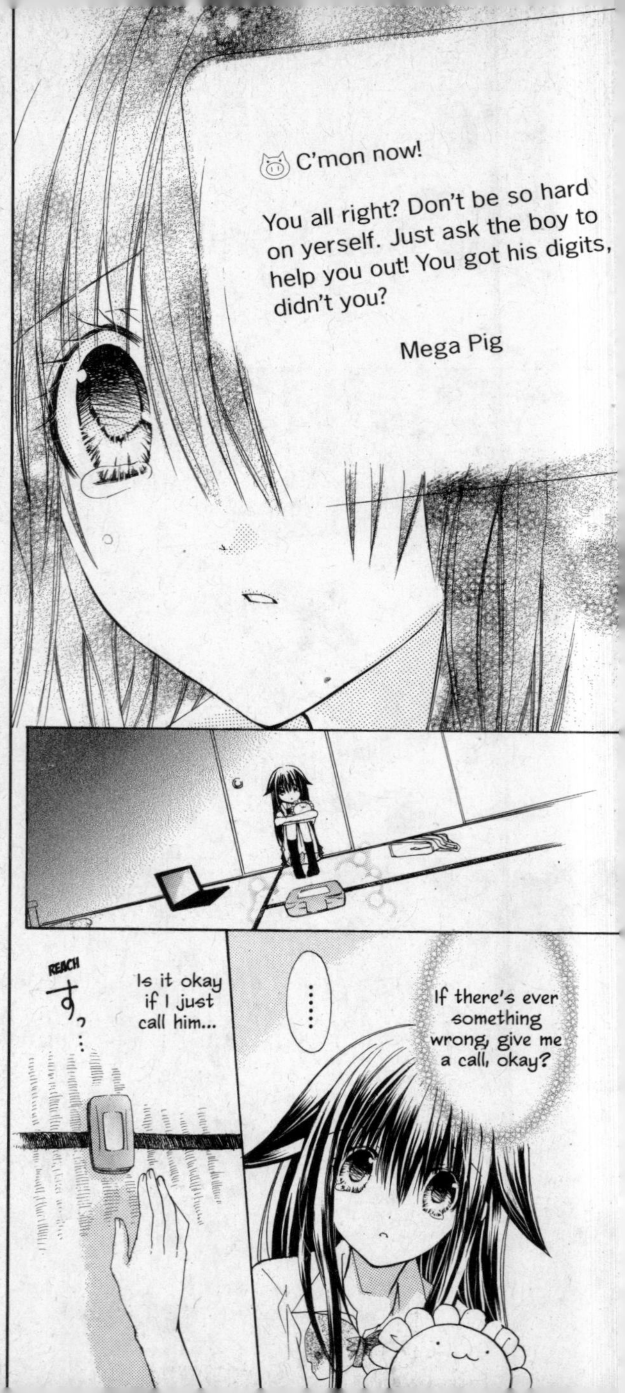
C'mon now!
You all right? Don't be so hard on yerself. Just ask the boy to help you out! You got his digits, didn't you?
Mega Pig
If there's ever something wrong, give me a call, okay?
......
Is it okay if I just call him...
REACH
す

Mahimahi

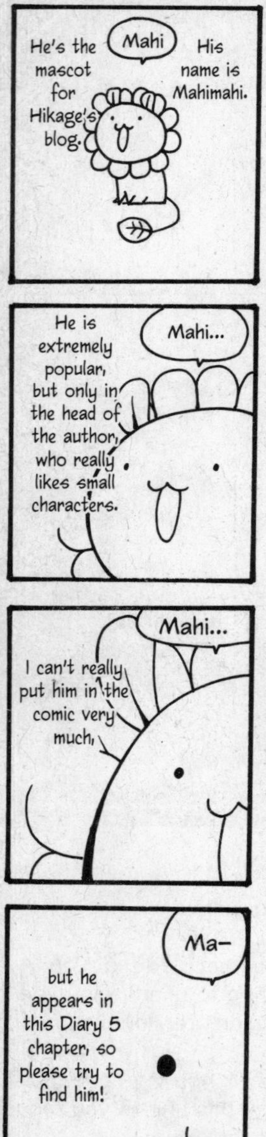
Mahi
His name is Mahimahi.
He's the mascot for Hikage's blog.
Mahi...
He is extremely popular, but only in the head of the author, who really likes small characters.
Mahi...
I can't really put him in the comic very much,
Ma-
but he appears in this Diary 5 chapter, so please try to find him!

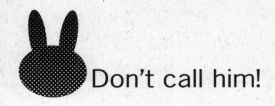

Don't call him!

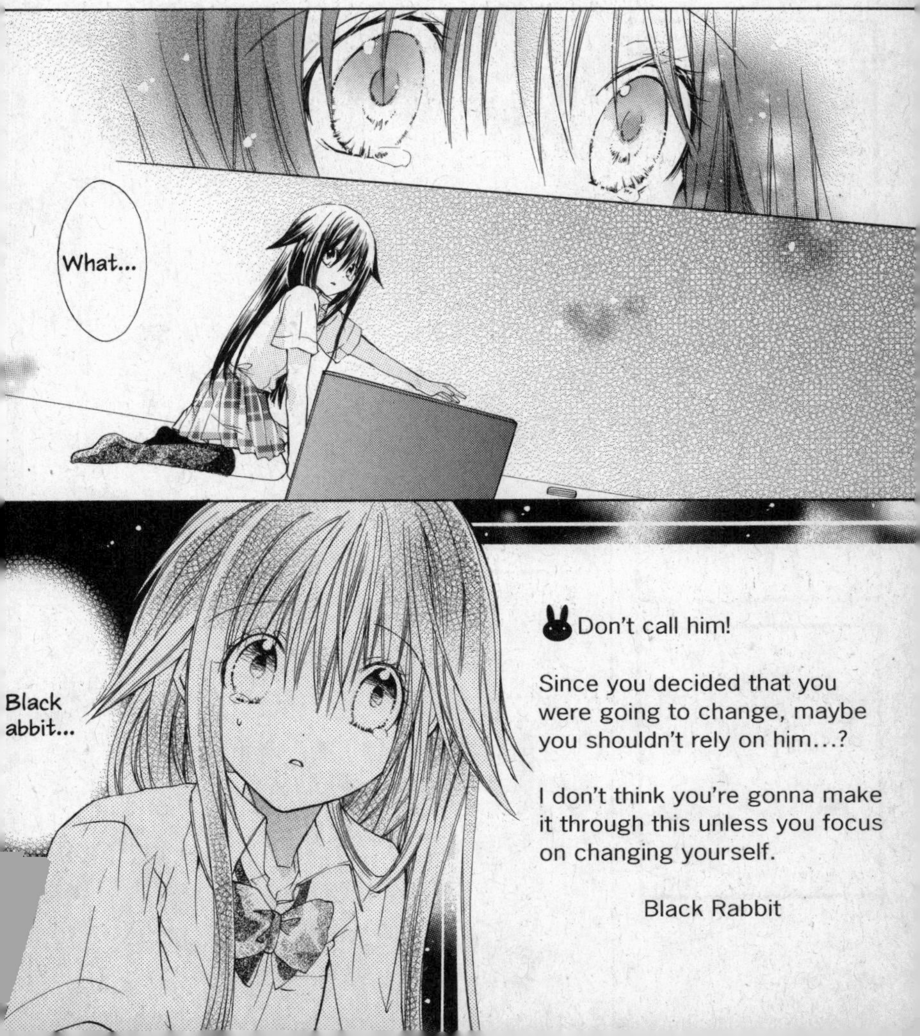
What...
Don't call him!
Since you decided that you were going to change, maybe you shouldn't rely on him...?
I don't think you're gonna make it through this unless you focus on changing yourself.
Black Rabbit
Black abbit...

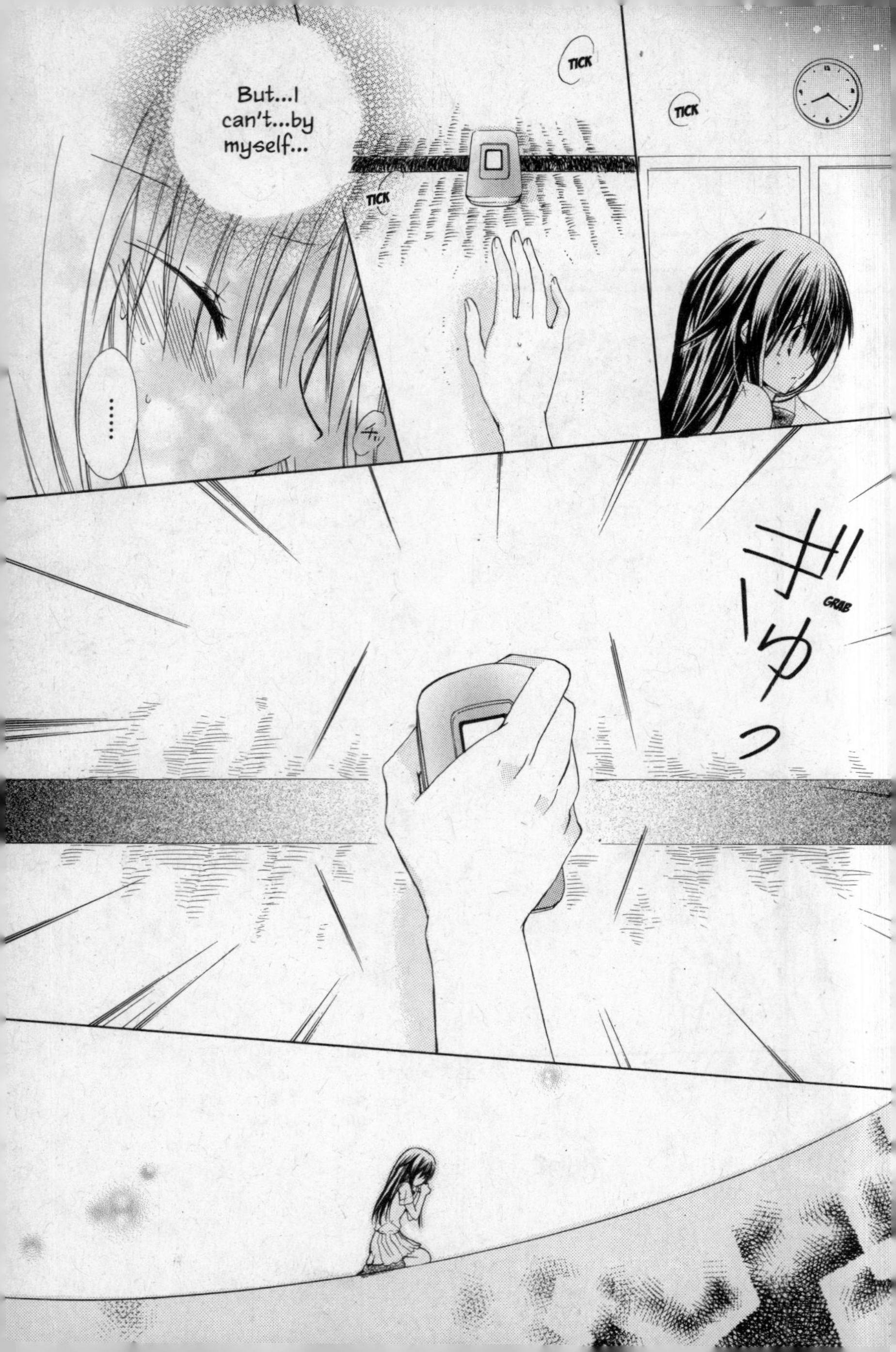
TICK
TICK
TICK
But...I can't...by myself...
......
ぎゅっ
GRAB

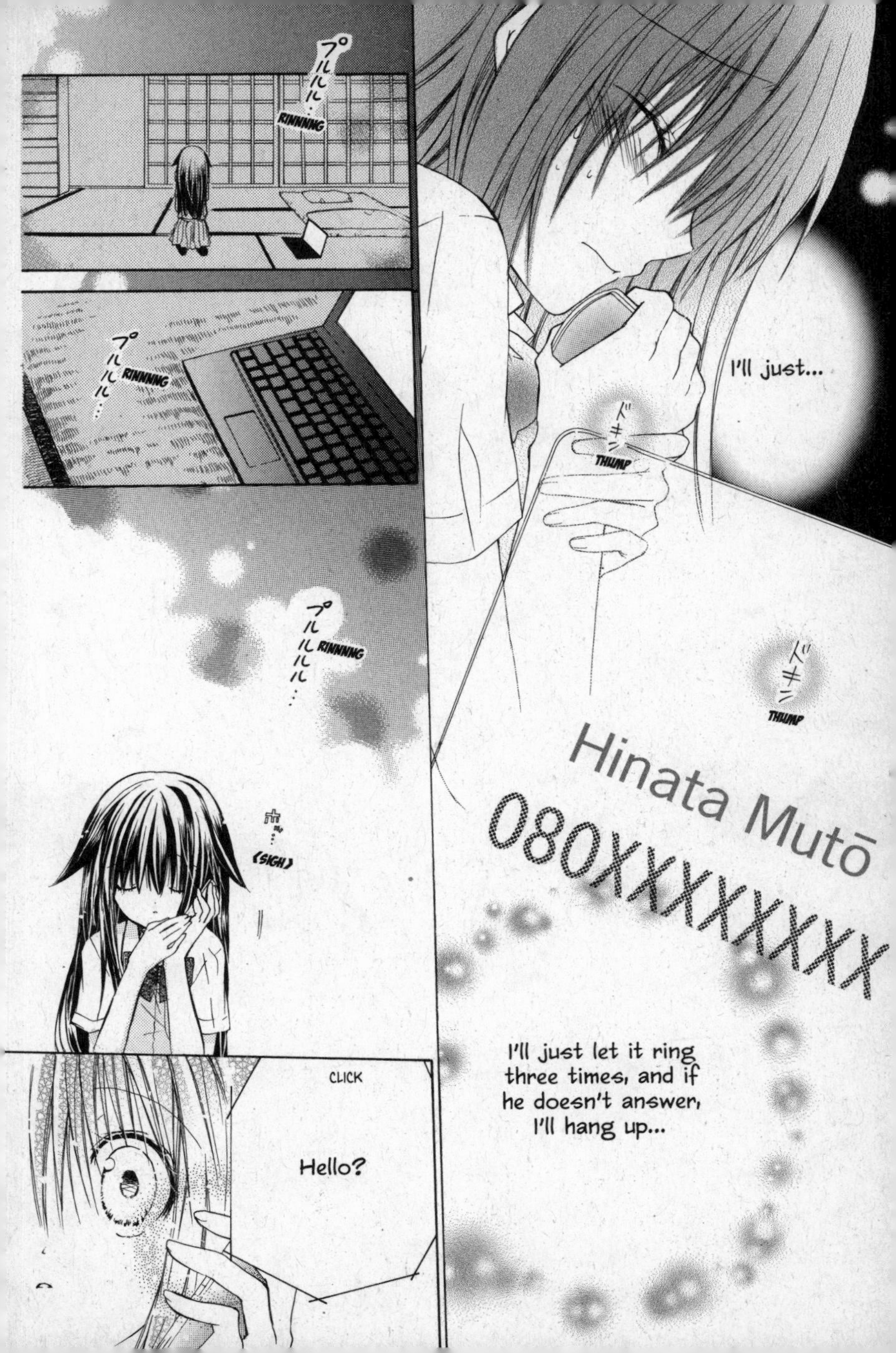
I'll just...
ドキン
THUMP
ドキン
THUMP
Hinata Mutō
080XXXXXXXX
I'll just let it ring three times, and if he doesn't answer, I'll hang up...
プルルル…
RINNNNG
プルルル…
RINNNNG
プルルル…
RINNNNG
(SIGH)
CLICK
Hello?

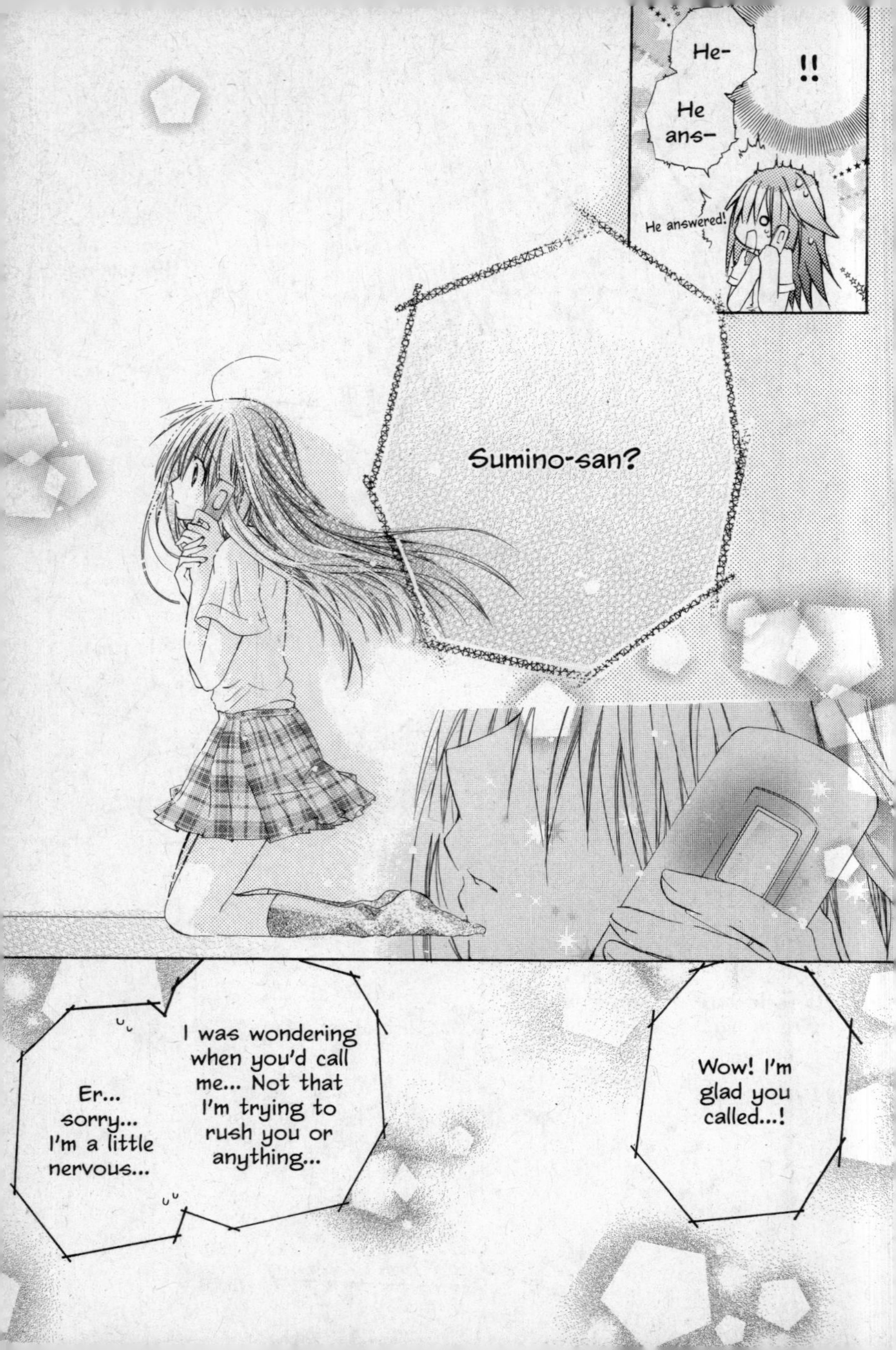
!!
He-
He ans-
He answered!
Sumino-san?
Wow! I'm glad you called...!
I was wondering when you'd call me... Not that I'm trying to rush you or anything...
Er... sorry... I'm a little nervous...

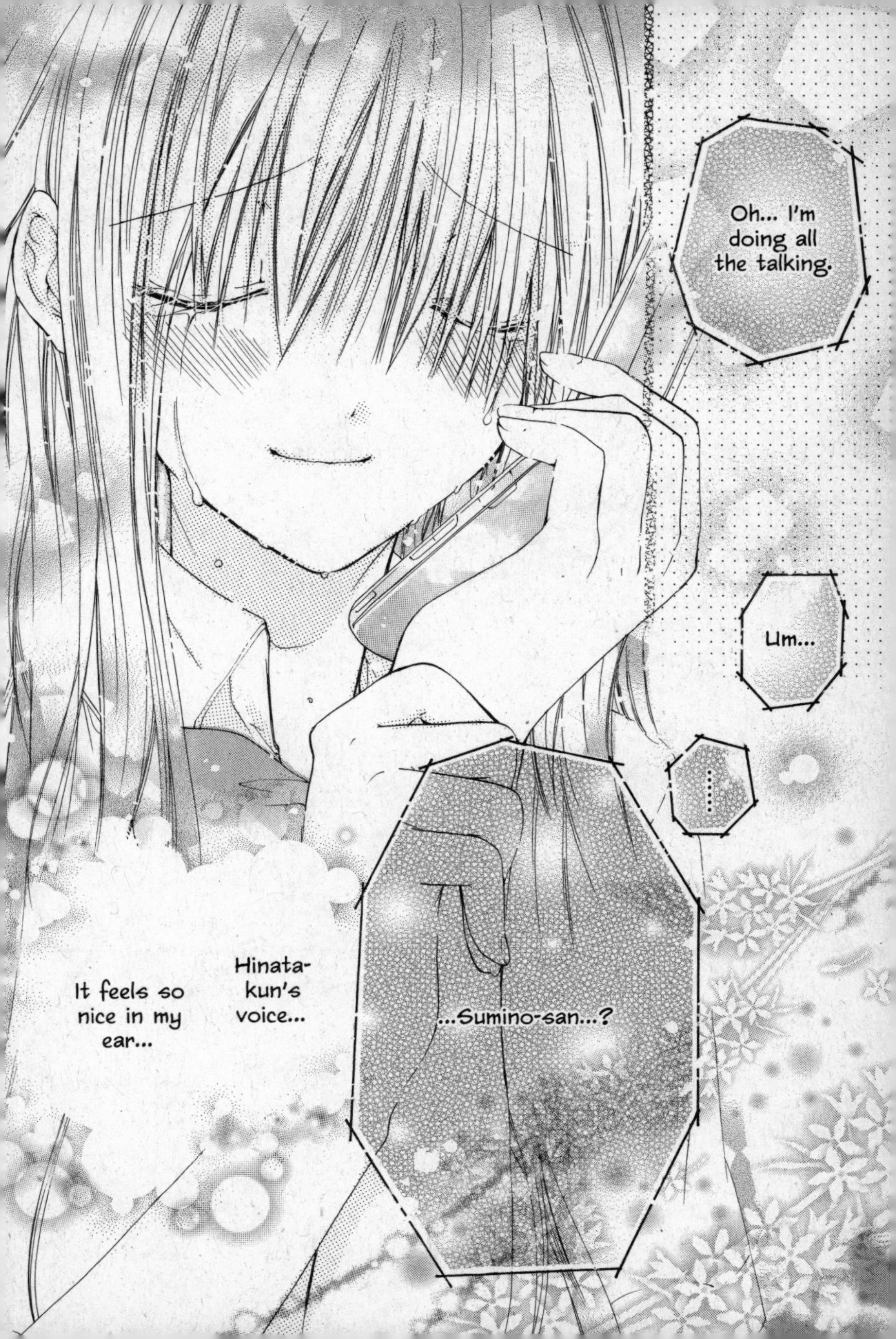

Oh... I'm doing all the talking.
Um...
......
...Sumino-san...?
Hinata-kun's voice...
It feels so nice in my ear...

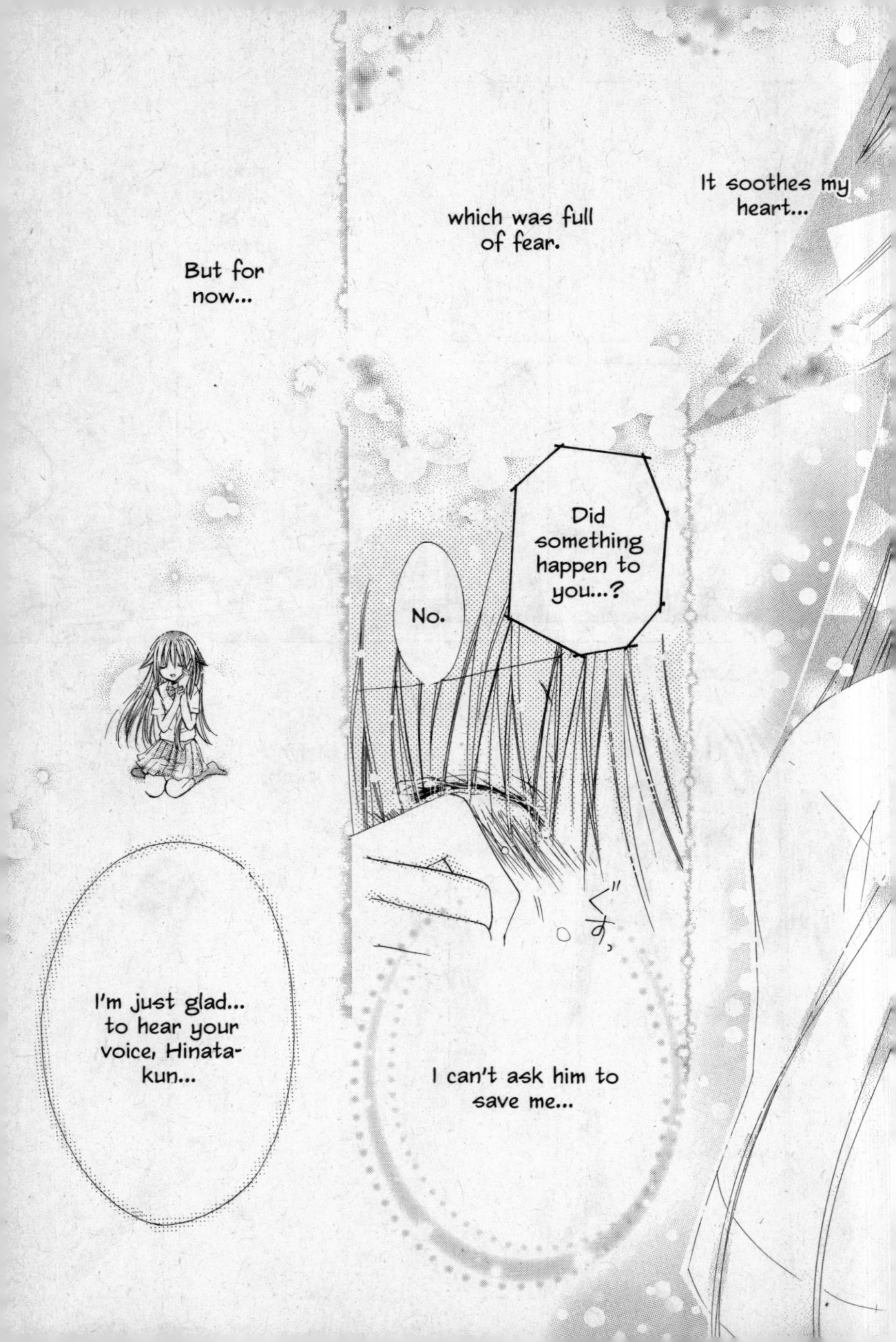

It soothes my heart...
which was full of fear.
Did something happen to you...?
No.
ぐす
I can't ask him to save me...
But for now...
I'm just glad... to hear your voice, Hinata-kun...

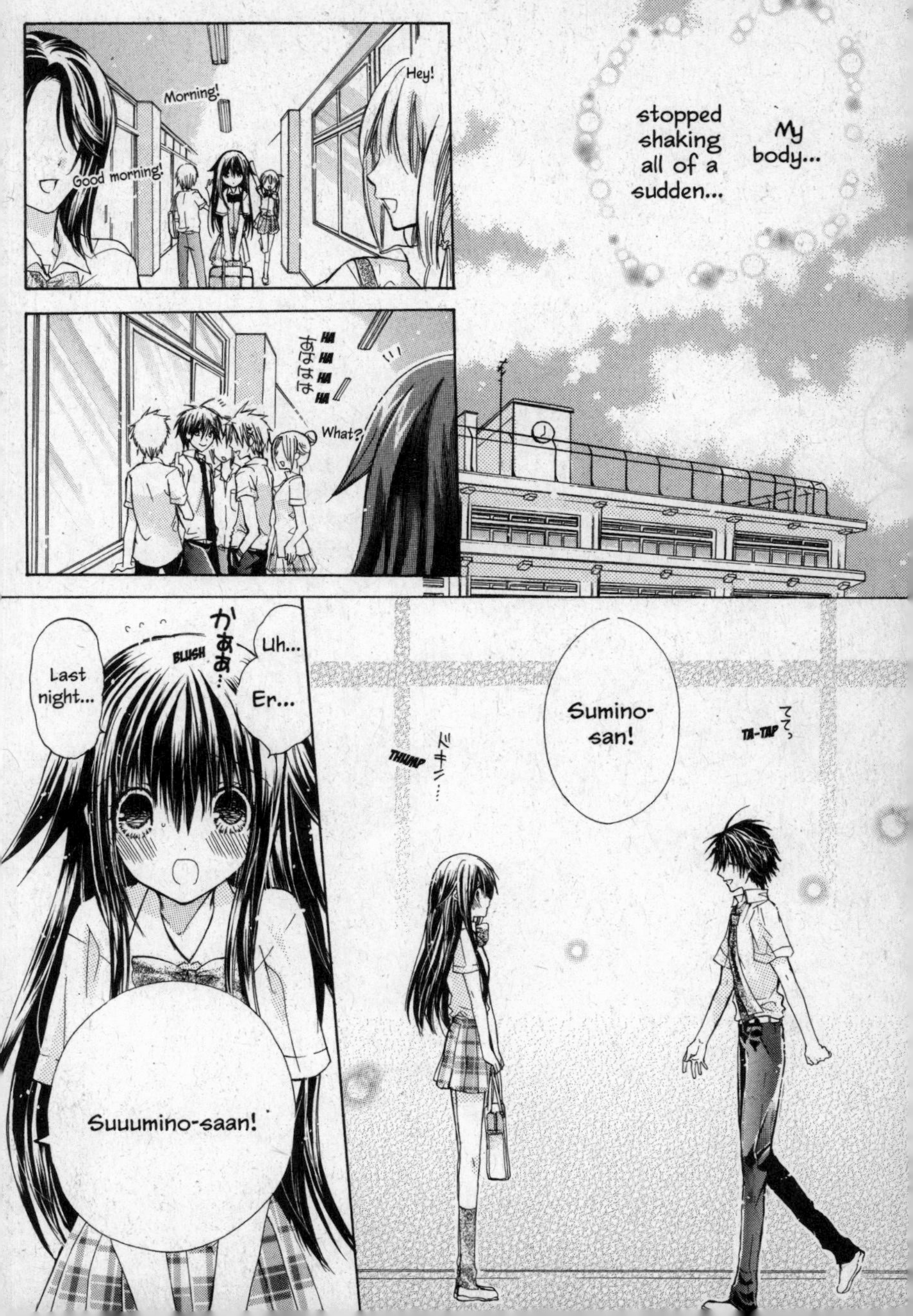
My body...
stopped shaking all of a sudden...
Hey!
Morning!
Good morning!
HA HA HA HA あははは
What?
TA-TAP てて
Sumino-san!
THUMP ドキン...
Uh...
Er...
BLUSH かぁぁ...
Last night...
Suuumino-saan!

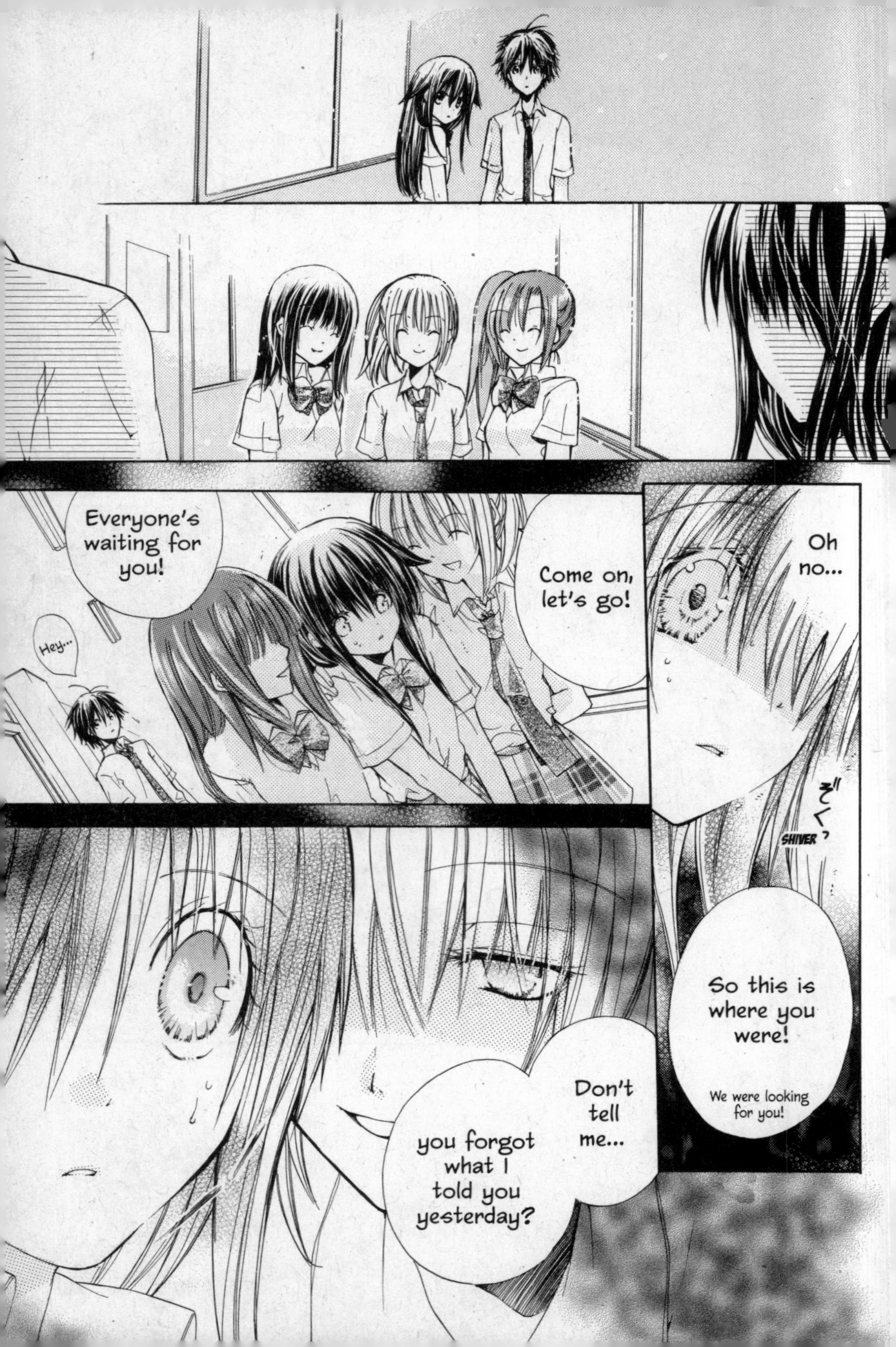
Oh no...
ぞくっ
SHIVER
Come on, let's go!
Everyone's waiting for you!
Hey...
So this is where you were!
We were looking for you!
Don't tell me...
you forgot what I told you yesterday?

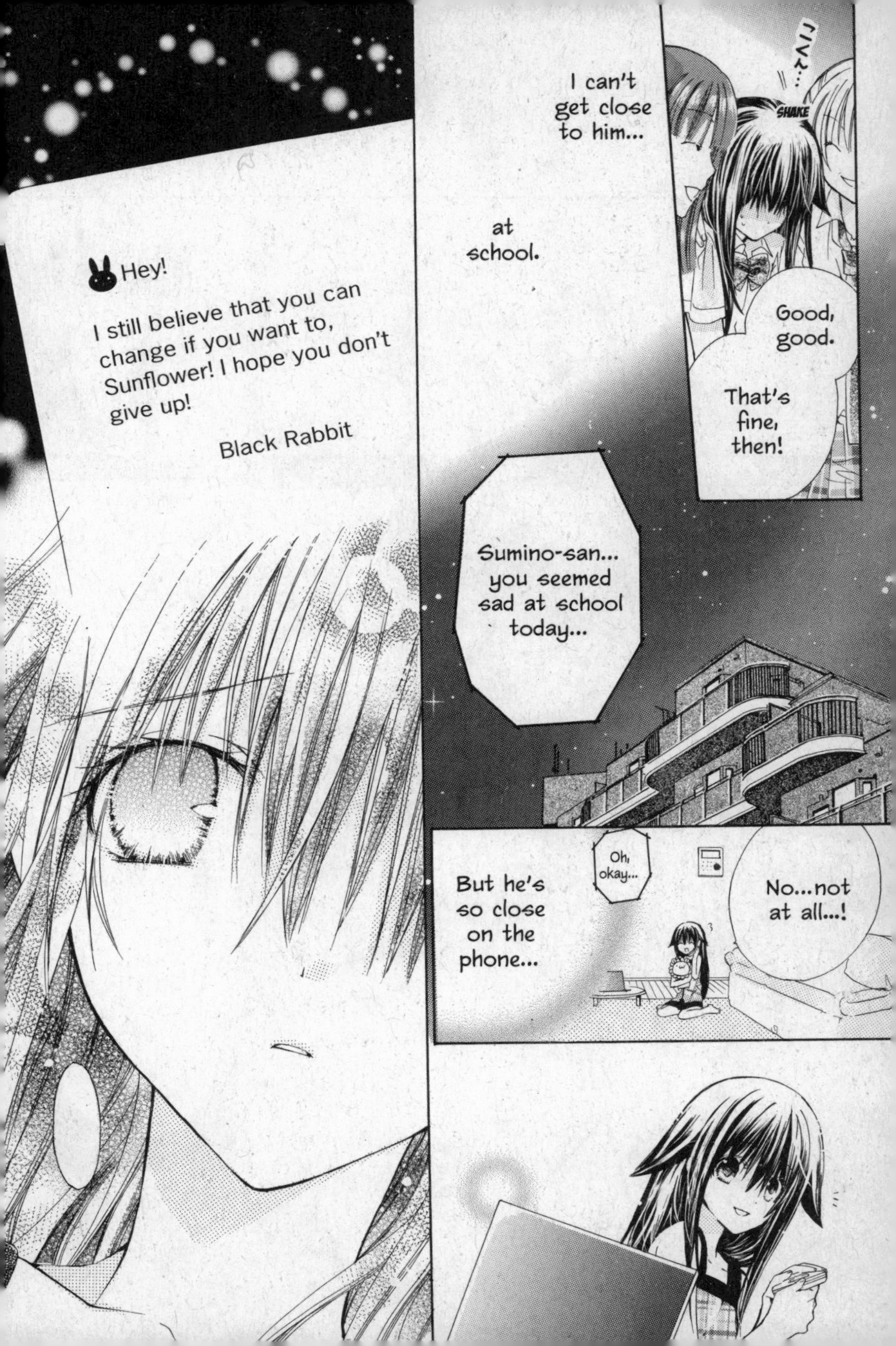

こくん…
SHAKE
Good, good.
That's fine, then!
I can't get close to him...
at school.
Sumino-san... you seemed sad at school today...
No...not at all...!
Oh, okay...
But he's so close on the phone...
Hey!
I still believe that you can change if you want to, Sunflower! I hope you don't give up!
Black Rabbit

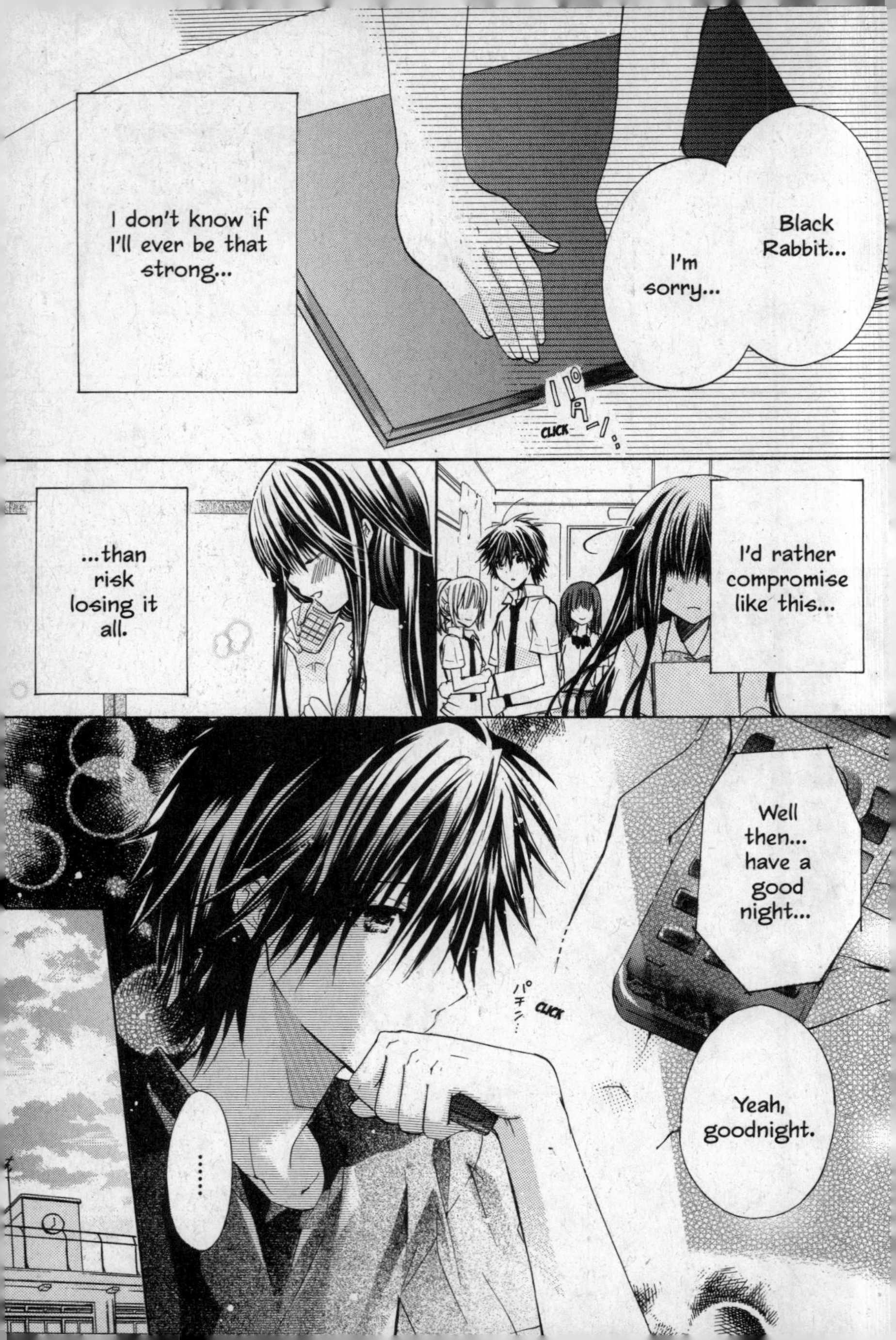
Black Rabbit... I'm sorry...
CLICK
I don't know if I'll ever be that strong...
I'd rather compromise like this...
...than risk losing it all.
Well then... have a good night...
CLICK
Yeah, goodnight.
......

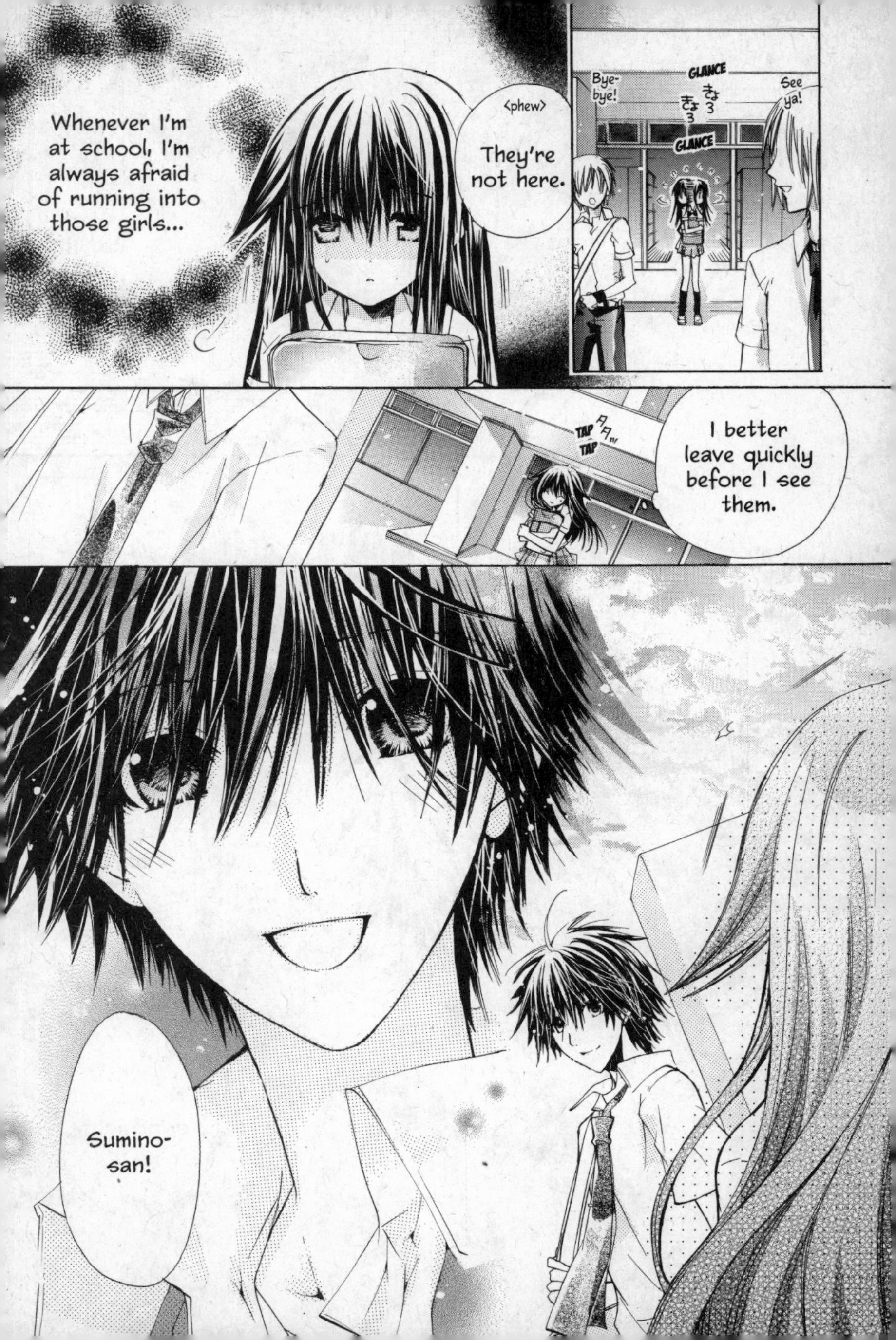
See ya!
GLANCE
きょろ きょろ
Bye-bye!
GLANCE
<phew>
They're not here.
Whenever I'm at school, I'm always afraid of running into those girls...
I better leave quickly before I see them.
タタ
TAP TAP
Sumino-san!

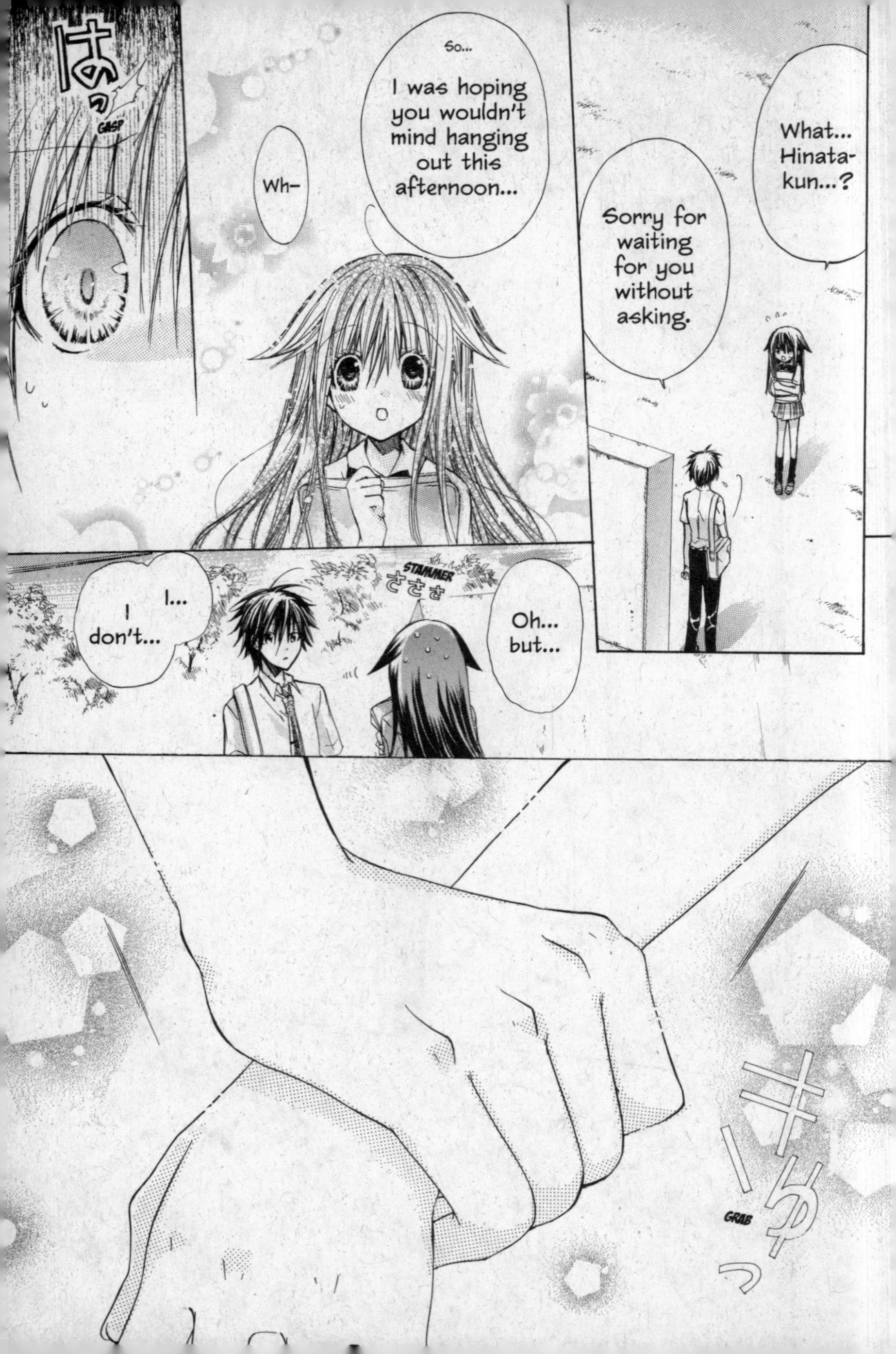

What... Hinata-kun...?
Sorry for waiting for you without asking.
So... I was hoping you wouldn't mind hanging out this afternoon...
Wh-
はっ
GASP
Oh... but...
さささ
STAMMER
I... I don't...
GRAB

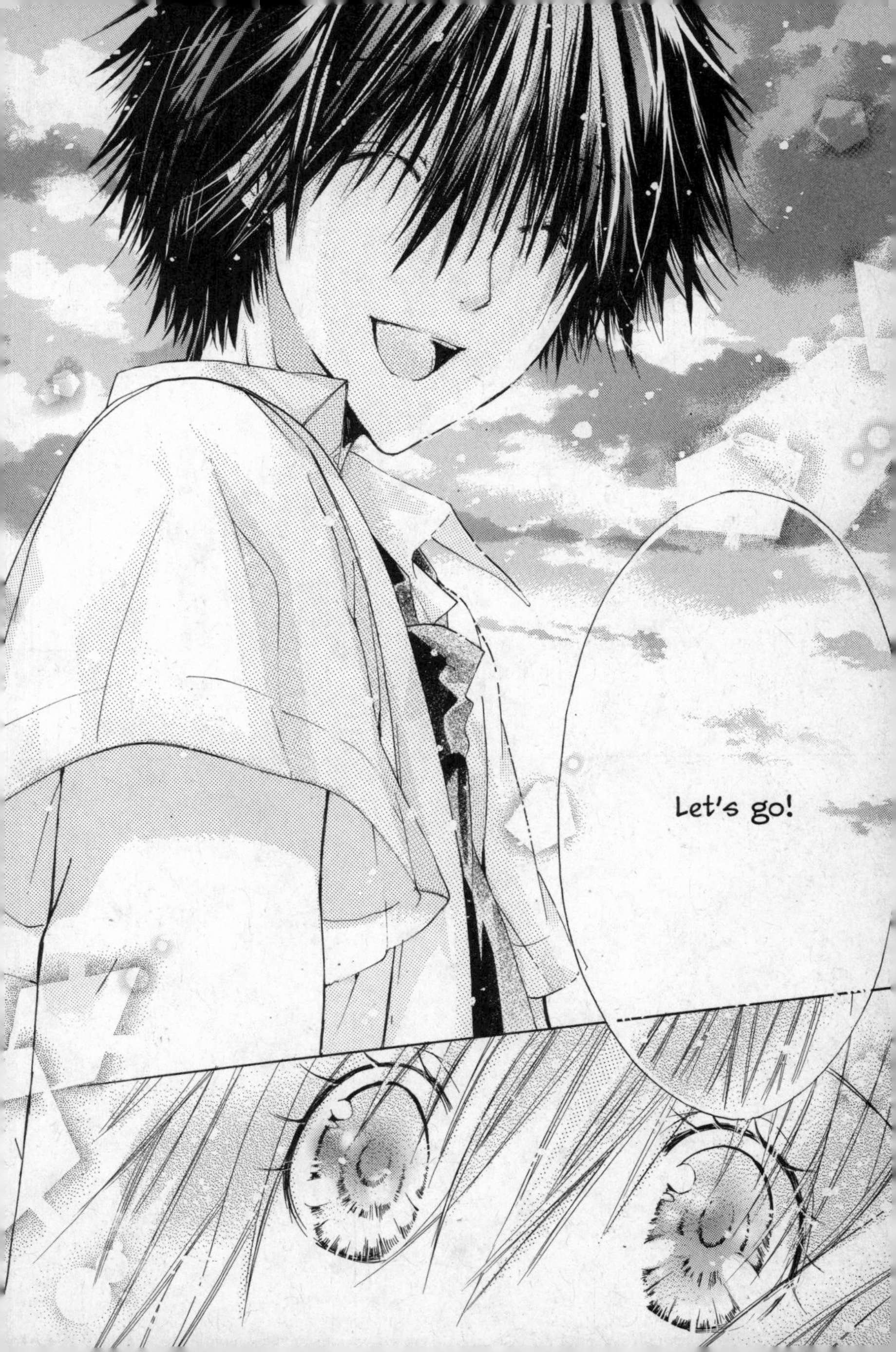
Let's go!

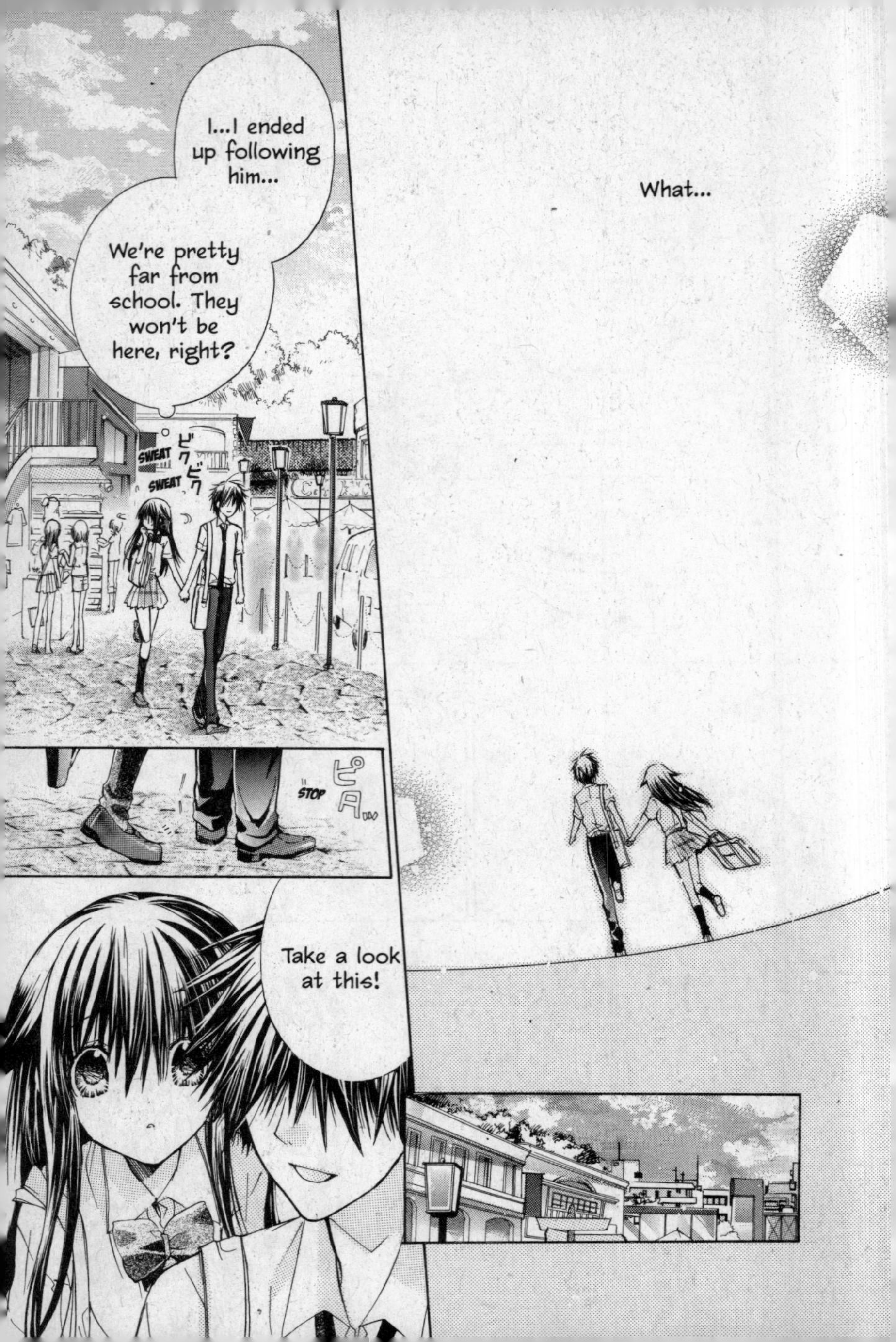
What...
I...I ended up following him...
We're pretty far from school. They won't be here, right?
SWEAT SWEAT
ビクビク
STOP
ピタ
Take a look at this!

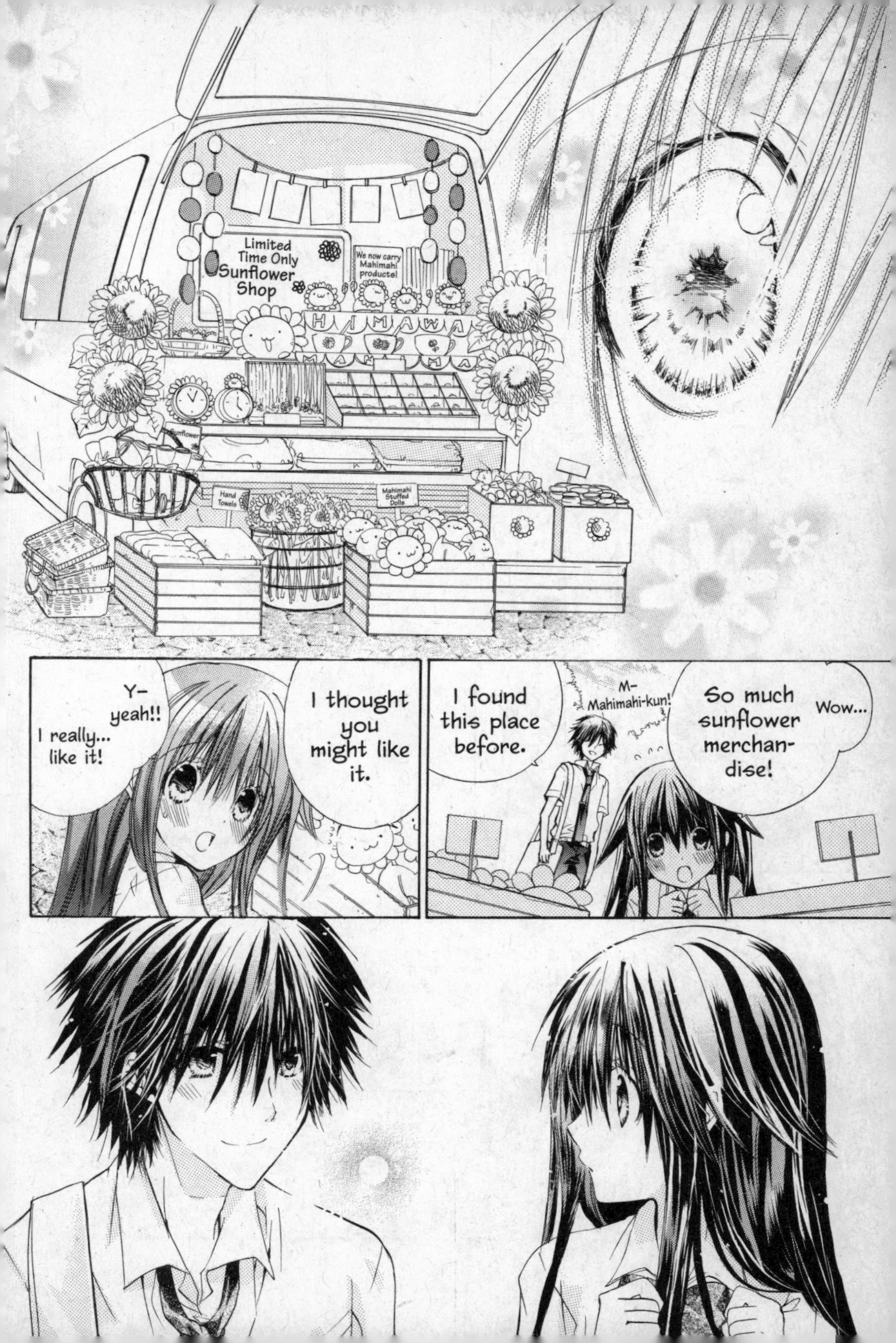
Limited Time Only Sunflower Shop
We now carry Mahimahi products!
Sunflower
Hand Towels
Mahimahi Stuffed Dolls
Wow...
So much sunflower merchan-dise!
M- Mahimahi-kun!
I found this place before.
I thought you might like it.
Y- yeah!! I really... like it!

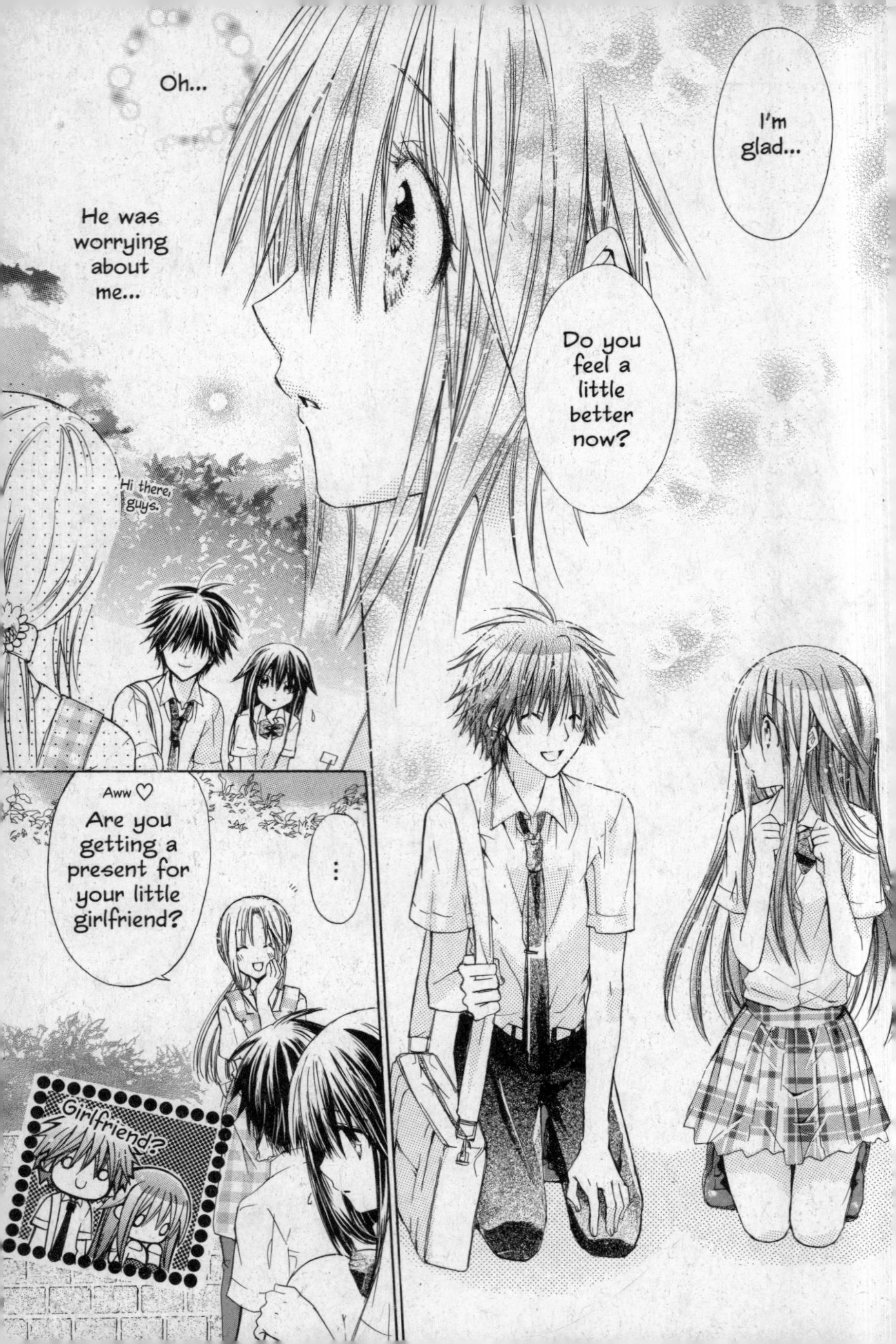

I'm glad...
Do you feel a little better now?
Oh...
He was worrying about me...
Hi there, guys.
...
Aww ♡ Are you getting a present for your little girlfriend?
Girlfriend?

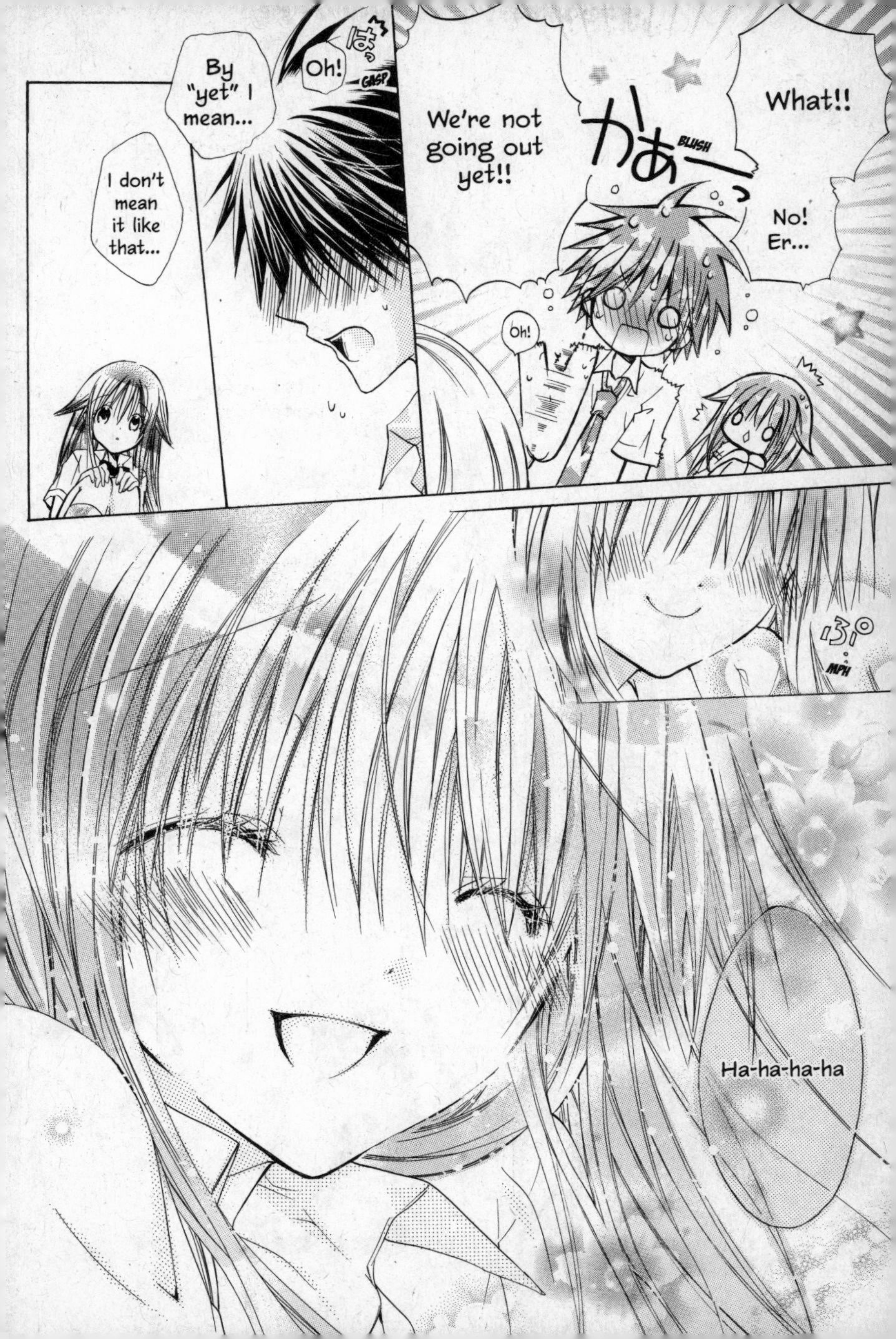
What!!
No! Er...
かあー BLUSH
We're not going out yet!!
Oh!
はっ GASP
Oh!
By "yet" I mean...
I don't mean it like that...
MPH
Ha-ha-ha-ha

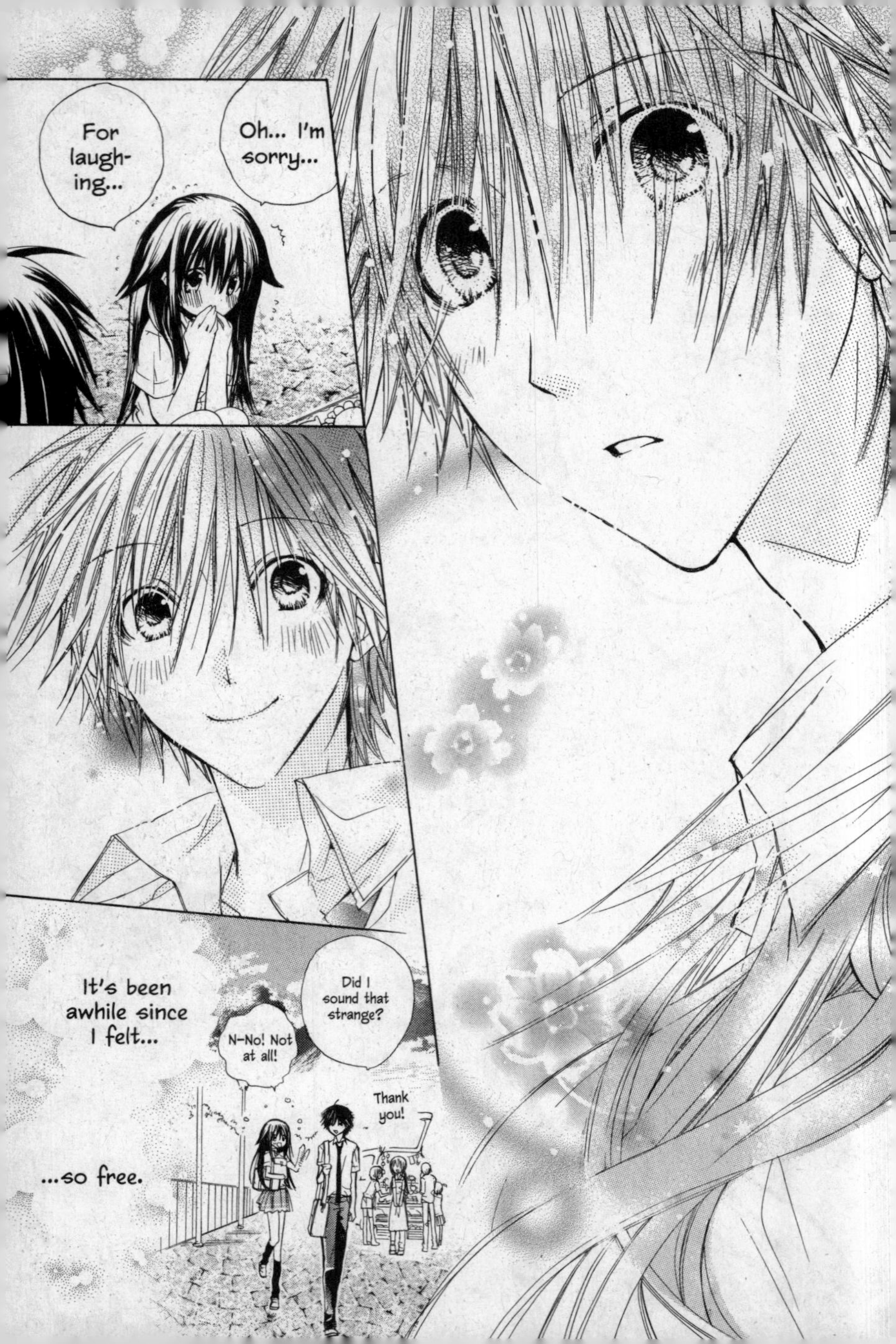
Oh... I'm sorry...
For laughing...
Did I sound that strange?
N-No! Not at all!
Thank you!
It's been awhile since I felt...
...so free.

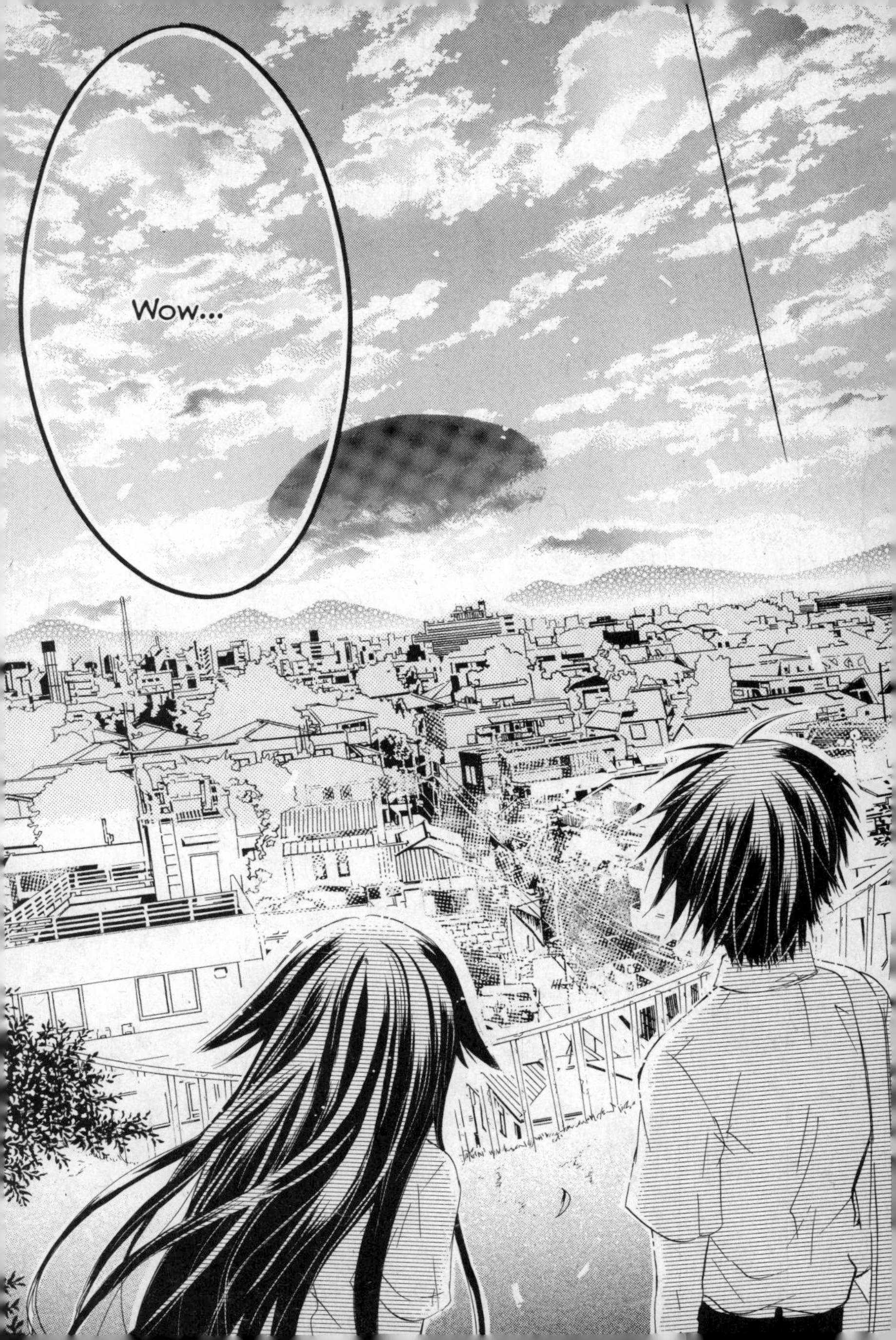
Wow...

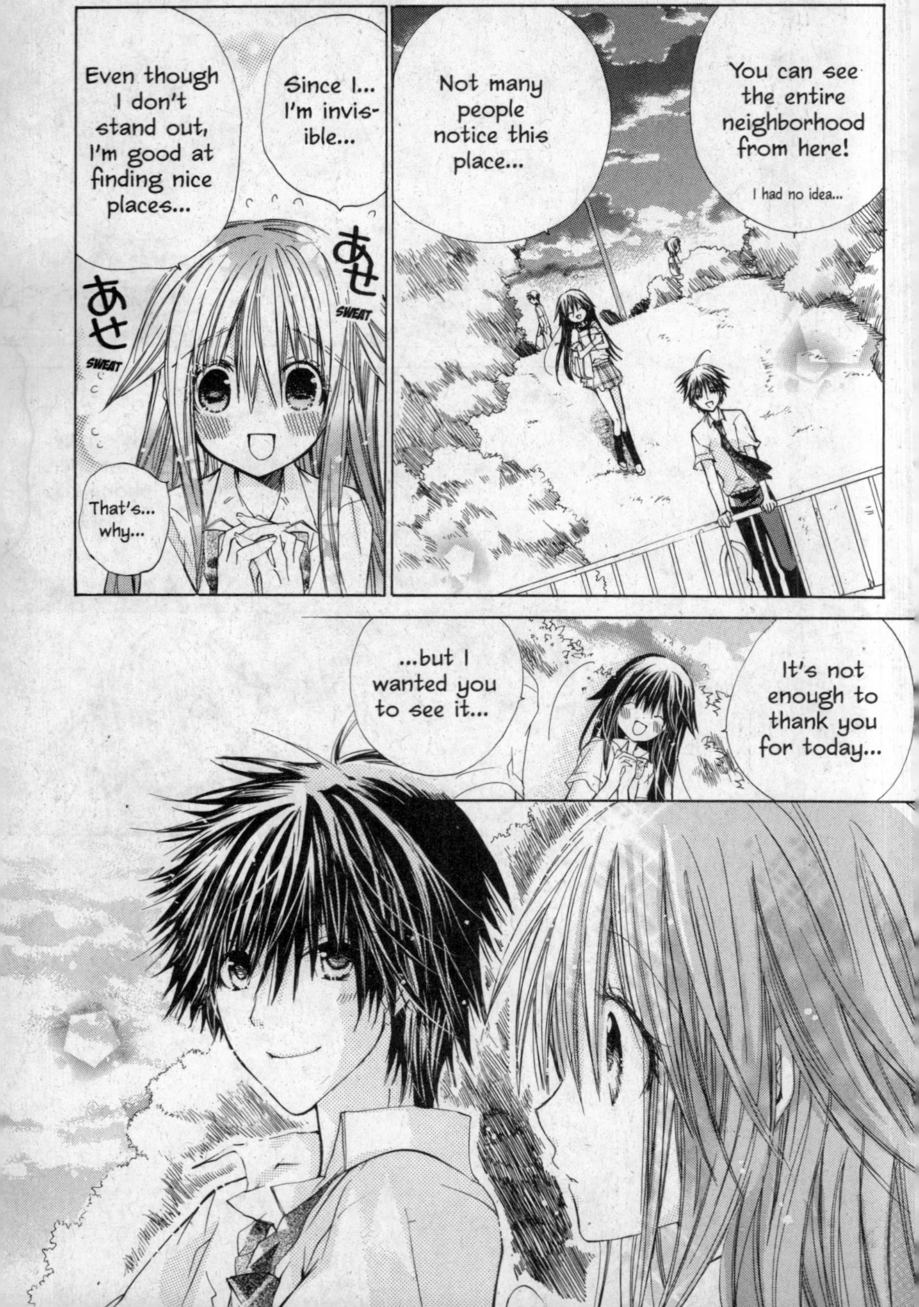
You can see the entire neighborhood from here!
I had no idea...
Not many people notice this place...
Since I... I'm invisible...
あせ
SWEAT
Even though I don't stand out, I'm good at finding nice places...
あせ
SWEAT
That's... why...
It's not enough to thank you for today...
...but I wanted you to see it...

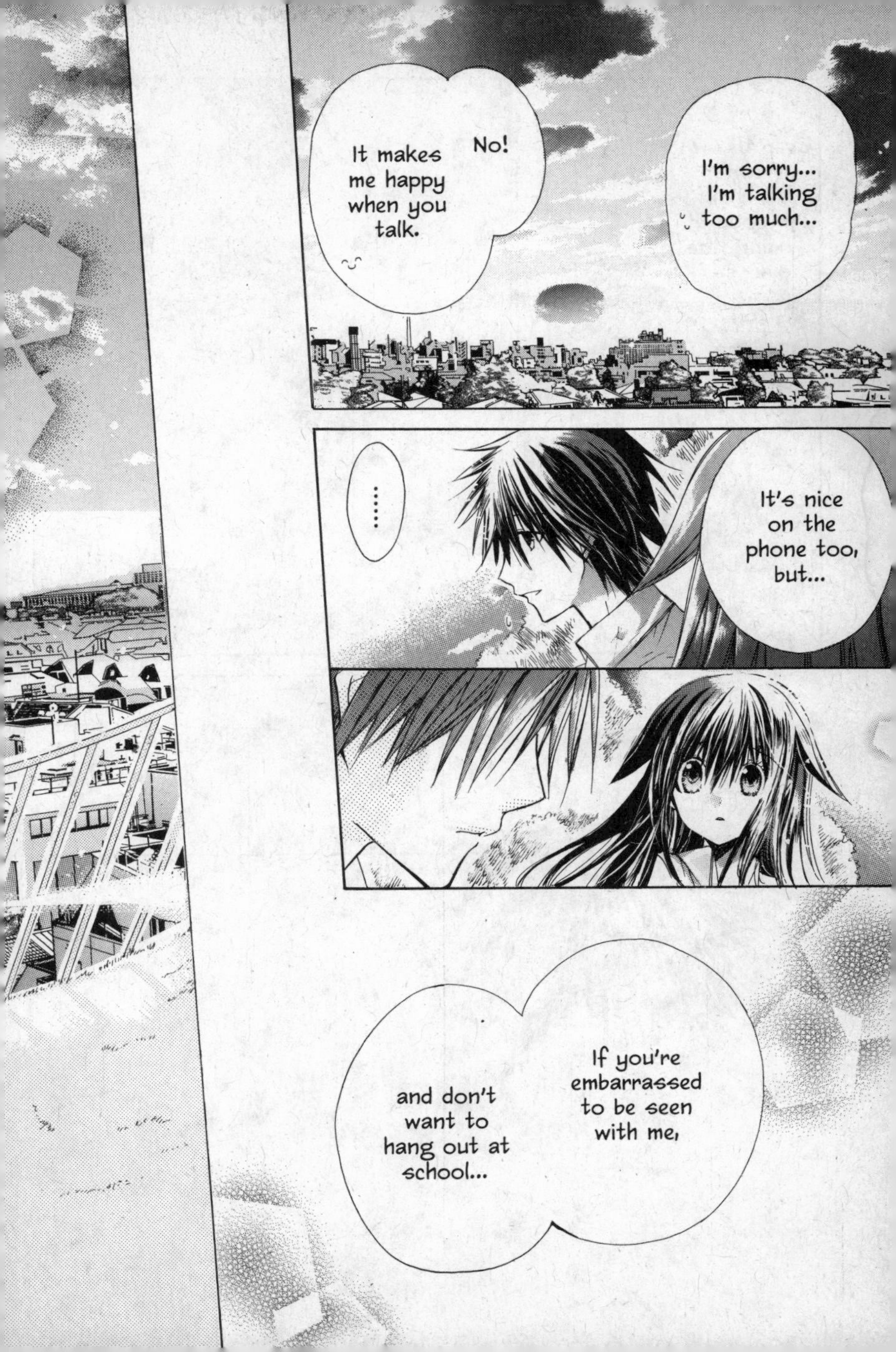
I'm sorry... I'm talking too much...
No!
It makes me happy when you talk.
It's nice on the phone too, but...
......
If you're embarrassed to be seen with me,
and don't want to hang out at school...

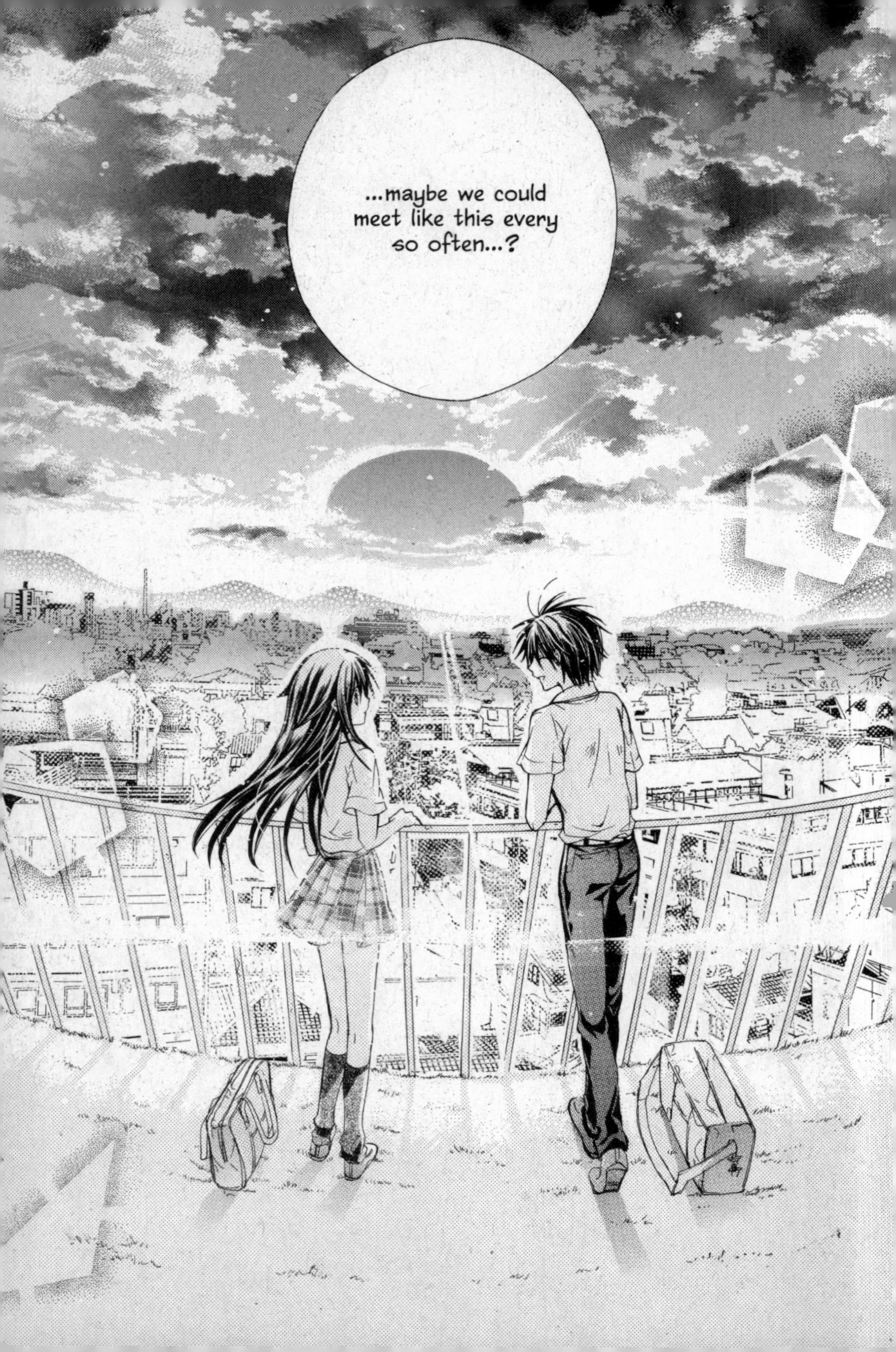
...maybe we could meet like this every so often...?

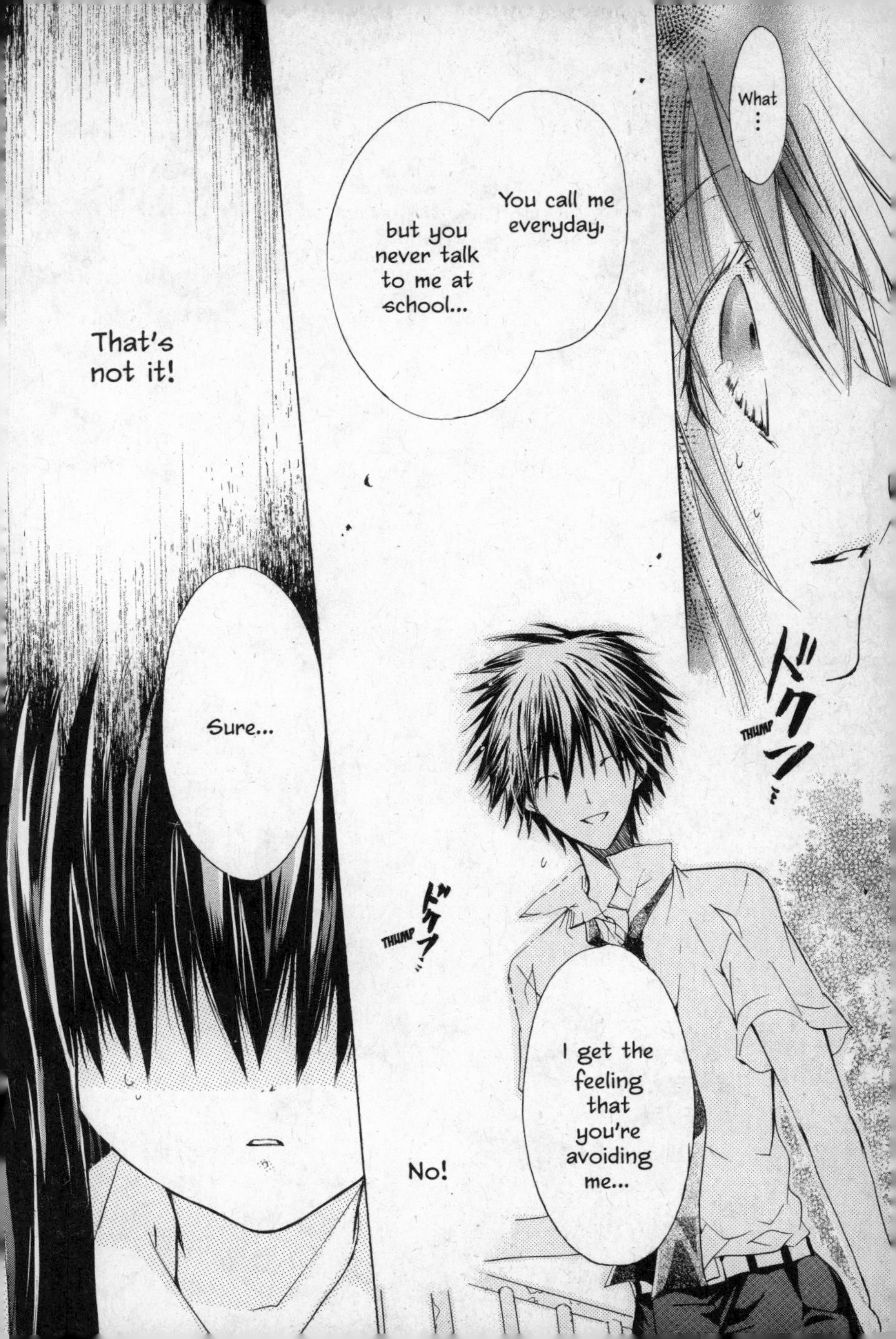
What...
THUMP
You call me everyday,
but you never talk to me at school...
I get the feeling that you're avoiding me...
THUMP
No!
That's not it!
Sure...

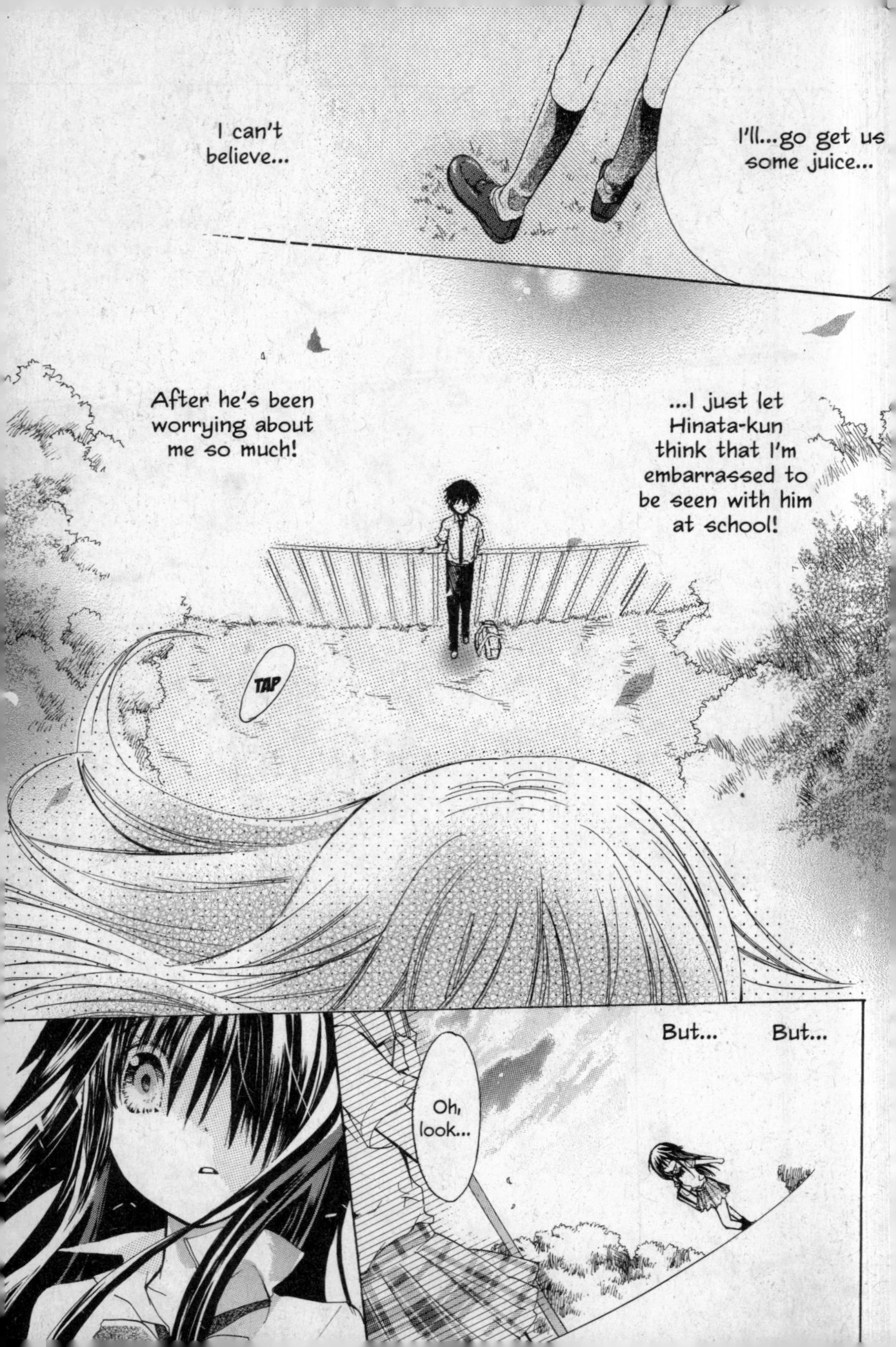
I'll...go get us some juice...
I can't believe...
...I just let Hinata-kun think that I'm embarrassed to be seen with him at school!
After he's been worrying about me so much!
TAP
But...
But...
Oh, look...

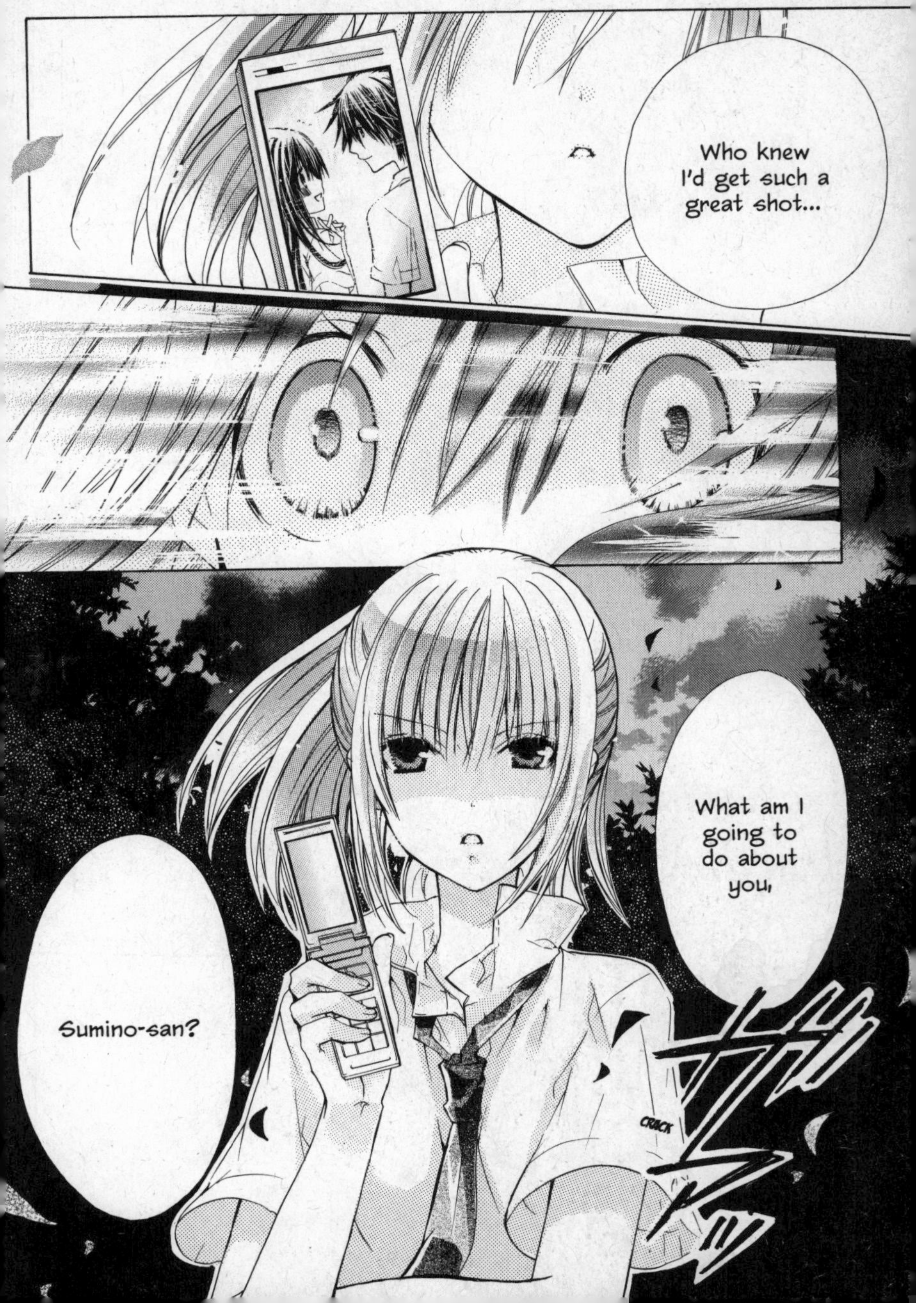
Who knew I'd get such a great shot...
What am I going to do about you,
Sumino-san?
CRACK

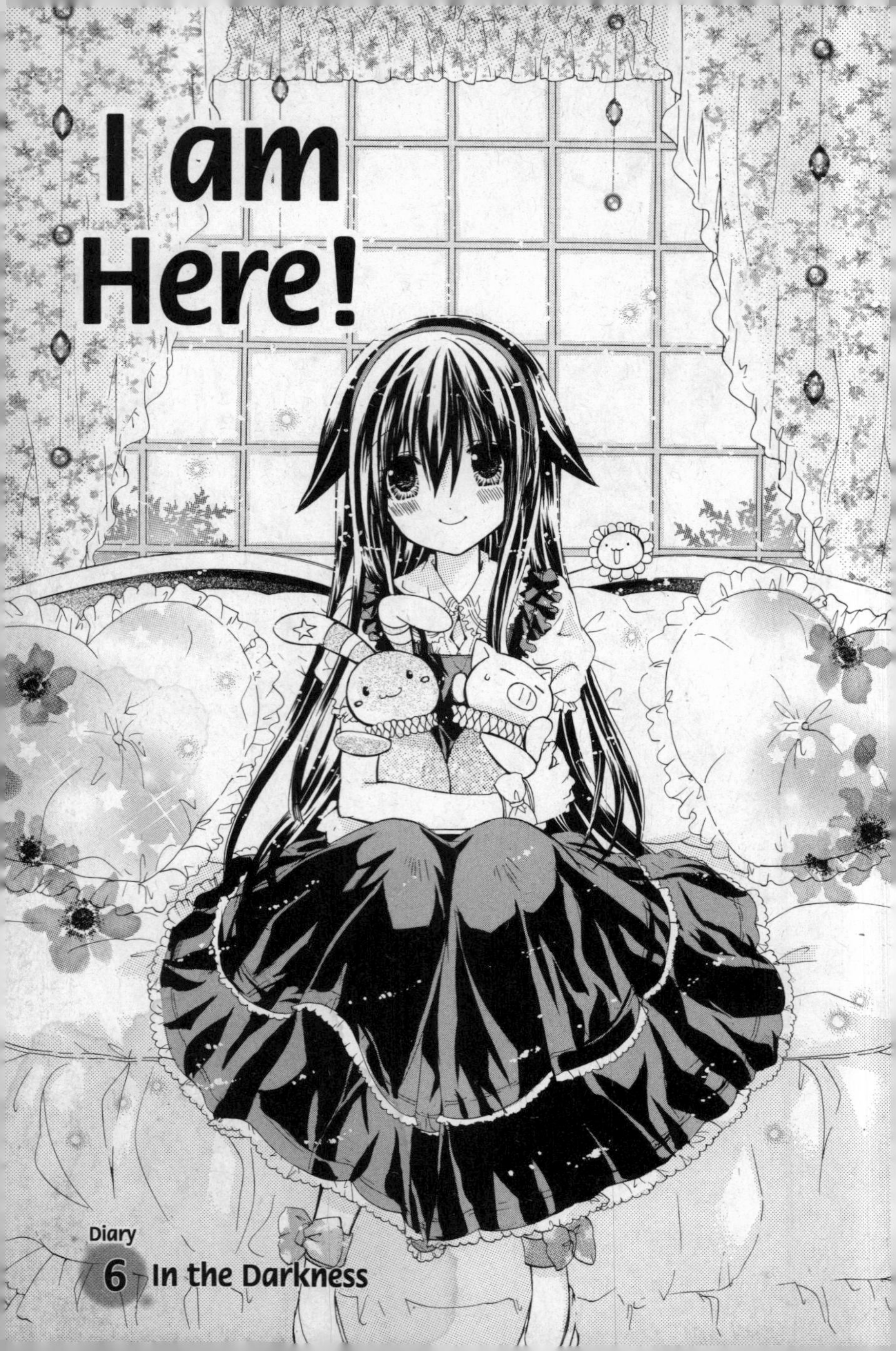
I am Here!
Diary
6 In the Darkness

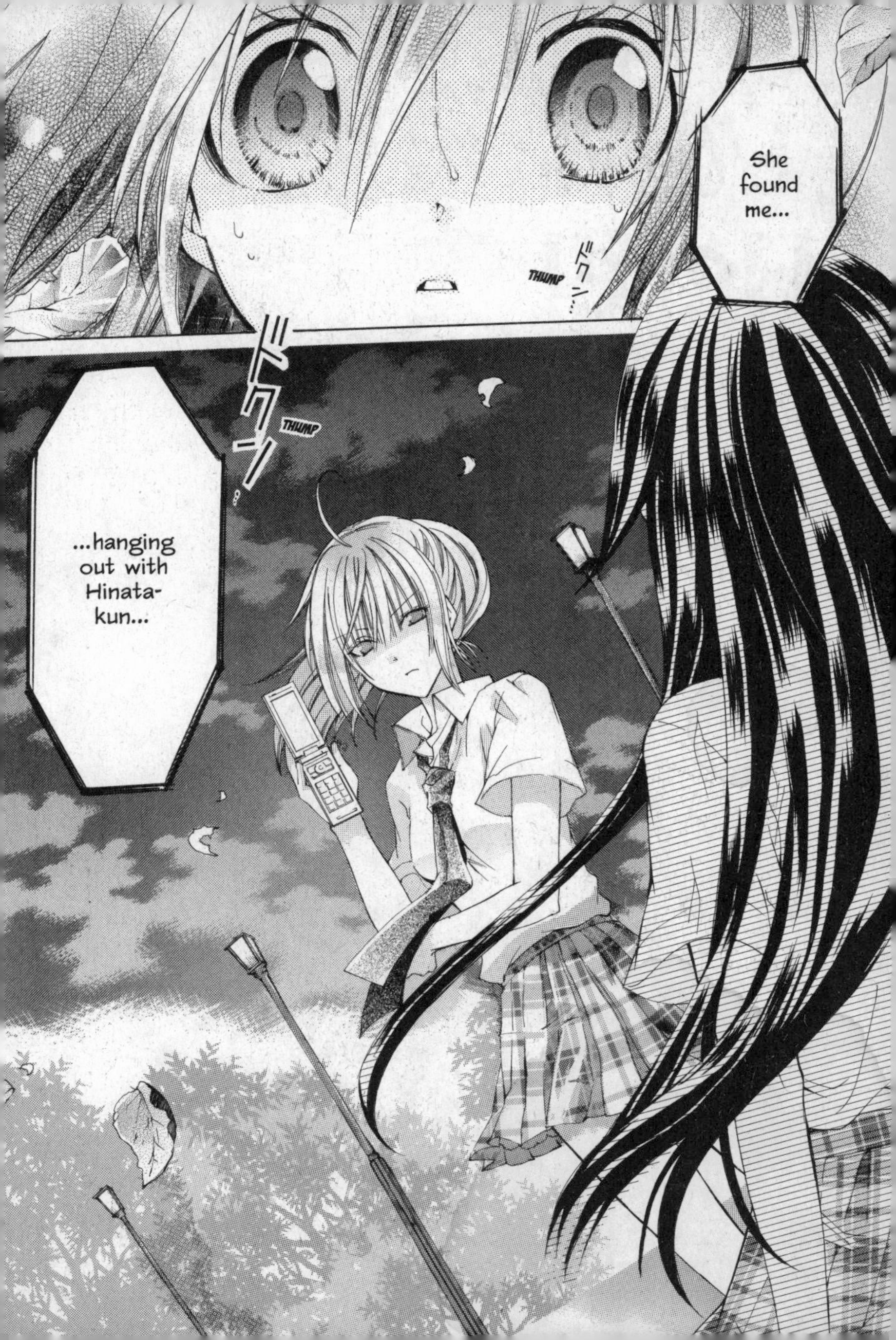
She found me...
THUMP
THUMP
...hanging out with Hinata-kun...

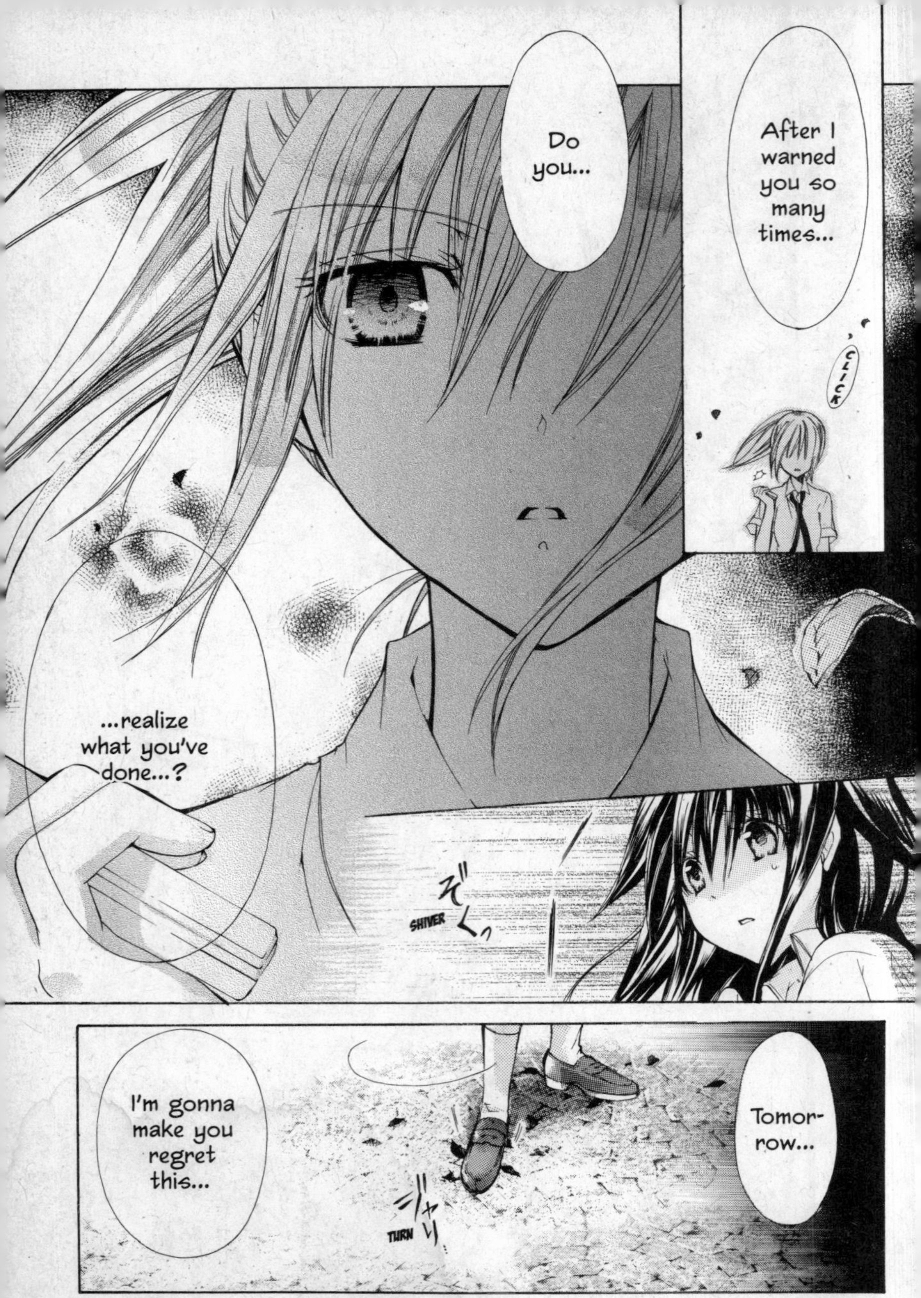
After I warned you so many times...
CLICK
Do you...
...realize what you've done...?
ぞくっ
SHIVER
Tomor-row...
I'm gonna make you regret this...
ジャリ
TURN

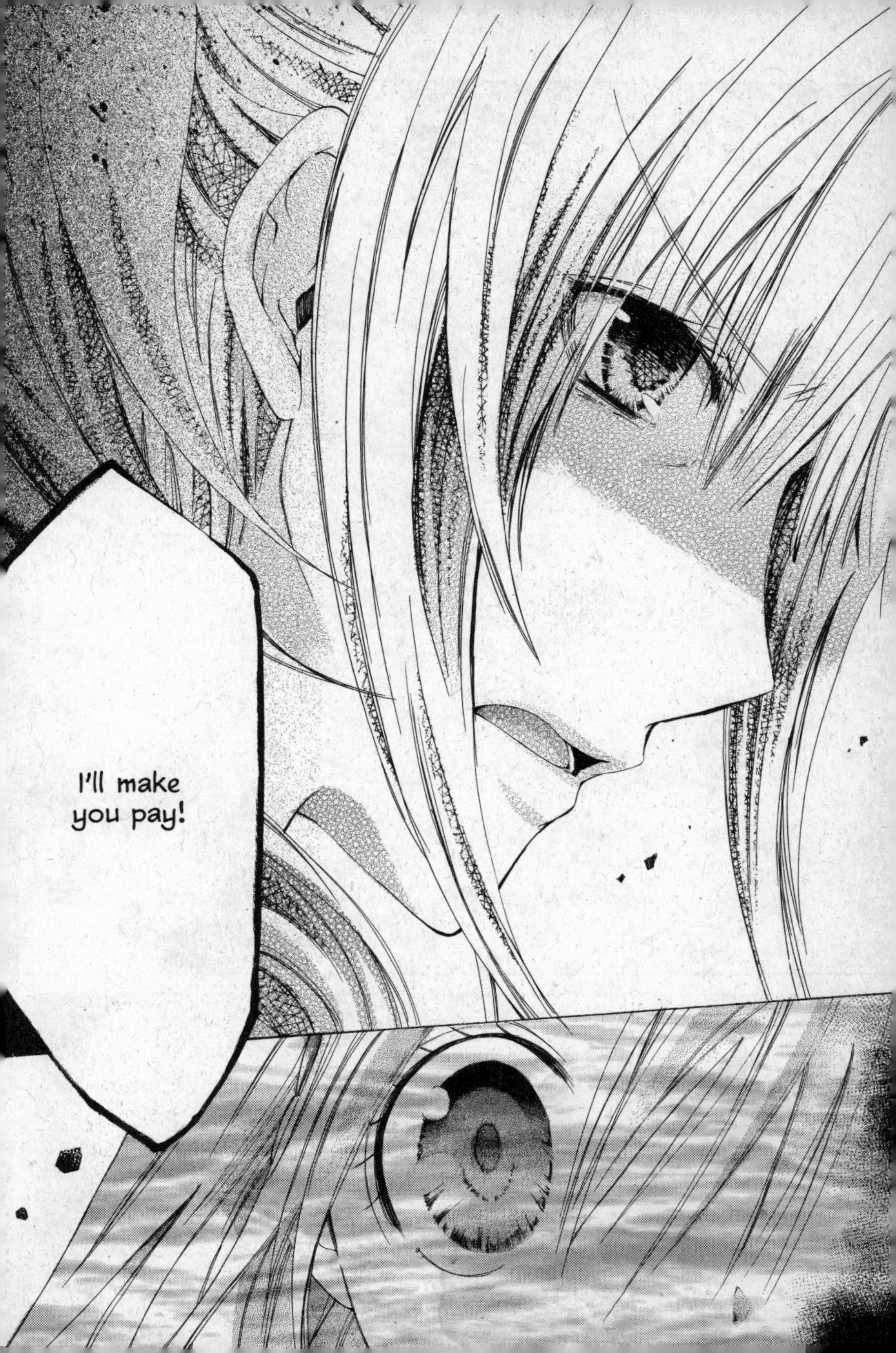
I'll make you pay!

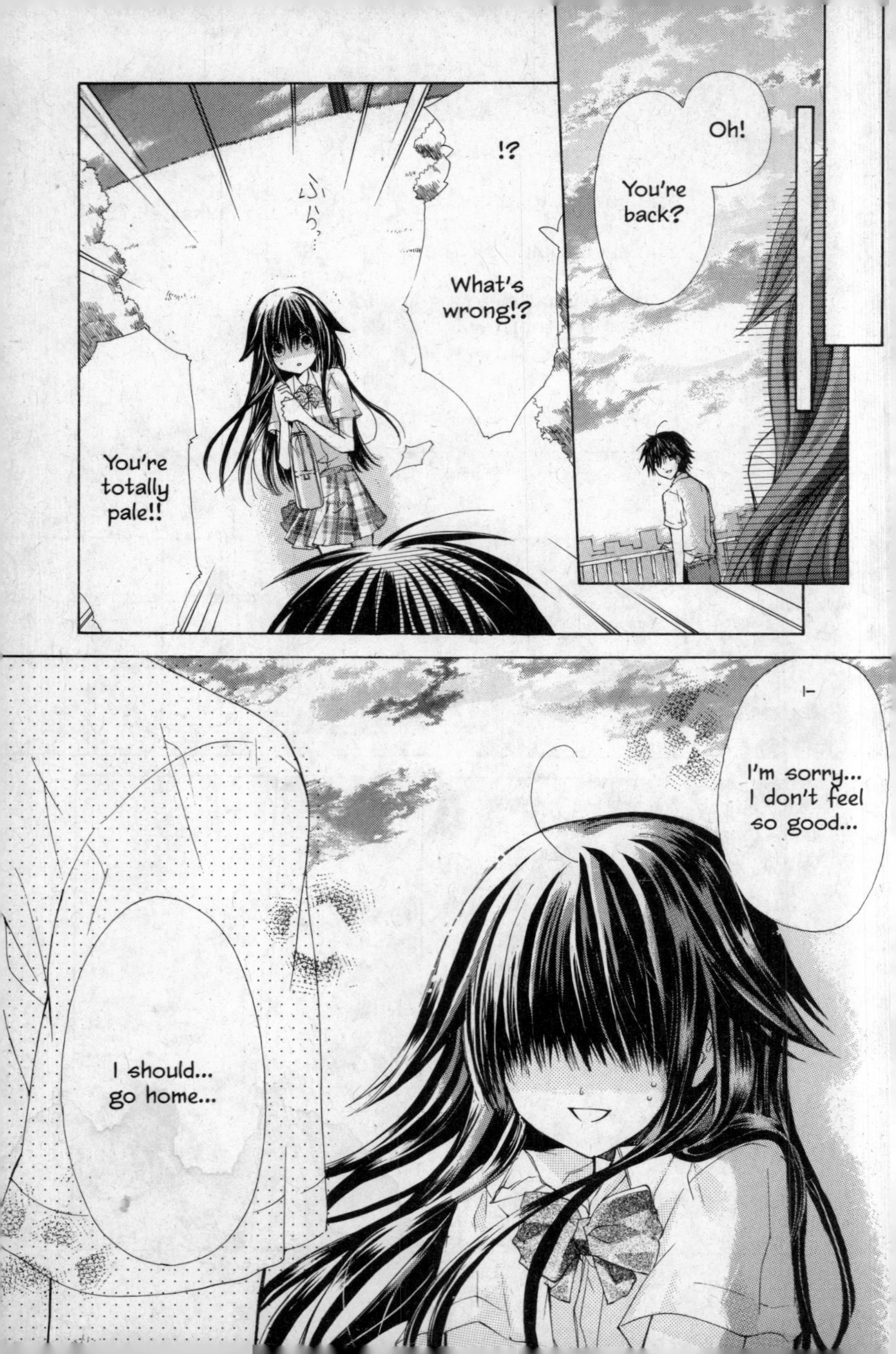
Oh!
You're back?
!?
ふらっ…
What's wrong!?
You're totally pale!!
I–
I'm sorry... I don't feel so good...
I should... go home...

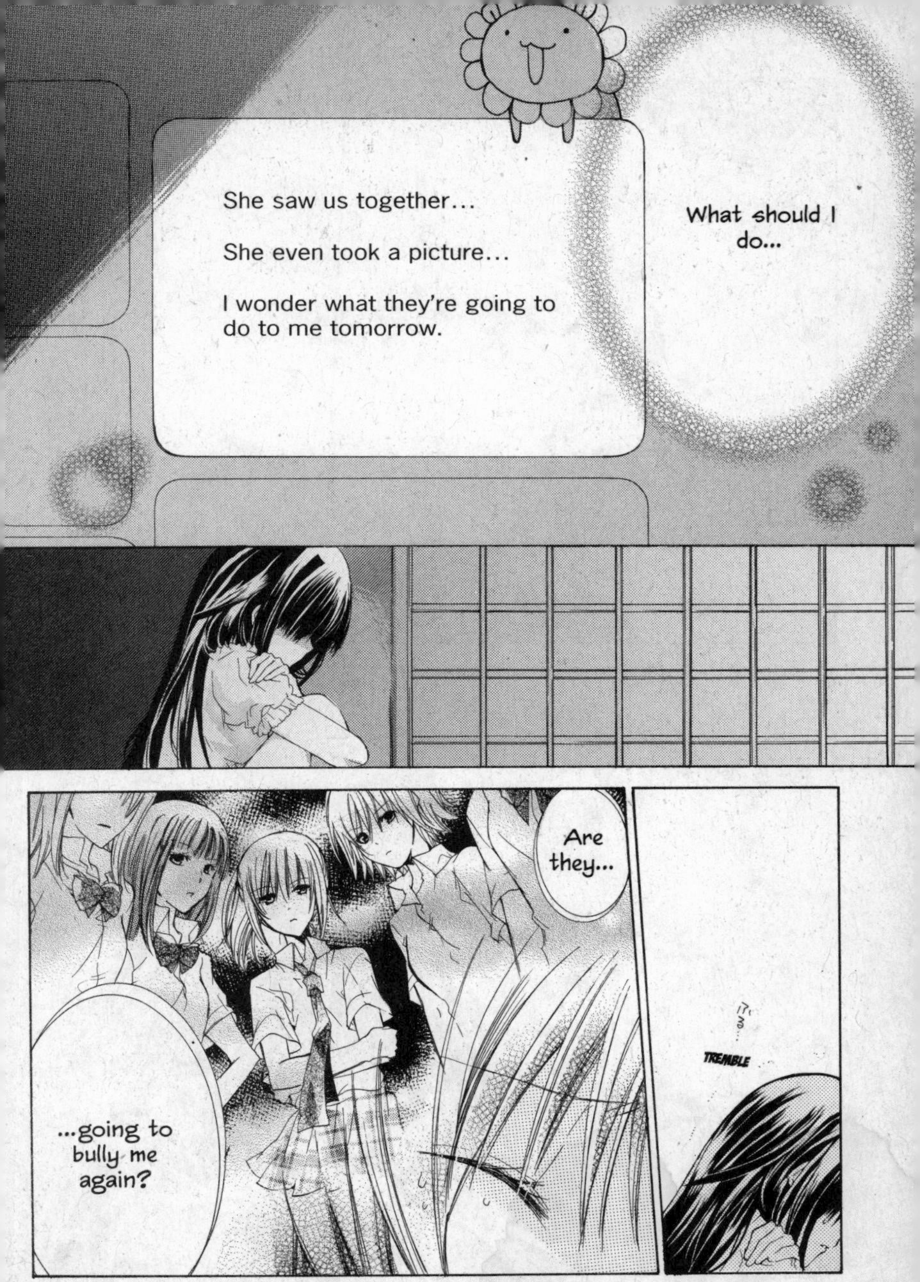
She saw us together...
She even took a picture...
I wonder what they're going to do to me tomorrow.
What should I do...
TREMBLE
Are they...
...going to bully me again?

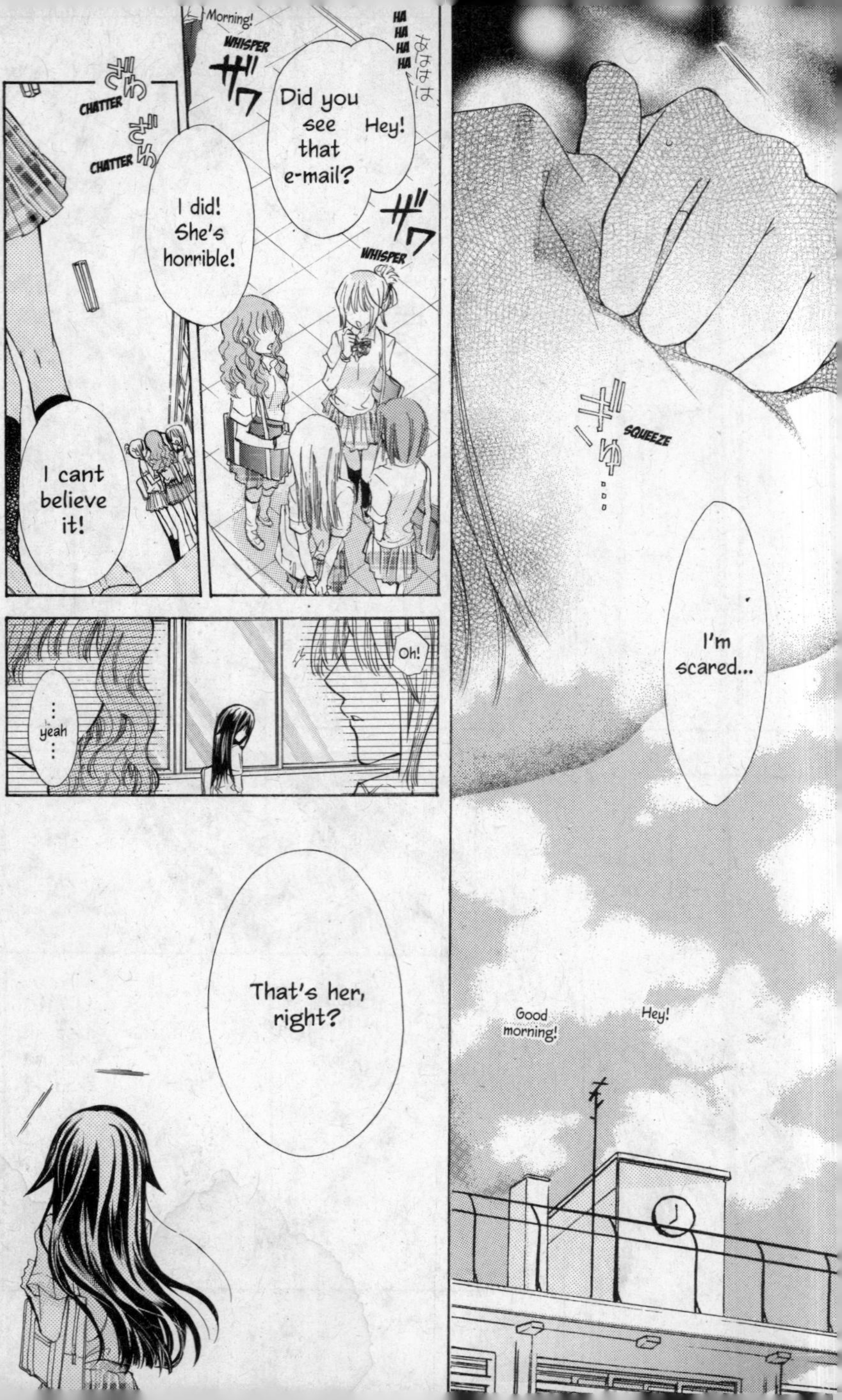

ギゅ…
SQUEEZE
I'm scared...
Hey!
Good morning!
あははは
HA HA HA HA
Hey!
Did you see that e-mail?
ザワ
WHISPER
Morning!
ザワ
WHISPER
ざわざわ
CHATTER
CHATTER
I did! She's horrible!
I cant believe it!
Oh!
...yeah...
That's her, right?

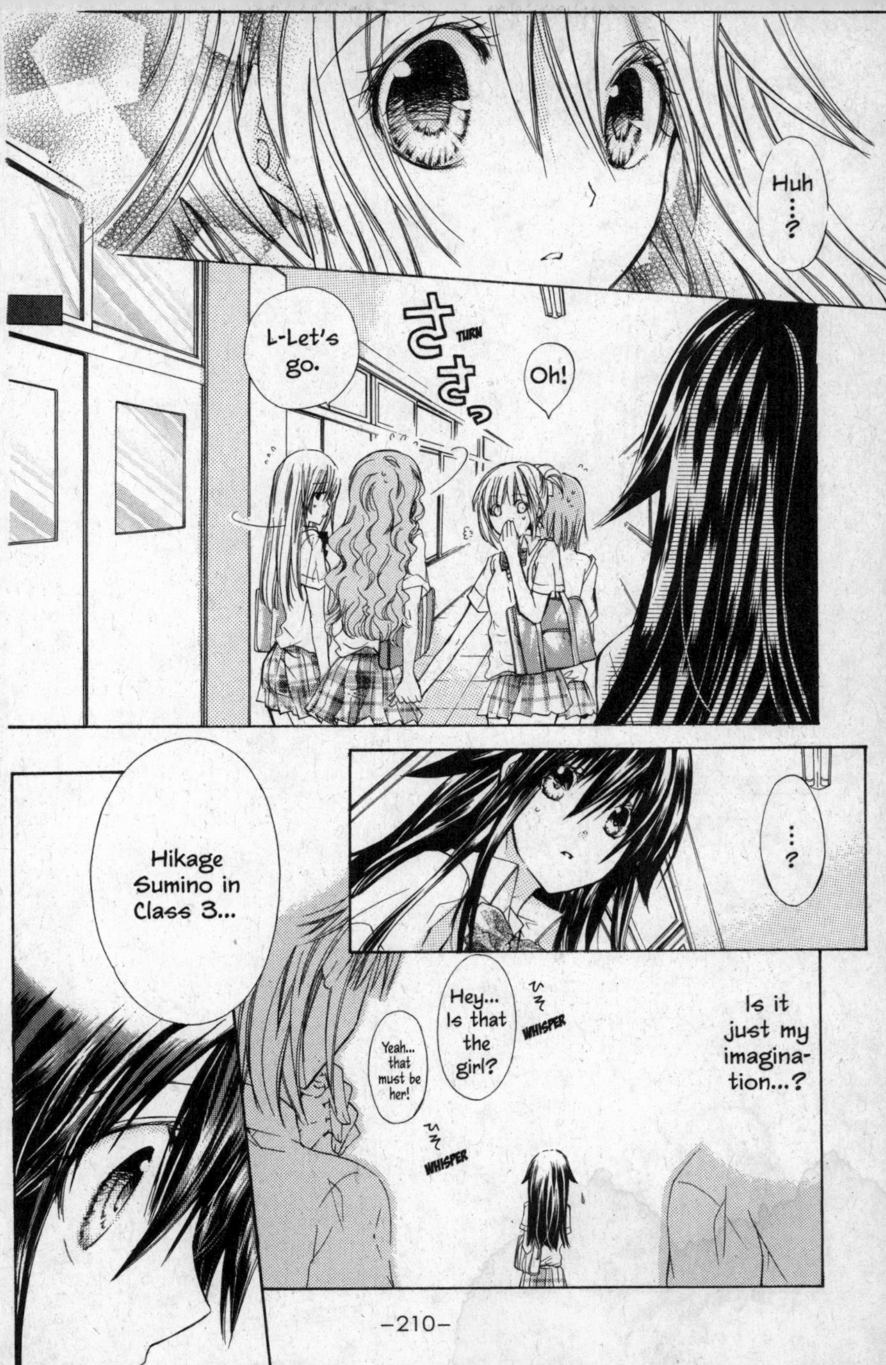
Huh...?
Oh!
さっ TURN
L-Let's go.
...?
Is it just my imagination...?
ひそ WHISPER
Hey... Is that the girl?
Yeah... that must be her!
ひそ WHISPER
Hikage Sumino in Class 3...

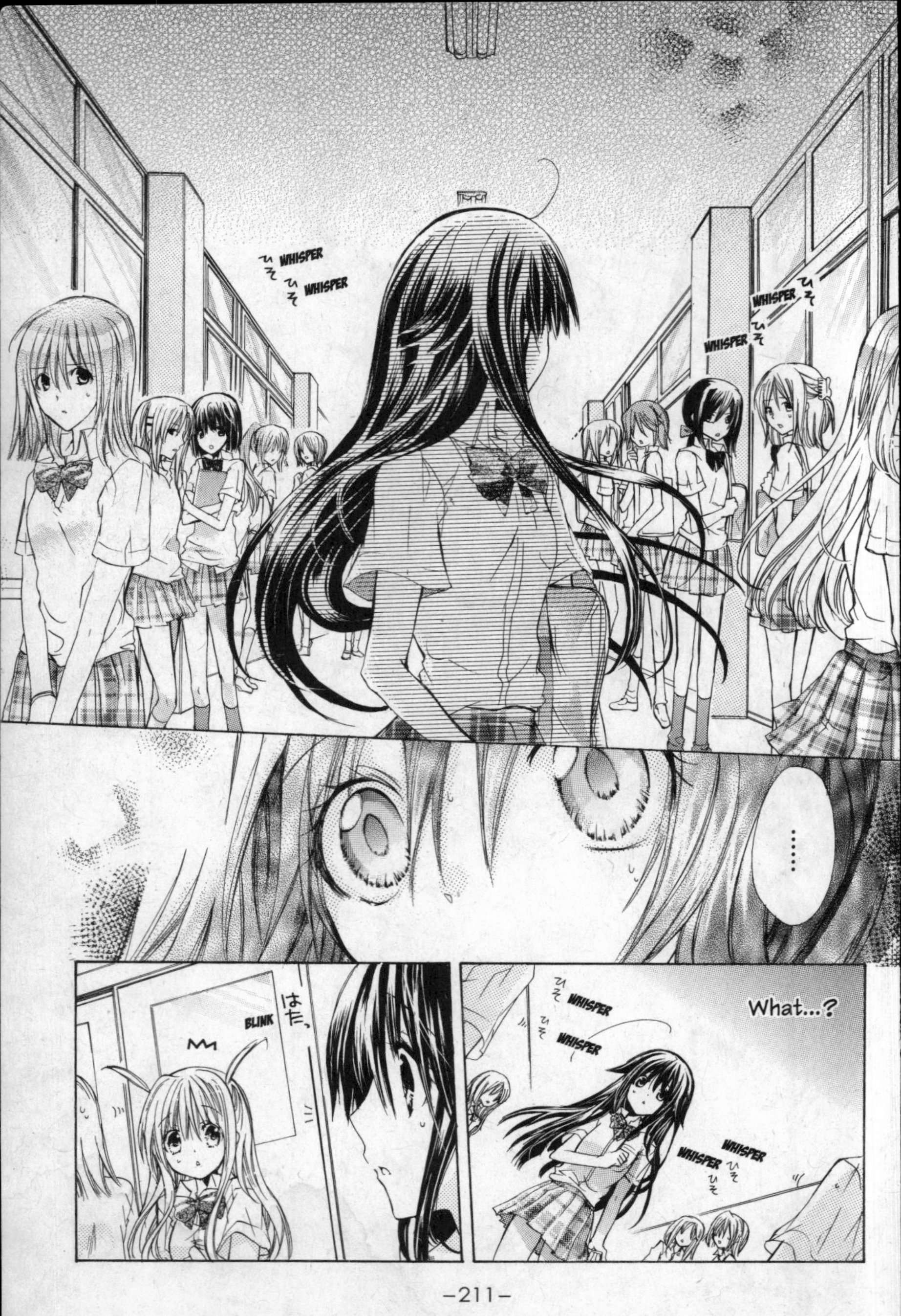
WHISPER ひそ
WHISPER ひそ
ひそ WHISPER
ひそ WHISPER
......
What...?
ひそ WHISPER
ひそ WHISPER
WHISPER ひそ
WHISPER ひそ
はたっ
BLINK

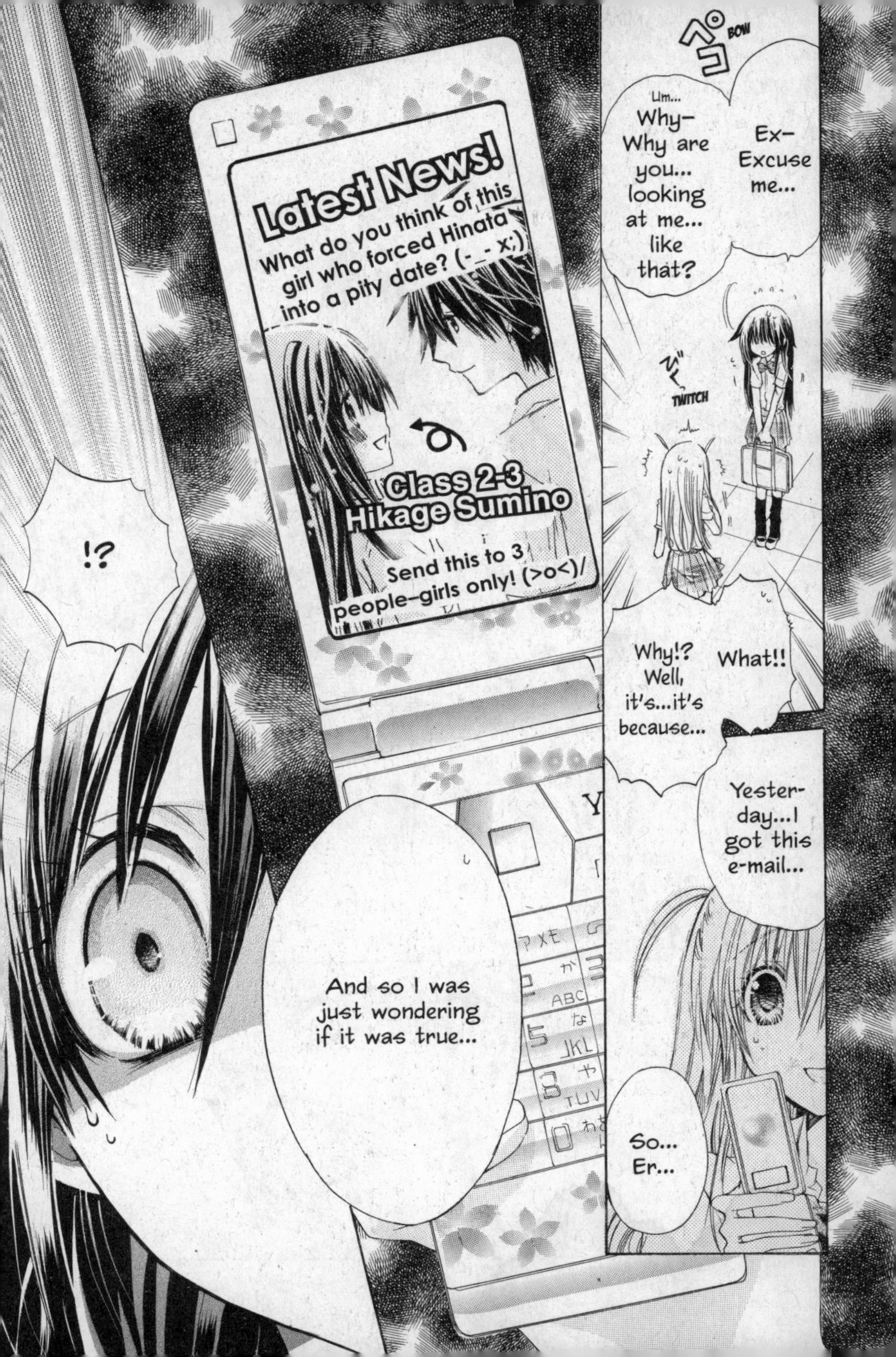
BOW
Ex– Excuse me...
Um... Why– Why are you... looking at me... like that?
TWITCH
What!!
Why!? Well, it's...it's because...
Yester-day...I got this e-mail...
So... Er...
Latest News!
What do you think of this girl who forced Hinata into a pity date? (-_- x;)
Class 2-3 Hikage Sumino
Send this to 3 people–girls only! (>o<)/
!?
And so I was just wondering if it was true...

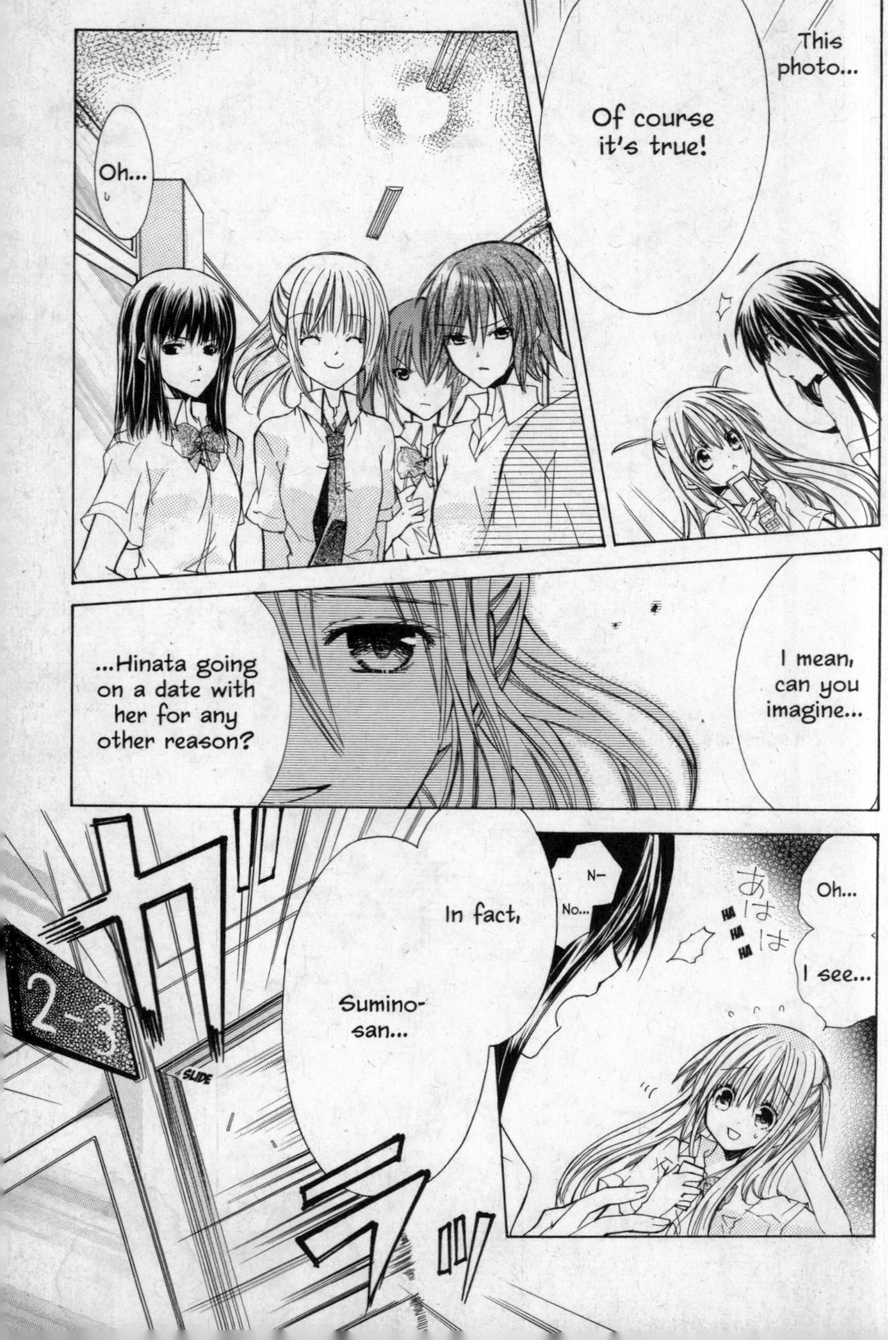
This photo...
Of course it's true!
Oh...
I mean, can you imagine...
...Hinata going on a date with her for any other reason?
Oh...
I see...
あはは
HA HA HA
N-
No...
In fact,
Sumino-san...
2-3
SLIDE

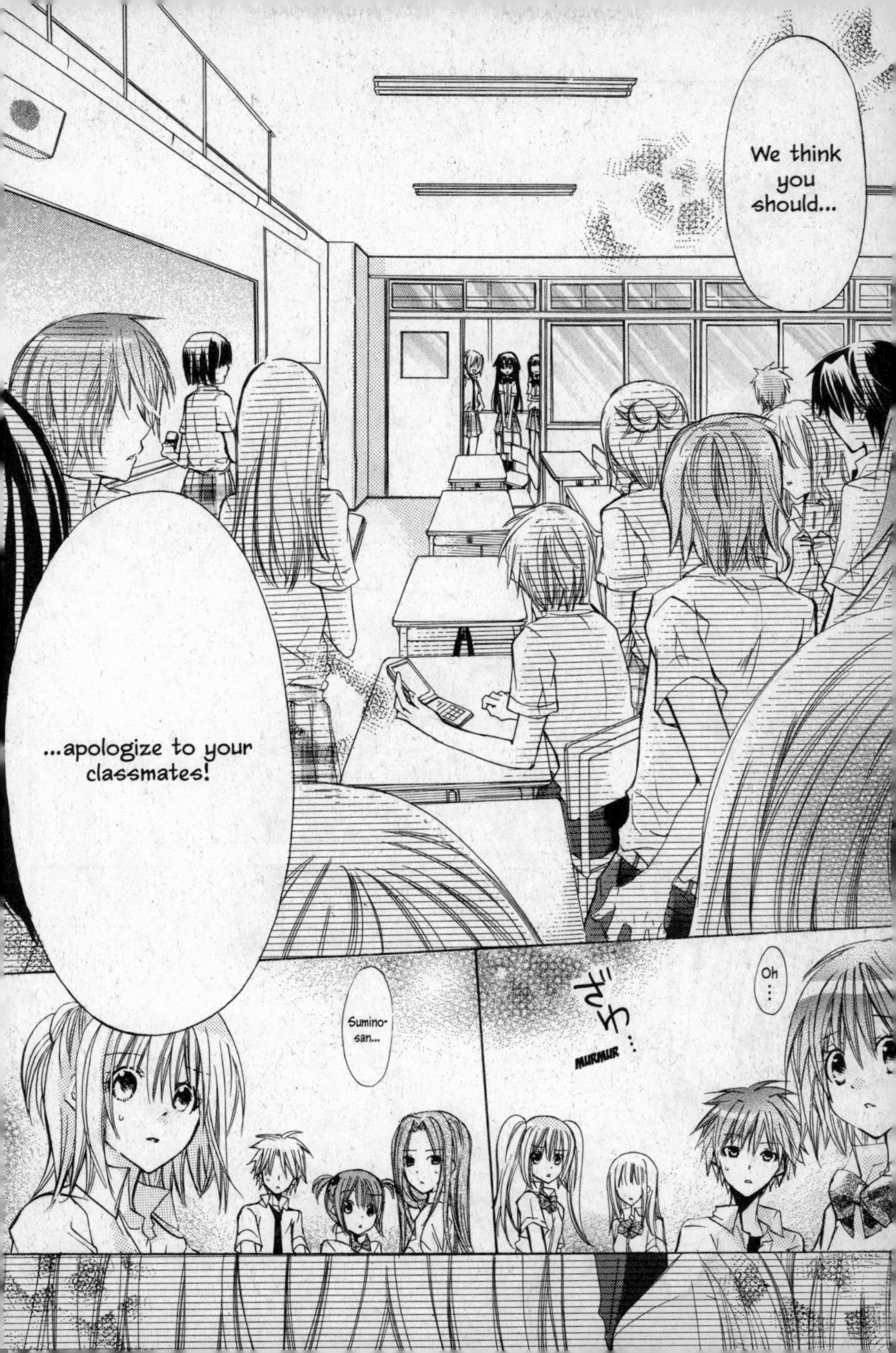
We think you should...
...apologize to your classmates!
Oh...
ざわ…
MURMUR
Sumino-san...

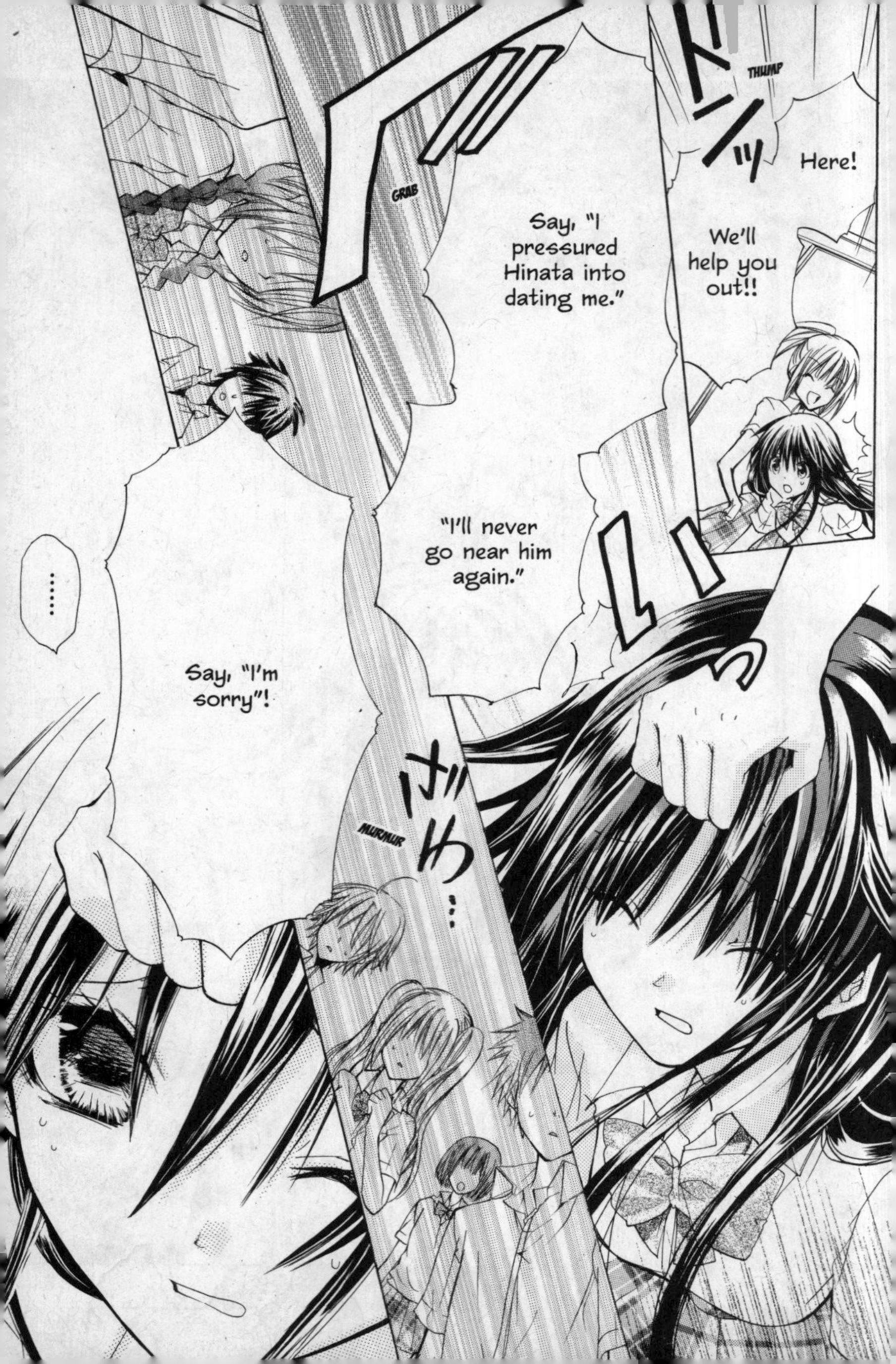
THUMP
Here!
We'll help you out!!
GRAB
Say, "I pressured Hinata into dating me."
"I'll never go near him again."
Say, "I'm sorry"!
......
MURMUR

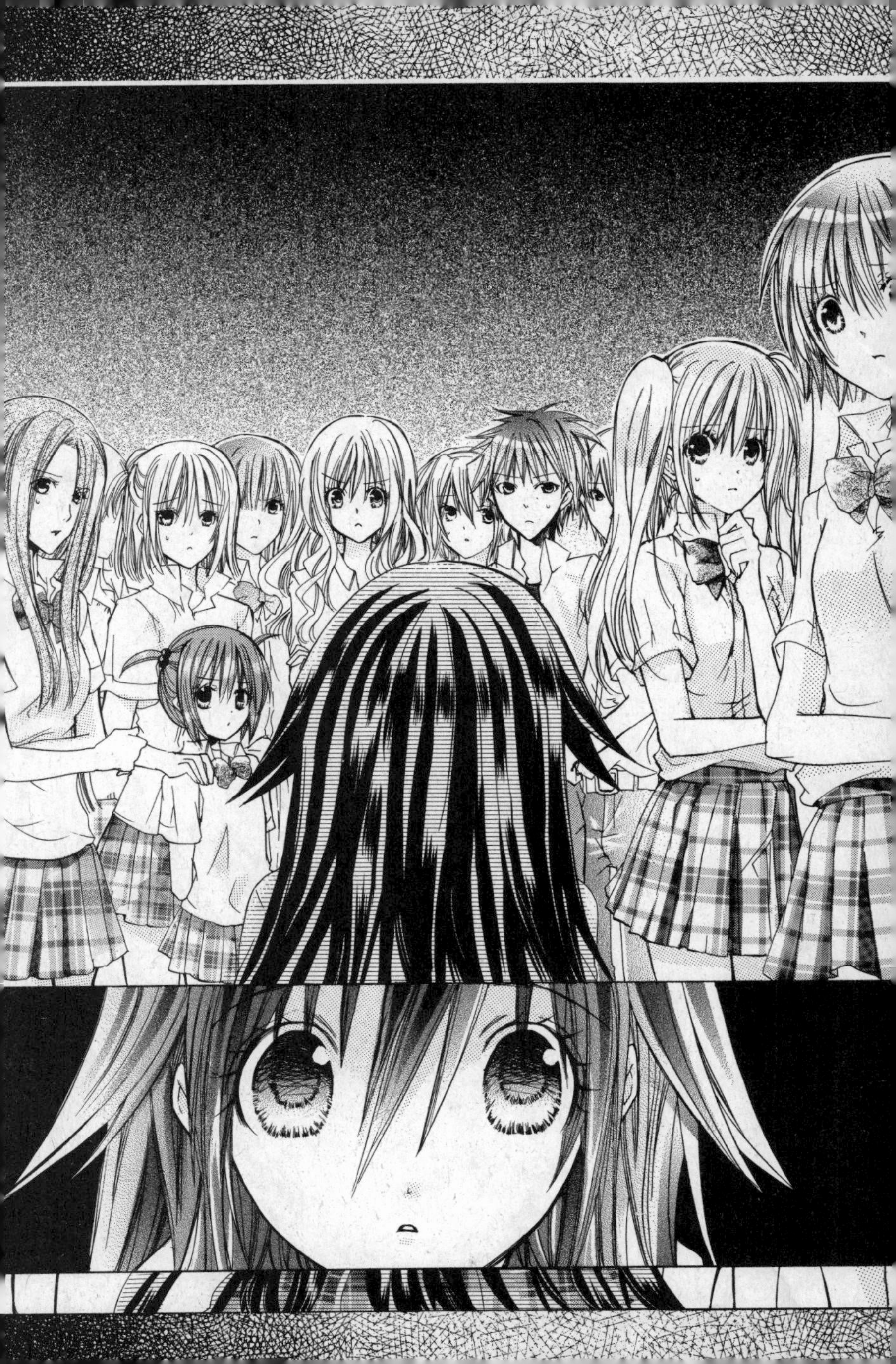

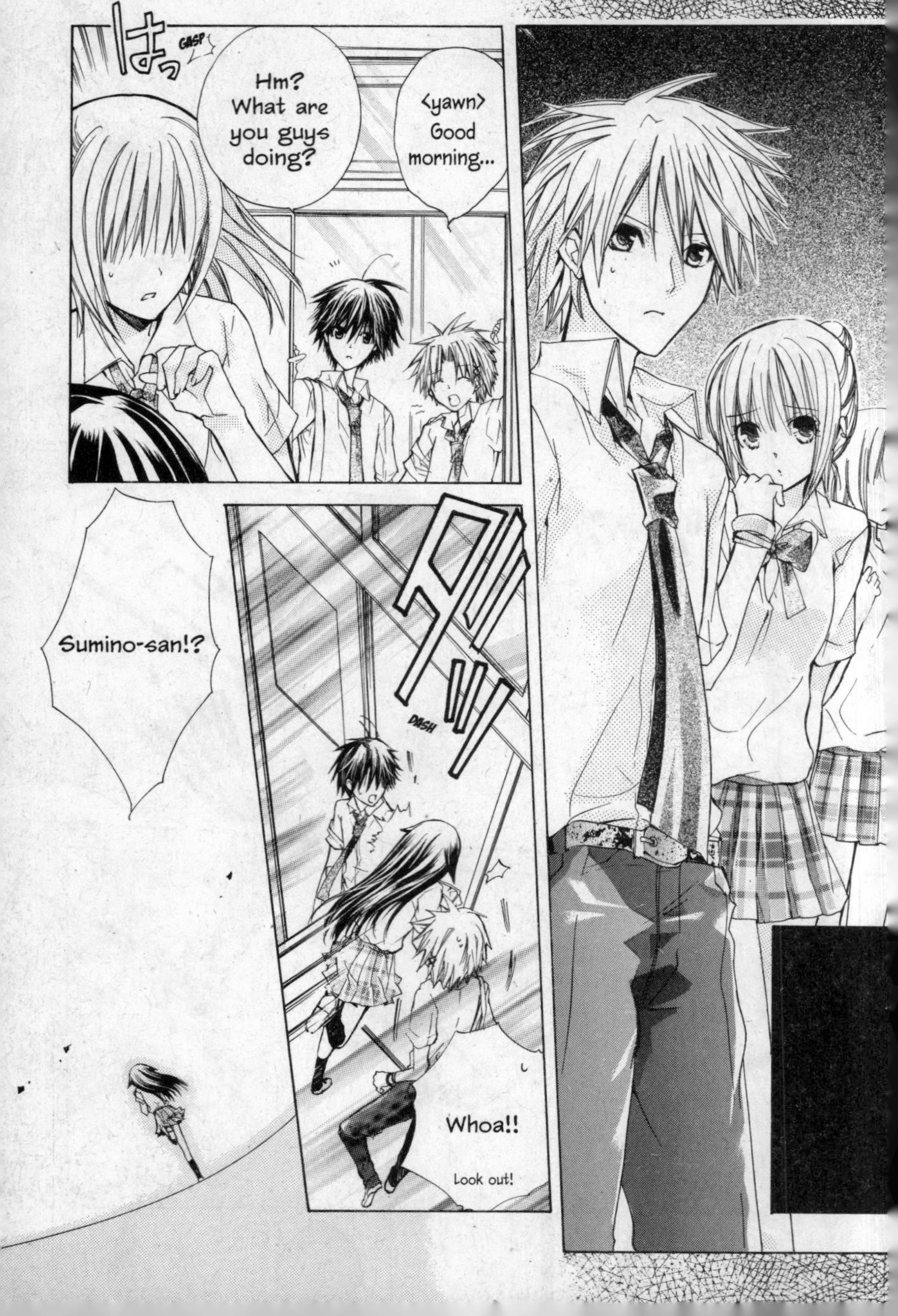
<yawn> Good morning...
Hm? What are you guys doing?
はっ
GASP
DASH
Whoa!!
Look out!
Sumino-san!?

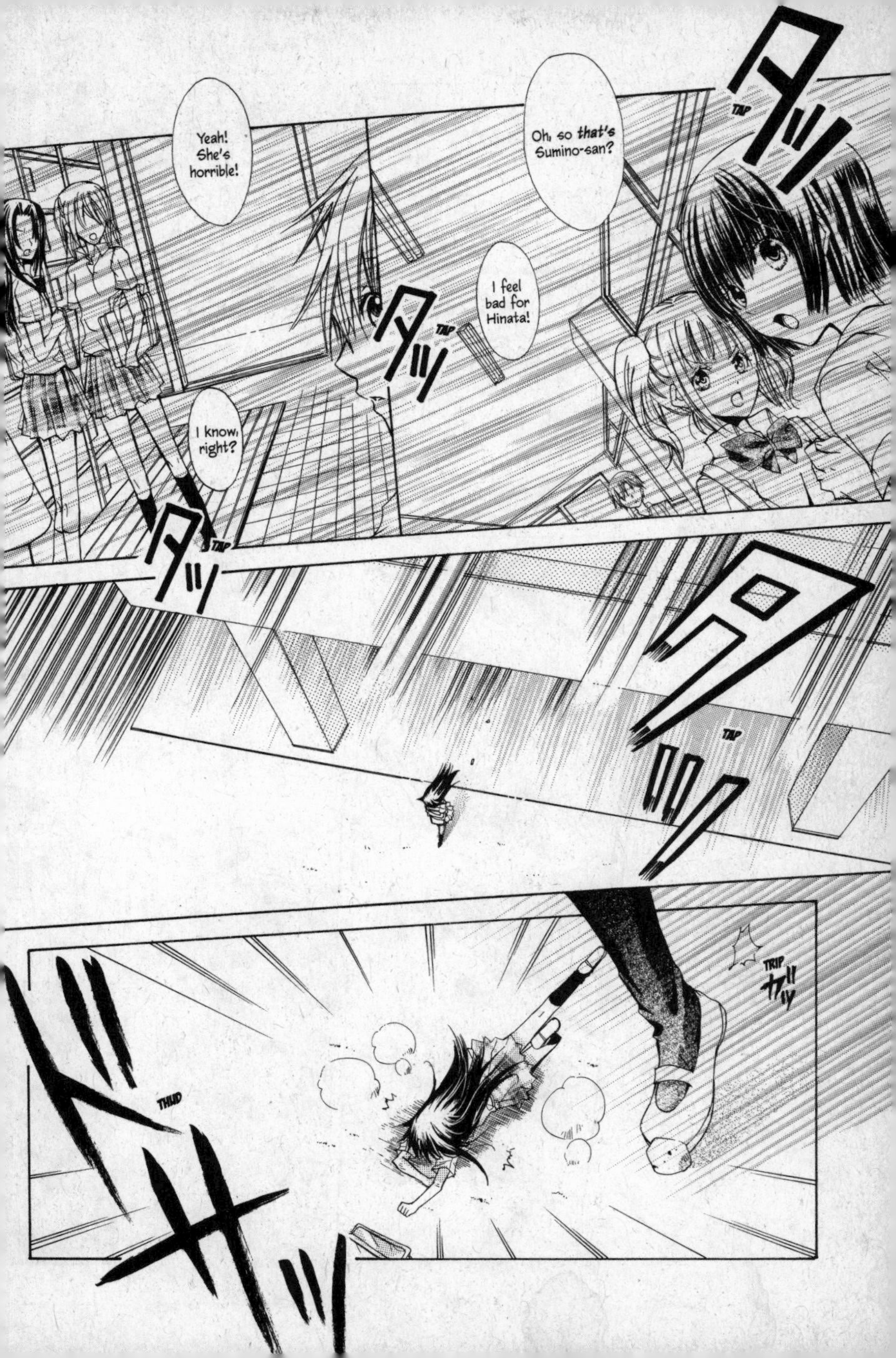

TAP
Oh, so *that's* Sumino-san?
I feel bad for Hinata!
TAP
Yeah! She's horrible!
I know, right?
TAP
TAP
TRIP
THUD

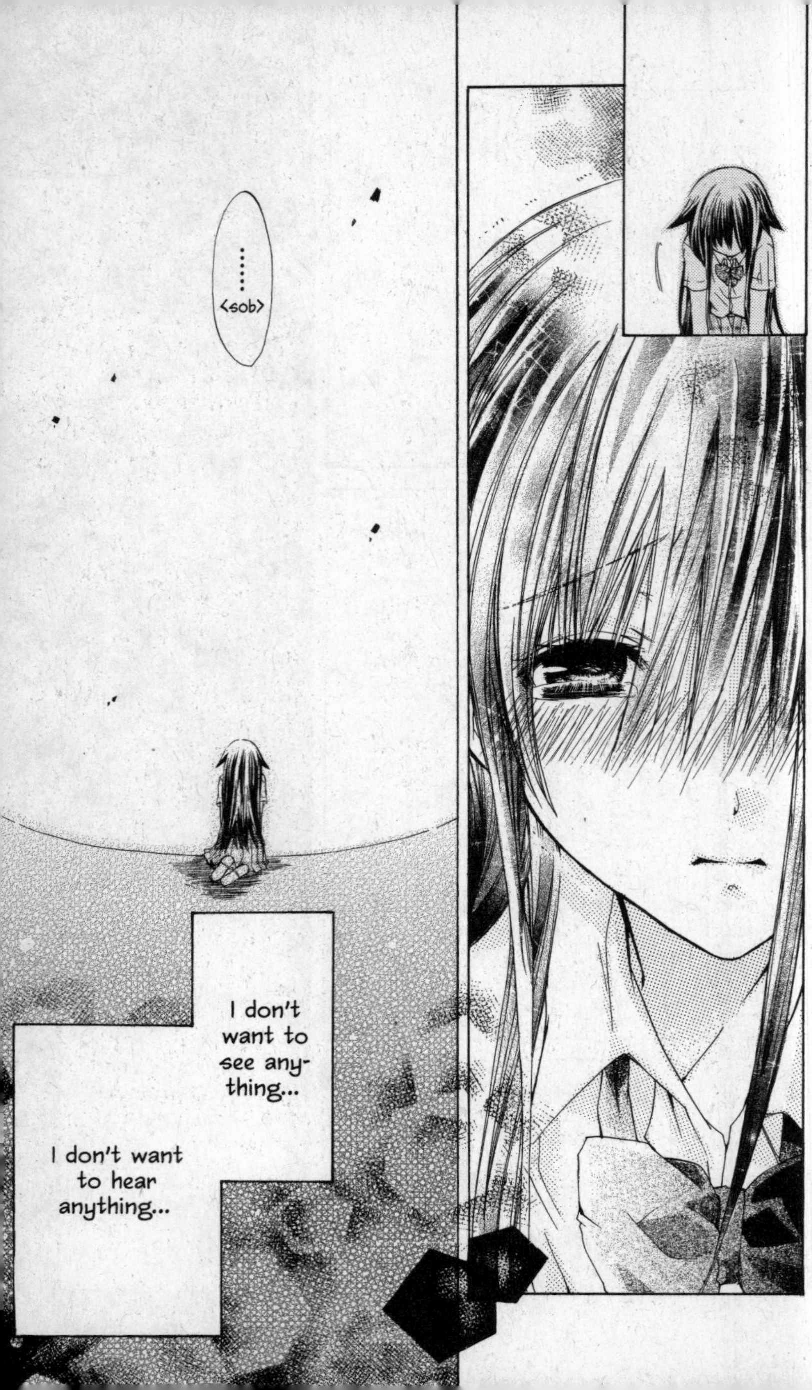
......
<sob>
I don't want to see any-thing...
I don't want to hear anything...

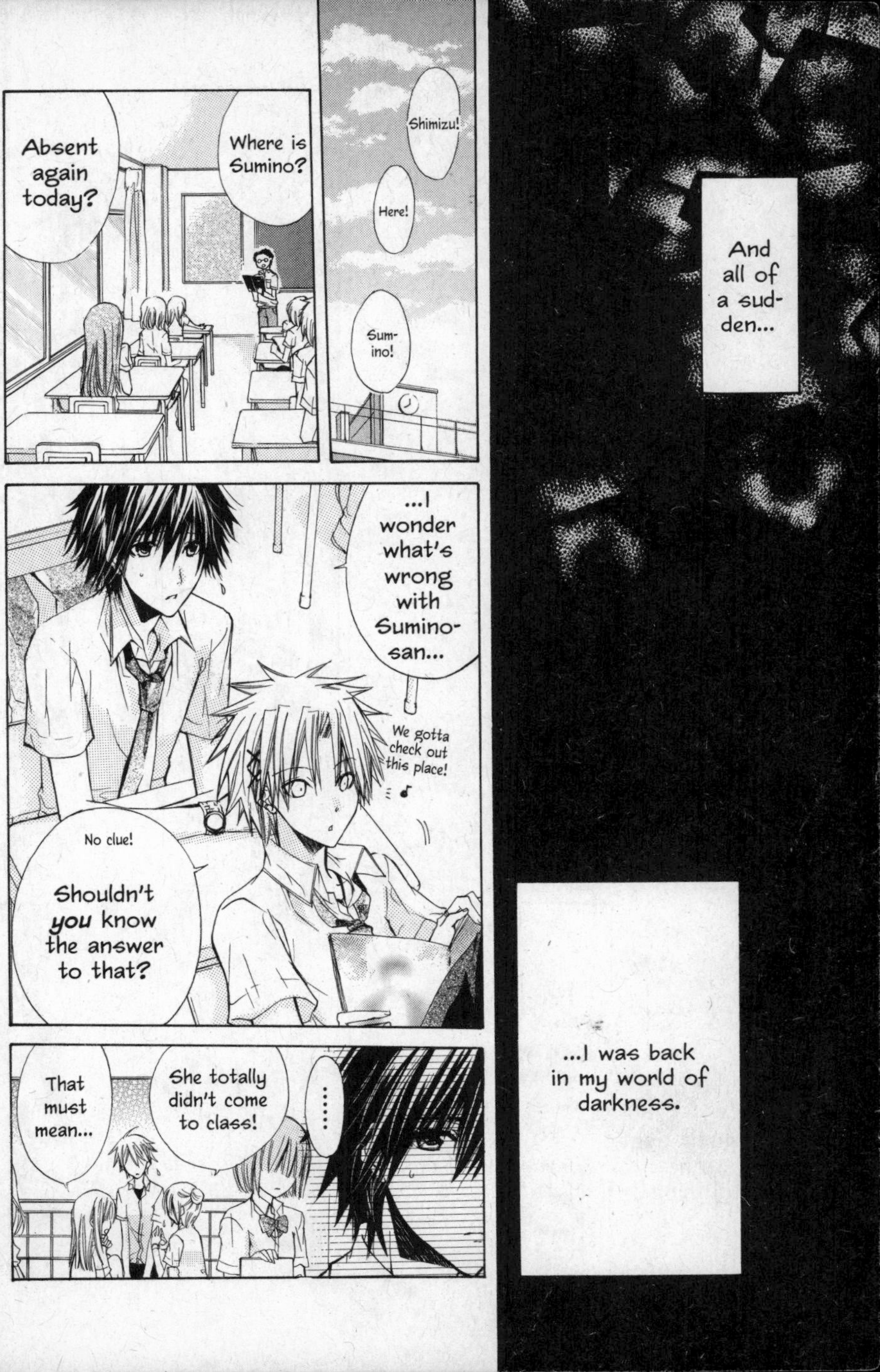
And all of a sud-den...
...I was back in my world of darkness.
Shimizu!
Here!
Sum-ino!
Where is Sumino?
Absent again today?
...I wonder what's wrong with Sumino-san...
We gotta check out this place!
No clue!
Shouldn't *you* know the answer to that?
......
She totally didn't come to class!
That must mean...

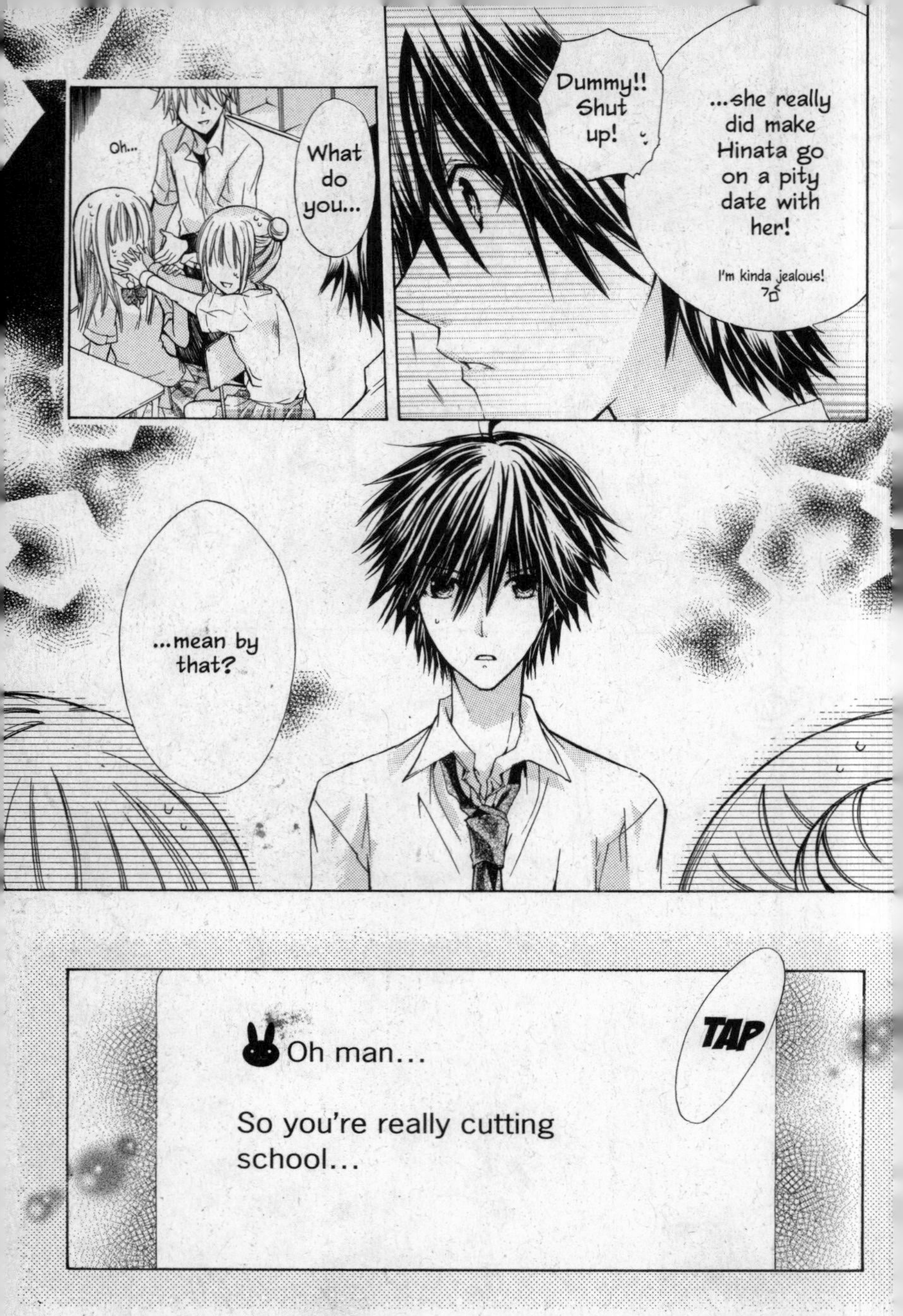
...she really did make Hinata go on a pity date with her!
I'm kinda jealous!
Dummy!! Shut up!
What do you...
Oh...
...mean by that?
TAP
Oh man...
So you're really cutting school...

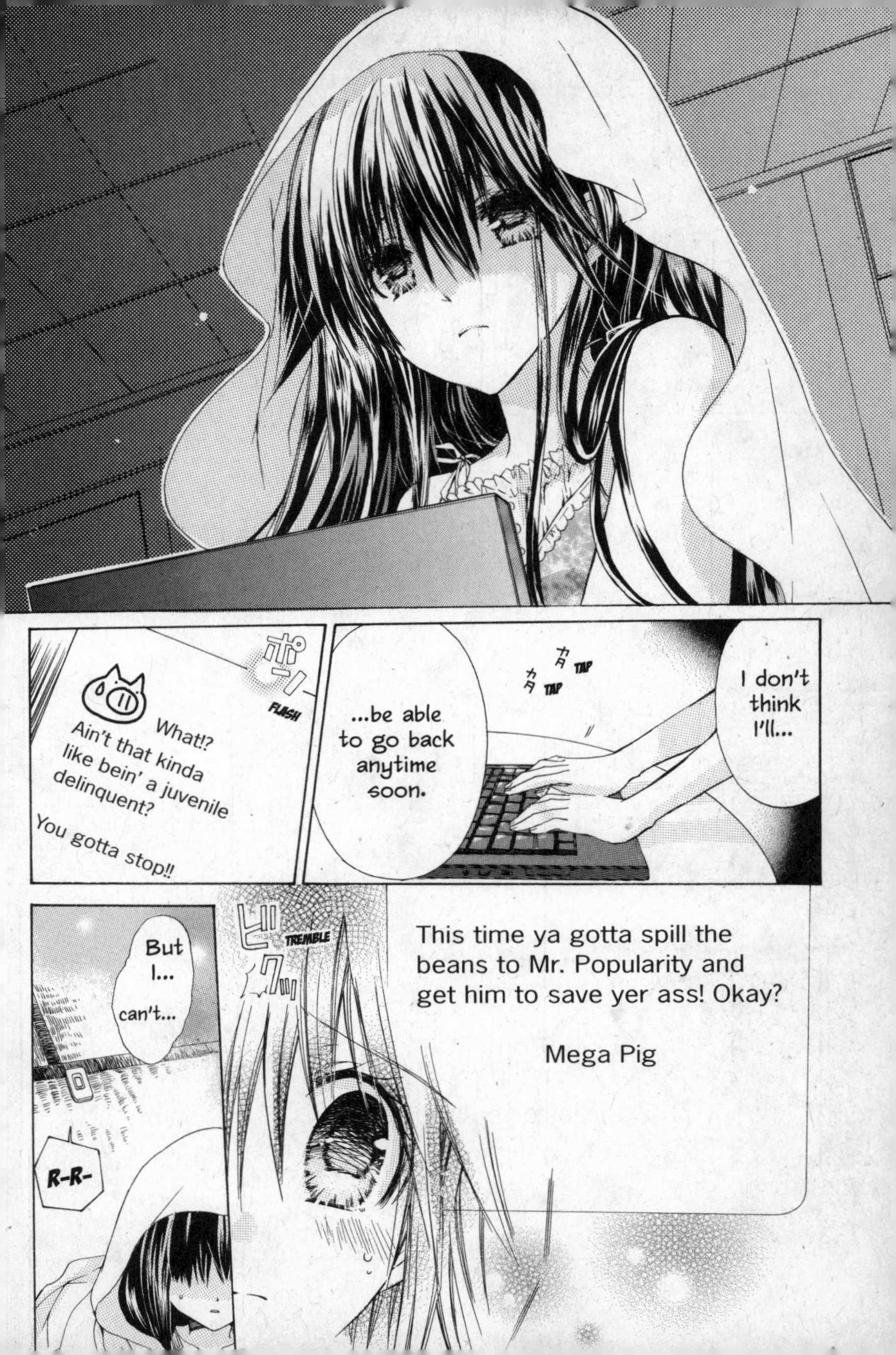
I don't think I'll...
TAP TAP
...be able to go back anytime soon.
FLASH
What!? Ain't that kinda like bein' a juvenile delinquent?
You gotta stop!!
TREMBLE
This time ya gotta spill the beans to Mr. Popularity and get him to save yer ass! Okay?
Mega Pig
But I... can't...
R-R-

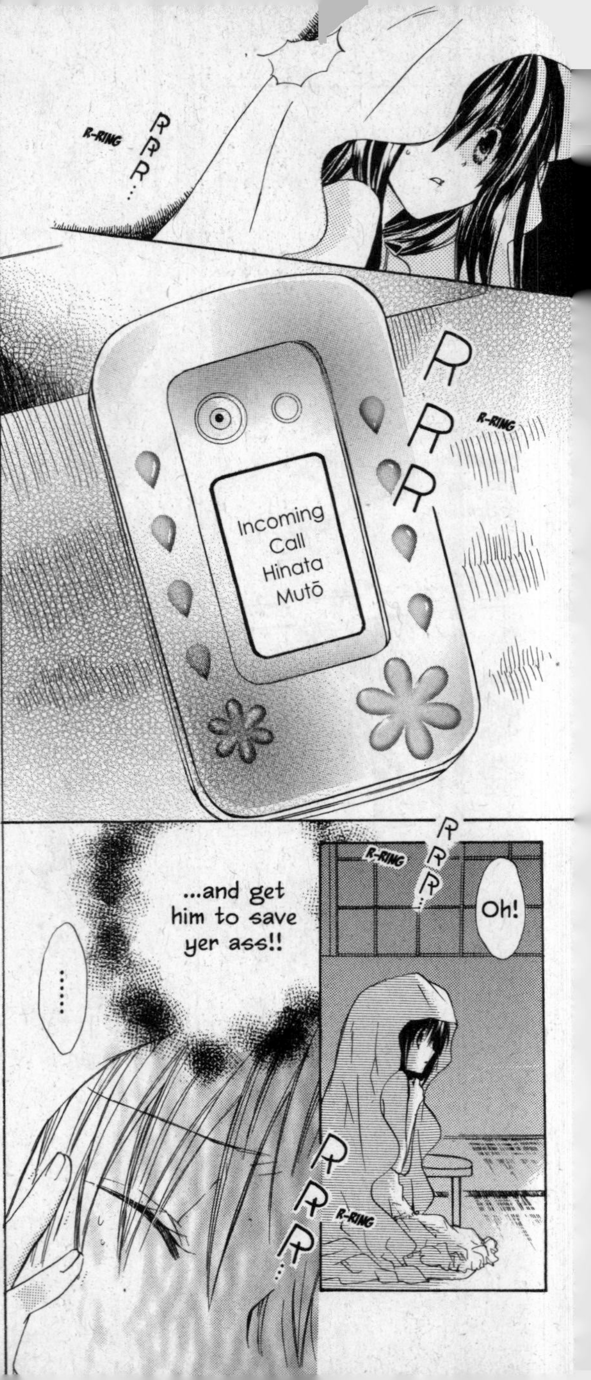
RRR...
R-RING
RRR
R-RING
Incoming Call Hinata Mutō
RRR...
R-RING
Oh!
...and get him to save yer ass!!
......
RRR...
R-RING

A No-Good Conversation

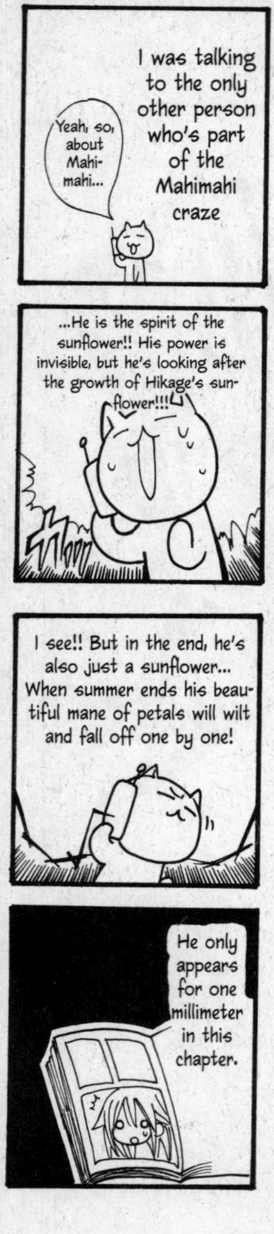
I was talking to the only other person who's part of the Mahimahi craze
Yeah, so, about Mahi-mahi...
...He is the spirit of the sunflower!! His power is invisible, but he's looking after the growth of Hikage's sun-flower!!!
I see!! But in the end, he's also just a sunflower... When summer ends his beau-tiful mane of petals will wilt and fall off one by one!
He only appears for one millimeter in this chapter.

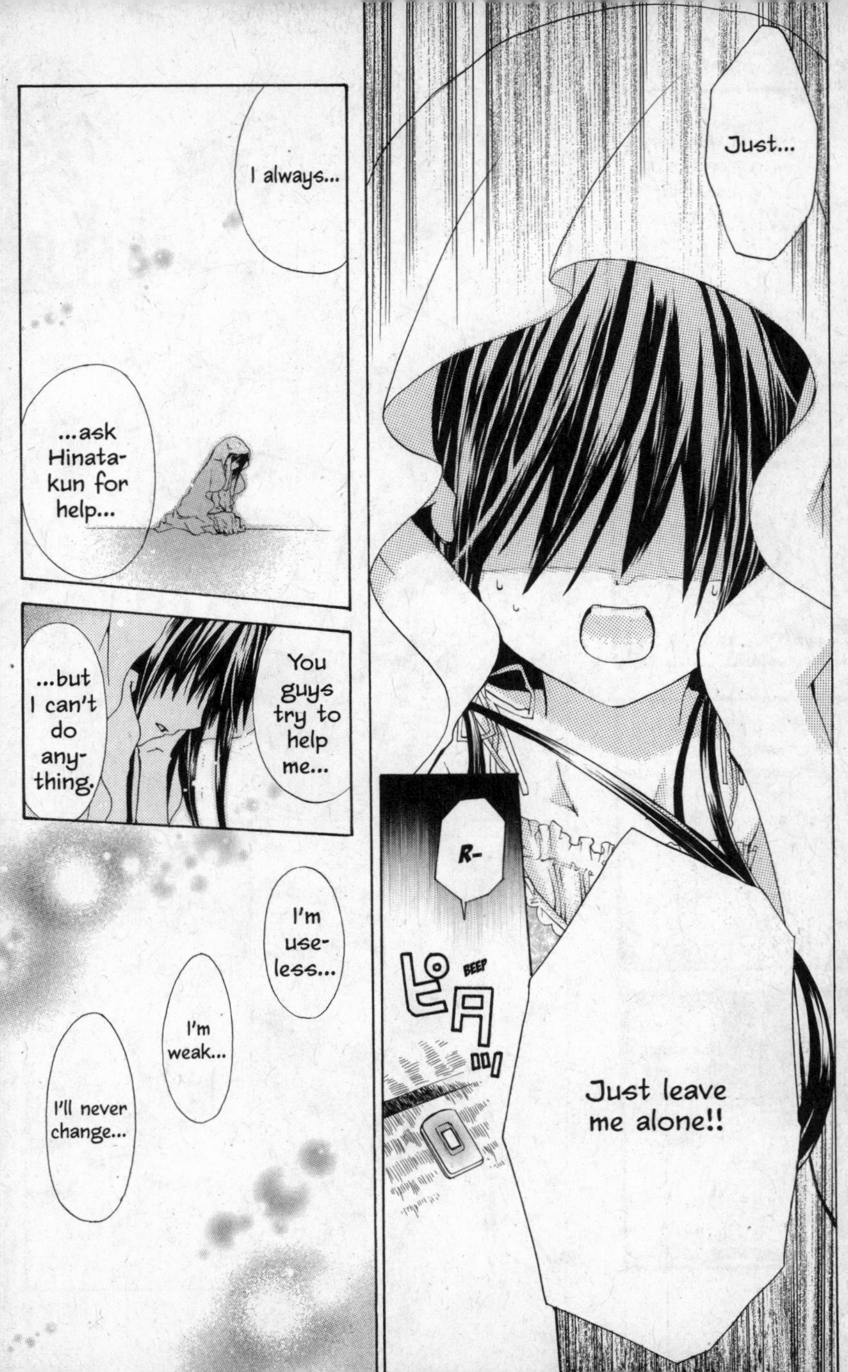
Just...
R-
BEEP
Just leave me alone!!
I always...
...ask Hinata-kun for help...
You guys try to help me...
...but I can't do anything.
I'm useless...
I'm weak...
I'll never change...

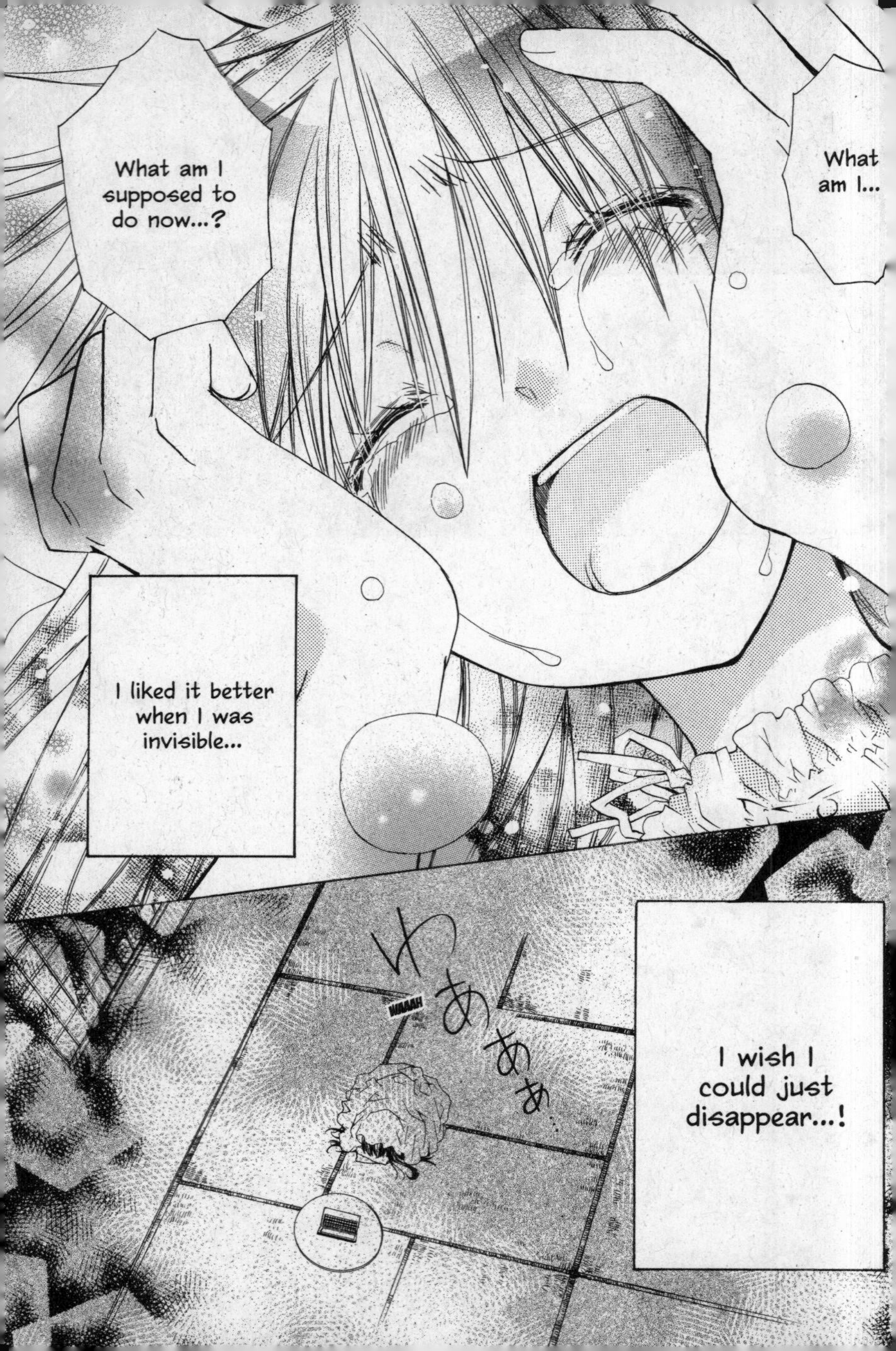
What am I...
What am I supposed to do now...?
I liked it better when I was invisible...
I wish I could just disappear...!
わあああ
WAAAH

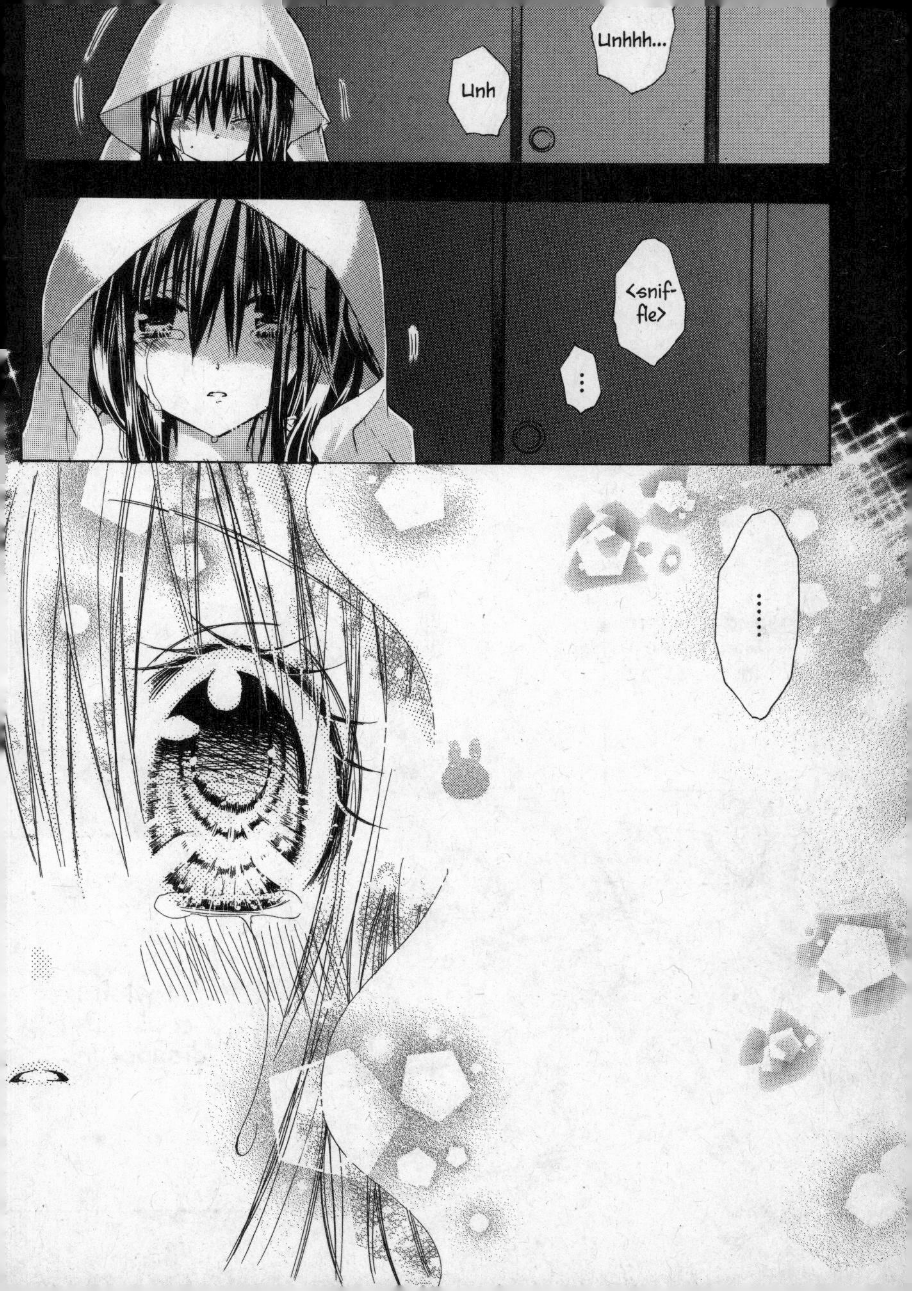
Unhhh...
Unh
<snif-fle>
...
......

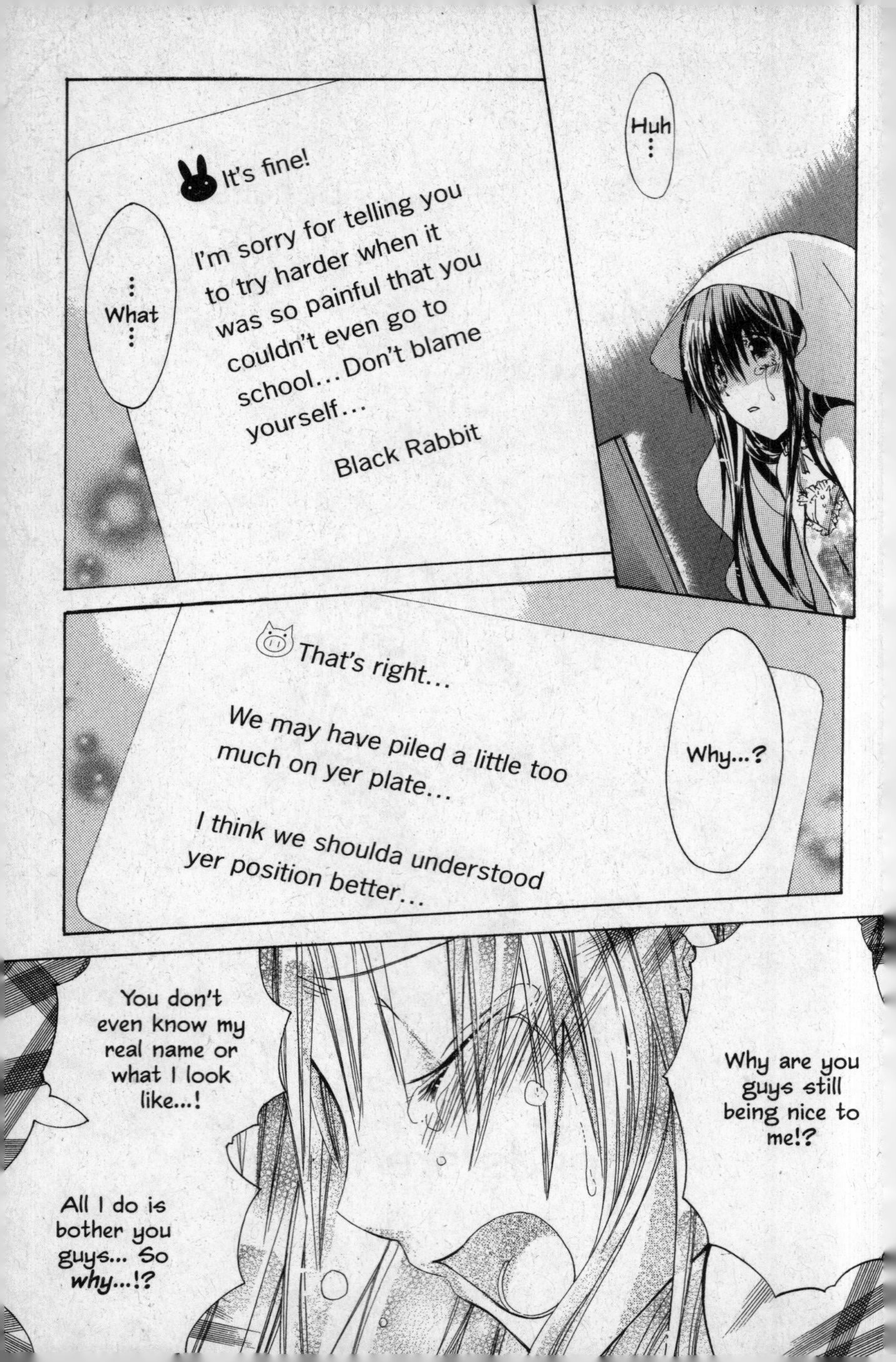
Huh...
It's fine!
I'm sorry for telling you to try harder when it was so painful that you couldn't even go to school... Don't blame yourself...
Black Rabbit
...What...
That's right...
We may have piled a little too much on yer plate...
I think we shoulda understood yer position better...
Why...?
Why are you guys still being nice to me!?
You don't even know my real name or what I look like...!
All I do is bother you guys... So *why*...!?

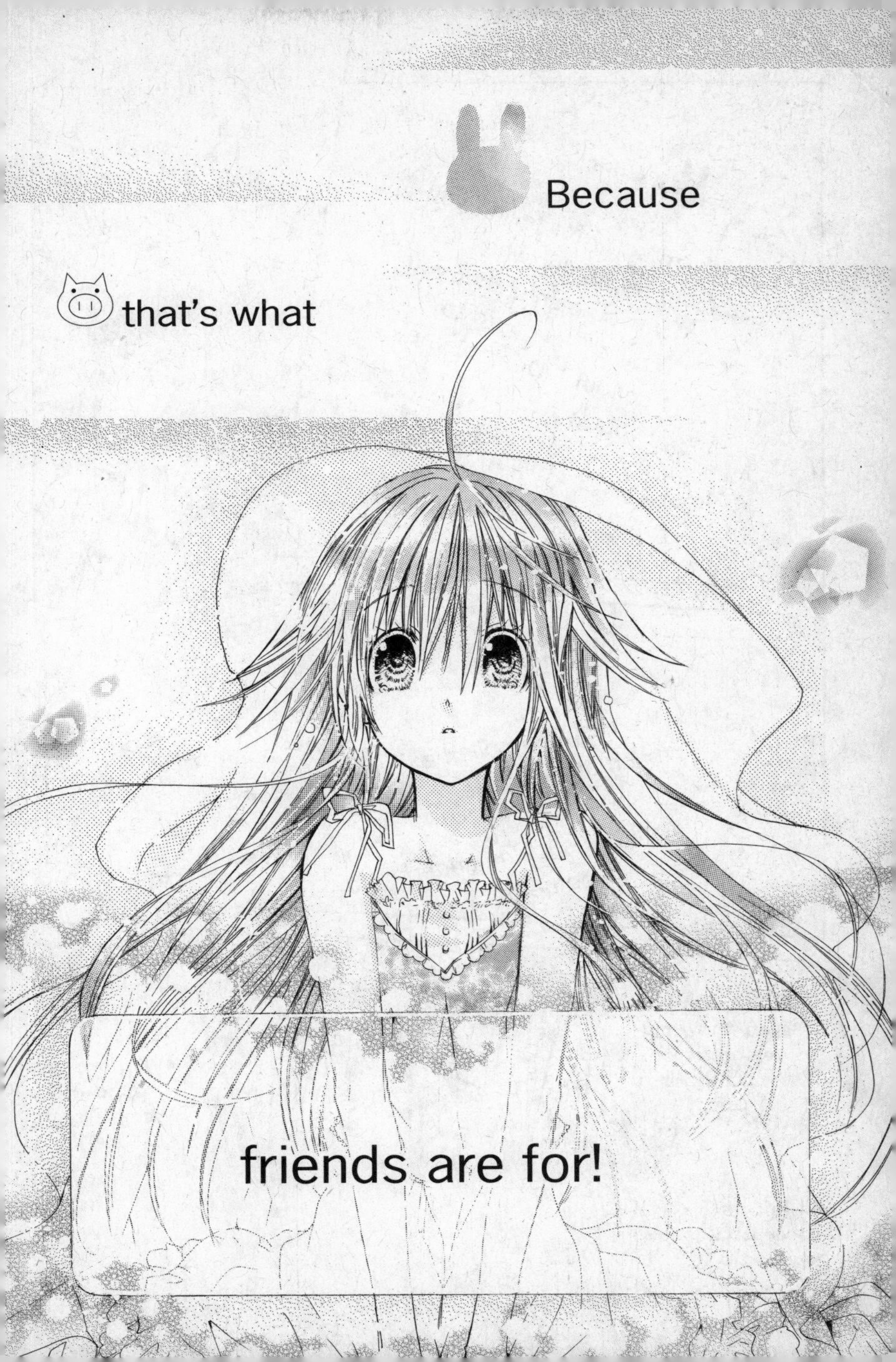
Because
that's what
friends are for!

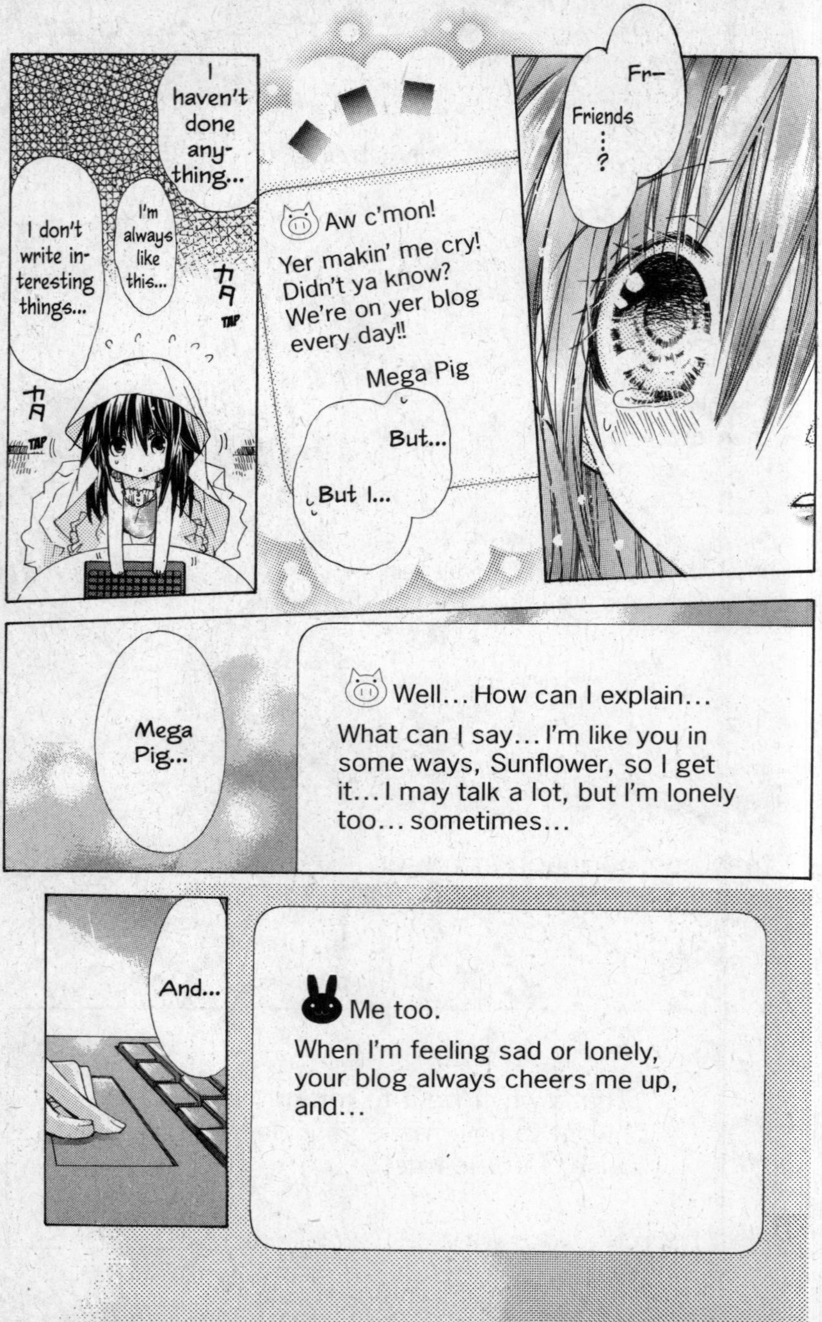
Fr— Friends...?
Aw c'mon!
Yer makin' me cry! Didn't ya know? We're on yer blog every day!!
Mega Pig
But...
But I...
I haven't done anything...
I'm always like this...
I don't write interesting things...
カタ
TAP
カタ
TAP
Well... How can I explain...
What can I say... I'm like you in some ways, Sunflower, so I get it... I may talk a lot, but I'm lonely too... sometimes...
Mega Pig...
Me too.
When I'm feeling sad or lonely, your blog always cheers me up, and...
And...

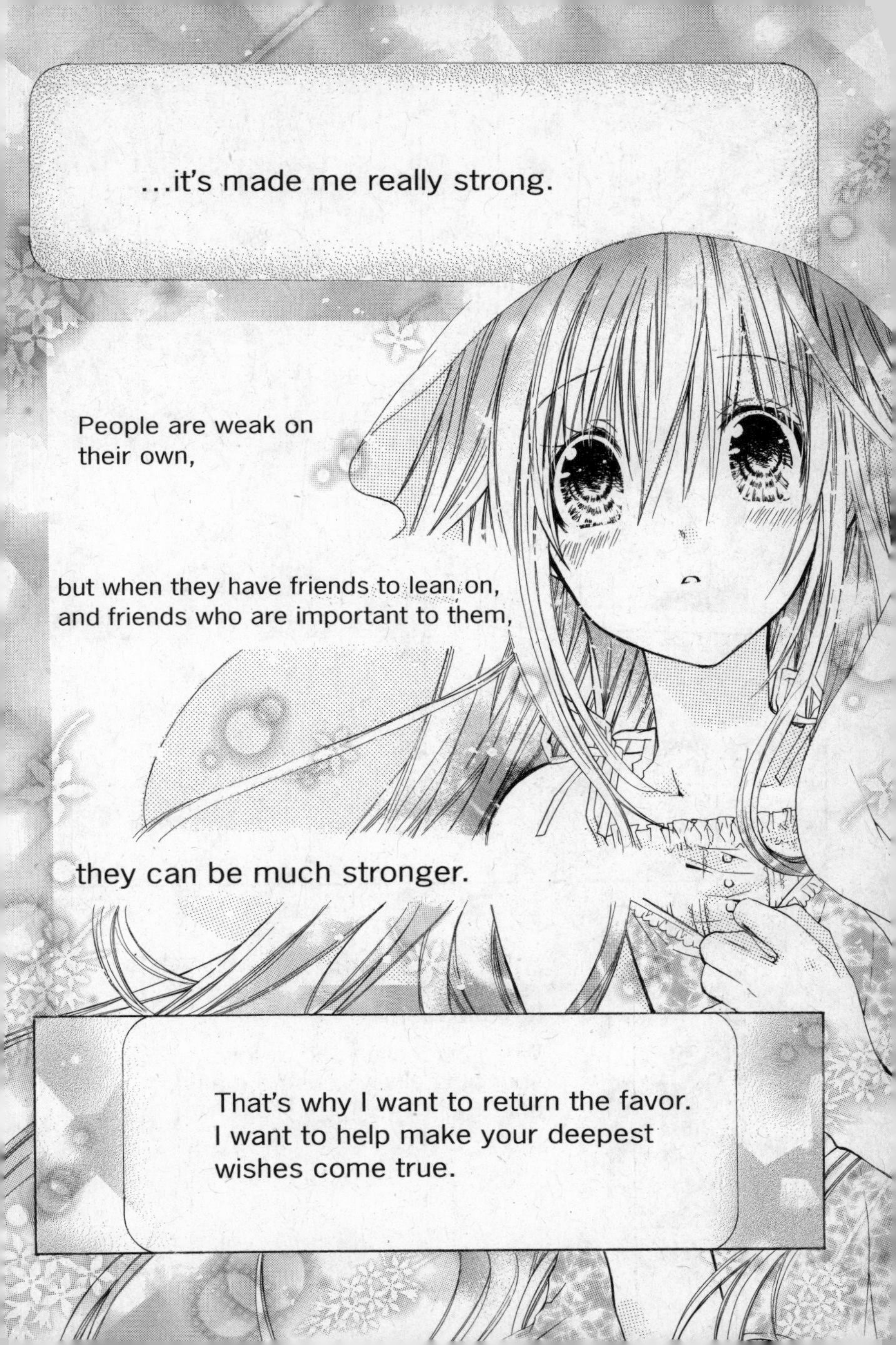
...it's made me really strong.
People are weak on their own,
but when they have friends to lean on, and friends who are important to them,
they can be much stronger.
That's why I want to return the favor. I want to help make your deepest wishes come true.

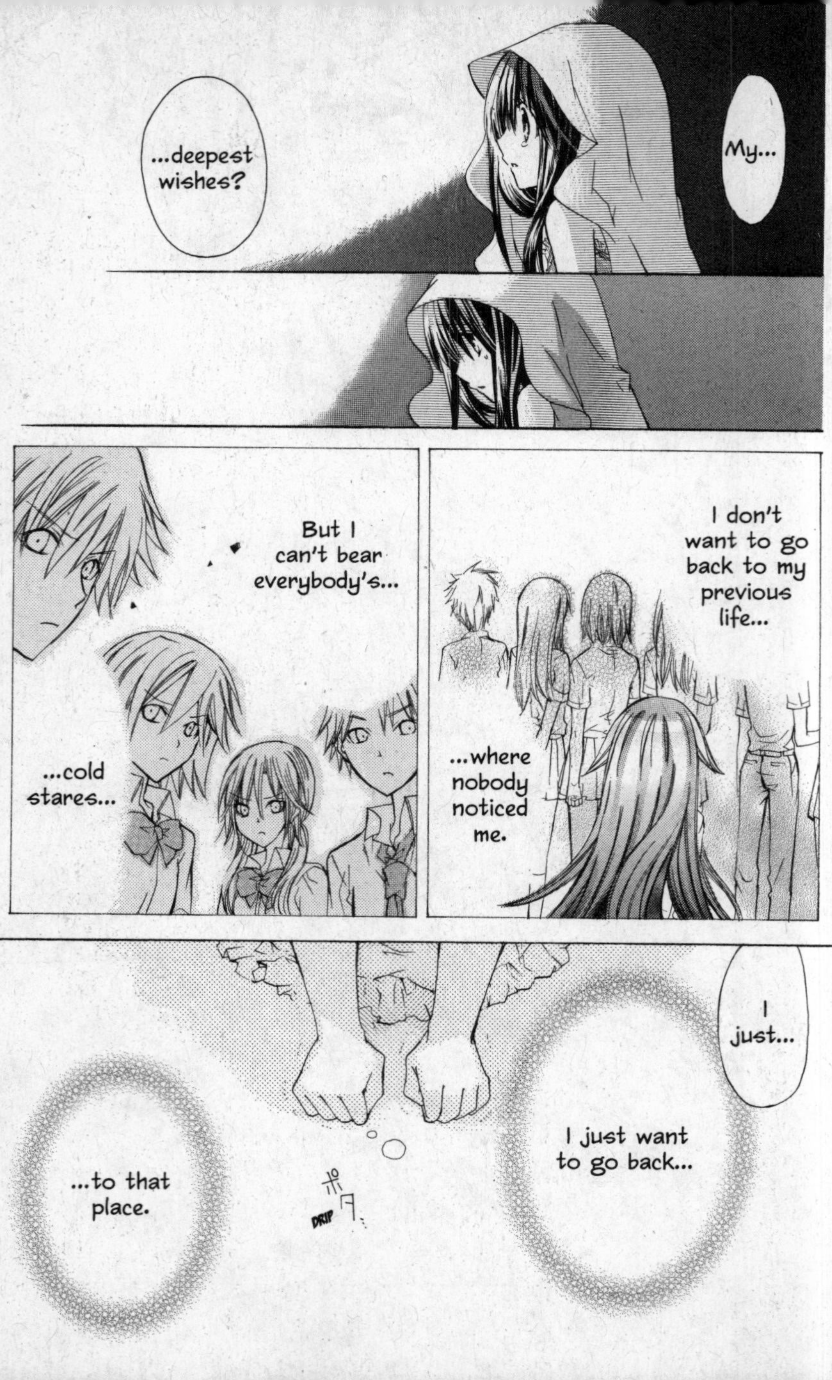
My...
...deepest wishes?
I don't want to go back to my previous life...
...where nobody noticed me.
But I can't bear everybody's...
...cold stares...
I just...
I just want to go back...
DRIP
...to that place.

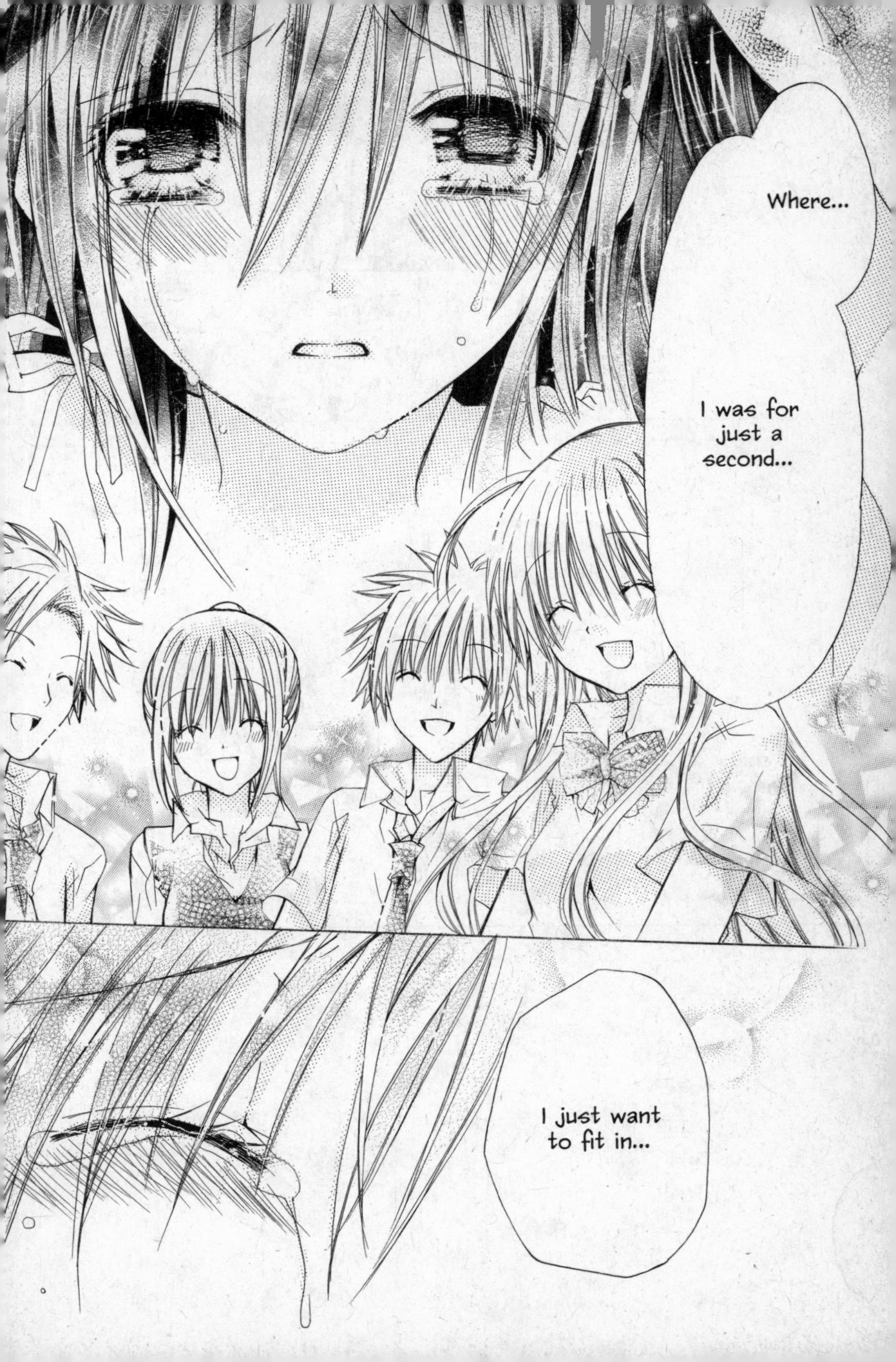
Where... I was for just a second...
I just want to fit in...

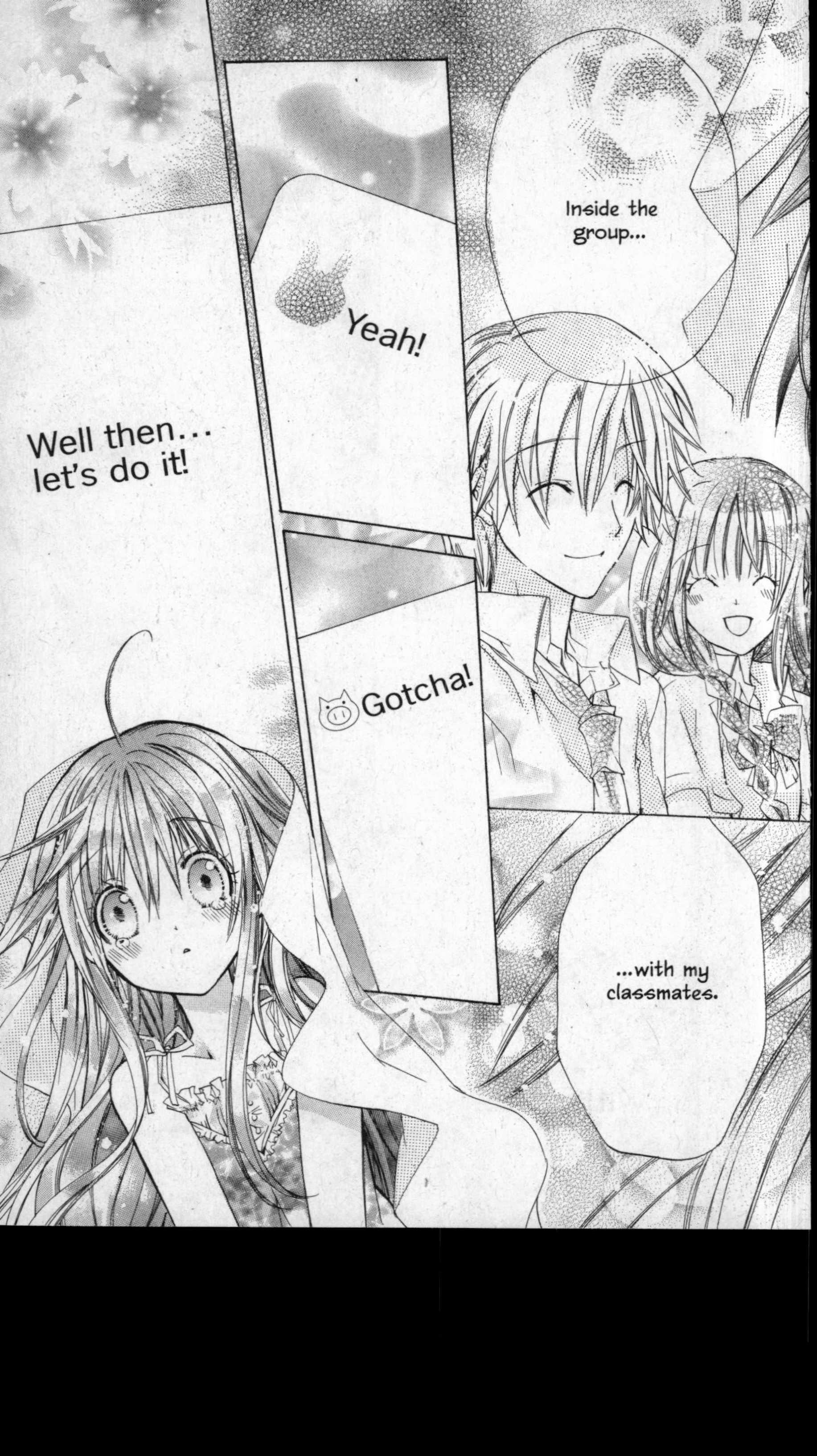
Inside the group...
Yeah!
Gotcha!
...with my classmates.
Well then... let's do it!

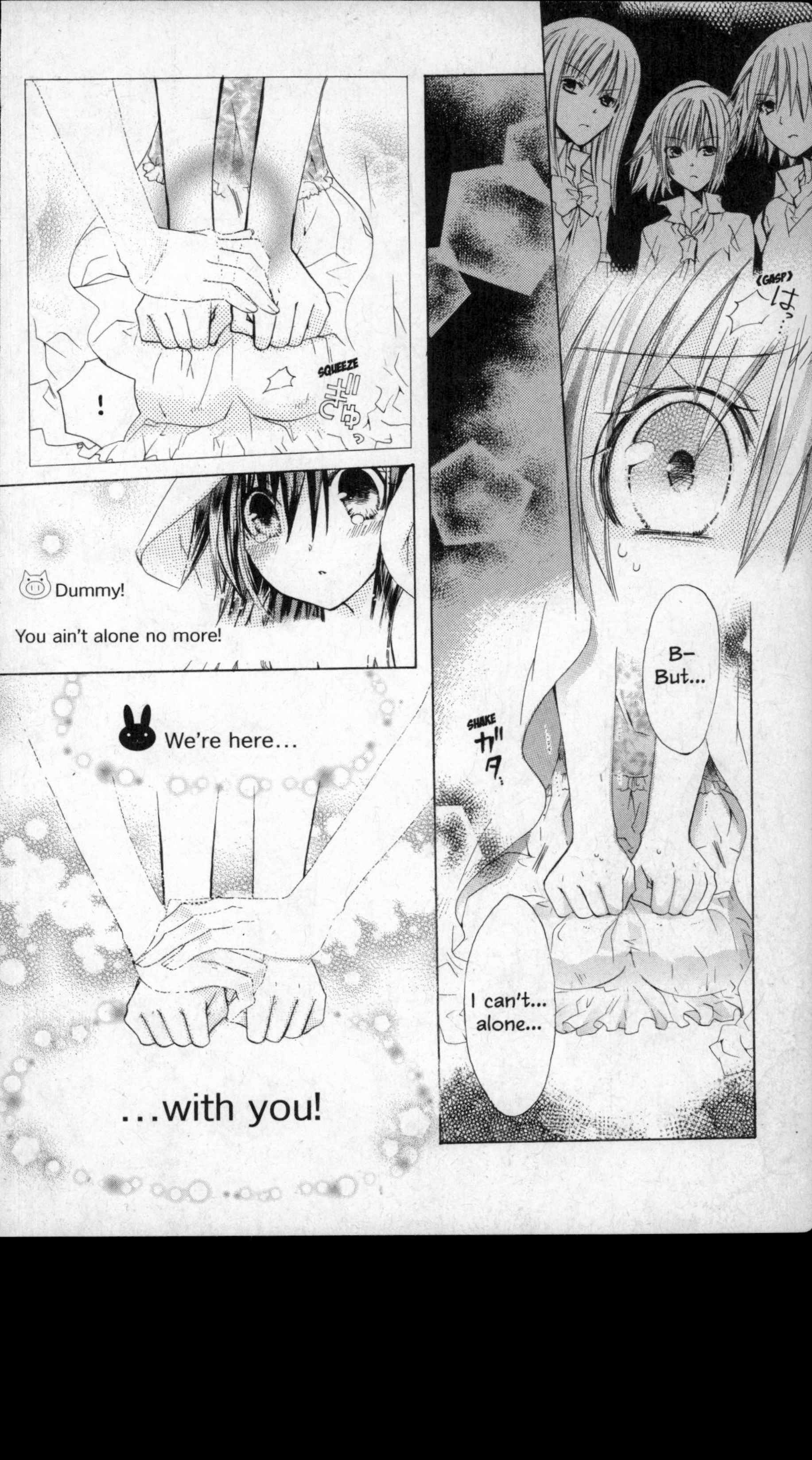
《GASP》
はっ…
B–
But…
SHAKE
ガタ
I can't…
alone…
SQUEEZE
ぎゅっ
!
Dummy!
You ain't alone no more!
We're here…
…with you!

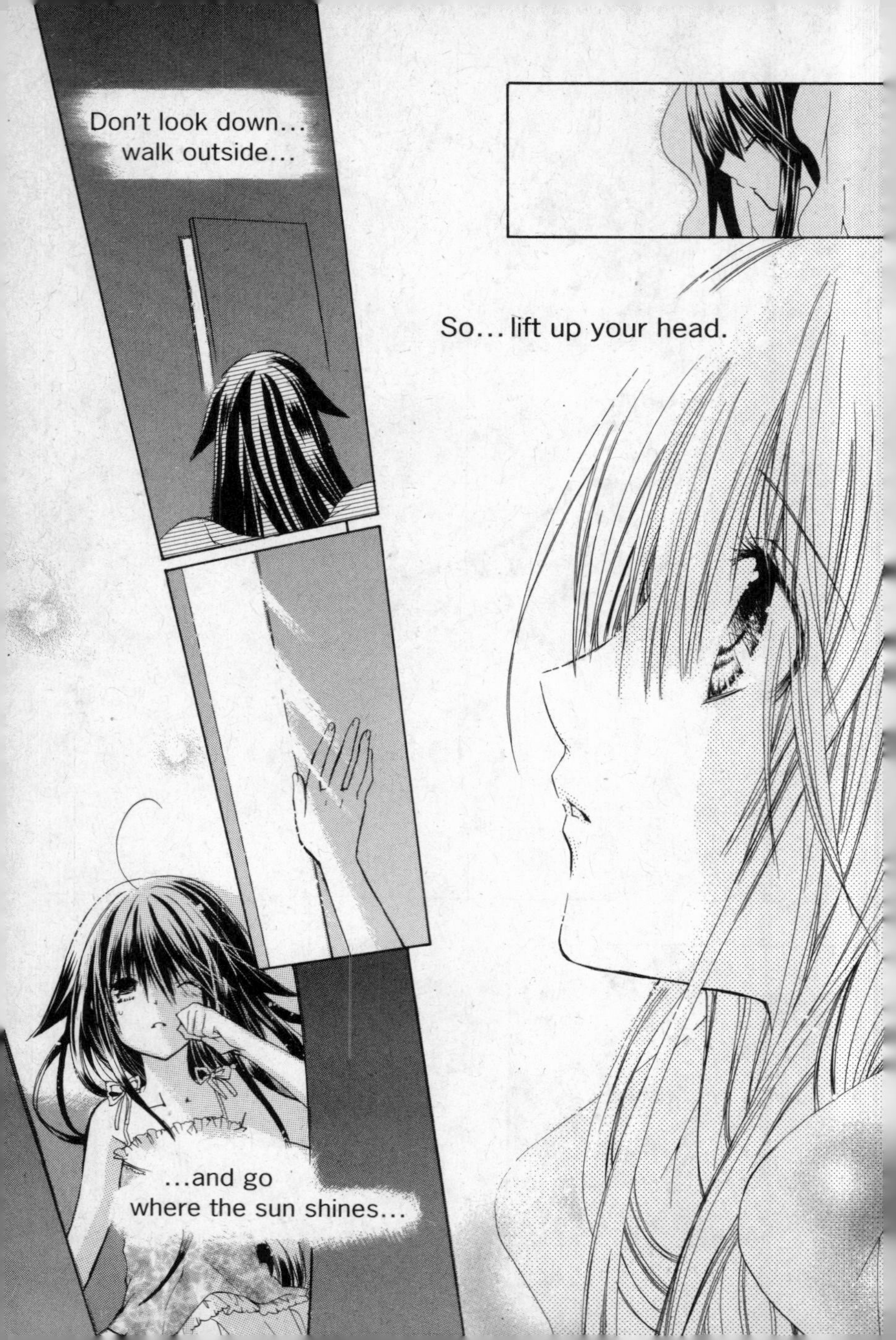
So... lift up your head.
Don't look down...
walk outside...
...and go
where the sun shines...

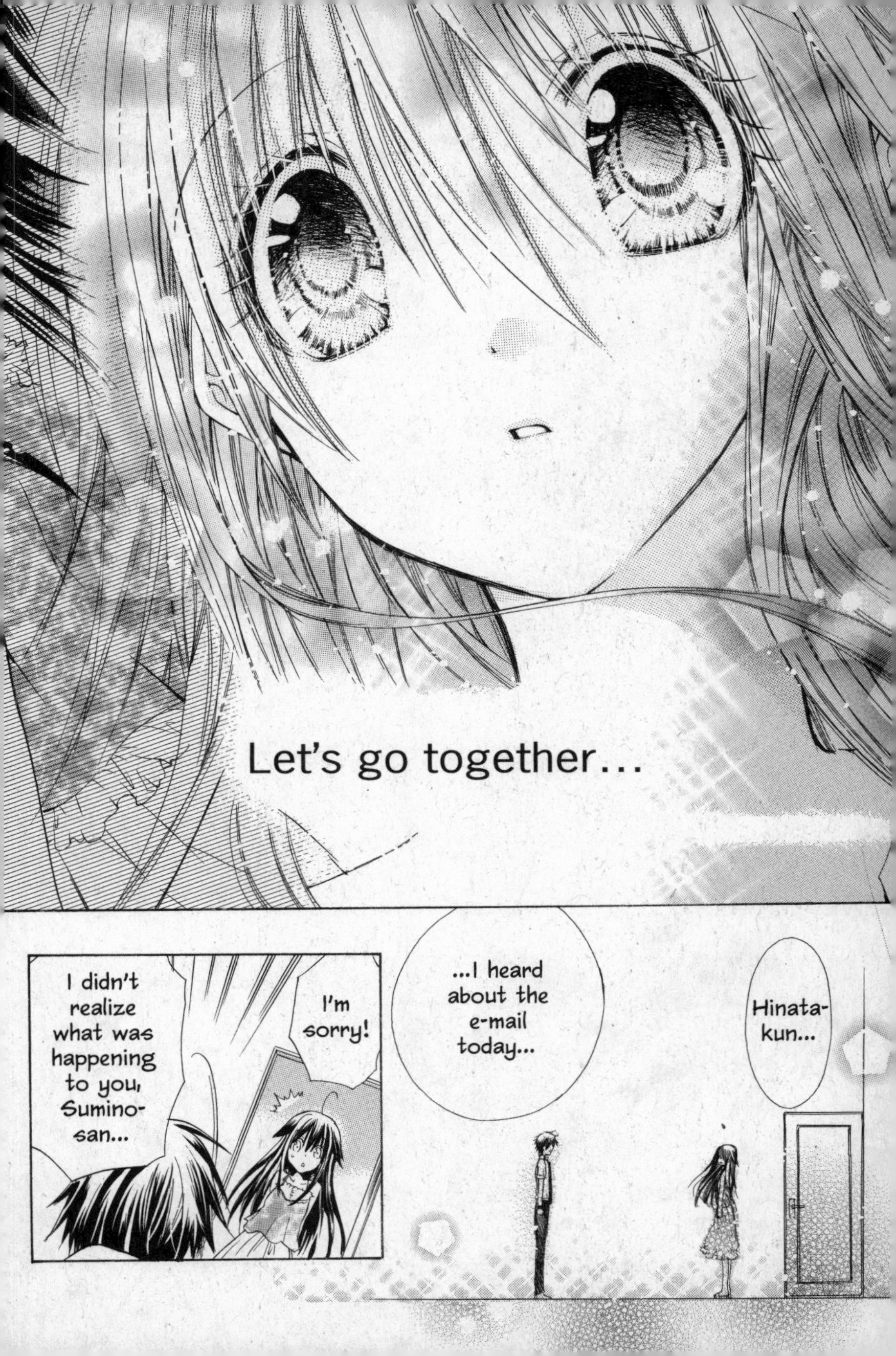
Let's go together...
Hinata-kun...
...I heard about the e-mail today...
I'm sorry!
I didn't realize what was happening to you, Sumino-san...

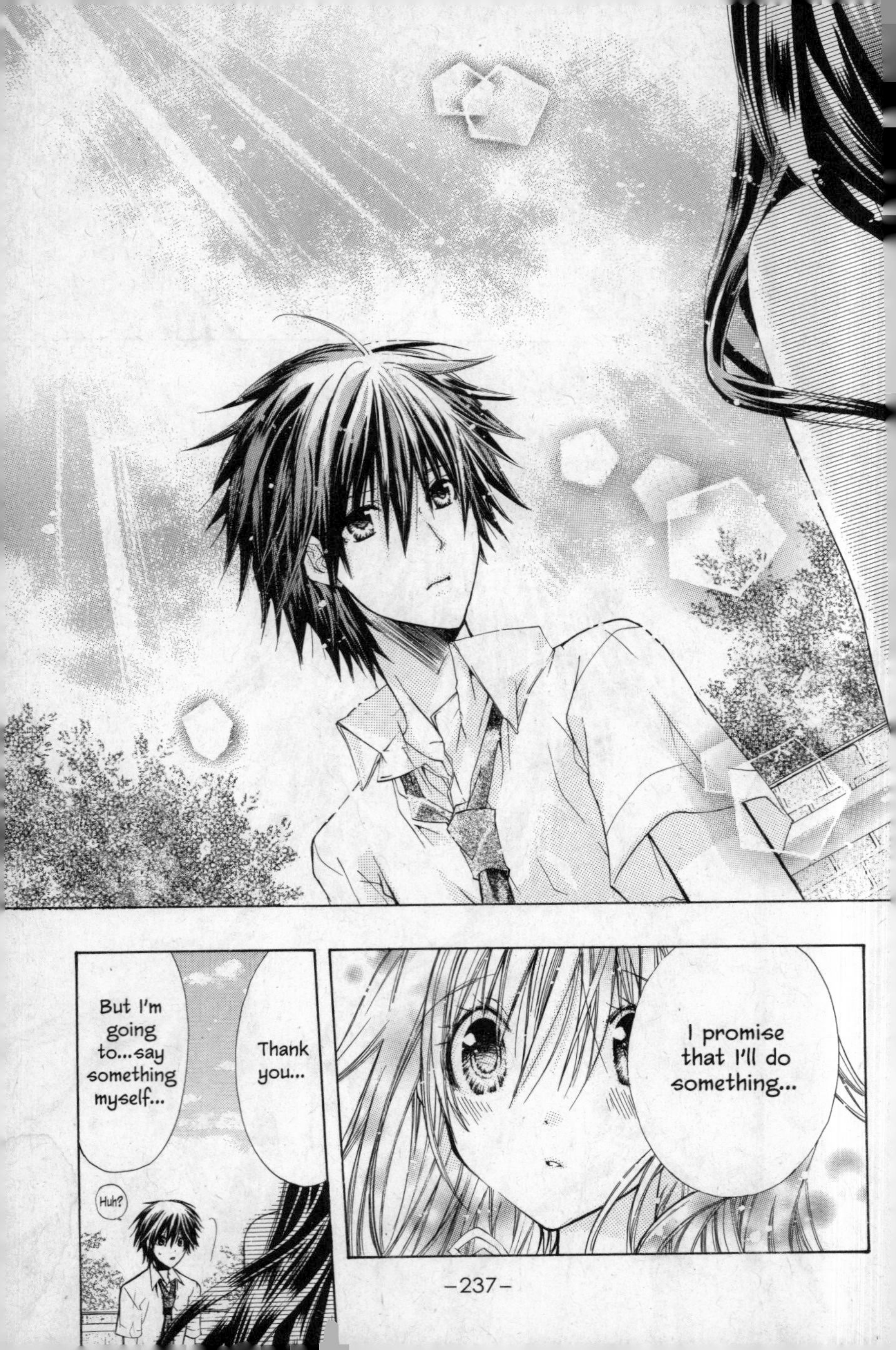
I promise that I'll do something...
Thank you...
But I'm going to...say something myself...
Huh?

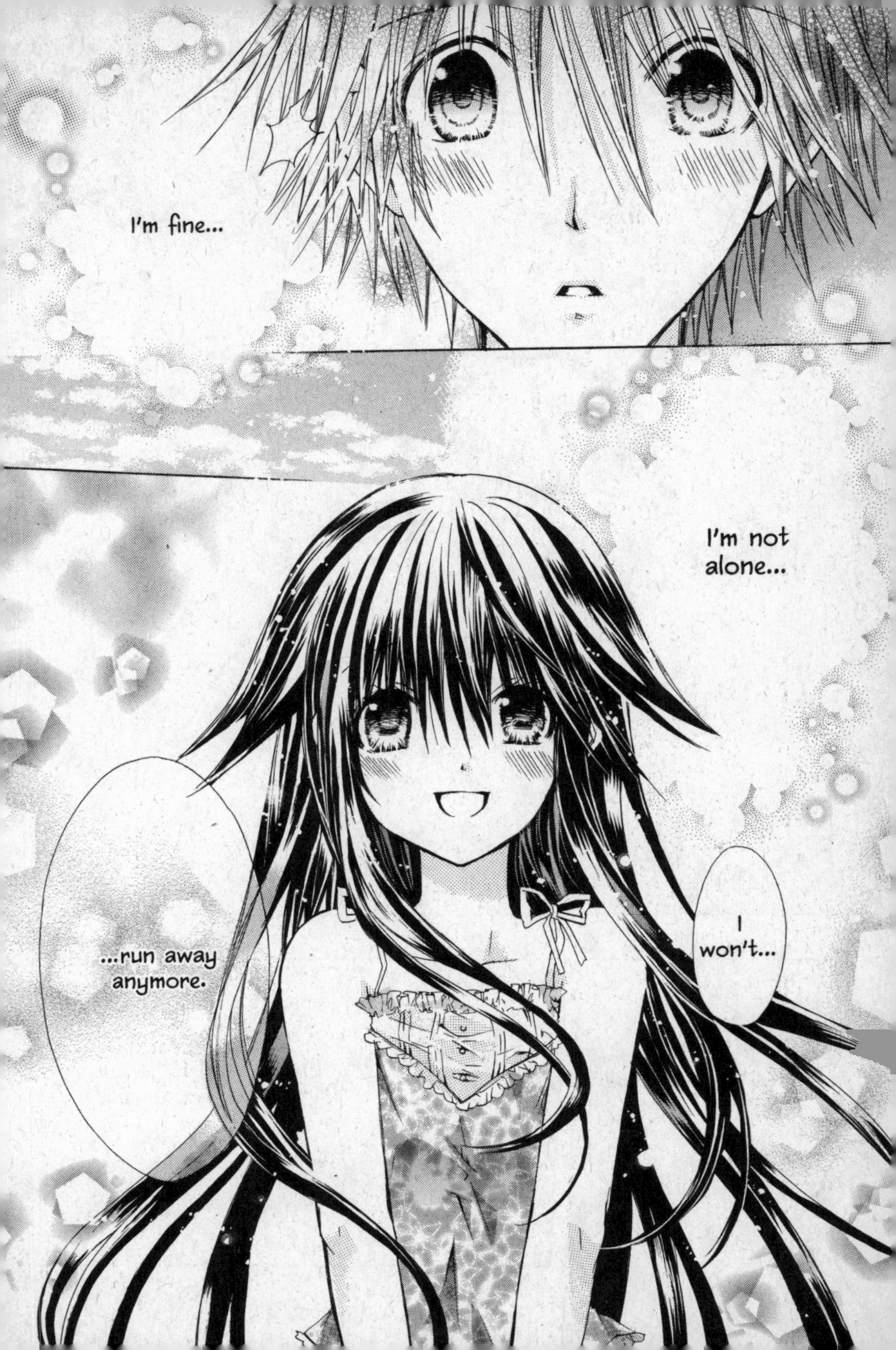
I'm fine...
I'm not alone...
I won't...
...run away anymore.

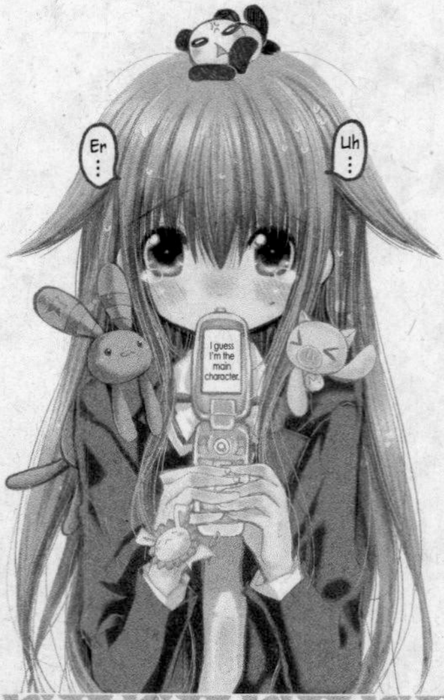
Uh…
Er…
I guess I'm the main character.

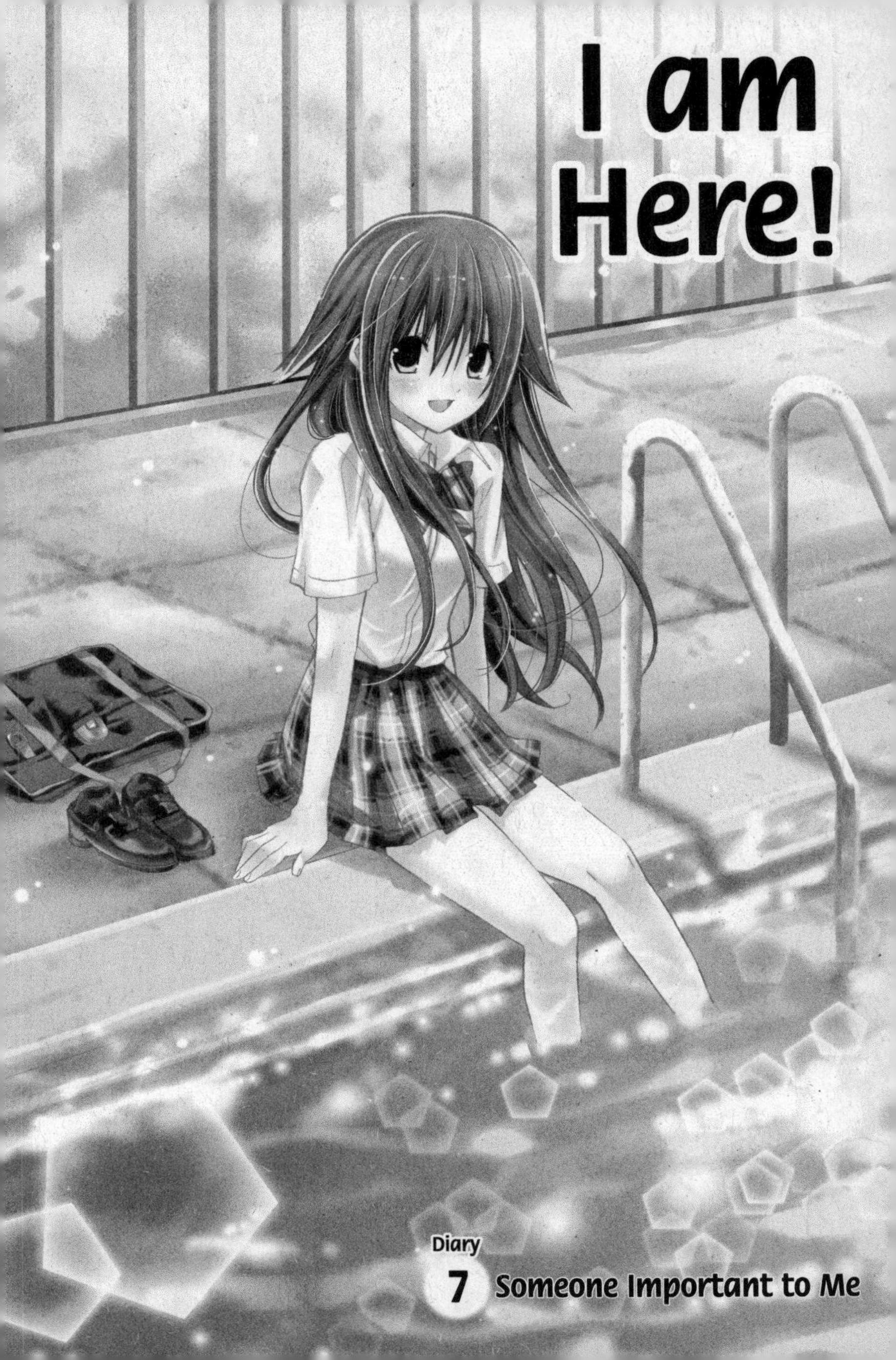
I am Here!
Diary
7 Someone Important to Me

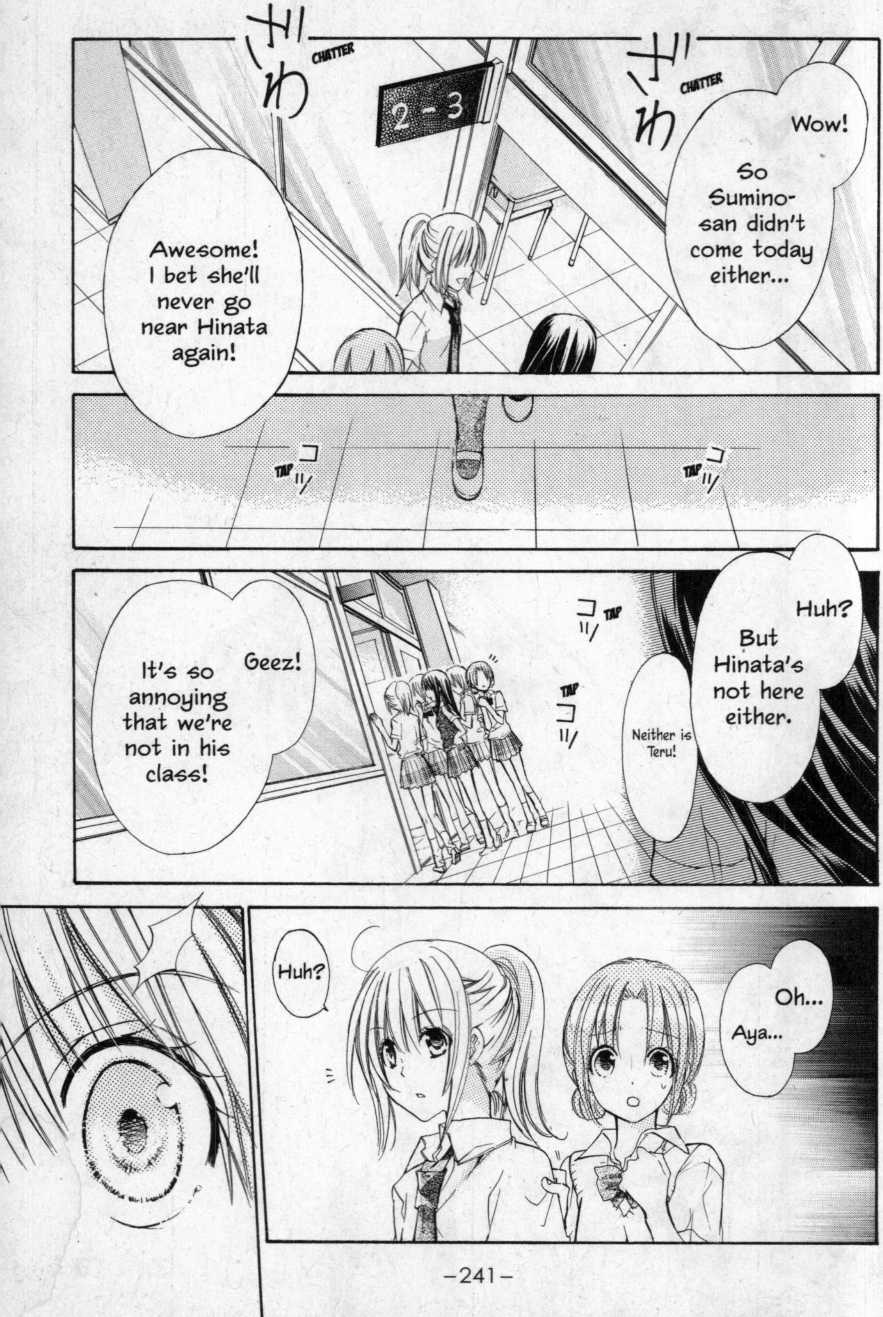
ざわ
CHATTER
Wow!
So Sumino-san didn't come today either...
2-3
ざわ
CHATTER
Awesome! I bet she'll never go near Hinata again!
コツ
TAP
コツ
TAP
Huh?
But Hinata's not here either.
Neither is Teru!
コツ
TAP
コツ
TAP
Geez!
It's so annoying that we're not in his class!
Oh...
Aya...
Huh?

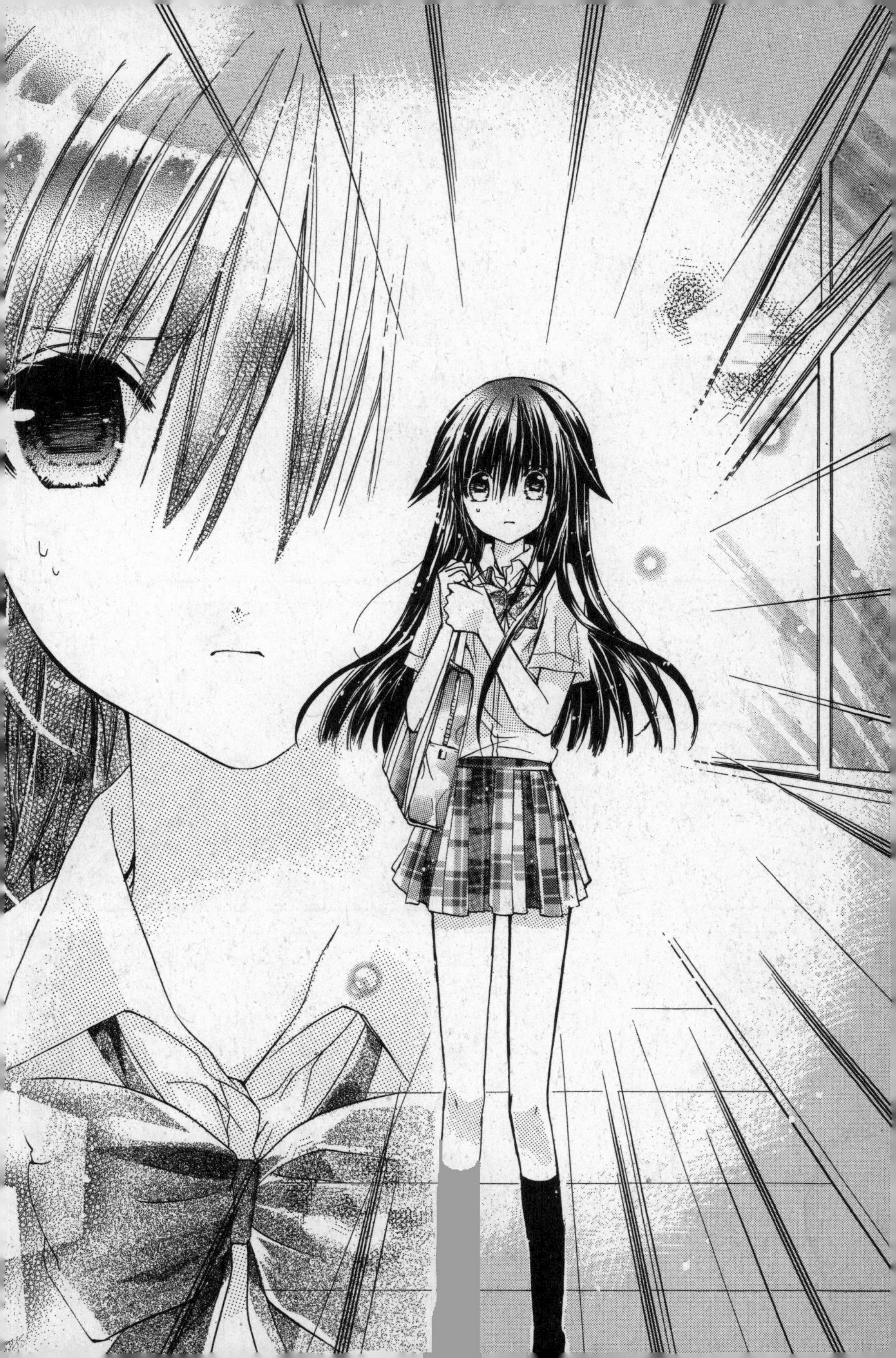

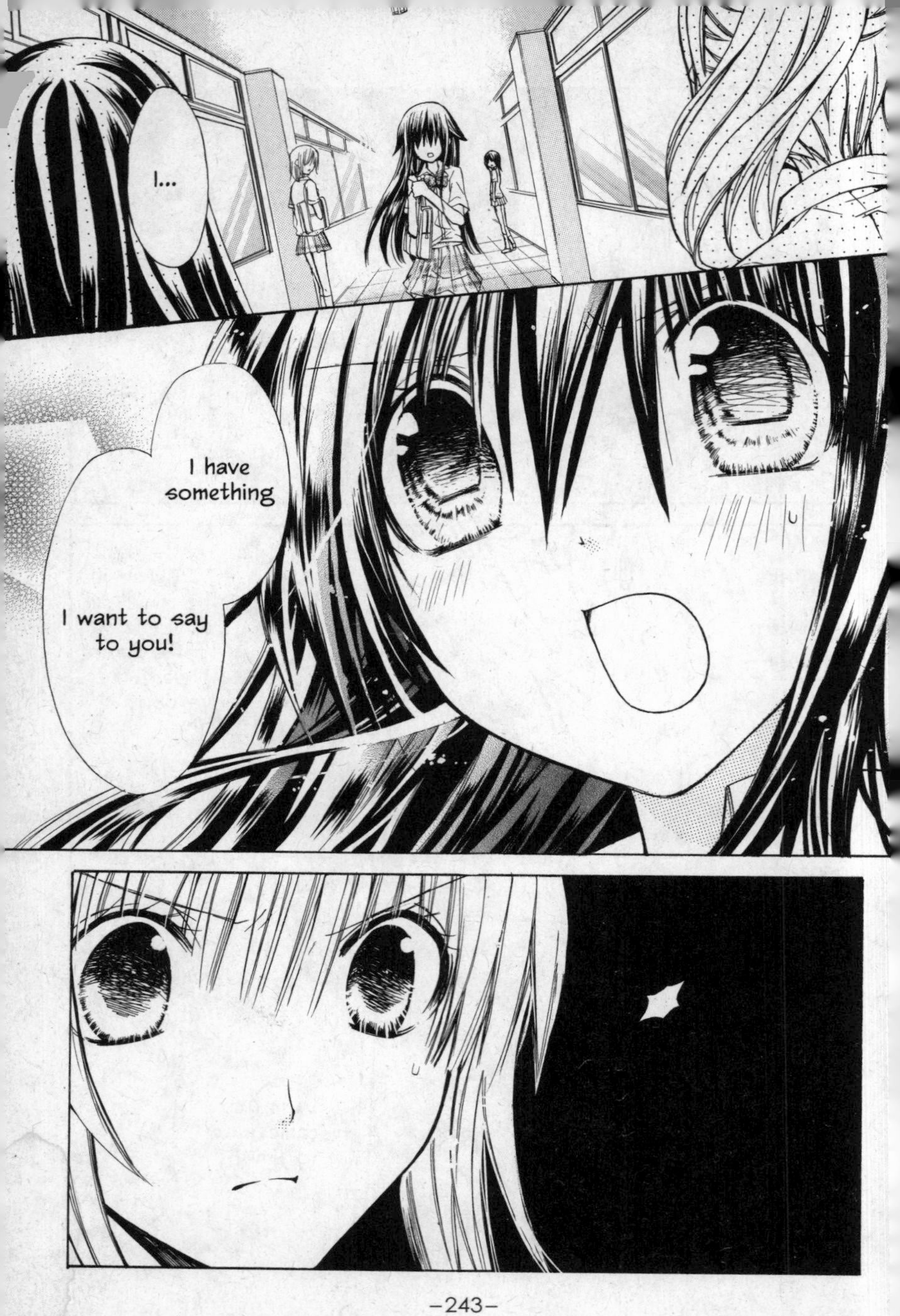
I...
I have something I want to say to you!

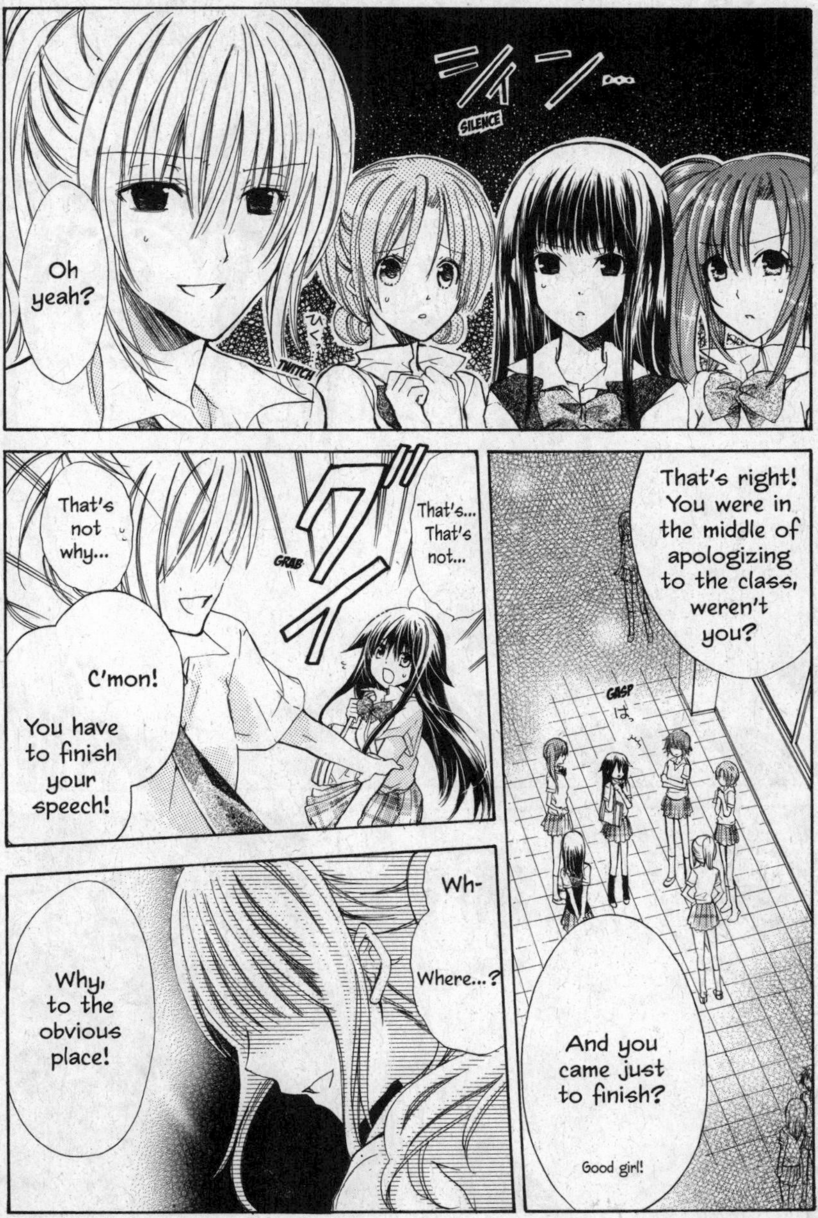
シィーン…
SILENCE
Oh yeah?
ひくっ
TWITCH
That's right! You were in the middle of apologizing to the class, weren't you?
GASP
は
And you came just to finish?
Good girl!
グイ
GRAB
That's... That's not...
That's not why...
C'mon!
You have to finish your speech!
Wh-
Where...?
Why, to the obvious place!

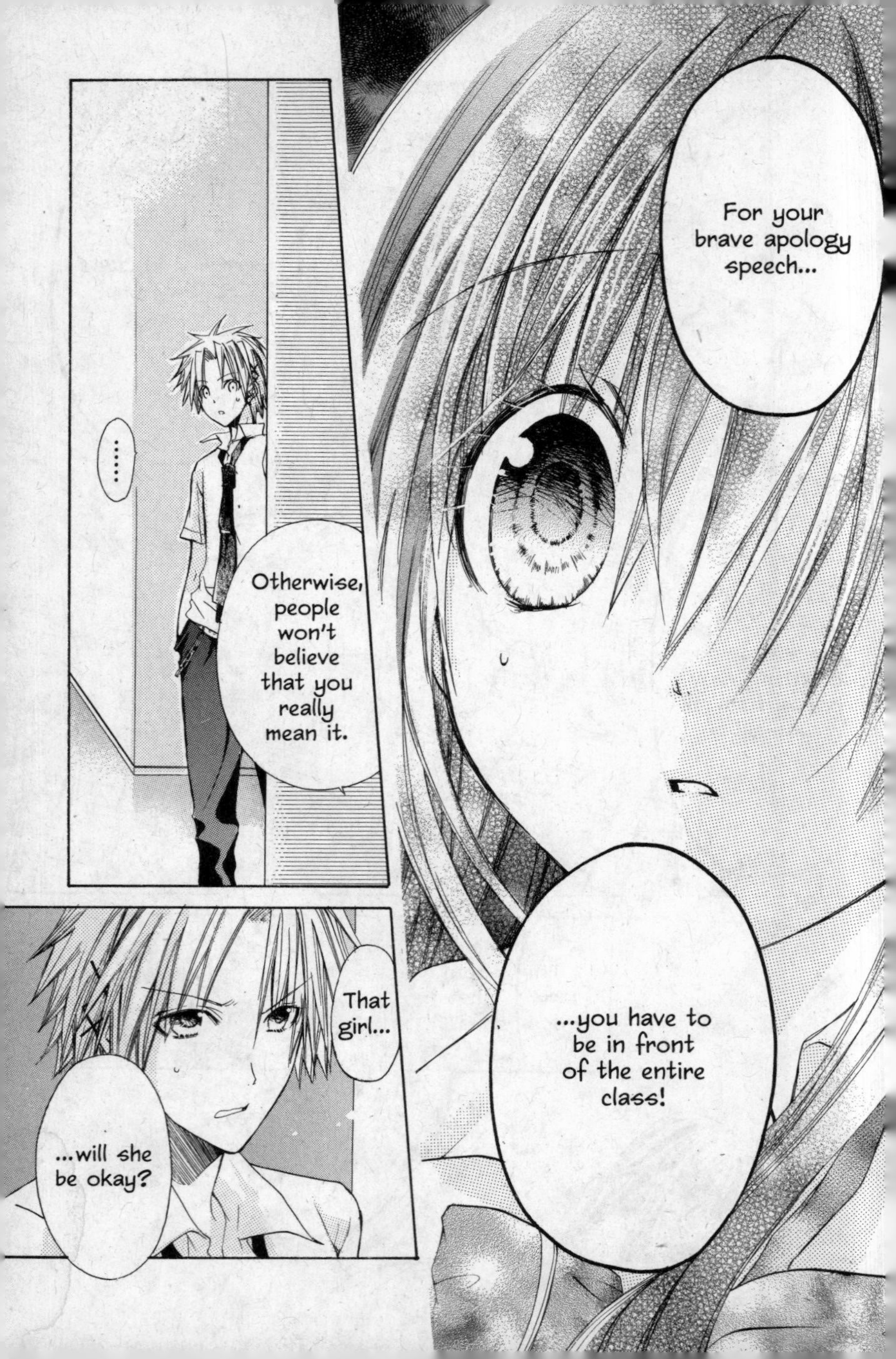
For your brave apology speech...
...you have to be in front of the entire class!
Otherwise, people won't believe that you really mean it.
......
That girl...
...will she be okay?

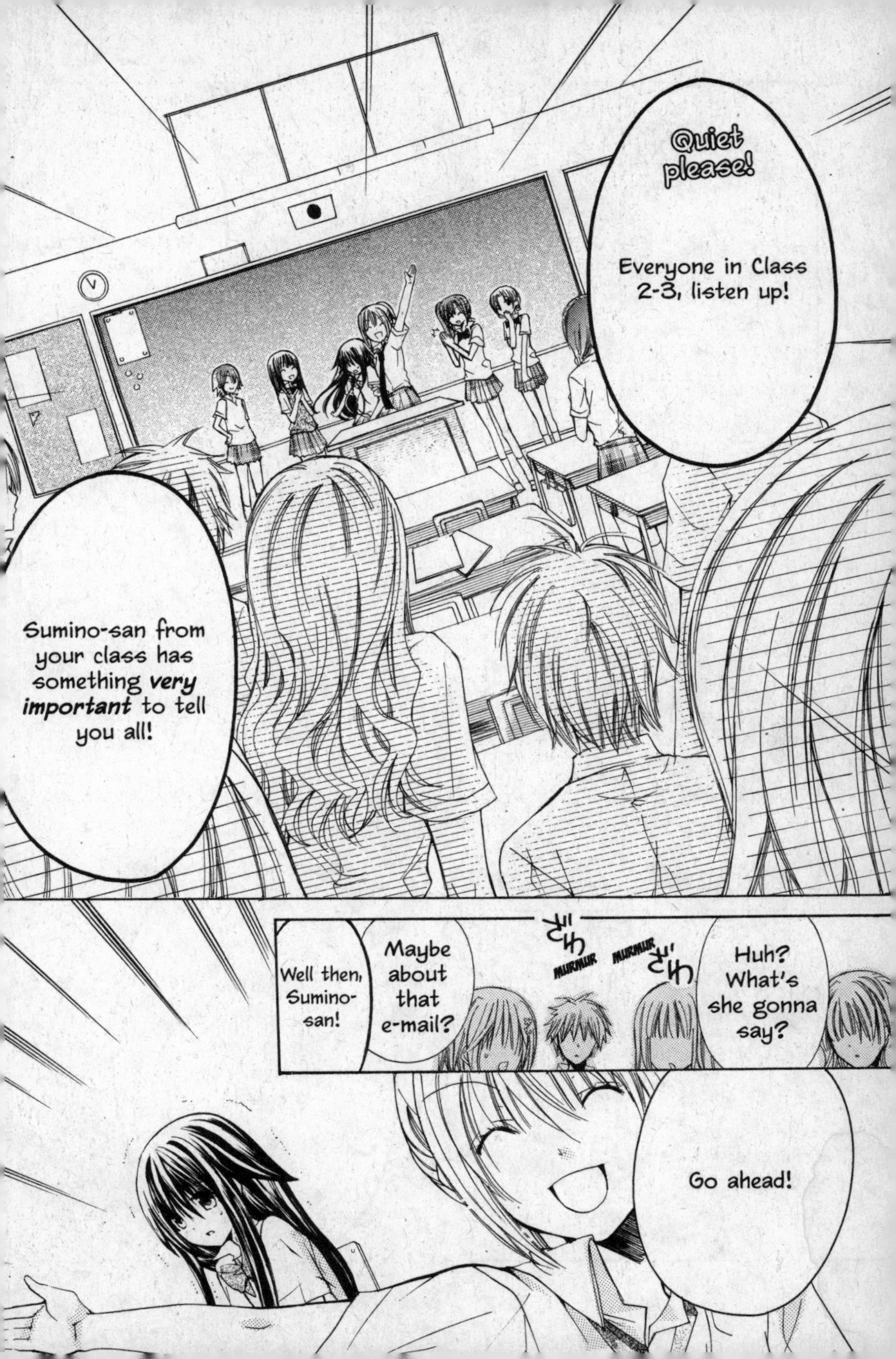
Quiet please!
Everyone in Class 2-3, listen up!
Sumino-san from your class has something *very important* to tell you all!
Huh? What's she gonna say?
ざわ MURMUR
ざわ MURMUR
Maybe about that e-mail?
Well then, Sumino-san!
Go ahead!

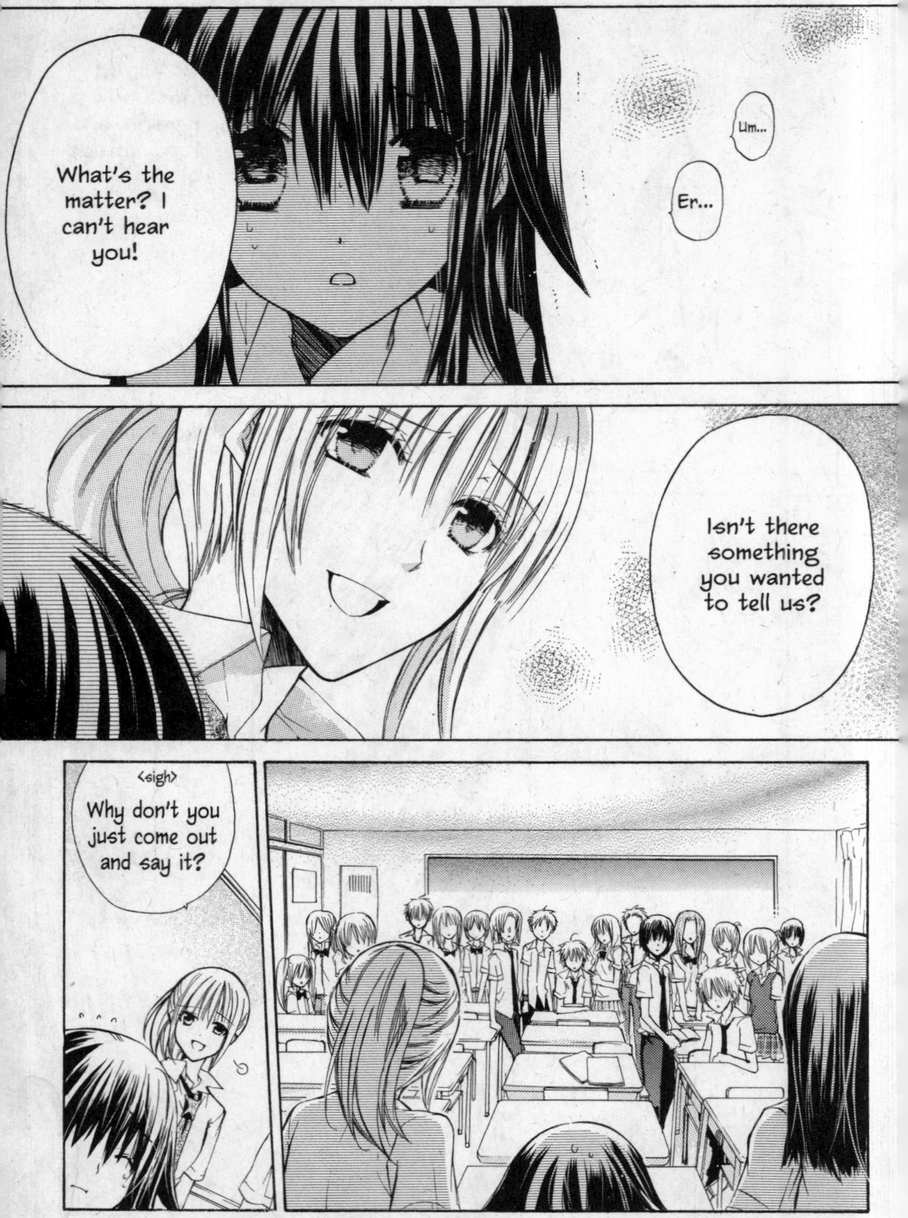
Um...
Er...
What's the matter? I can't hear you!
Isn't there something you wanted to tell us?
<sigh>
Why don't you just come out and say it?

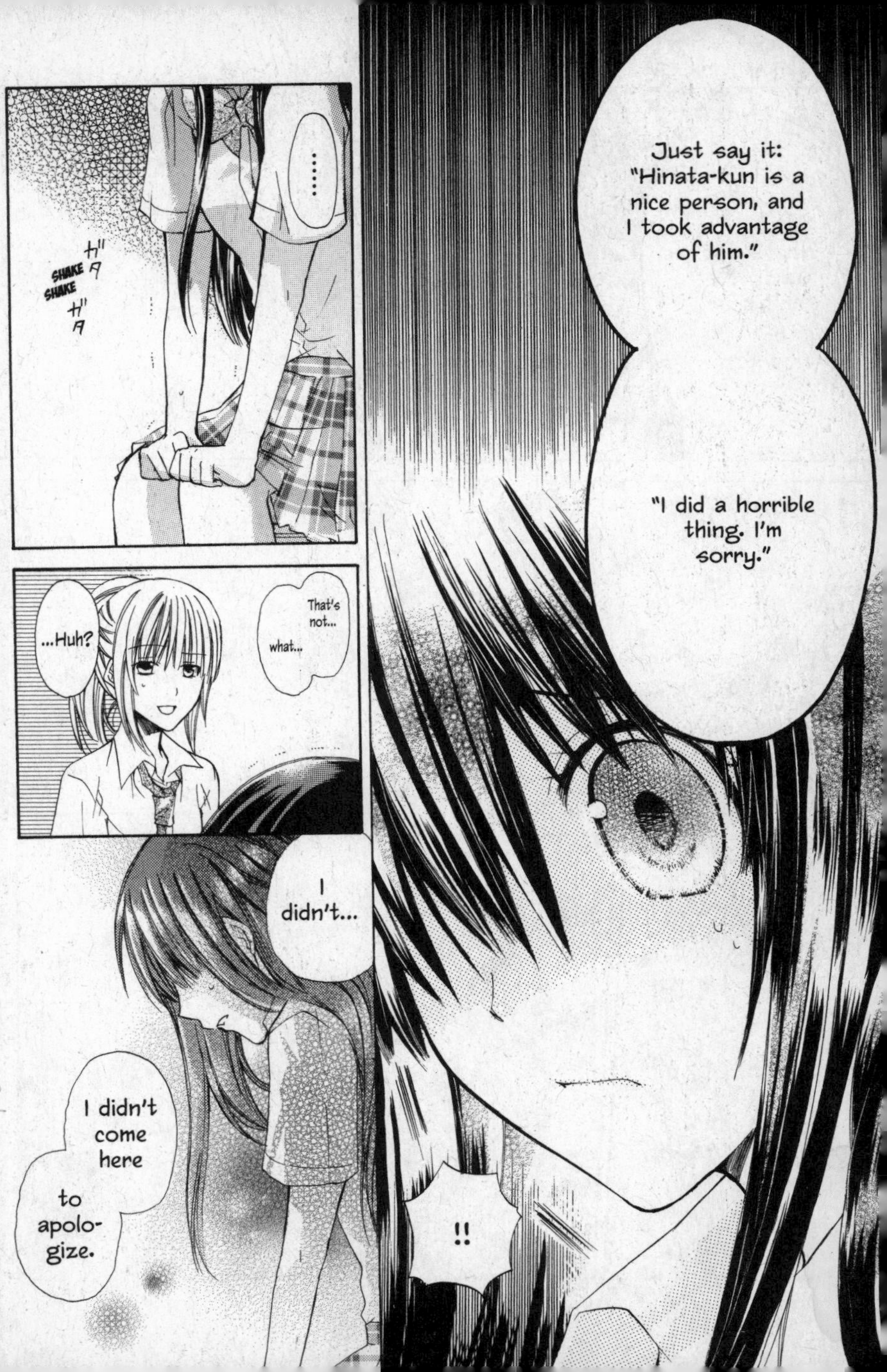
Just say it: "Hinata-kun is a nice person, and I took advantage of him."
"I did a horrible thing. I'm sorry."
!!
......
SHAKE SHAKE
ガタ ガタ
That's not... what...
...Huh?
I didn't...
I didn't come here to apologize.

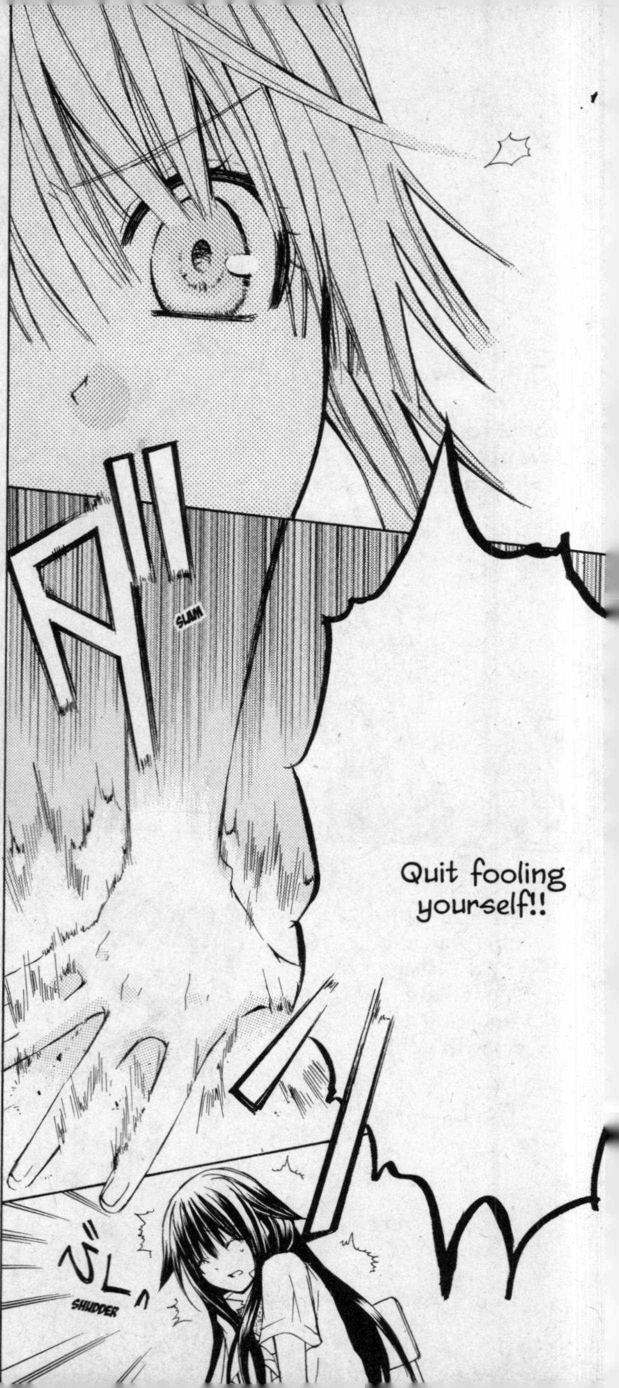
SLAM
Quit fooling yourself!!
SHUDDER

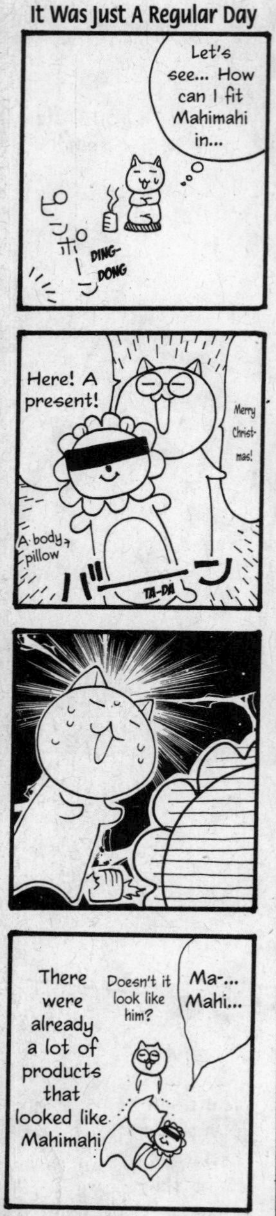
It Was Just A Regular Day
Let's see... How can I fit Mahimahi in...
ピンポーン
DING-DONG
Here! A present!
Merry Christmas!
A body pillow
バーン
TA-DA
Ma-... Mahi...
Doesn't it look like him?
There were already a lot of products that looked like Mahimahi

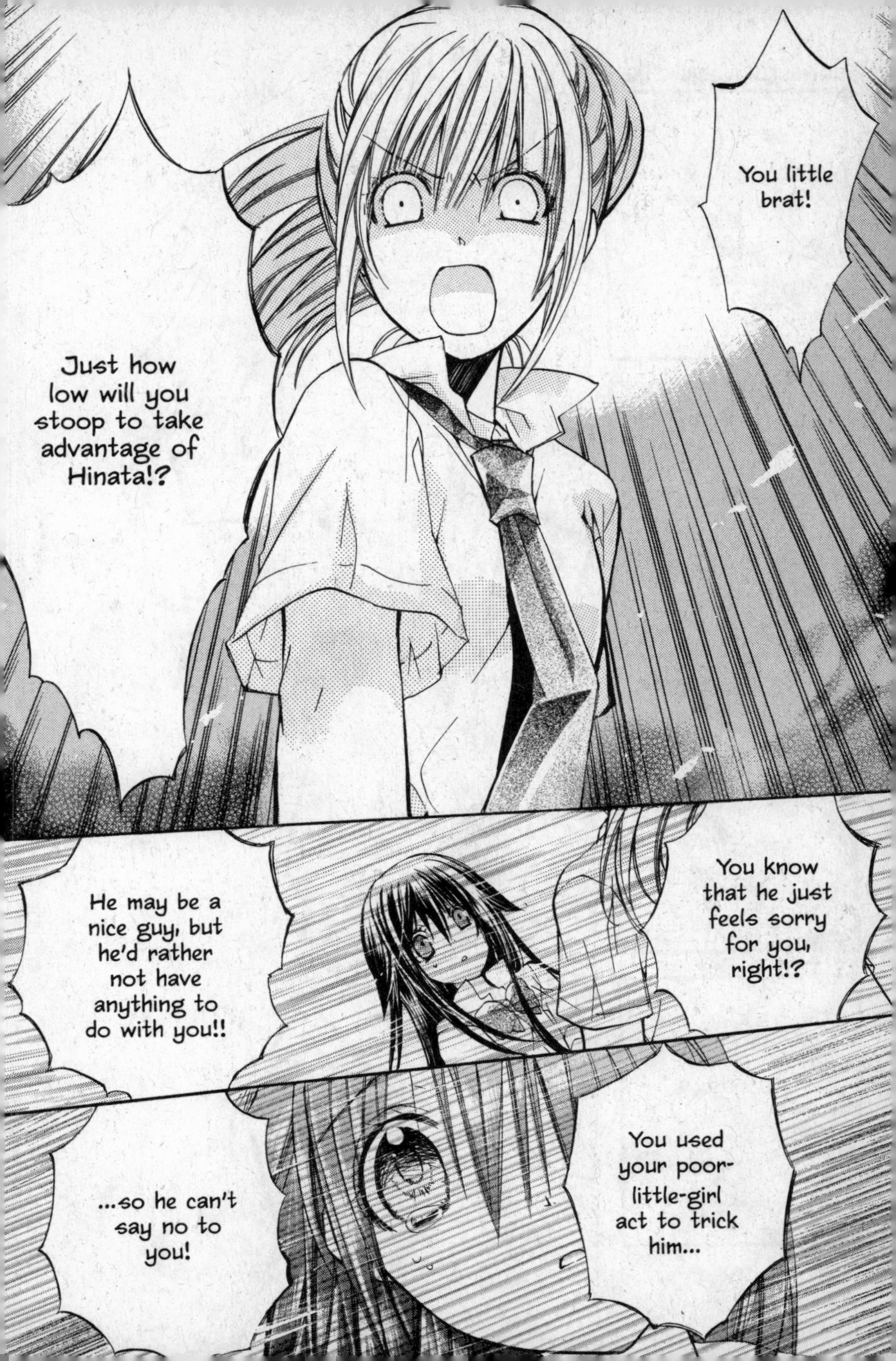
You little brat!
Just how low will you stoop to take advantage of Hinata!?
You know that he just feels sorry for you, right!?
He may be a nice guy, but he'd rather not have anything to do with you!!
You used your poor-little-girl act to trick him...
...so he can't say no to you!

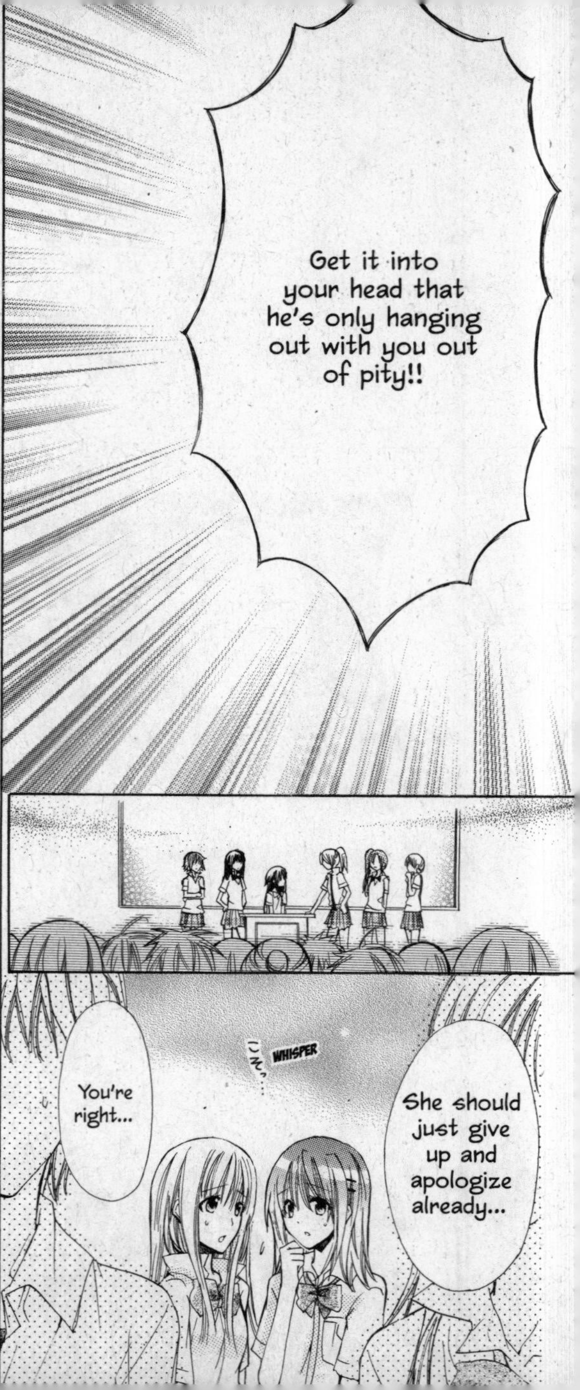
Get it into your head that he's only hanging out with you out of pity!!
She should just give up and apologize already...
WHISPER
You're right...

A Shock

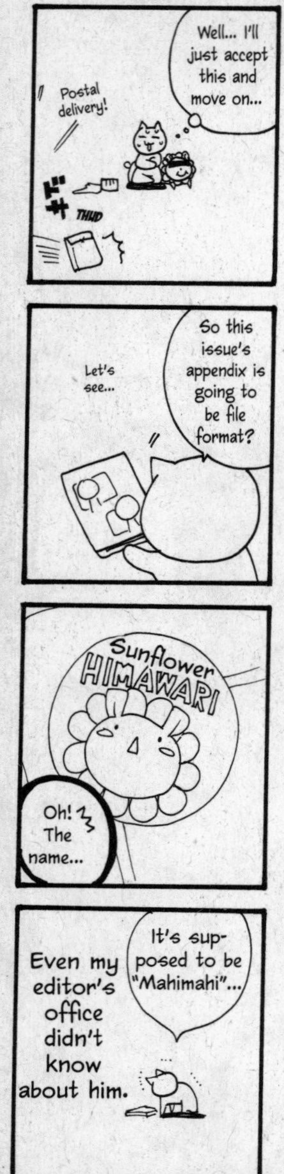
Well... I'll just accept this and move on...
Postal delivery!
THUD
So this issue's appendix is going to be file format?
Let's see...
Sunflower
HIMAWARI
Oh! The name...
It's sup-posed to be "Mahimahi"...
Even my editor's office didn't know about him.

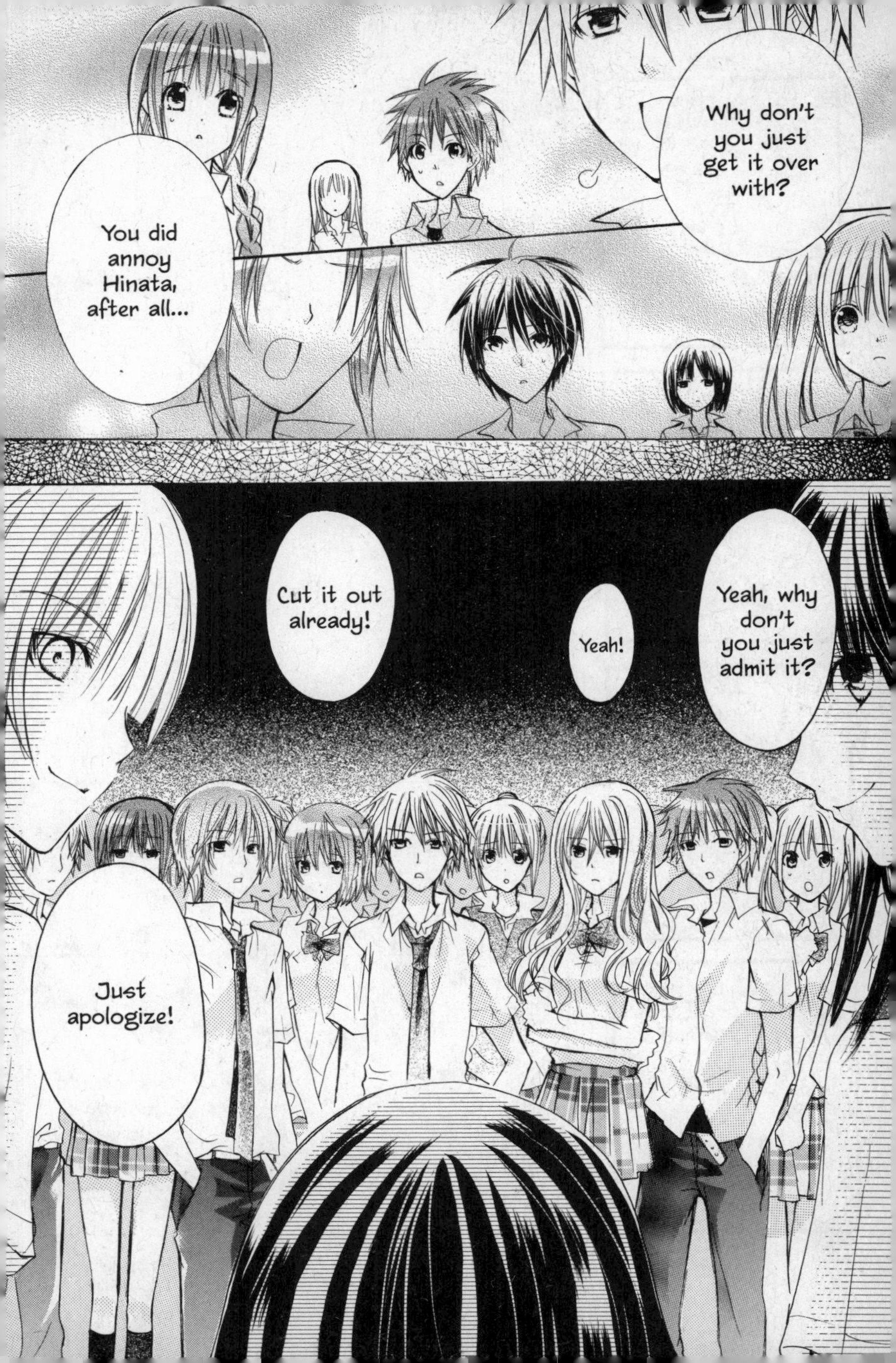
Why don't you just get it over with?
You did annoy Hinata, after all...
Yeah, why don't you just admit it?
Yeah!
Cut it out already!
Just apologize!

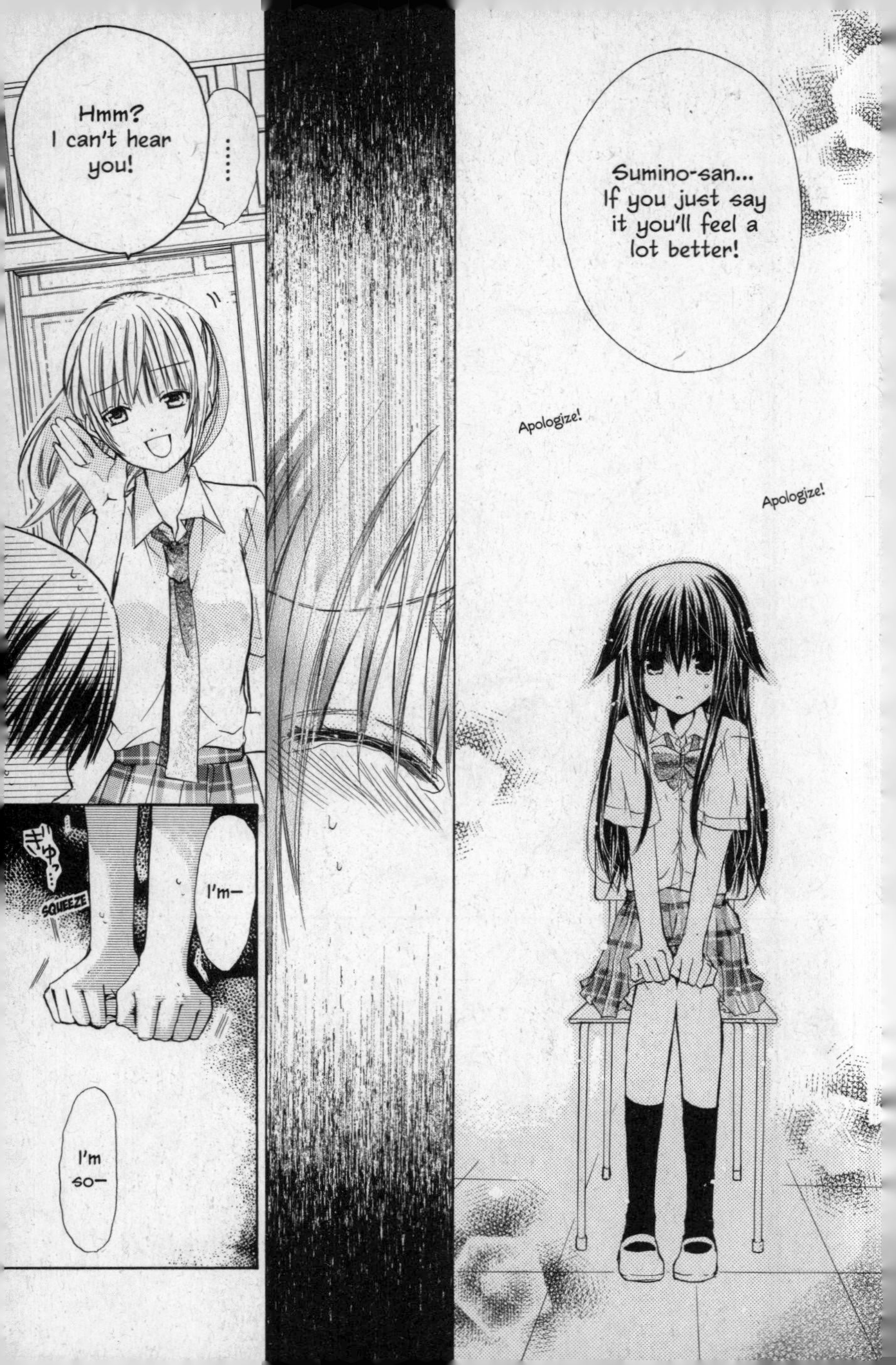
Sumino-san... If you just say it you'll feel a lot better!
Apologize!
Apologize!
Hmm? I can't hear you!
......
I'm—
SQUEEZE
I'm so—

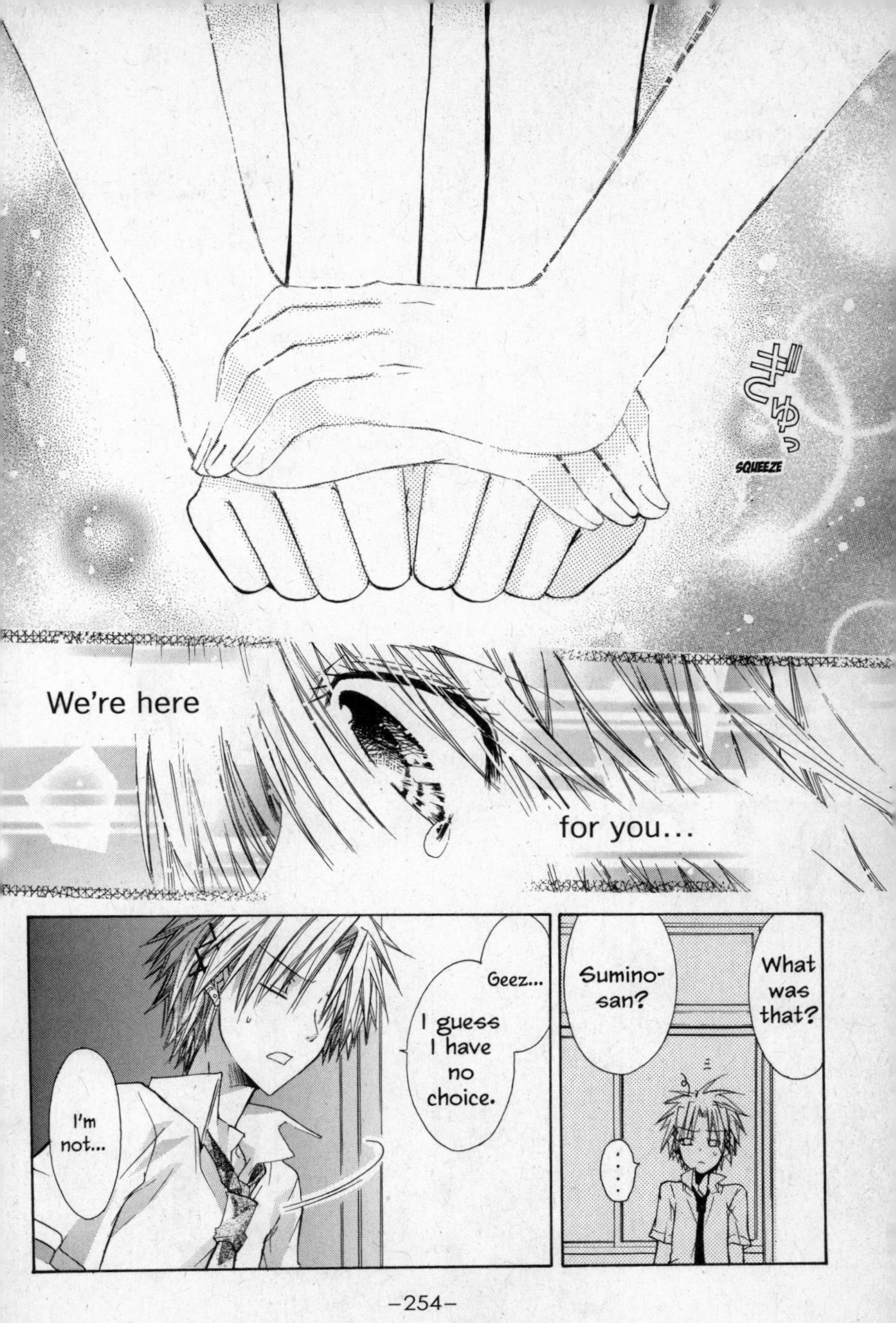
ぎゅっ
SQUEEZE
We're here
for you...
What was that?
Sumino-san?
...
Geez...
I guess I have no choice.
I'm not...

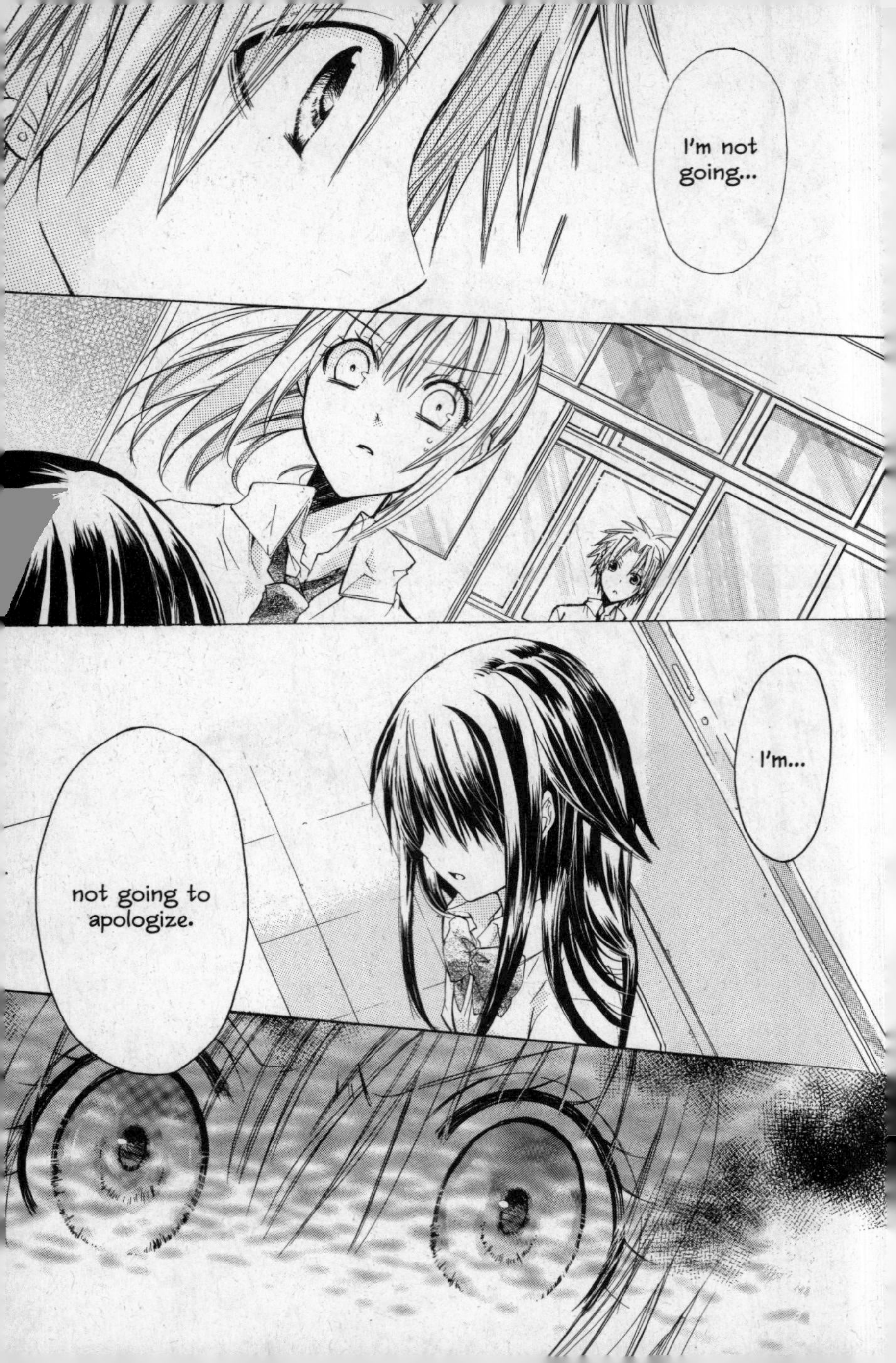
I'm not going...
I'm...
not going to apologize.

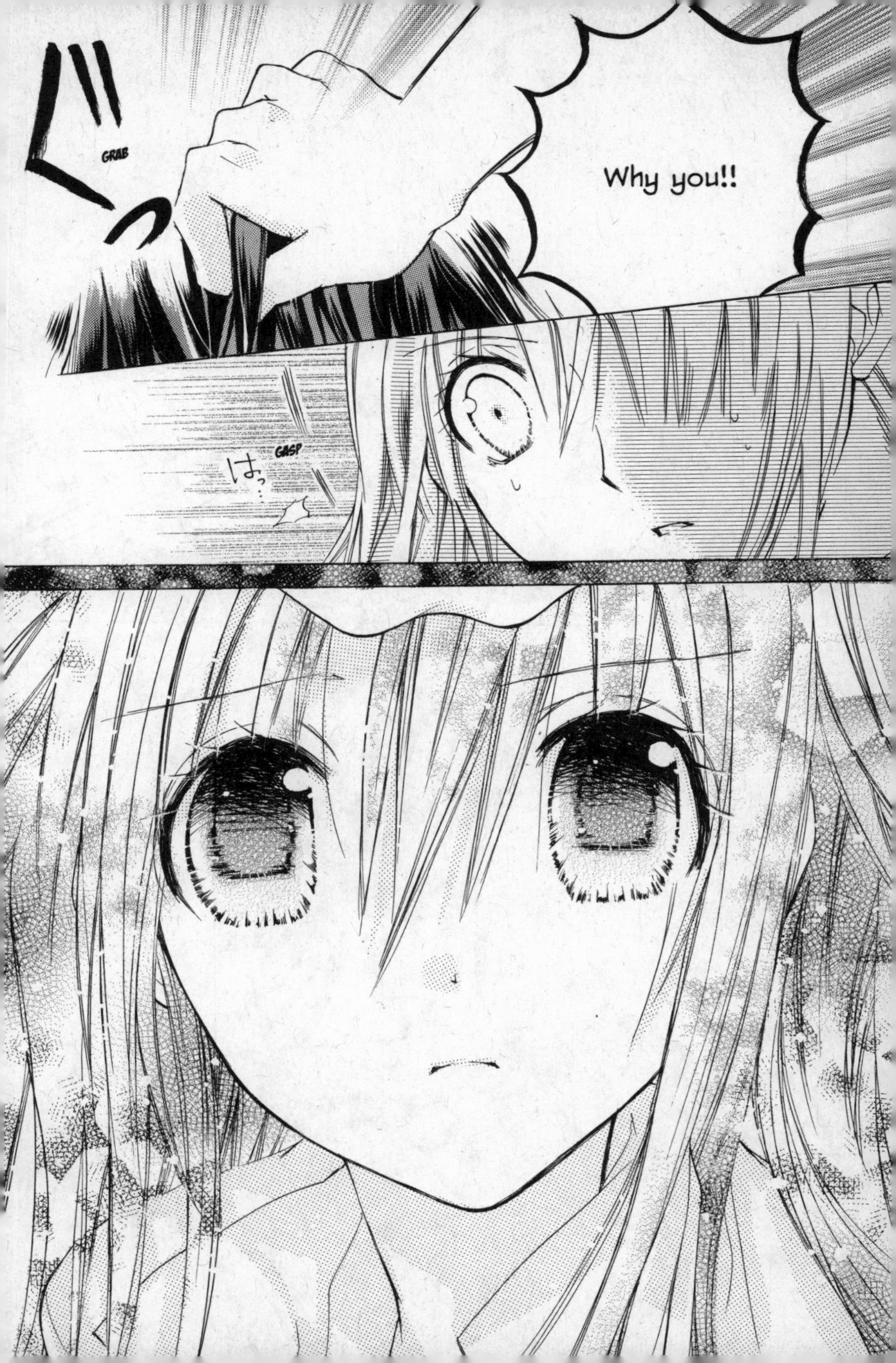

Why you!!
GRAB
GASP
はっ…

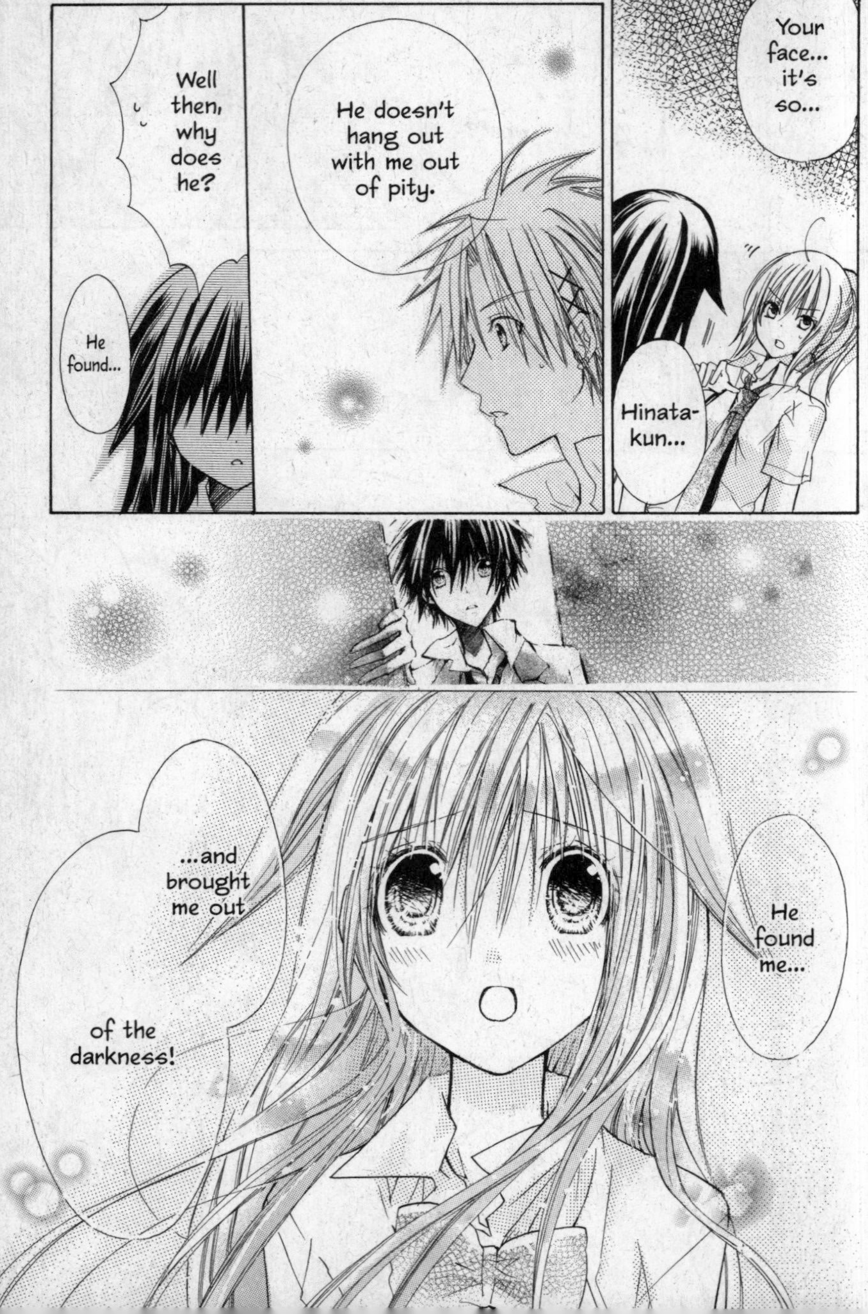
Your face... it's so...
Hinata-kun...
He doesn't hang out with me out of pity.
Well then, why does he?
He found...
He found me...
...and brought me out
of the darkness!

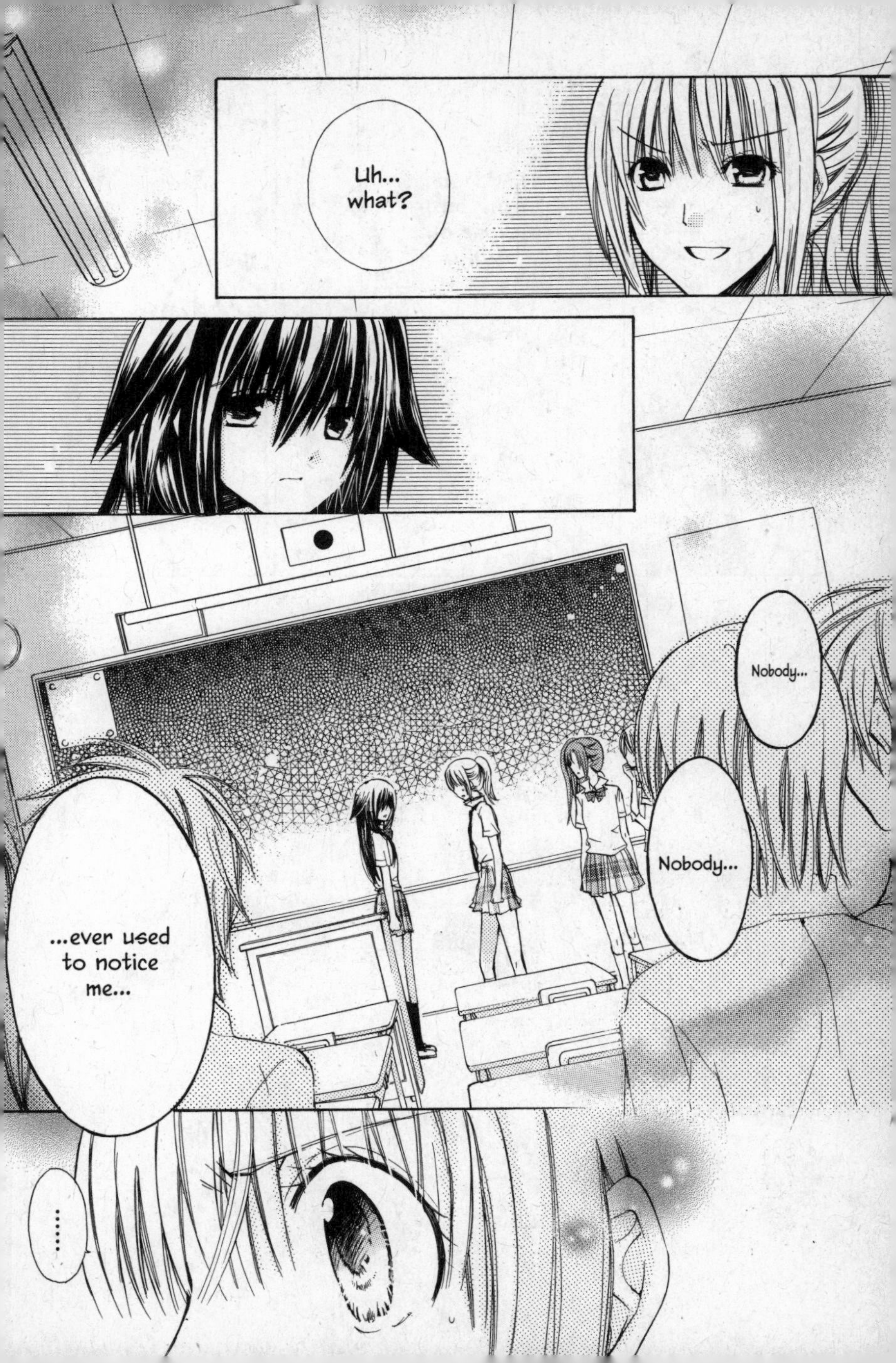

Uh... what?
Nobody...
Nobody...
...ever used to notice me...
......

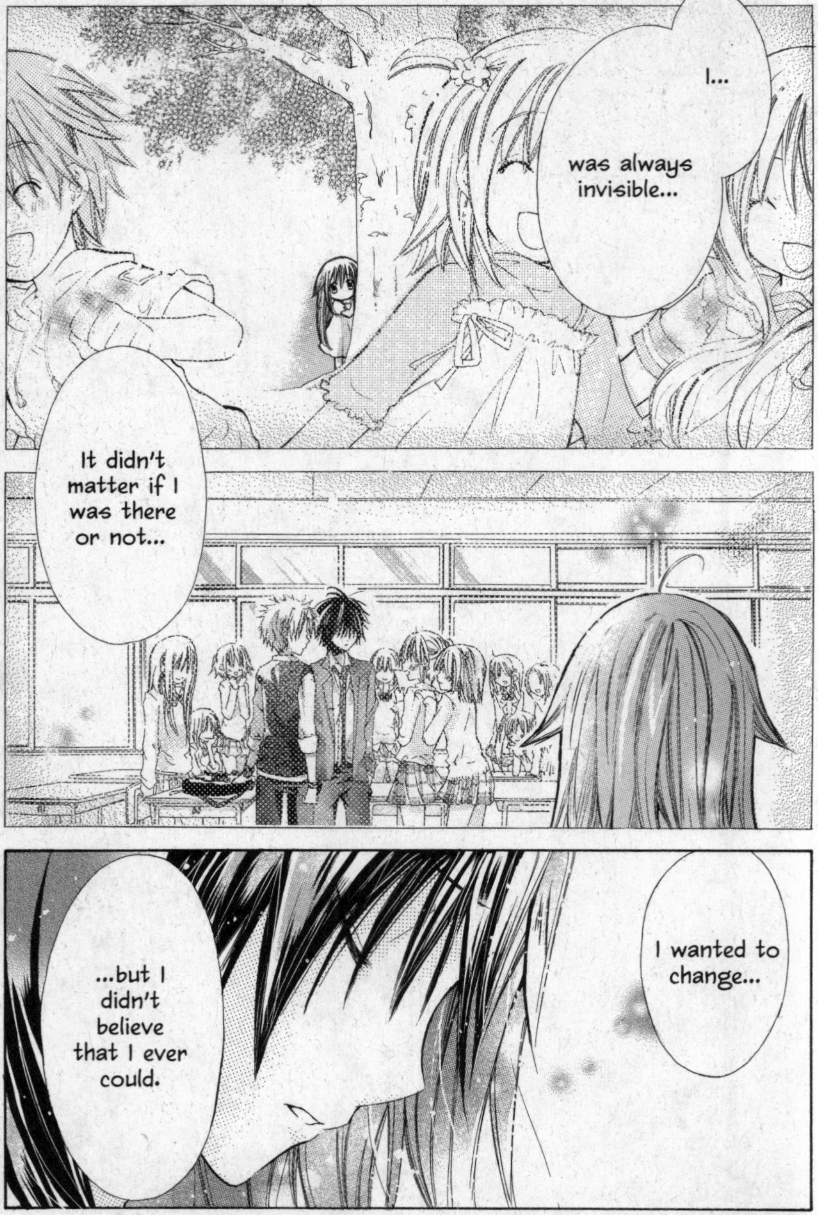
I...
was always invisible...
It didn't matter if I was there or not...
I wanted to change...
...but I didn't believe that I ever could.

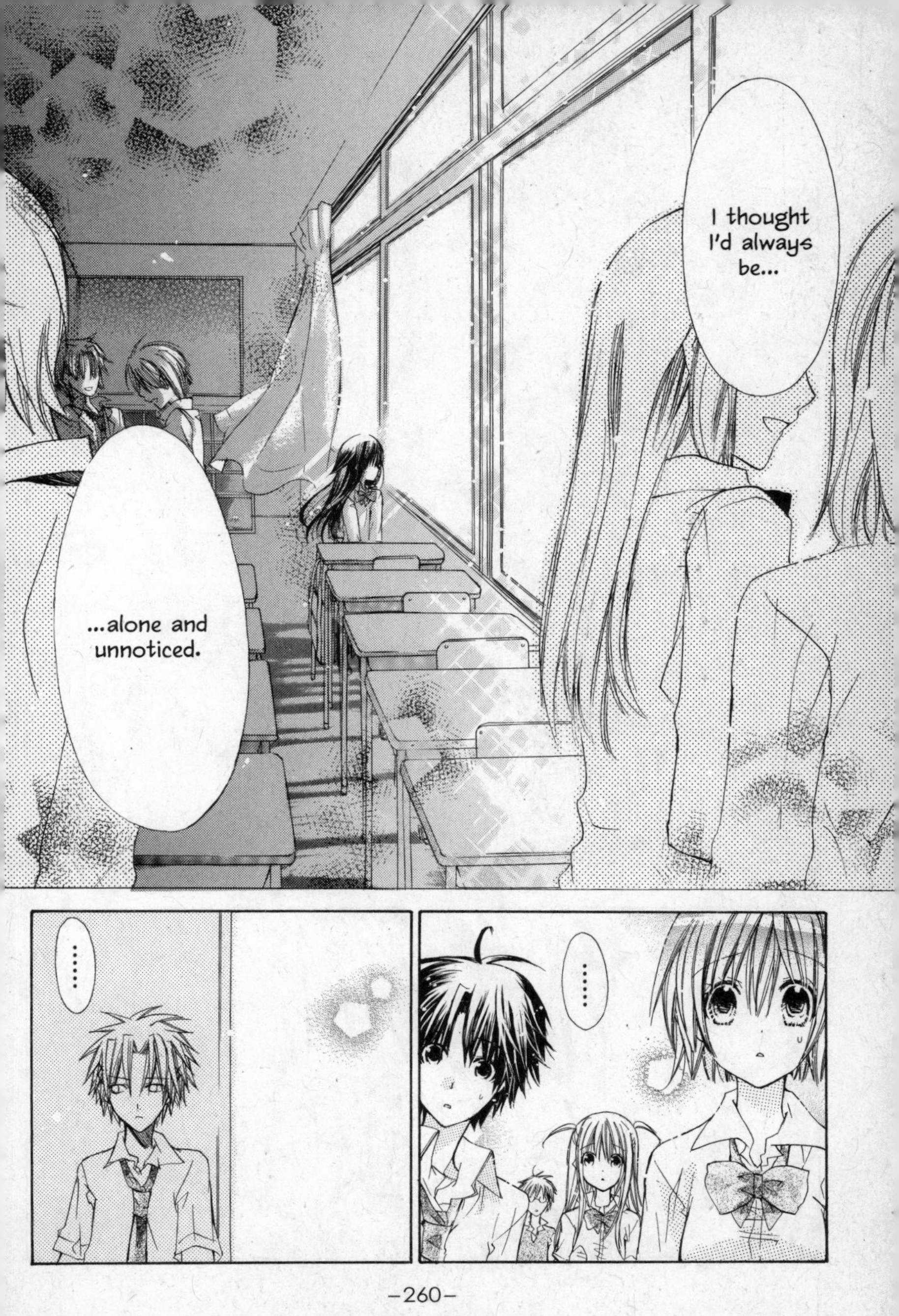
I thought I'd always be...
...alone and unnoticed.
......
......

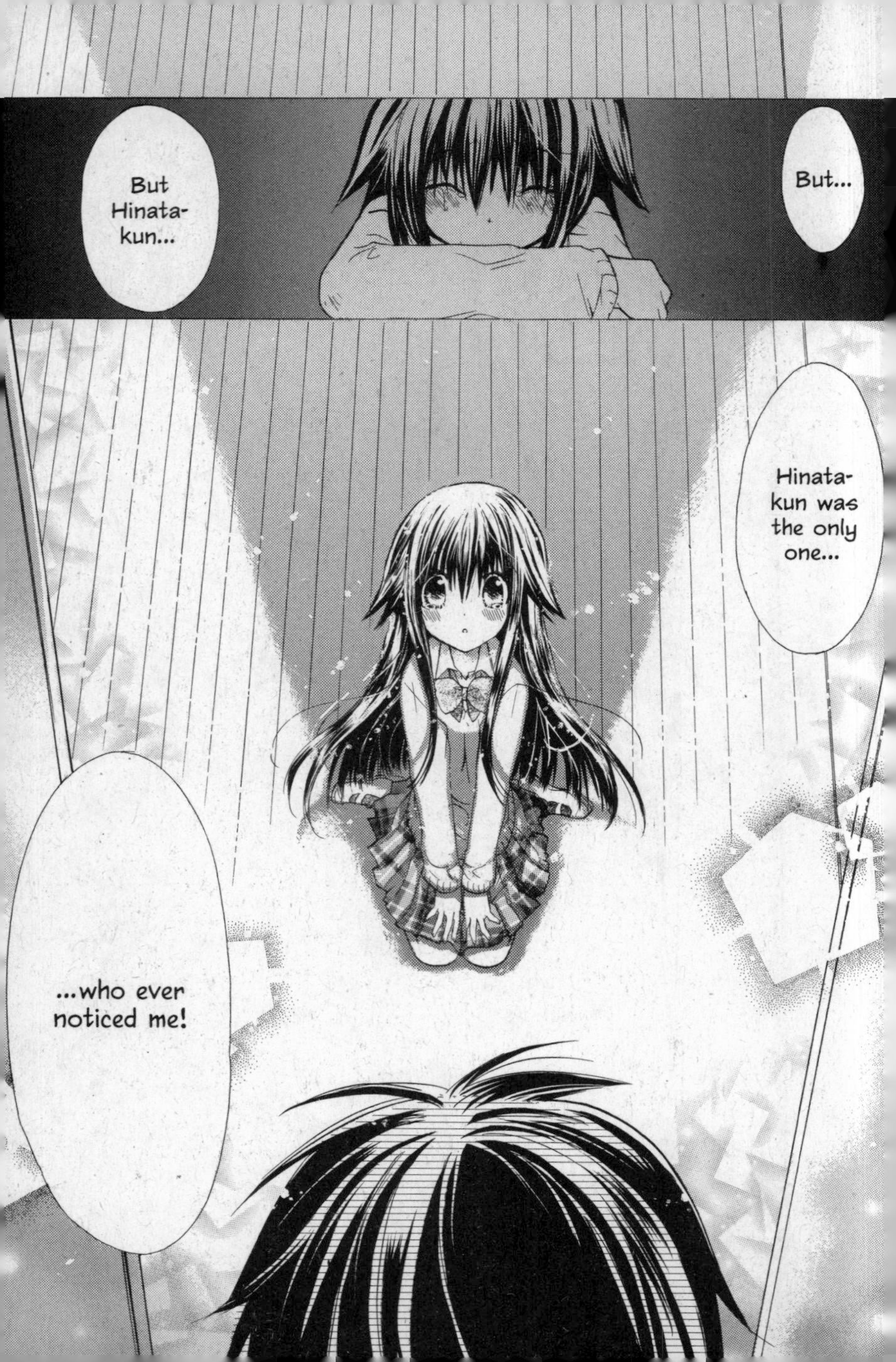
But...
But Hinata-kun...
Hinata-kun was the only one...
...who ever noticed me!

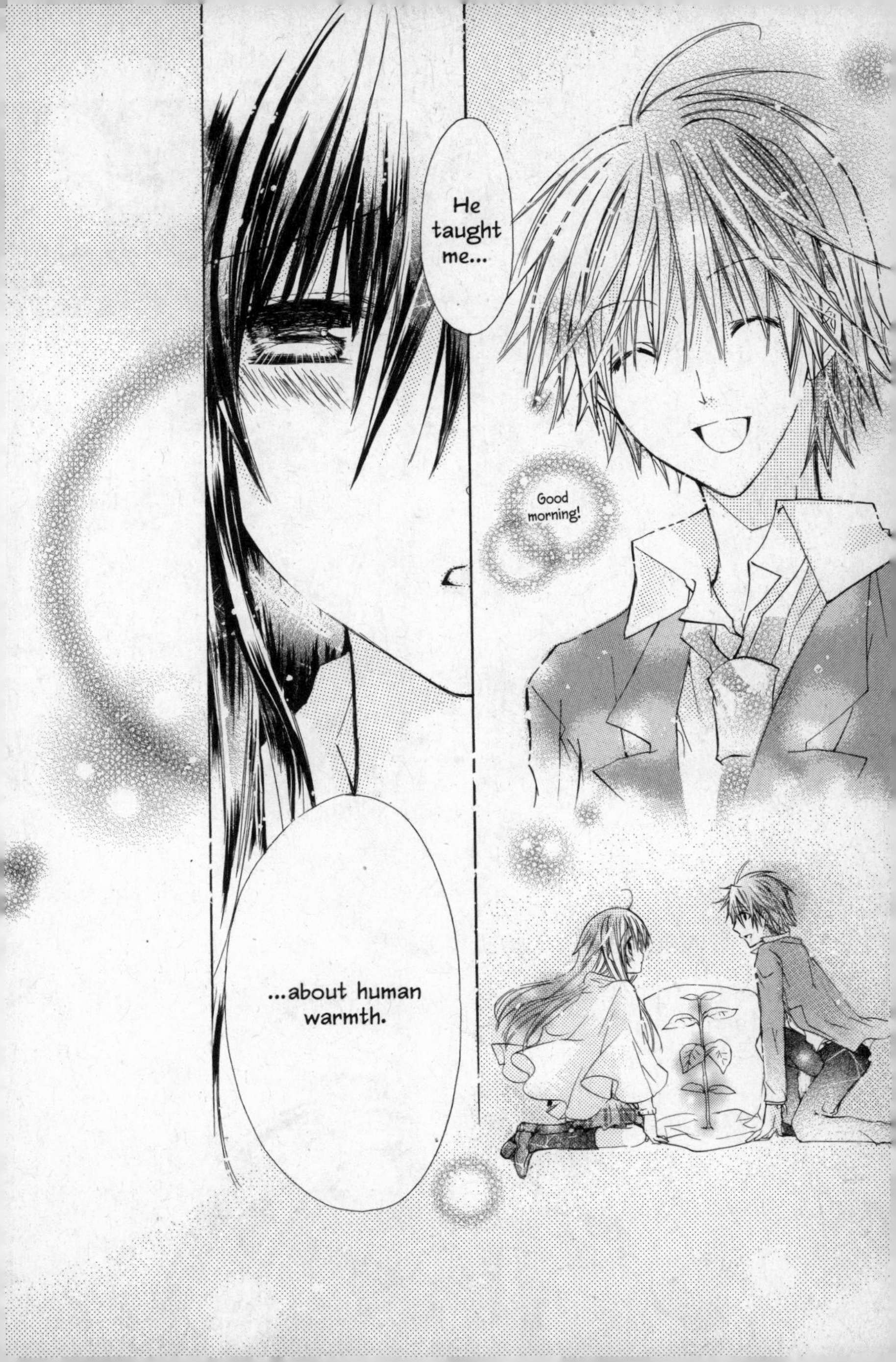
He taught me...
Good morning!
...about human warmth.

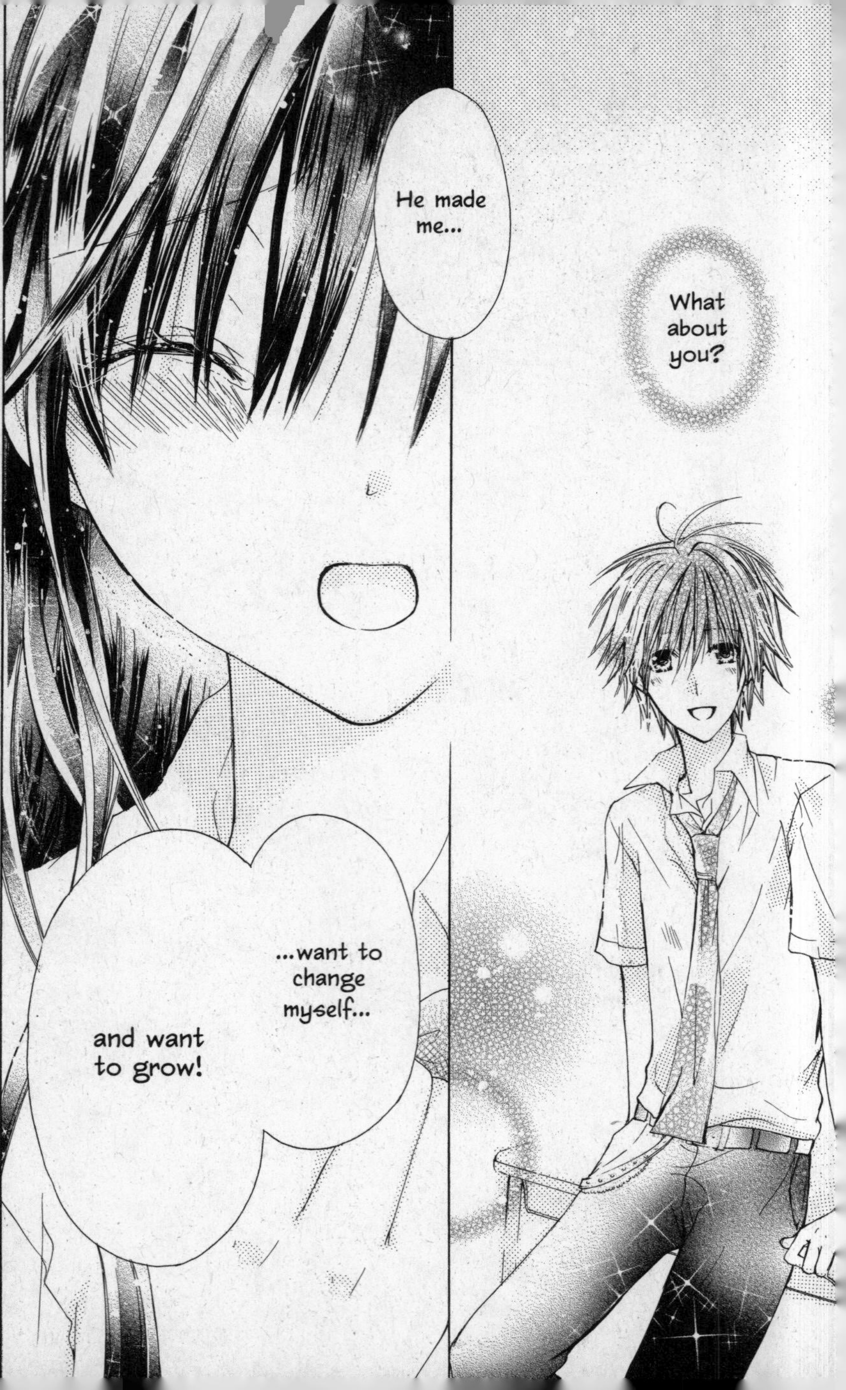
What about you?
He made me...
...want to change myself...
and want to grow!

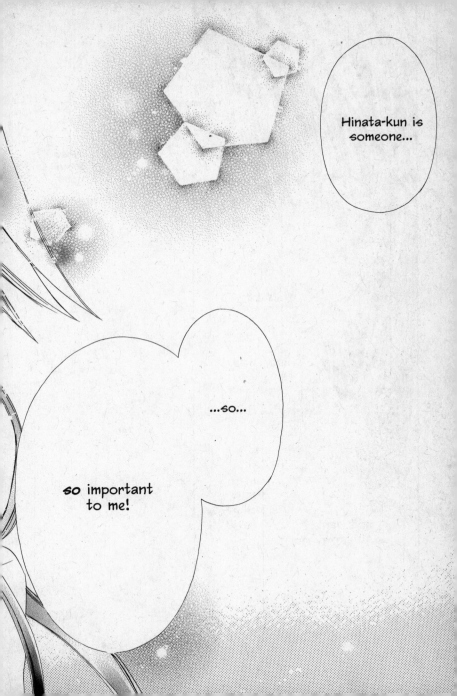

Hinata-kun is someone...

...so...

so important to me!

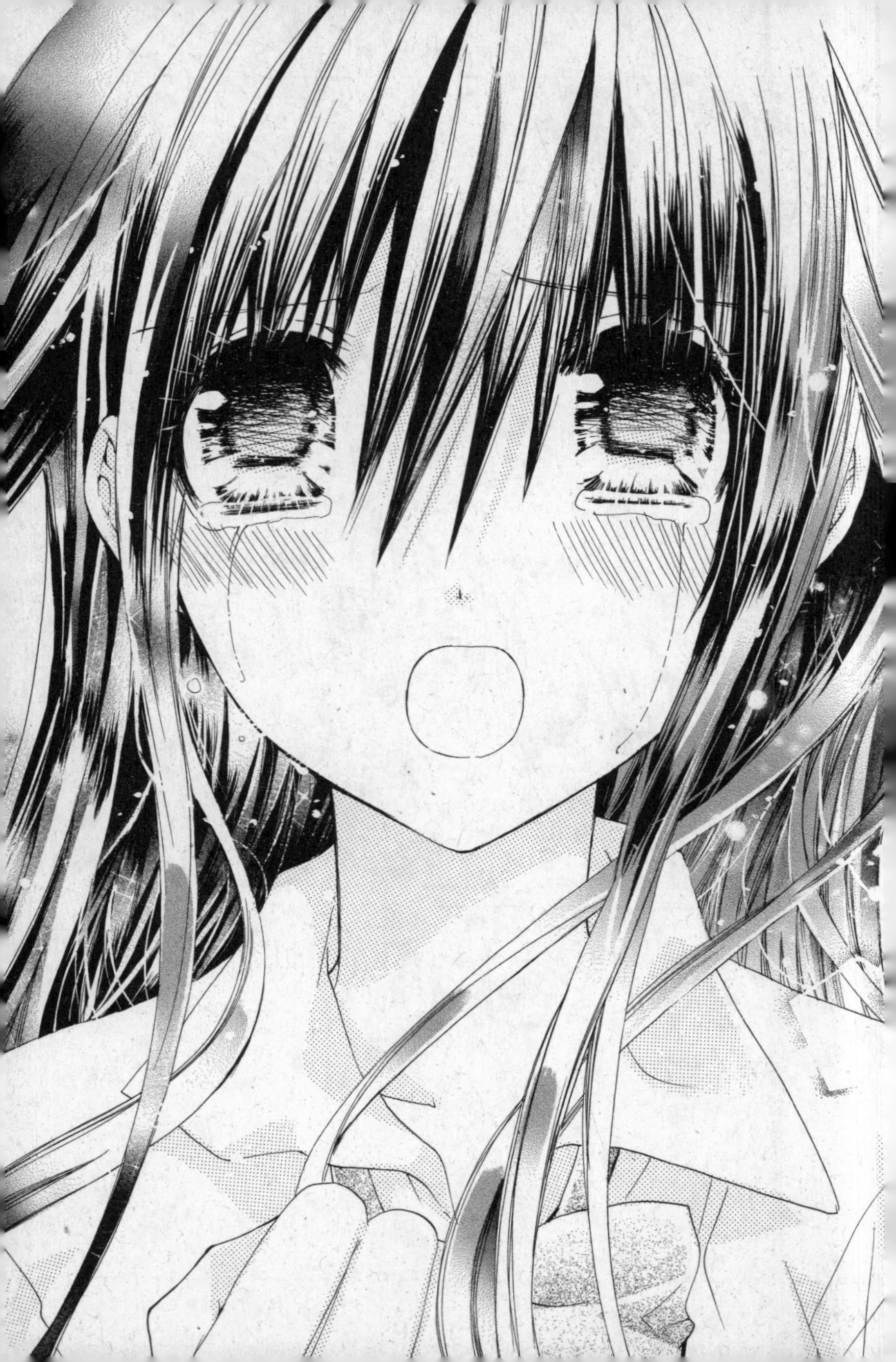

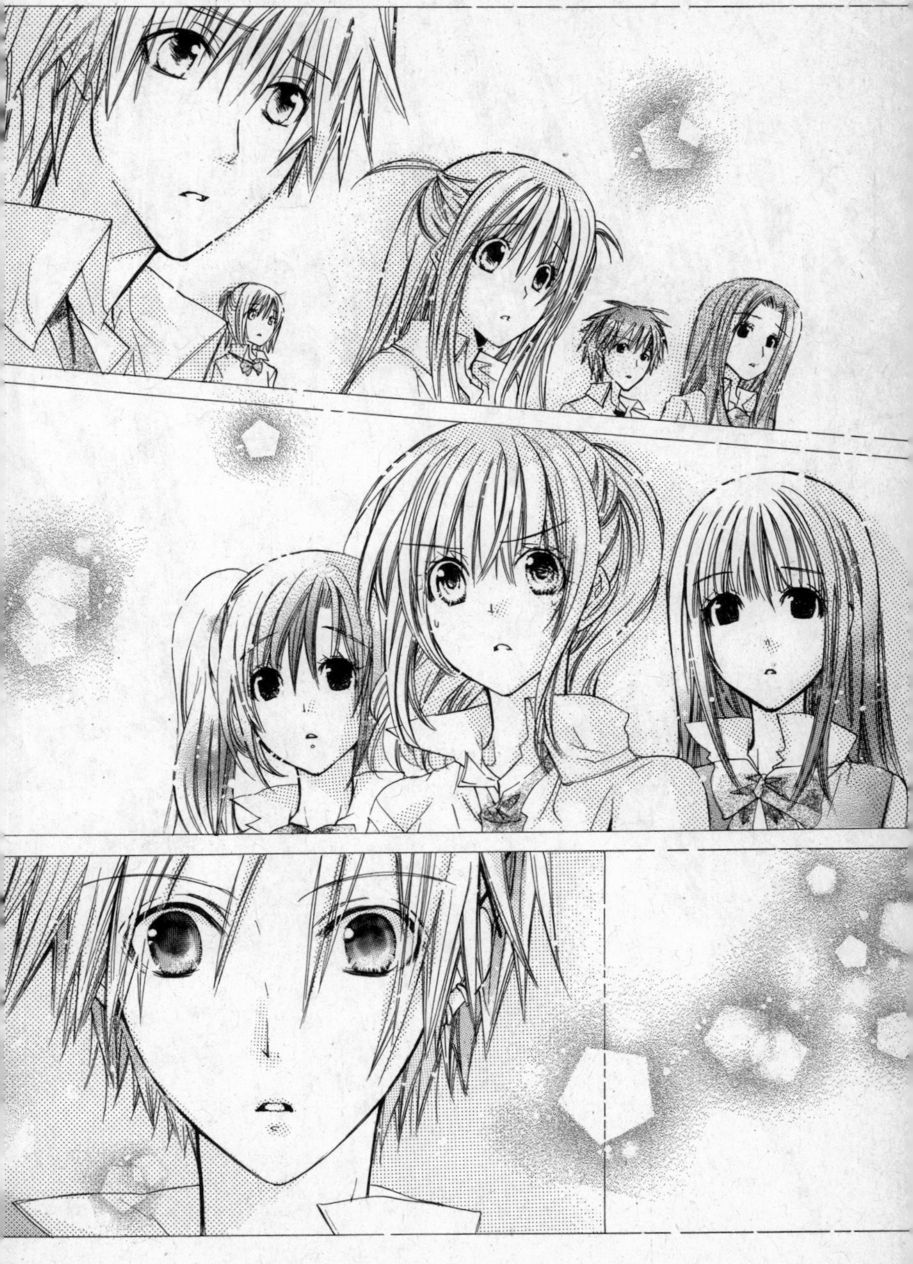

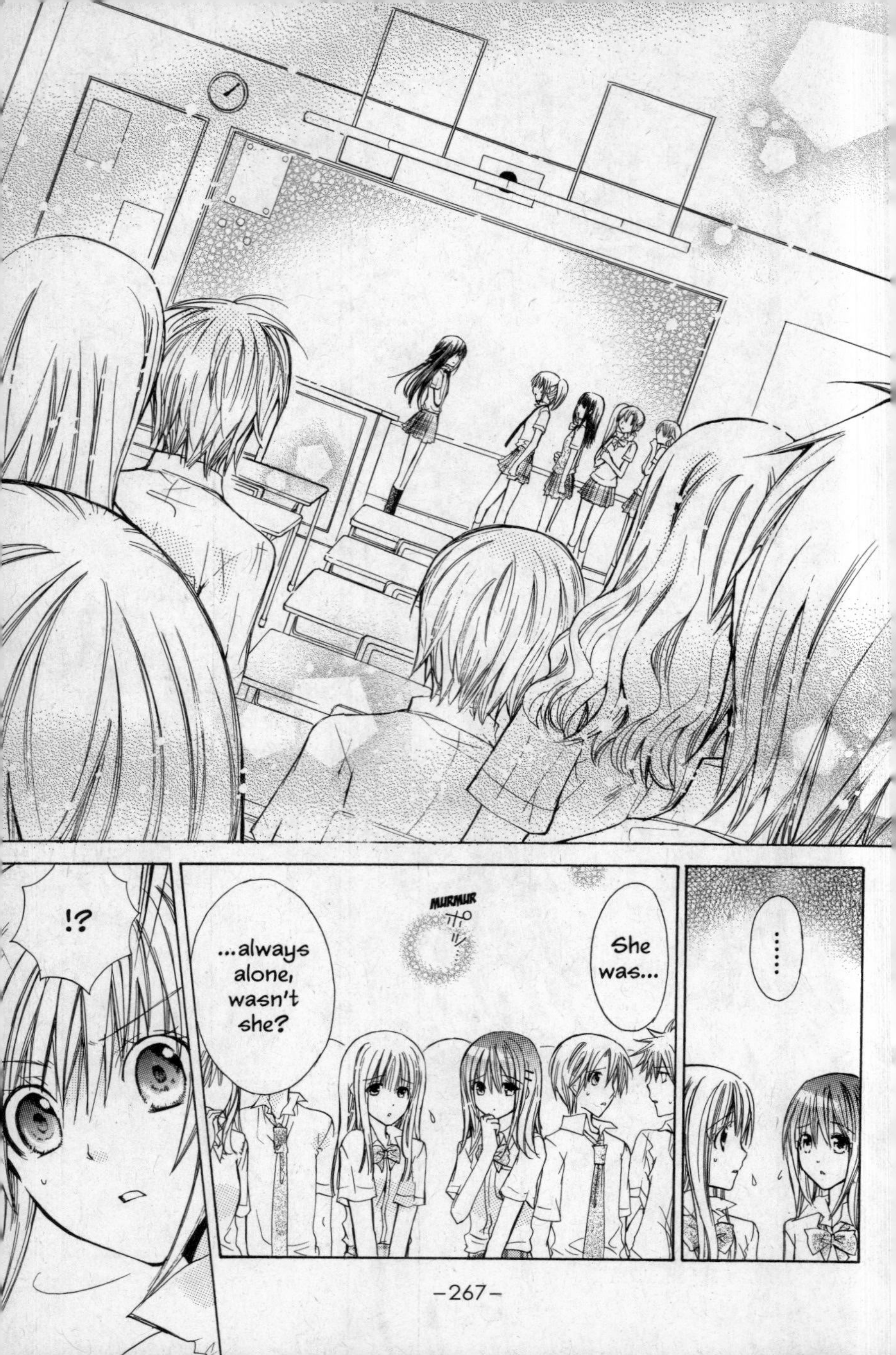
......
She was...
MURMUR
...always alone, wasn't she?
!?

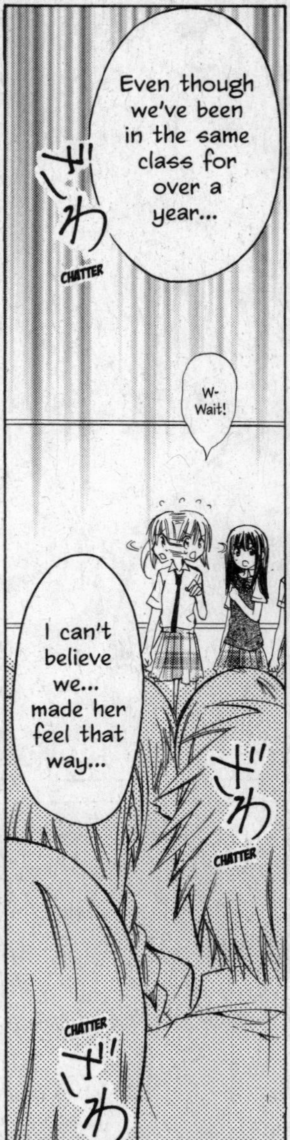
Even though we've been in the same class for over a year...
ざわ
CHATTER
W-Wait!
I can't believe we... made her feel that way...
ざわ
CHATTER
CHATTER
ざわ
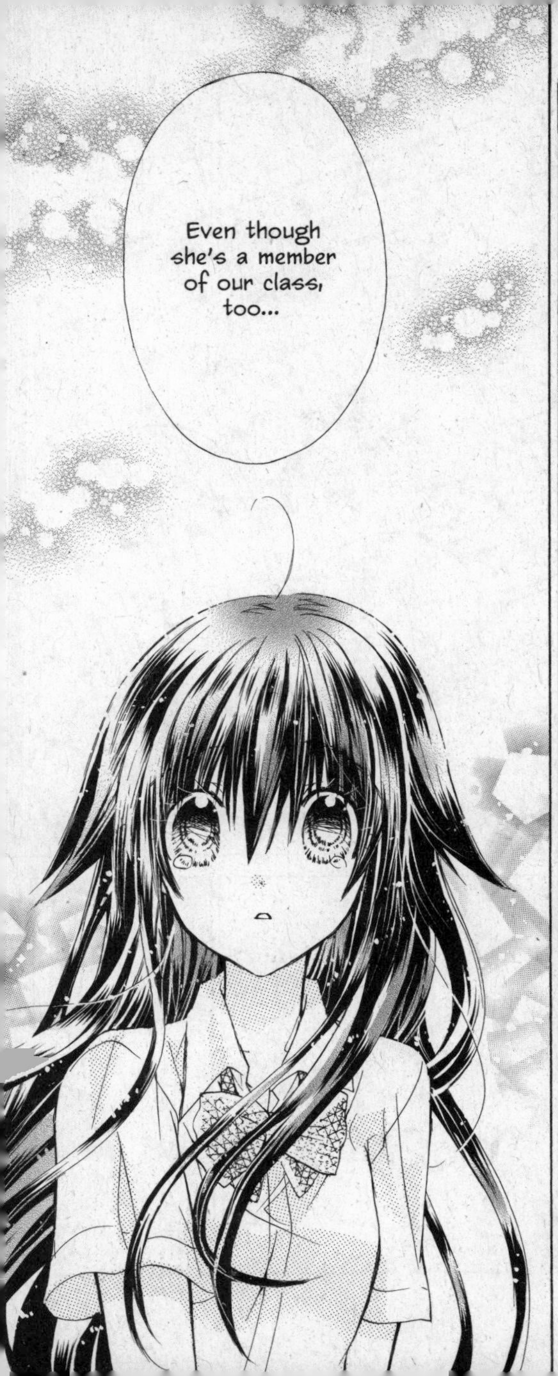
Even though she's a member of our class, too...

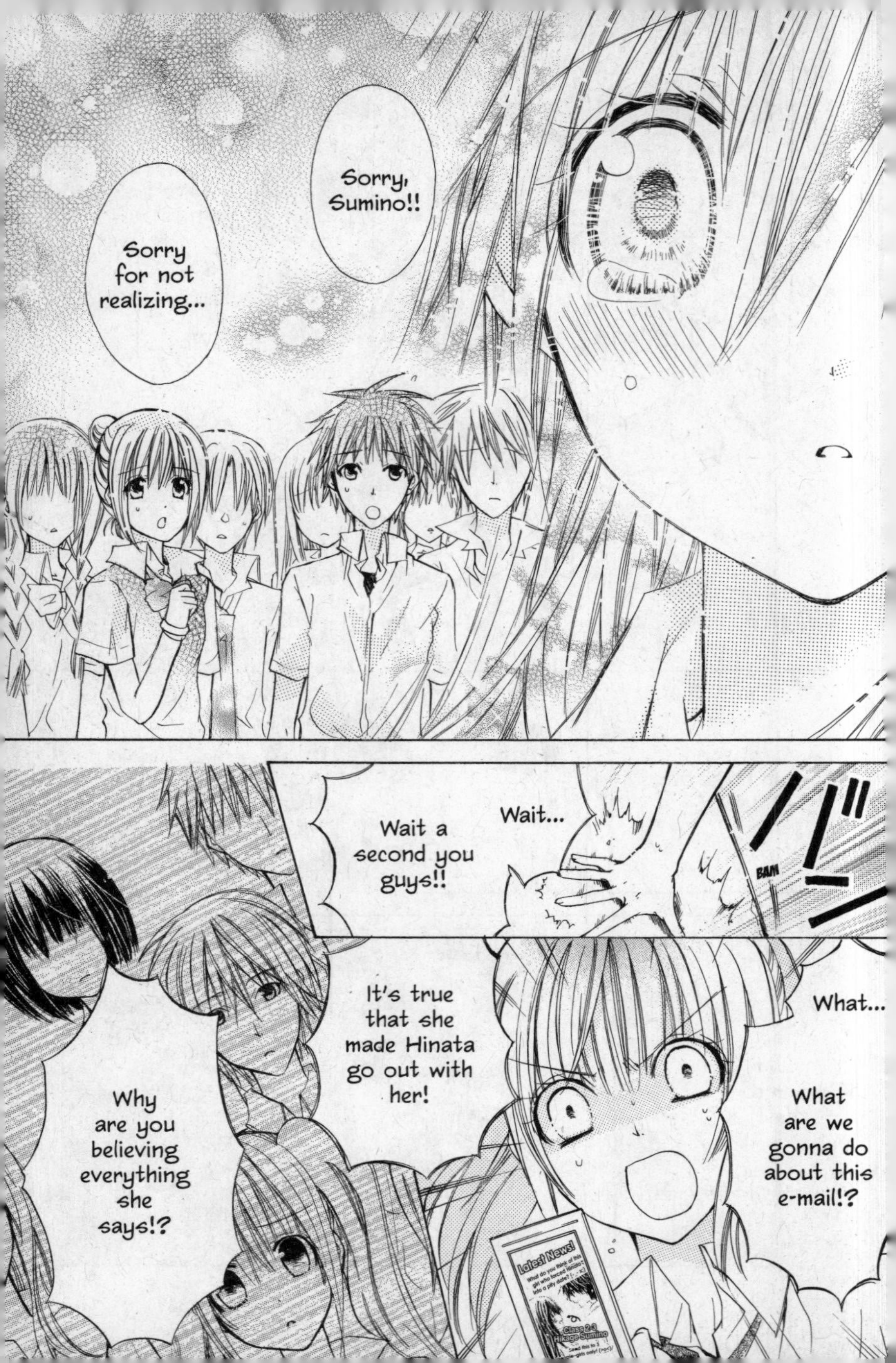
Sorry, Sumino!!
Sorry for not realizing...
BAM
Wait...
Wait a second you guys!!
What...
What are we gonna do about this e-mail!?
Latest News!
What do you think of this girl who forced Hinata into a pity date?
Class 2-3 Hikage Sumino
It's true that she made Hinata go out with her!
Why are you believing everything she says!?

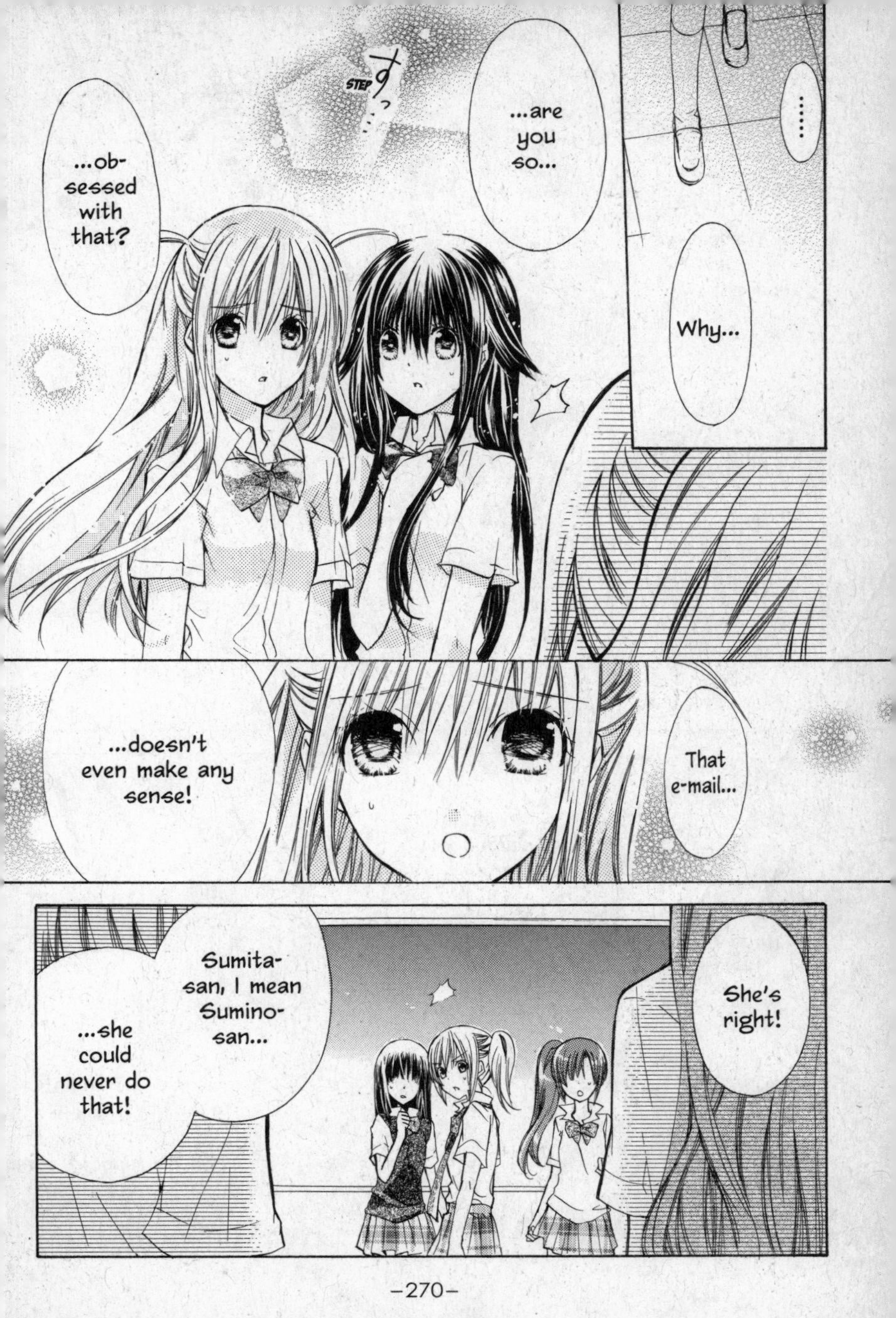
......
Why...
...are you so...
STEP
すっ
...ob-sessed with that?
That e-mail...
...doesn't even make any sense!
She's right!
Sumita-san, I mean Sumino-san...
...she could never do that!

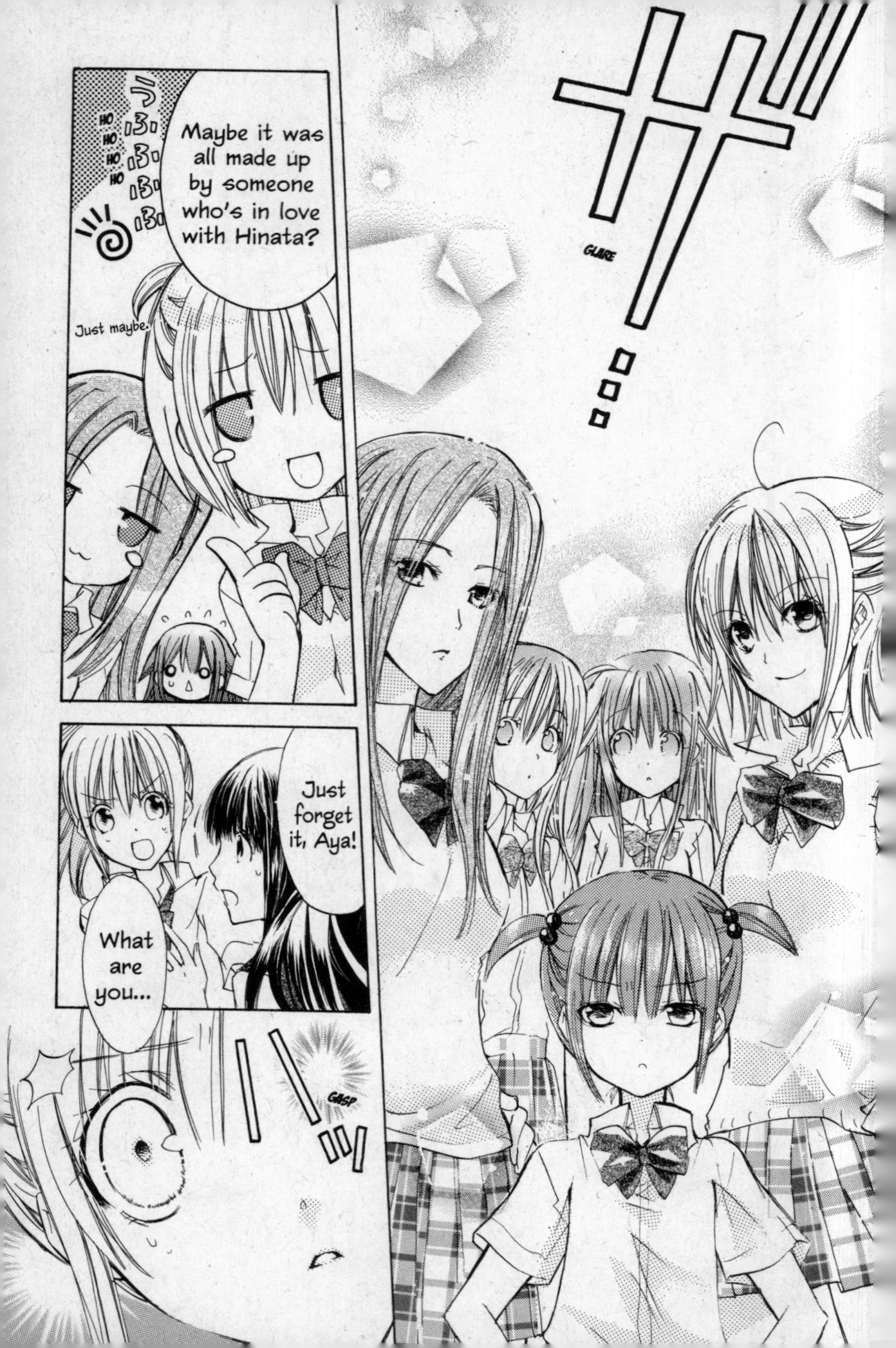
GLARE
...
HO HO HO HO
Maybe it was all made up by someone who's in love with Hinata?
Just maybe.
Just forget it, Aya!
What are you...
GASP

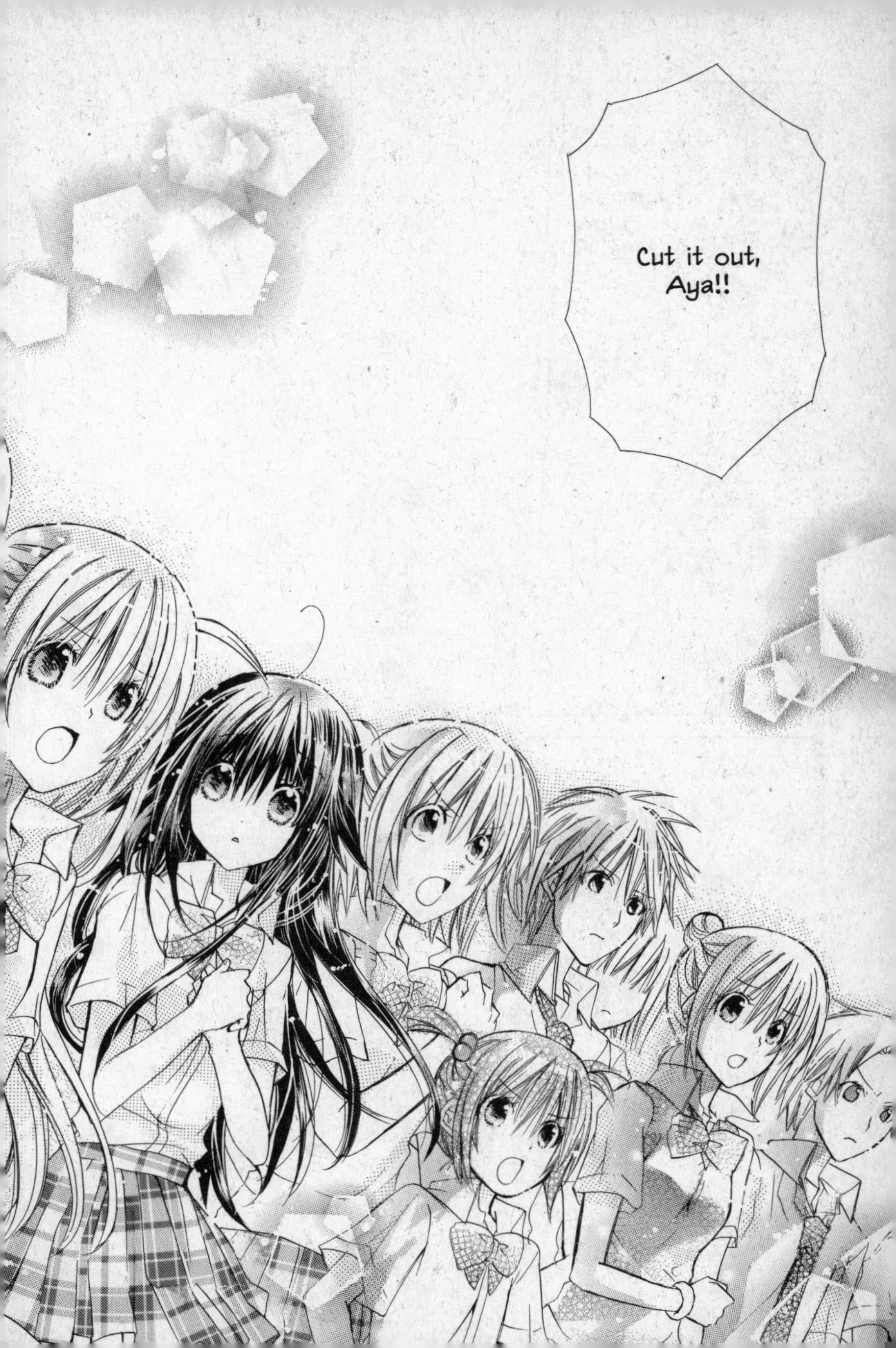
Cut it out, Aya!!

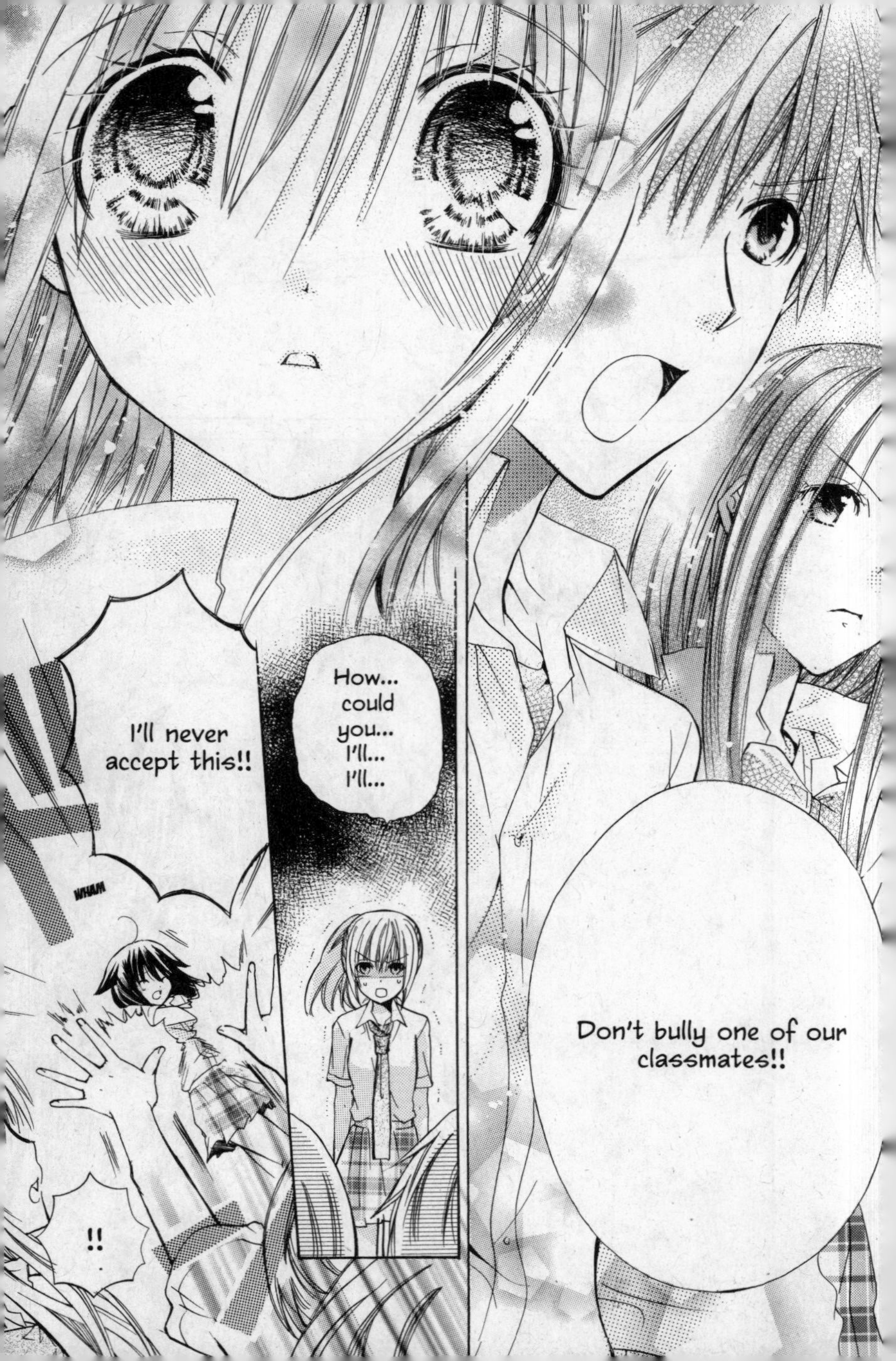
Don't bully one of our classmates!!
How... could you... I'll... I'll...
I'll never accept this!!
WHAM
!!

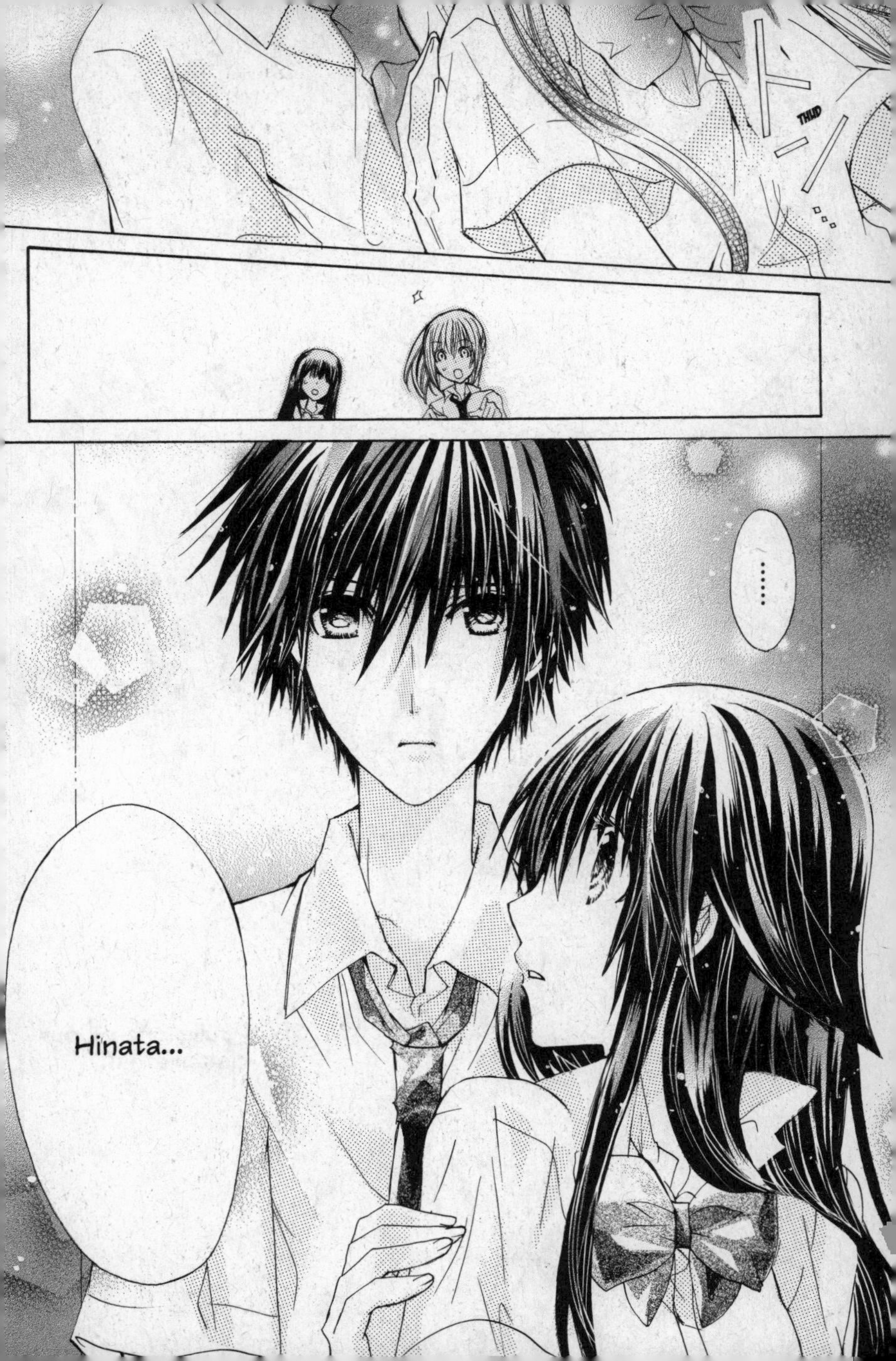
THUD
......
Hinata...

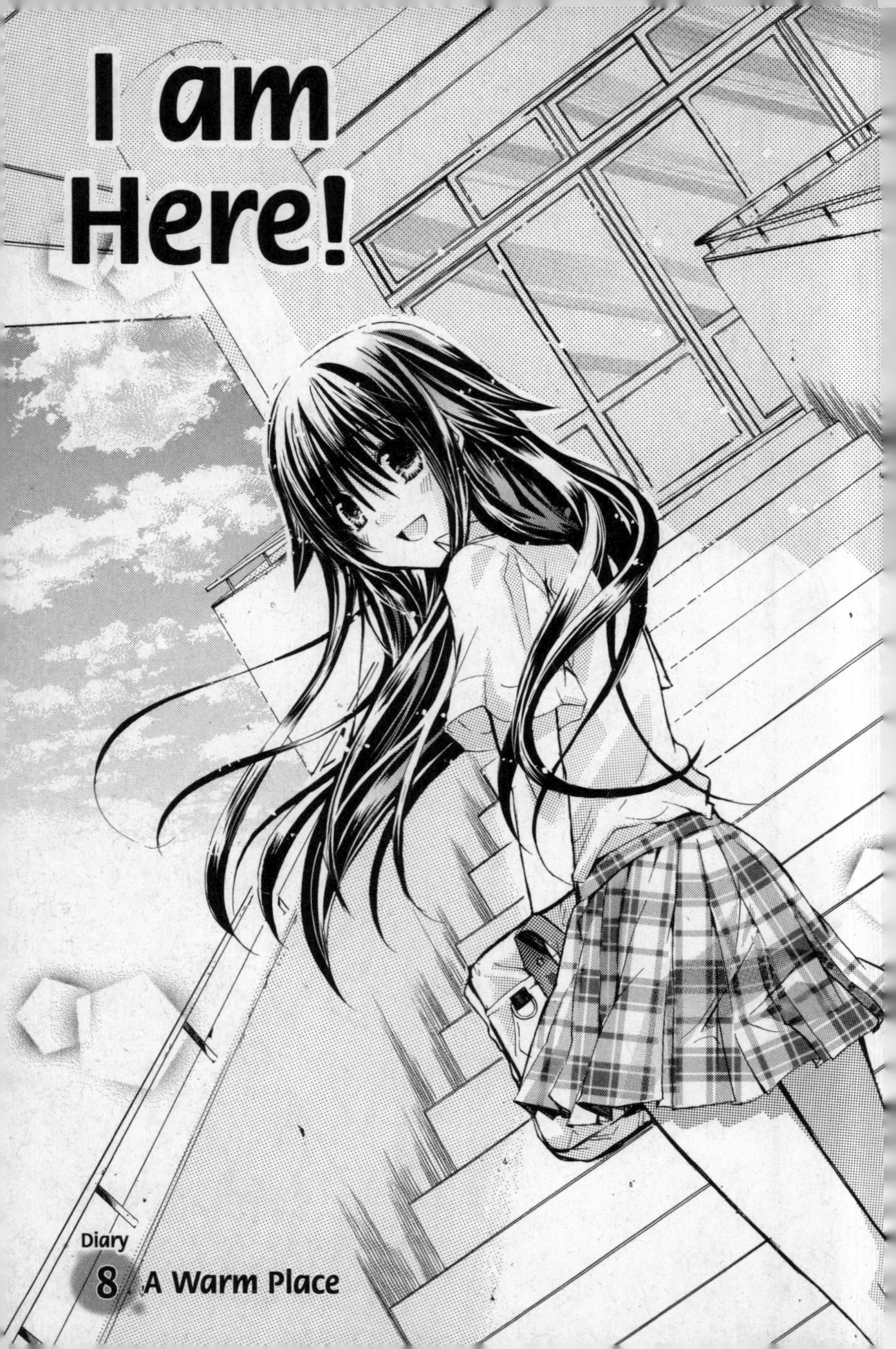
I am Here!
Diary 8 A Warm Place

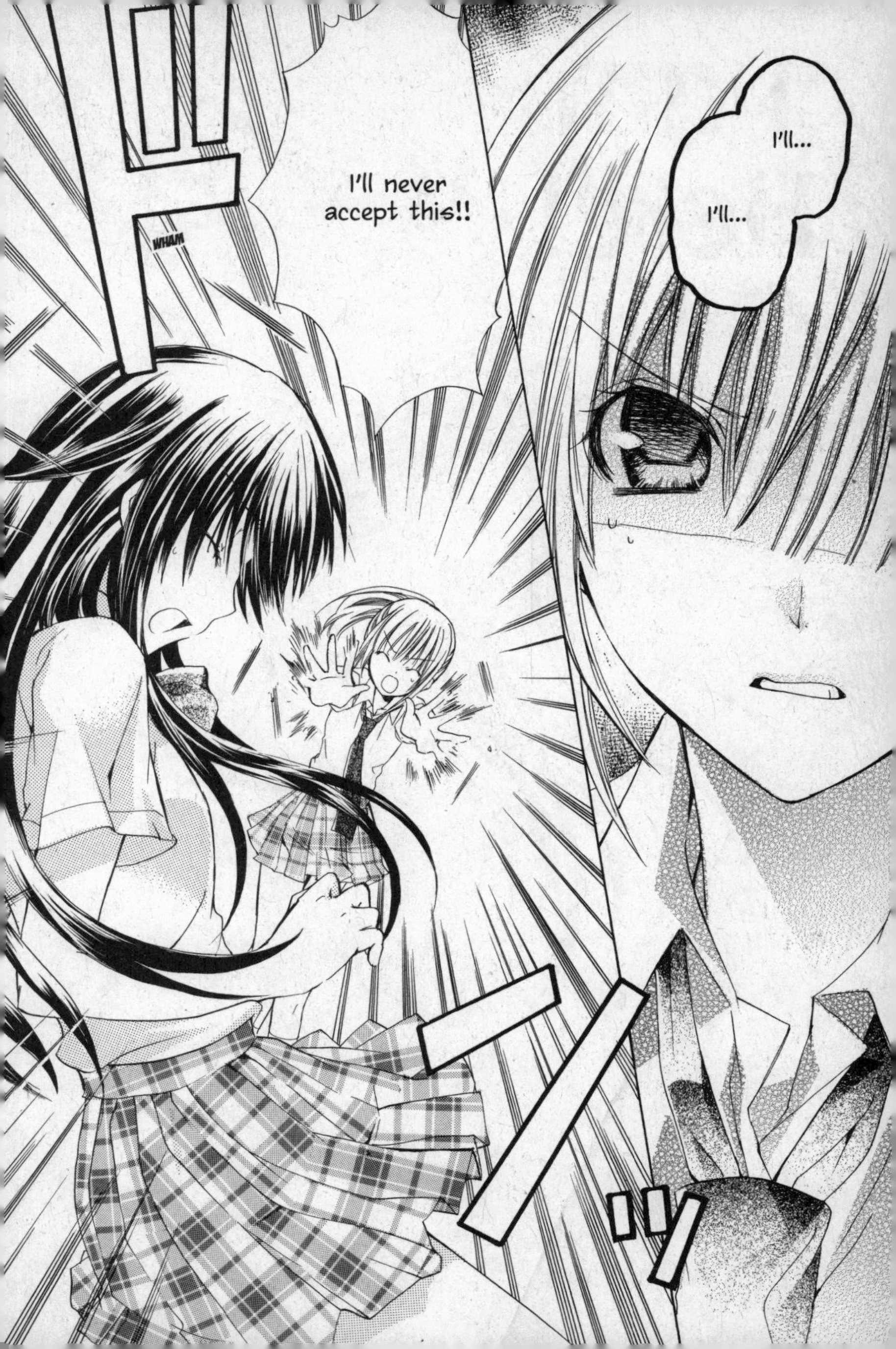
I'll...
I'll...
I'll never accept this!!
WHAM

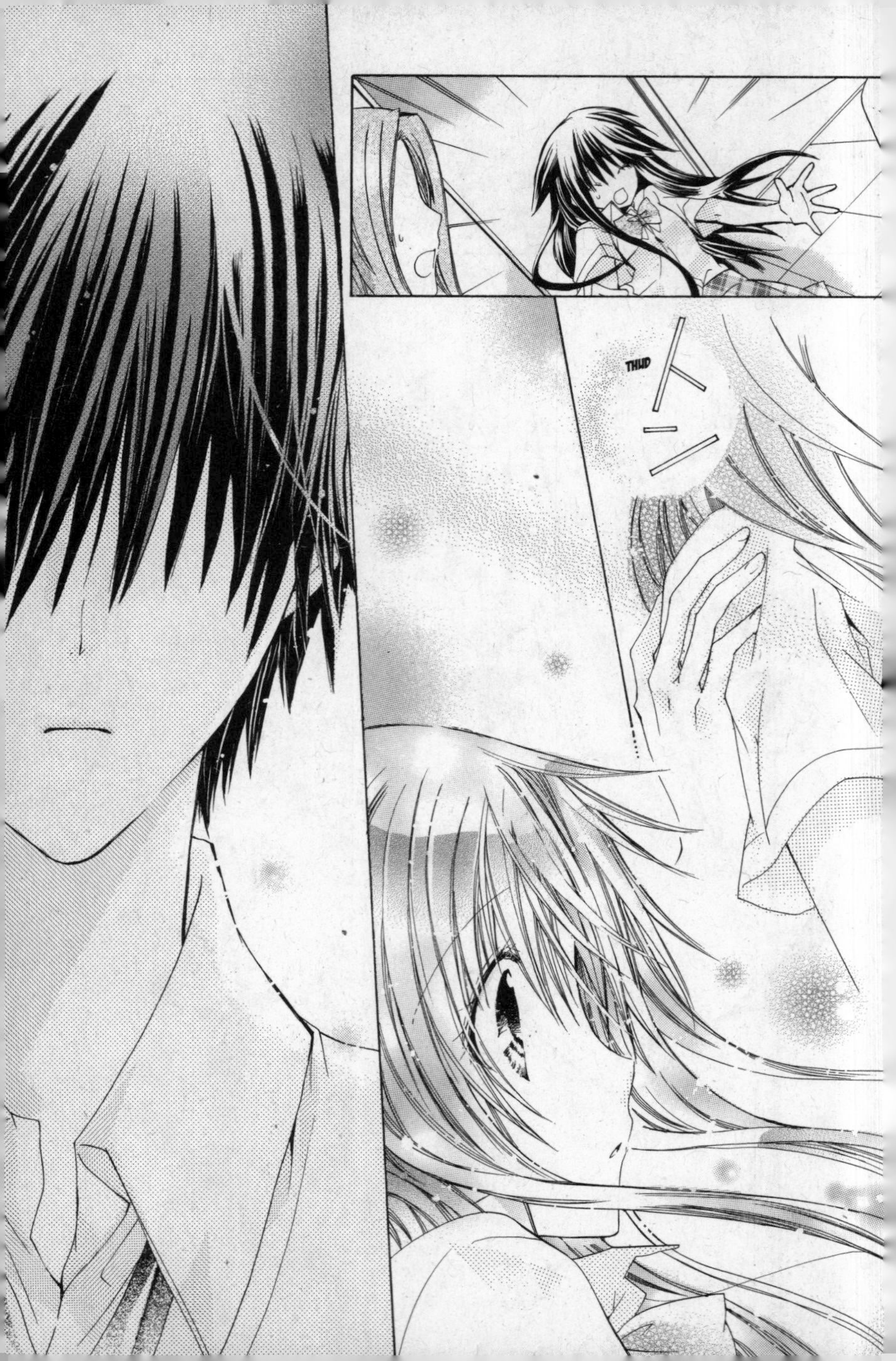
THUD

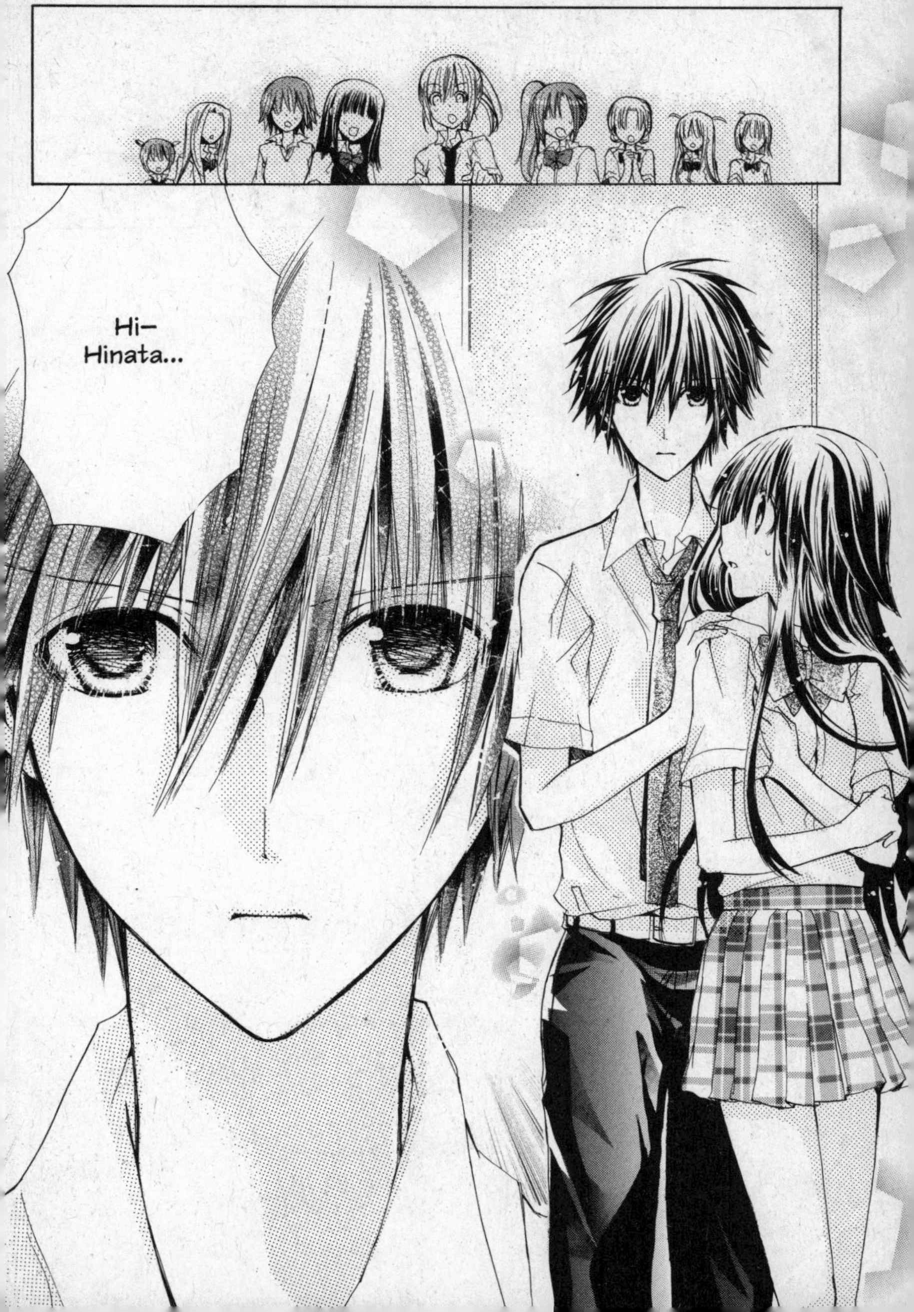
Hi-
Hinata...

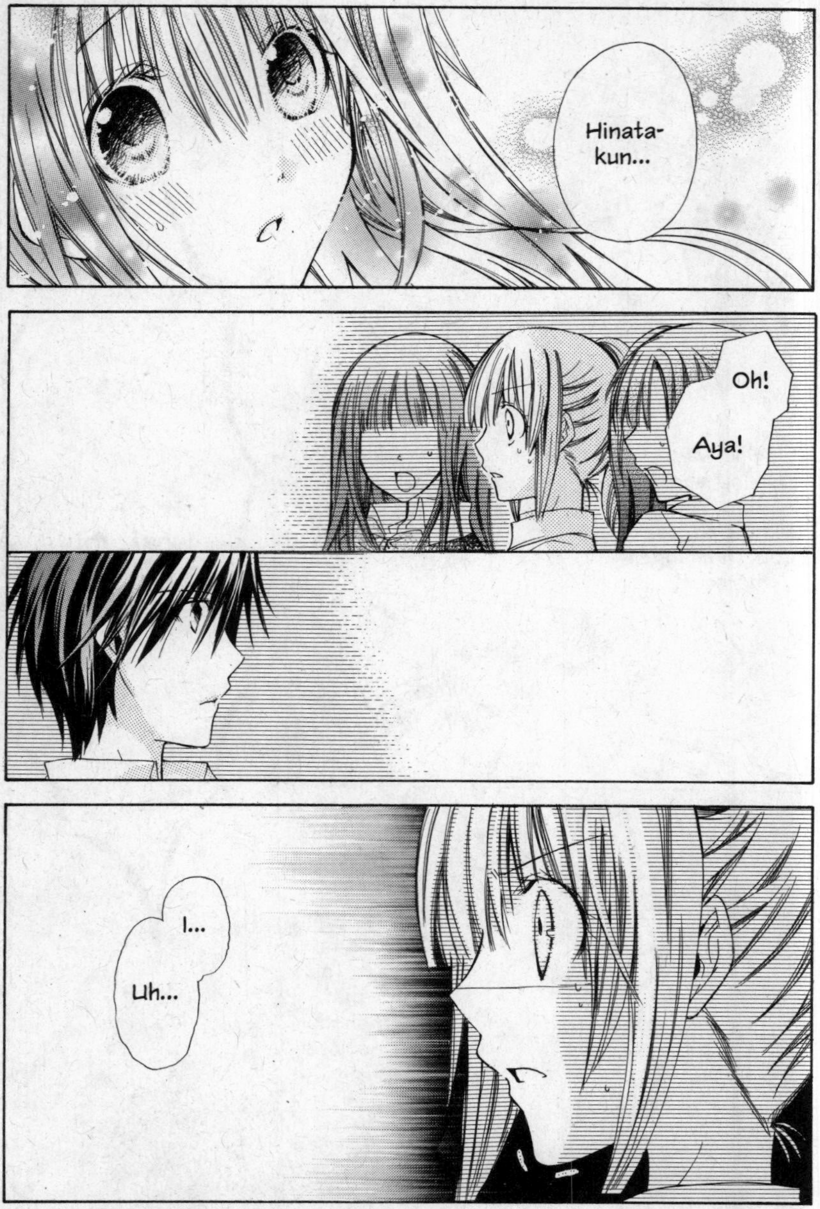
Hinata-kun...
Oh!
Aya!
I...
Uh...

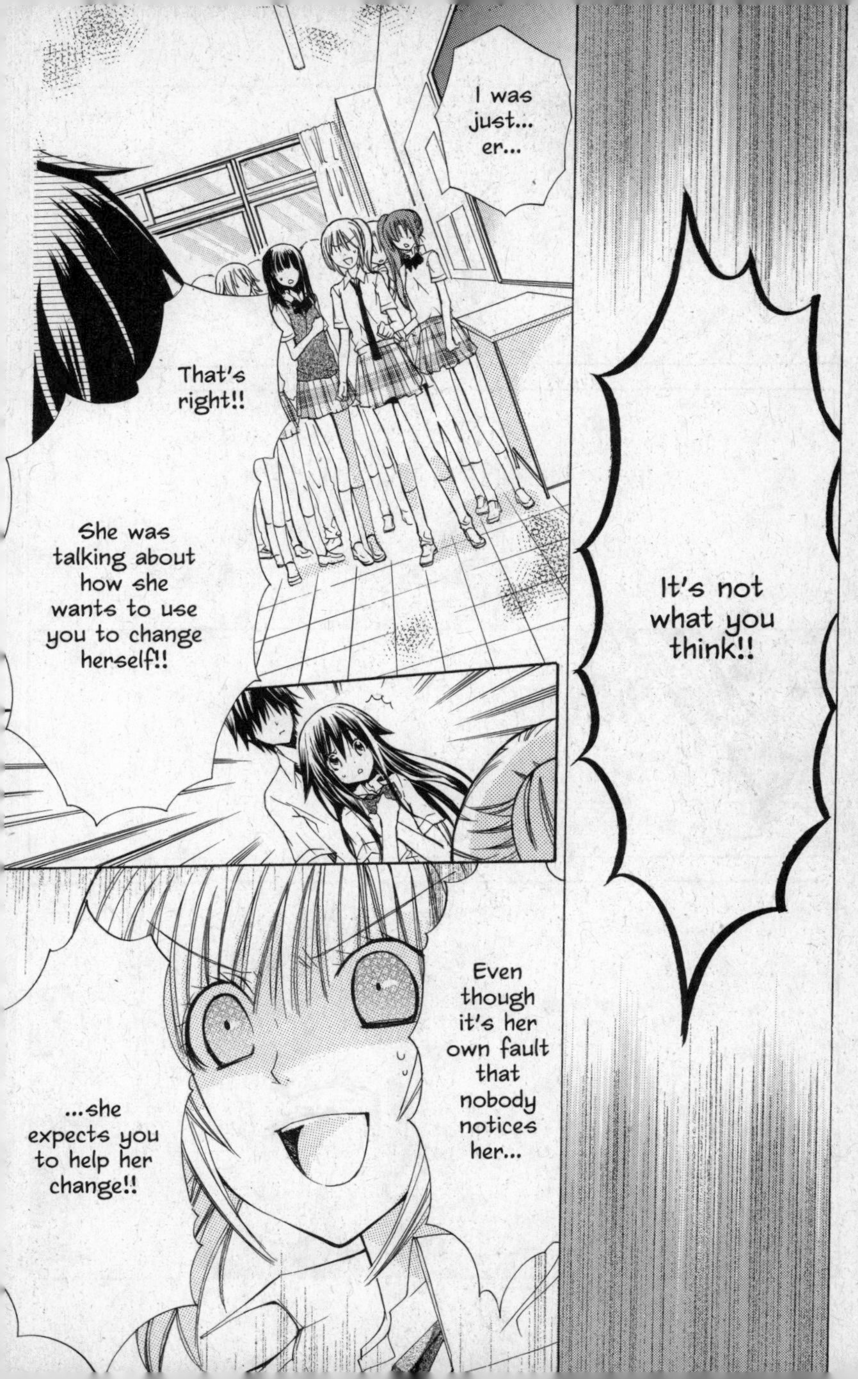

It's not what you think!!
I was just... er...
That's right!!
She was talking about how she wants to use you to change herself!!
Even though it's her own fault that nobody notices her...
...she expects you to help her change!!

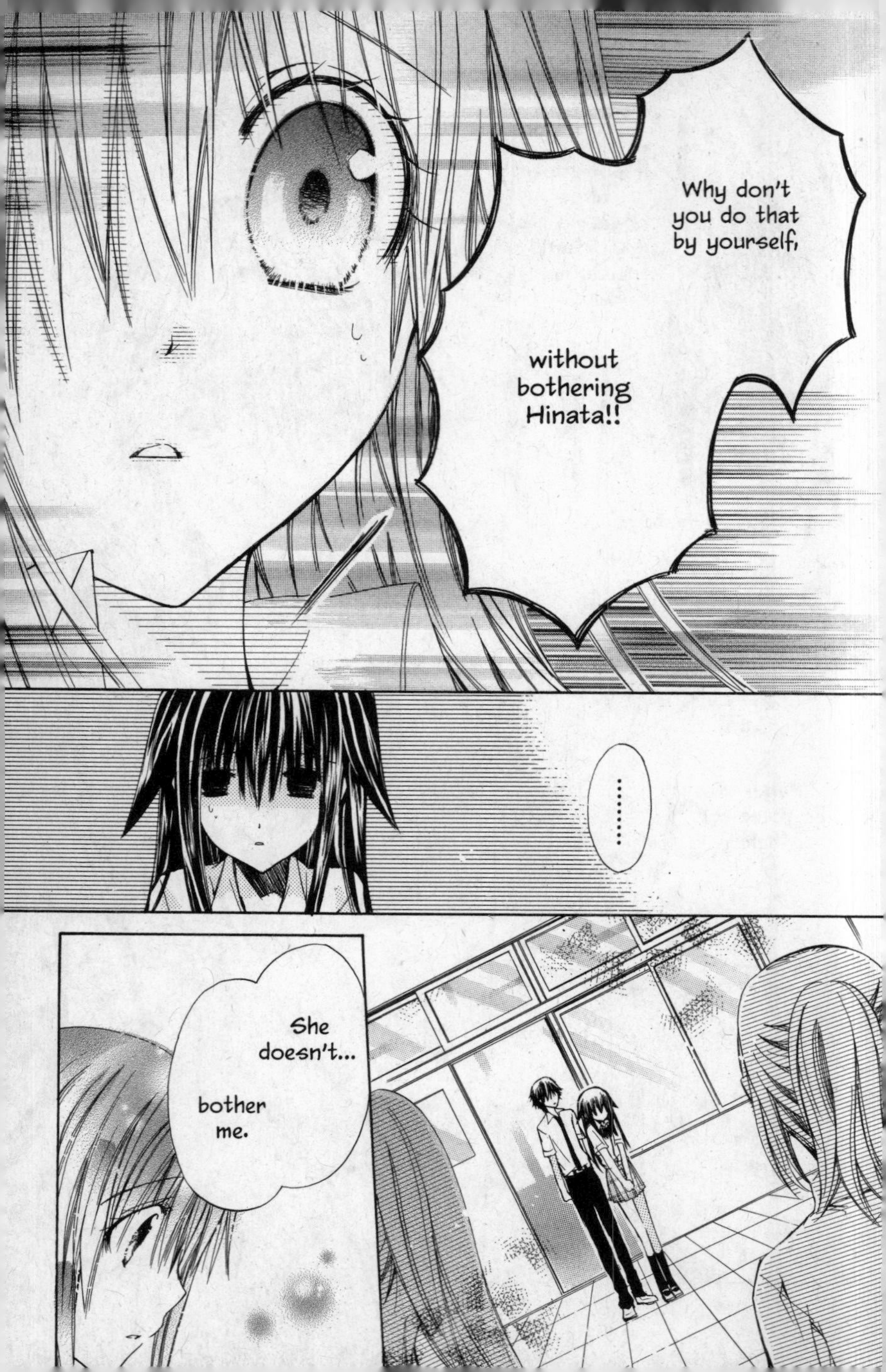
Why don't you do that by yourself,
without bothering Hinata!!
......
She doesn't...
bother me.

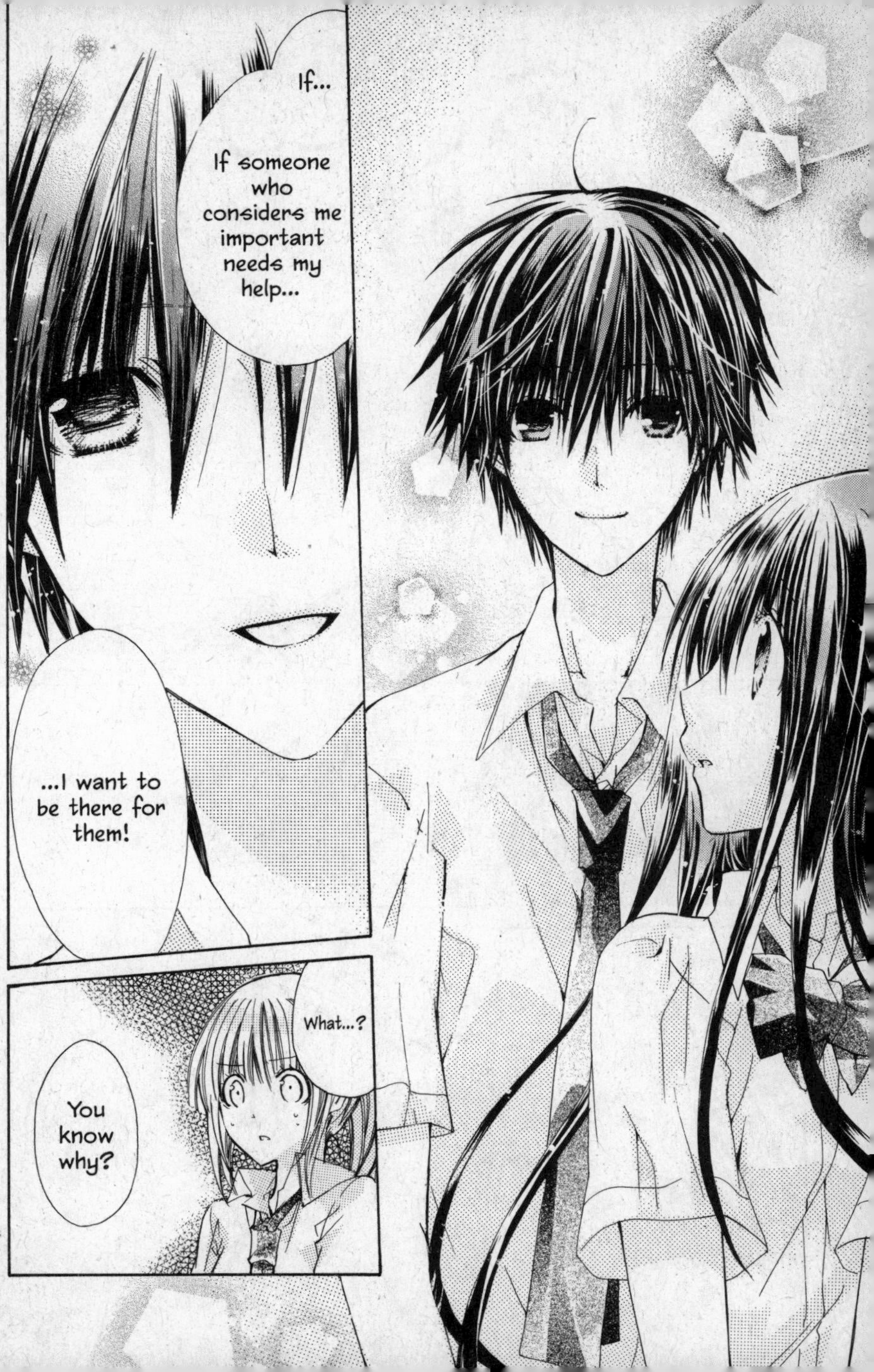
If...
If someone who considers me important needs my help...
...I want to be there for them!
What...?
You know why?

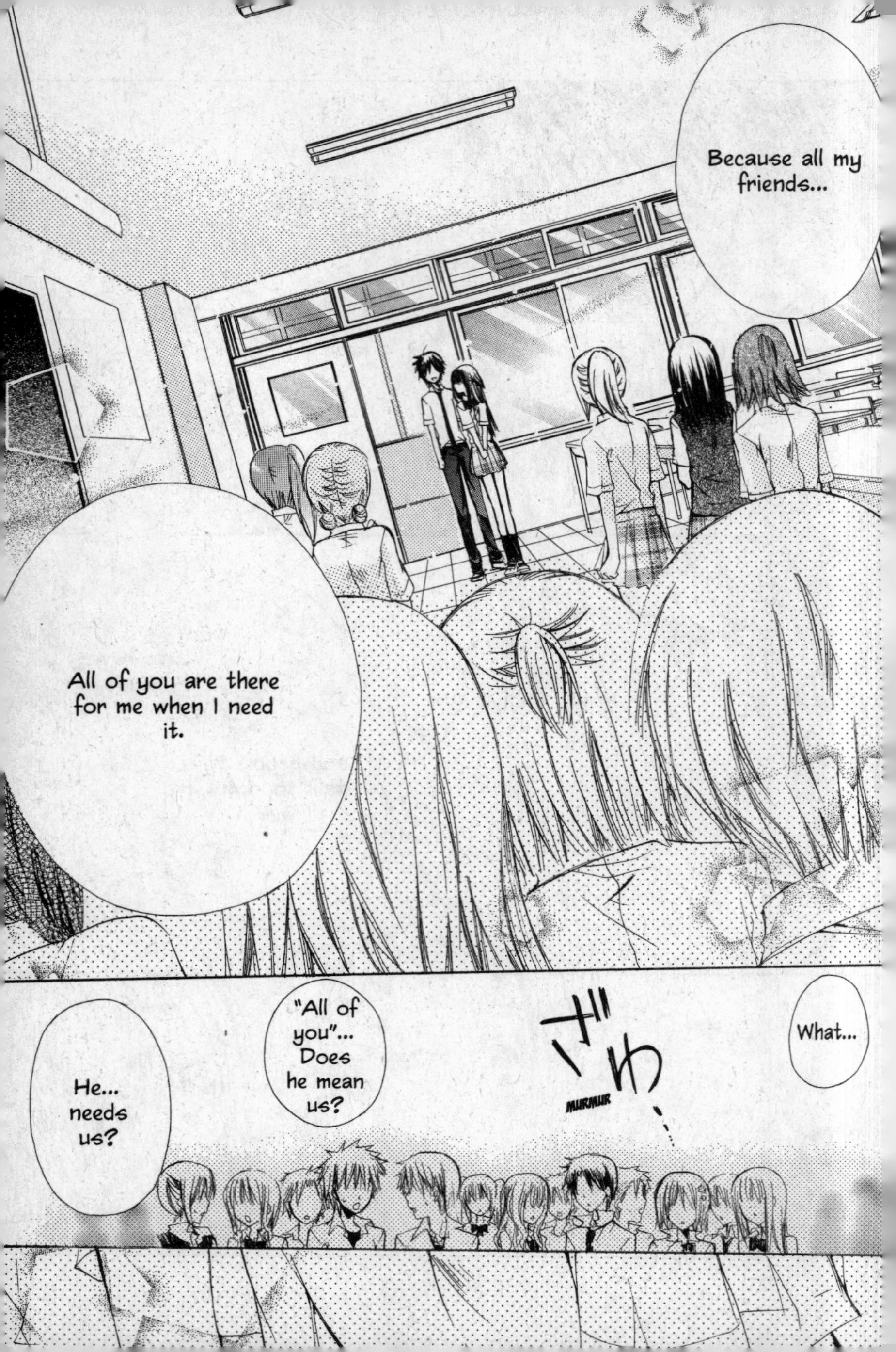
Because all my friends...
All of you are there for me when I need it.
What...
ざわ
MURMUR
"All of you"... Does he mean us?
He... needs us?

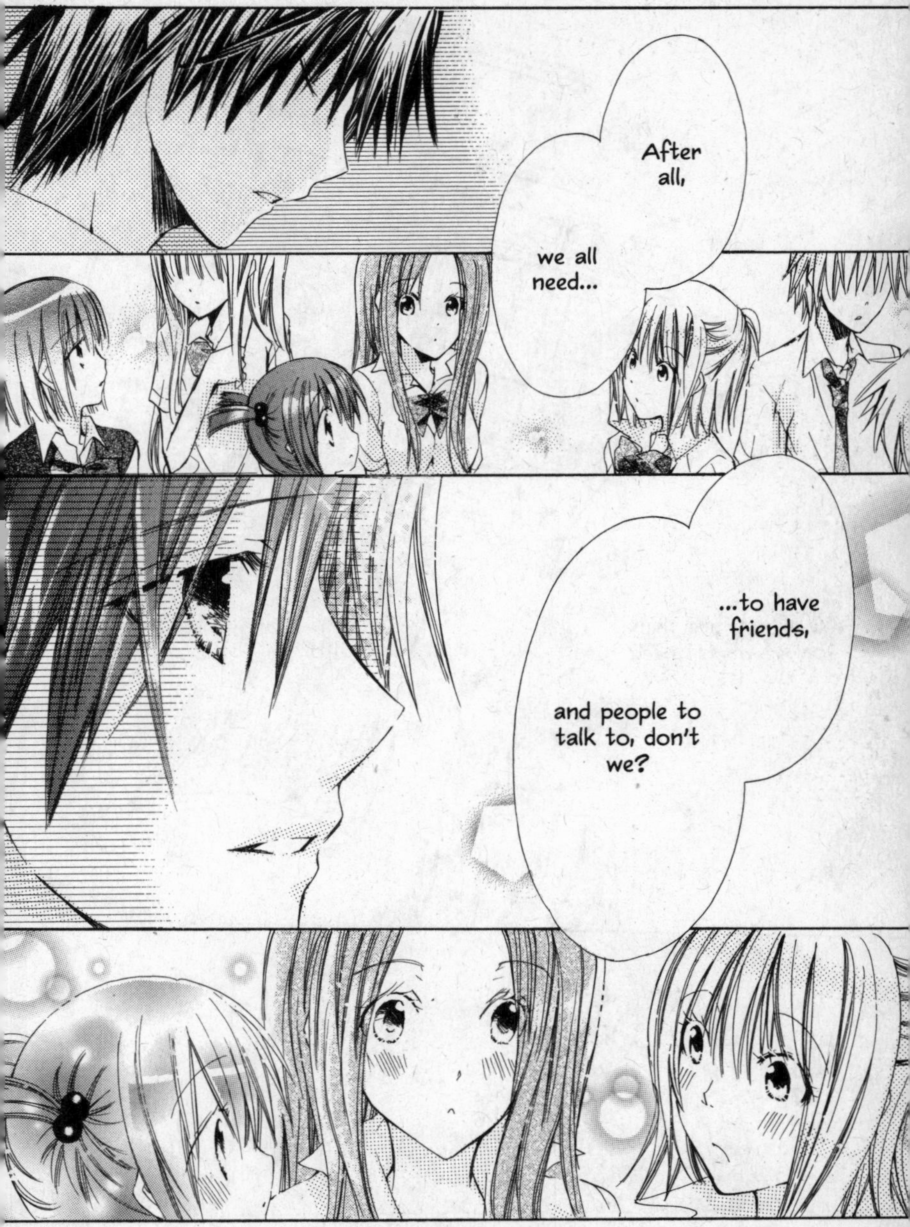
After all,
we all need...
...to have friends,
and people to talk to, don't we?

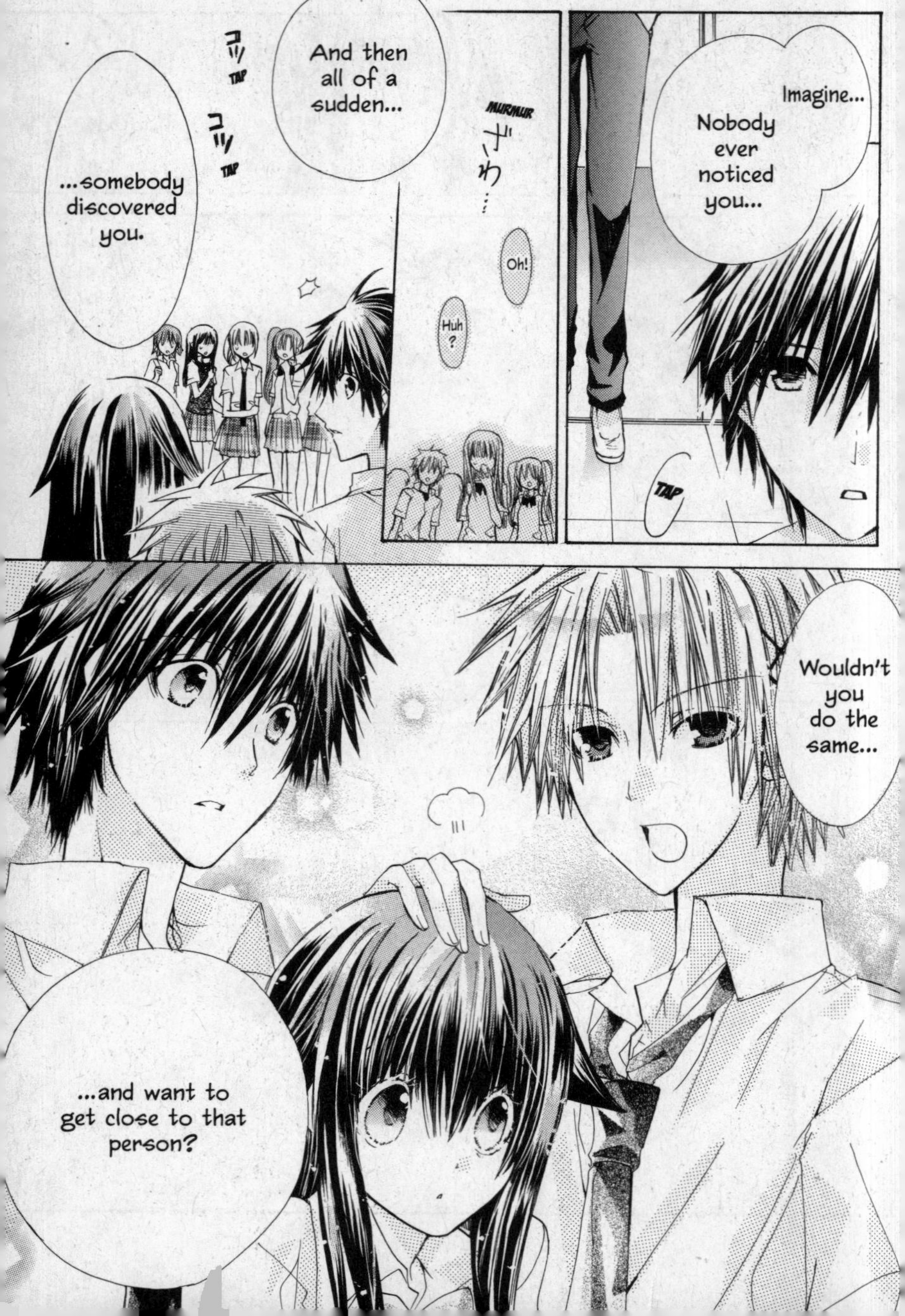
Imagine...
Nobody ever noticed you...
TAP
ざわ…
MURMUR
Oh!
Huh?
And then all of a sudden...
コツ
TAP
コツ
TAP
...somebody discovered you.
Wouldn't you do the same...
...and want to get close to that person?

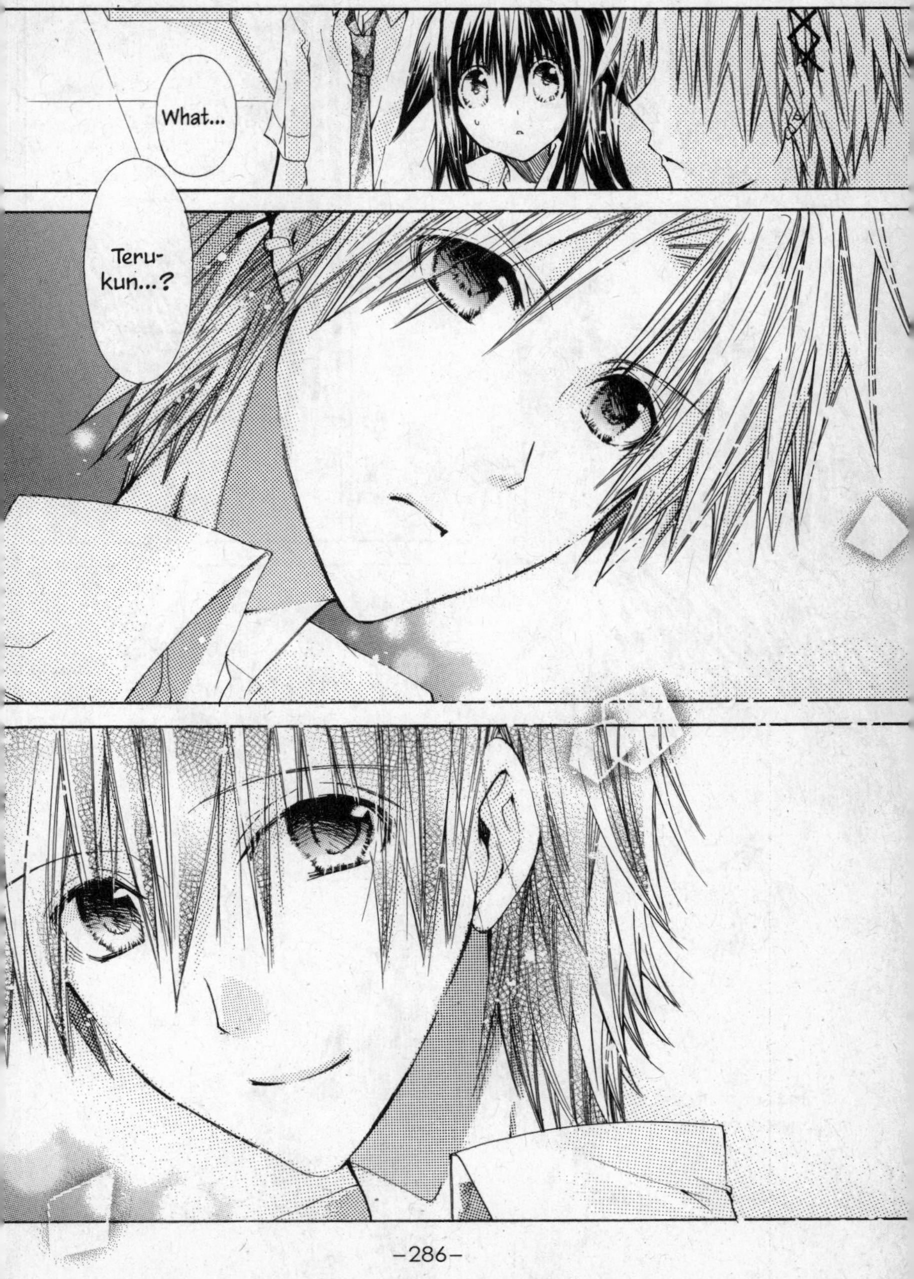
What...
Teru-kun...?

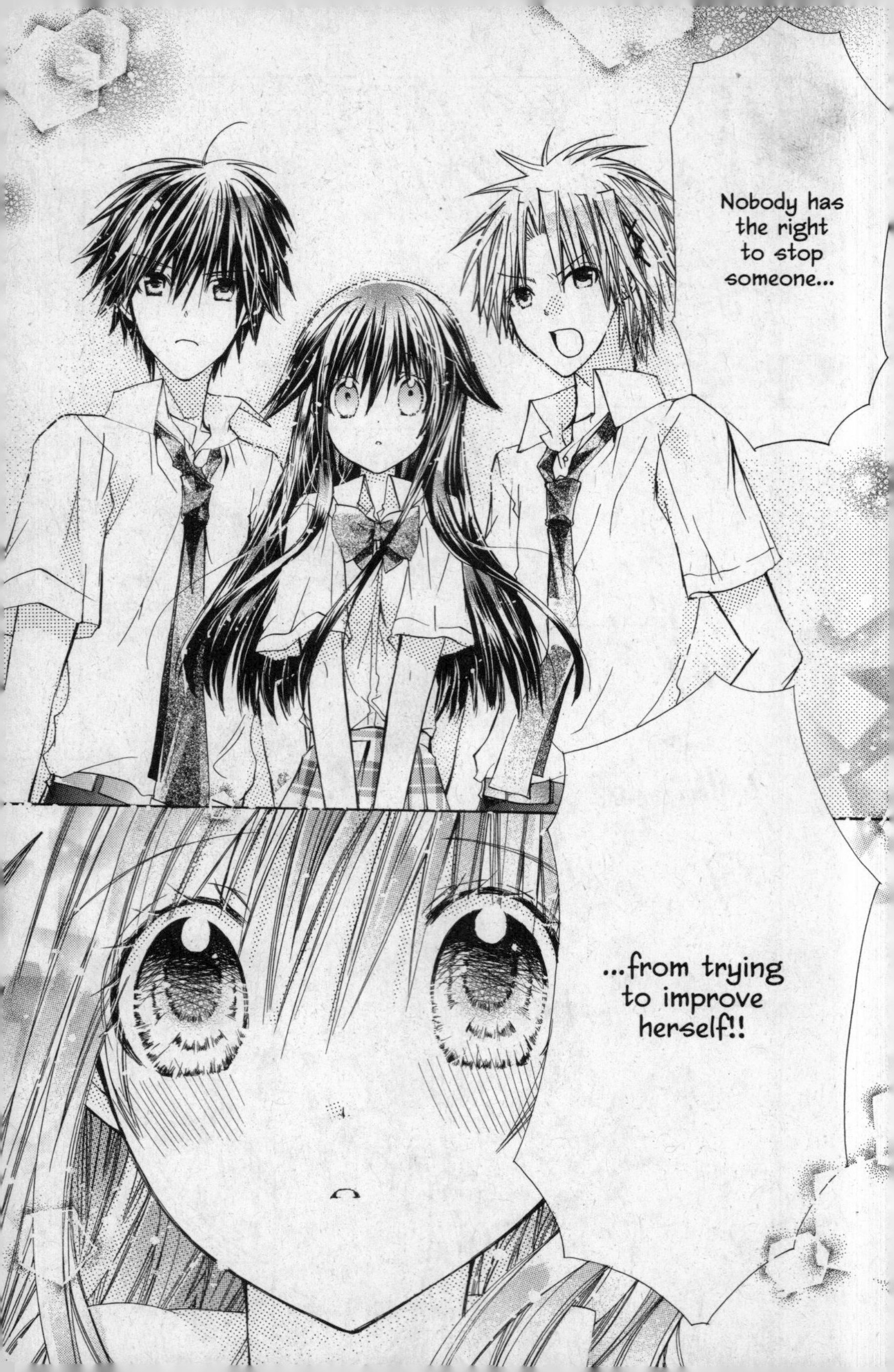
Nobody has the right to stop someone...
...from trying to improve herself!!

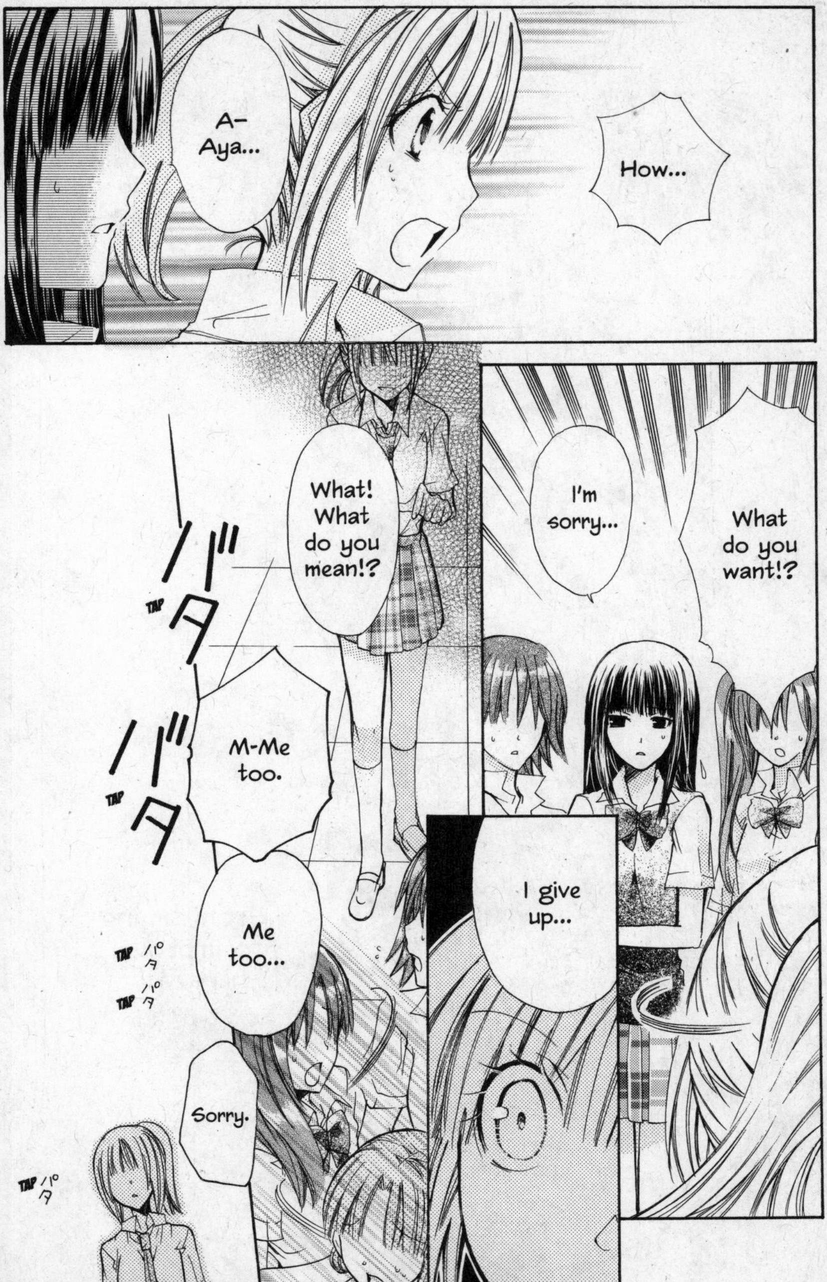
How...
A- Aya...
What do you want!?
I'm sorry...
I give up...
What! What do you mean!?
バタ
TAP
M-Me too.
バタ
TAP
Me too...
パタ
TAP
パタ
TAP
Sorry.
パタ
TAP

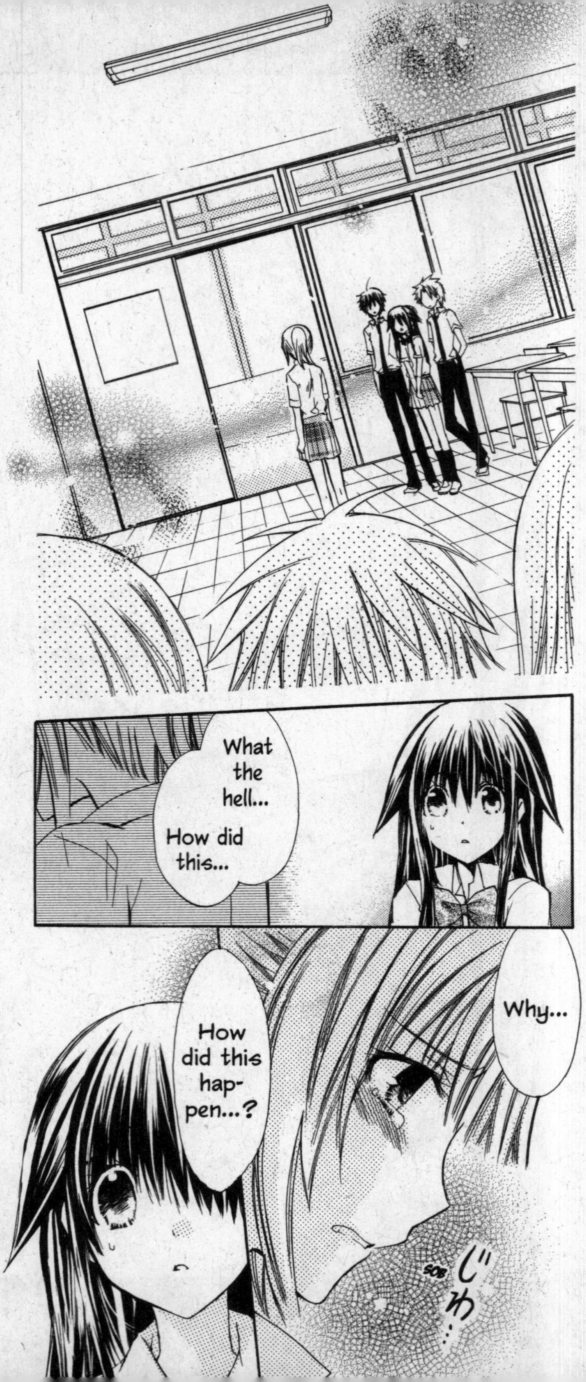
What the hell...
How did this...
Why...
How did this hap-pen...?
SOB
じわ…

Since You Demanded

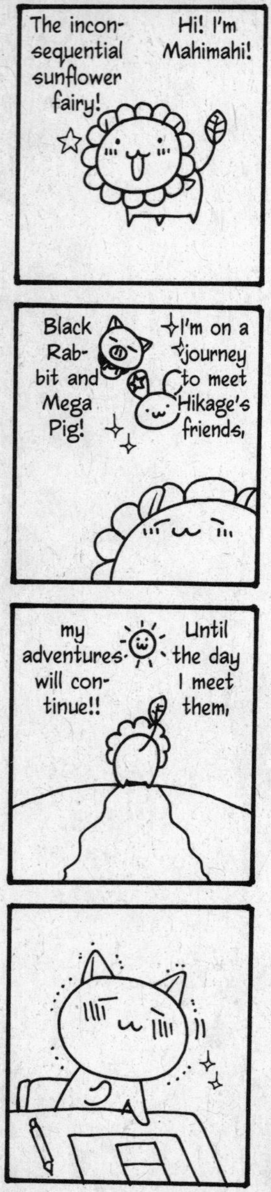
Hi! I'm Mahimahi!
The incon-sequential sunflower fairy!
I'm on a journey to meet Hikage's friends,
Black Rab-bit and Mega Pig!
Until the day I meet them,
my adventures will con-tinue!!

I gave it a try

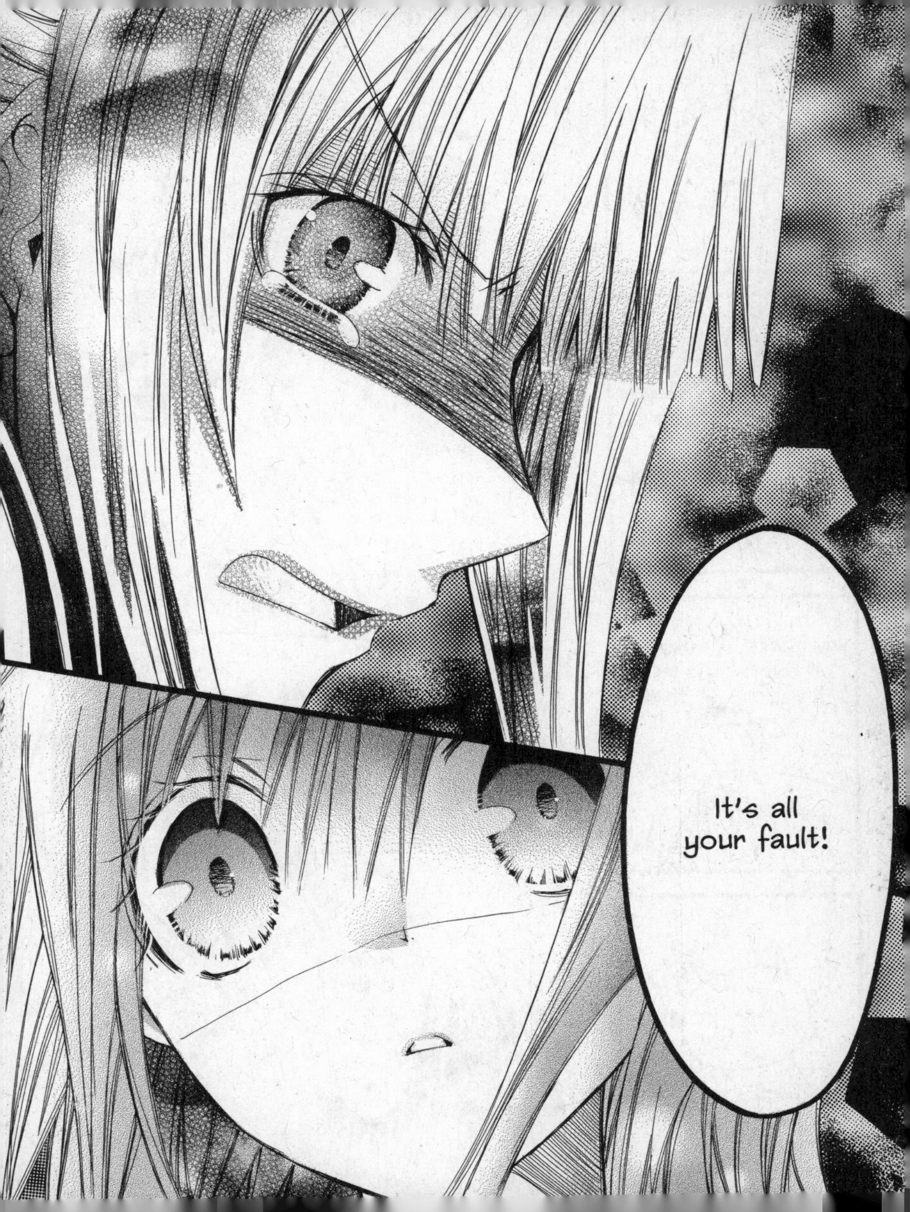
It's all your fault!

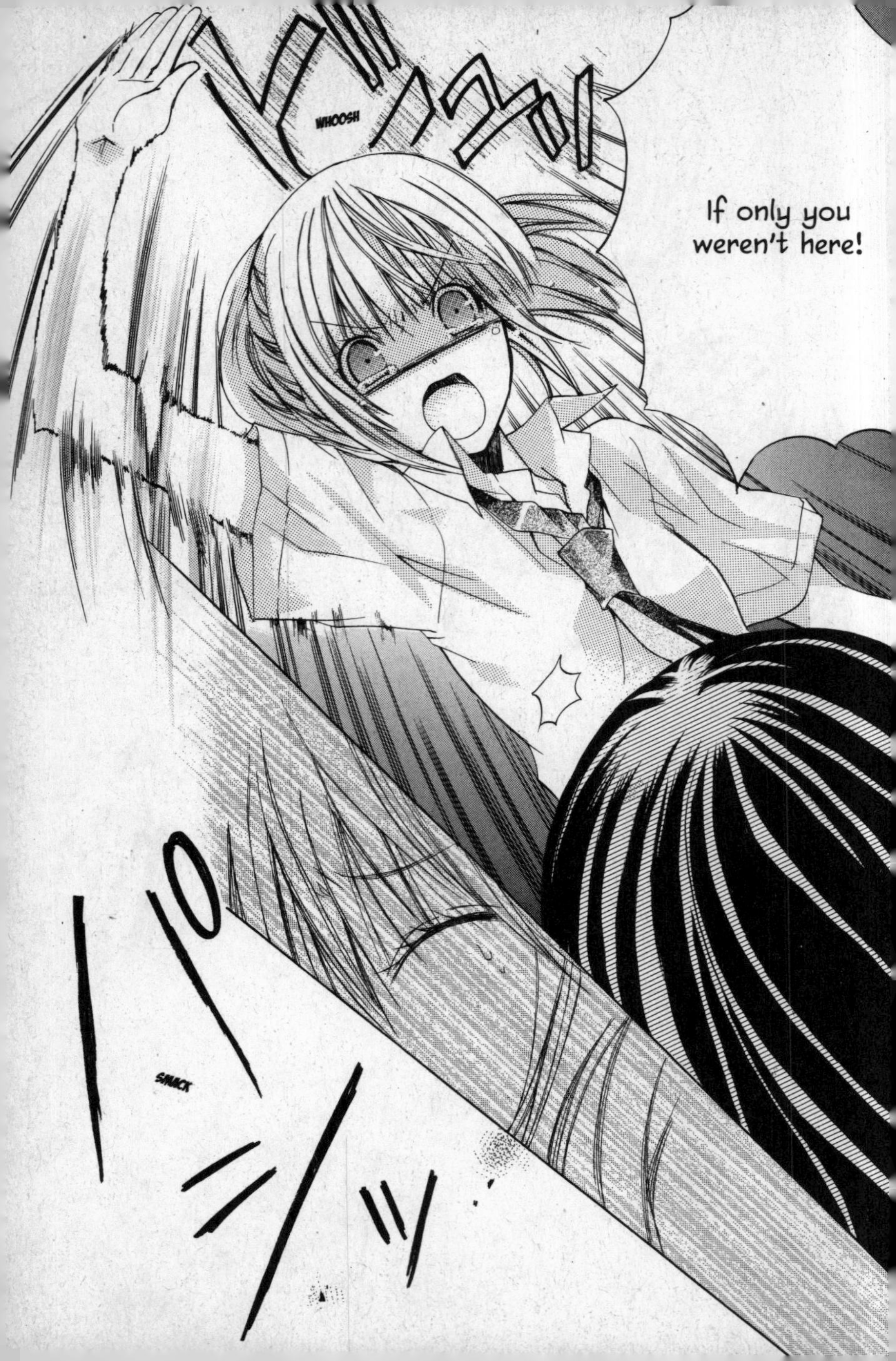
If only you weren't here!
WHOOSH
SMACK

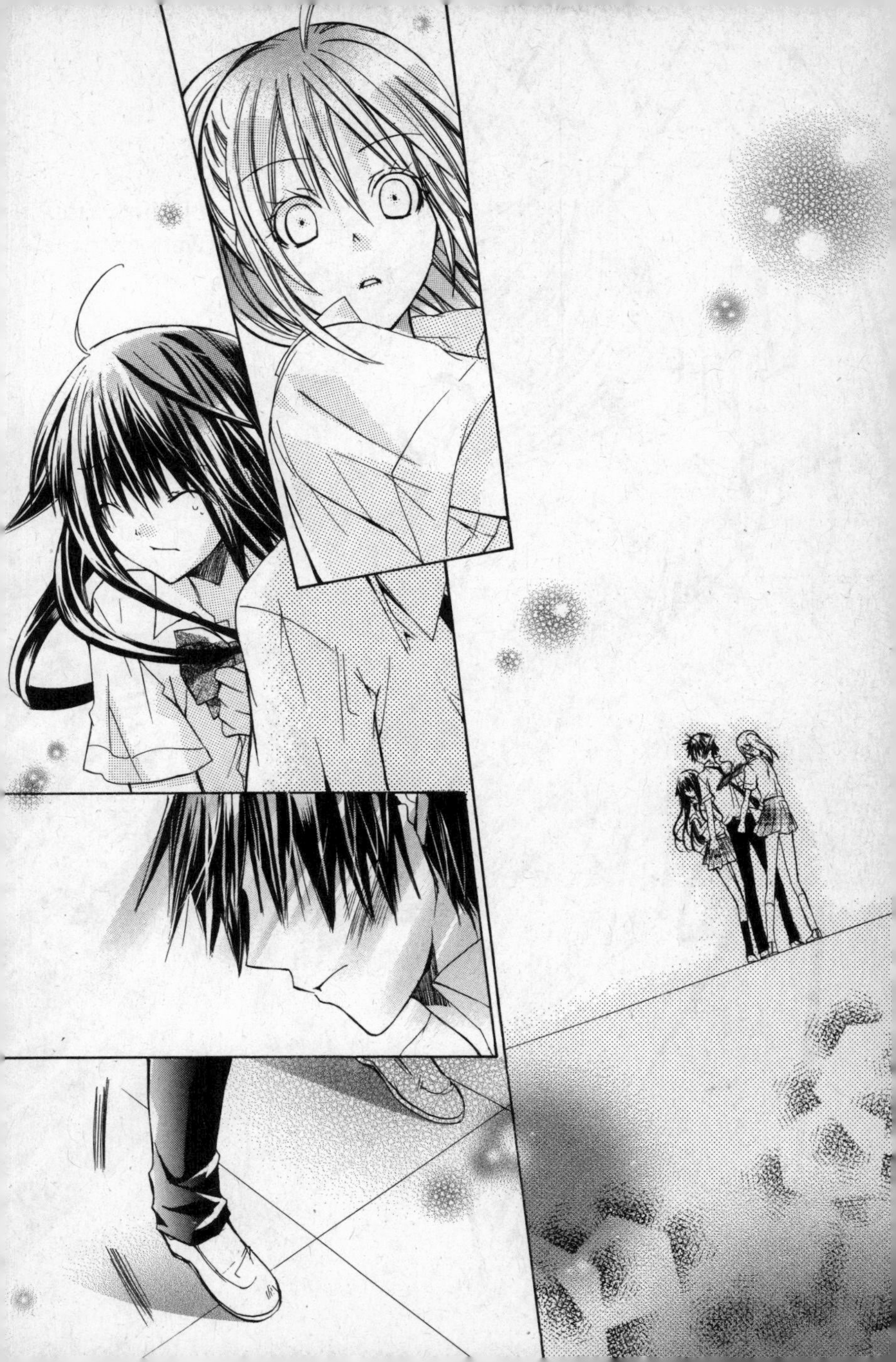

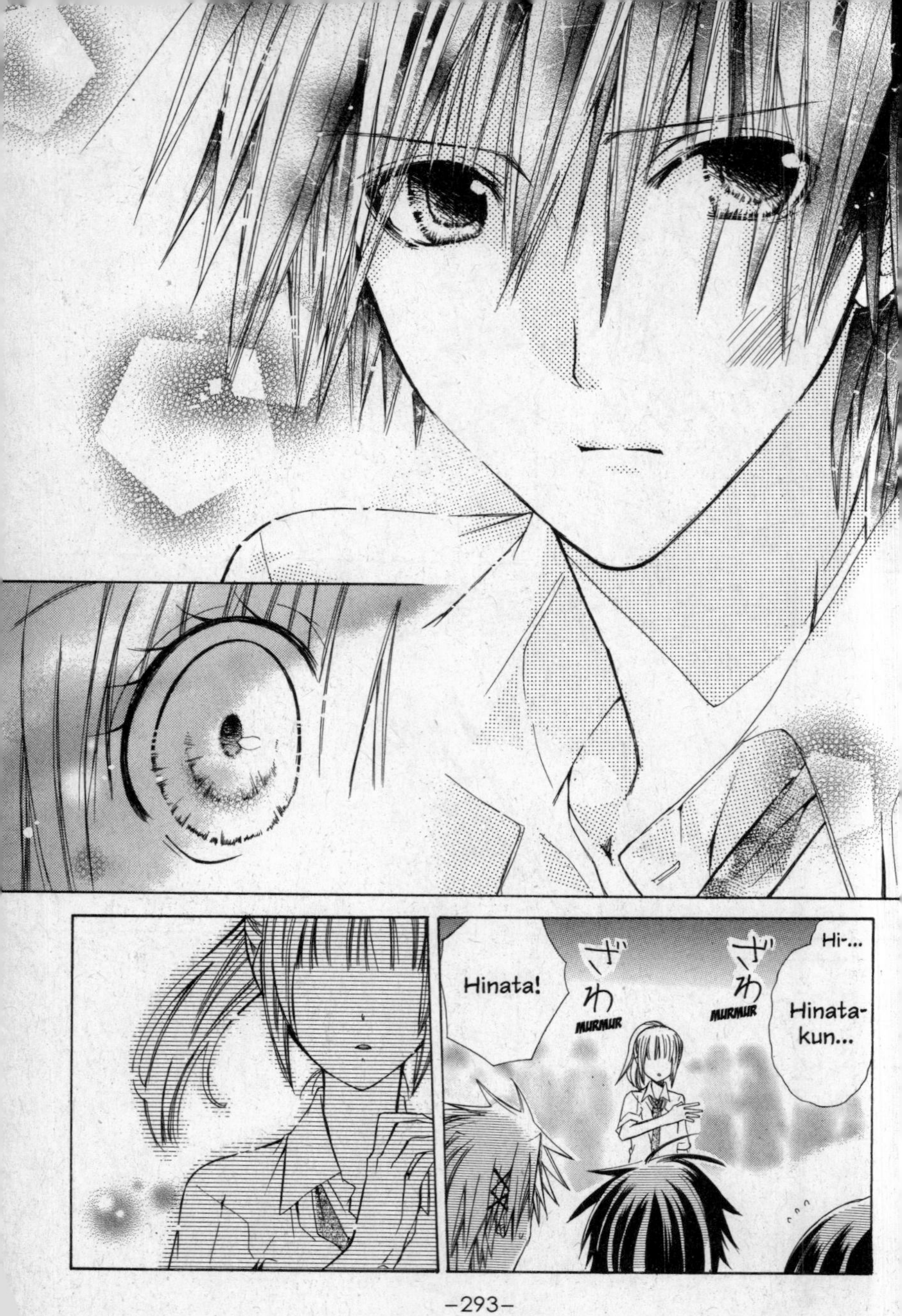
Hi-... Hinata-kun...
ざわ
MURMUR
ざわ
MURMUR
Hinata!

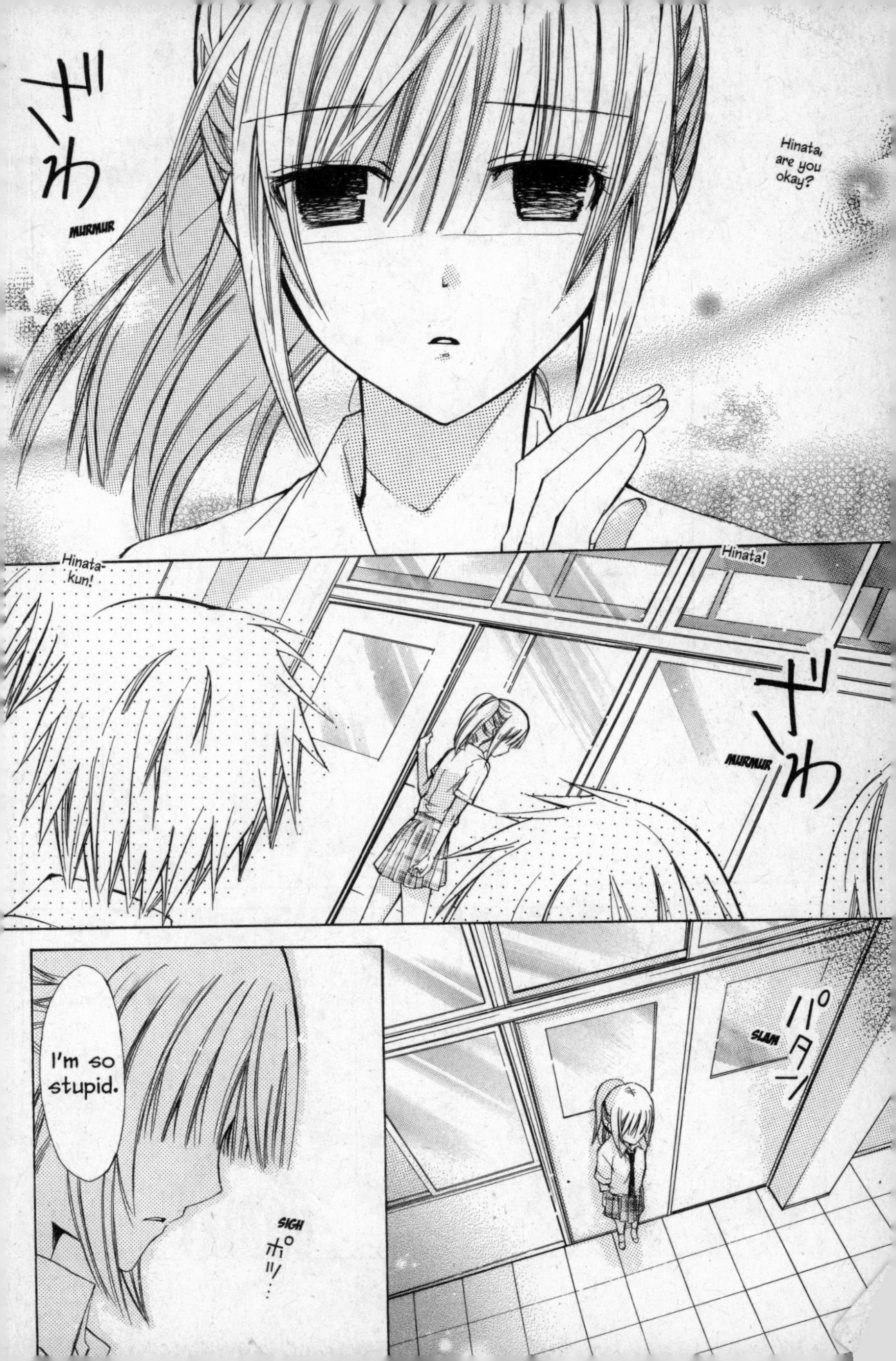
Hinata, are you okay?
ざわ
MURMUR
Hinata!
ざわ
MURMUR
Hinata-kun!
パタン
SLAM
I'm so stupid.
ポツ…
SIGH

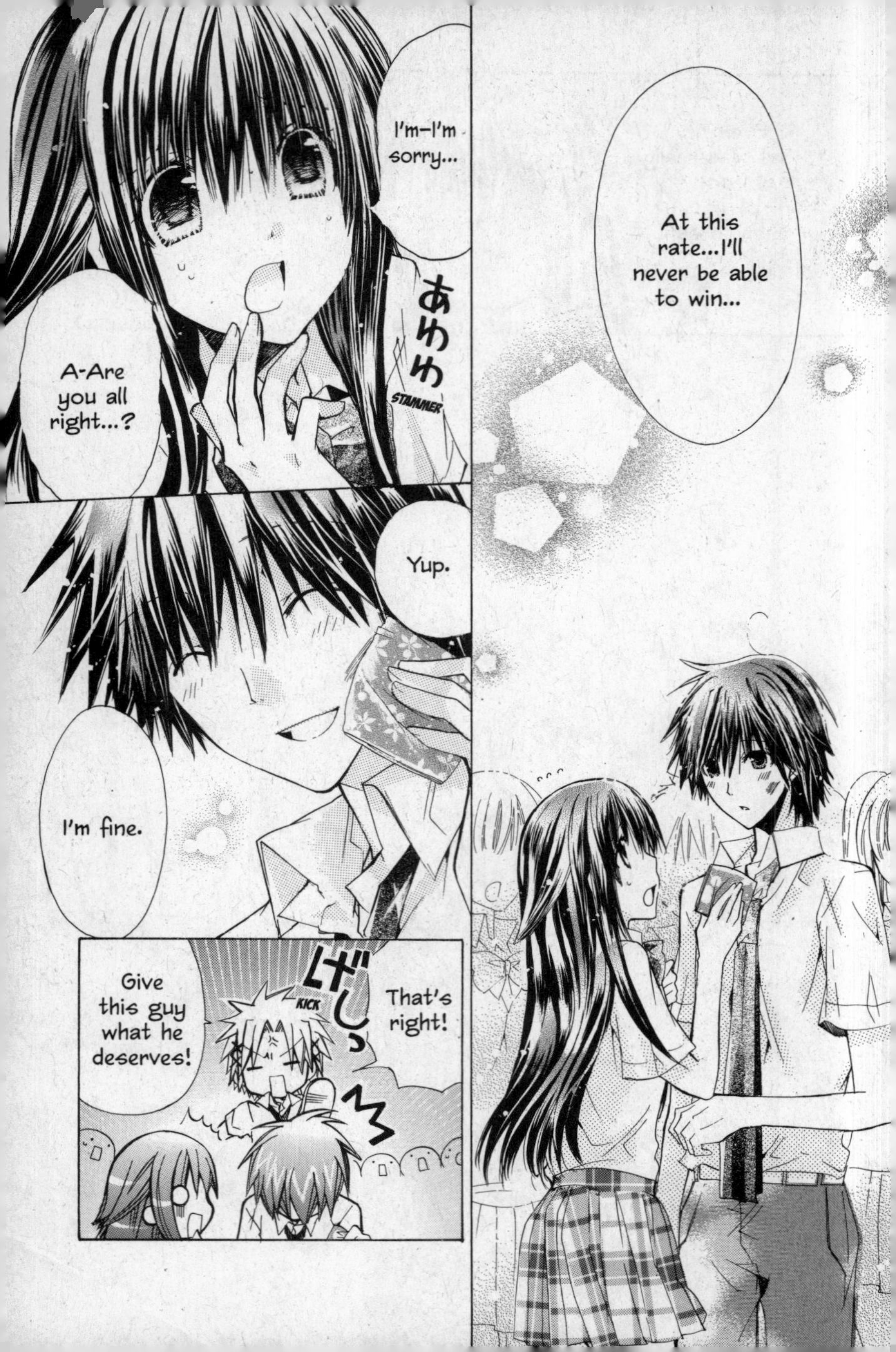
At this rate...I'll never be able to win...
I'm-I'm sorry...
あわわ
STAMMER
A-Are you all right...?
Yup.
I'm fine.
That's right!
げしっ
KICK
Give this guy what he deserves!

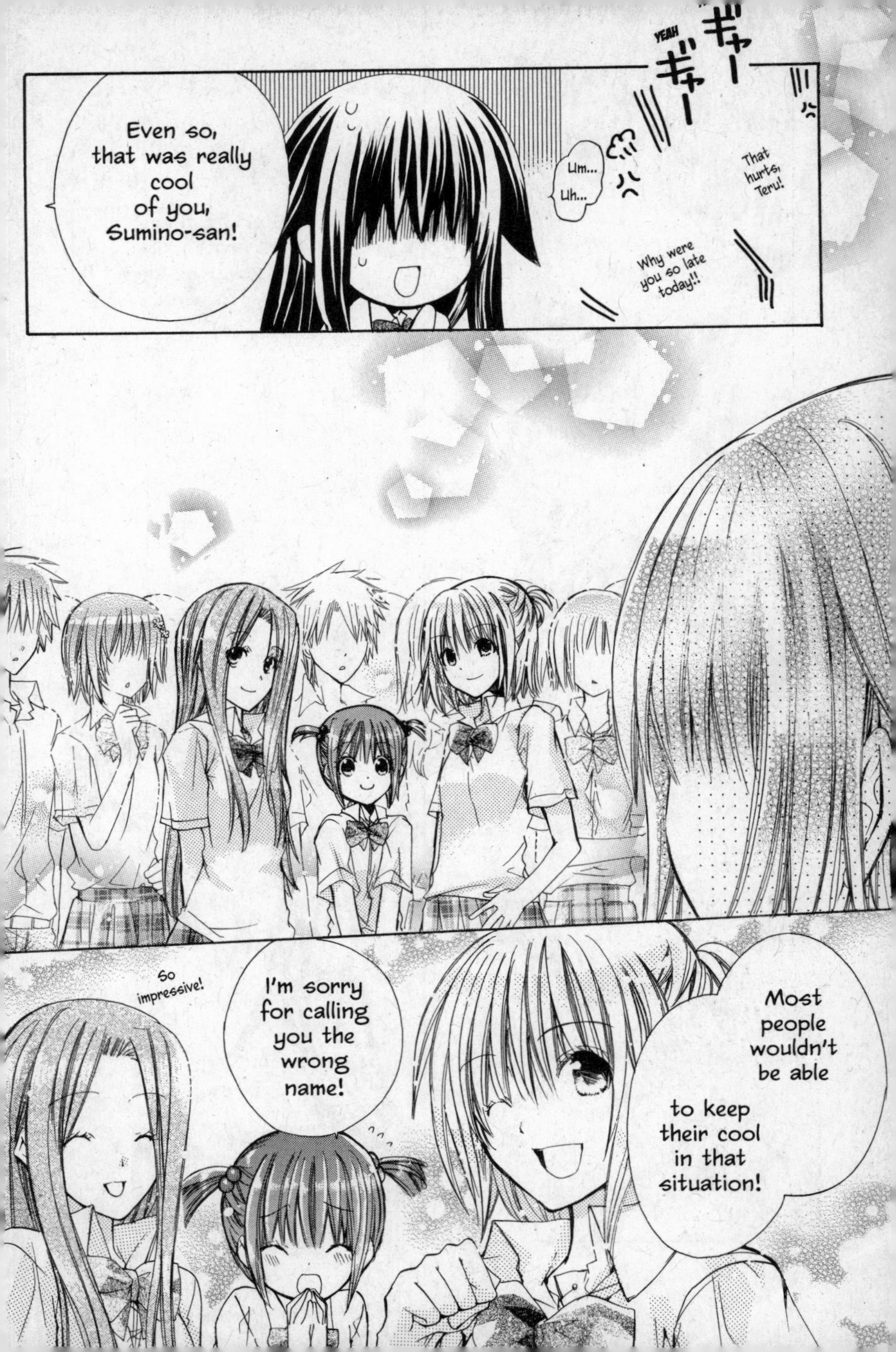
ギャーギャー
YEAH
That hurts, Teru!
Why were you so late today!!
Um... Uh...
Even so, that was really cool of you, Sumino-san!
Most people wouldn't be able to keep their cool in that situation!
I'm sorry for calling you the wrong name!
So impressive!

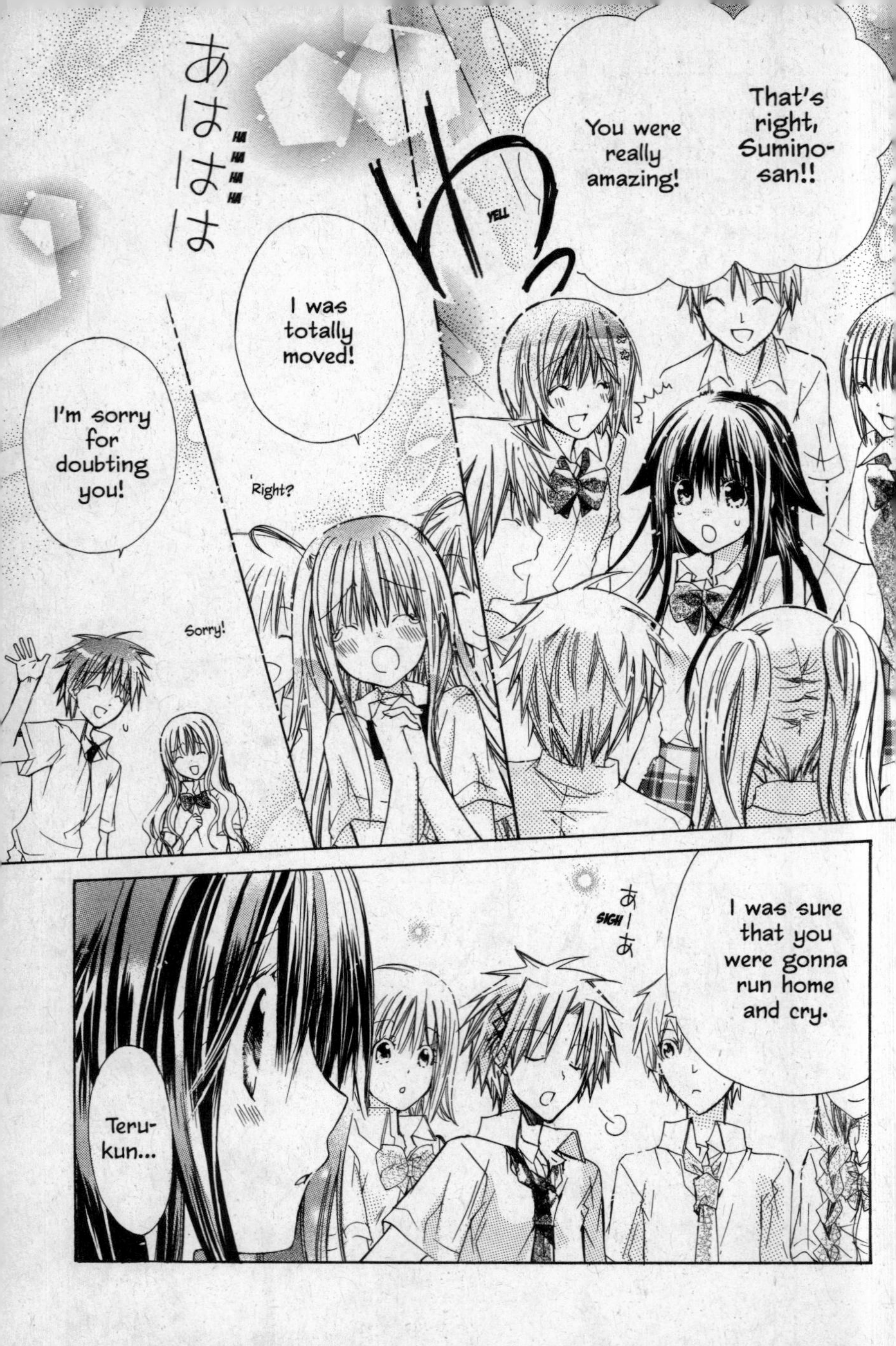
That's right, Sumino-san!!
You were really amazing!
YELL
I was totally moved!
あははは
HA HA HA HA
Right?
I'm sorry for doubting you!
Sorry!
I was sure that you were gonna run home and cry.
あーあ
SIGH
Teru-kun...

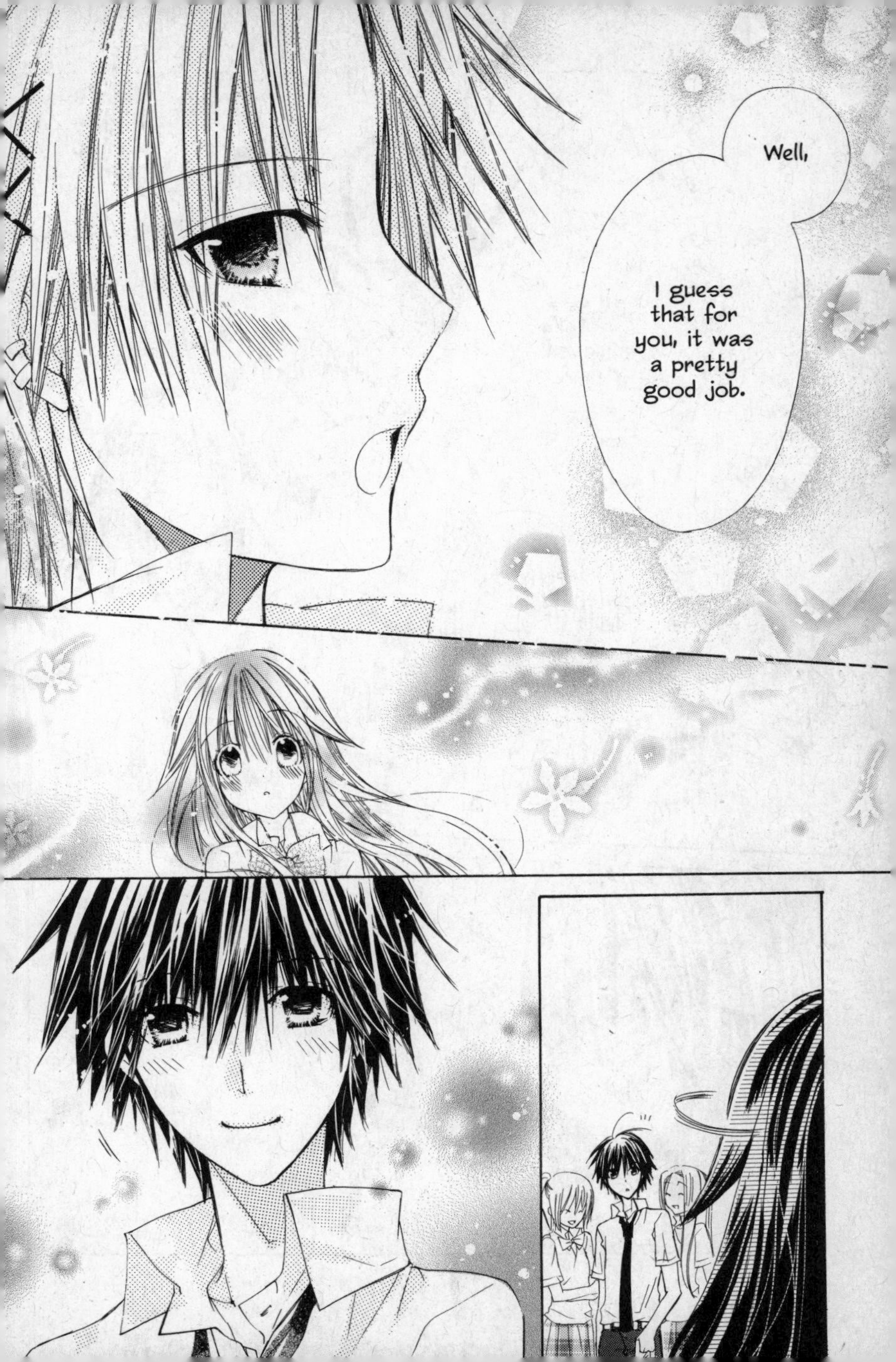
Well,
I guess that for you, it was a pretty good job.

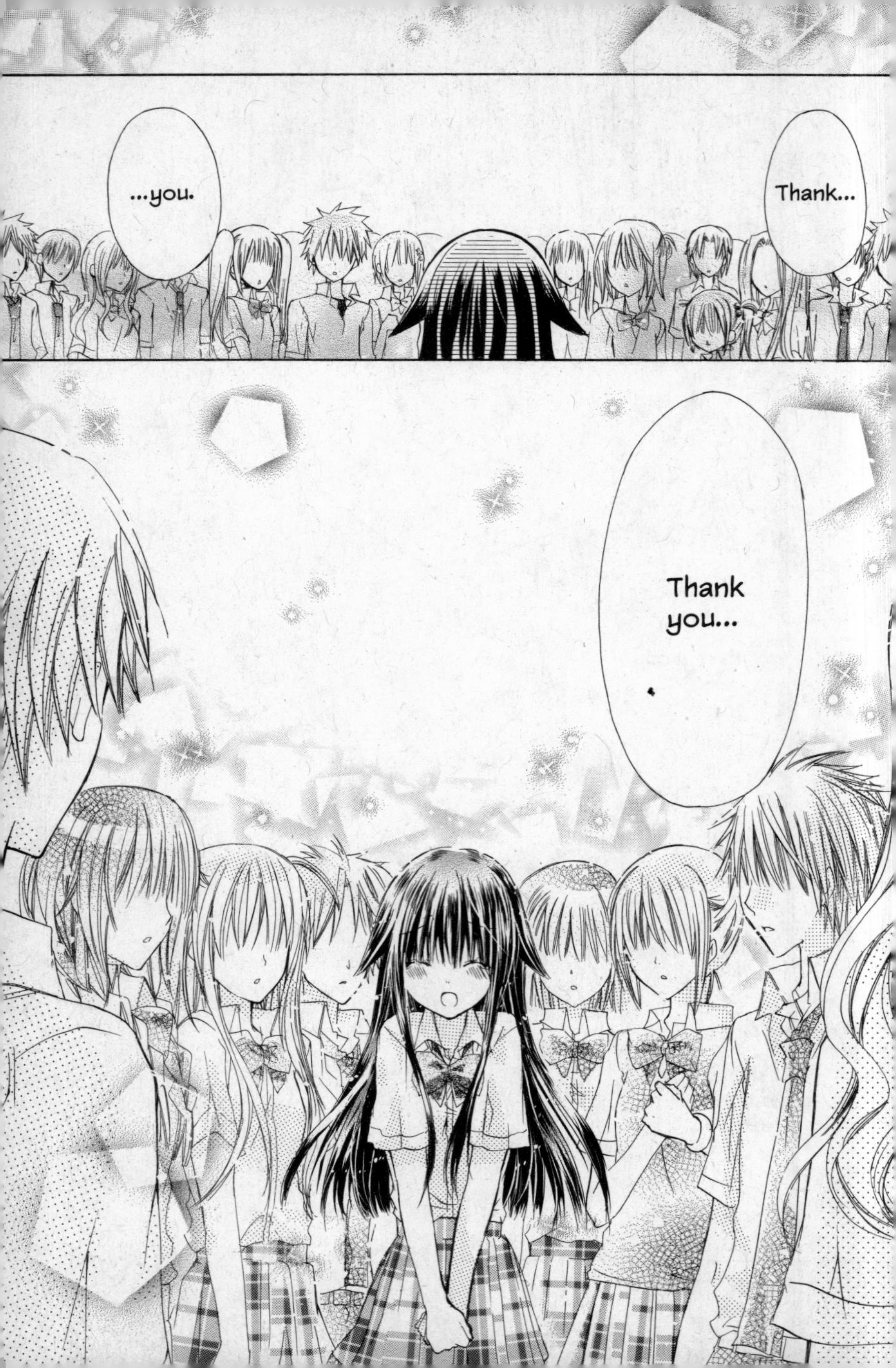
Thank...
...you.
Thank you...

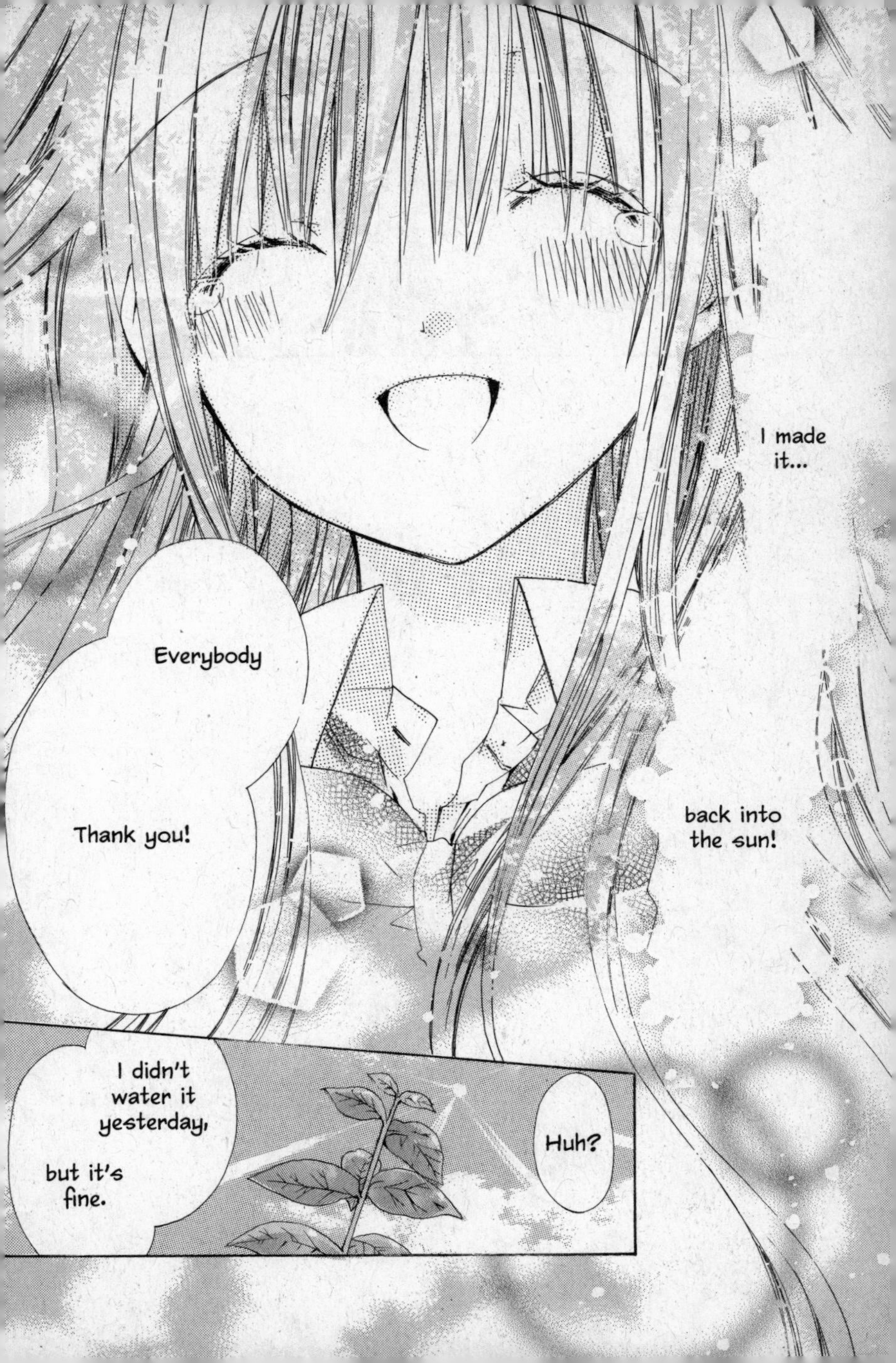
I made it...
back into the sun!
Everybody
Thank you!
Huh?
I didn't water it yesterday,
but it's fine.

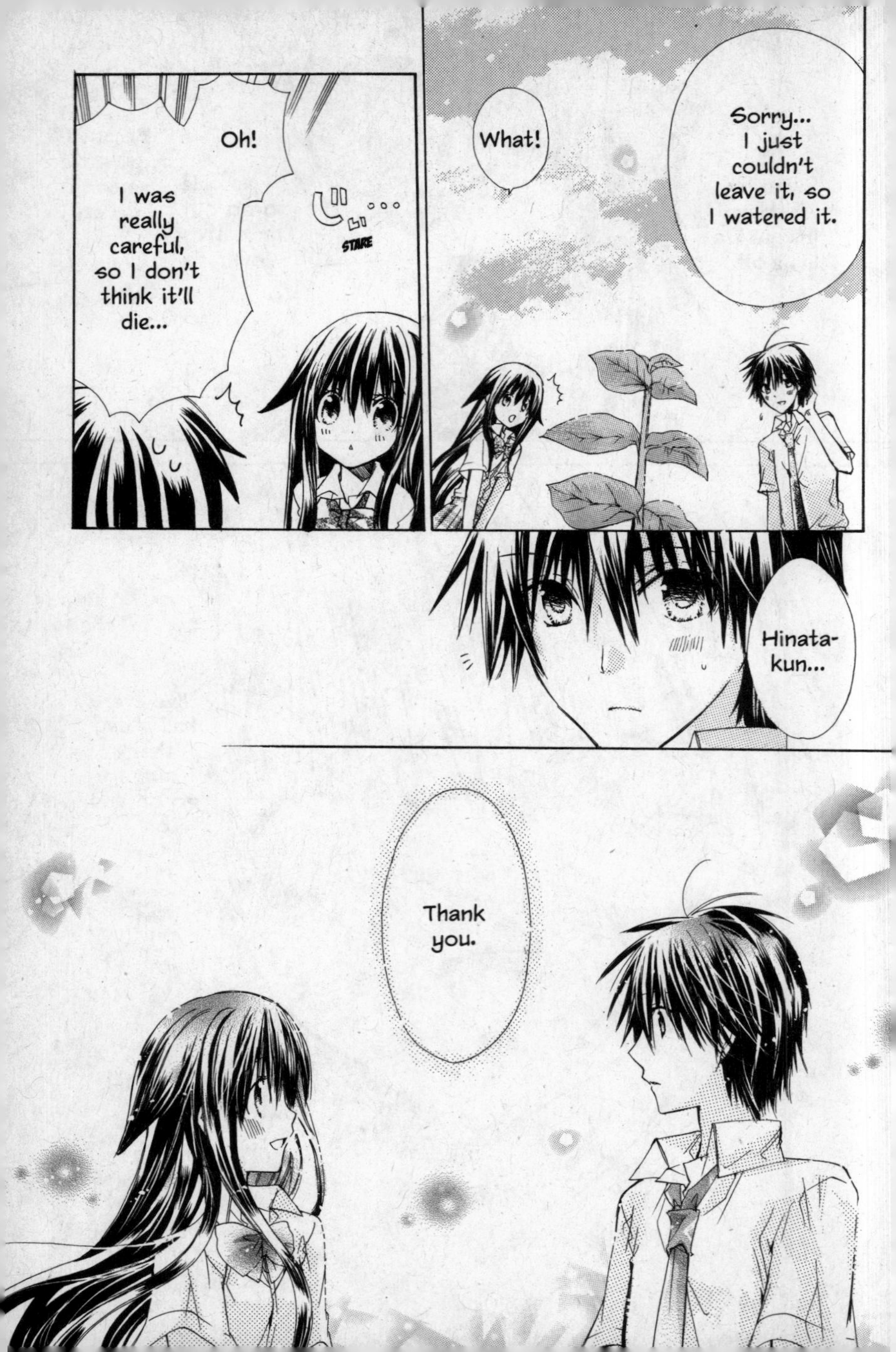
Sorry... I just couldn't leave it, so I watered it.
What!
Oh!
STARE
I was really careful, so I don't think it'll die...
Hinata-kun...
Thank you.

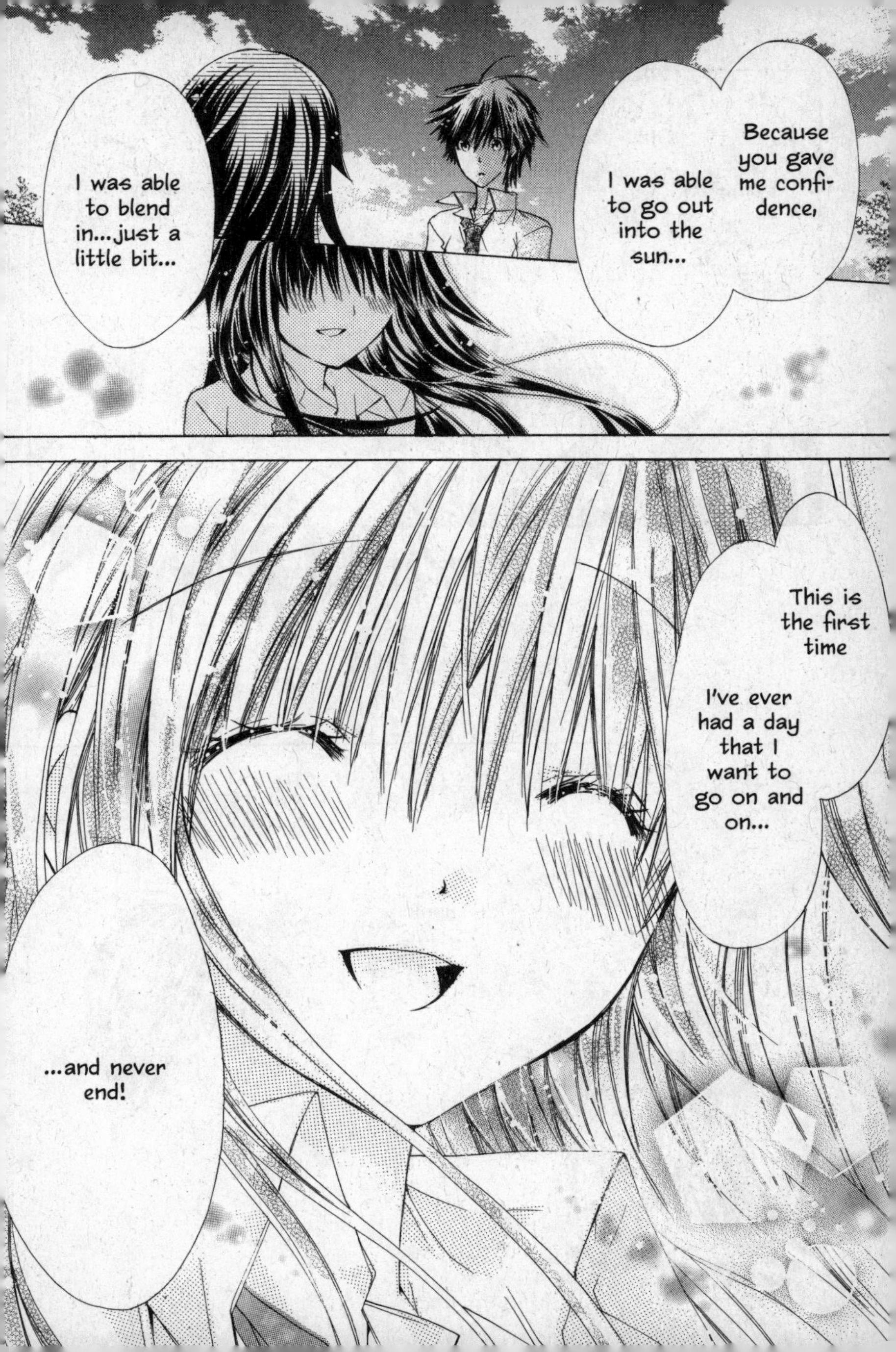
Because you gave me confi-dence,
I was able to go out into the sun...
I was able to blend in...just a little bit...
This is the first time
I've ever had a day that I want to go on and on...
...and never end!

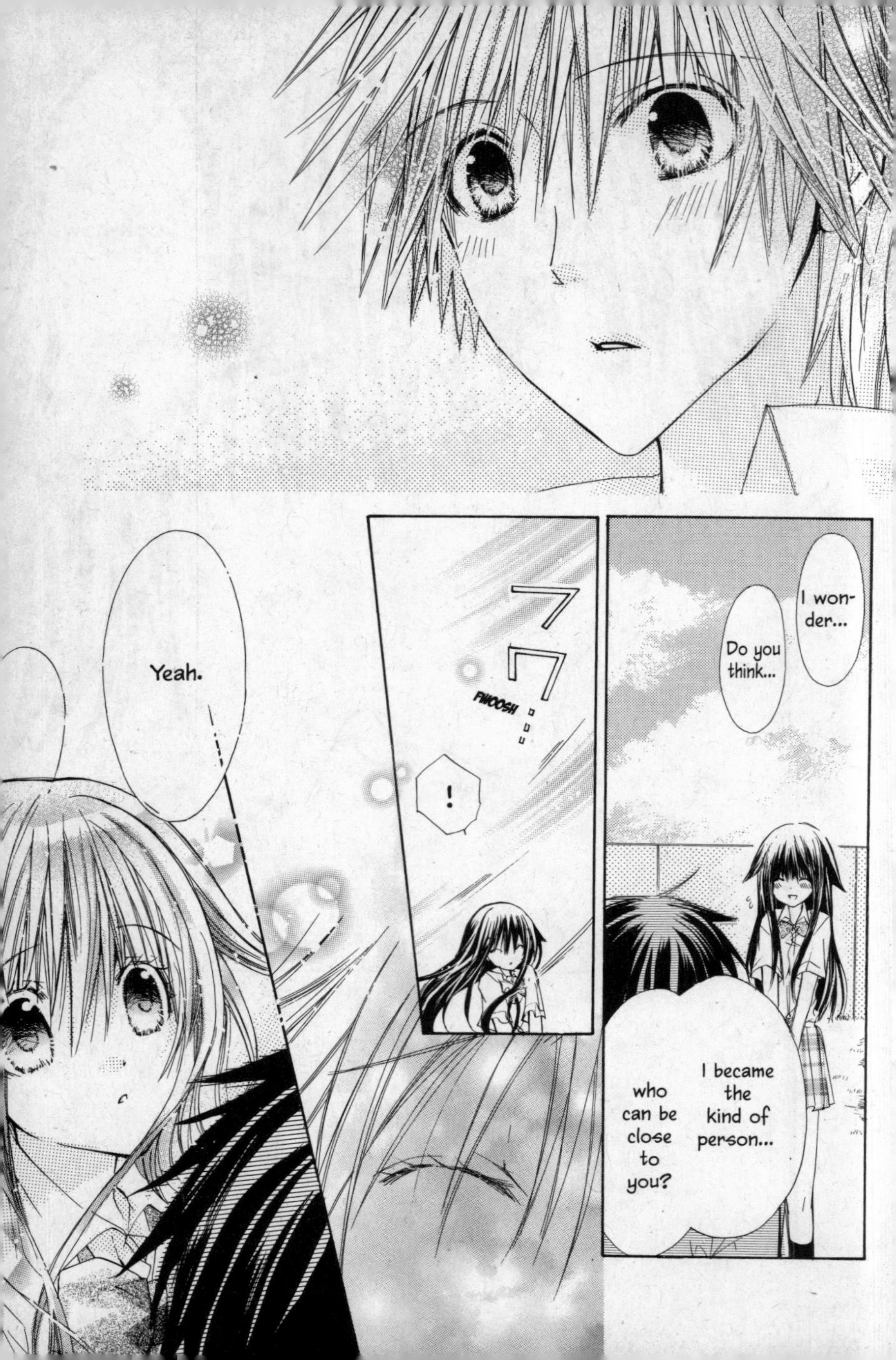
I won-der...
Do you think...
I became the kind of person...
who can be close to you?
FWOOSH
!
Yeah.

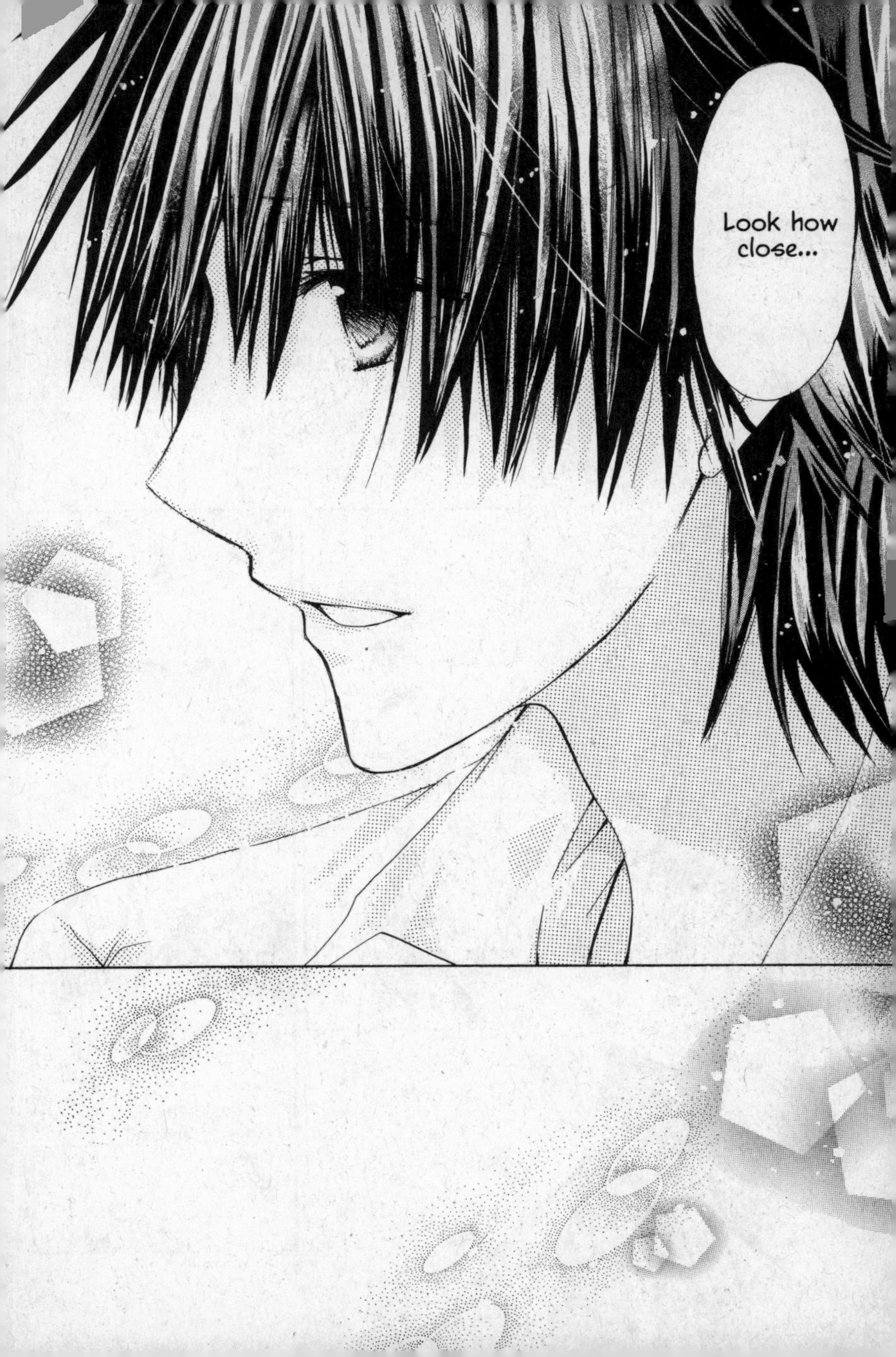
Look how close...

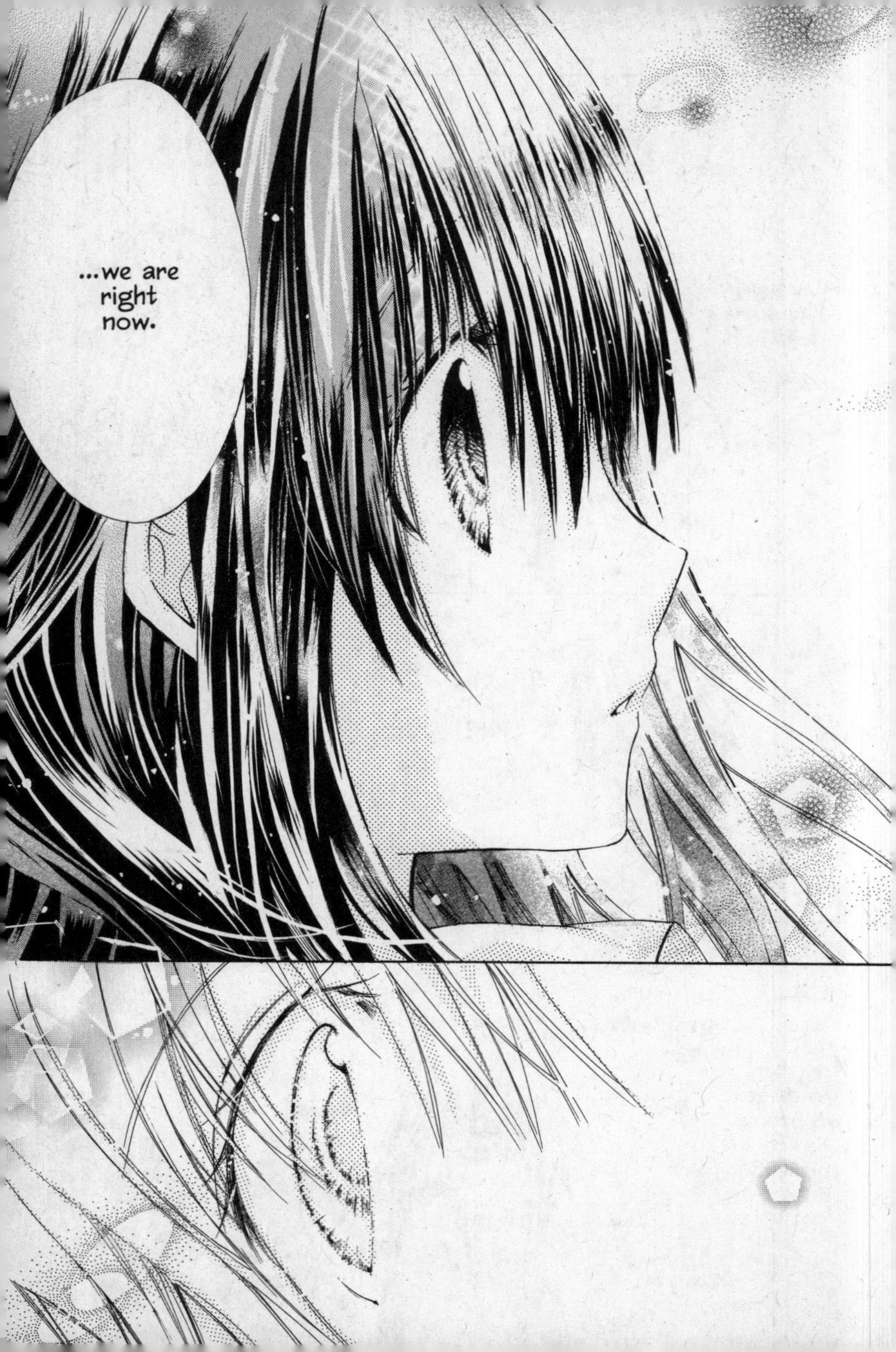
...we are right now.

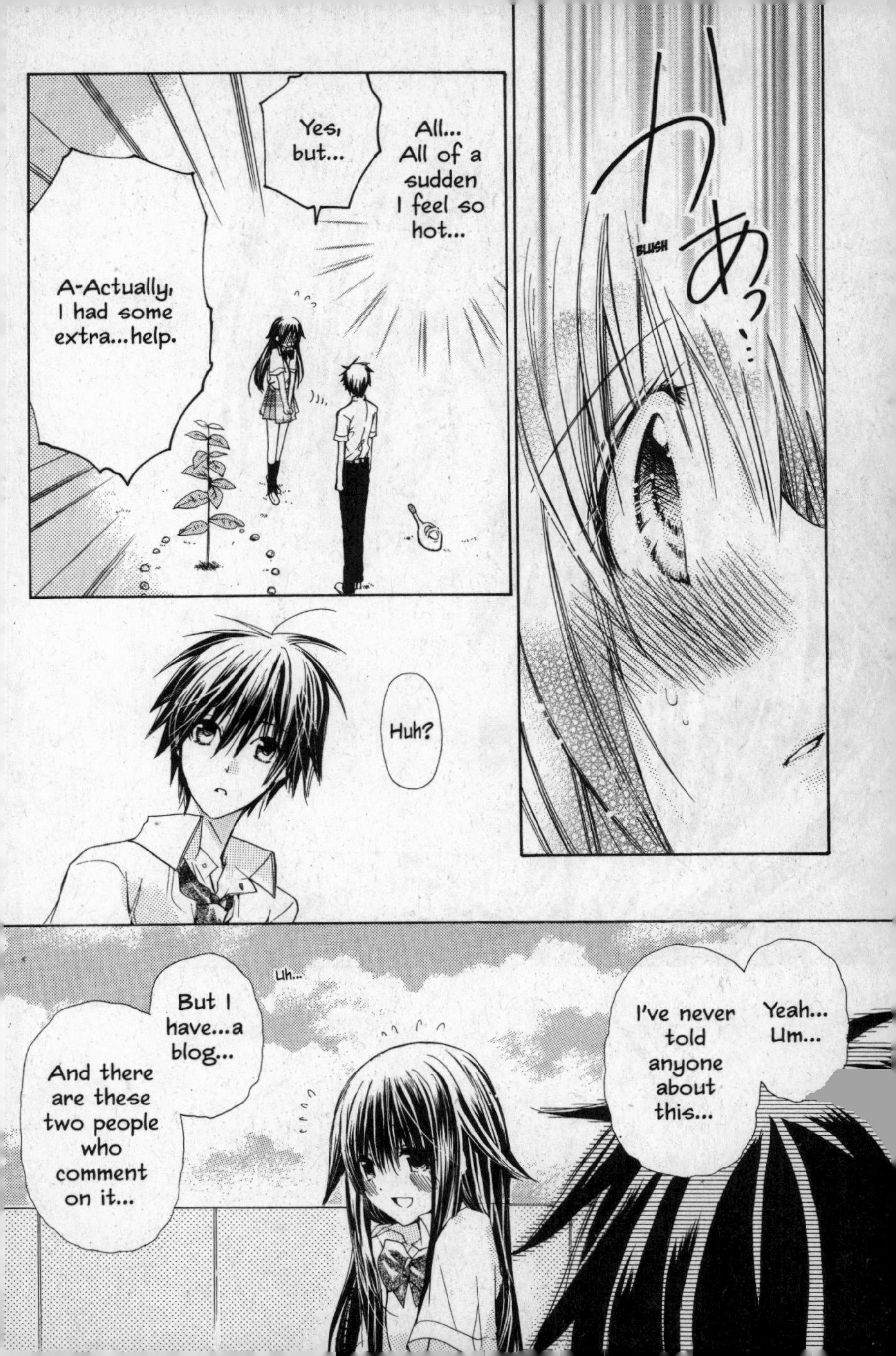
わあっ…
BLUSH
All... All of a sudden I feel so hot...
Yes, but...
A-Actually, I had some extra...help.
Huh?
Yeah... Um...
I've never told anyone about this...
Uh...
But I have...a blog...
And there are these two people who comment on it...

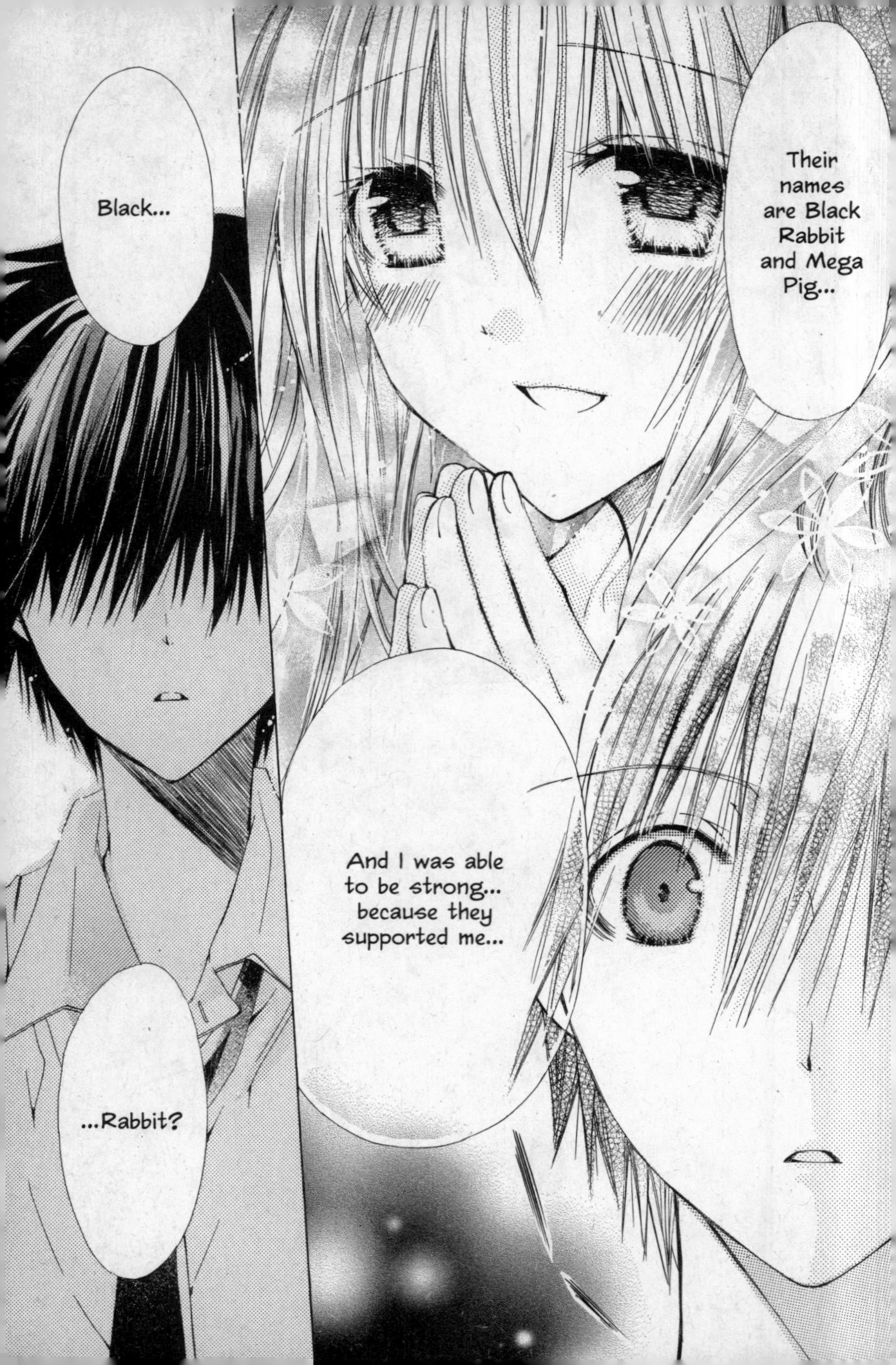
Their names are Black Rabbit and Mega Pig...
And I was able to be strong... because they supported me...
Black...
...Rabbit?

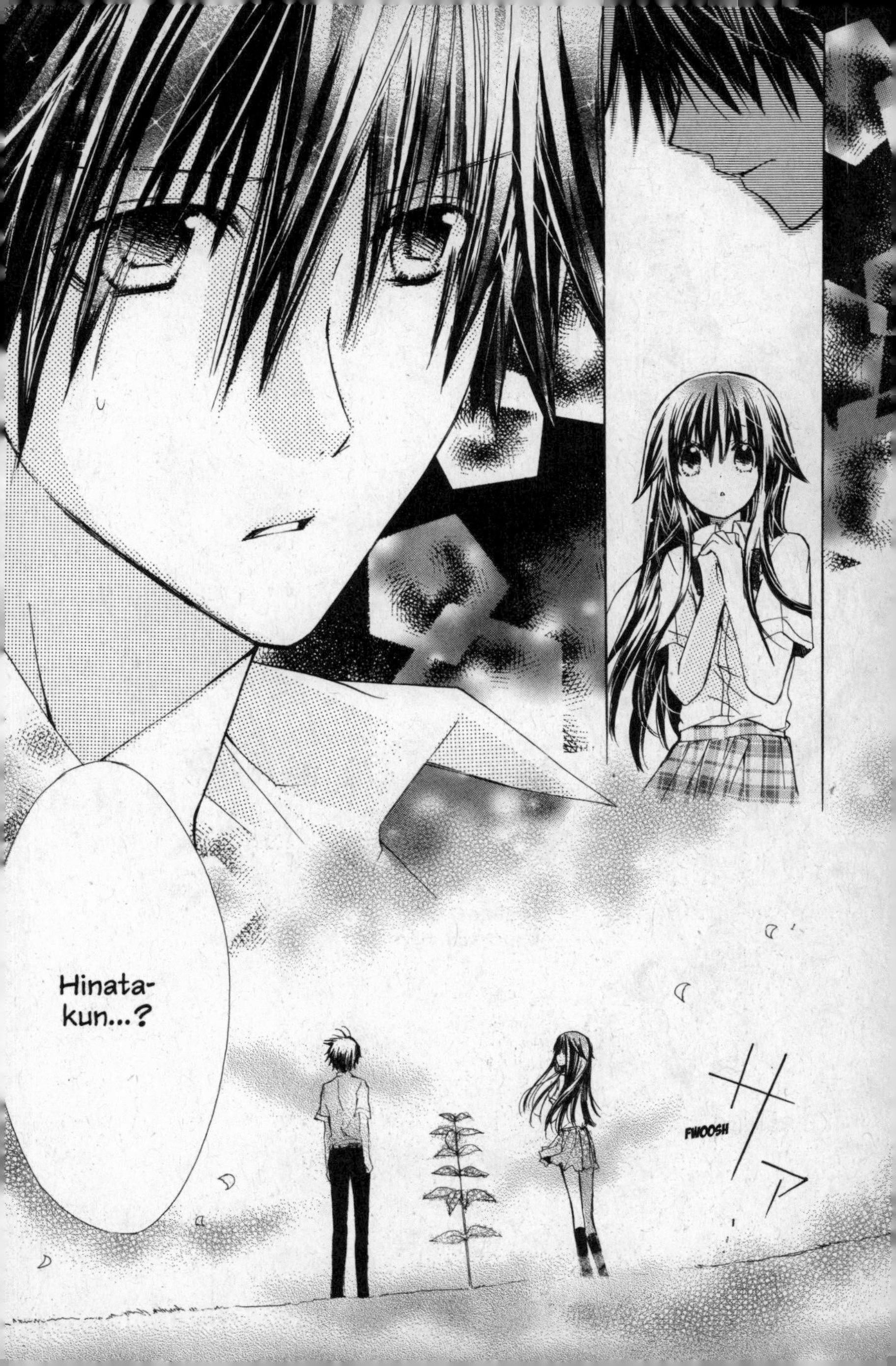
Hinata-kun...?
FWOOSH

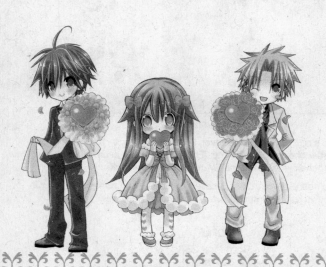

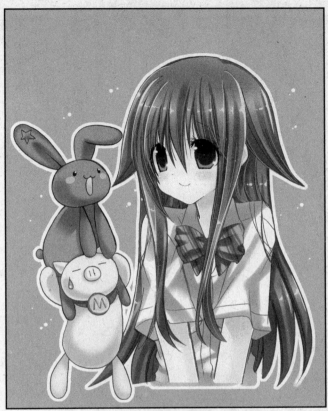

Hi, everyone!

While it's not quite Hikage-level, I remember that I had a homeroom teacher who called me "Endō-san" and a cram-school teacher who called me "Mae-chan" by mistake.

There's something about being called by the wrong name that goes beyond sad...it's more agonizing.

PROFILE
Born May 23
Gemini
Blood Type B

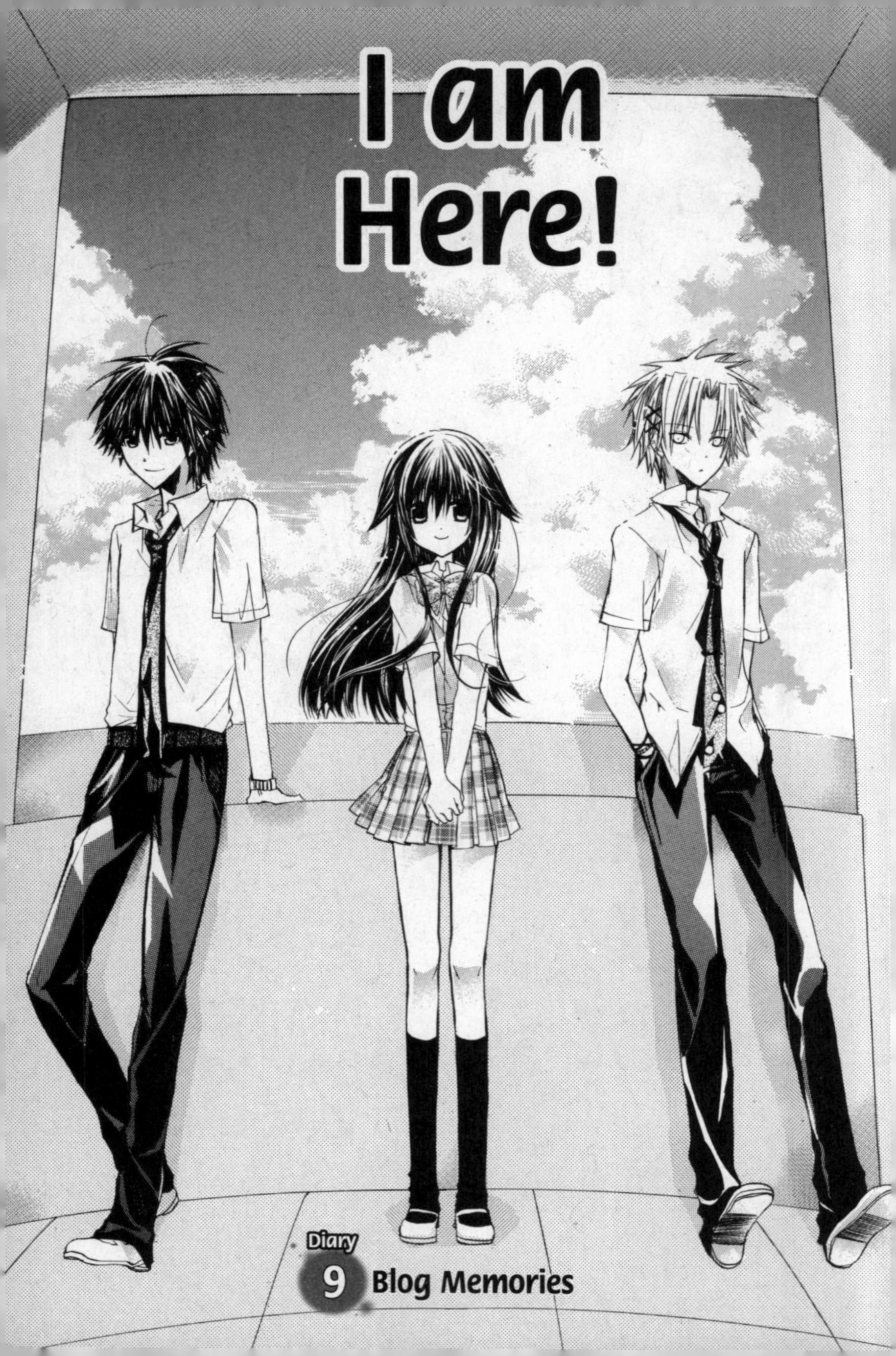
I am Here!
Diary 9 Blog Memories

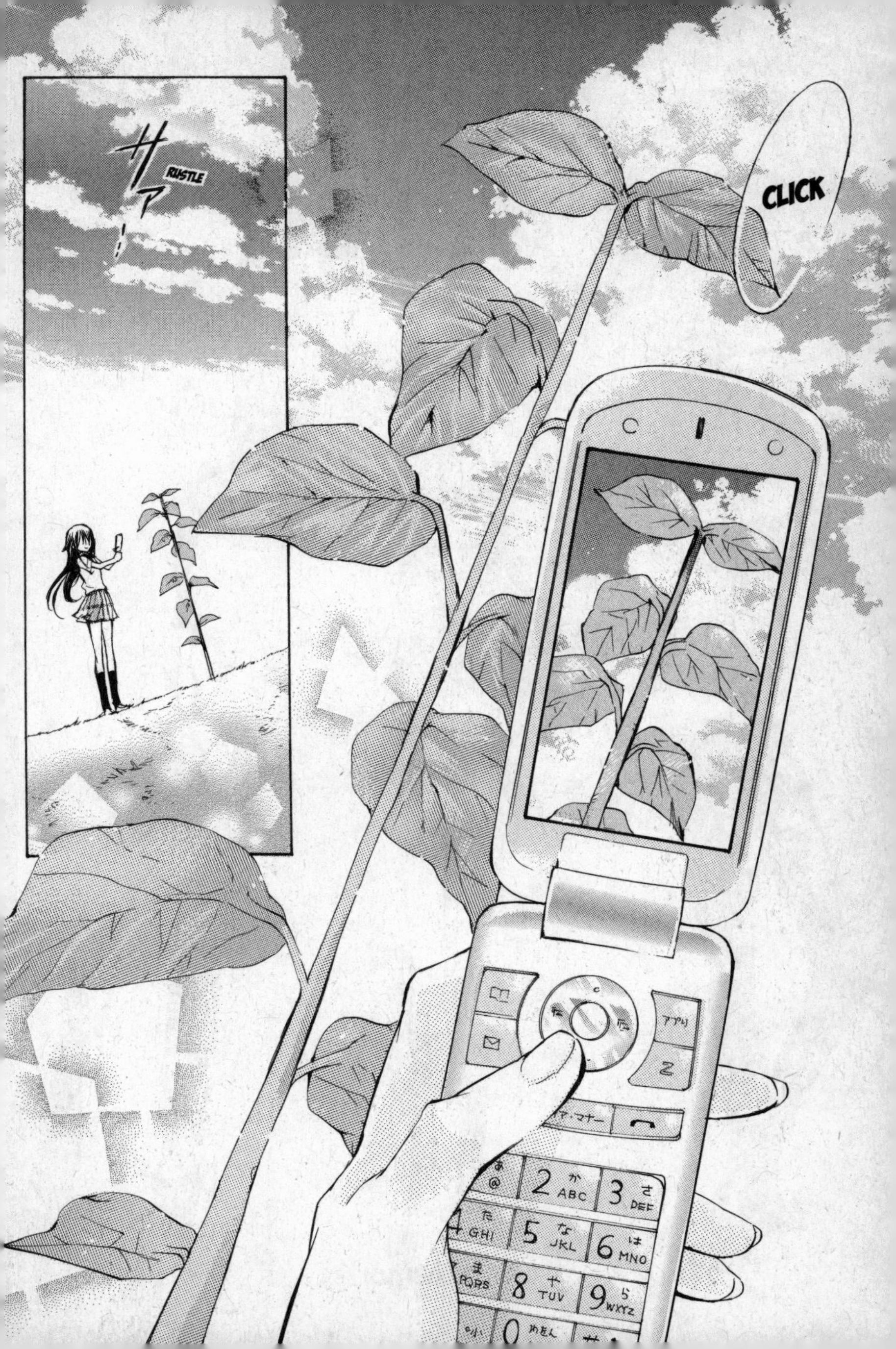
CLICK
サァ!
RUSTLE

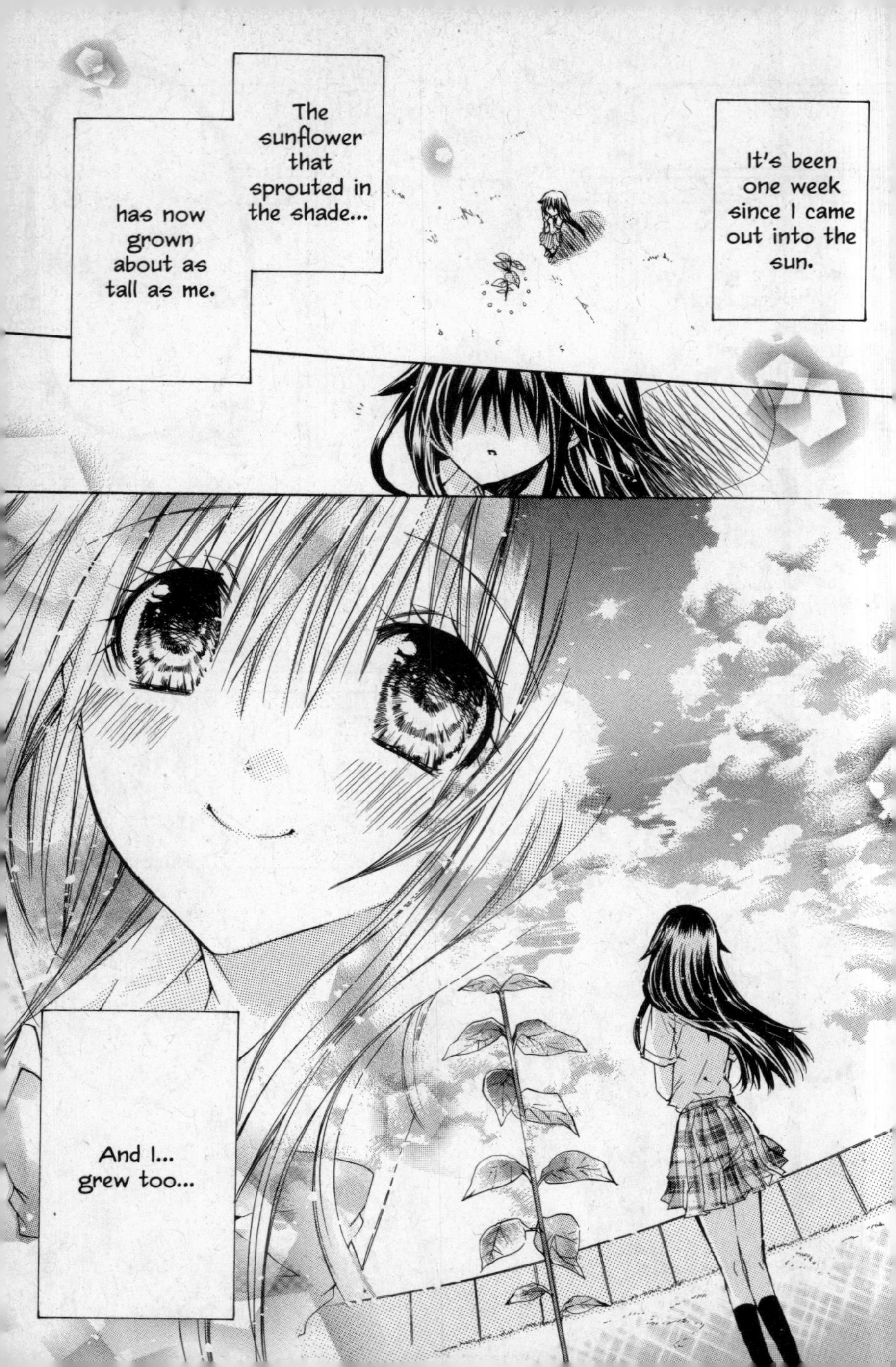
It's been one week since I came out into the sun.
The sunflower that sprouted in the shade...
has now grown about as tall as me.
And I... grew too...

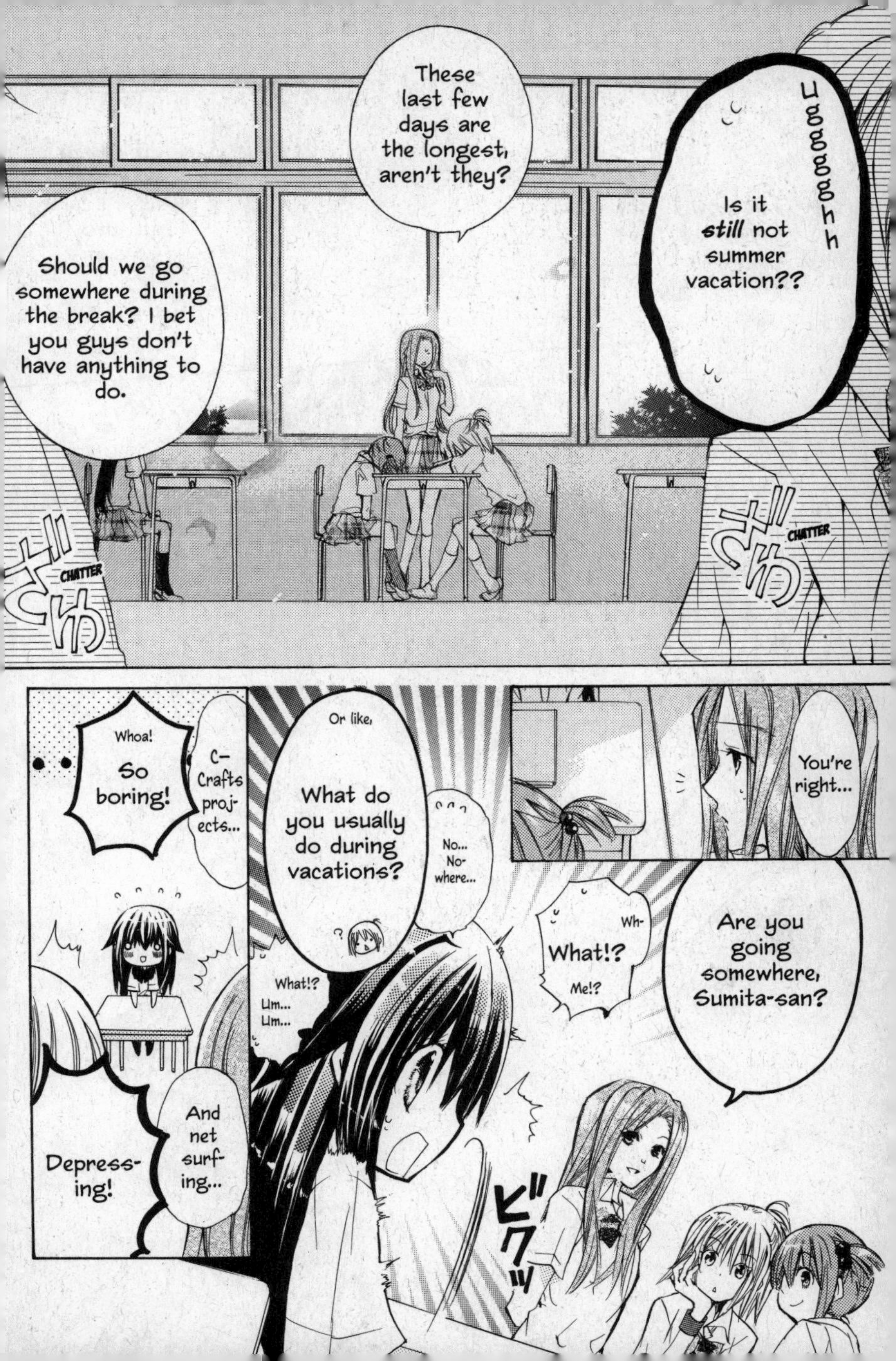
Uggggghh
Is it *still* not summer vacation??
These last few days are the longest, aren't they?
ざわ
CHATTER
Should we go somewhere during the break? I bet you guys don't have anything to do.
ざわ
CHATTER
You're right...
Are you going somewhere, Sumita-san?
Wh- What!? Me!?
ビクッ
Or like, What do you usually do during vacations?
No... No-where...
What!? Um... Um...
C- Crafts proj-ects...
Whoa! So boring!
And net surf-ing...
Depress-ing!

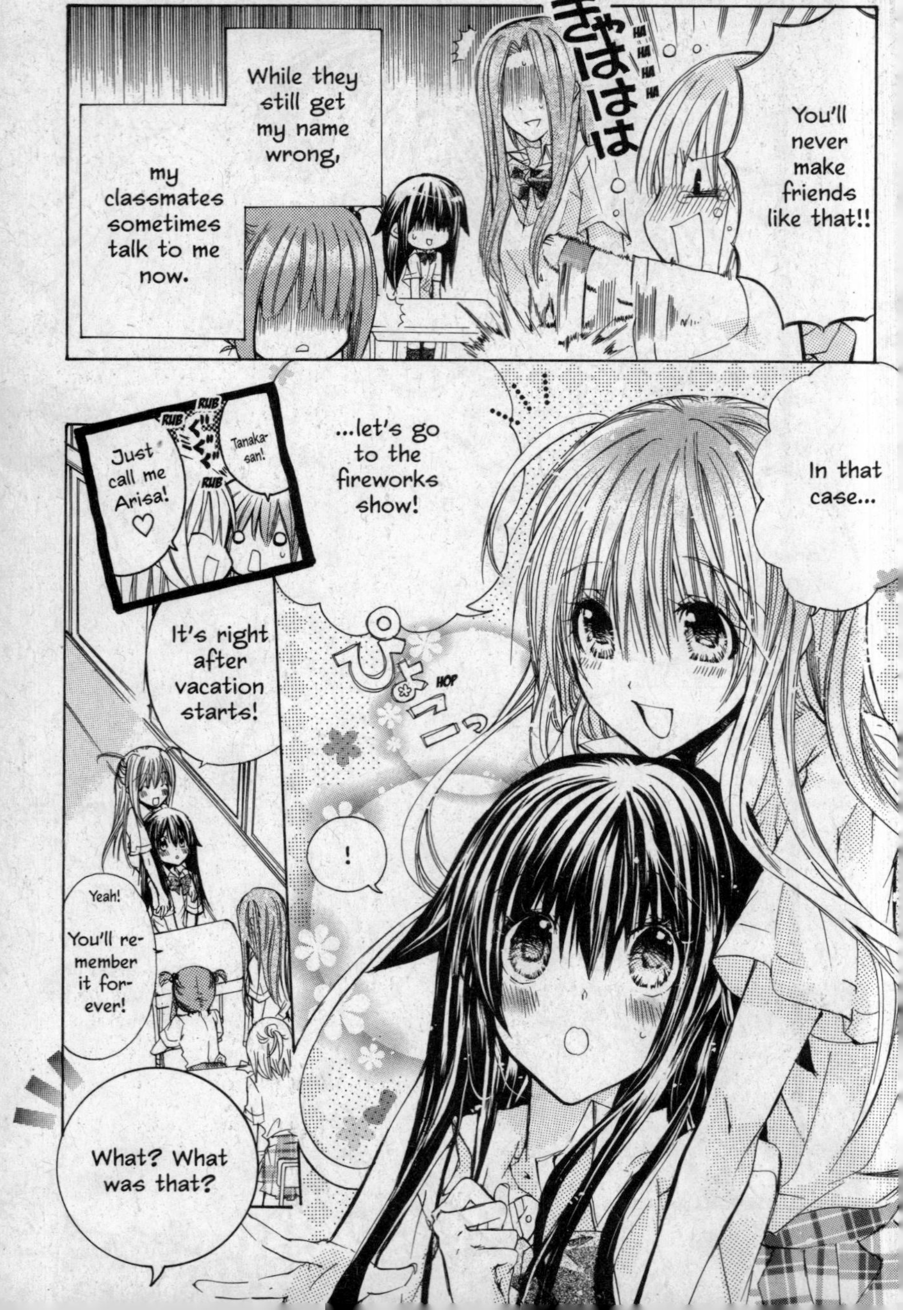
ぎゃははは
HA HA HA HA
You'll never make friends like that!!
While they still get my name wrong,
my classmates sometimes talk to me now.
In that case...
...let's go to the fireworks show!
RUB RUB RUB
Tanaka-san!
Just call me Arisa! ♡
It's right after vacation starts!
ぴょこっ
HOP
!
Yeah!
You'll re-member it for-ever!
What? What was that?

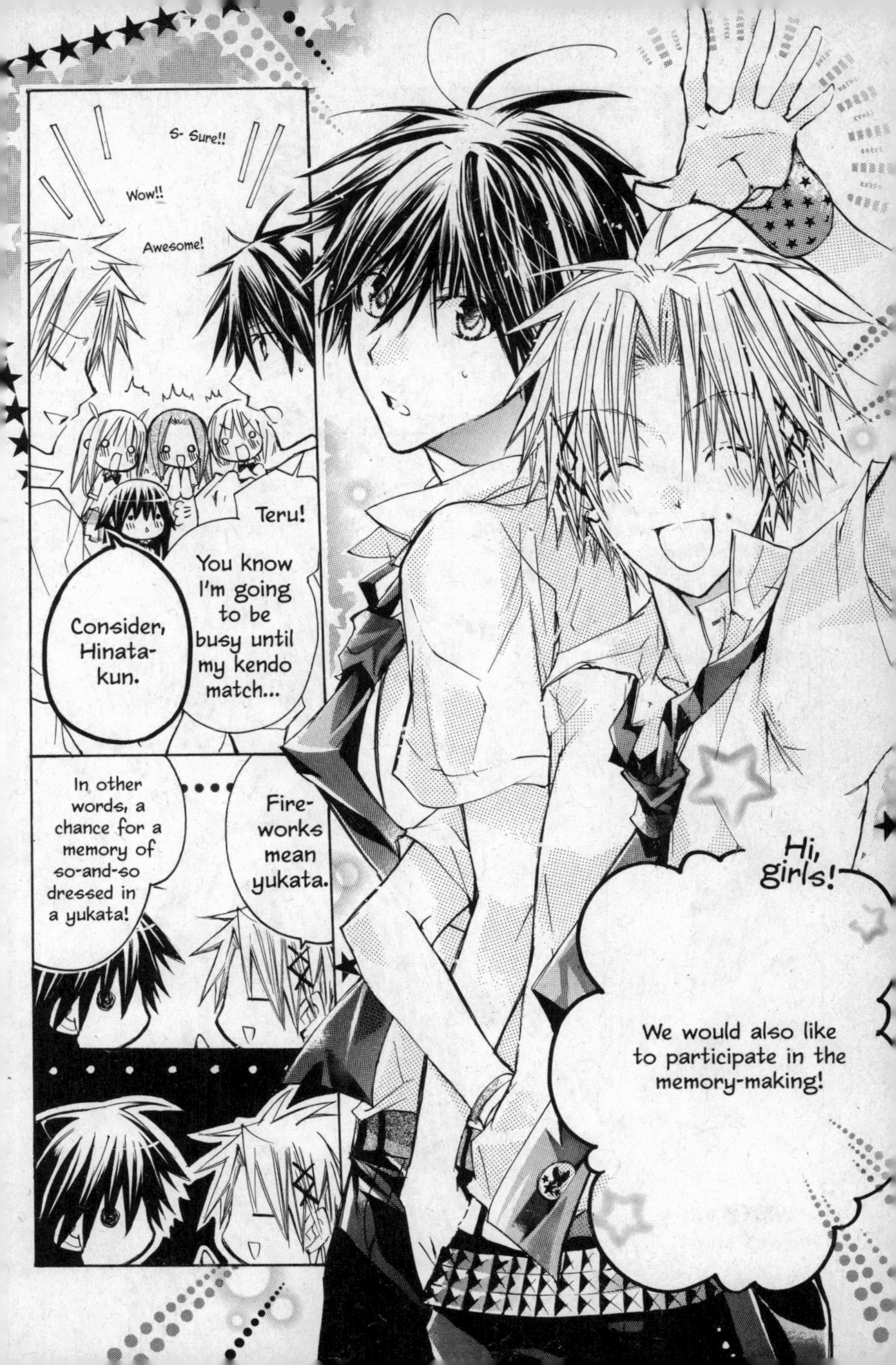
Hi, girls!
We would also like to participate in the memory-making!
S- Sure!!
Wow!!
Awesome!
Teru!
You know I'm going to be busy until my kendo match...
Consider, Hinata-kun.
Fire-works mean yukata.
In other words, a chance for a memory of so-and-so dressed in a yukata!
....

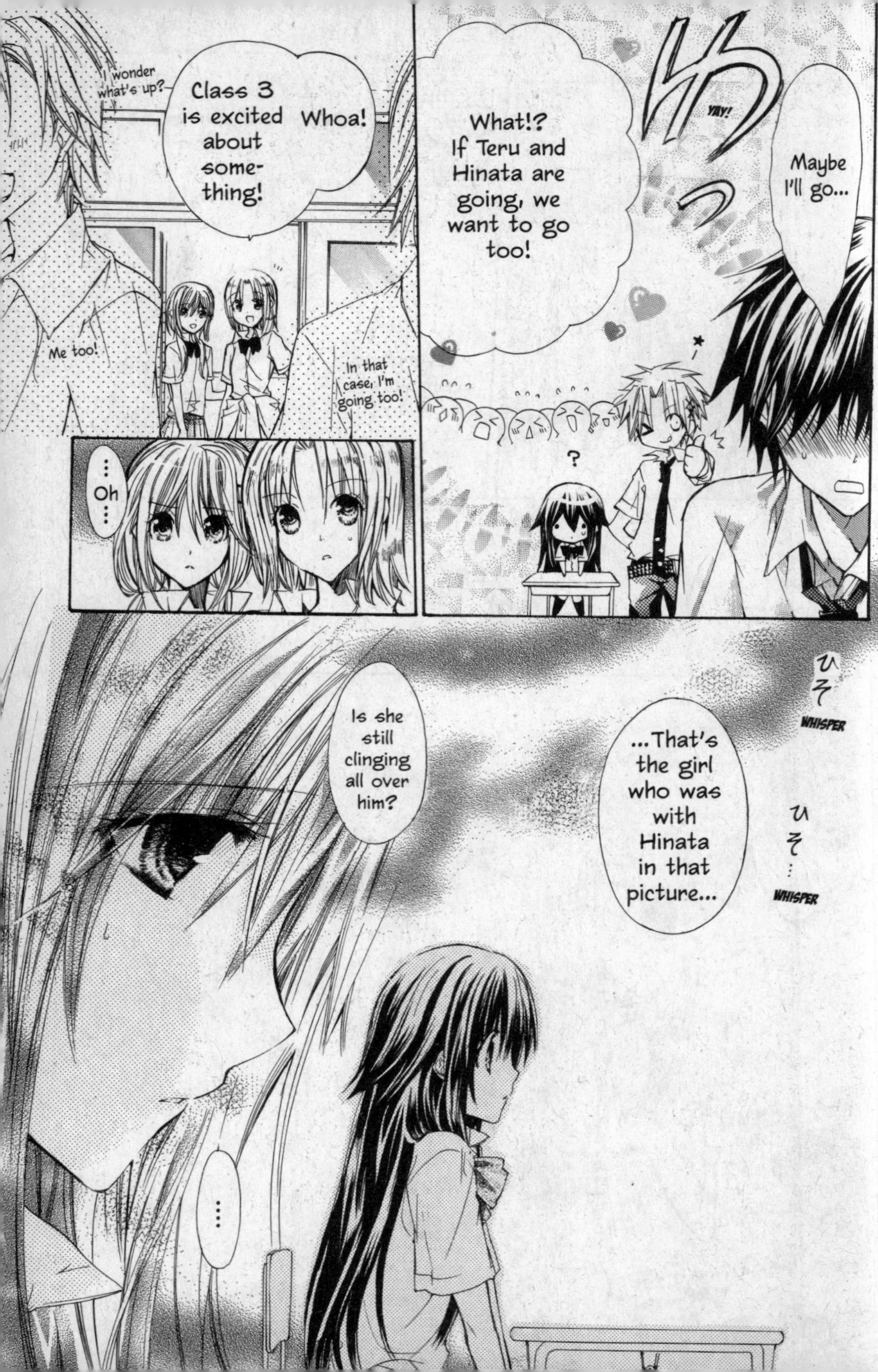
わっ
YAY!
Maybe I'll go...
What!? If Teru and Hinata are going, we want to go too!
Whoa!
Class 3 is excited about some-thing!
I wonder what's up?
In that case, I'm going too!
Me too!
...Oh...
ひそ
WHISPER
...That's the girl who was with Hinata in that picture...
ひそ...
WHISPER
Is she still clinging all over him?
...

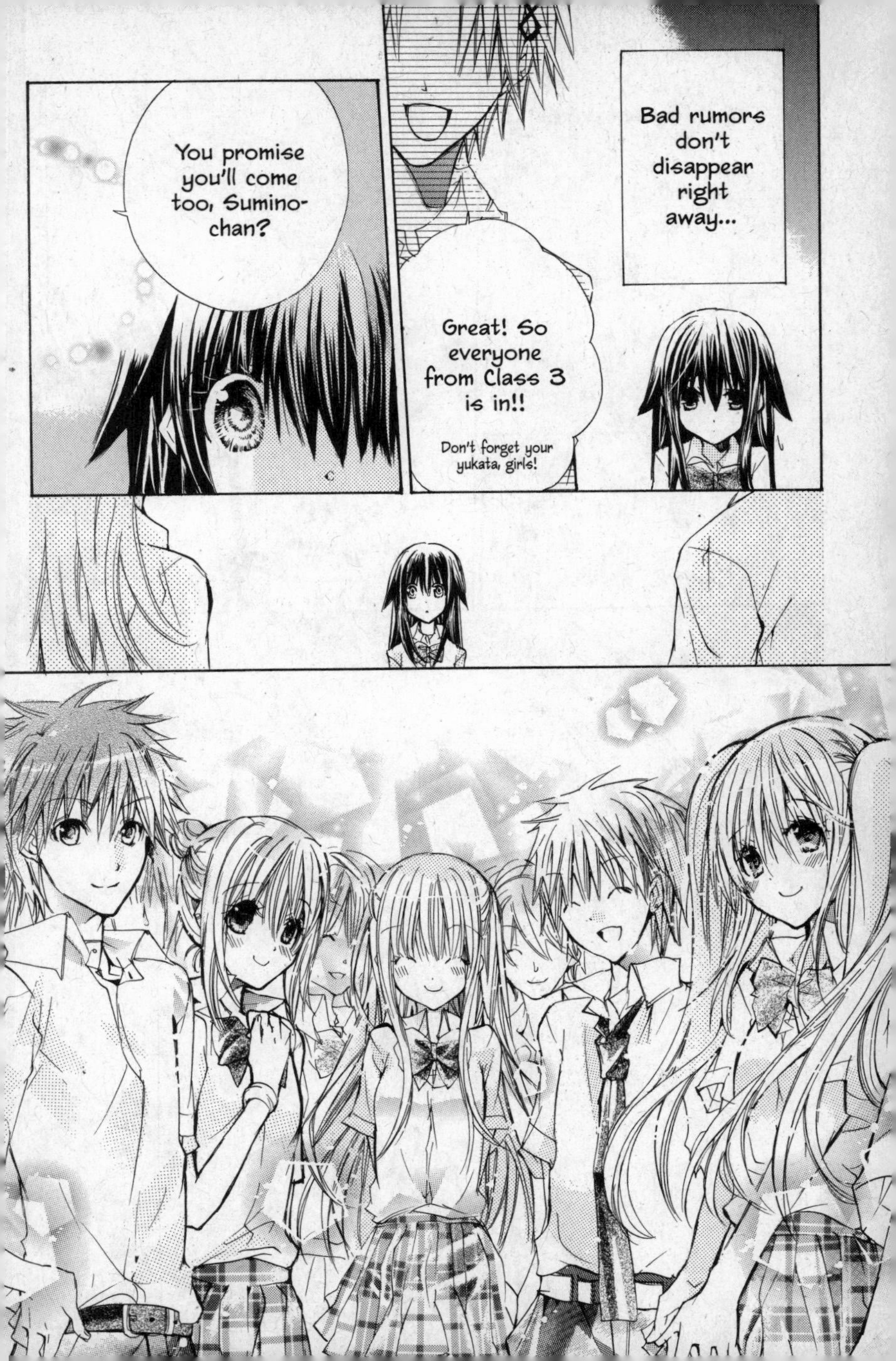
Bad rumors don't disappear right away...
Great! So everyone from Class 3 is in!!
Don't forget your yukata, girls!
You promise you'll come too, Sumino-chan?

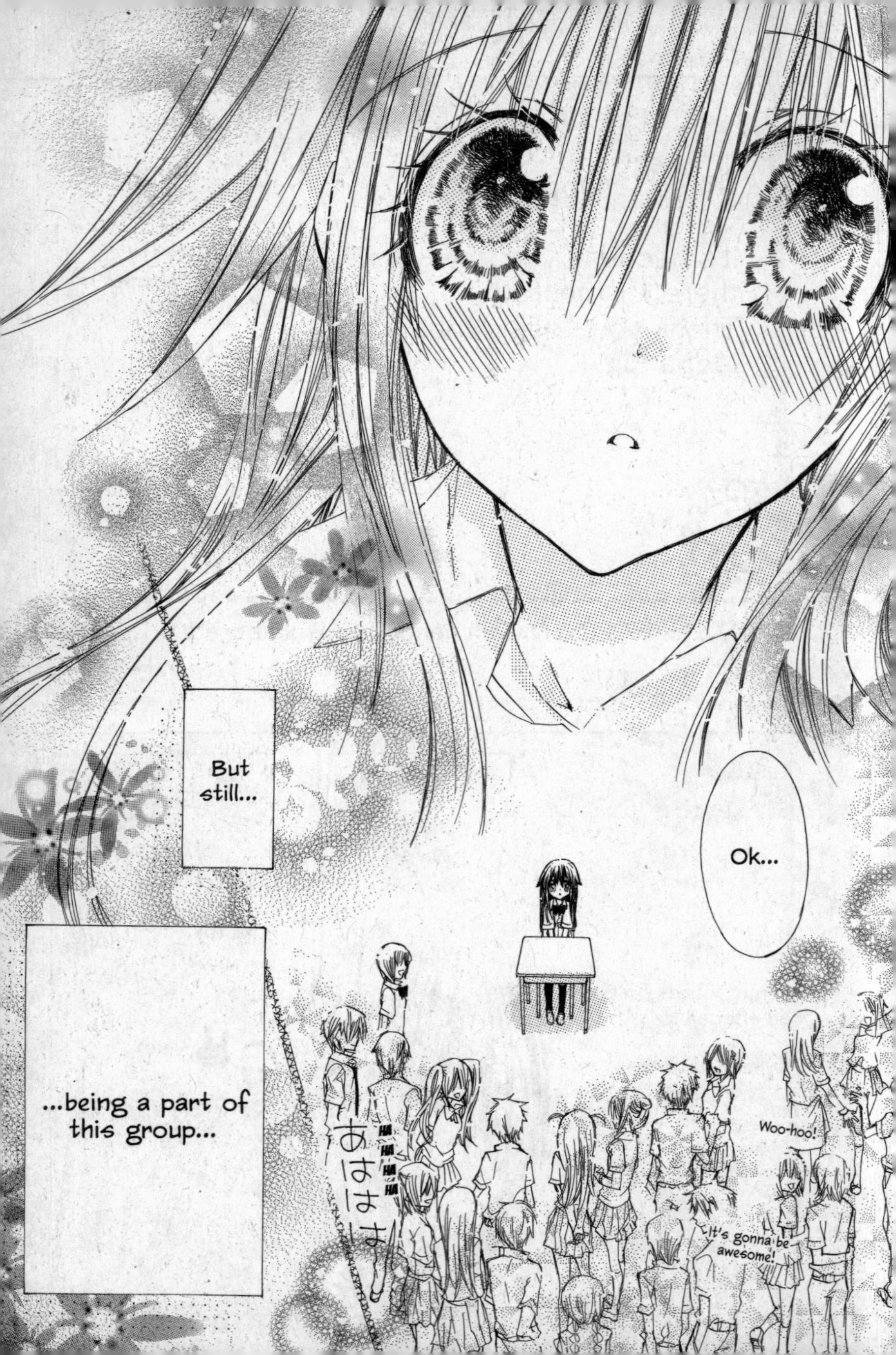
Ok...
But still...
Woo-hoo!
It's gonna be awesome!
HA HA HA HA
あははは
...being a part of this group...

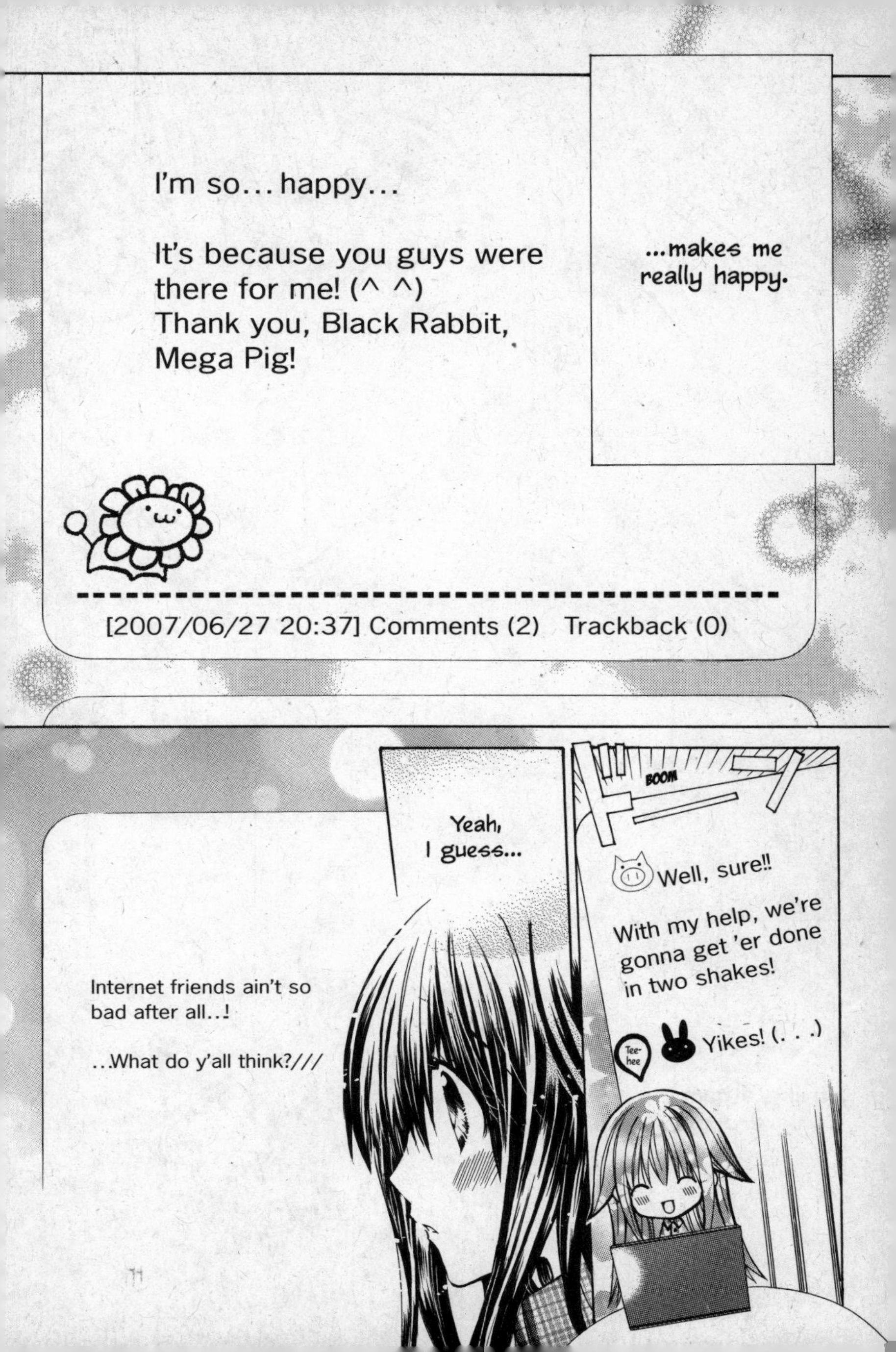
...makes me really happy.
I'm so... happy...
It's because you guys were there for me! (^ ^)
Thank you, Black Rabbit, Mega Pig!
[2007/06/27 20:37] Comments (2) Trackback (0)
BOOM
Well, sure!!
With my help, we're gonna get 'er done in two shakes!
Tee-hee
Yikes! (. . .)
Yeah, I guess...
Internet friends ain't so bad after all..!
...What do y'all think?///

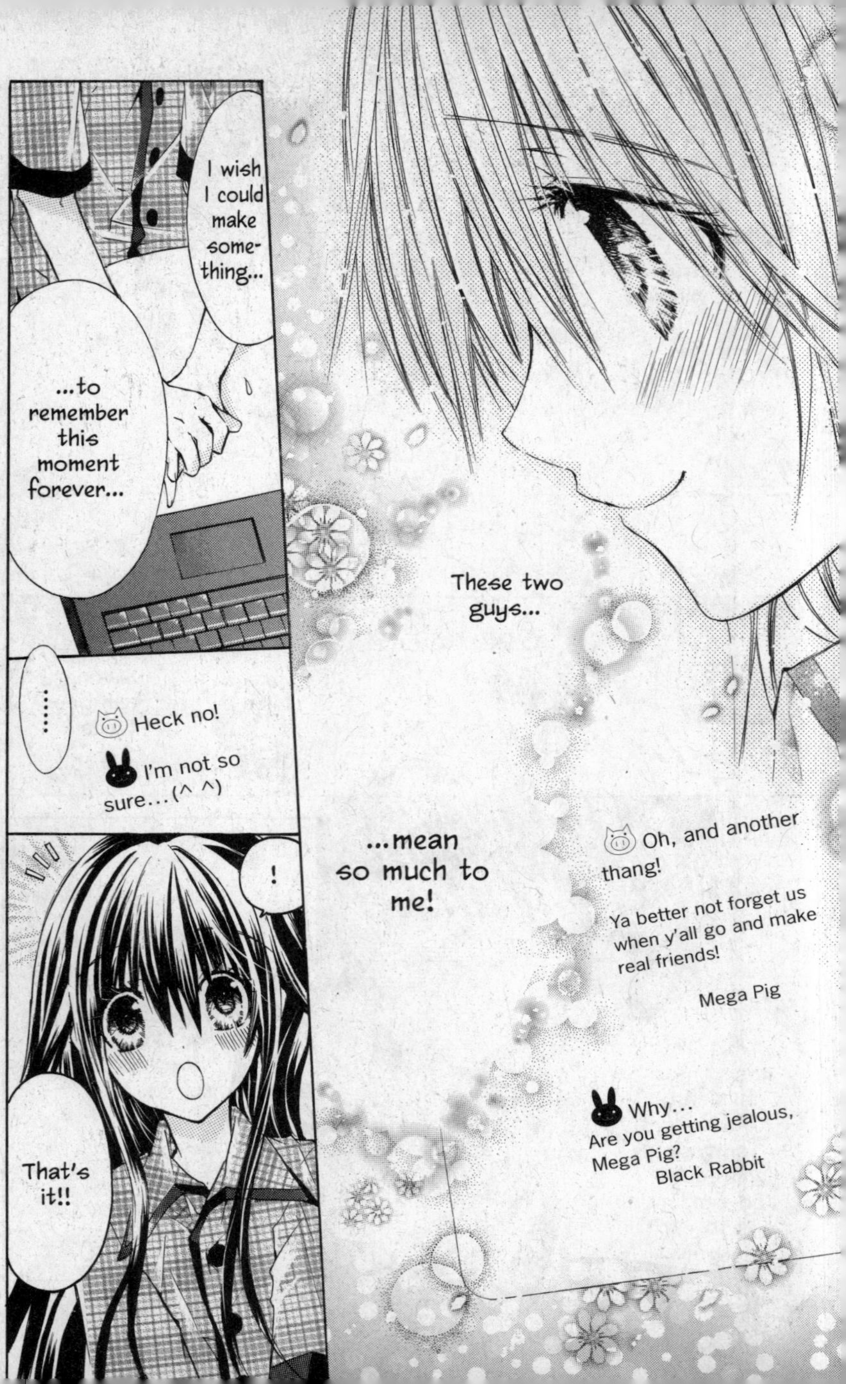
These two guys...
...mean so much to me!
Oh, and another thang!
Ya better not forget us when y'all go and make real friends!
Mega Pig
Why...
Are you getting jealous, Mega Pig?
Black Rabbit
I wish I could make some-thing...
...to remember this moment forever...
......
Heck no!
I'm not so sure... (^ ^)
!
That's it!!

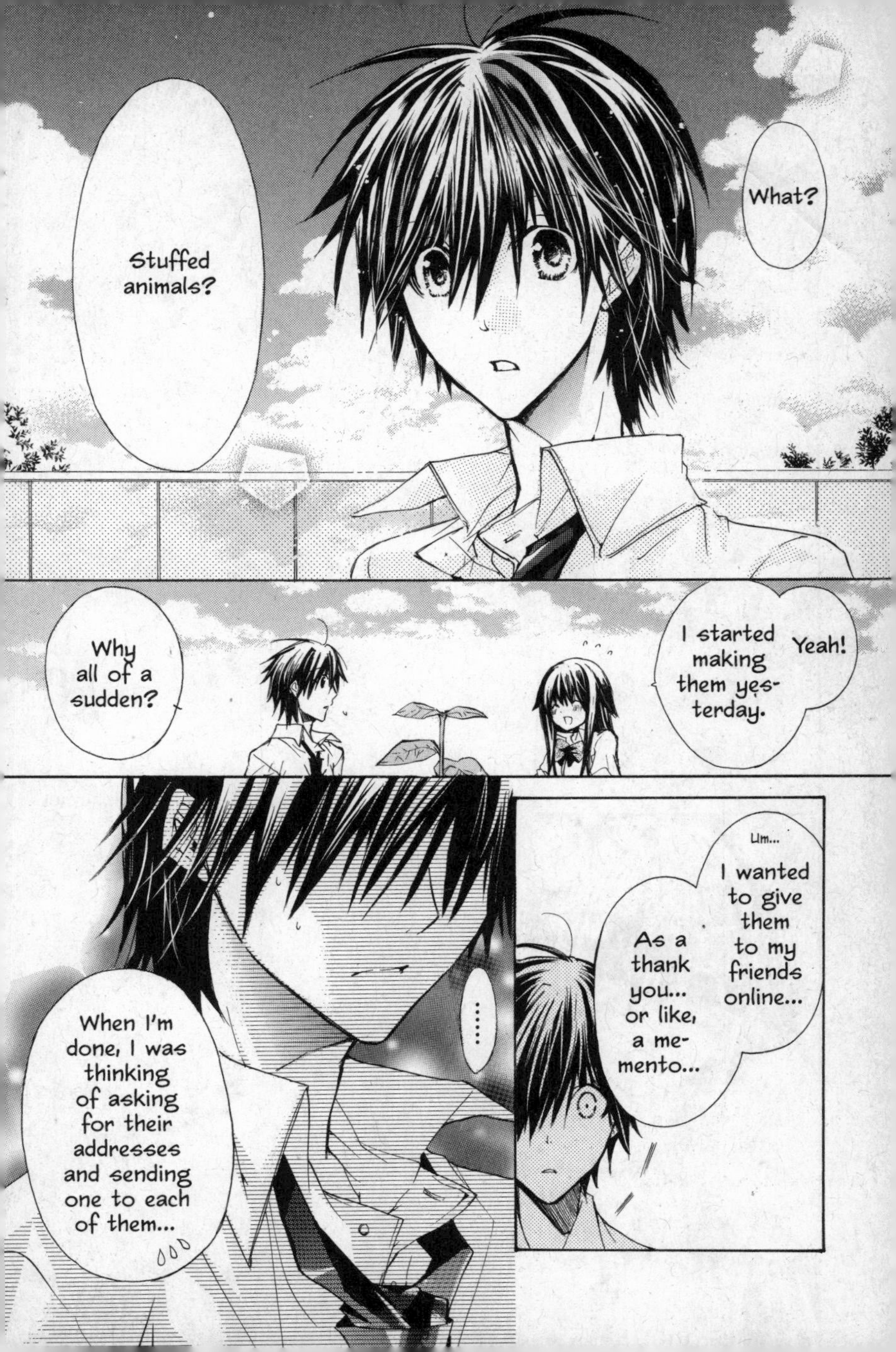
What?
Stuffed animals?
Yeah!
I started making them yes-terday.
Why all of a sudden?
Um... I wanted to give them to my friends online...
As a thank you... or like, a me-mento...
......
When I'm done, I was thinking of asking for their addresses and sending one to each of them...

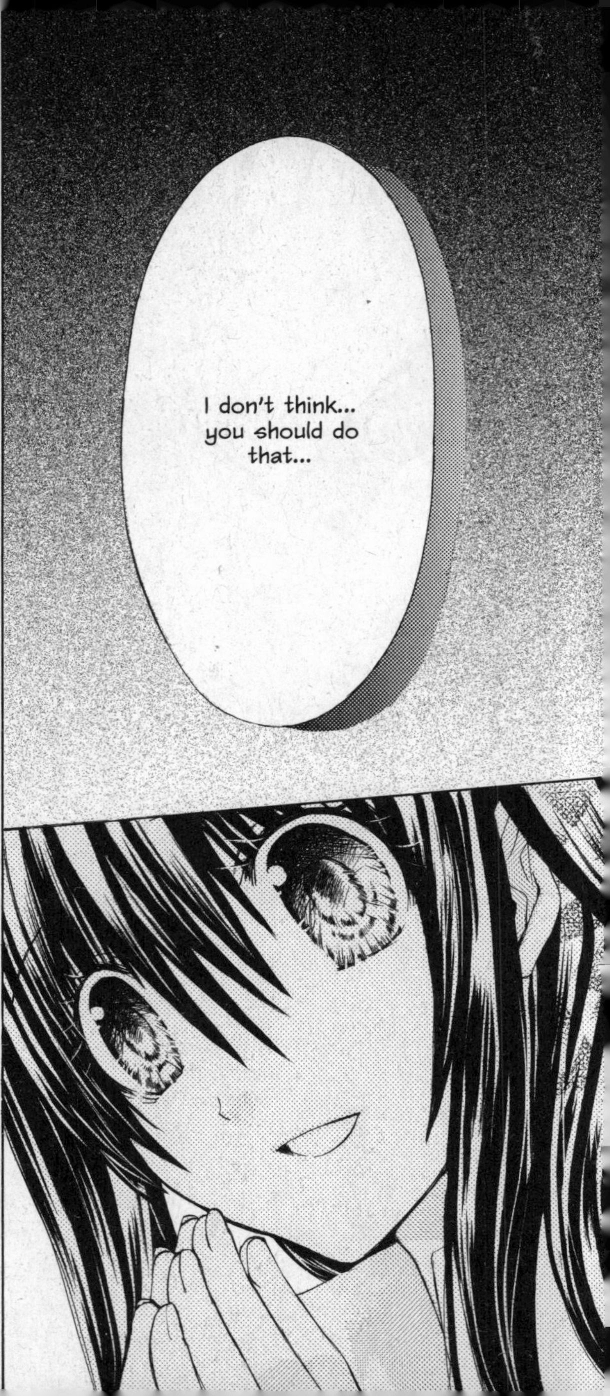
I don't think... you should do that...

The Adventures of Mahimahi 2

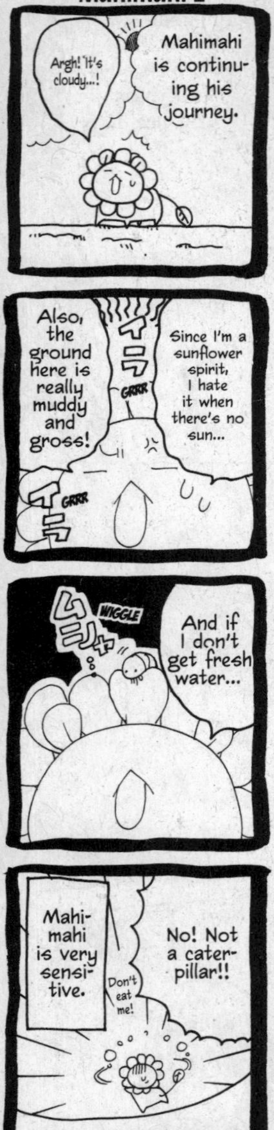
Mahimahi is continuing his journey.
Argh! It's cloudy...!
Since I'm a sunflower spirit, I hate it when there's no sun...
Also, the ground here is really muddy and gross!
GRRR
GRRR
And if I don't get fresh water...
WIGGLE
No! Not a caterpillar!!
Mahimahi is very sensitive.
Don't eat me!

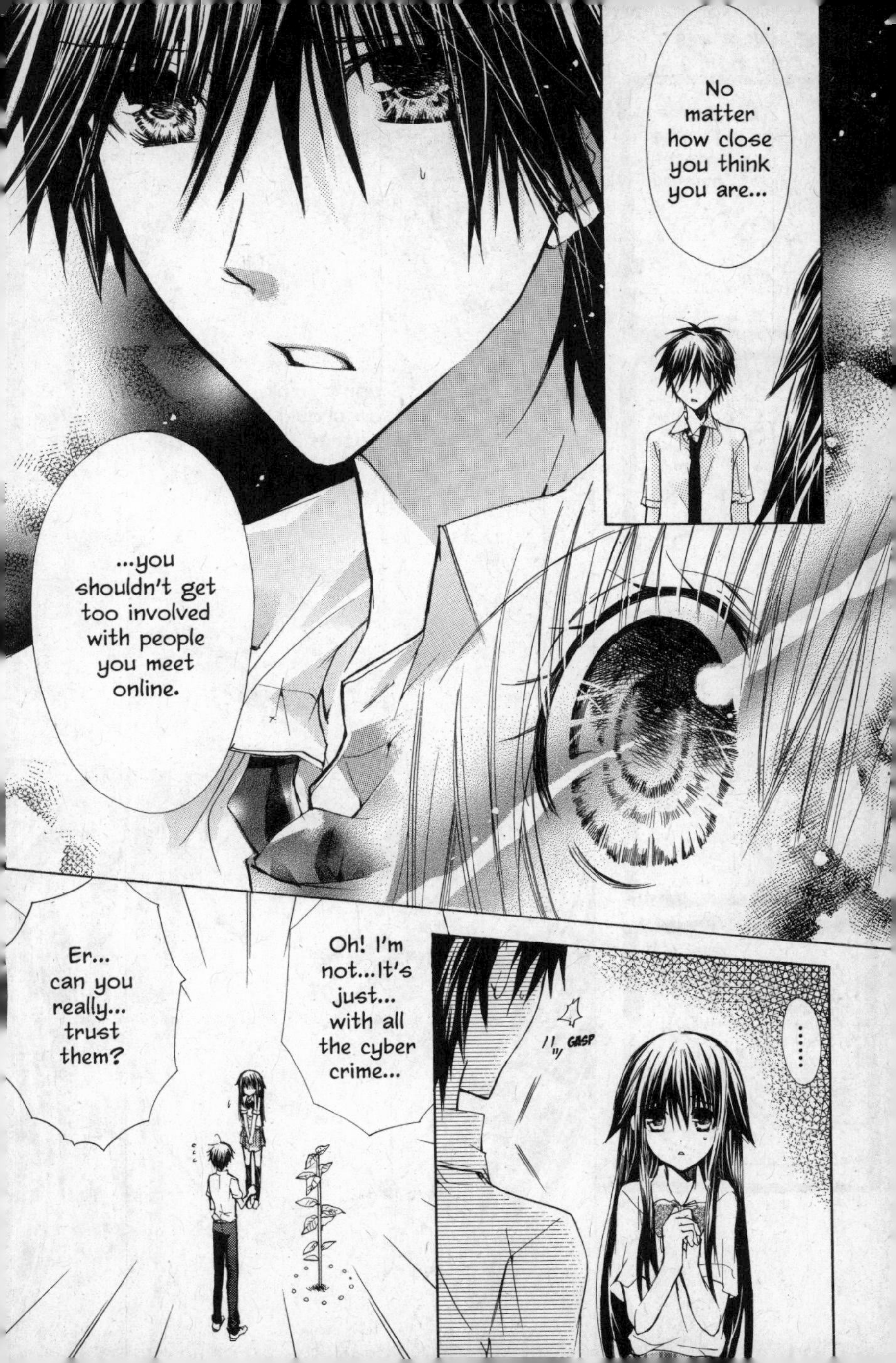
No matter how close you think you are...
...you shouldn't get too involved with people you meet online.
GASP
......
Oh! I'm not...It's just... with all the cyber crime...
Er... can you really... trust them?

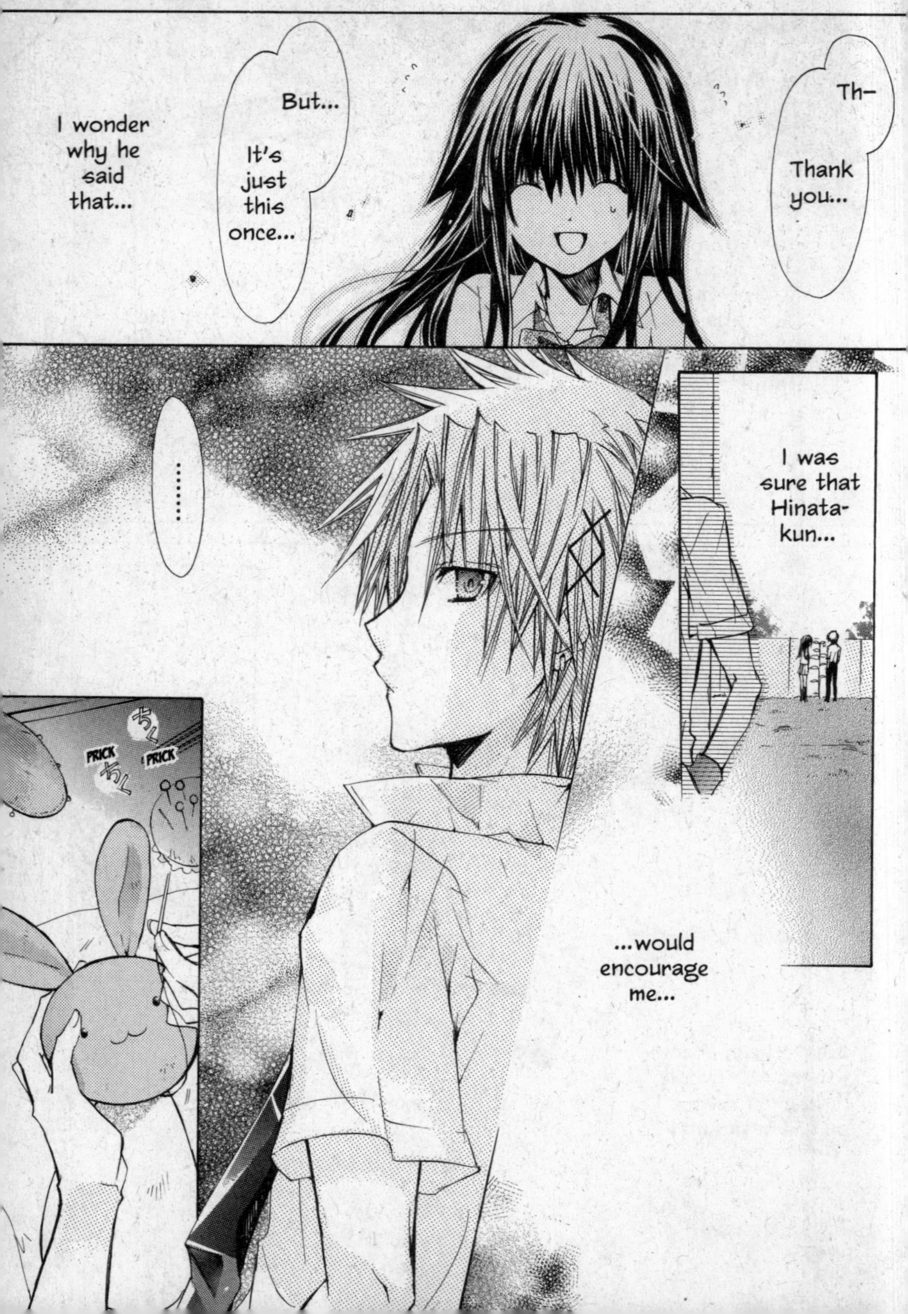
Th-
Thank you...
But...
It's just this once...
I wonder why he said that...
I was sure that Hinata-kun...
......
...would encourage me...
PRICK
PRICK

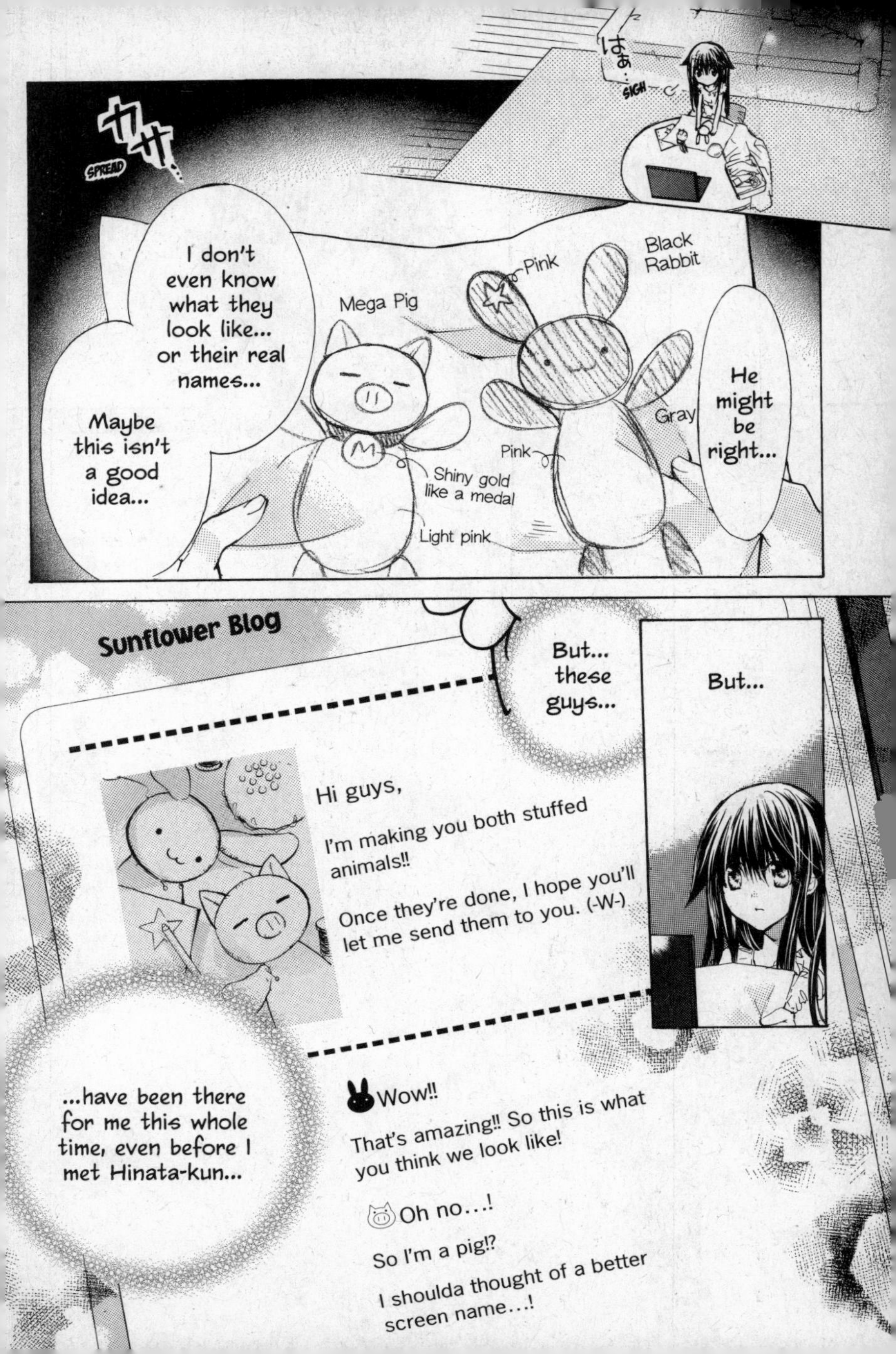
はぁ…
SIGH
カサ
SPREAD
He might be right...
Black Rabbit
Pink
Gray
Pink
Mega Pig
Shiny gold like a medal
Light pink
I don't even know what they look like... or their real names...
Maybe this isn't a good idea...
But...
But... these guys...
Sunflower Blog
Hi guys,
I'm making you both stuffed animals!!
Once they're done, I hope you'll let me send them to you. (-W-)
...have been there for me this whole time, even before I met Hinata-kun...
Wow!!
That's amazing!! So this is what you think we look like!
Oh no…!
So I'm a pig!?
I shoulda thought of a better screen name…!

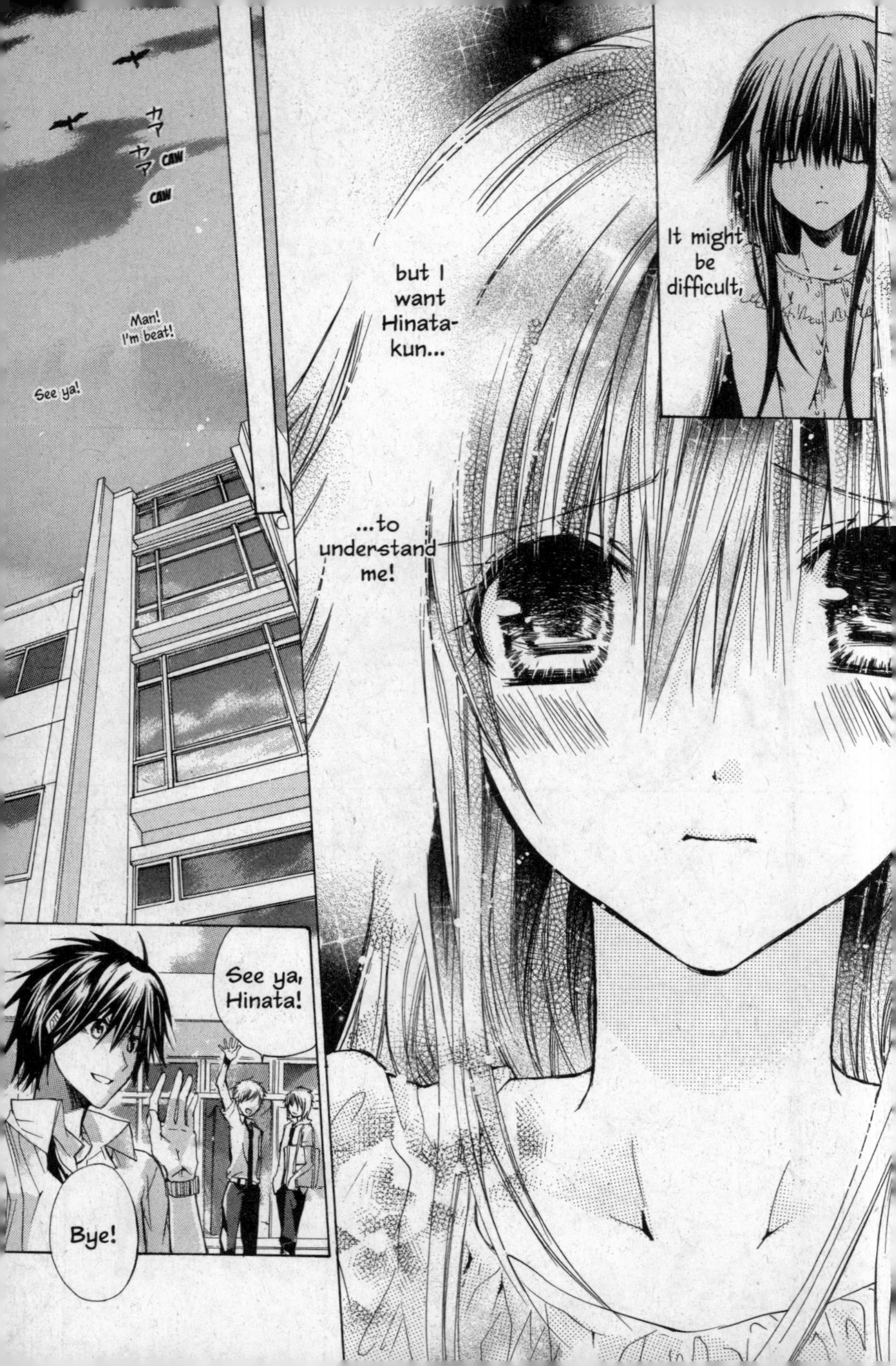
It might be difficult,
but I want Hinata-kun...
...to understand me!
カア カア
CAW
CAW
Man! I'm beat!
See ya!
See ya, Hinata!
Bye!

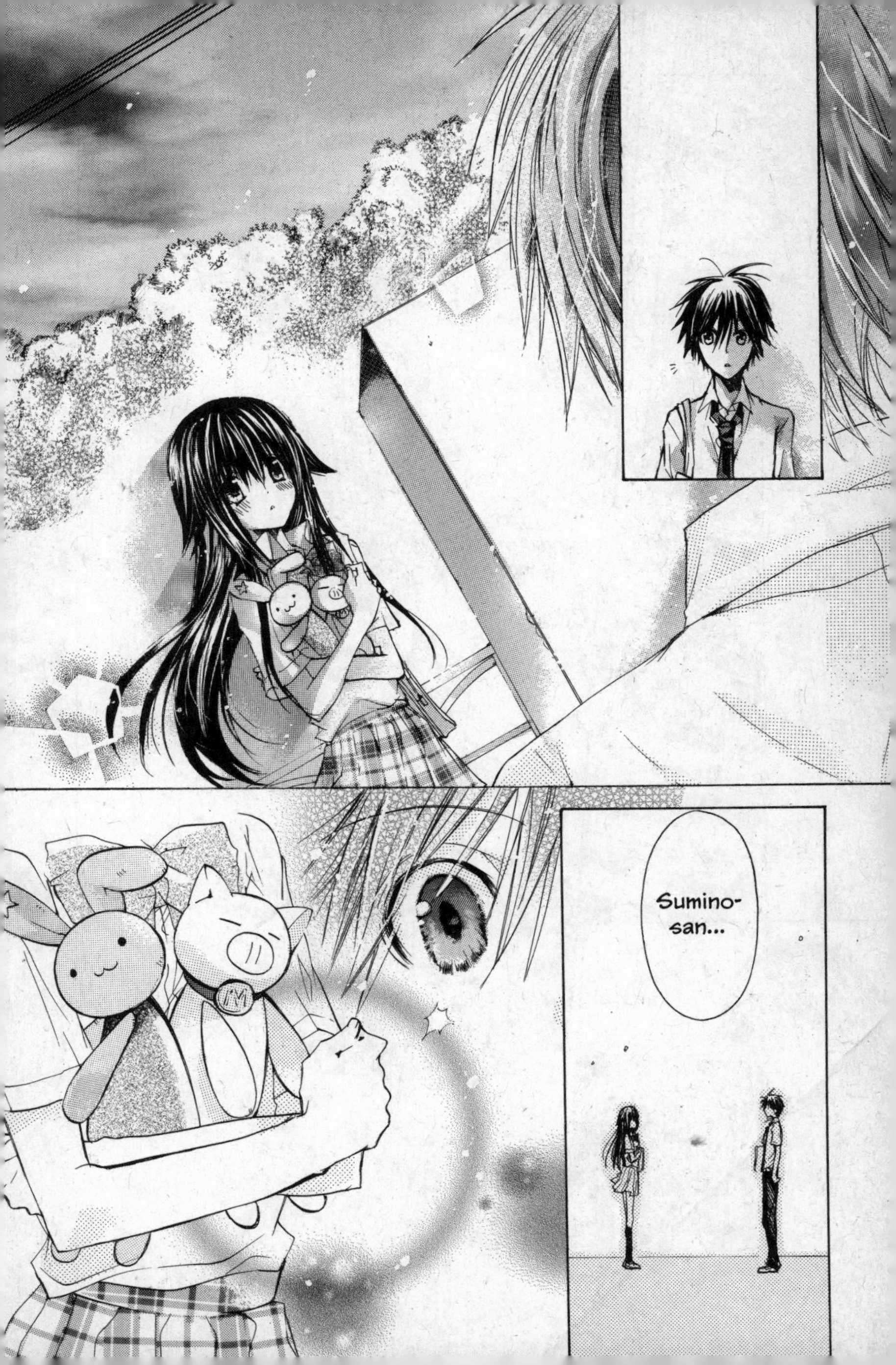
Sumino-san...

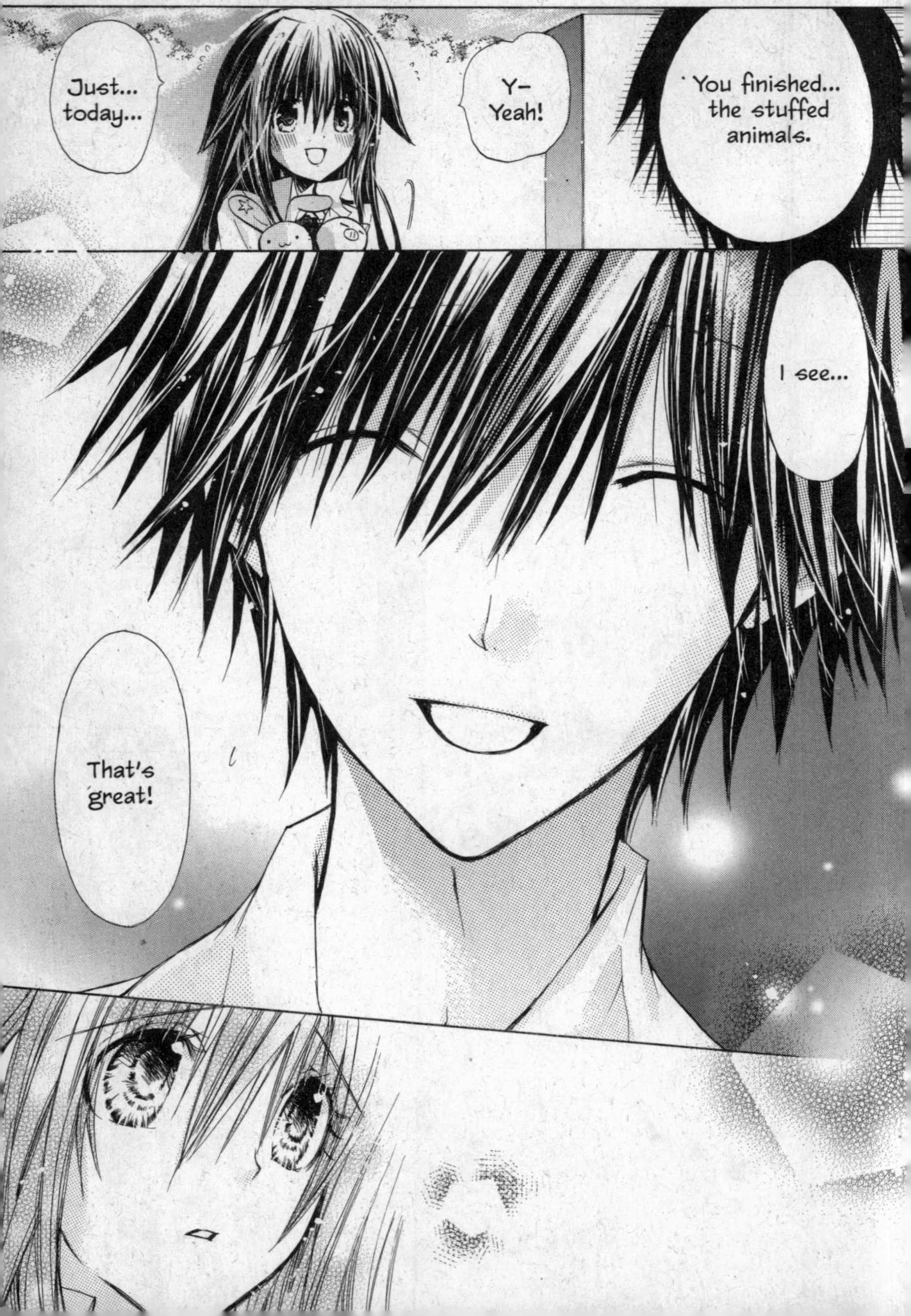
You finished... the stuffed animals.
Y- Yeah!
Just... today...
I see...
That's great!

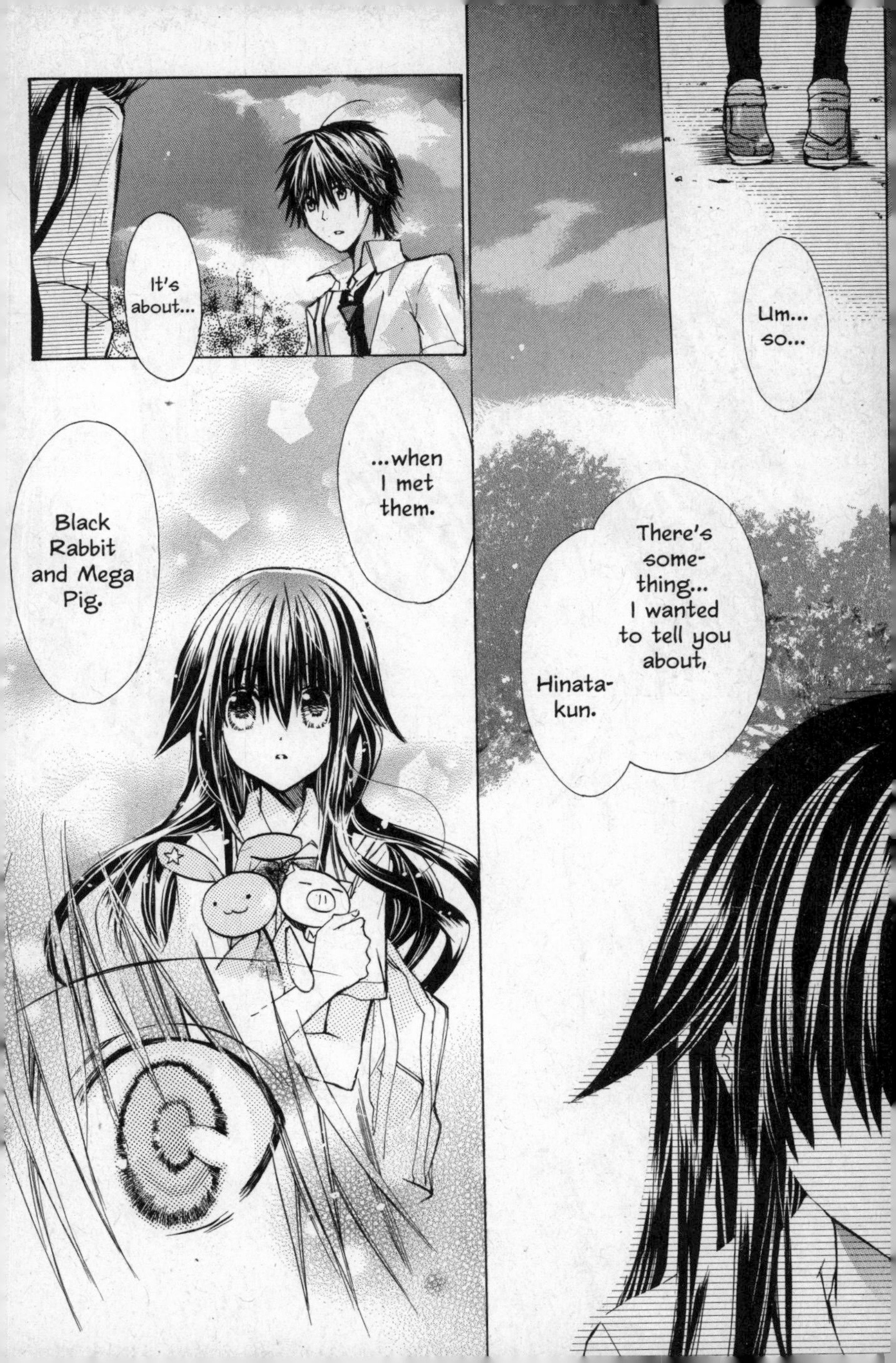
Um... so...
There's some-thing... I wanted to tell you about, Hinata-kun.
It's about...
...when I met them.
Black Rabbit and Mega Pig.

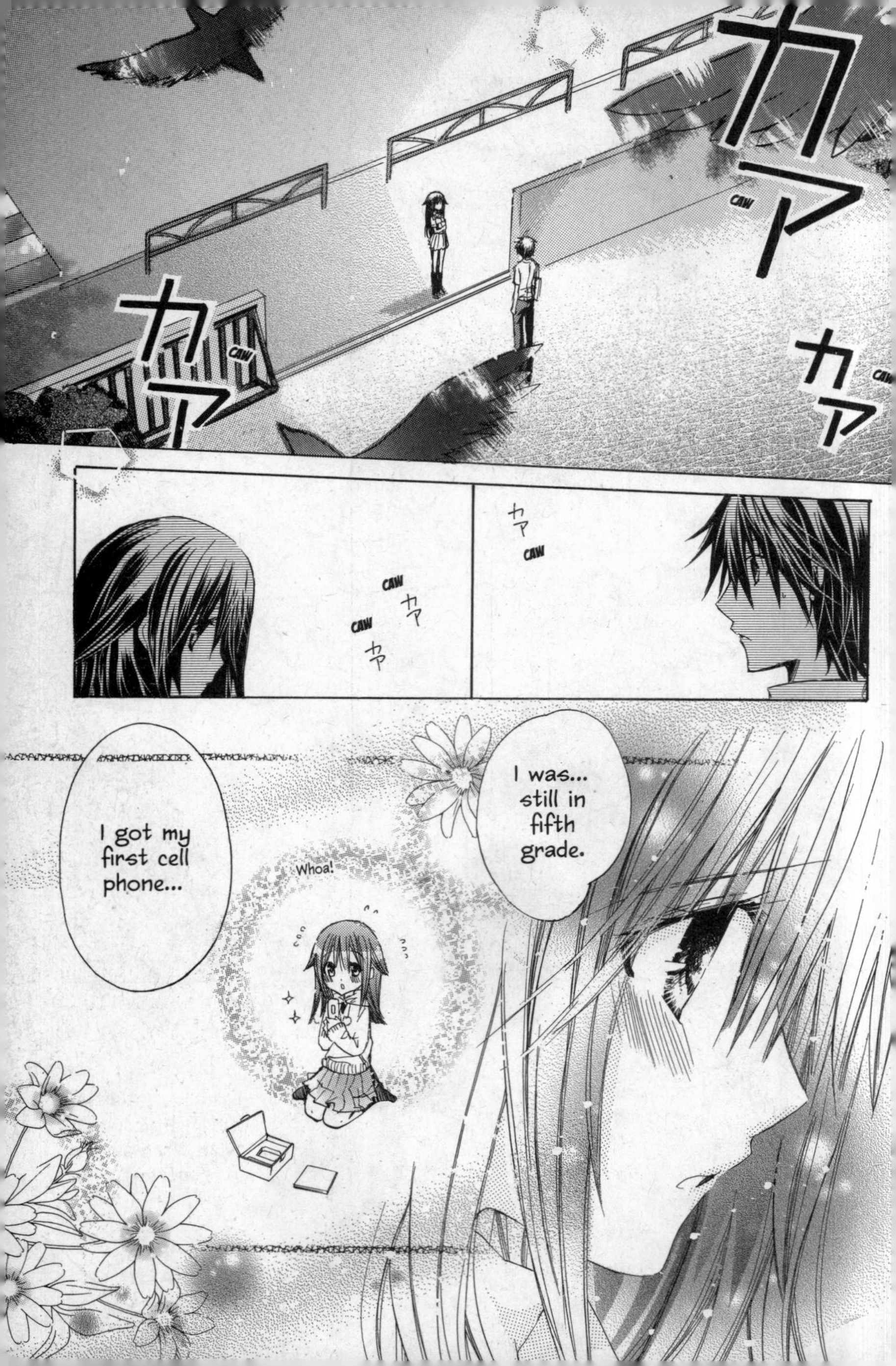

カァー
CAW
カァ
CAW
カァ
CAW
カァ
CAW
CAW
カァ
CAW
カ
I was... still in fifth grade.
Whoa!
I got my first cell phone...

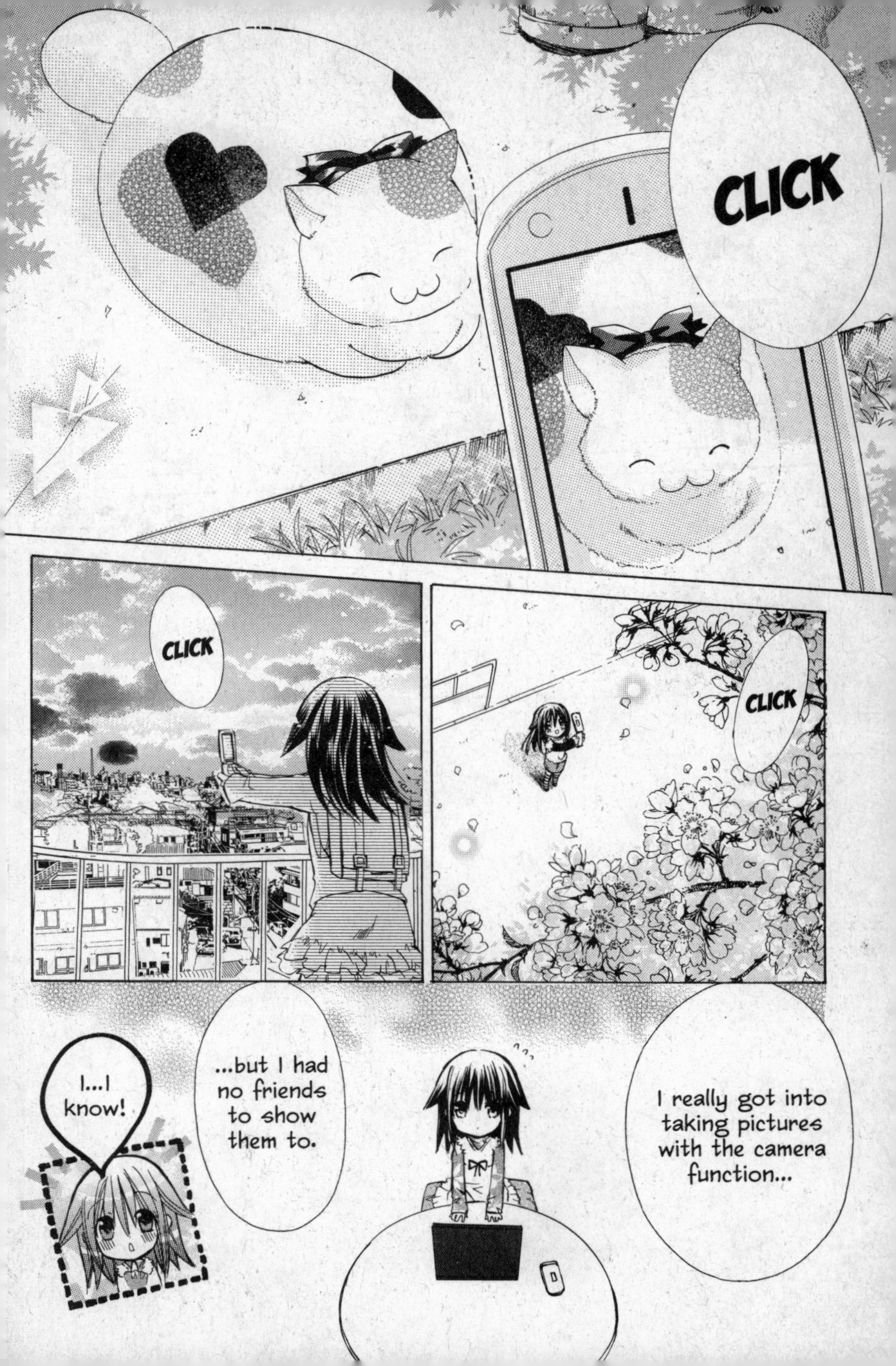
CLICK
CLICK
CLICK
I really got into taking pictures with the camera function...
...but I had no friends to show them to.
I...I know!

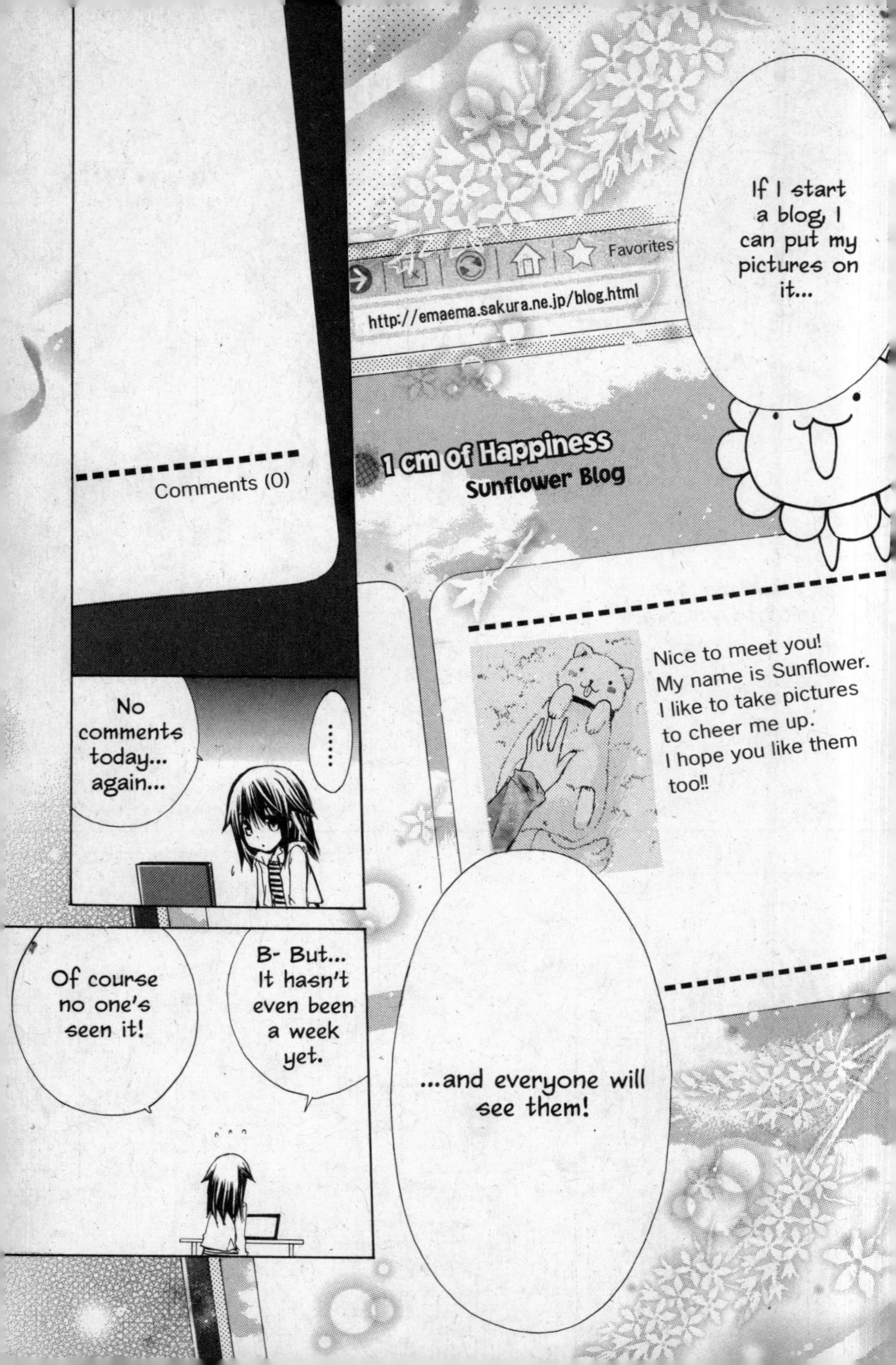
If I start a blog, I can put my pictures on it...
Favorites
http://emaema.sakura.ne.jp/blog.html
1 cm of Happiness
Sunflower Blog
Nice to meet you! My name is Sunflower. I like to take pictures to cheer me up. I hope you like them too!!
...and everyone will see them!
Comments (0)
......
No comments today... again...
B- But... It hasn't even been a week yet.
Of course no one's seen it!

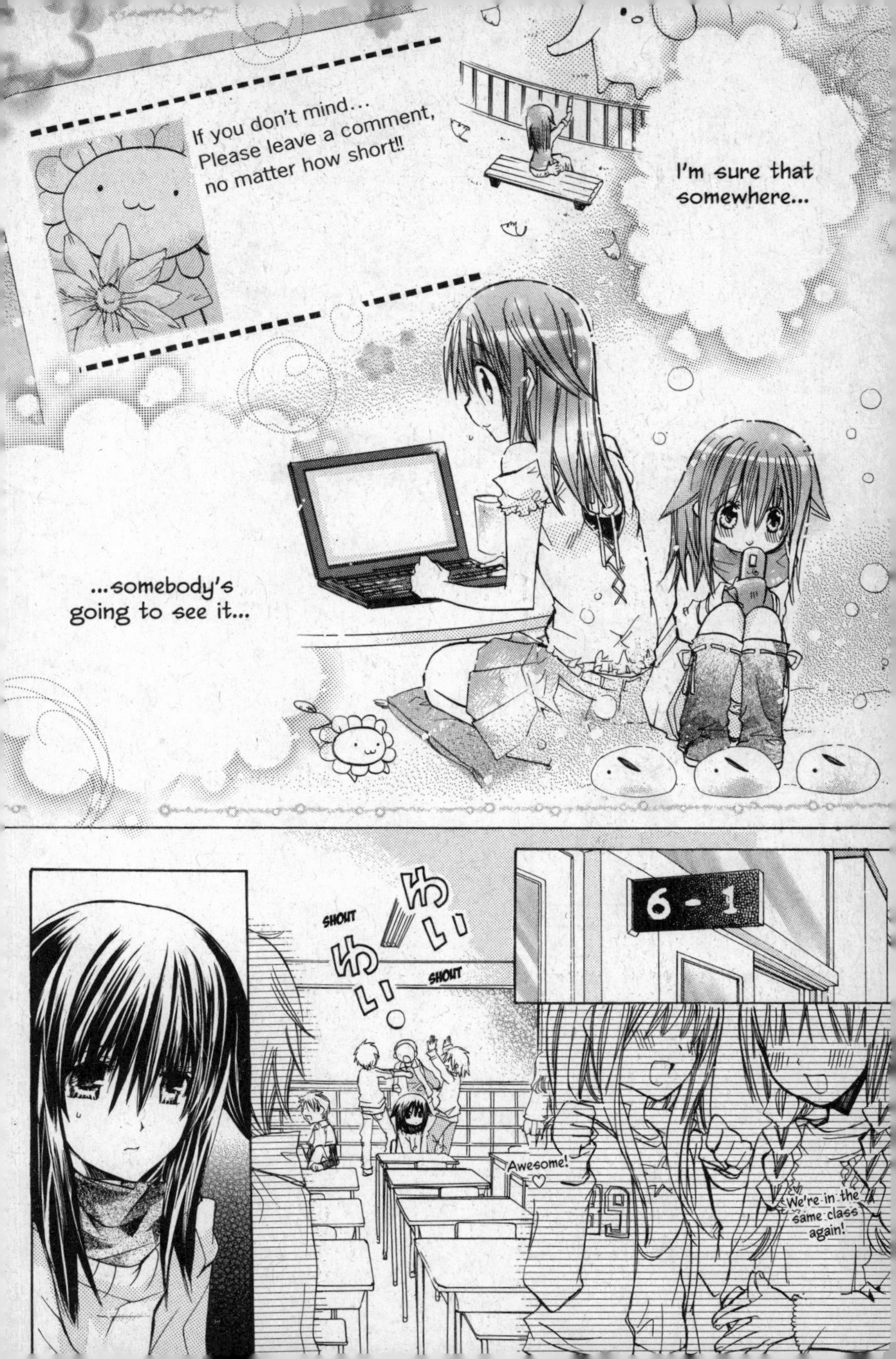
I'm sure that somewhere...
If you don't mind...
Please leave a comment,
no matter how short!!
...somebody's going to see it...
6-1
We're in the same class again!
Awesome!
SHOUT
わい
SHOUT
わい

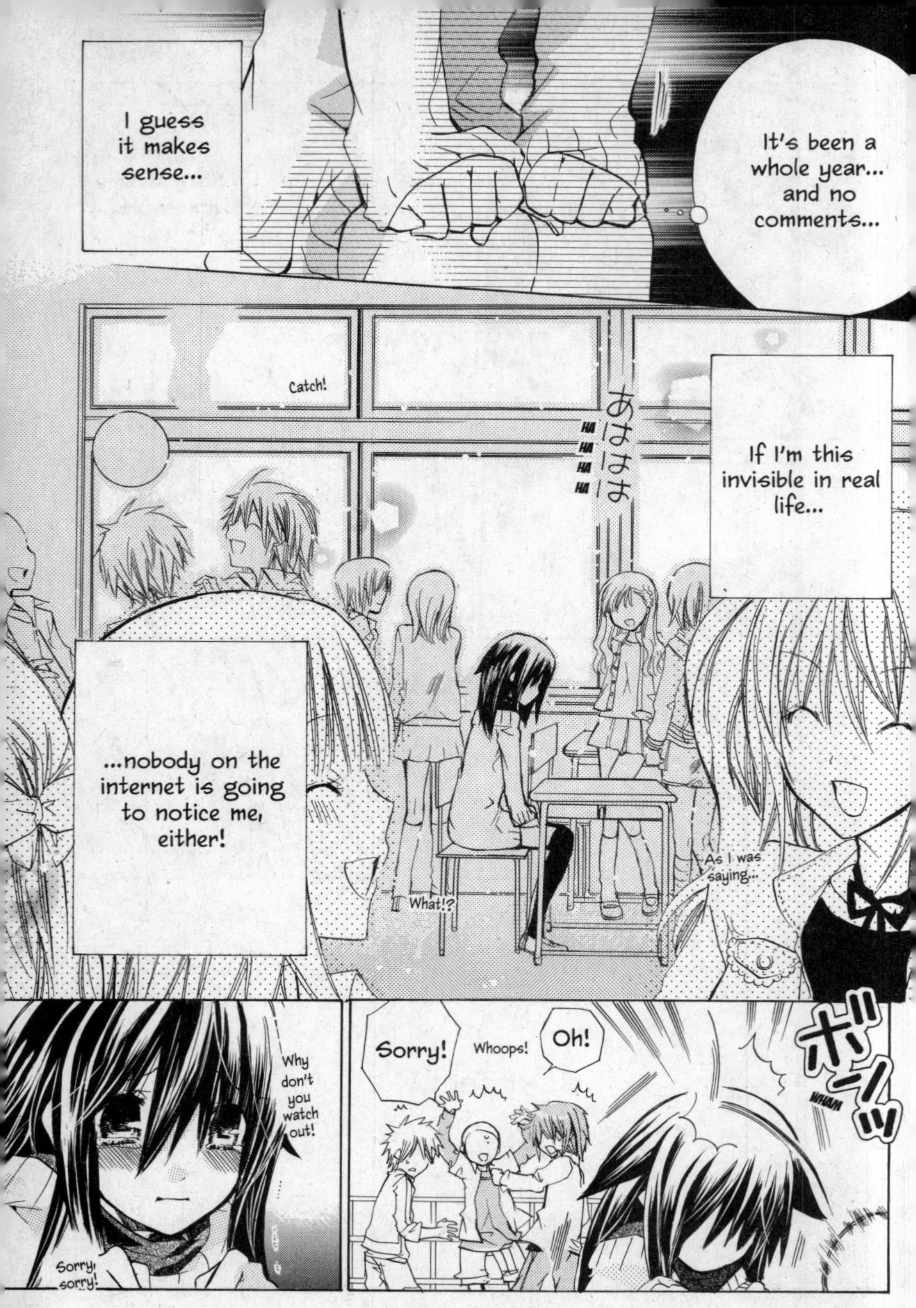
It's been a whole year... and no comments...
I guess it makes sense...
If I'm this invisible in real life...
あははは
HA HA HA HA
Catch!
As I was saying...
What!?
...nobody on the internet is going to notice me, either!
ボーッ
WHAM
Oh!
Whoops!
Sorry!
Why don't you watch out!
Sorry, sorry!

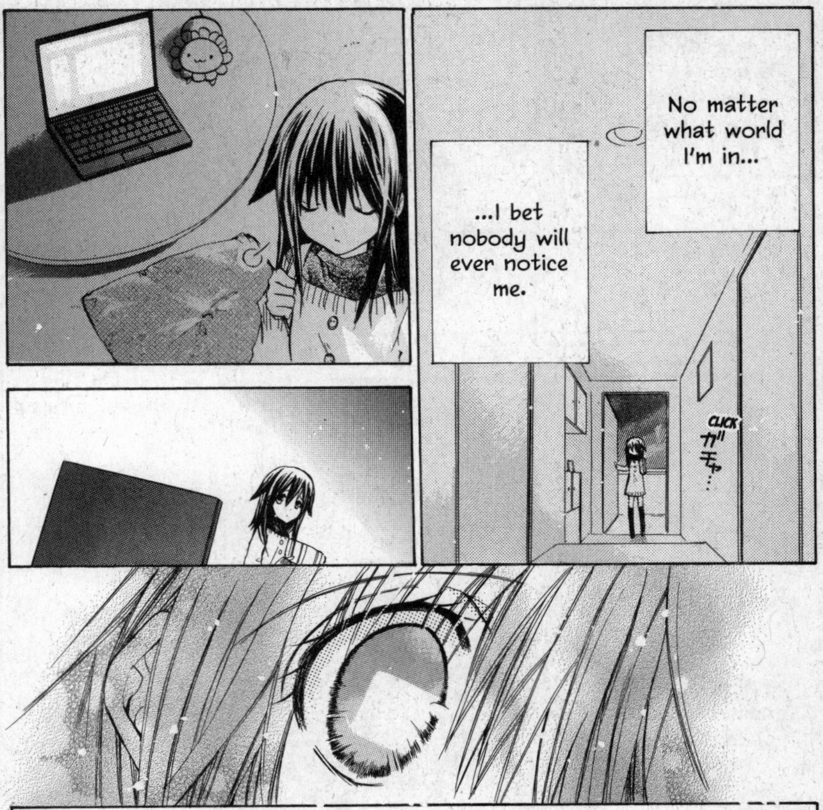
No matter what world I'm in...
...I bet nobody will ever notice me.
CLICK
ガチャ…

Comment (1)

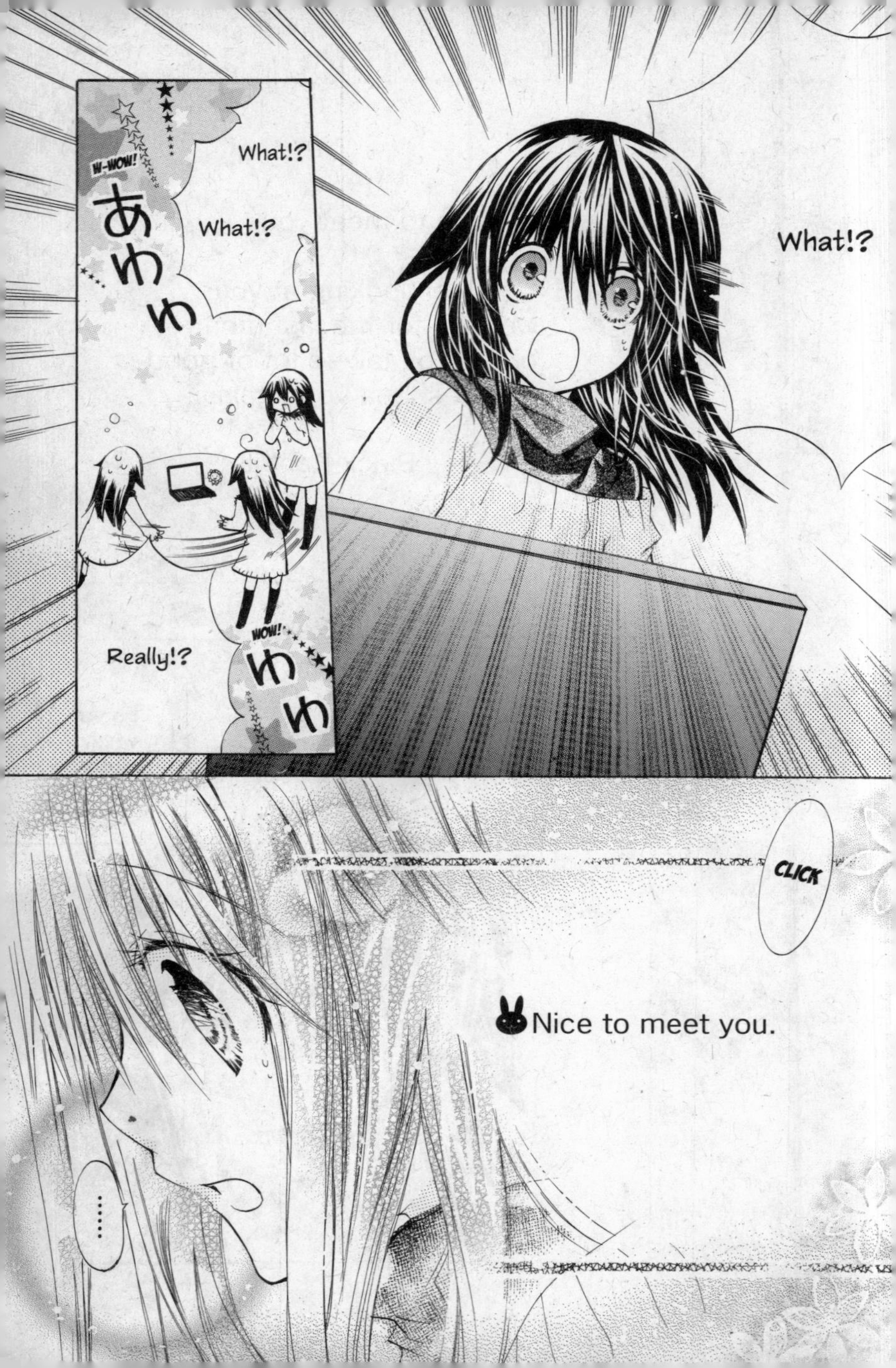
What!?
What!?
W-WOW!
あわわ
What!?
WOW!
わわ
Really!?
CLICK
Nice to meet you.
......

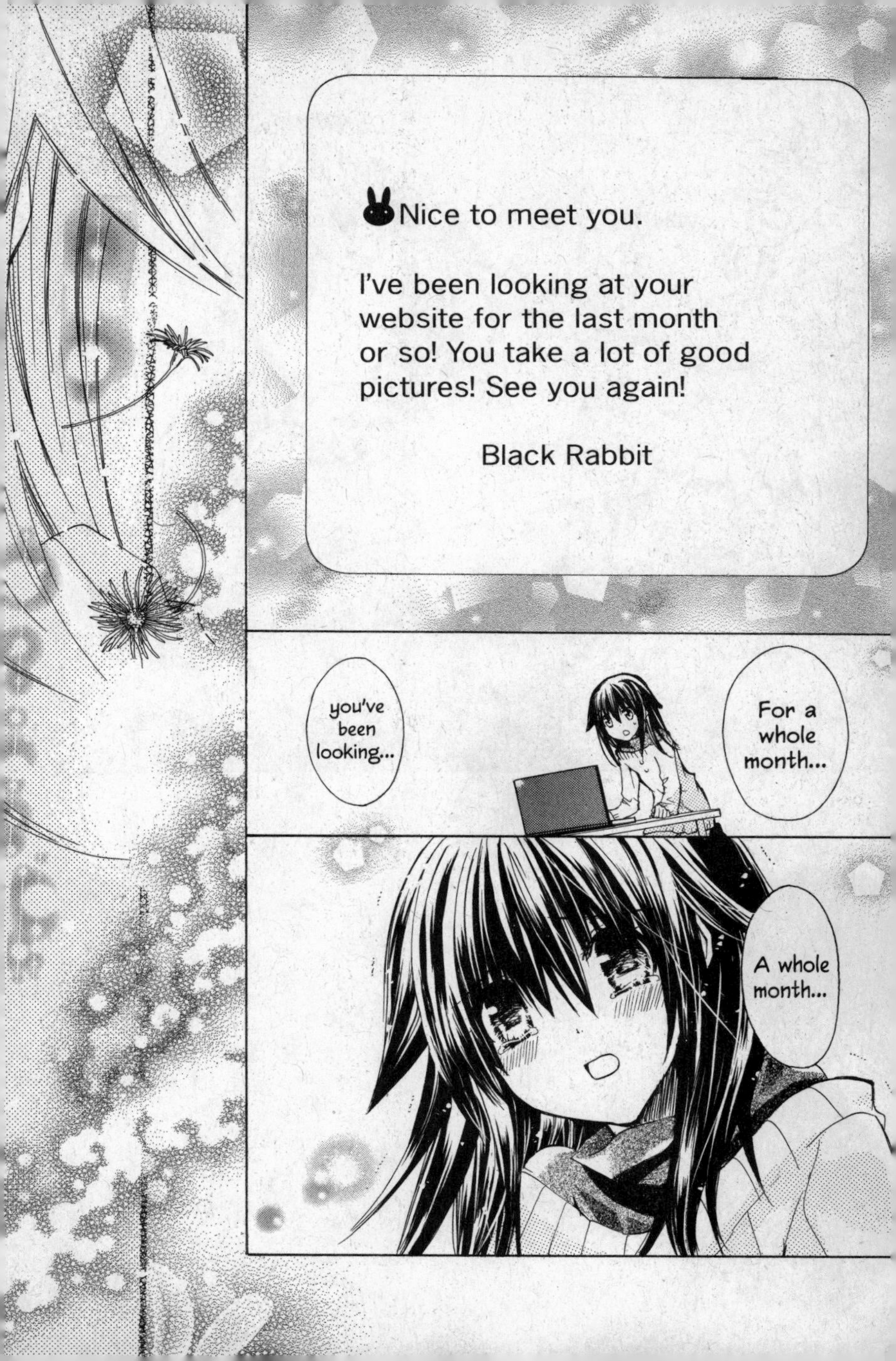
Nice to meet you.
I've been looking at your website for the last month or so! You take a lot of good pictures! See you again!
Black Rabbit
For a whole month...
you've been looking...
A whole month...

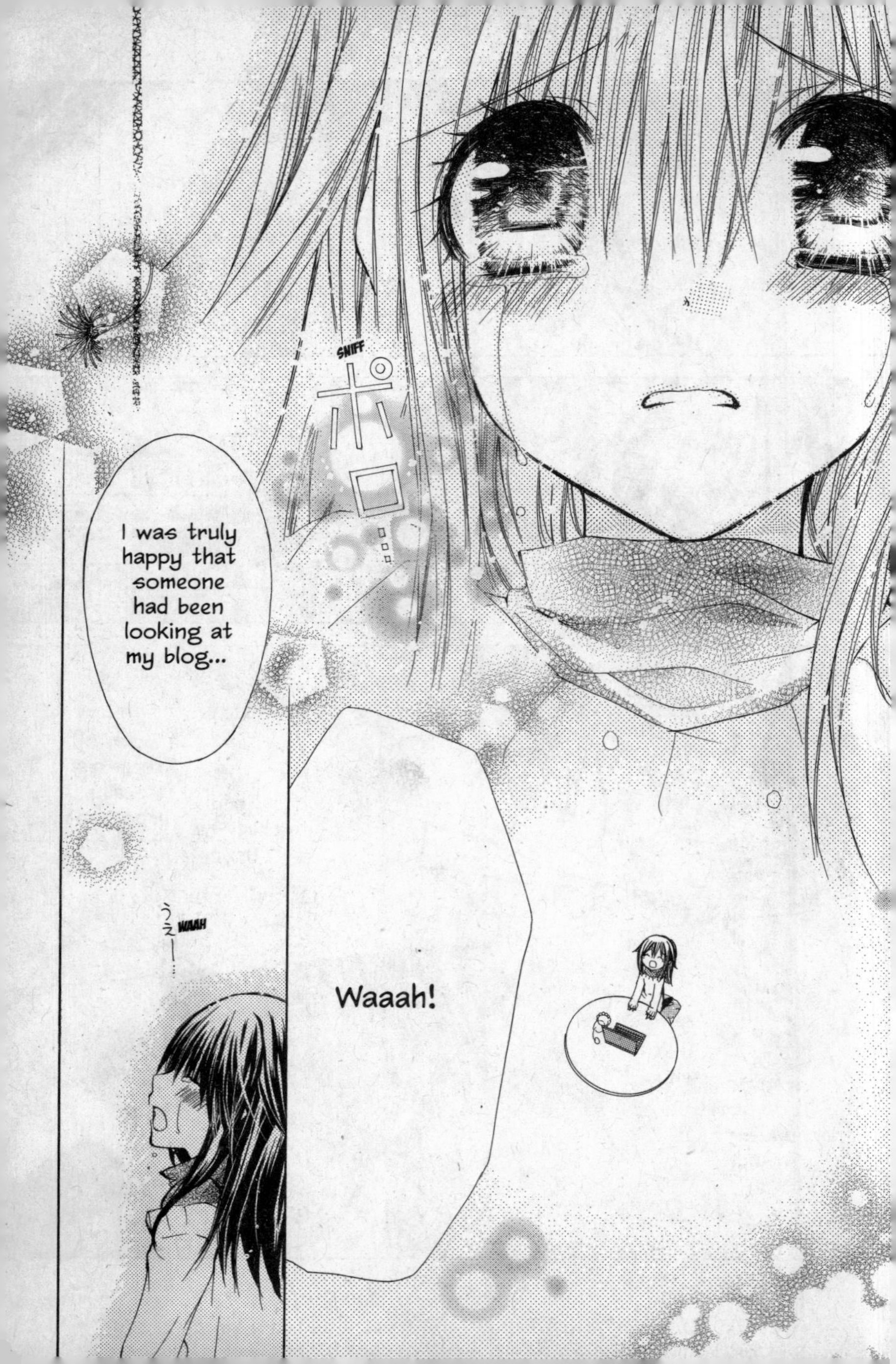
SNIFF
ポロ…
Waaah!
I was truly happy that someone had been looking at my blog...
WAAH
うえー…

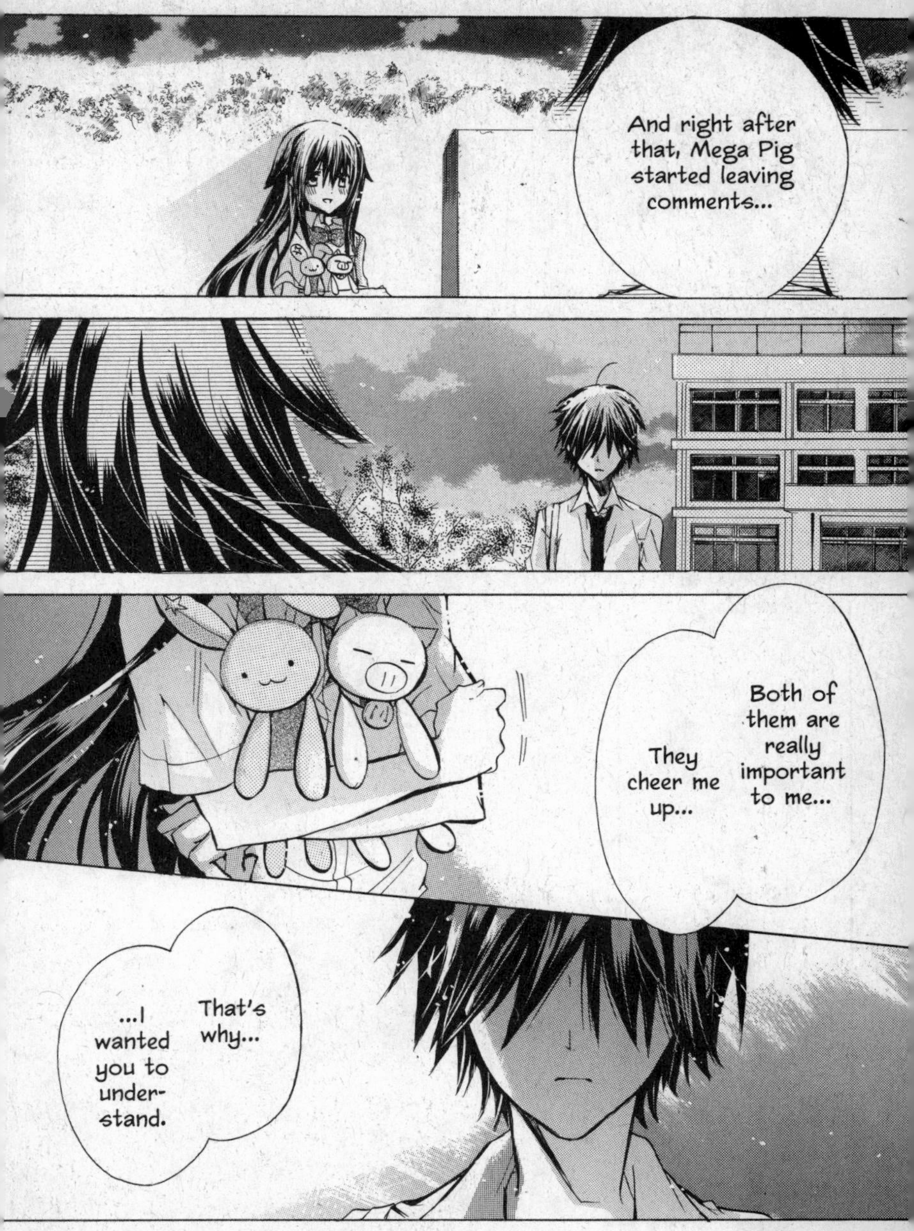
And right after that, Mega Pig started leaving comments...
Both of them are really important to me...
They cheer me up...
That's why...
...I wanted you to understand.

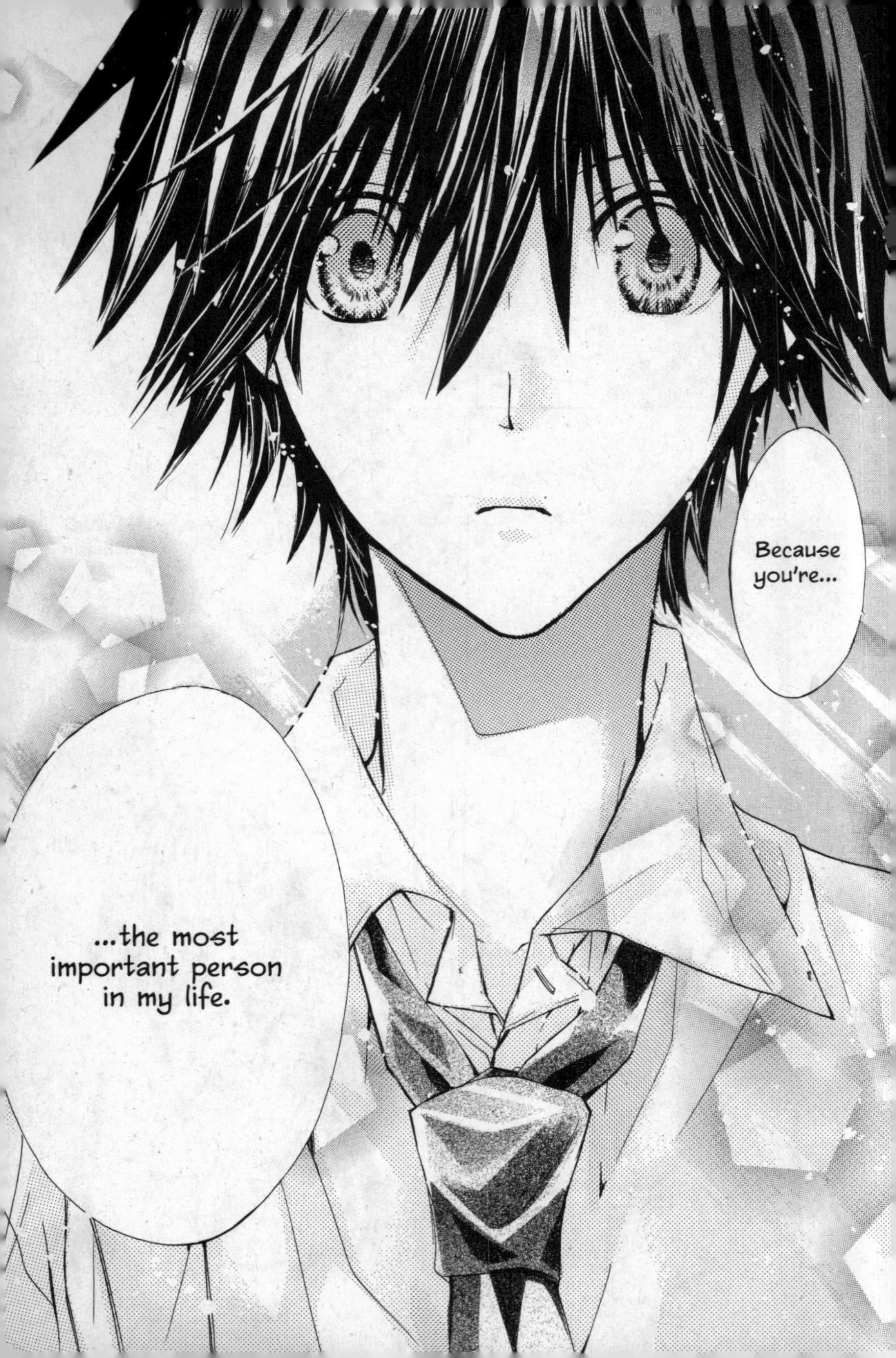
Because you're...
...the most important person in my life.

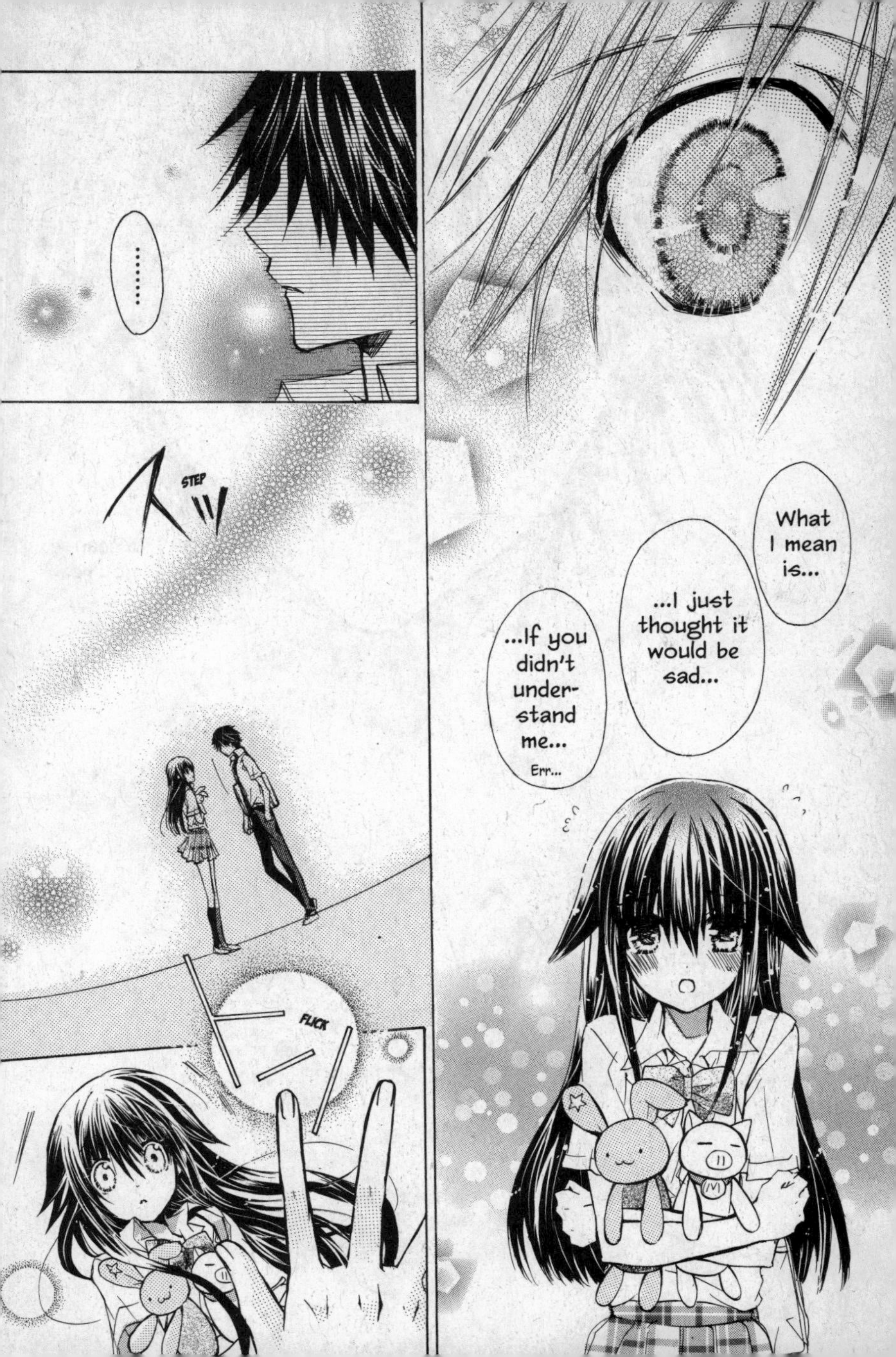
What I mean is...
...I just thought it would be sad...
...If you didn't under-stand me...
Err...
......
STEP
FLICK

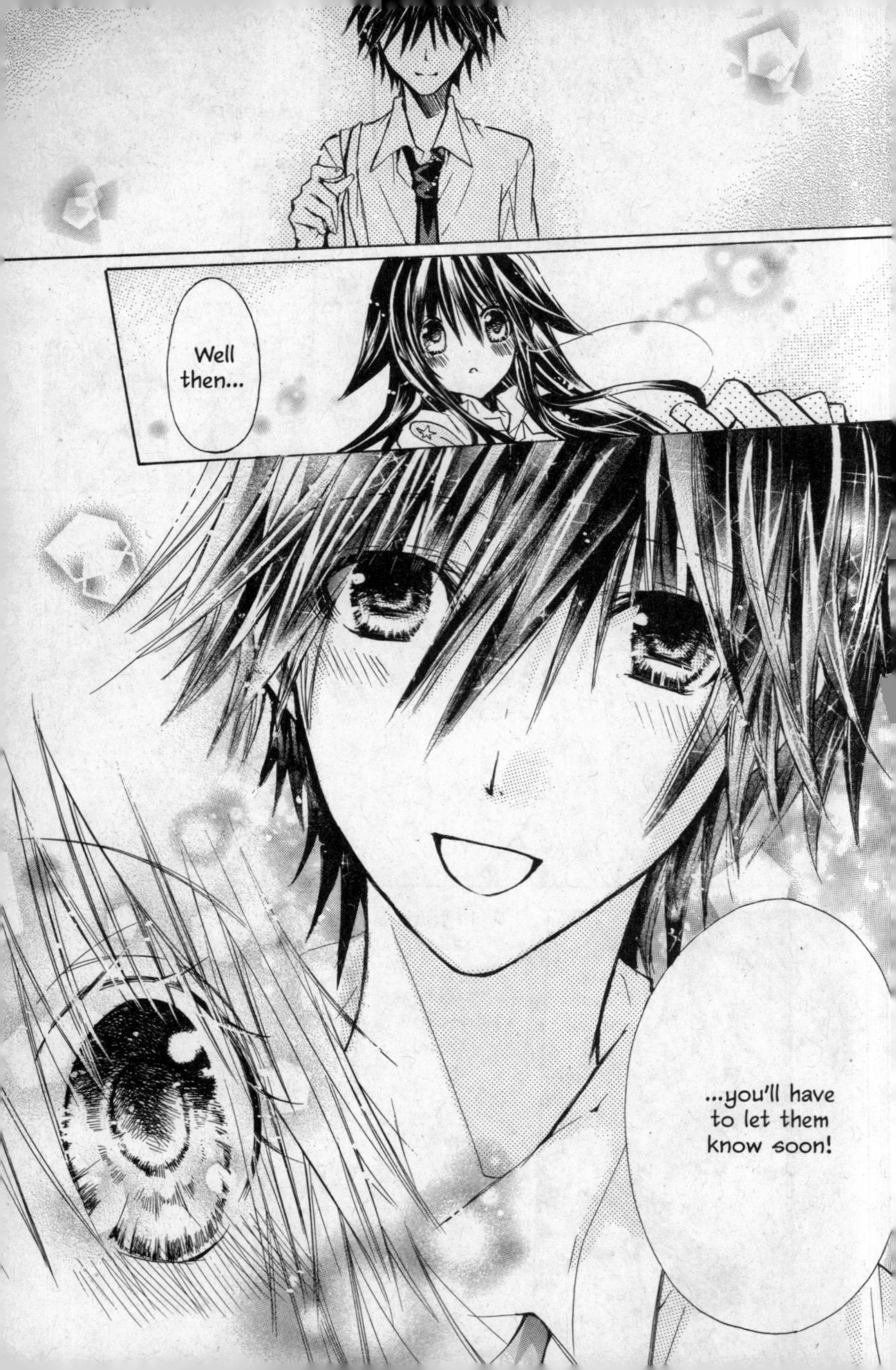
Well then...
...you'll have to let them know soon!

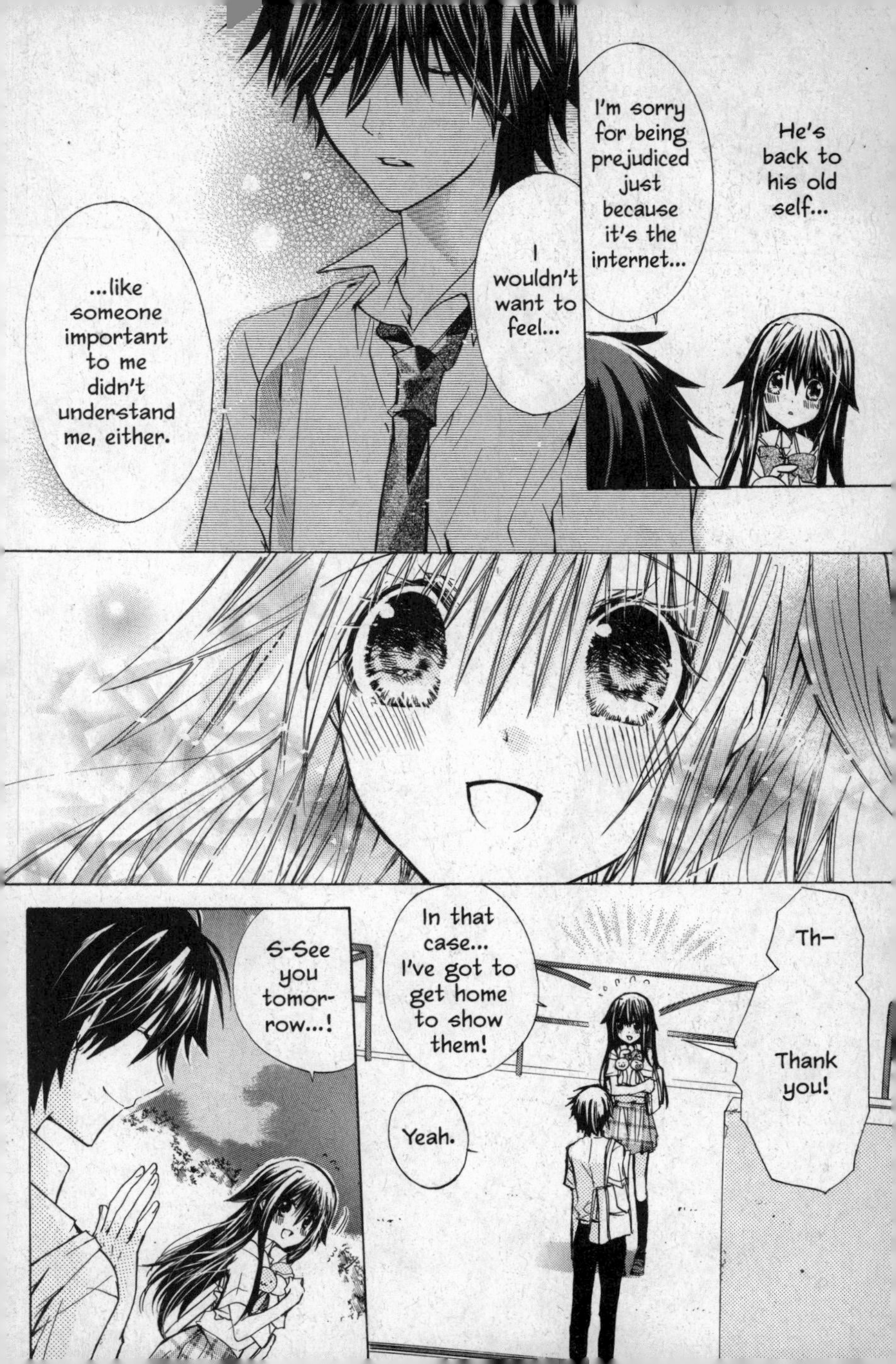

He's back to his old self...
I'm sorry for being prejudiced just because it's the internet...
I wouldn't want to feel...
...like someone important to me didn't understand me, either.
Th-
Thank you!
In that case... I've got to get home to show them!
Yeah.
S-See you tomor-row...!

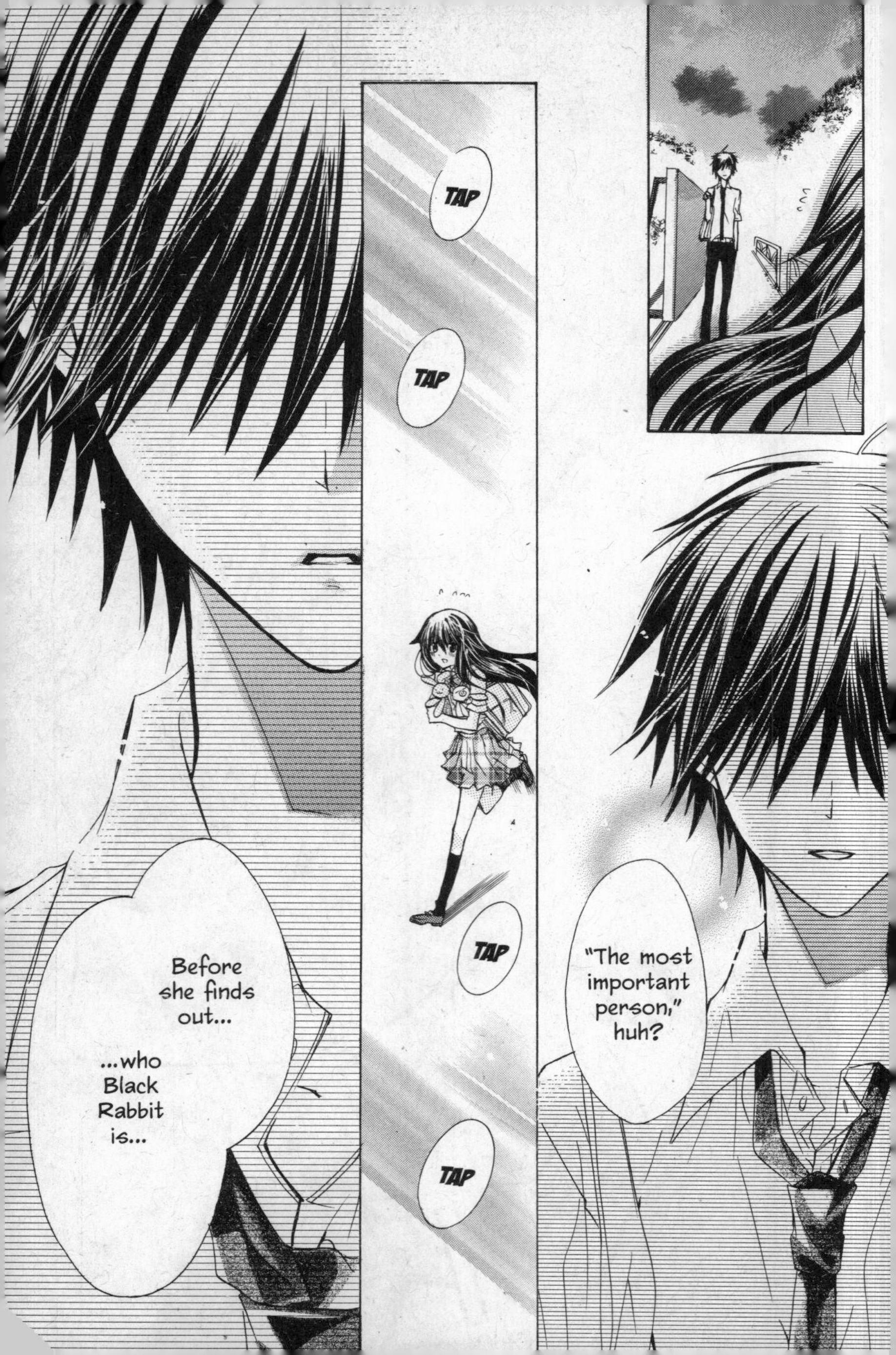
"The most important person," huh?
TAP
TAP
TAP
TAP
Before she finds out...
...who Black Rabbit is...

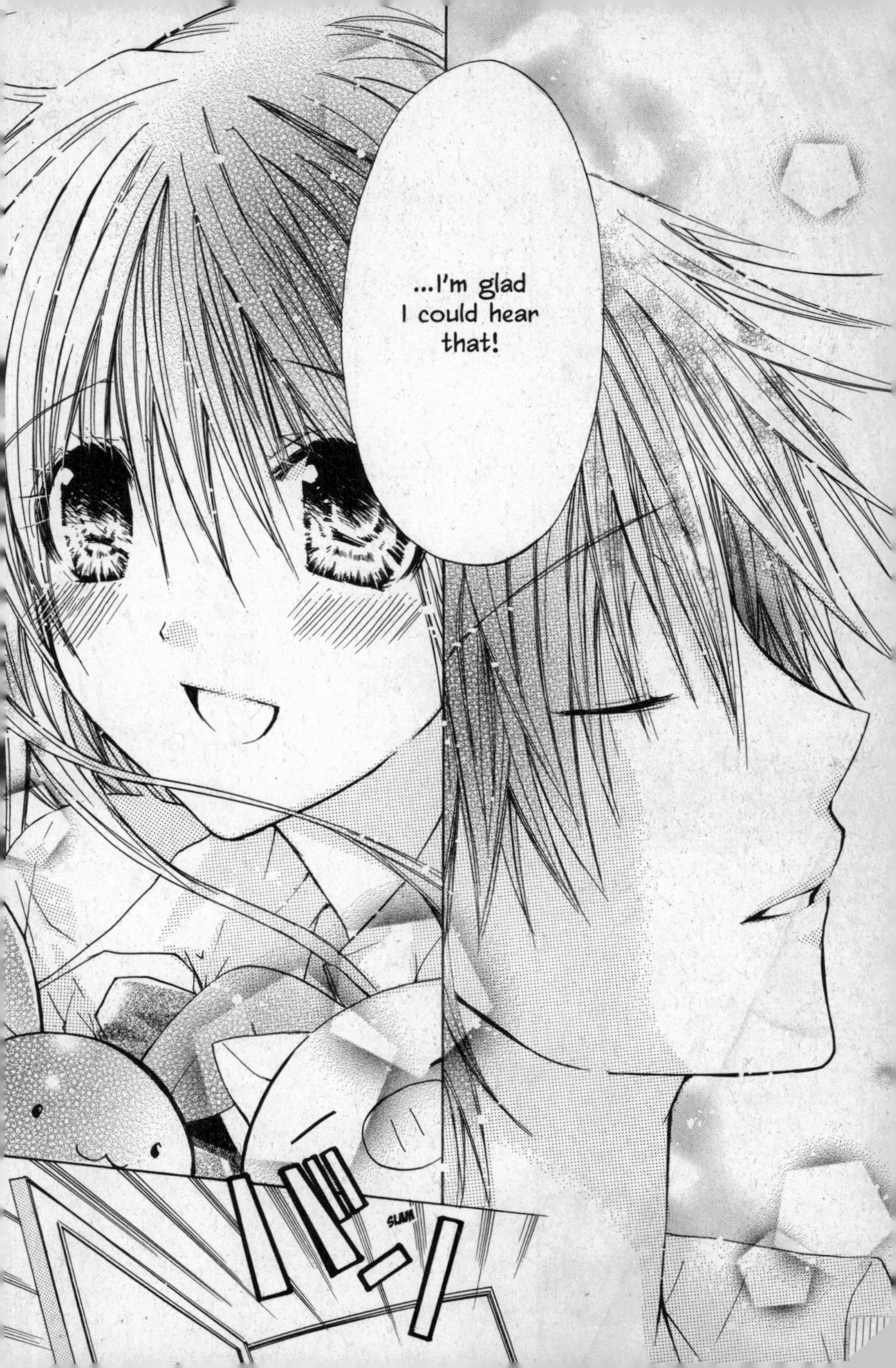
...I'm glad I could hear that!
SLAM

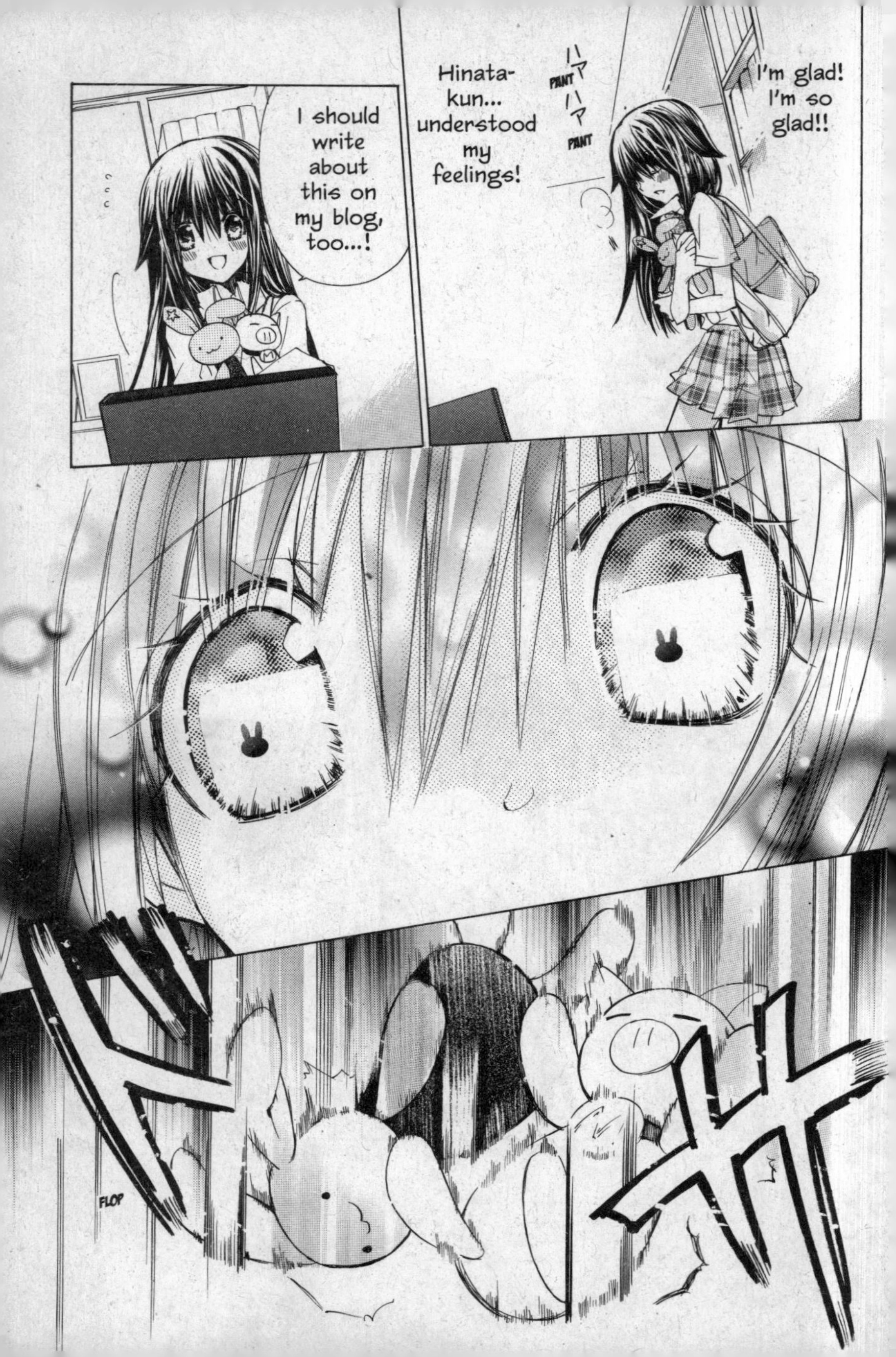
I'm glad! I'm so glad!!
PANT
PANT
Hinata-kun... understood my feelings!
I should write about this on my blog, too...!
FLOP

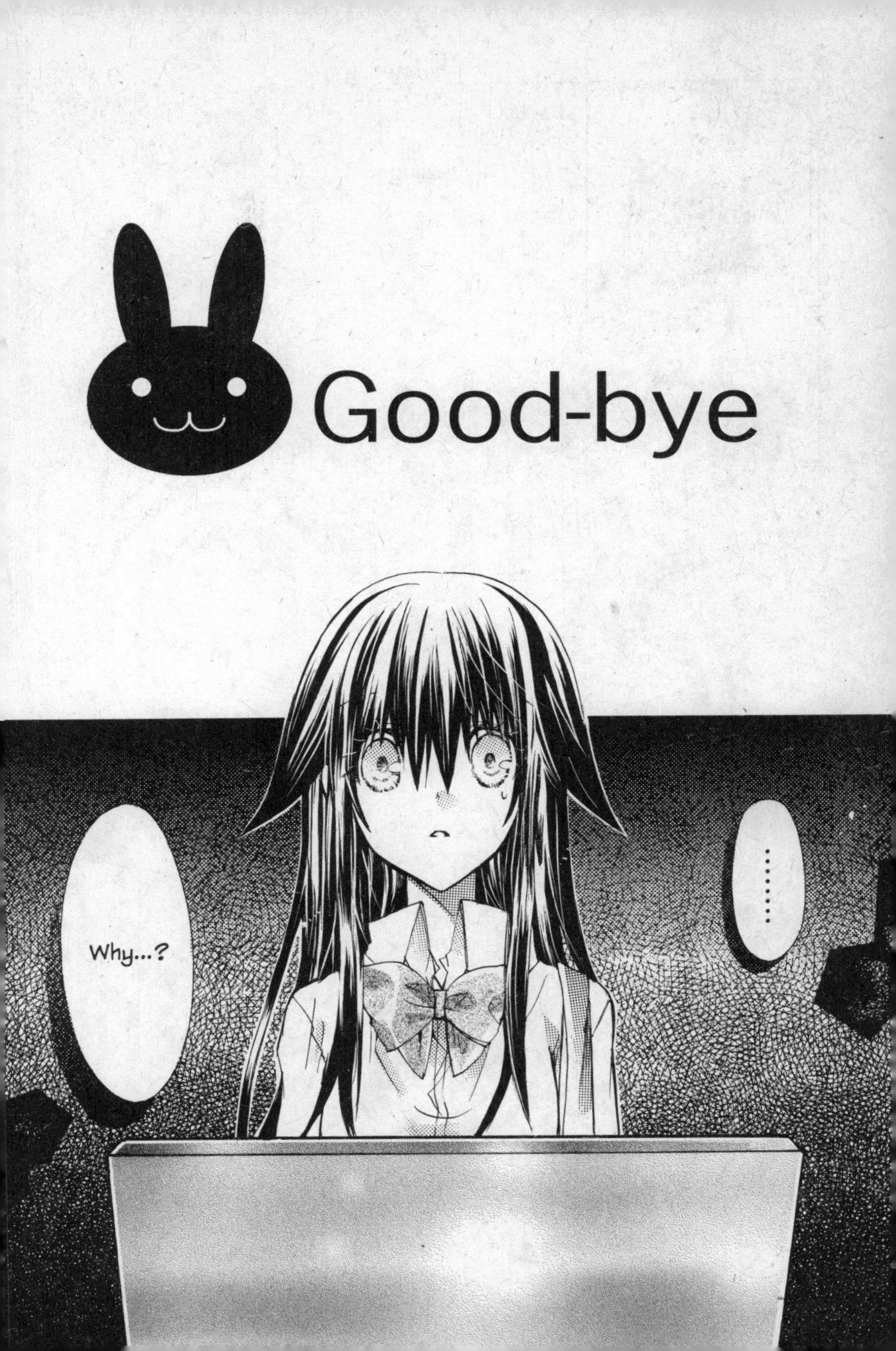
Good-bye
......
Why...?

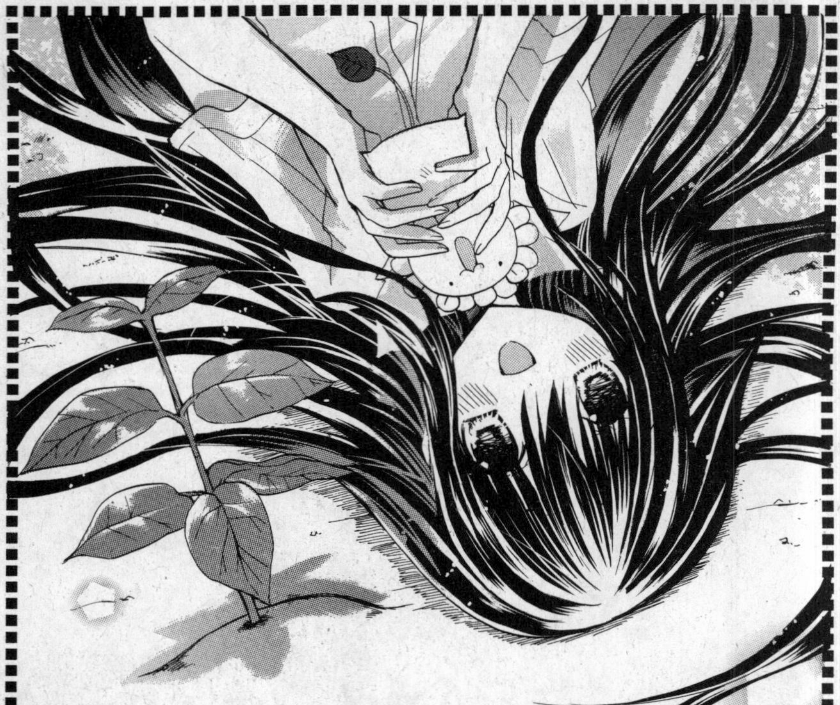

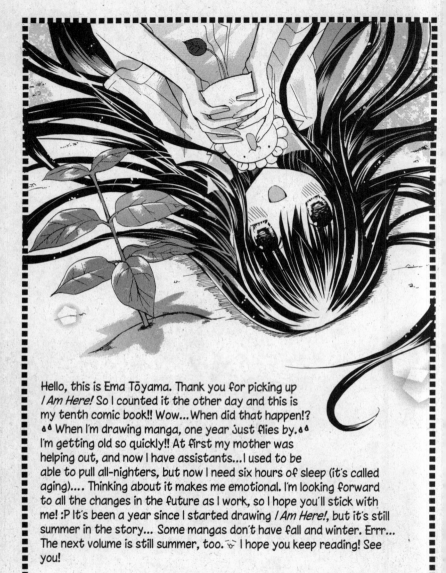

Hello, this is Ema Tōyama. Thank you for picking up *I Am Here!* So I counted it the other day and this is my tenth comic book!! Wow... When did that happen!? When I'm drawing manga, one year just flies by. I'm getting old so quickly!! At first my mother was helping out, and now I have assistants... I used to be able to pull all-nighters, but now I need six hours of sleep (it's called aging).... Thinking about it makes me emotional. I'm looking forward to all the changes in the future as I work, so I hope you'll stick with me! :P It's been a year since I started drawing *I Am Here!*, but it's still summer in the story... Some mangas don't have fall and winter. Errr... The next volume is still summer, too. I hope you keep reading! See you!

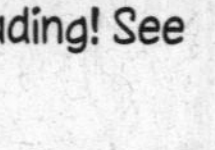

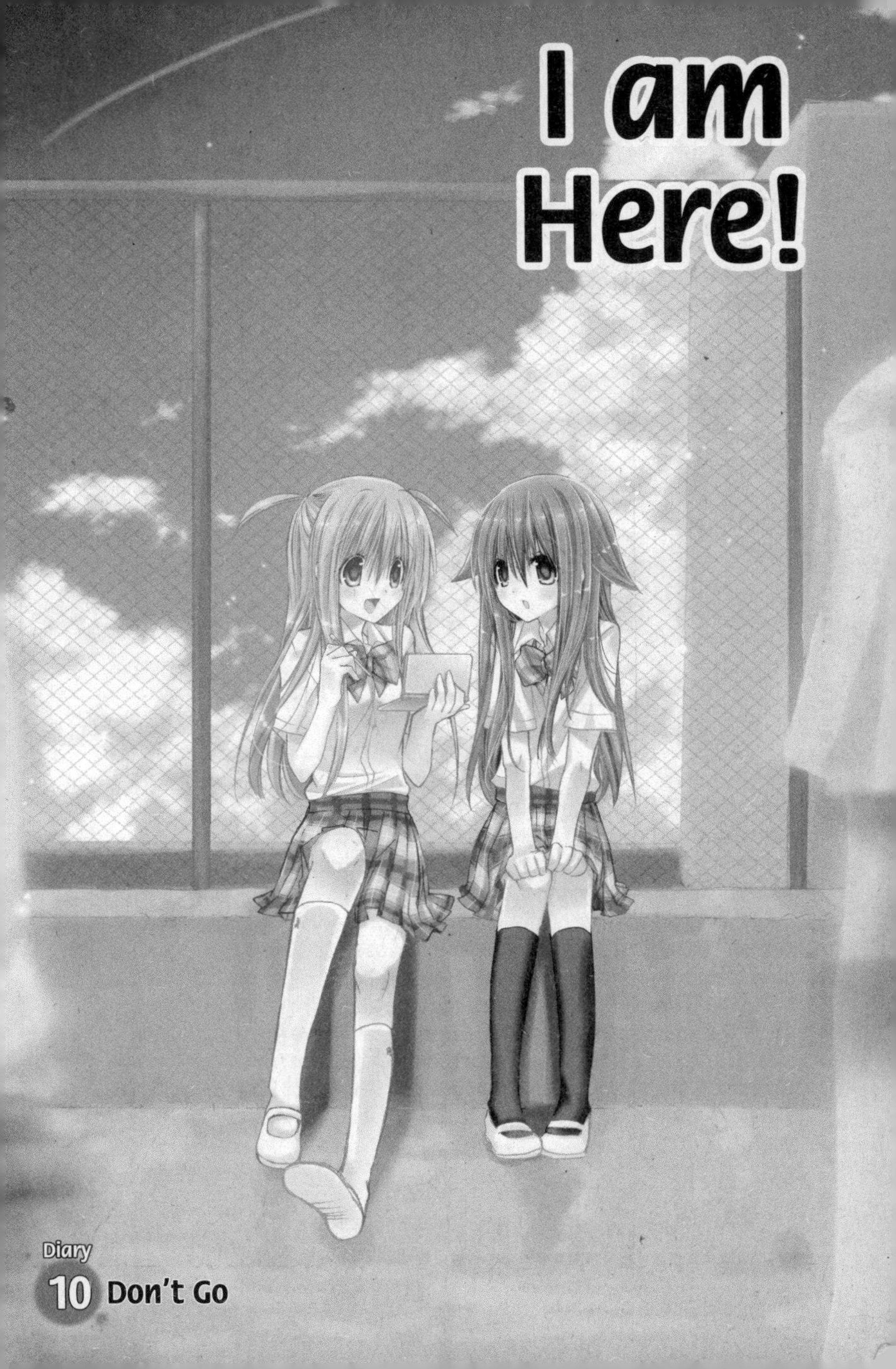
I am Here!
Diary
10 Don't Go

Good-bye

I'm sorry to say this so suddenly.

I've decided to stop visiting your
blog after today.

Now that you've found your
sunshine, I'm sure you'll be fine
without me, Sunflower.

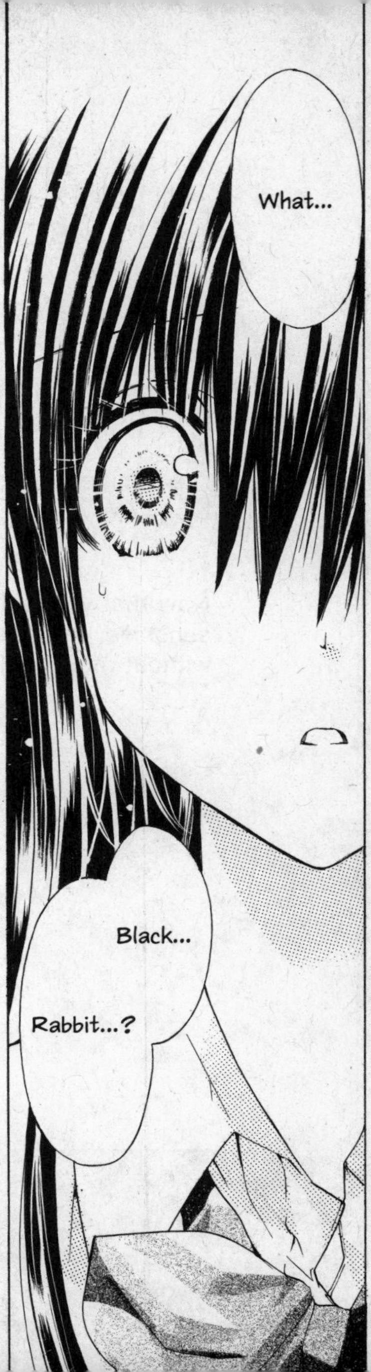
What...
Black...
Rabbit...?

I had so much fun spending time with you and Mega Pig.

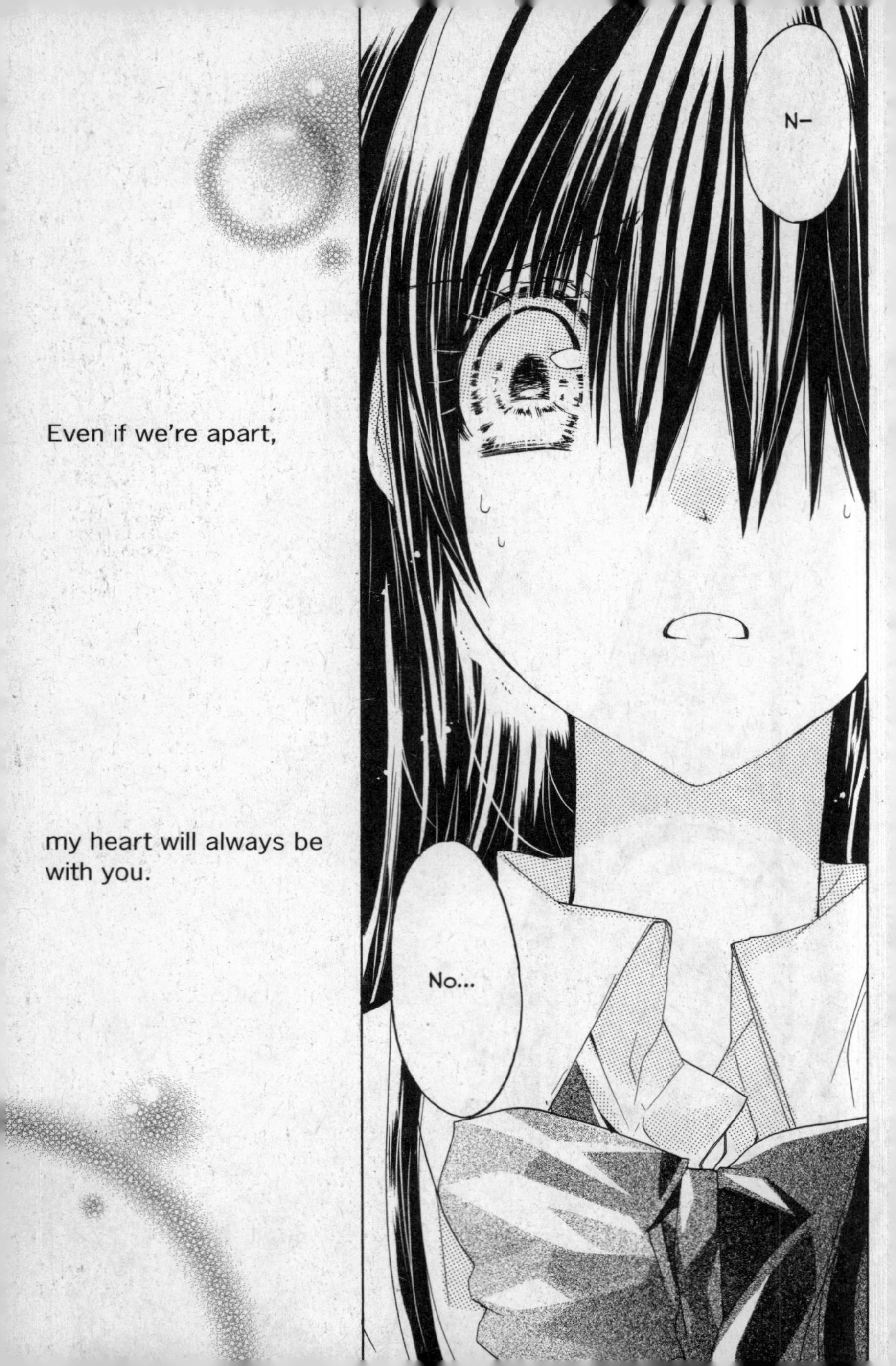
N–
No...
Even if we're apart,
my heart will always be with you.

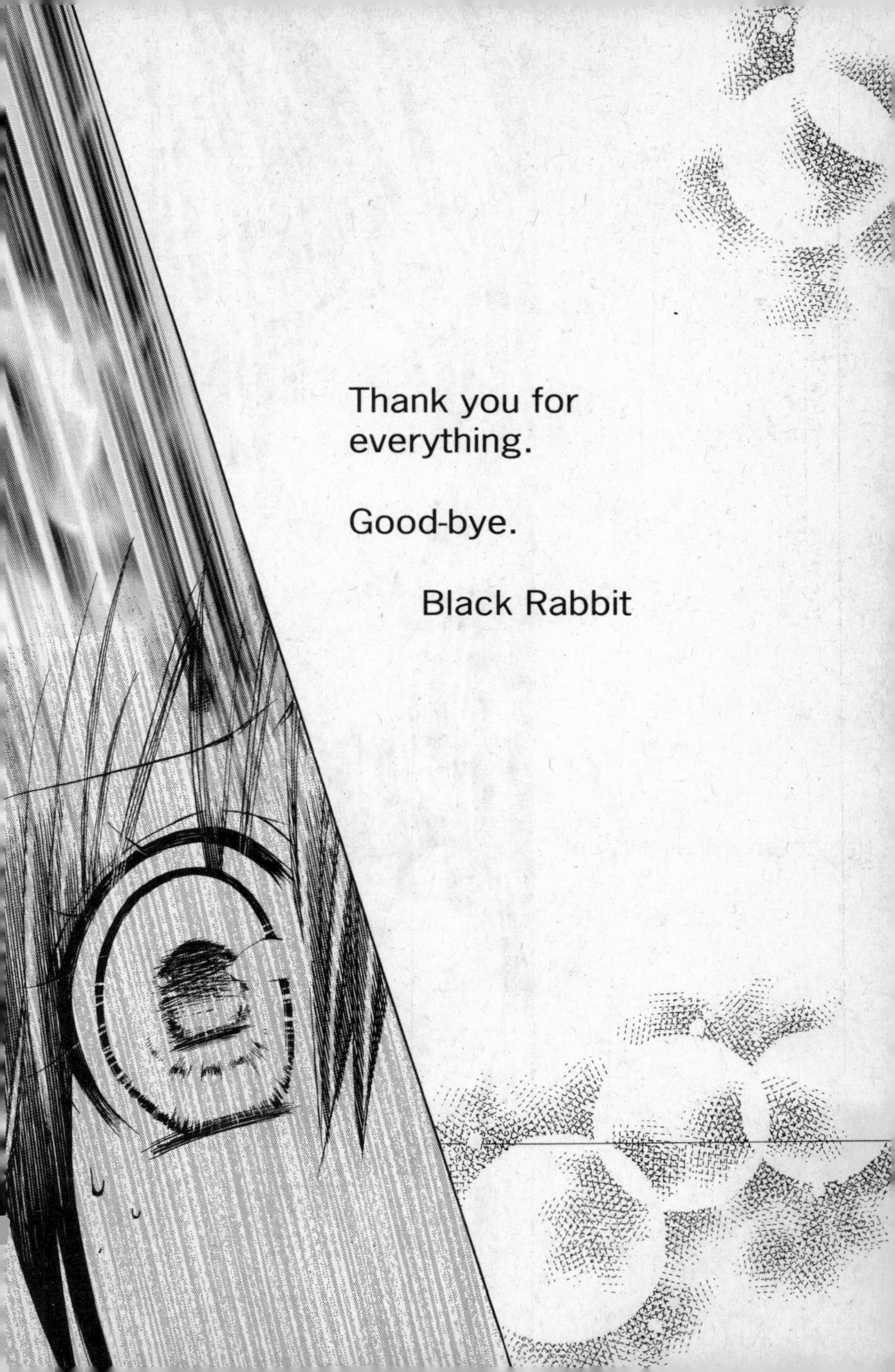
Thank you for everything.
Good-bye.
Black Rabbit

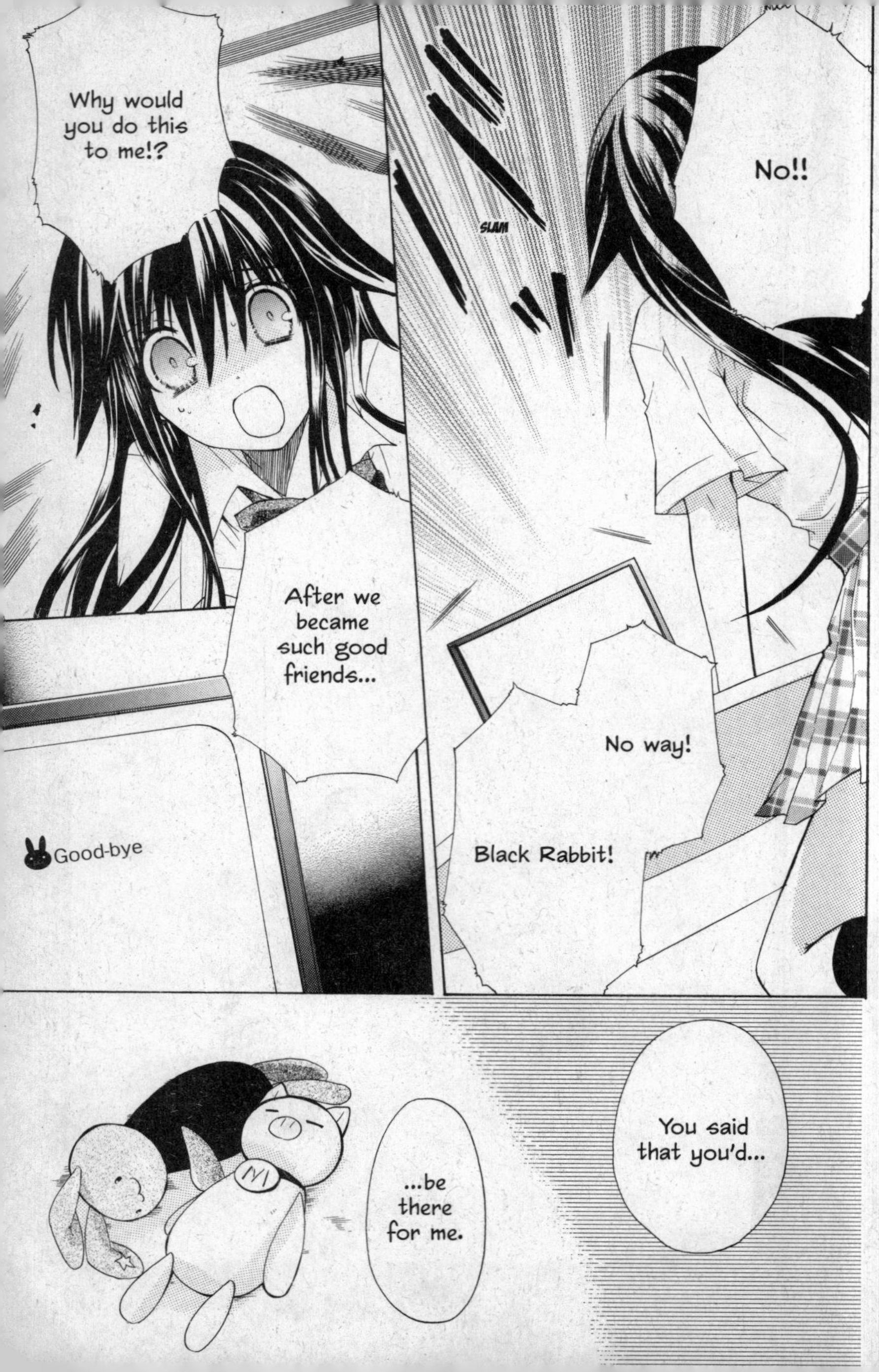
No!!
SLAM
No way!
Black Rabbit!
Why would you do this to me!?
After we became such good friends...
Good-bye
You said that you'd...
...be there for me.

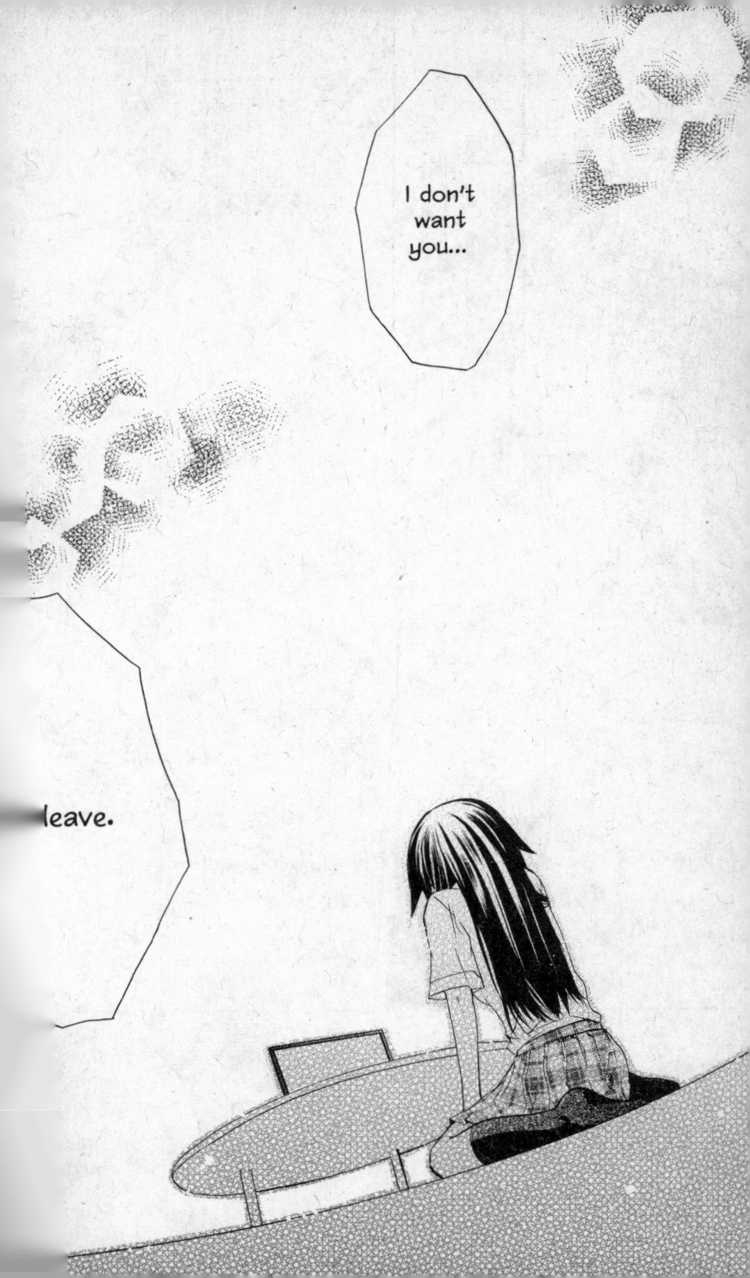
I don't want you...
leave.

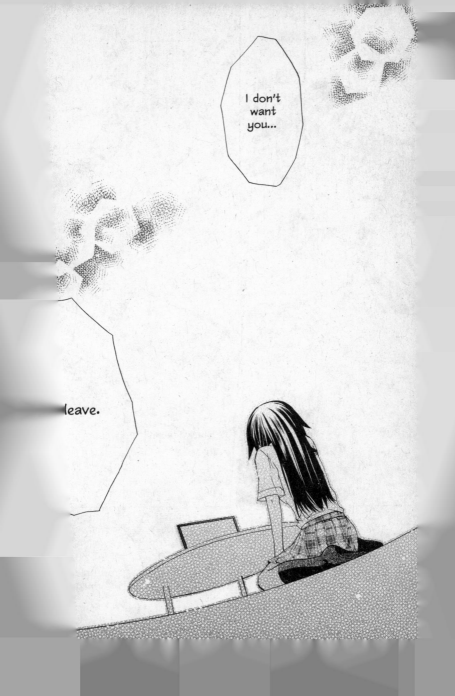

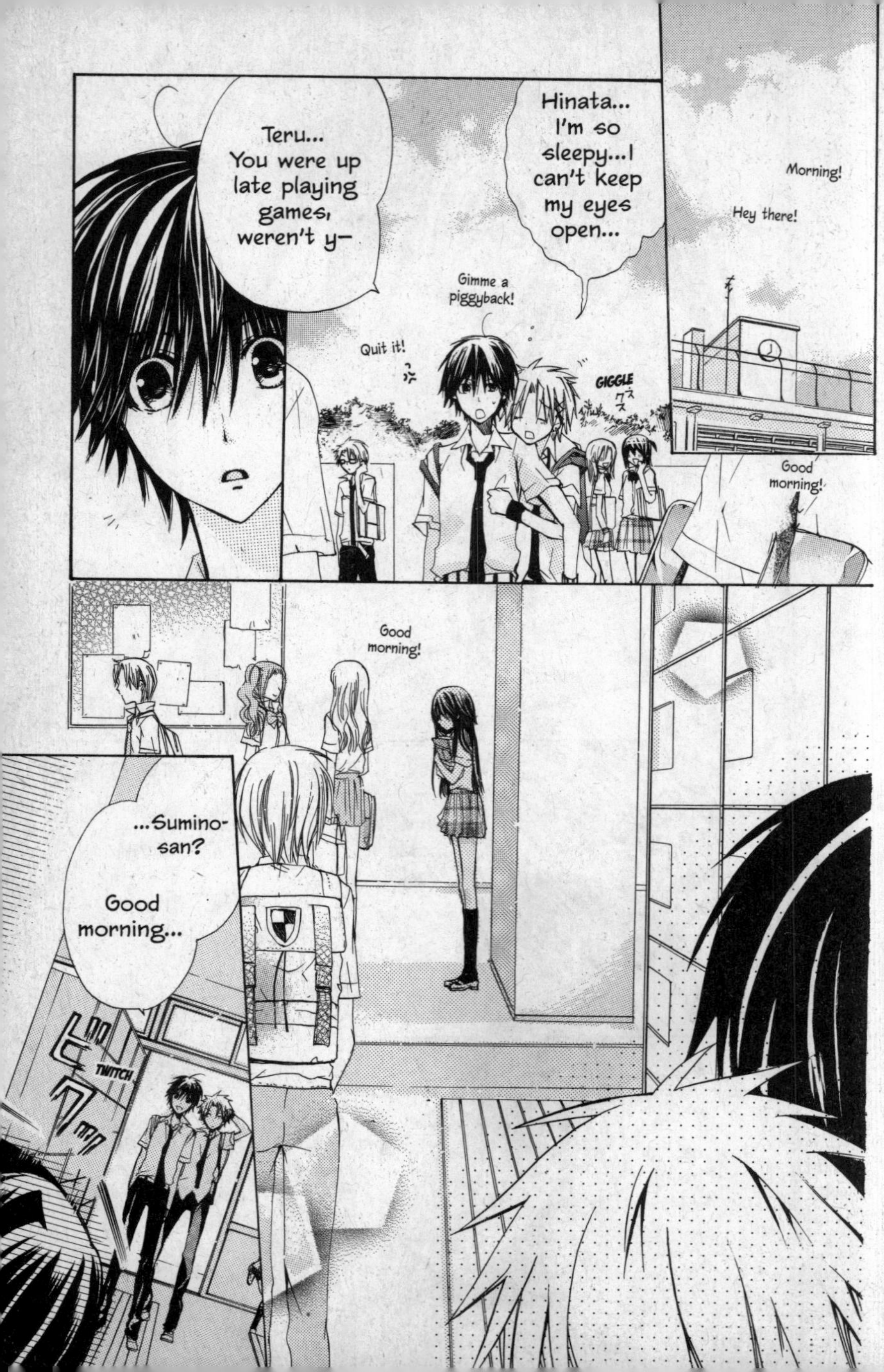
Morning!
Hey there!
Good morning!
Hinata... I'm so sleepy...I can't keep my eyes open...
Gimme a piggyback!
GIGGLE
Quit it!
Teru... You were up late playing games, weren't y—
Good morning!
...Sumino-san?
Good morning...
TWITCH

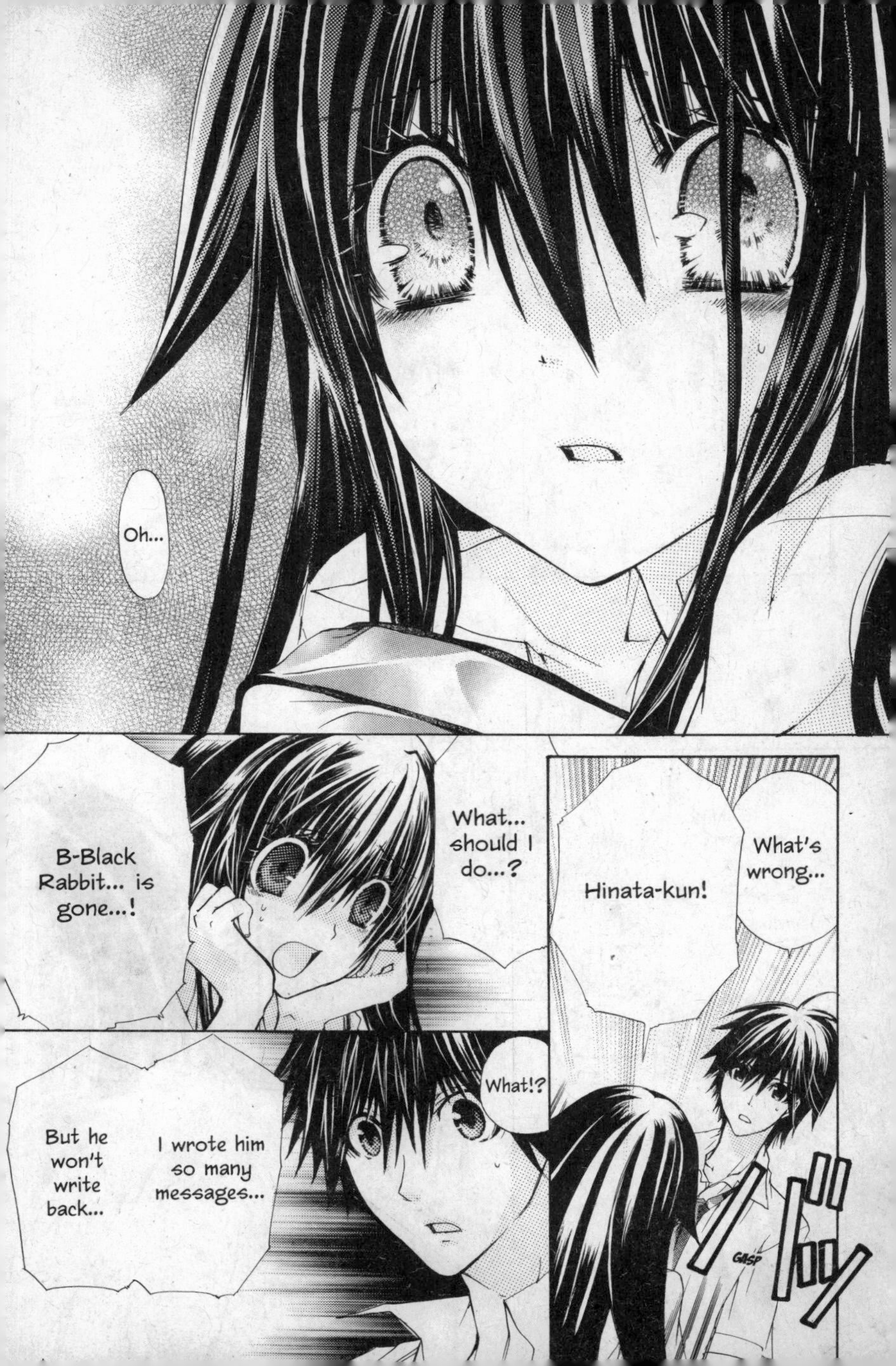
Oh...
What's wrong...
Hinata-kun!
GASP
What... should I do...?
B-Black Rabbit... is gone...!
What!?
I wrote him so many messages...
But he won't write back...

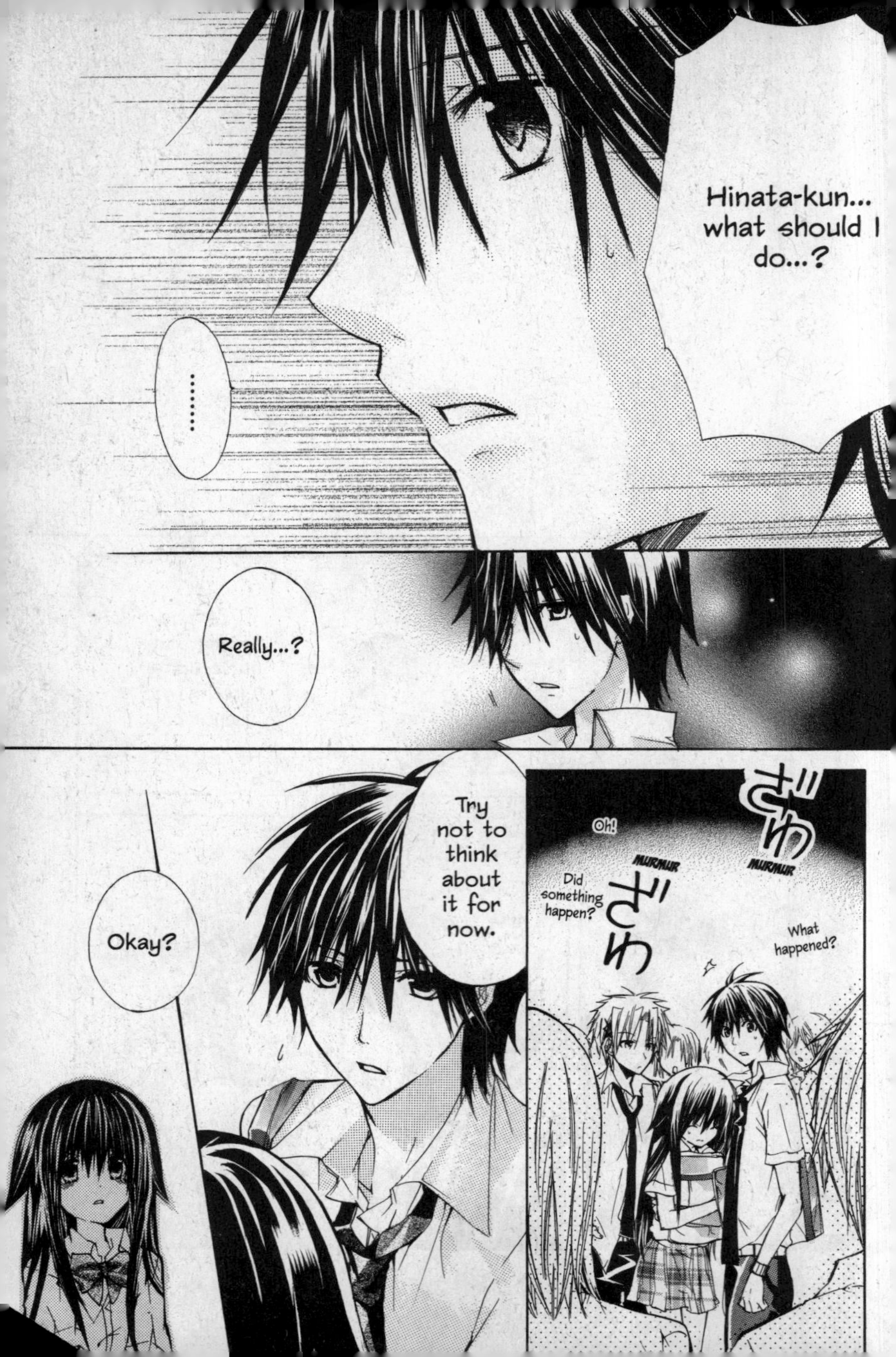

Hinata-kun... what should I do...?
....
Really...?
ざわ
MURMUR
Oh!
MURMUR
Did something happen?
ざわ
What happened?
Try not to think about it for now.
Okay?

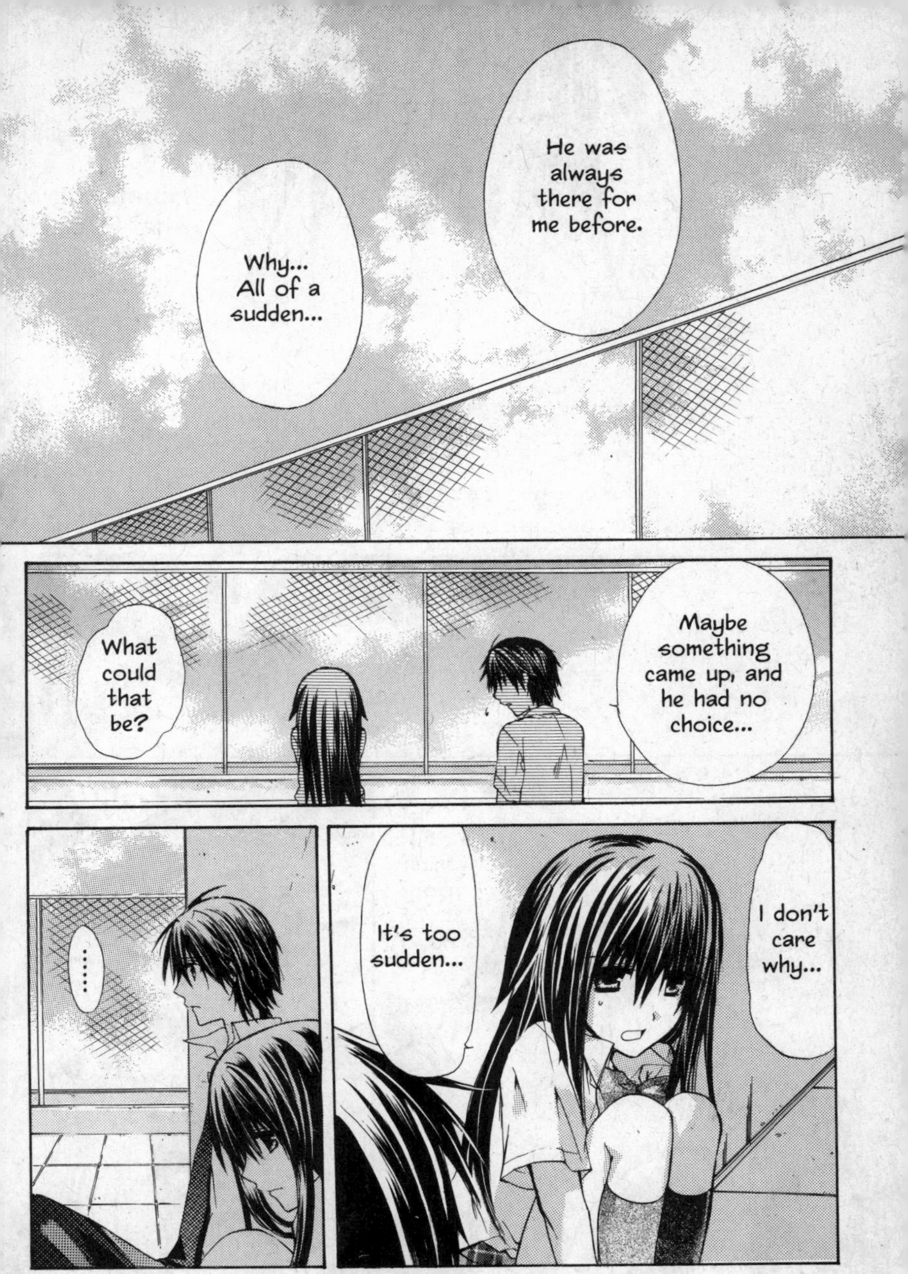
He was always there for me before.
Why... All of a sudden...
Maybe something came up, and he had no choice...
What could that be?
I don't care why...
It's too sudden...
......

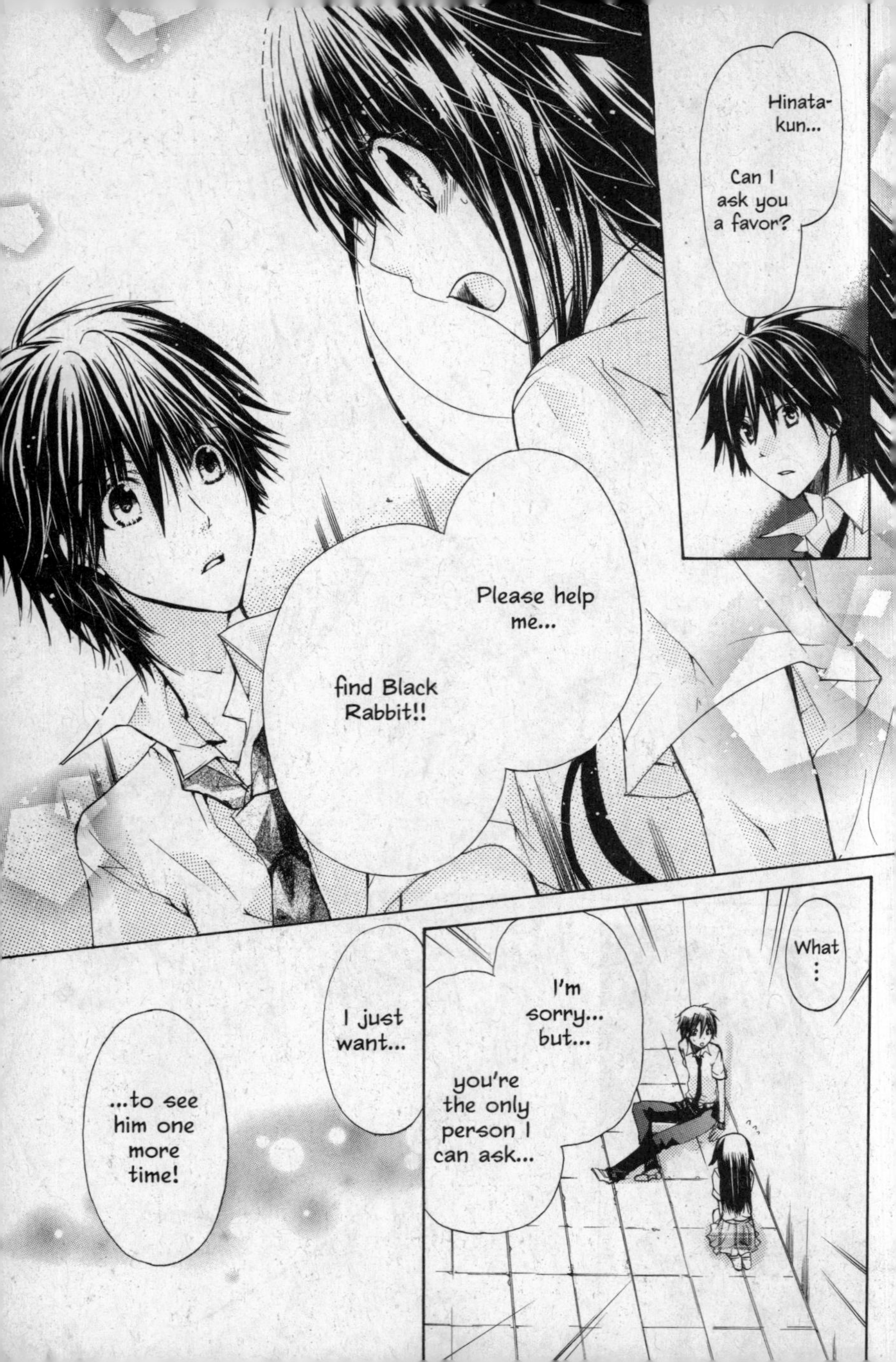
Hinata-kun...
Can I ask you a favor?
Please help me...
find Black Rabbit!!
What...
I'm sorry... but...
you're the only person I can ask...
I just want...
...to see him one more time!

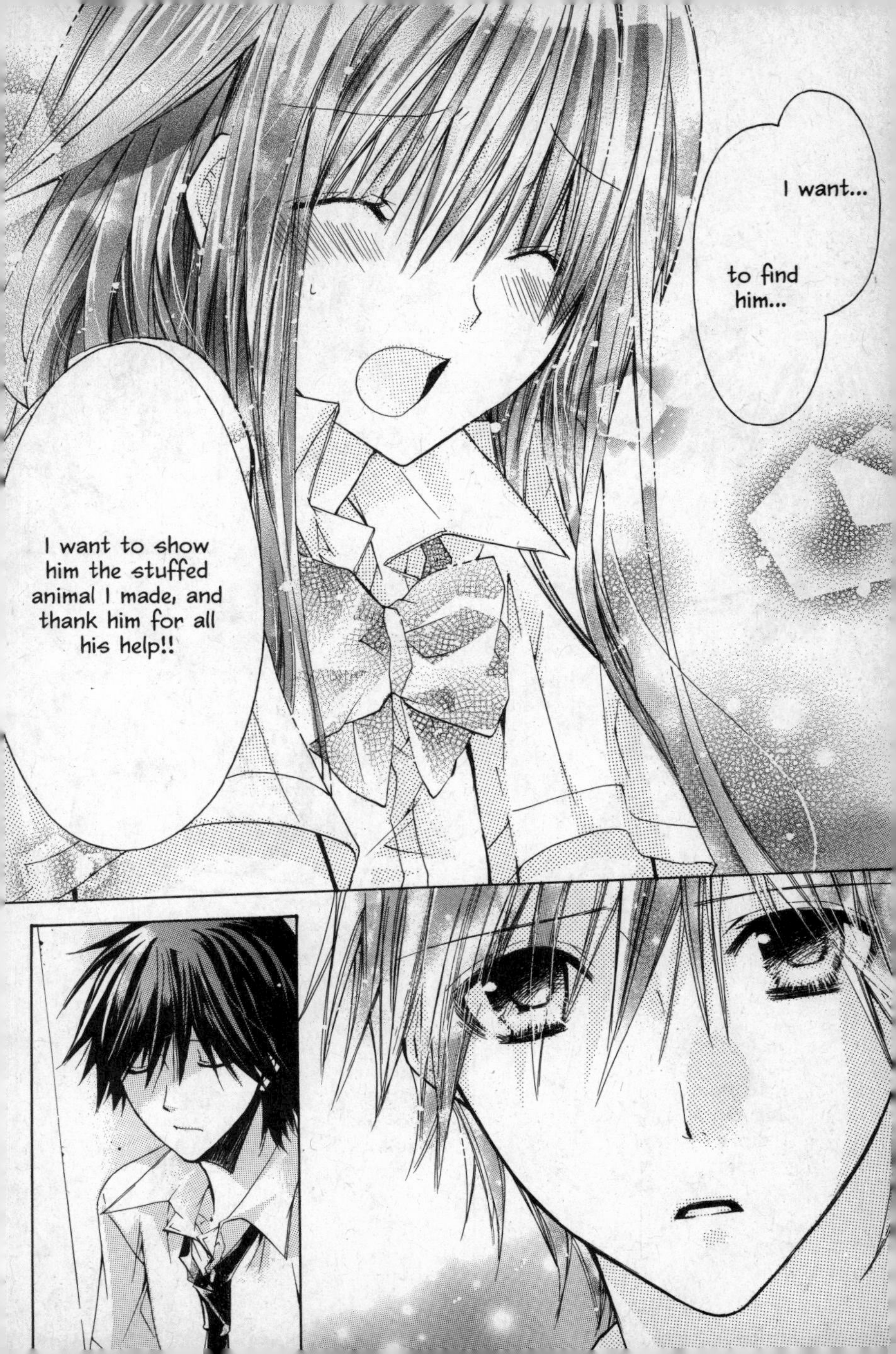
I want...
to find him...
I want to show him the stuffed animal I made, and thank him for all his help!!

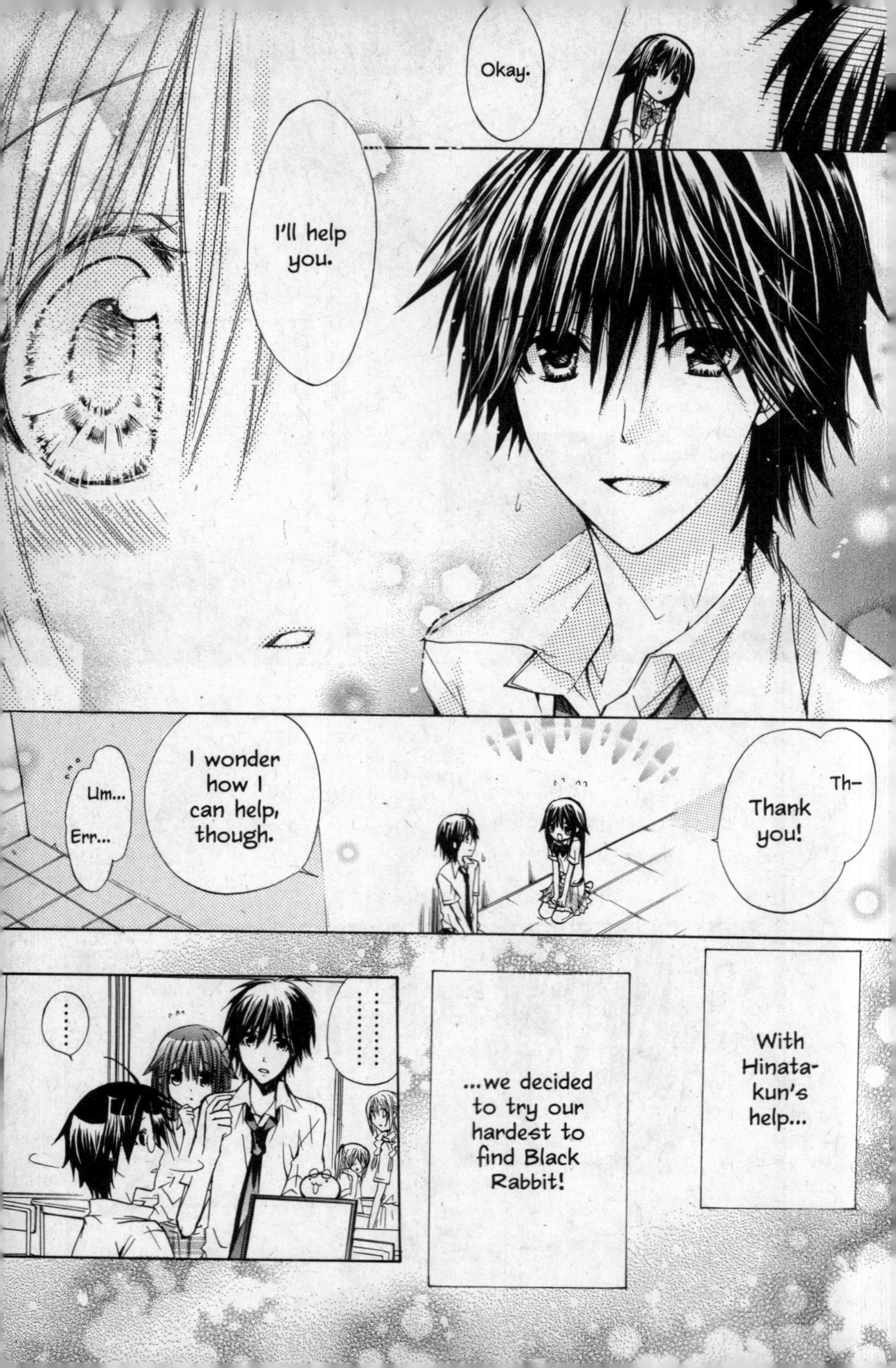

Okay.
I'll help you.
Th- Thank you!
I wonder how I can help, though.
Um... Err...
With Hinata-kun's help...
...we decided to try our hardest to find Black Rabbit!
......
.....

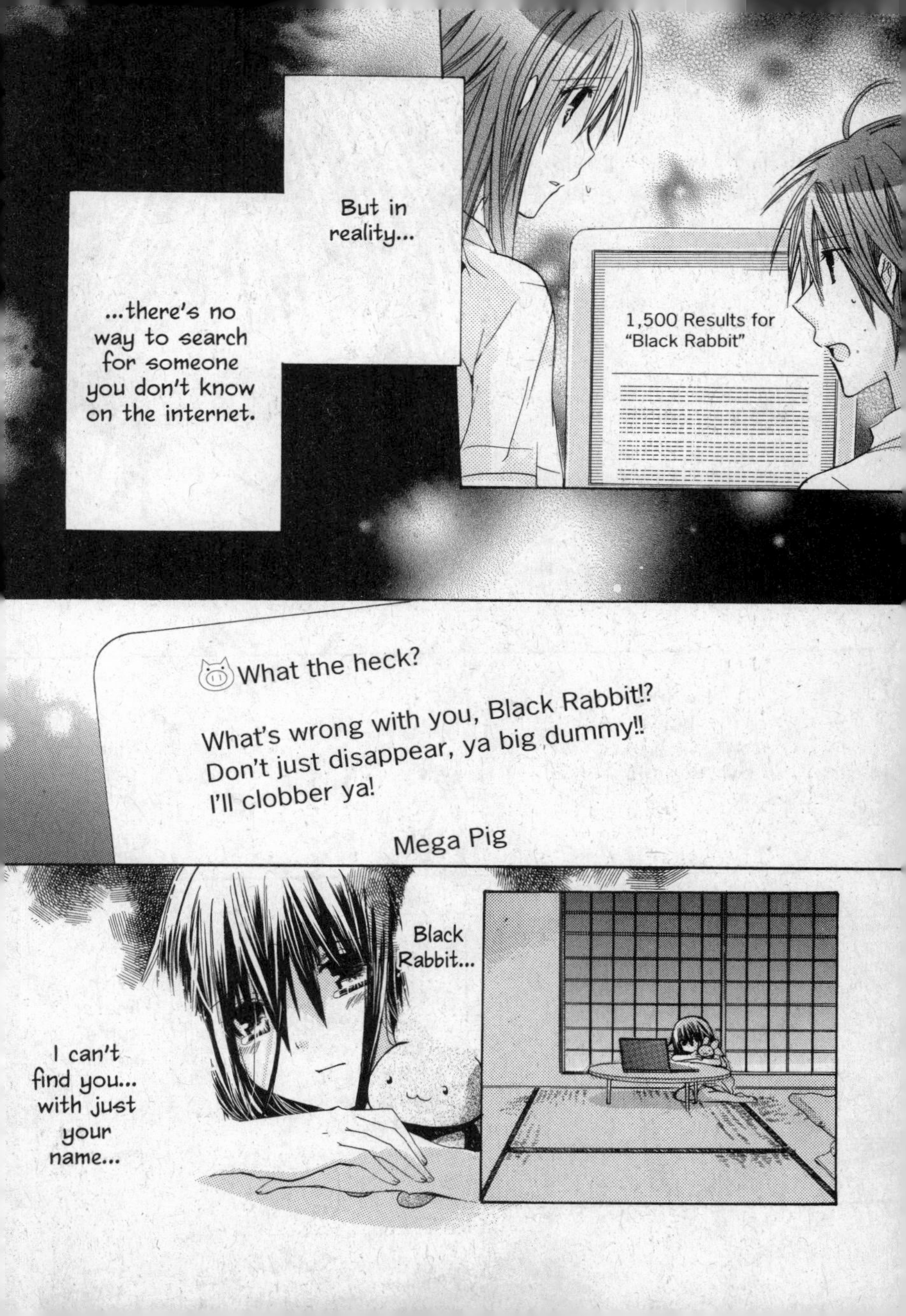

But in reality...
...there's no way to search for someone you don't know on the internet.
1,500 Results for "Black Rabbit"
What the heck?
What's wrong with you, Black Rabbit!? Don't just disappear, ya big dummy!! I'll clobber ya!
Mega Pig
Black Rabbit...
I can't find you... with just your name...

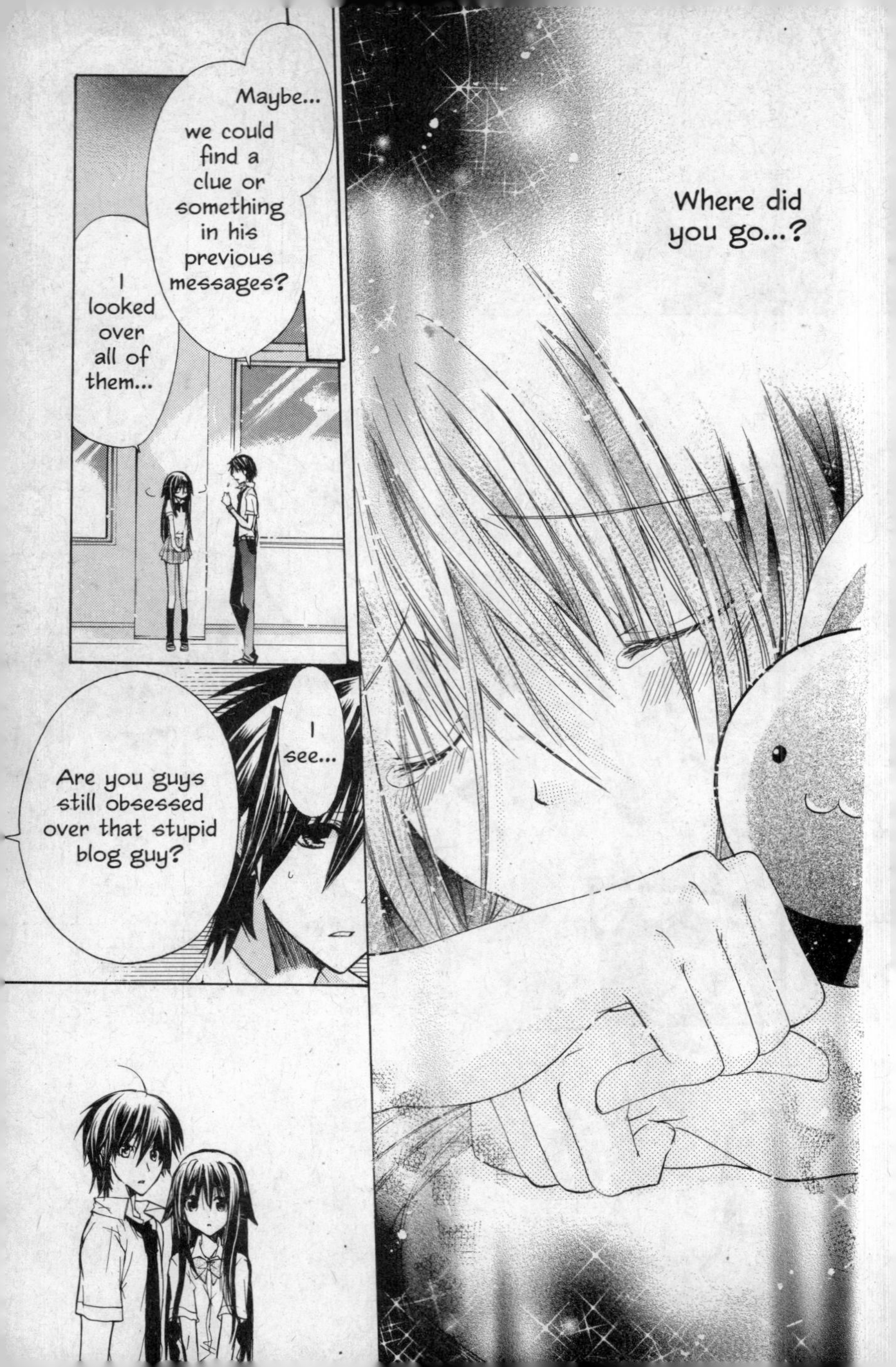

Where did you go...?
Maybe... we could find a clue or something in his previous messages?
I looked over all of them...
I see...
Are you guys still obsessed over that stupid blog guy?

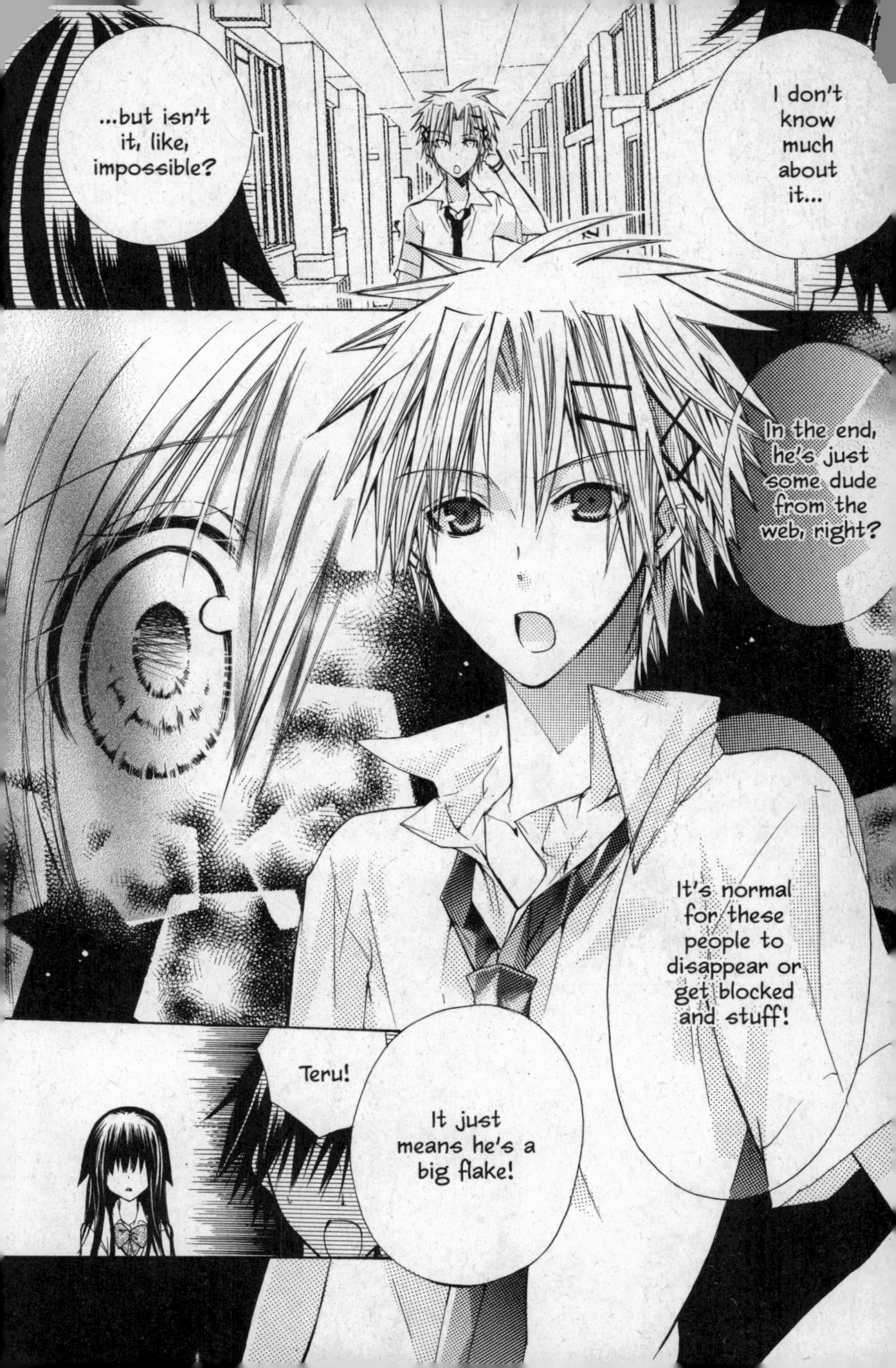
I don't know much about it...
...but isn't it, like, impossible?
In the end, he's just some dude from the web, right?
It's normal for these people to disappear or get blocked and stuff!
It just means he's a big flake!
Teru!

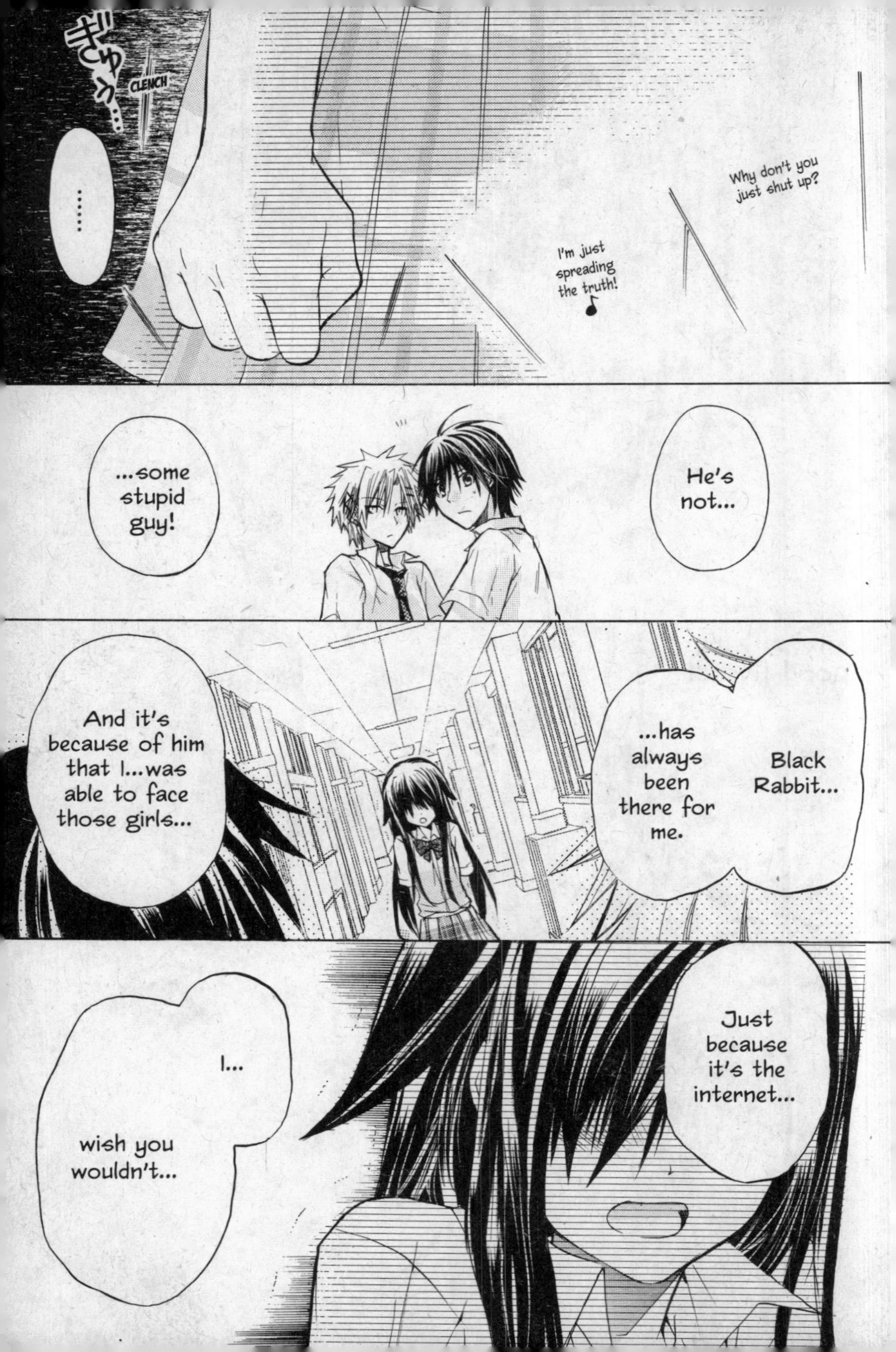
Why don't you just shut up?
I'm just spreading the truth! ♪
ぎゅう…
CLENCH
……
He's not...
...some stupid guy!
Black Rabbit...
...has always been there for me.
And it's because of him that I...was able to face those girls...
Just because it's the internet...
I...
wish you wouldn't...

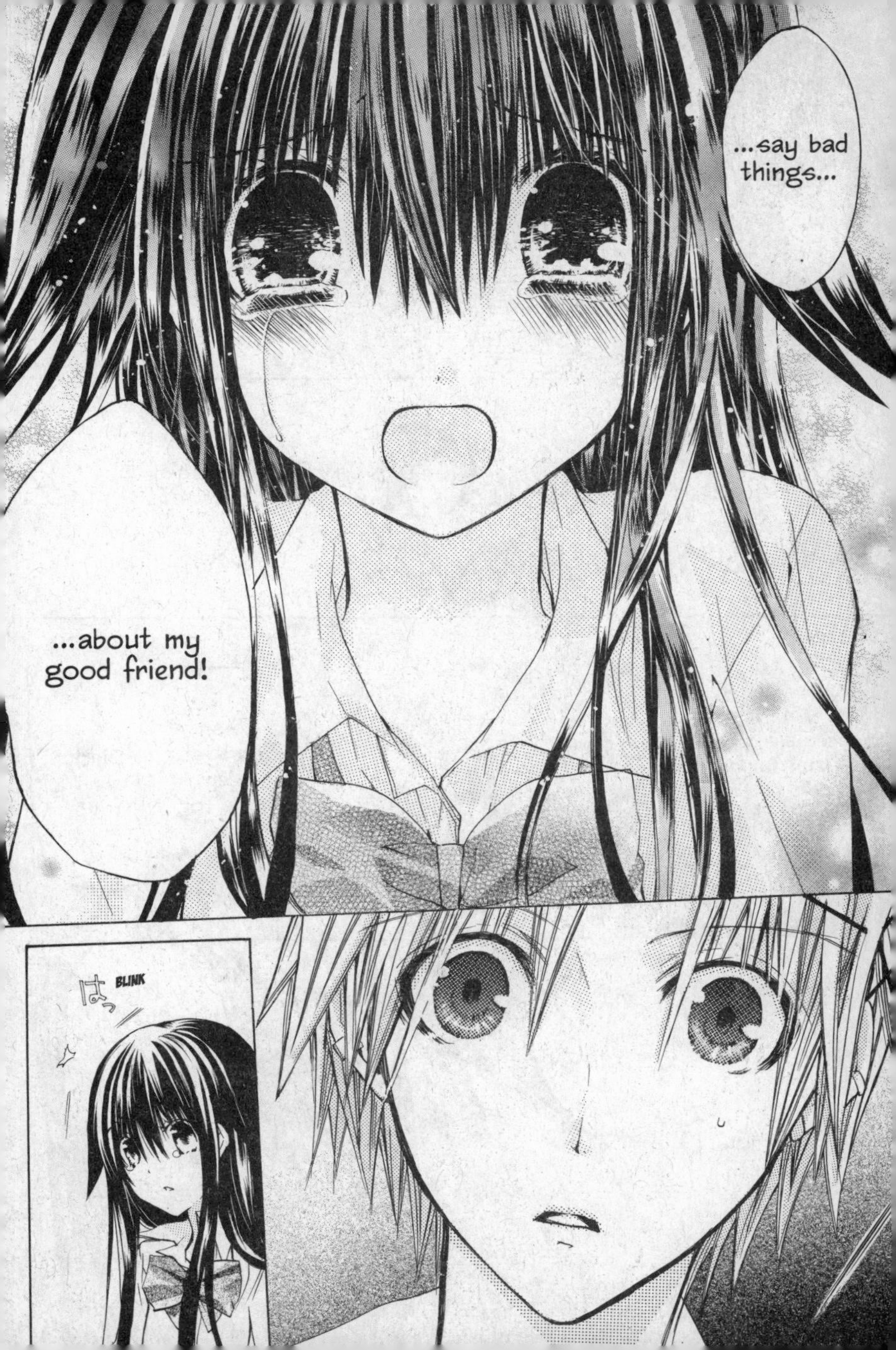
...say bad things...
...about my good friend!
BLINK
はっ

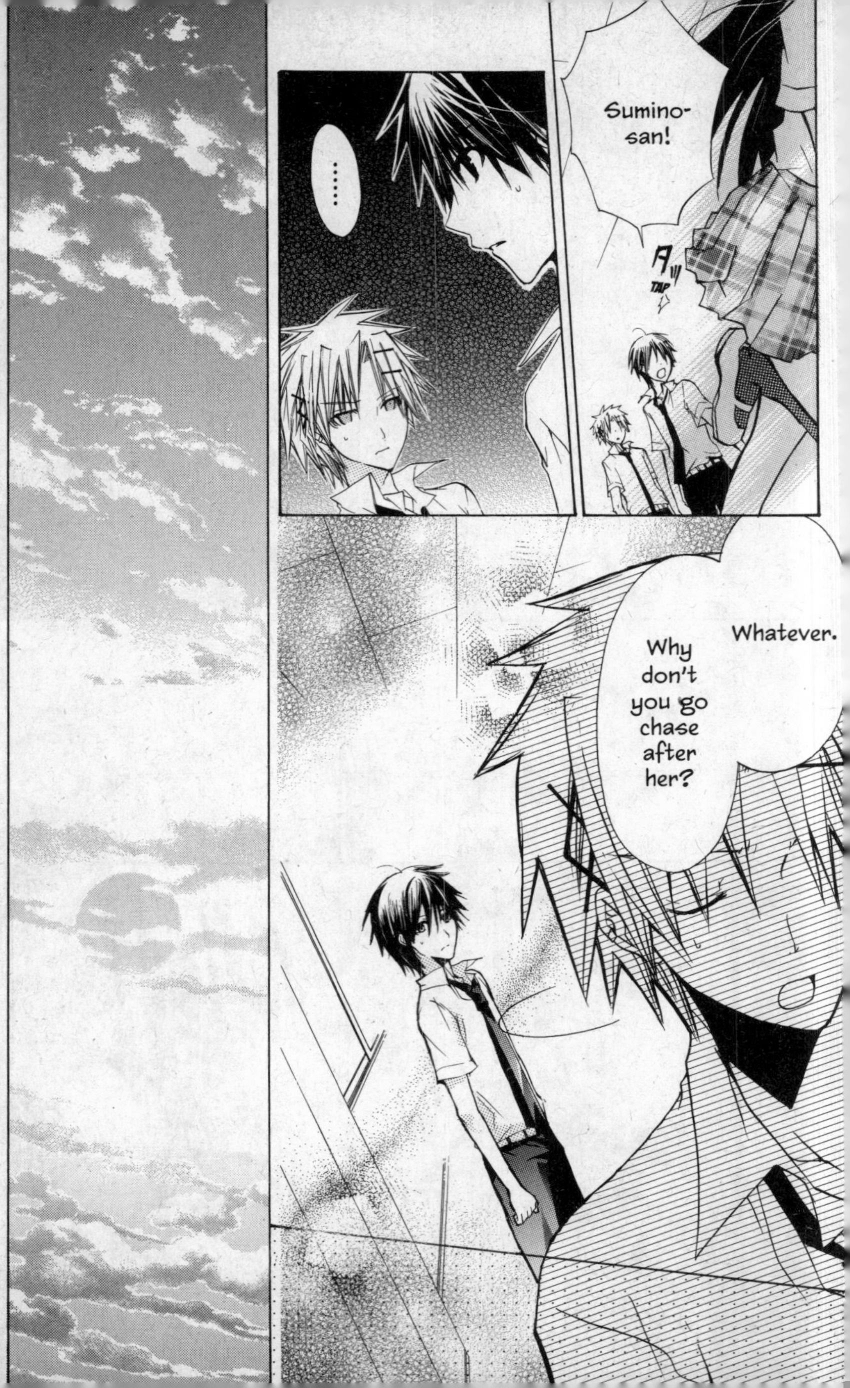
Sumino-san!
TAP
......
Whatever.
Why don't you go chase after her?

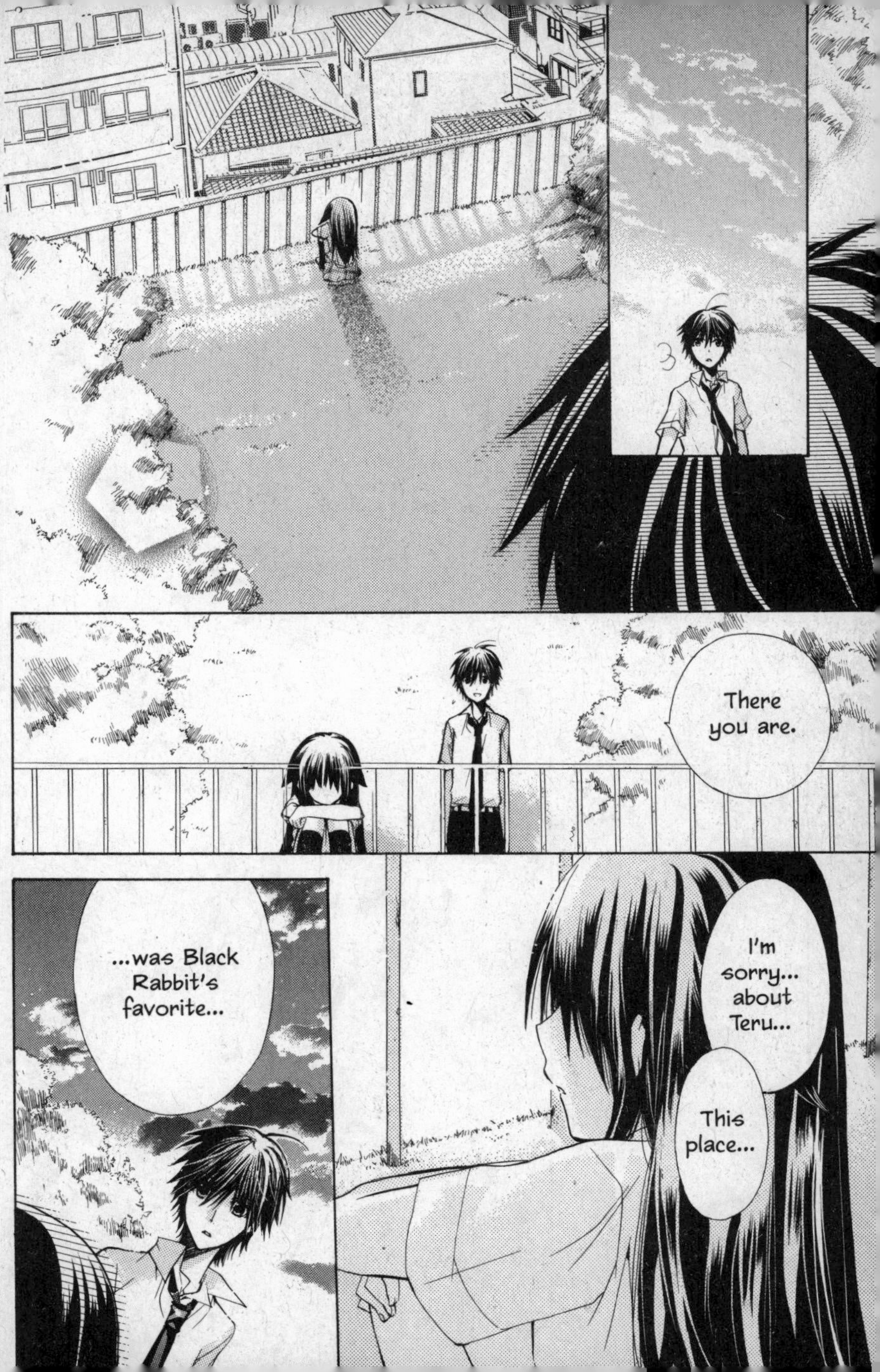
There you are.
I'm sorry... about Teru...
This place...
...was Black Rabbit's favorite...

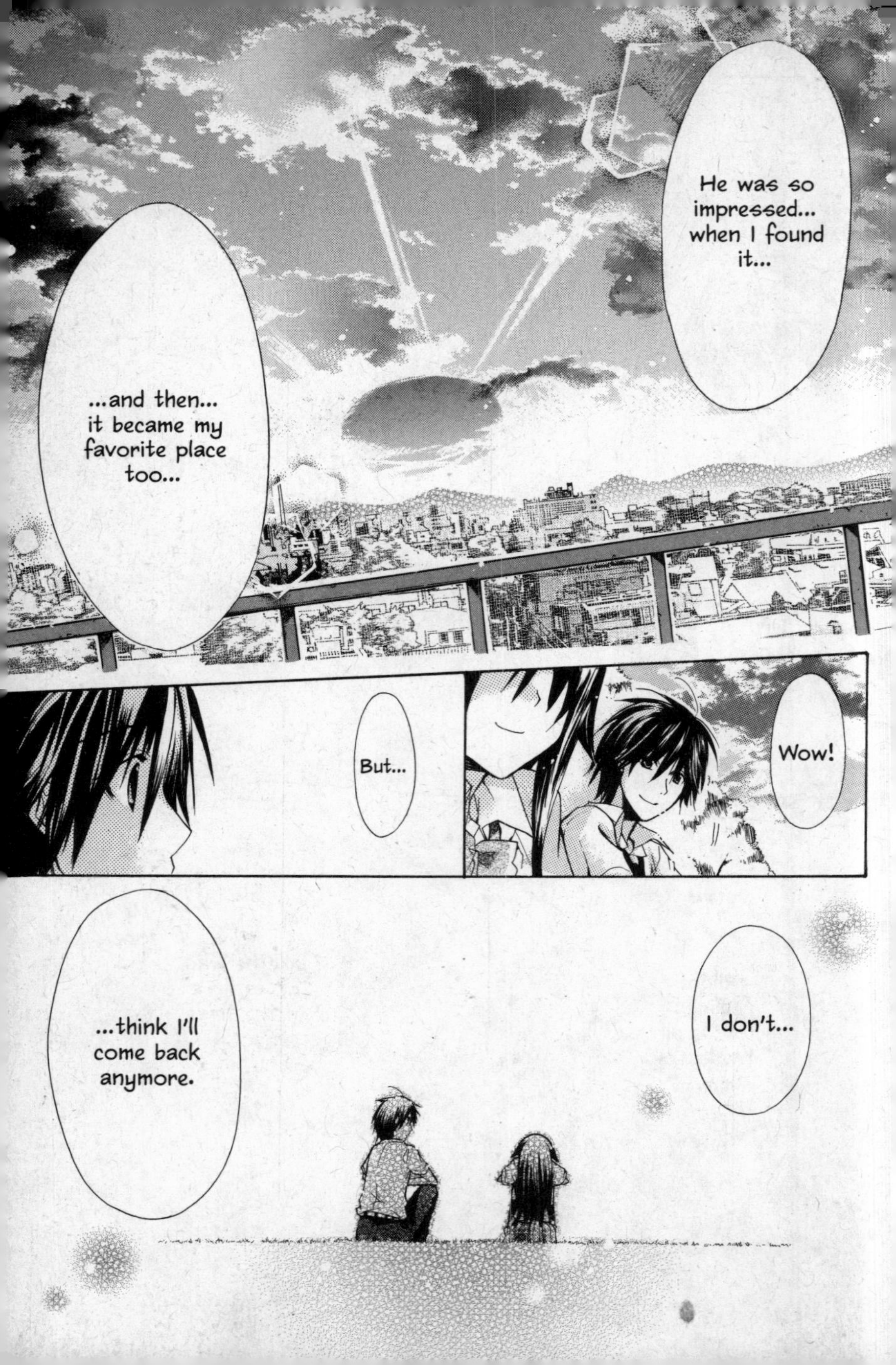
He was so impressed... when I found it...
...and then... it became my favorite place too...
Wow!
But...
I don't...
...think I'll come back anymore.

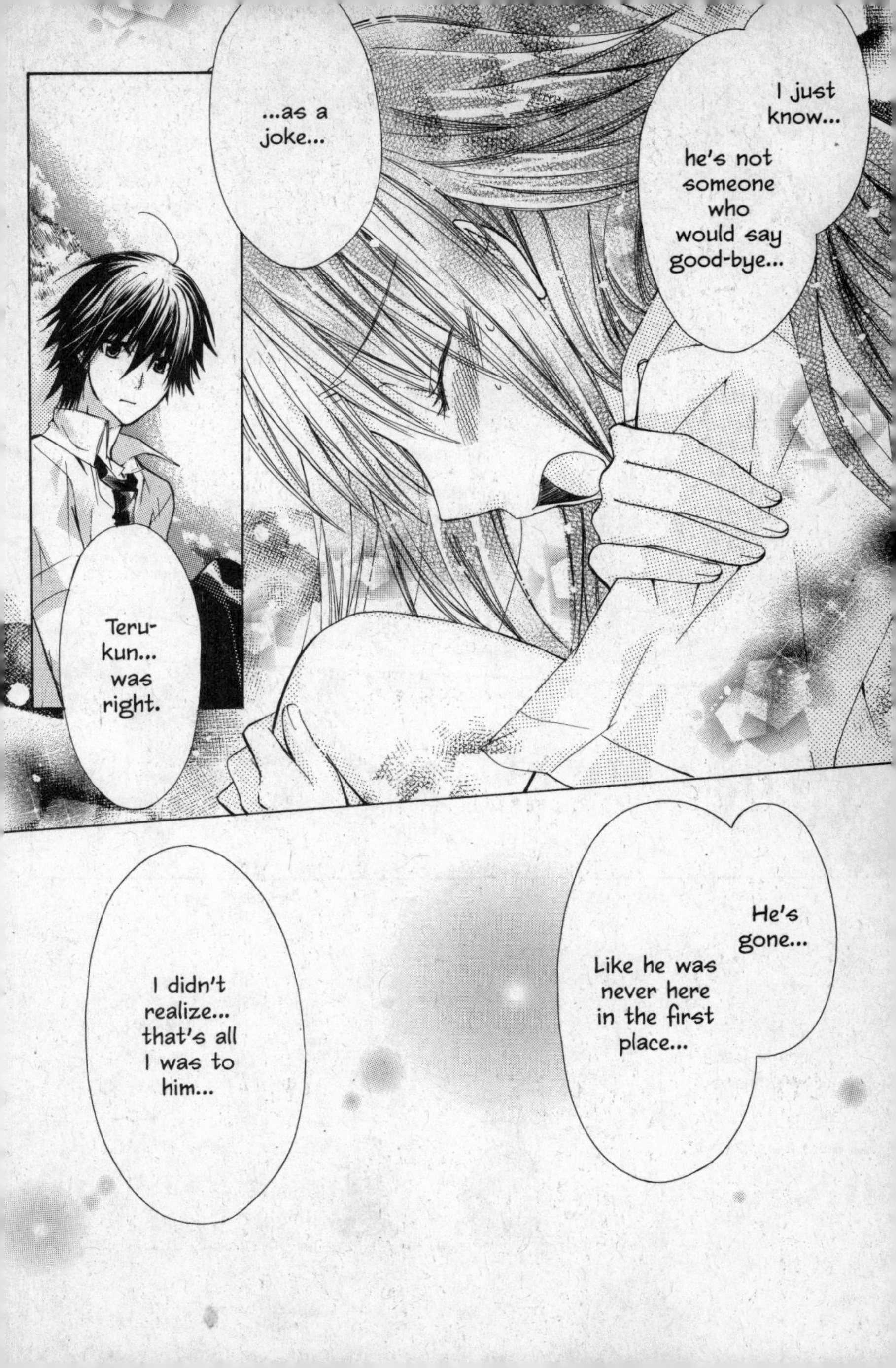

I just know... he's not someone who would say good-bye...
...as a joke...
Teru-kun... was right.
He's gone... Like he was never here in the first place...
I didn't realize... that's all I was to him...

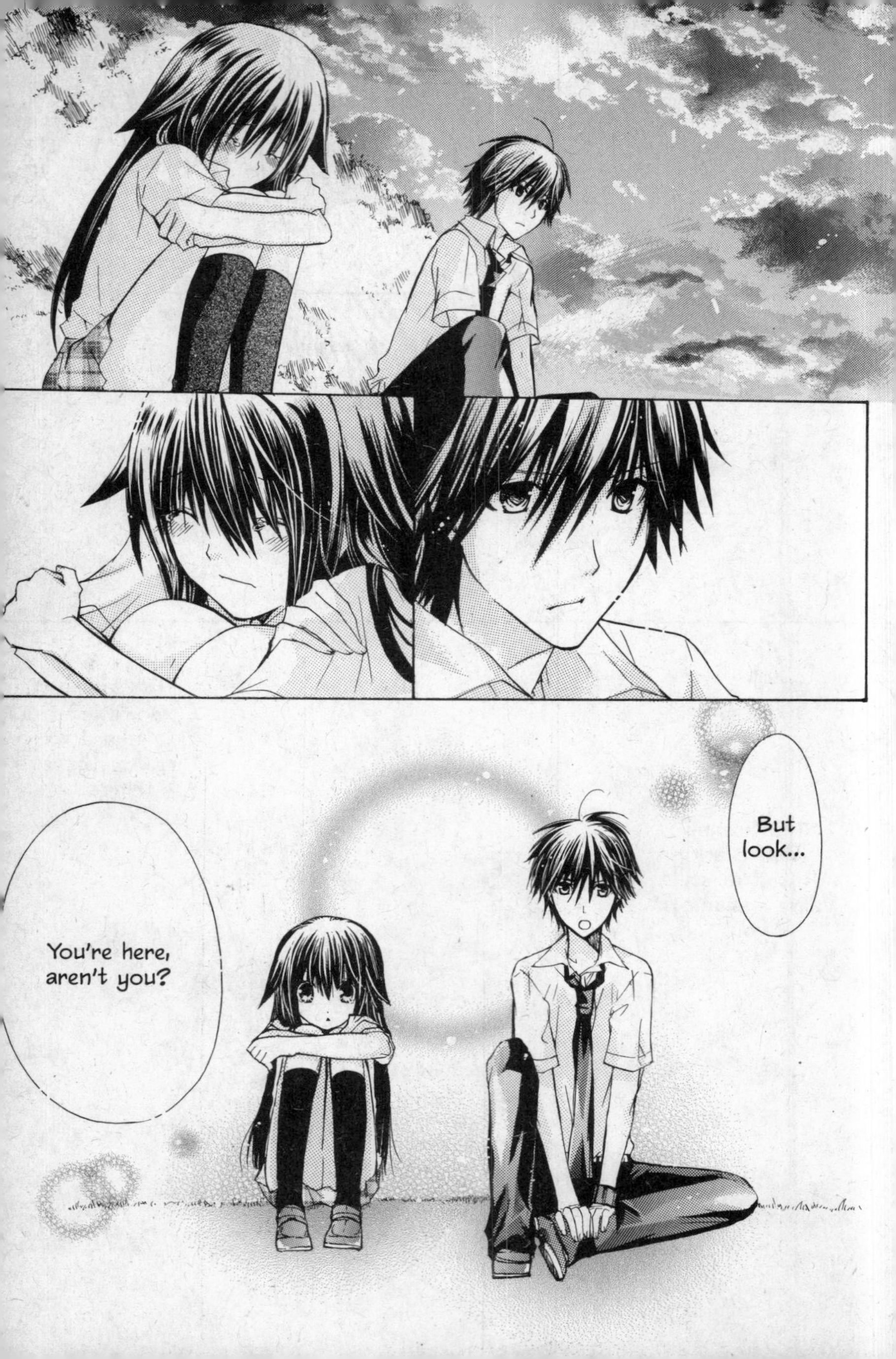
But look...
You're here, aren't you?

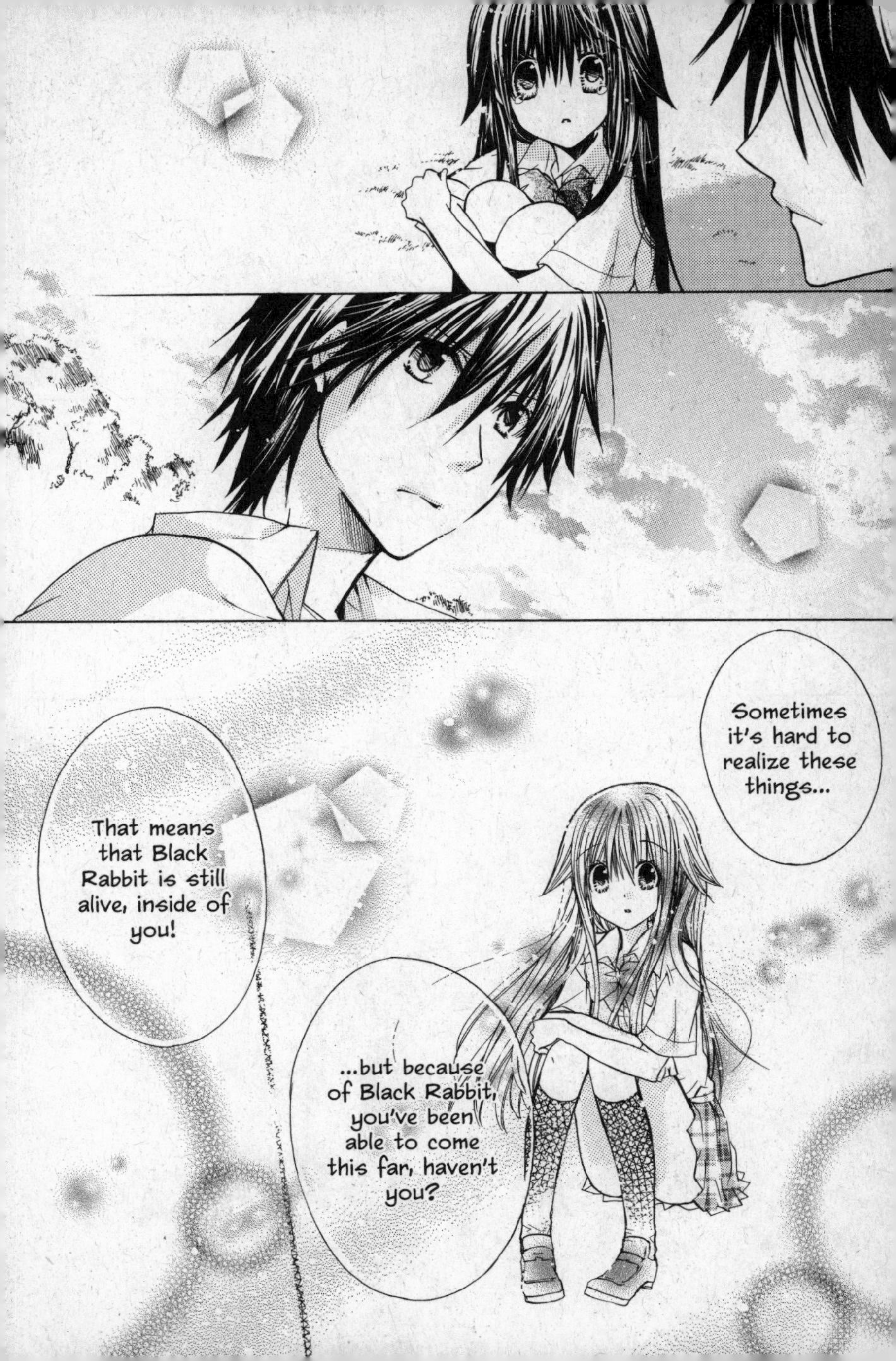

Sometimes it's hard to realize these things...
...but because of Black Rabbit, you've been able to come this far, haven't you?
That means that Black Rabbit is still alive, inside of you!

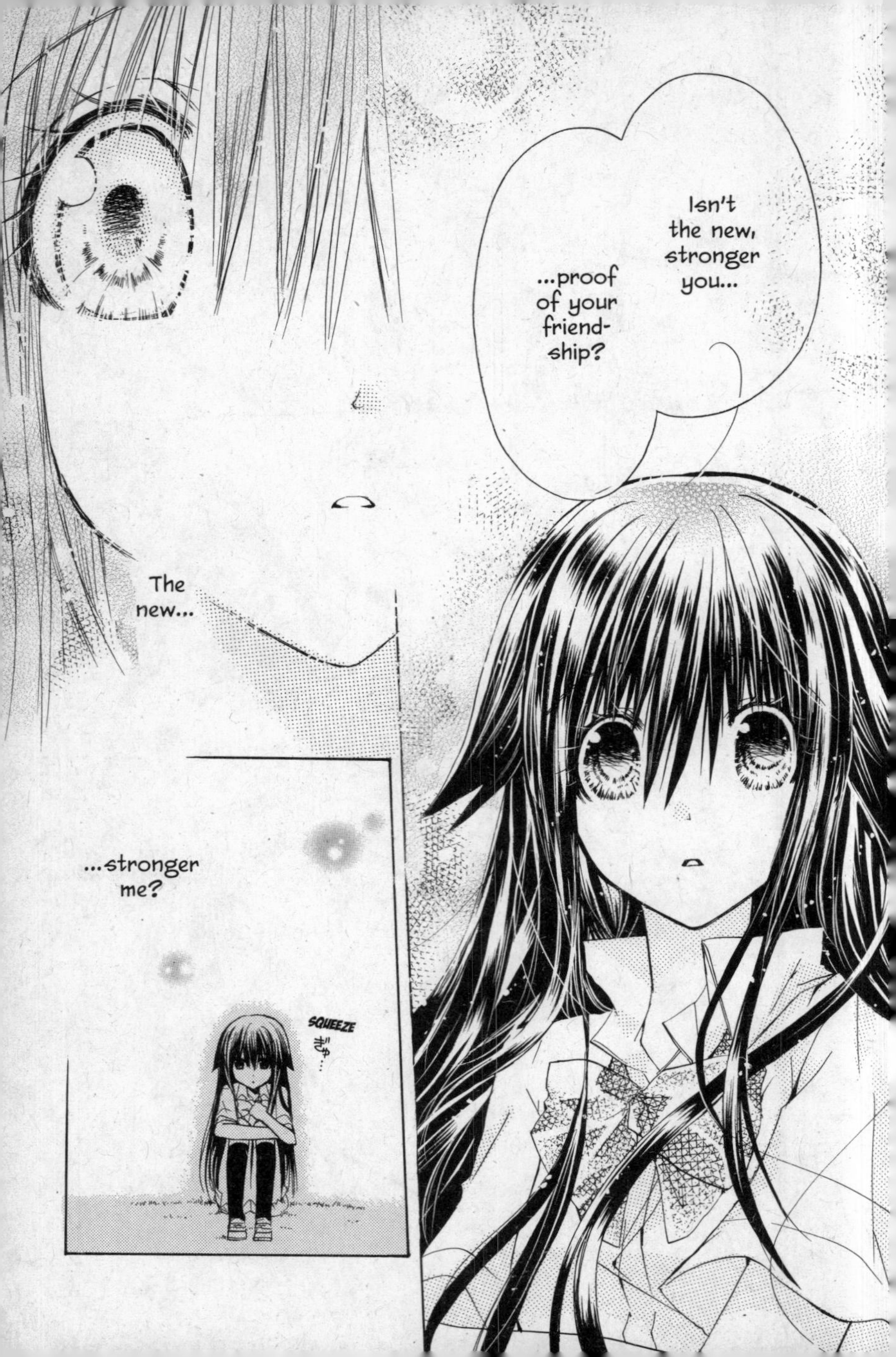
Isn't the new, stronger you...
...proof of your friendship?
The new...
...stronger me?
SQUEEZE
ぎゅ…

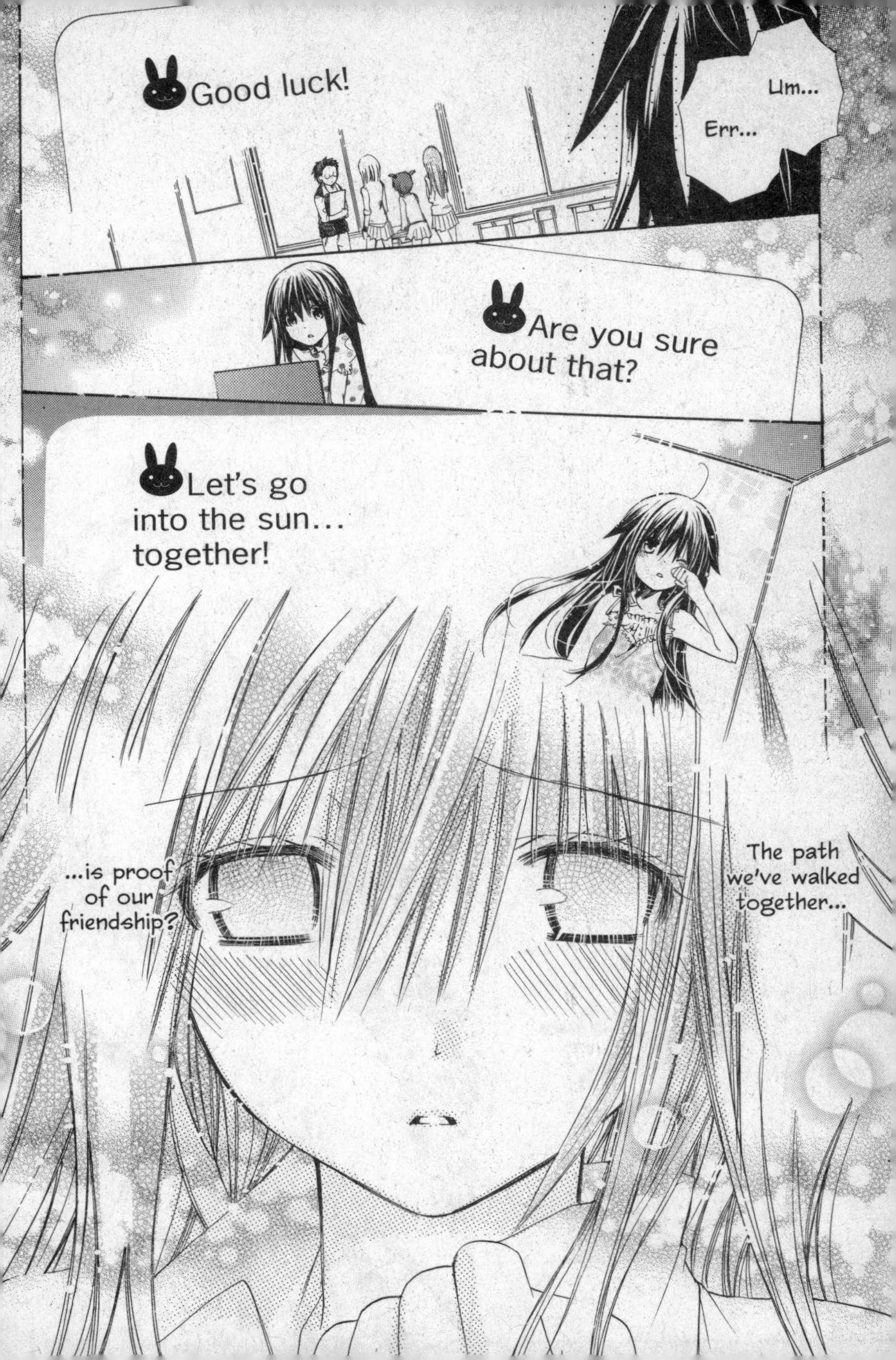

Um...
Err...
Good luck!
Are you sure about that?
Let's go into the sun... together!
The path we've walked together...
...is proof of our friendship?

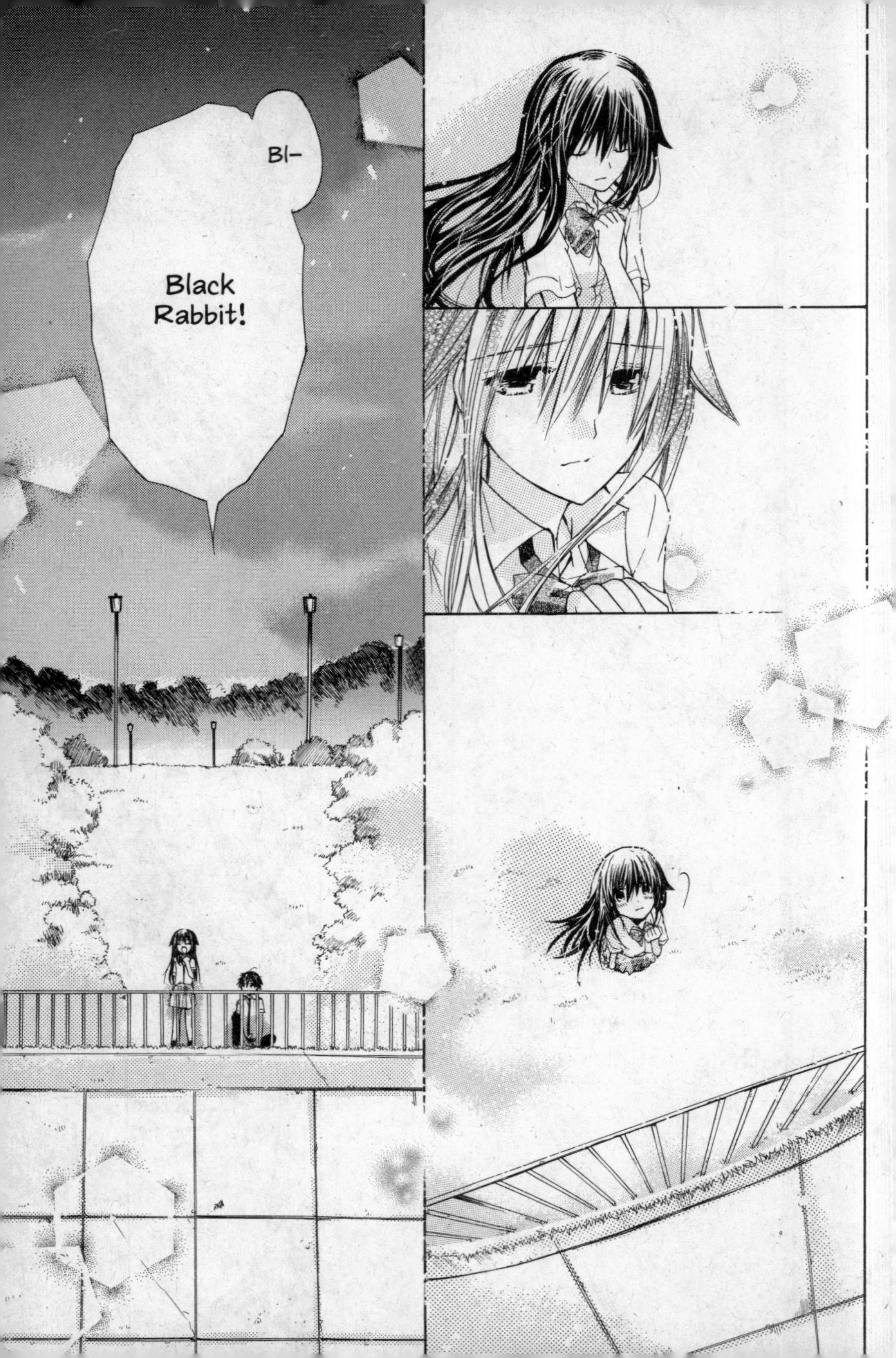
Bl-
Black Rabbit!

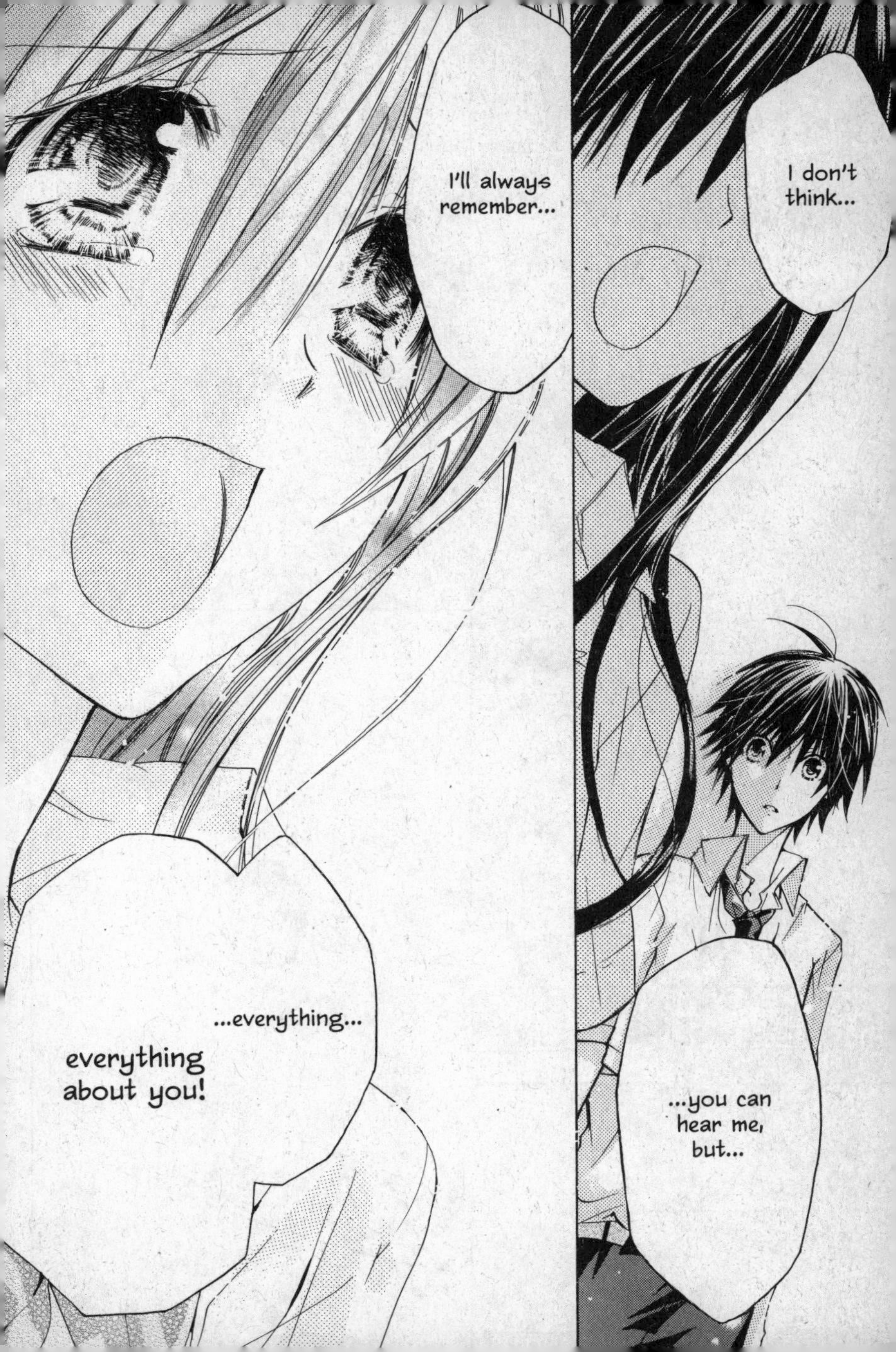
I don't think...
...you can hear me, but...
I'll always remember...
...everything...
everything about you!

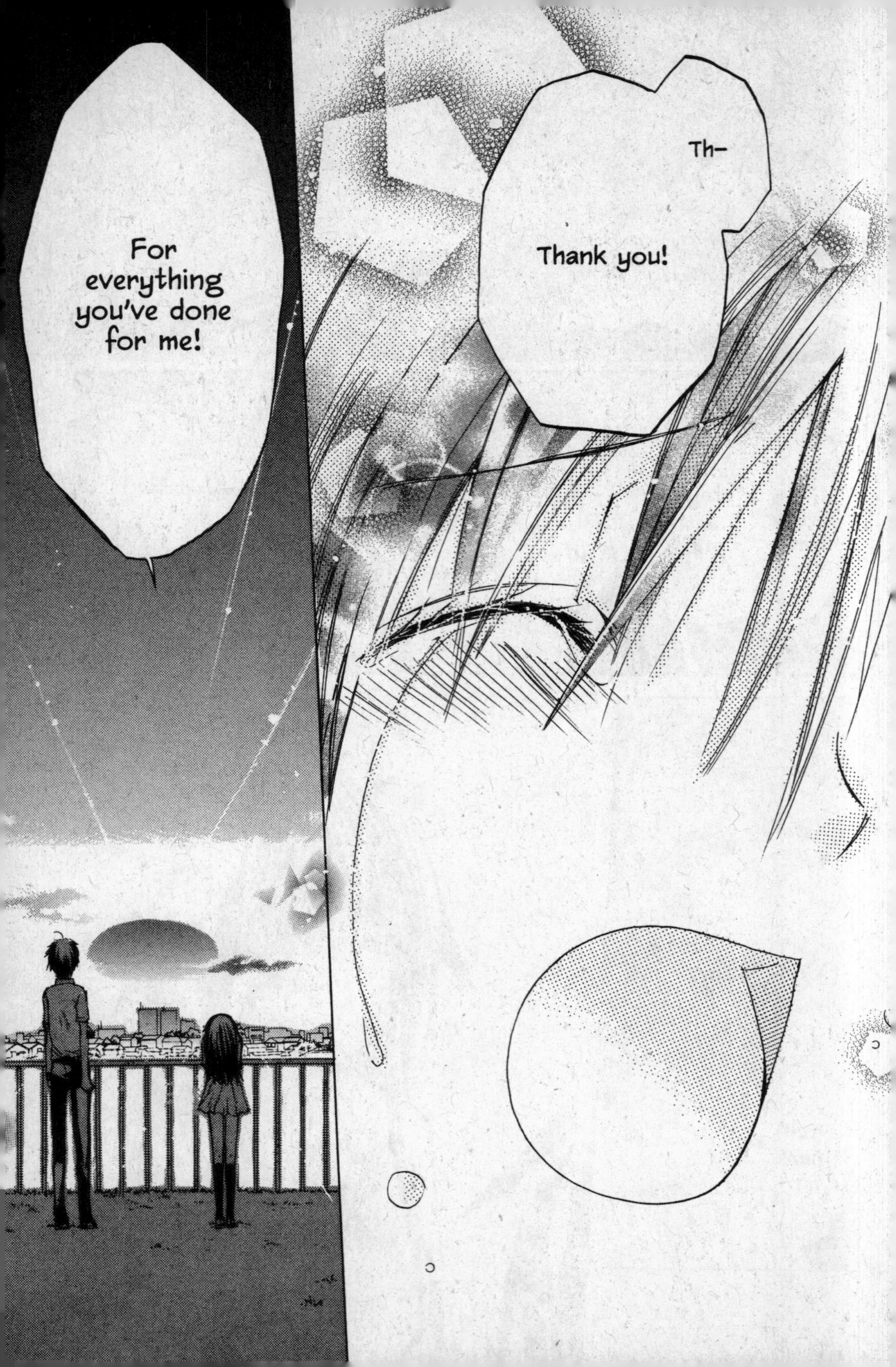
Th-
Thank you!
For everything you've done for me!

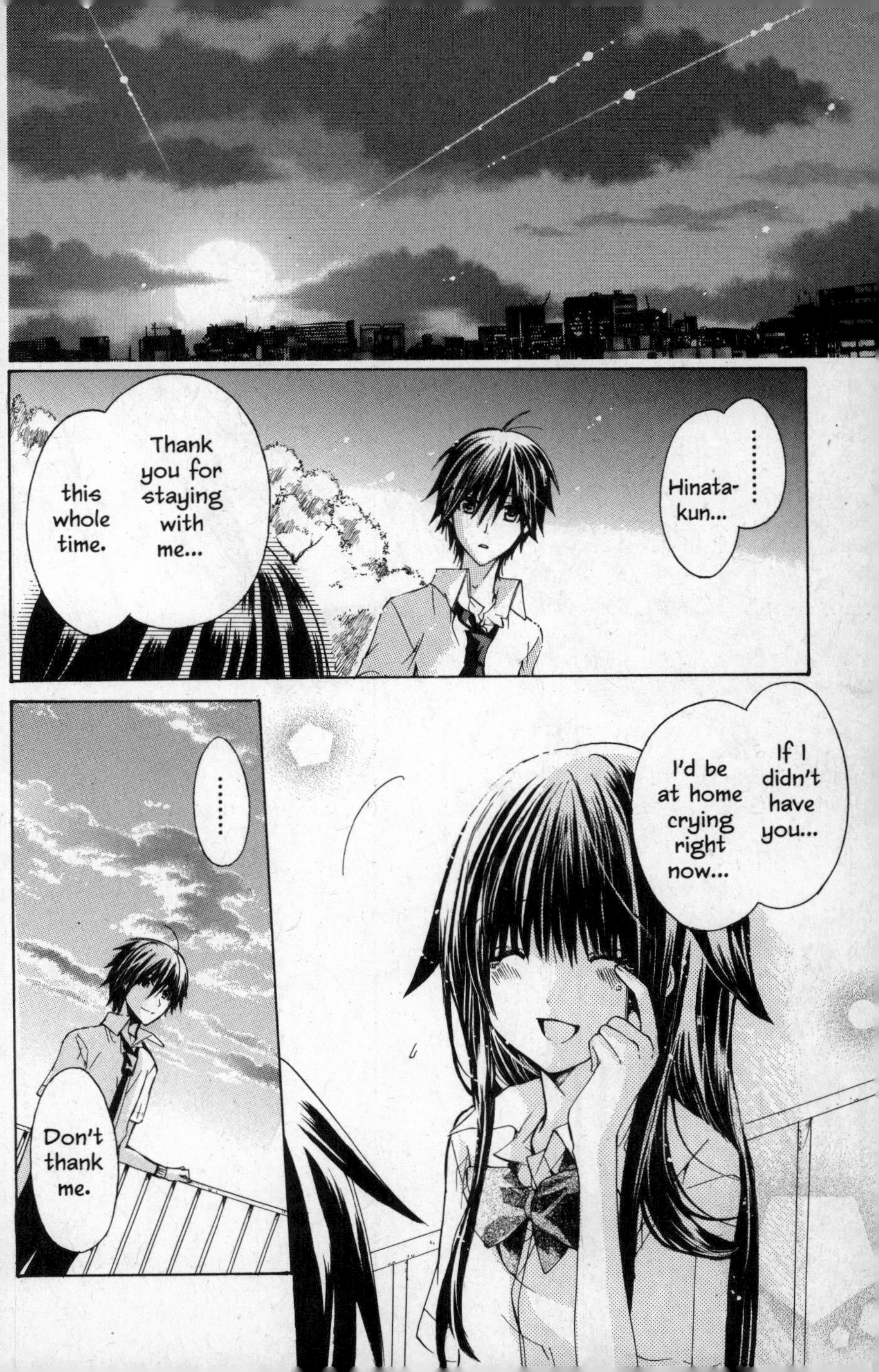

...... Hinata-kun...
Thank you for staying with me... this whole time.
If I didn't have you... I'd be at home crying right now...
......
Don't thank me.

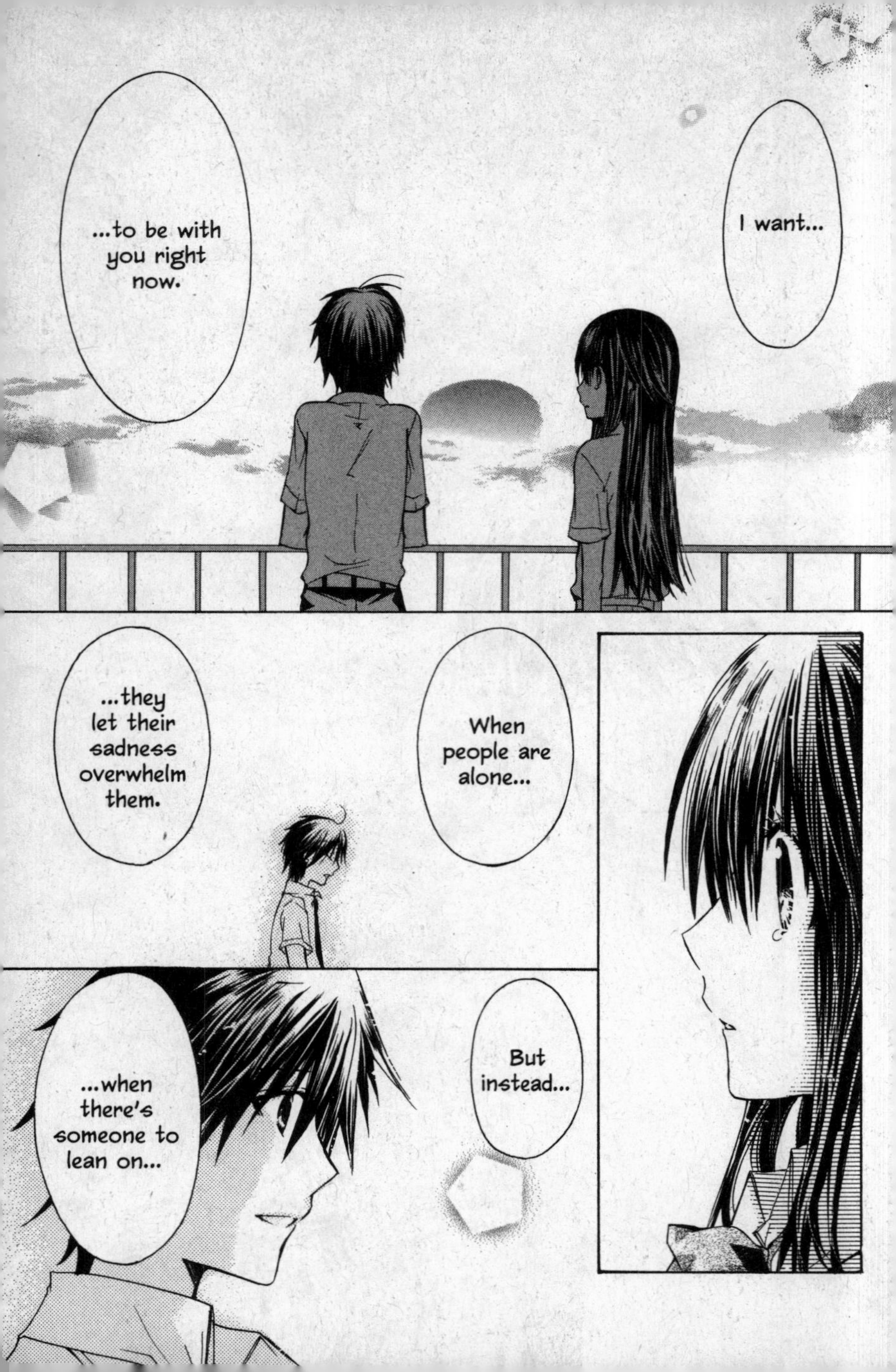
I want...
...to be with you right now.
When people are alone...
...they let their sadness overwhelm them.
But instead...
...when there's someone to lean on...

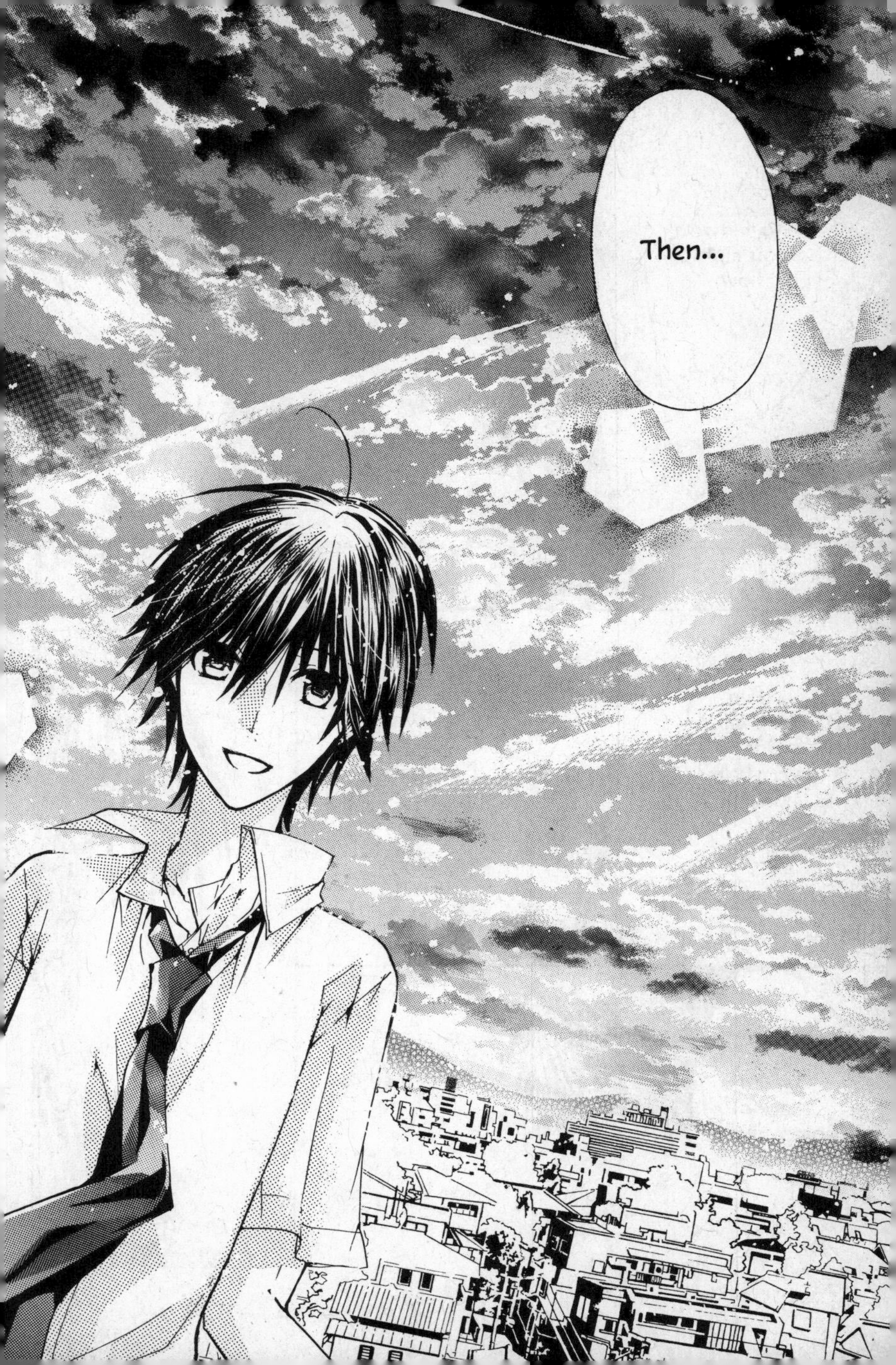
Then...

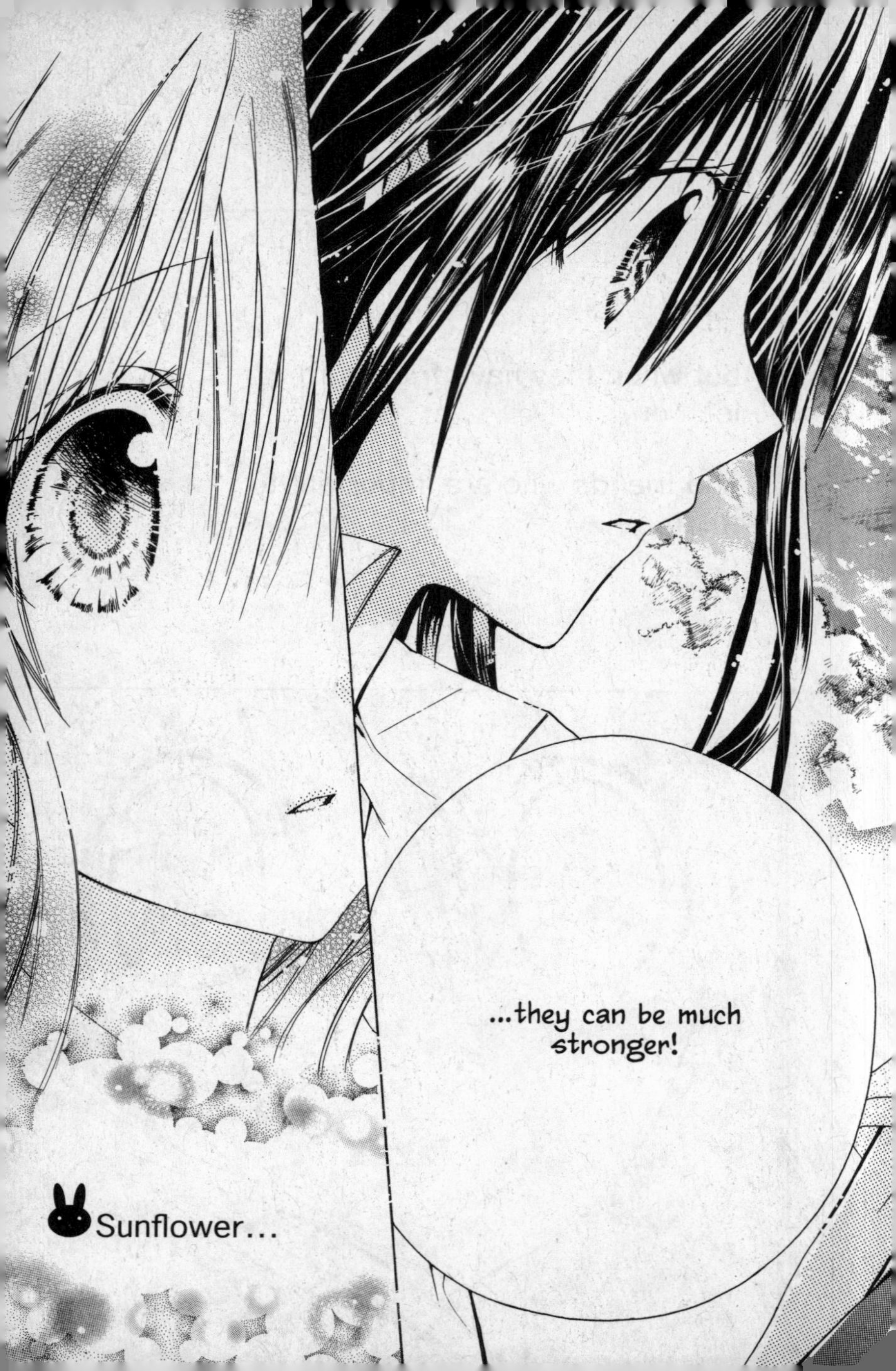
...they can be much stronger!
Sunflower...

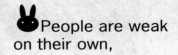People are weak
on their own,

but when they have friends to
lean on,

and friends who are important to
them,

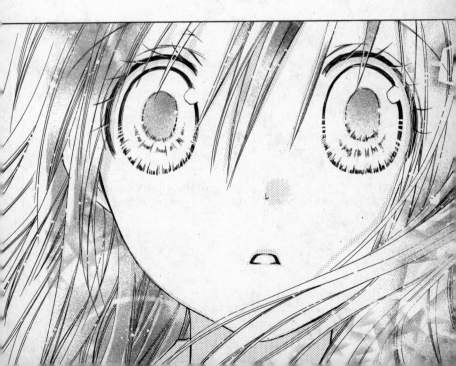

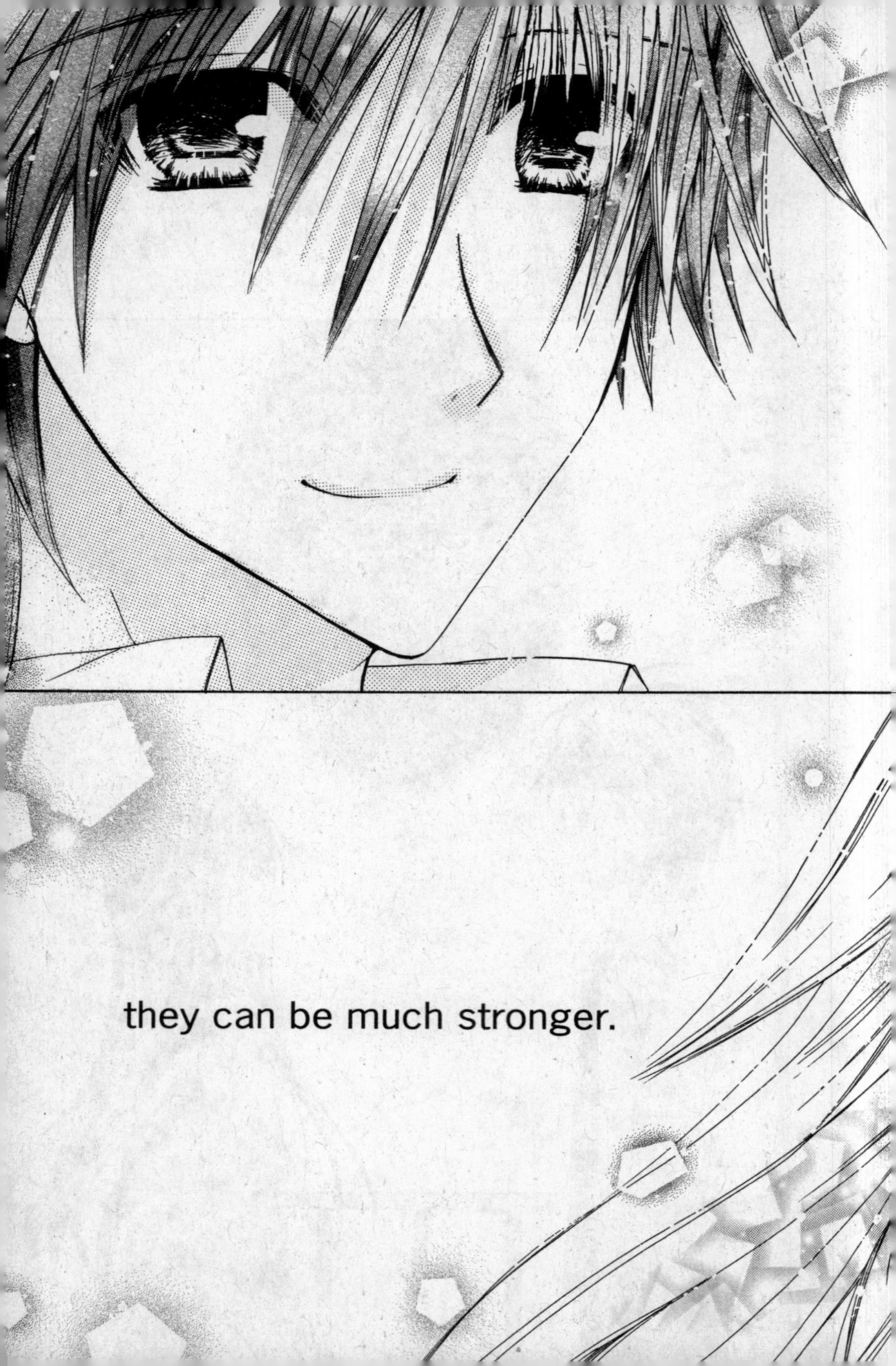
they can be much stronger.

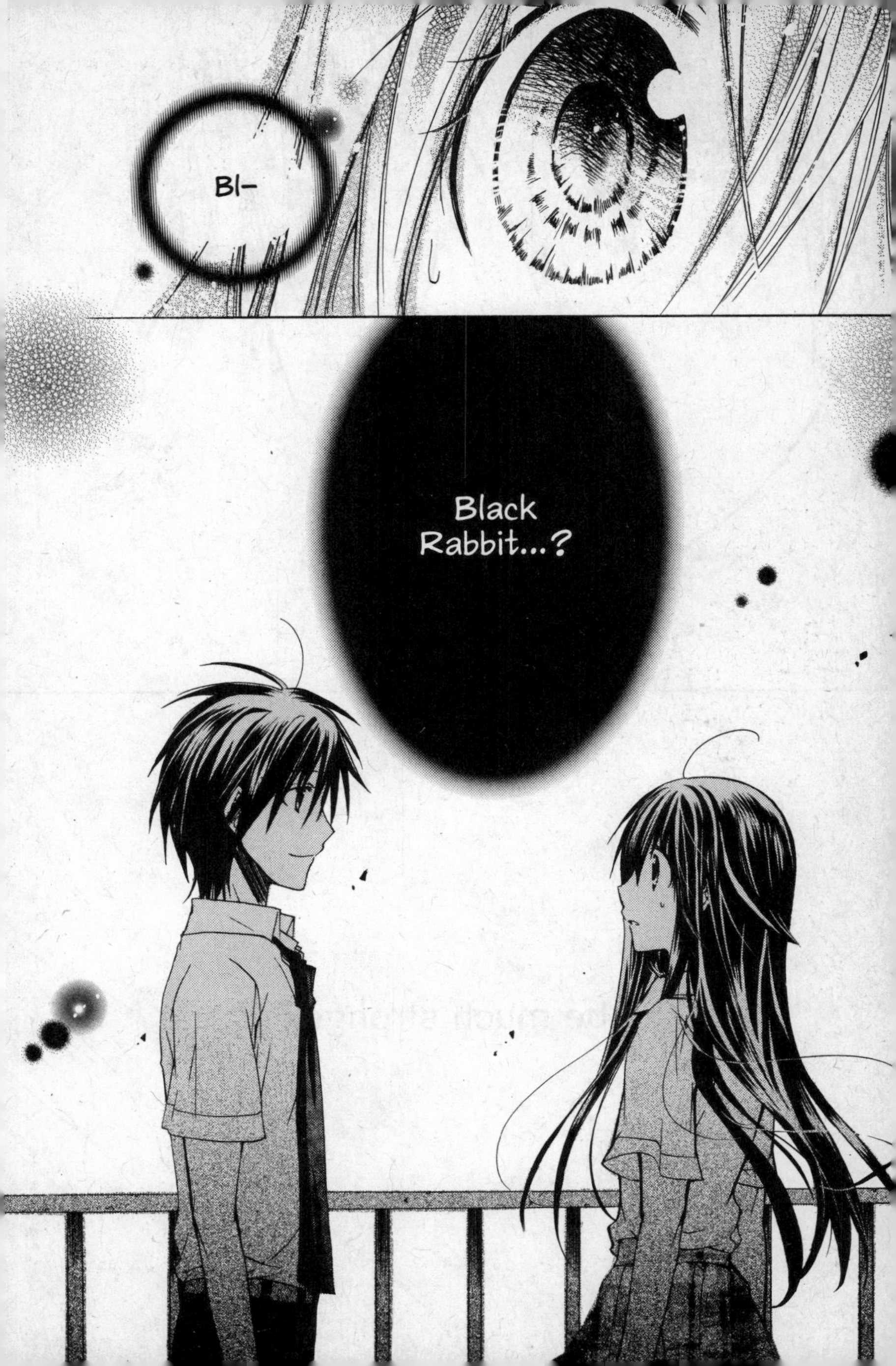
Bl-
Black Rabbit...?

Hello, this is Ema Tōyama. Thank you so much for reading *I Am Here!* How did you like it? This was my first manga with almost no funny scenes, and each episode was really hard for me to draw. But it also helped me learn how much fun it is to construct a story! Thank you to the Nakayoshi Editorial Department for making it possible for me to make this manga, to my editor who made it with me, and to everyone who read it! I hope to see you again in the next volume. See you!

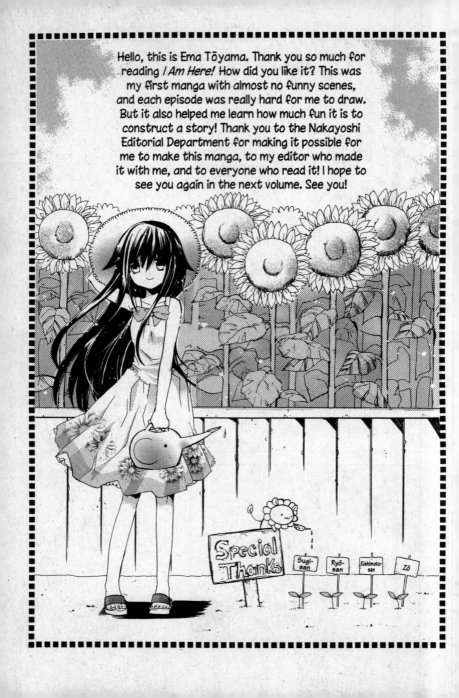

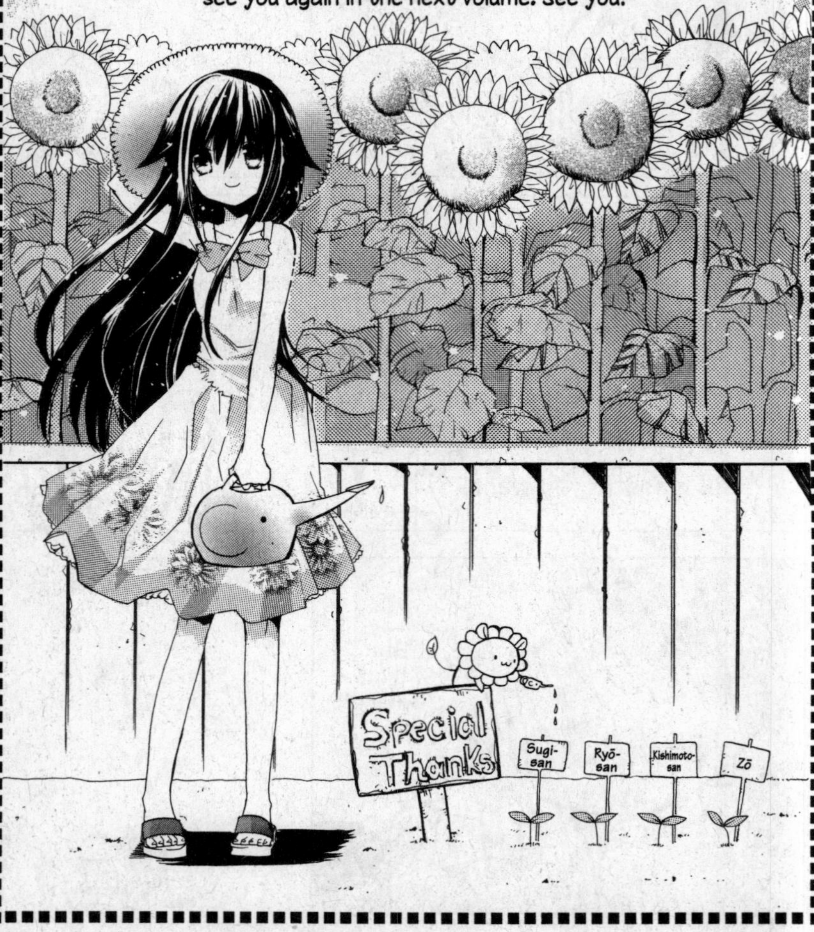
Special Thanks
Sugi-san
Ryō-san
Kishimoto-san
Zō

Special 1

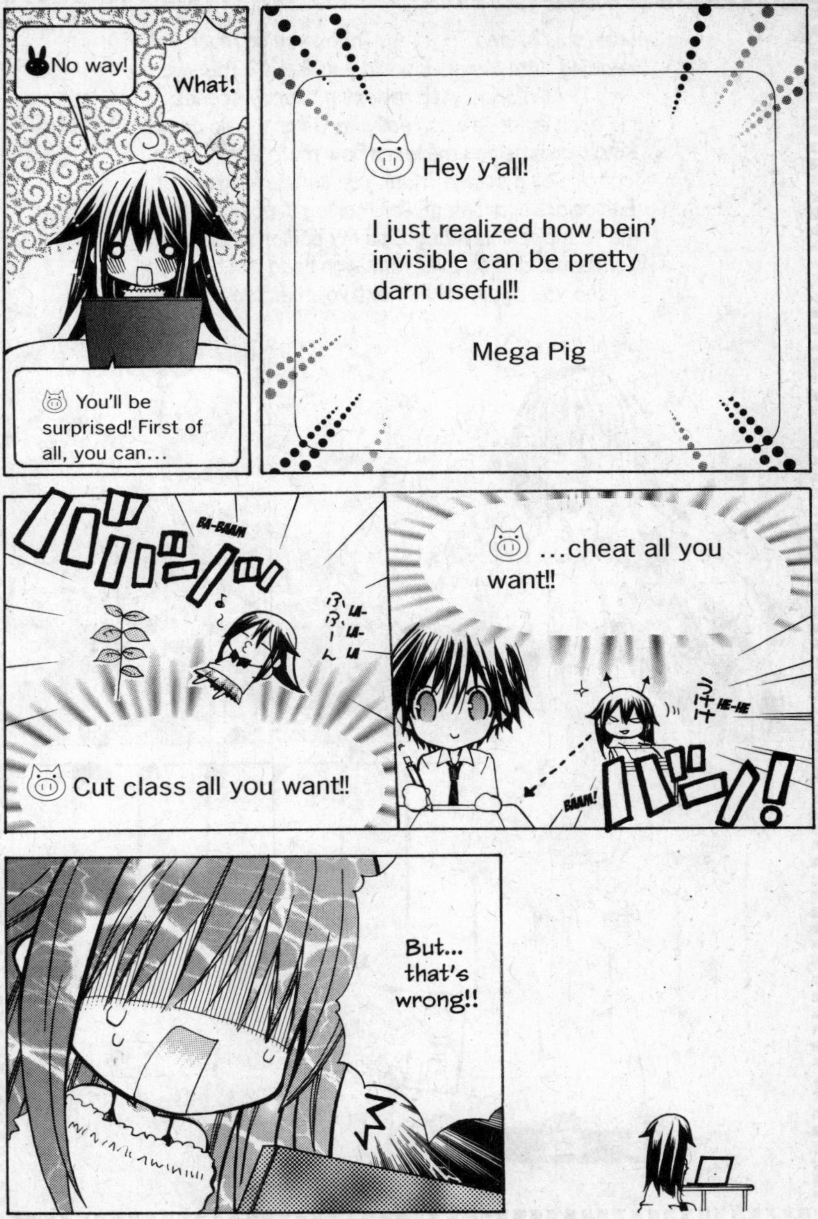

Hey y'all!
I just realized how bein' invisible can be pretty darn useful!!
Mega Pig
What!
No way!
You'll be surprised! First of all, you can…
…cheat all you want!!
うけけ
HE-HE
BAAM!
BA-BAAM
ふふーん
LA-LA-LA
Cut class all you want!!
But… that's wrong!!

Special 2

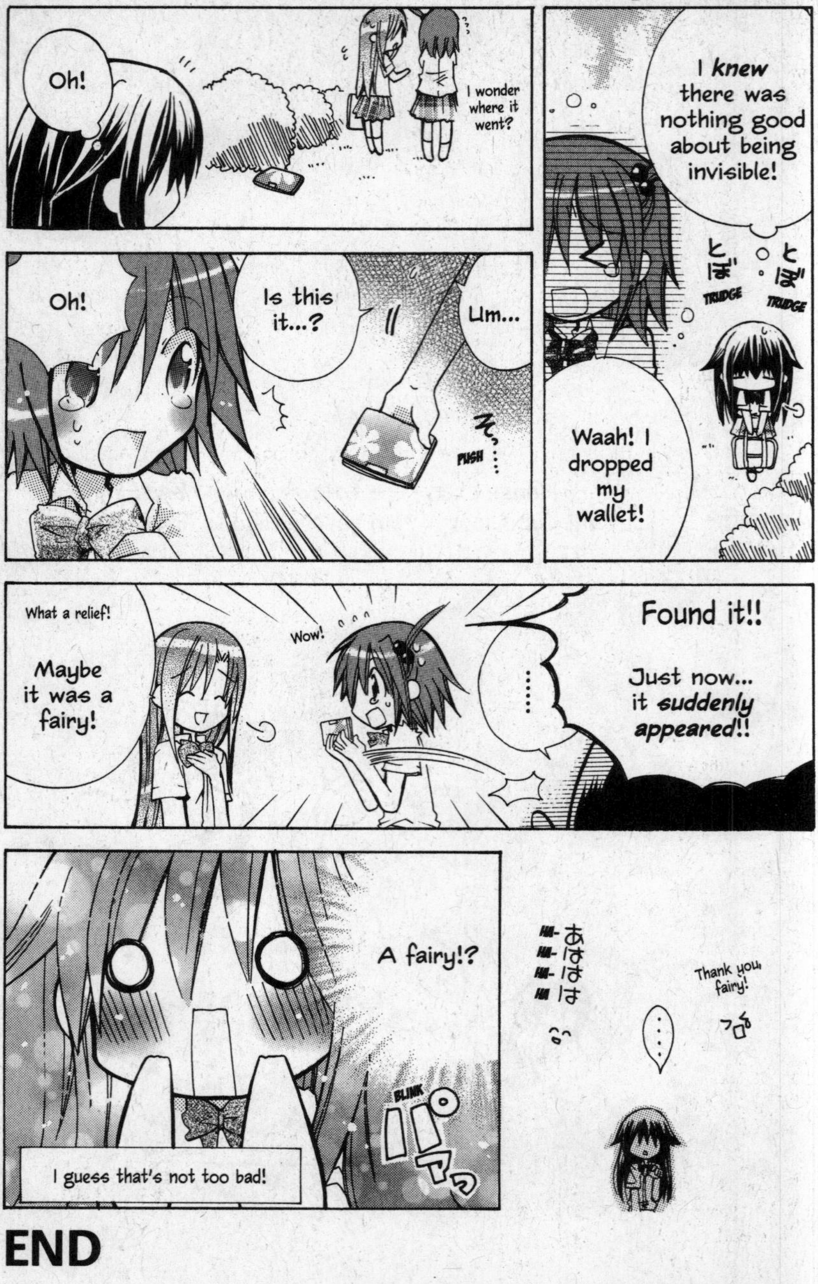
I *knew* there was nothing good about being invisible!
とぼ TRUDGE
とぼ TRUDGE
Waah! I dropped my wallet!
I wonder where it went?
Oh!
Um...
PUSH
Is this it...?
Oh!
Found it!!
Just now... it *suddenly appeared*!!
......
Wow!
What a relief!
Maybe it was a fairy!
Thank you, fairy!
....
あははは HA- HA- HA- HA
A fairy!?
BLINK
I guess that's not too bad!

END

Please enjoy the following *I Am Here Extra!* ♪
It's a story from before Hinata finds Hikage.

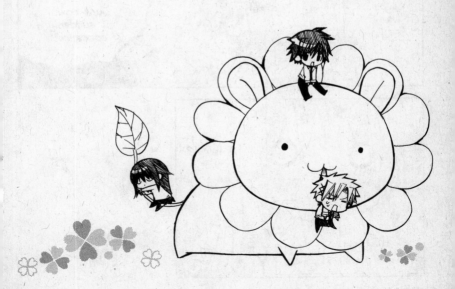

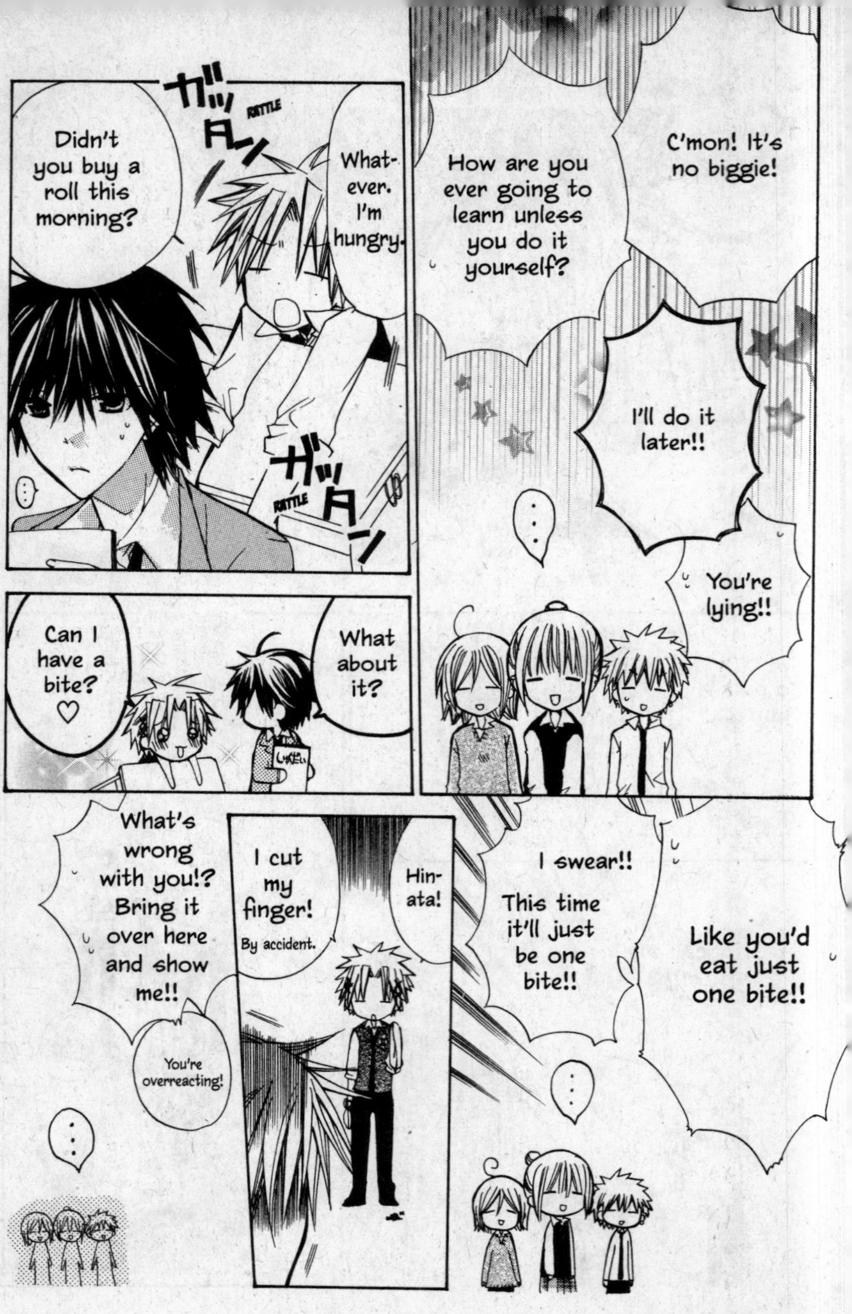
C'mon! It's no biggie!
How are you ever going to learn unless you do it yourself?
I'll do it later!!
…
You're lying!!
RATTLE
What-ever. I'm hungry.
Didn't you buy a roll this morning?
RATTLE
…
What about it?
Can I have a bite? ♡
Like you'd eat just one bite!!
I swear!!
This time it'll just be one bite!!
…
Hin-ata!
I cut my finger!
By accident.
What's wrong with you!? Bring it over here and show me!!
You're overreacting!
…

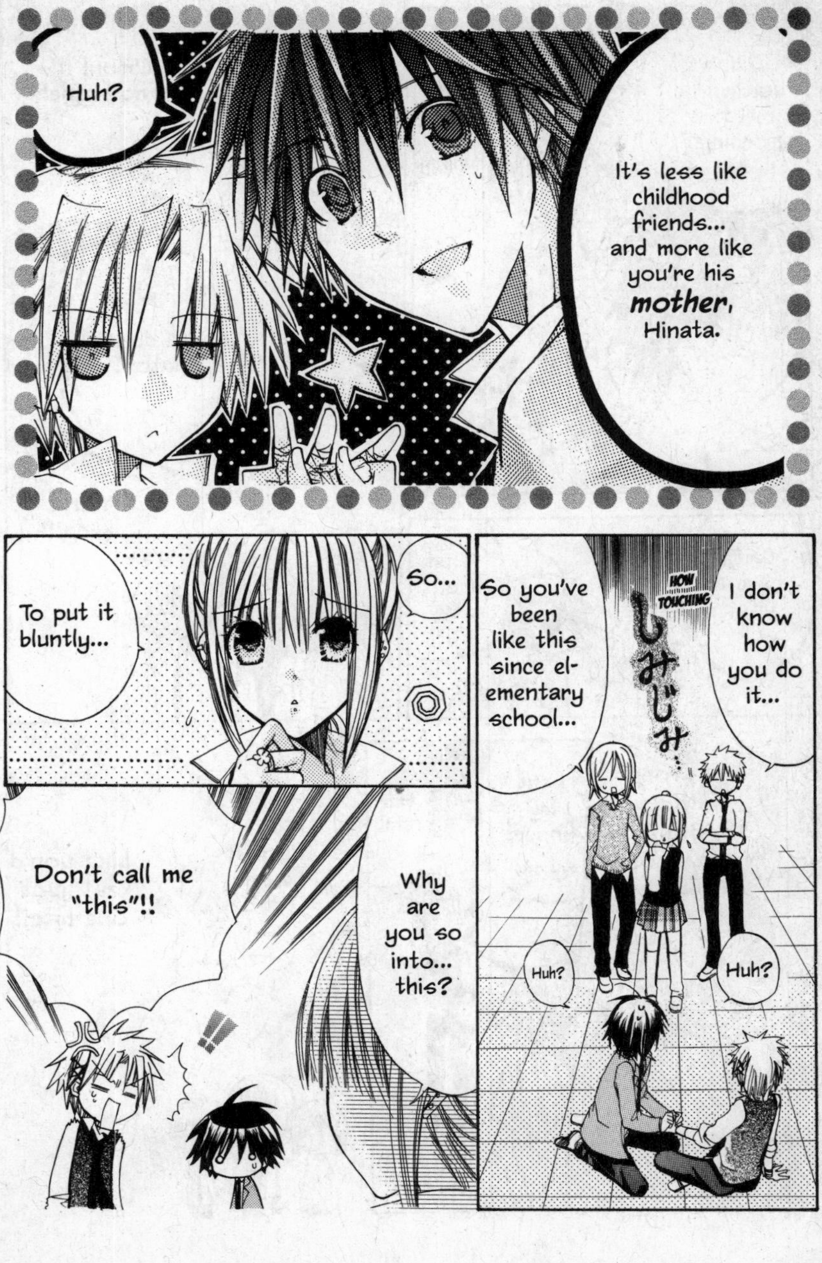
It's less like childhood friends... and more like you're his **mother**, Hinata.
Huh?
I don't know how you do it...
HOW TOUCHING
しみじみ…
So you've been like this since el-ementary school...
Huh?
Huh?
So...
To put it bluntly...
Why are you so into... this?
Don't call me "this"!!
!!

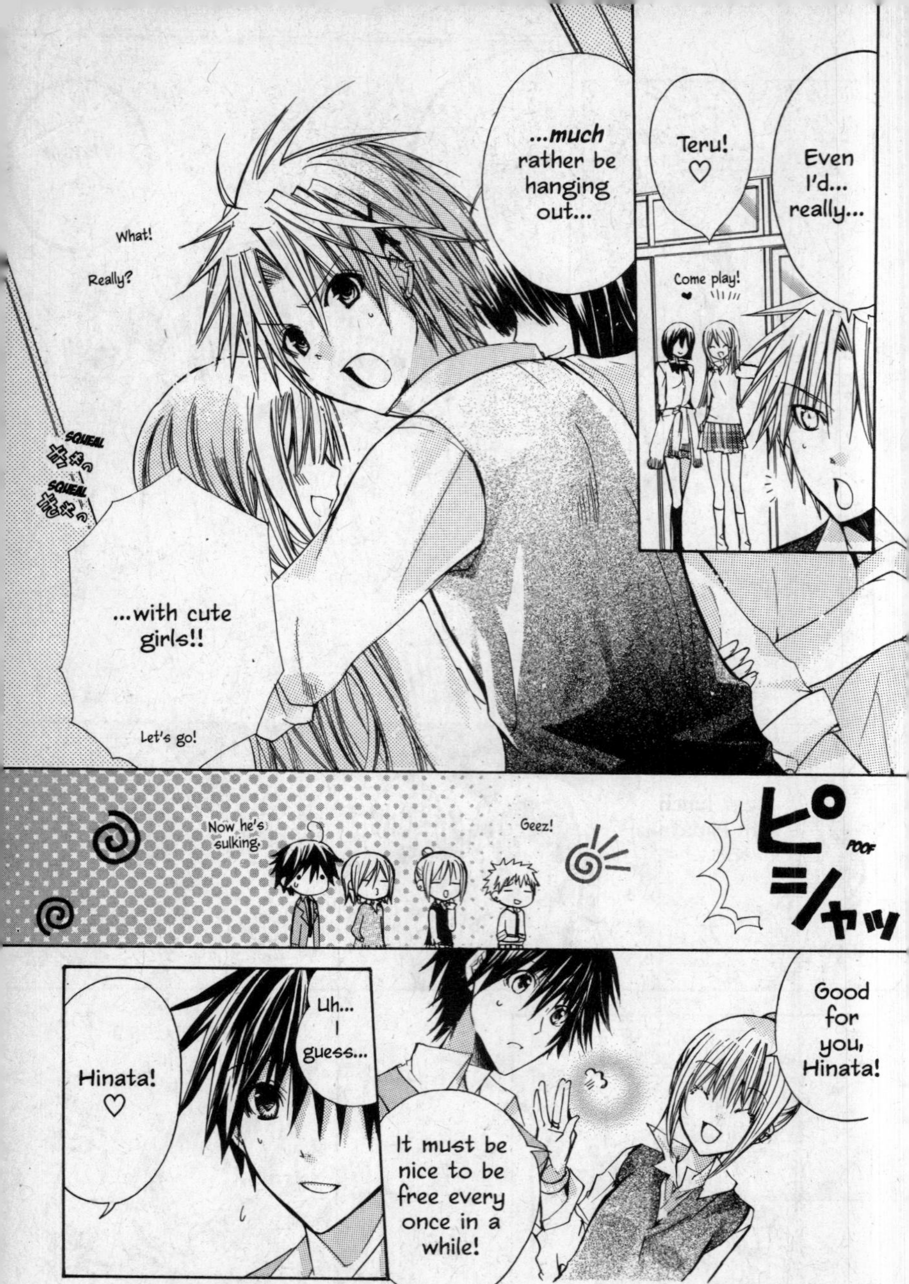
Even I'd... really...
Teru! ♡
Come play!
...much rather be hanging out...
What!
Really?
SQUEAL
SQUEAL
...with cute girls!!
Let's go!
ピシャッ
POOF
Geez!
Now he's sulking.
Good for you, Hinata!
It must be nice to be free every once in a while!
Uh... I guess...
Hinata! ♡

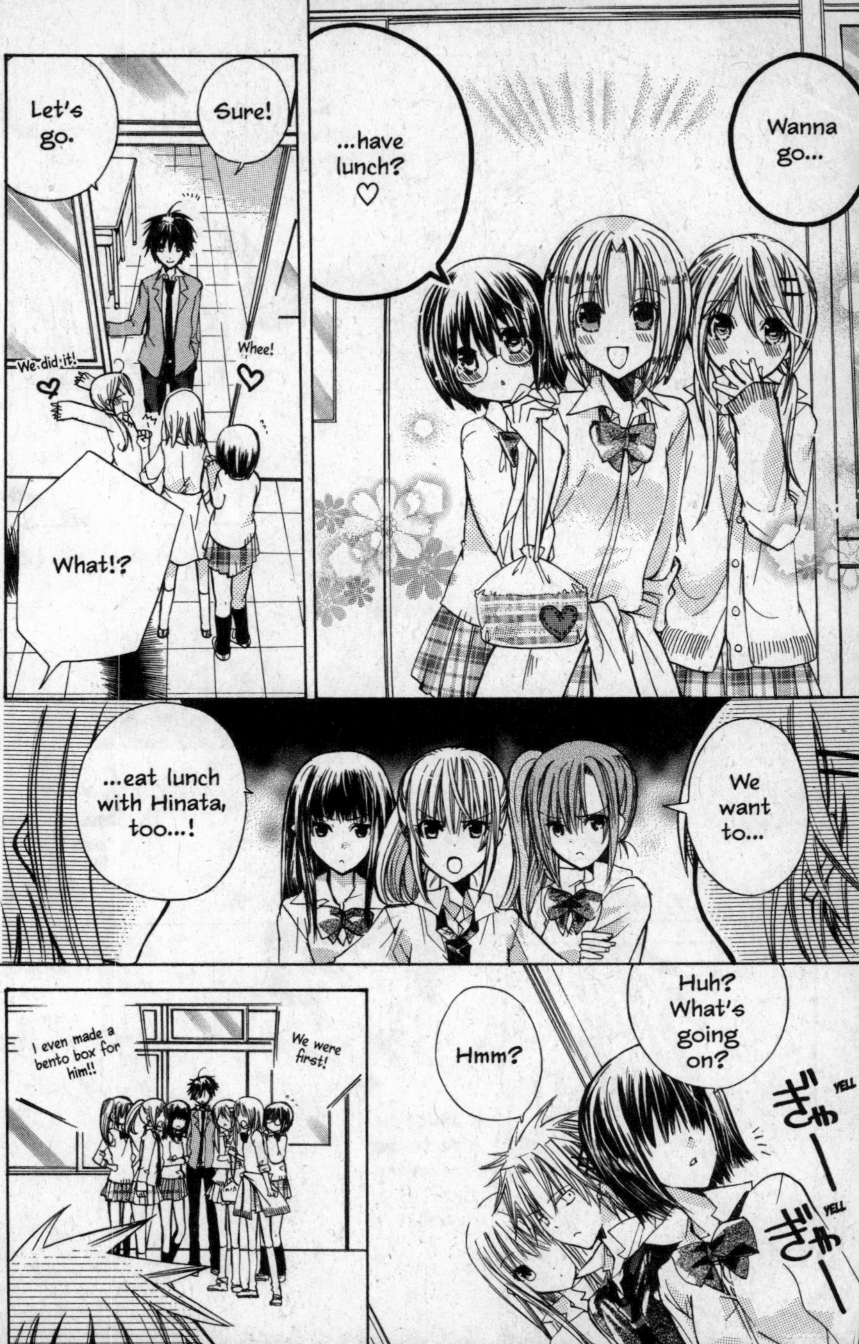
Wanna go...
...have lunch? ♡
Let's go.
Sure!
Whee! ♡
We did it! ♡
What!?
We want to...
...eat lunch with Hinata, too...!
ぎゃー YELL
ぎゃー YELL
Huh? What's going on?
Hmm?
We were first!
I even made a bento box for him!!

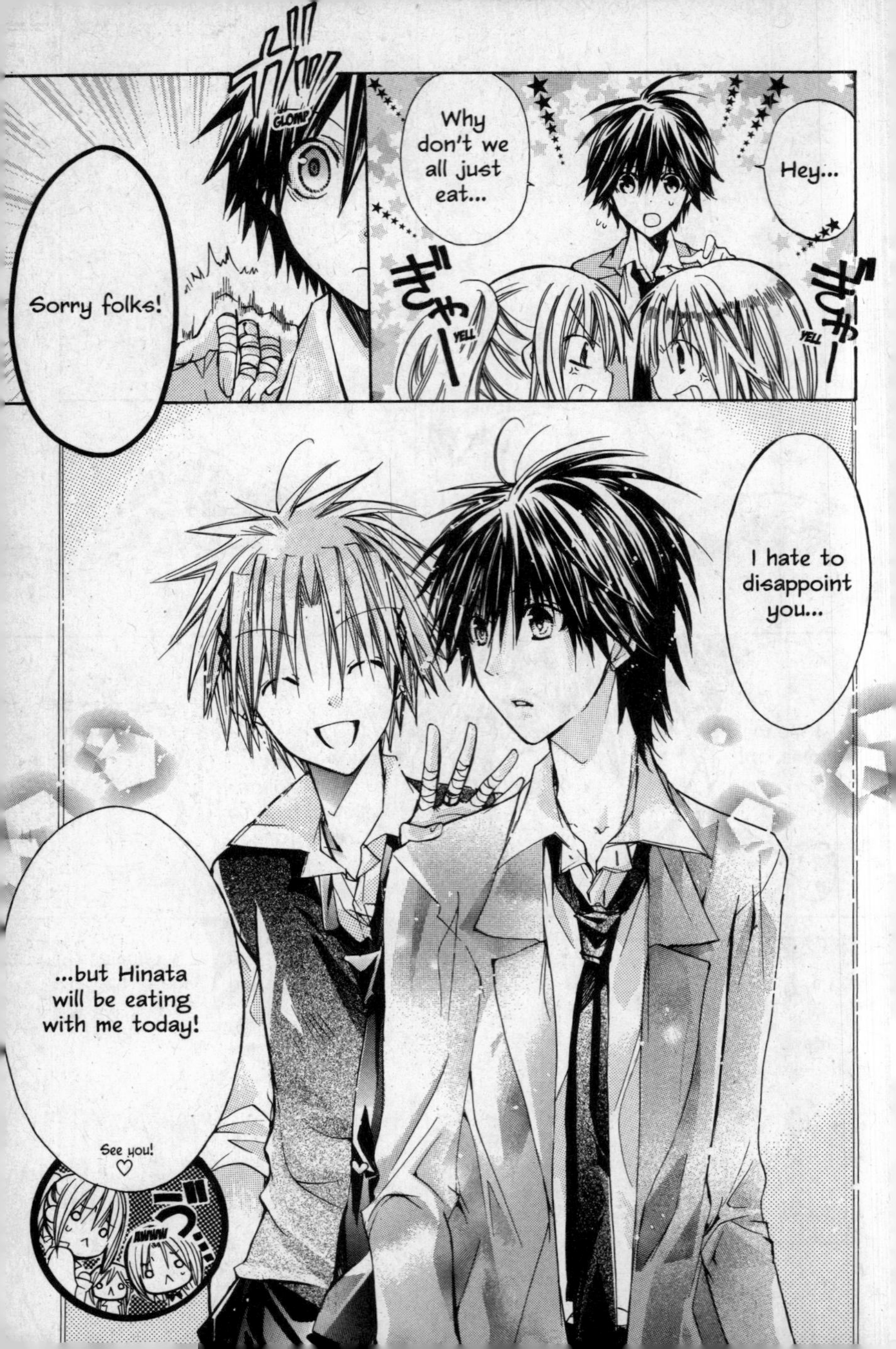
Hey...
Why don't we all just eat...
YELL
YELL
GLOMP
Sorry folks!
I hate to disappoint you...
...but Hinata will be eating with me today!
See you! ♡
AWWW

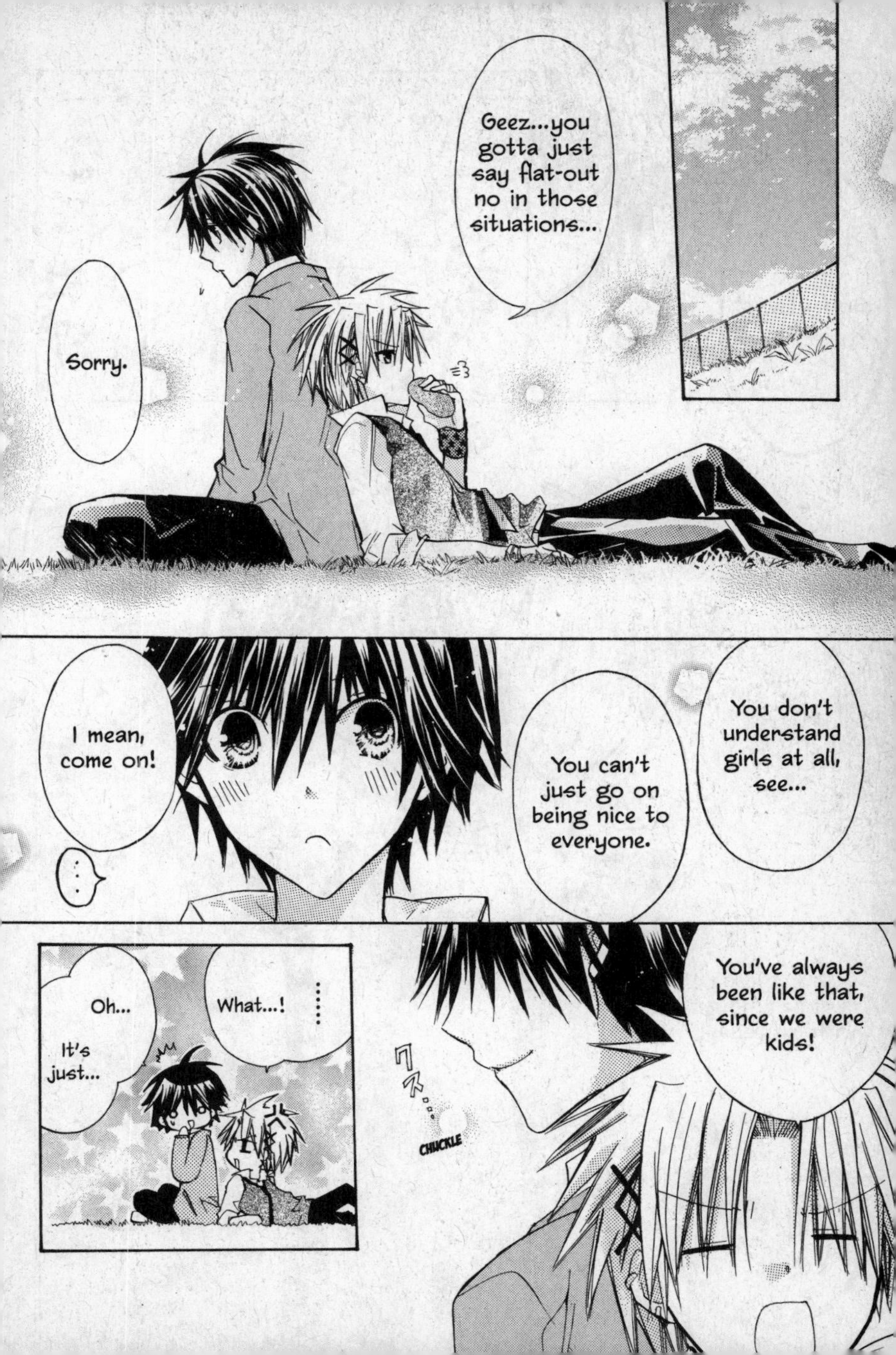

Geez...you gotta just say flat-out no in those situations...
Sorry.
You don't understand girls at all, see...
You can't just go on being nice to everyone.
I mean, come on!
...
You've always been like that, since we were kids!
クス...
CHUCKLE
......
What...!
Oh... It's just...

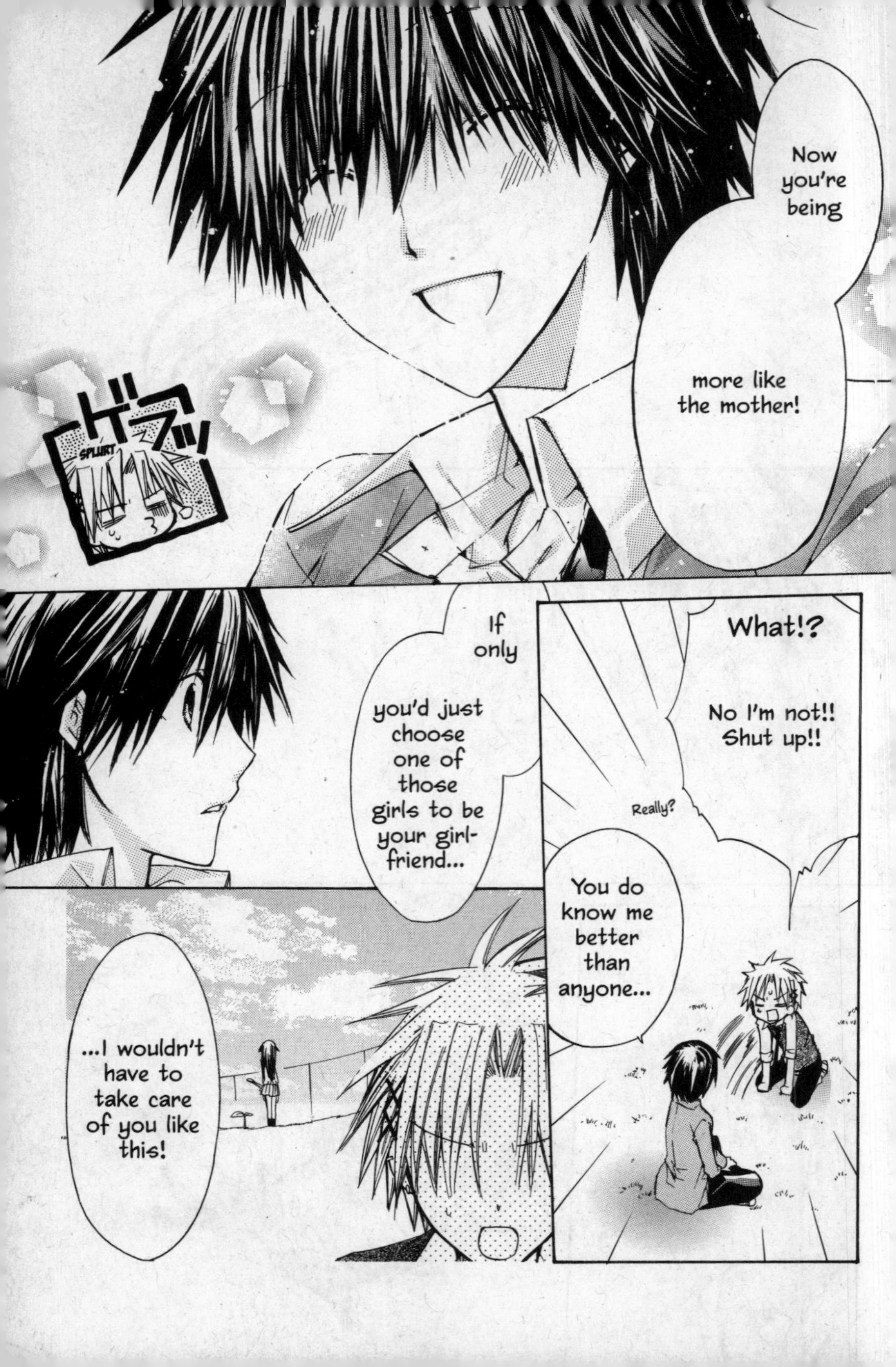
Now you're being
more like the mother!
ゲラッ
SPLURT
What!?
No I'm not!! Shut up!!
Really?
You do know me better than anyone...
If only
you'd just choose one of those girls to be your girl-friend...
...I wouldn't have to take care of you like this!

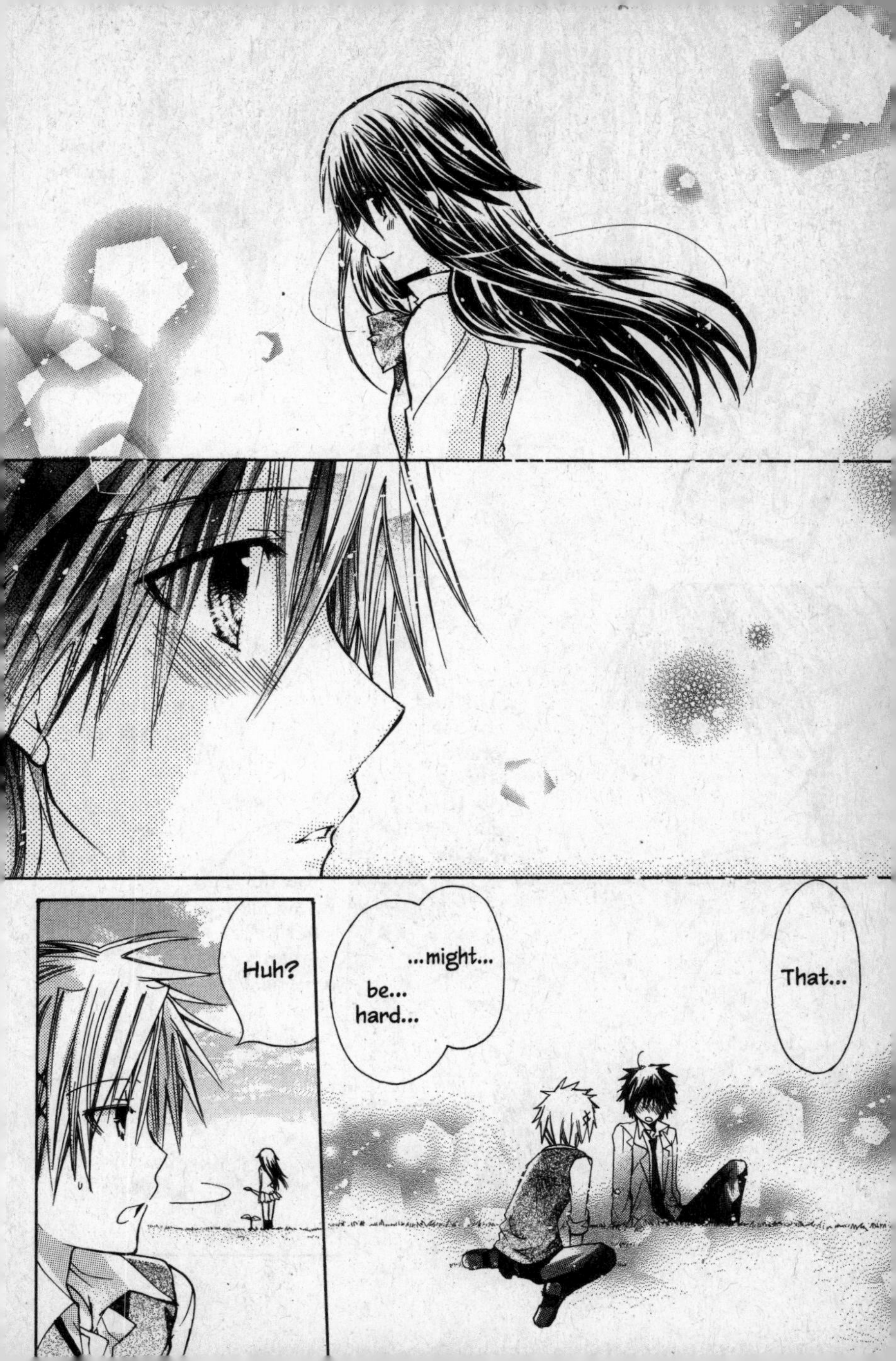
That...
...might... be... hard...
Huh?

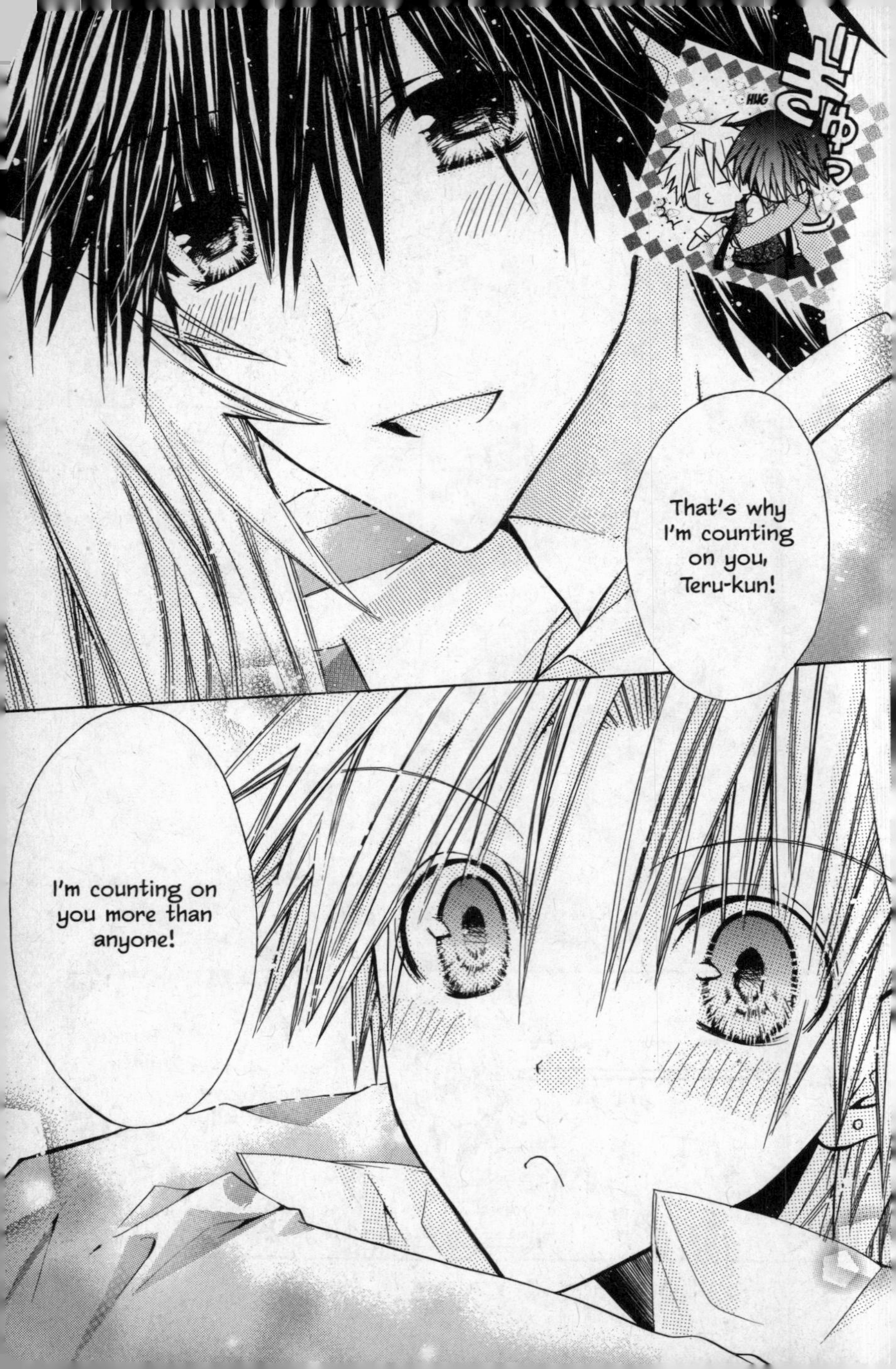
HUG
That's why I'm counting on you, Teru-kun!
I'm counting on you more than anyone!

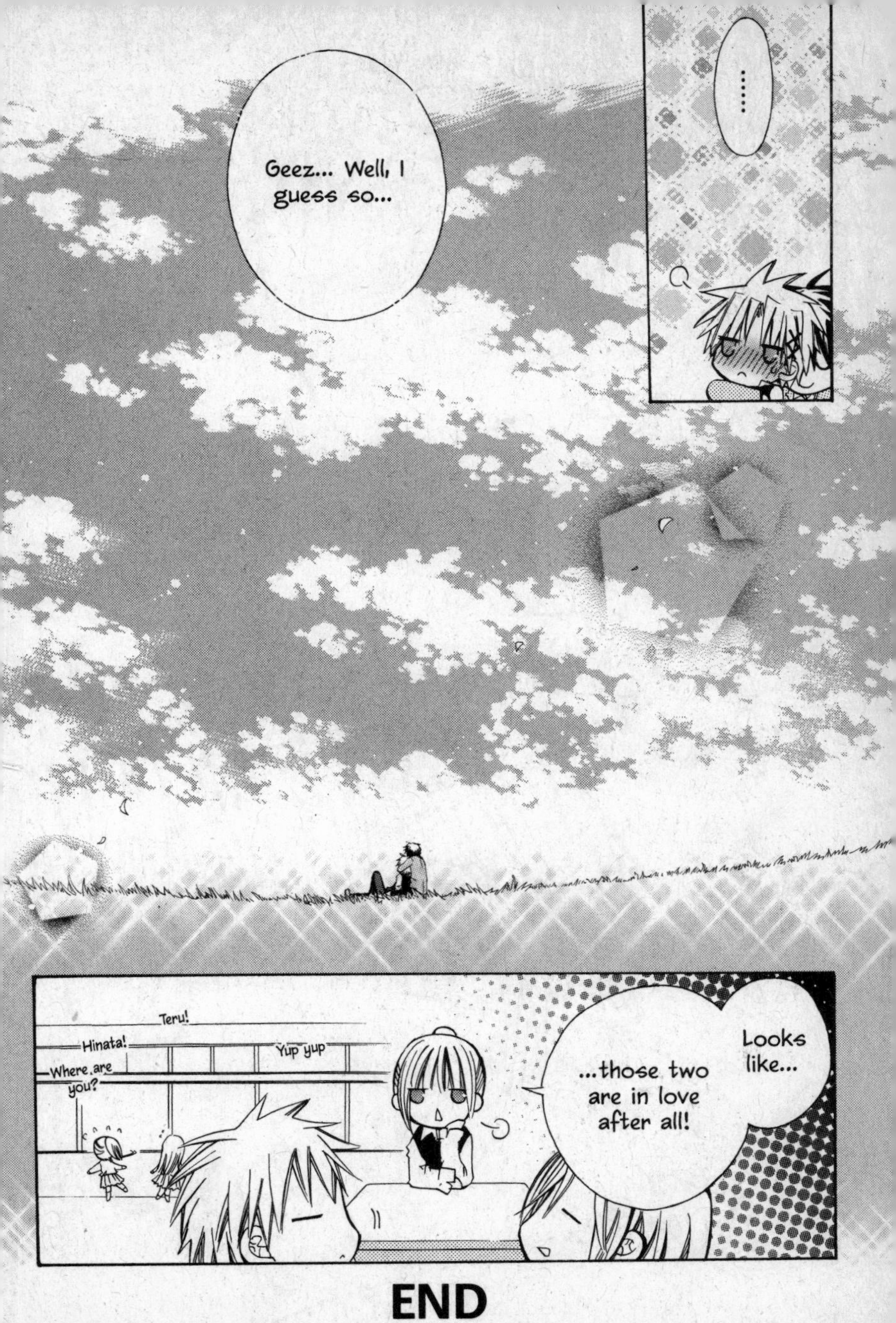
......
Geez... Well, I guess so...
Looks like...
...those two are in love after all!
Yup yup
Teru!
Hinata!
Where are you?

END

Translation Notes

Japanese is a tricky language for most Westerners, and translation is often more art than science. For your edification and reading pleasure, here are notes on some of the places where we could have gone in a different direction with our translation of the work, or where a Japanese cultural reference is used

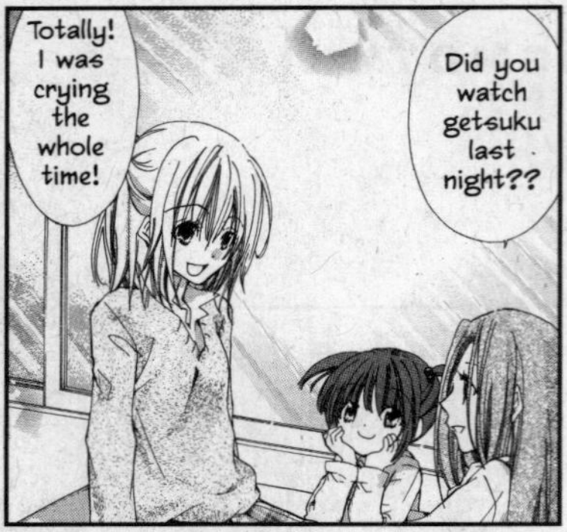
Did you watch getsuku last night??
Totally! I was crying the whole time!

Getsuku, page 5
Literally "Monday nine," getsuku is a general term for the drama that airs at 9 PM every Monday on Fuji TV, one of the major broadcasting companies in Japan. Hits in the past have included *Tokyo Love Story, The 101st Proposal,* and *Long Vacation.*

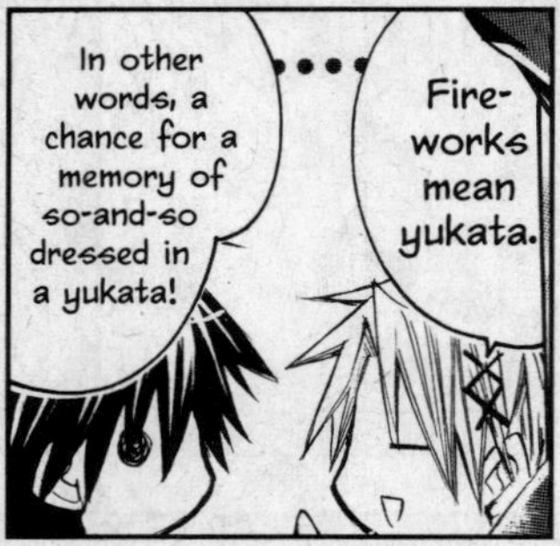
Fire-works mean yukata.
...
In other words, a chance for a memory of so-and-so dressed in a yukata!

***Yukata*, page 312**
A *yukata* is a summer kimono usually made of cotton. People wearing *yukata* are a common sight in Japan at fireworks displays, *bon-odori* festivals, and other summer events.

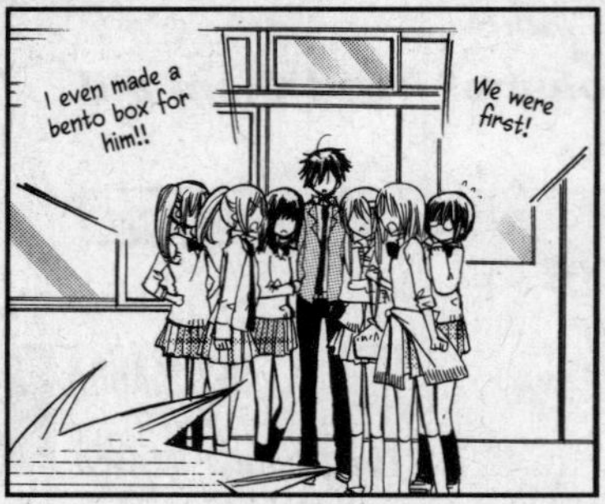
We were first!
I even made a bento box for him!!

Bento Box, page 393
A bento box is a single-portion takeout or home-packed meal common in Japanese cuisine. Commonly consisting of rice, fish or meat, and one or more pickled or cooked vegetable, it is common in manga for girls to make bento for boys who they like.

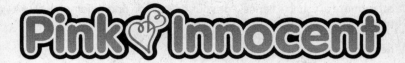
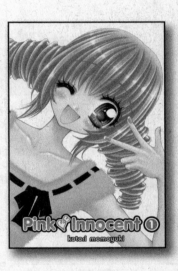
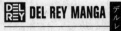

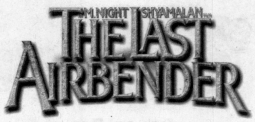

THE OFFICIAL GRAPHIC NOVELS OF THE BLOCKBUSTER FILM

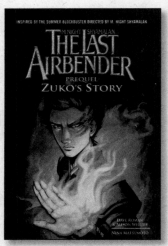

THE LAST AIRBENDER: PREQUEL: ZUKO'S STORY

WRITTEN BY DAVE ROMAN AND ALISON WILGUS
ILLUSTRATED BY NINA MATSUMOTO

Banished from the Fire Nation, Prince Zuko's only chance at redemption lies in finding the mystical Avatar who once kept the four nations in balance.

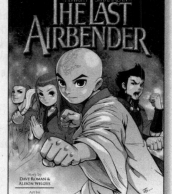

THE LAST AIRBENDER

WRITTEN BY DAVE ROMAN AND ALISON WILGUS
ILLUSTRATED BY JOON CHOI

It is Aang's destiny as the Avatar to bring balance to the world. But will even the powers of the last of the airbenders be enough to challenge the ruthless Fire Nation?

WWW.DELREYMANGA.COM

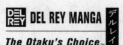

DEL REY MANGA デルレイ
The Otaku's Choice.™

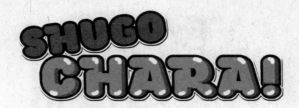
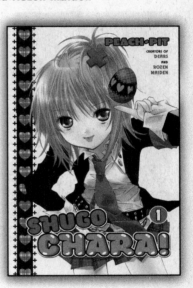
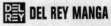

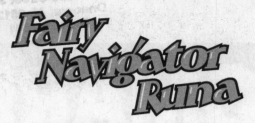

Fairy Navigator Runa

STORY BY MIYOKO IKEDA
ILLUSTRATIONS BY MICHIYO KIKUTA

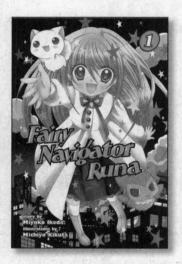

THE LEGENDARY CHILD

As a baby, Runa Rindō was left in front of a school for foster children, wearing a mysterious pendant. Now she's in fourth grade and strange things are starting to happen around her. It's only a matter of time before she discovers her secret powers—and her quest as the Legendary Fairy Child begins!

From the illustrator of *Mamotte! Lollipop*

Special extras in each volume! Read them all!

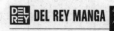

TOMARE!

[STOP!]

You are going the wrong way!

Manga is a completely different type of reading experience.

To start at the *beginning*, go to the *end*!

That's right! Authen[...] [...]anese way—
from right to left, exac[...] [...]oks are read.
It's easy to follow: Just [...] [...]ook, and read each
page—and each panel—[...] [...]ght side to the left side, starting at
the top right. Now you're experiencing manga as it was meant to be.